The Macedonian Phalanx

The Macedonian Phalanx

Equipment, Organization and Tactics from Philip and Alexander to the Roman Conquest

Richard Taylor

Pen & Sword
MILITARY

First published in Great Britain in 2020 by
Pen& Sword Military
An imprint of
Pen & Sword Books Ltd
Yorkshire– Philadelphia

Copyright © Richard Taylor 2020

ISBN 978 1 52674 815 7

A CIP catalogue record for this book is
available from the British Library.

Typeset in 11.5/14 Ehrhardt by Vman Infotech Pvt. Ltd.

Printed and bound in the UK by TJ Books Limited, Padstow, Cornwall.

Pen & Sword Books Limited incorporates the imprints of Atlas, Archaeology, Aviation,
Discovery, Family History, Fiction, History, Maritime, Military, Military Classics,
Politics, Select, Transport, True Crime, Air World, Frontline Publishing, Leo Cooper,
Remember When, Seaforth Publishing, The Praetorian Press, Wharncliffe Local
History, Wharncliffe Transport, Wharncliffe True Crime and White Owl.

For a complete list of Pen & Sword titles please contact
PEN & SWORD BOOKS LIMITED
47 Church Street, Barnsley, South Yorkshire, S70 2AS, England
E-mail: enquiries@pen-and-sword.co.uk
Website: www.pen-and-sword.co.uk

Or
PEN AND SWORD BOOKS
1950 Lawrence Rd, Havertown, PA 19083, USA
E-mail: Uspen-and-sword@casematepublishers.com
Website: www.penandswordbooks.com

Contents

Note on sources

The Macedonian phalanx came into being sometime in the mid-fourth century BC, and remained in use until the first century BC (all dates in this book are BC/BCE unless otherwise stated, and from here on I will omit the 'BC'). This is a period of Greek history which varies quite widely in terms of how well documented it is, particularly by literary historians. Even where complete literary histories exist, they are sometimes frustratingly vague or skirt over matters of detail we would love to know more about, but which might have been thought self-evident to contemporary readers. This means that we often have only hints or suggestions on many important topics, and there is much scope for interpretation and scholarly disagreement. In the account of the Macedonian phalanx that follows, I will spell out my own theories where I have formed them, but sometimes I can only outline conflicting interpretations and leave it up to the reader to make up their own minds.

In terms of literary sources (by which I mean continuous historical accounts written in antiquity, though sometimes hundreds of years after the period with which we are dealing), the invention of the phalanx falls sometime shortly after the conclusion of Xenophon's *Hellenica*, the last of the three major literary histories of ancient Greece by near-contemporary authors, that is Herodotus (the 'father of history'), Thucydides and Xenophon. For the next few decades we are dependent on the *Library of History* of Diodorus Siculus ('the Sicilian'), who, writing in the first century, compiled a history of the Greek and Roman world up to his time, which has survived in extensive fragments. Diodorus comes across as rather prone to filling in his battle accounts with cliched scenes, but, as the title of his work suggests, he used a variety of earlier books as his sources, and where these sources were eyewitness accounts, now themselves lost, their preservation in Diodorus is invaluable.

One of the best known users of the Macedonian phalanx was of course Alexander the Great, and for his reign we have a relative multiplicity of sources. As well as Diodorus' account, we have that of the Roman historian Quintus Curtius Rufus; both derive their work from Greek sources generally rather hostile to Alexander, and together making up what is now known as the 'Vulgate' tradition. In contrast, the *Anabasis of Alexander* by the Roman governor and historian Arrian, writing in the second century AD, made use of the contemporary histories of Alexander written by two of his generals, Ptolemy and Aristobolus. Much more sympathetic to Alexander, these accounts also preserve much useful military detail, meaning that, although Arrian was writing hundreds of years later, his work is of the greatest value for understanding Alexander's army. Alexander is also one of the many historical figures from this period included in the *Parallel Lives* of Plutarch, a Greek historian of the late first and early second century AD, who wrote potted biographies of notable figures from Greek and Roman history. Plutarch showed no great interest in military matters and his biographies were intended to entertain as much as to inform, but for some periods he is pretty much all we have.

After Alexander, for parts of the next two decades we have the account of Diodorus, who based this part of his history on the very well regarded, but now lost, history of Hieronymus of Cardia, an eyewitness to and participant in the Wars of the Successors, in which armies based around the Macedonian phalanx fought each other for control of Alexander's empire. But from the end of the fourth century we enter a period of relative darkness, with no surviving historical account until, in the last quarter of the third century, the great *History* of Polybius begins. Polybius was a Greek statesman of the second century, and thus an eyewitness to the time of the defeat of the Macedonian phalanx by the legions of Rome, and a major purpose of his account was to explain to his Greek readers how the Romans came to dominate their world. As such, Polybius includes essential detail on the phalanx, and his thoughts on the subject will be encountered frequently in this book. Alongside Polybius we have the Latin work *From the Foundation of the City* by Titus Livius ('Livy'), which, as the name suggests, covered the entire history of Rome up to his time (late first century). Livy does not have a great reputation as a historian of military matters, but he preserves useful earlier sources, including Polybius, so that in some cases where the account of Polybius is lost, the gaps can be filled in from Livy. Following the end of Polybius' account, though, we are again rather in the dark, relying on Livy and Plutarch for accounts of matters involving Rome. There are a few other literary historians who preserve scraps of information about the phalanx, whom we will encounter in the following pages – in particular, authors of the Roman period (Frontinus and Polyaenus being the surviving examples) made collections of 'stratagems', clever ploys and tricks for use by generals, by trawling through earlier historical accounts, and often some useful fragments are preserved amongst these.

Alongside the literary histories, there is another and rather unique source of written evidence, in the form of the various tactical manuals, or *Tactica* (in Latin sometimes *Ars Tactica*, in Greek *Techne Taktike*). In the period of the existence of the Macedonian phalanx, written accounts of how to equip, organize and drill an army began to be composed – and as might be expected, these provide a rich and invaluable source of information on the subject. Detailed tactical information on military matters of this sort is exceptionally rare in any period of history before the modern era (for the Roman legions, for example, we are reduced to piecing together scraps of information from other sources). Unfortunately the earliest of these *Tactica* that has survived, that of Asclepiodotus, was written at a time (in the first century) when the phalanx was no longer widely used, and the subject had become one of chiefly academic interest (as it is now), a matter (perhaps) for philosophers not generals. Asclepiodotus' work is accordingly rather looked down on now, along with those of two later Roman authors, Arrian (the same as the historian of Alexander) and Aelian, who wrote very similar accounts (perhaps derived from a common source). But while the *Tactica* can tend to the pedantic, I believe they preserve accurate and essential information on the use of the phalanx, and we will be hearing much more from them in the following pages.

So much for the literary sources. Other written evidence is available in the form of the numerous official inscriptions and, in the case of the Ptolemaic kingdom in Egypt, exceedingly numerous and often unofficial papyri which have survived. Naturally, such sources are more useful for some sorts of information than for others, and their survival can be patchy and random. Military matters, battle accounts and drill are not well recorded in them, but they do give us names and ranks and essential information about internal organization and recruitment in the Hellenistic kingdoms. Such scraps can supplement what we can glean from the literary accounts.

Aside from such written accounts, archaeology offers another source of information on the phalanx. Broadly speaking, there are two types of evidence available: firstly, actual pieces of equipment used by the phalanx, such as shields, spears and swords; and secondly, depictions in art of men bearing such equipment. Both types of evidence are reasonably plentiful, especially due to the phenomenon of the 'Macedonian tomb' – from around the fourth to the second centuries, notable Macedonians were buried in richly decorated barrel-vaulted tombs, several of which have been excavated; some contain actual pieces of equipment, buried with their owner, and most contain rich wall paintings, often of the deceased in military garb. In addition, there are (small) depictions on coins and tombstones and other types of material evidence which will come into play in the following chapters.

All this evidence cumulatively allows us to piece together a fairly detailed picture of the Macedonian phalanx, though there remain many points of obscurity and dispute. In the pages that follow I will aim to set out the evidence as it is known to us and to discuss the various interpretations.

For translations, I have usually used the Loeb edition translations where they are available, sometimes slightly modified to make the translation more literal or to render a technical term more accurately (translators can be rather loose in their use of military terminology, especially weapon names). For Polybius, I have used both the Loeb (Paton) and Shuckburgh translations, preferring whichever seems more literal.

Because not all readers will be familiar with either ancient Greek or Greek characters, I also transliterate some of the most important words and phrases into Latin script. So far as proper names are concerned, I generally use the Anglicized form where one exists (such as Philip and Alexander for Philippos and Alexandros), or the Latinized where a Latin form is widely used or familiar (for example Coenus and Asclepiodotus for Koinos and Asklepiodotos); for lesser known names (such as Andromachos or Menedemos), I give a direct transliteration. I cannot claim total consistency in this, using the form of the name that seems most convenient (to me). Technical terms (such as unit and weapon names) I have transliterated (and rendered in italics at least on first appearance), except where noted.

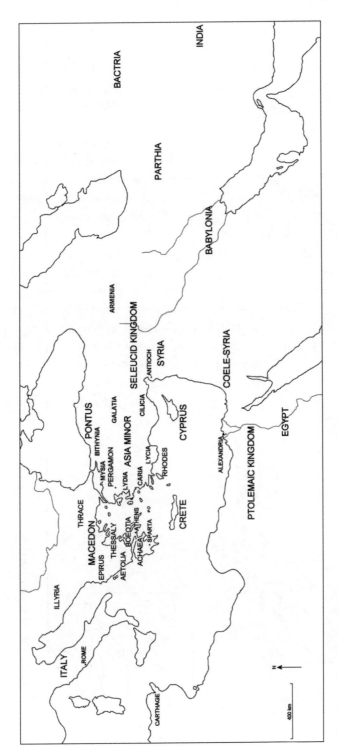

Fig. 1.1. General map.

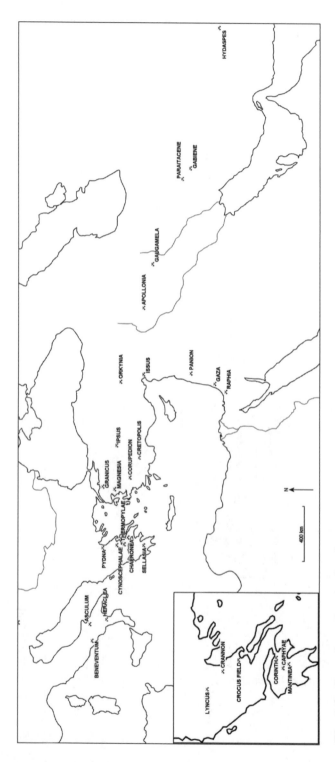

Fig. 1.2. Location of major battles.

Chapter 1

Origins

The story of how Philip II established the small kingdom of Macedon as the dominant power in Greece, and of how his even more famous son Alexander III ('the Great') conquered the whole of the Achaemenid Persian Empire and beyond, is well known. Alexander's conquests ushered in a period of three centuries (the Hellenistic Age) in which Greco-Macedonian kingdoms were established throughout the Near and Middle East, from the Mediterranean to the borders of India, initiating a unique flourishing of Greek culture (albeit sometimes viewed as inferior to the earlier glories of the Classical period that preceded it) that lasted until overwhelmed by the rising power of Rome. Central to Philip's rise to power, to Alexander's spectacular conquests and to the dominance of vast areas by the kings who followed them was the Macedonian army (or in the case of the new kingdoms, armies created following the Macedonian model); and central to the success of the Macedonian army was the Macedonian phalanx, that is to say, the heavy infantry of the Macedonian and Hellenistic kingdoms. Before the Roman legions rose to prominence as the dominant heavy infantry force of the ancient world, the Macedonian phalanx occupied a comparable place of honour, and it was the defeat of the phalanx at the hands of the legions that brought about the final decline and subjugation of the Greek-speaking world – and with it the end of the political and cultural dominance of Greece.

This book is an attempt to provide a comprehensive, if at times necessarily high-level, analysis of the rise, dominance and decline of the Macedonian phalanx, to describe what the phalanx was and how it functioned, examine why it was so spectacularly successful and discover why in the end it fell before the might of Rome.

Definition of terms

Before considering the origins of the Macedonian phalanx, we should be clear about terminology, starting with the phrase 'Macedonian phalanx' itself. What exactly is meant by this?

Firstly, 'Macedonian'. This means, simply enough, from Macedon or Macedonia. The ancient Greek name was Macedonia (Μακεδονία) – in English, the forms Macedon and Macedonia are both used, largely interchangeably, though sometimes Macedon is used for the kingdom and Macedonia for the geographical area. In this book I will use the form Macedon, to make clear that it is the ancient kingdom being referred to, not the modern country (the former Yugoslav republic, as of the time of writing called 'North Macedonia', which lies somewhat to the north of ancient Macedon), nor the region of northern Greece, which more closely matches the boundaries of the ancient kingdom. This being a work of ancient history, it is to be understood that the name Macedon in this book refers always to the ancient kingdom, and I do not have anything to say about the controversies surrounding the modern uses of the name.[1]

Macedon lay on the coastal plains between Thessaly to the south (with Mount Olympus on the border) and Thrace to the east, and extended (to a greater or lesser extent, depending on the current political strength of the kingdom) into the mountainous inland regions running north and west from the coast. The Macedonians had much in common ethnically and culturally with their neighbours to the south in the rest of Greece. Exactly how much they had in common was a matter of some dispute at the time; it seems that Macedonians generally considered themselves to be part of the wider Greek world, though lower-class Macedonians (the serfs and peasants who made up the bulk of the population) may have been more different culturally. There was perhaps a distinct Macedonian language, or maybe a very strong dialect of Greek, at any rate different enough to be largely incomprehensible to southern Greek speakers.[2]

At this period, of course, the notion of 'Greekness' was rather different from what we are used to today in the era of nation states. The Greek world was divided into numerous small, competing political units – in southern Greece particularly, the familiar city-states (such as Athens and Sparta), with larger leagues or confederacies often centred around a powerful city (such as the Boeotian League, headed by Thebes). A Greek citizen's first loyalty was to his home state (usually his city) rather than to any wider Greek 'nation'. Greeks did see themselves as different from (and largely superior to) non-Greek-speaking outsiders ('barbarians' – a term indicating foreign-sounding language rather than savagery), and faced with an outside threat – such as the Persian invasions of the early fifth century – Greeks could unite and form common cause against the enemy, though there were probably nearly as many Greek speakers (including the Macedonians) who joined the Persians as fought against them.

But the notion of any unified Greek nation was wholly alien at the time, and the cities, leagues and kingdoms were as much defined by their differences as by their shared 'Greekness'. In the course of the fourth century, a greater sense of pan-Hellenism was starting to develop, but this was in continued opposition to the outside enemy (Persia) rather than due to any great desire for political unity.[3]

In the context of this divided Greek world, the Macedonians were on one level just another Greek state; though, somewhat unusually, a monarchy spread over a relatively wide geographical area rather than a democratic or oligarchic city state. But the southern Greeks had traditionally seen the Macedonians as being rather backward and uncultured – not least in retaining their monarchical traditions – and being to a greater or lesser extent outsiders. This was a view that some upper-class Macedonians, and in particular many of the kings, fought to correct by enthusiastically embracing and promoting southern Greek culture, though it is doubtful just how far down the social ladder this penetrated. Even among the aristocracy there was a great attachment to a traditional way of life, centred around fighting, hunting, heavy drinking and sexual licence (at least as described by censorious southern Greeks), partly inspired (ironically enough) by identification with the heroic values to be found in the great Greek epic and origin myth, Homer's *Iliad*. The Macedonians' relationship to the Greeks of the south is perhaps analogous to the historical relationship between Scotland and England. On the one hand, the two are ethnically and culturally closely related, with a common language and culture, and, to a varying degree, joined by a shared sense of Britishness (at least since the union of the two kingdoms). On the other, English and Scots remain distinct, proud of their different heritage, and retain a sense of political and cultural difference. In Scotland as in Macedon, there was also a distinction between the upper social levels (and Lowlanders), who more fully adopted English/British culture, and the lower classes (and Highlanders), who retained a greater cultural difference and their own distinct language, and were sometimes viewed as being somewhat backward by English and Lowland Scots alike. Macedon too had its Highlanders – who may have formed the core of its phalanx as we shall see – possibly with their own language, and Macedon retained its own traditions, even as it adopted Greek literature and philosophy and led a pan-Hellenic campaign against the 'barbarian' enemy. In the course of this book I will sometimes use 'Macedonian' in opposition to 'Greek', to distinguish between the Macedonians and the Greeks of the southern mainland and islands. This should not be taken to imply that the Macedonians were not themselves also Greek, but reflects genuine differences in traditions, self-image and status which were clearly important at the time.

Next, the phalanx. 'Phalanx' was a Greek word of uncertain etymology (it may originally have meant 'log' or 'roller'), which had for some centuries been used to describe a close-order formation of heavy infantry (that is, infantry with shields and armour who fight hand-to-hand rather than with missiles), formed up several (typically eight) ranks deep and in a solid more-or-less continuous block, hundreds of men wide. The origins of the phalanx – the formation and the word – are uncertain and the subject of much debate. Homer, the first great writer of Greek literature, author of the *Iliad* and *Odyssey* (I am assuming for the sake of simplicity that there was a single author, rather than a more dispersed oral tradition), who held a place in Greek literature similar to that occupied by the *Bible* and Shakespeare in English, used the word 'phalanx' (in the singular) in his accounts of combat before the walls of Troy only once, though he did use the plural, *phalanges*, a number of times to refer to bodies of men. Indeed, combat in his day (or in the day to which his writings referred back) seems to have involved looser, more open-order formations of infantry (although as we will see, the later Greeks did not see it this way). At some point between the eighth century BC (when Homer may have been writing) and the fifth century (the time of the Persian Wars), social, political and (to some extent) technological changes in Greece caused the decline of the chariot-borne warrior backed up by more or less disorganized bands of warriors on foot, as described by Homer, and the rise of the phalanx, a unified body of close-order heavy infantry, who formed up together, stood together and fought together, the embodied, armed citizenry of their home state. There are disagreements among scholars about the date at which these changes happened and their causes, but whatever the details, the overall picture is clearly established that by the end of the fifth century – when the two victors in the war against Persia, Athens and Sparta, fought a costly and disastrous war against each other – Greek infantry of the major (city-) states were heavily armed infantry – *hoplitai* in Greek, known in English as 'hoplites'. They had large shields (typically a metre across), lesser or greater amounts of bronze armour (at the least, a bronze helmet, though body armour and greaves/leg guards were also often worn) and wielded a spear, around two metres long, in one hand. Infantry armed this way were too ponderous to move rapidly or to cross rough terrain with ease, and could be vulnerable to missile-armed opponents able to shoot from a distance and retire, or to take cover in rough ground. But formed up shoulder to shoulder (or shield to shield), in large formations many ranks deep, such infantry could defeat any opponent, Greek or non-Greek, in pitched battle on the open field. Experience in the Persian Wars, when at the start of the fifth century the Persian kings

Darius I and Xerxes attempted to subjugate the Greek mainland, had shown that Greek hoplites formed up in a phalanx were masters of the battlefield. With success came demand; Persian kings did not repeat their attempt to conquer Greece, but hired large numbers of Greek mercenary hoplites for their civil wars and, in due course, to oppose the pan-Hellenic invasion under Alexander the Great, while hoplite phalanx armies contested all the major battles of the fifth and fourth centuries in which the Greek city-states fought, ultimately fruitlessly, for domination.[4]

It is important to keep in mind, though, that 'phalanx' was not (just) a technical term for this particular formation. Ancient Greek tended to be more free and easy with technical terminology than we might like, and to use the same word for different (if similar) things, rather than devising new words for new phenomena. Thus 'phalanx' could be used for any infantry formation, not just one made up of hoplites or equivalent close-order heavy infantry, and could be used to mean just 'line of battle' (sometimes as opposed to cavalry or light skirmisher forces outside of the main line). The Macedonian phalanx was a special variant of the earlier hoplite formation, but it could also mean just the Macedonian line of battle, and not every time the word is found in our sources does it carry a particular technical meaning. For the purposes of this book, unless stated otherwise, 'phalanx' means specifically the close-order heavy infantry formation.[5]

So a phalanx is a heavy infantry formation of multiple ranks, and the Macedonian phalanx is the type of phalanx particularly associated with and used by the Macedonians. As we will see in the following chapters, there are a number of special features of the Macedonian phalanx (not all of which, in my view, are actually real). While discussion of the details of each of these features will be the subject of the rest of this book, it is worth setting out here what may be taken as the orthodox modern view of the nature of the Macedonian phalanx, and what made it different from the Greek phalanx (or phalanxes) that preceded it. So, the Macedonian phalanx is distinctive for:

- being particularly close order and/or 'heavy' (the meaning of this word in this context will be considered later); the Greek phalanx presumably used a more open order in comparison, and/or was less 'heavy'.
- using a longer spear than the Greek hoplite, long enough that it needed to be held in both hands rather than wielded one-handed. The length of this spear varied (and is subject to some uncertainty and much debate), and was called by the Macedonians a *sarisa* or *sarissa* (the single 's' is the more usual Greek spelling, but in English it is usually written with

two, and as this is an Anglicized version of the word, I will use the plural sarissas).

- using a smaller shield than the Greek hoplite's shield, necessitated by the two-handed grip of the spear (and perhaps by the close-order formation). This shield was (it is usually argued) called a *pelte* (or *pelta*, there being two dialect variants of the word), a term which in Greek was applied to any small or light shield, as opposed to *aspis*, which is the normal Greek word for the large shields carried by classical hoplites.

- possessing a particularly high standard of drill, necessitated by and enabling the close order and use of the cumbersome long sarissa. Greek hoplites, in contrast, were (with some exceptions, notably the Spartans) generally undrilled citizen militias called up only for short campaigns, and neither professional nor highly trained.

- being rendered, by virtue of the close-order of the formation and long spear, particularly ponderous on the battlefield, unable to manoeuvre effectively and liable to fall into disorder on difficult terrain. Greek phalanxes also performed badly on rough ground, but this feature is thought to be taken to an extreme by the Macedonian phalanx.

I will be examining – and in some cases questioning – this view of the Macedonian phalanx in the following chapters. But this overall picture of a unique Macedonian phalanx, distinct from the hoplite phalanx that preceded it, seems clear enough. This phalanx was sometimes called by ancient historians 'the Macedonian phalanx' or, more frequently, the phrase 'armed in the Macedonian fashion' was used – it being understood in both cases that this implied a particular formation, tactic and method of arming that was consistent across the whole of the period under consideration, from the invention of the Macedonian phalanx in the fourth century until its demise during the second and first centuries (the extent to which it is true that the nature of the phalanx was consistent across this period will be one of the issues examined in this chapter and the next). The men making up the Macedonian phalanx tend, in modern parlance, to be called 'phalangites', and this term does have a basis in ancient Greek, as they are sometimes called *phalangitai*. Among modern authors, 'phalangite' is often used in distinction to 'hoplite', the earlier large shield and short spear-wielding infantry of the Greek city states. This distinction of terms is not found in ancient authors, as the members of the Macedonian phalanx were often also called *hoplitai* (the word being simply the general Greek term for heavy infantry, literally 'armed men' or 'men-at-arms'), as well as a selection of other terms including 'peltasts', that is 'small–shield–carriers' (*peltastai*) and 'sarissa-carriers' (*sarisophoroi*). In this book I will generally use 'phalangites' to refer to the members of the Macedonian phalanx, those armed in the Macedonian fashion, and 'hoplites' to refer to Greek infantry armed in the traditional manner, but it should be borne in mind that these terms do not necessarily accurately reflect their ancient Greek usage.

Historical background

The history of the Macedonian phalanx is in many ways also the history of Macedonian imperialism and of the Hellenistic world which Macedonian expansion created. This book looks at the phalanx thematically, so it will be useful to have in mind an overview of the history of the period to understand how the story of the phalanx fits into the history of the age. Those who are already familiar with the historical background may wish to skip this section.

The Macedonian phalanx was created in the kingdom of Macedon, by the Macedonian king Philip II. Philip came to the throne of Macedon in 359, at a time when the Greek city-states were still vying for supremacy and none, despite the defeat of Athens by Sparta in the Peloponnesian War at the end of the fifth century, was predominant. The Persian Empire, which had invaded Greece at the start of the fifth century, made no attempt to invade again, but maintained an interest in Greek affairs, frequently intervening financially and diplomatically to further its own interests. Macedon, meanwhile, was, as usual in its history up to this point, struggling against its inherent weaknesses – an underdeveloped economy, rural society, hostile and aggressive neighbours, a powerful and unruly aristocracy and a royal family beset by disputed accessions and assassinations.

Philip II's prospects looked bleak at the start of his reign, but in a remarkable period of twenty-four years he turned around his own and his kingdom's fortunes. The hostile neighbouring tribes were first bought off, then defeated, Macedonian territory was extended, the economy was transformed (not least by the fortuitous discovery of rich silver mines) and the process of moving from a predominantly rural to a more urban society was set in hand with the foundation of new cities. Economic and social development made possible the transformation of the Macedonian army, with the phalanx at its heart. This greatly improved army allowed Philip first to defend the kingdom from its hostile neighbours, then to end southern Greek interference in Macedonian affairs, and finally, by defeating two of the most powerful city-states, Athens and Thebes, at the Battle of Chaeronea (338), to achieve what none of the Greek city-states had been able to, establishing himself in a pre-eminent position in Greece at the head of the League of Corinth, organized with a view to invading the Persian Empire itself.

At the peak of his success, Philip fell victim to the enduring Macedonian curse of assassination (in 336), and it was left to his son Alexander ('the Great') to bring his plans to fulfilment. Using the firm foundation and outstanding army Philip had created, Alexander launched the planned invasion of Persia. First defeating a local Persian army in Asia Minor at the Battle of the Granicus (334), Alexander marched on into Asia, defeating a Persian royal army under King Darius III at the Battle of Issus (333), subduing the coastal cities and making himself Pharaoh of Egypt. Marching into the heart of the empire, Alexander defeated Darius again at the Battle of Gaugamela (331) and thus became ruler of the Persian Empire. Not satisfied with these successes, Alexander pressed on through modern Iran, Afghanistan and Pakistan, defeated an Indian king at the Battle of the Hydaspes (326) and was turned back only when his army, exhausted by years of non-stop campaigning, refused to go on any further. Alexander returned to Babylon, where he died (of fever probably, but possibly assassinated) aged 33, without an heir.

The Macedonian army thus found itself in the heart of a newly conquered empire, with no clear successor to the throne, and commanded by a group of highly capable and profoundly ambitious generals who were suddenly at liberty to carve out their own kingdoms. The following twenty-five years or so were occupied by the wars of the so-called Successors, in what was in effect a vast and sprawling Macedonian civil war, as the generals sought either to establish themselves as successor to Alexander or to find some portion of the empire they could rule. At the same time, some Greek cities, notably Athens in the Lamian War, attempted unsuccessfully to throw off Macedonian domination. Numerous battles were fought across Asia – notably Paraitacene (317), Gabene (316), Gaza (312) and Ipsus (301) – with these all contested between the most ambitious of the Successors, Antigonus Monophthalmus ('One-Eyed') and his son Demetrius Poliorcetes ('The Besieger') and a coalition of generals opposed to them. At Ipsus, Antigonus was finally defeated and killed, and from the endless wars emerged three more or less stable kingdoms. In Macedon, Demetrius' son Antigonus Gonatas made himself king after defeating a devastating Gallic invasion from the north which had overrun Macedon and much of Greece, and founded the Antigonid dynasty. In Asia, the Seleucid kingdom founded by the general Seleucus was centred on Syria, and included at one time or another most of Asia Minor and much of the territory in Asia of the old Persian Empire. Meanwhile in Egypt, Ptolemy founded a kingdom based around the ancient Pharaonic kingdom, centred on the most famous and long-lasting of Alexander the Great's many city foundations, Alexandria-in-Egypt.

While the history of Alexander and the Successors is one of interminable warfare, behind the scenes the processes of urbanization and social and economic development started by Philip in Macedon were continued on a vastly greater scale in the conquered territories. Alexander founded numerous cities throughout his new empire, and under the Successors and the new kingdoms, these cities multiplied and expanded as a wave of emigration from Macedon and Greece allowed the Seleucid and Ptolemaic kings, in particular, to establish a Greco-Macedonian urban population to secure their rule over their new territories. Along with this expansion came a new flowering of Greek culture, creating what is now known as the Hellenistic Age.

These three major kingdoms co-existed in a state of hostile rivalry for the next century, a period that is largely obscure due to the paucity of literary historical sources, though notable was a further attempt by Athens and other Greek cities to end the Macedonian dominance of Greece in the Chremonidean War. The late third century sees the return of detailed accounts of events with the writings of Polybius. At this time, the Seleucid and Ptolemaic kingdoms were, as usual, engaged in hostilities over control of the territories of the Mediterranean seaboard; defeat of the Seleucid king Antiochus III at the Battle of Raphia (217) led him to turn east instead, and to campaign with some success to re-establish firm control over the eastern territories he nominally ruled. Meanwhile in Macedon, the Antigonid king Antigonus Doson was, again as usual, trying to maintain Macedonian influence over the still-independent and still-squabbling city-states of Greece, defeat of the Spartans at the Battle of Sellasia (222) marking a short-lived highpoint for Macedonian endeavours in this regard.

Meanwhile, in the West was emerging a new threat that would eventually put an end to the Hellenistic Age. Greek armies had already encountered Rome in the early third century when Pyrrhus, King of Epirus (the home of Alexander the Great's mother Olympias), tried to intervene in Italian affairs in favour of the southern Italian Greek colonies, which were alarmed by the rising power of Rome. Pyrrhus won a succession of increasingly costly ('Pyrrhic') victories over Roman armies before losing heart and returning home. Rome then was preoccupied for several decades with a colossal fight to the death, known as the Punic Wars, with its North African rival Carthage. Carthage looked to be on top when its greatest general, Hannibal, led an army (including, memorably, a force of elephants) across the Alps into Italy and won a succession of battles, but the Romans did not know when they were beaten, fought on and eventually defeated Hannibal and Carthage at the Battle of Zama (202) in Africa.

The Antigonid Macedonian king Philip V had unwisely taken an interest in this conflict, backing Hannibal when he looked to be on top. With Carthage defeated, Rome set out on a new quest to ensure that no other rival power existed which could, even in theory, pose the sort of threat that Carthage had. Macedon came first, and a Roman army, using Greek league and city rivalries as a pretext, invaded Greece and inflicted a devastating defeat on Philip's army at the Battle of Cynoscephalae (197), establishing a pattern that was to be repeated several times over the next century and a half. Antiochus III, returned from his successes in the East and looking to take advantage of Macedon's defeat, marched into Greece, to be summarily ejected following defeat by a Roman army at Thermopylae (191) – at the site of the famous last stand of the 300 Spartans against Persia three centuries earlier – and then being defeated again in Asia Minor at the Battle of Magnesia (190). The resultant peace settlement restricted the Seleucid kingdom to its Syrian heartland, and it began a long decline as the familiar pattern of disputed succession, assassination and civil war bled the kingdom of its strength.

In Asia Minor, some of the traditionally independent city-states themselves grew, briefly, to major power status, with Rhodes and Pergamon in particular flourishing – the latter under the Attalid line of kings – but their power and independence was possible only with Rome's indulgence. Rome preferred not to allow any potential rival power to exist, so in turn they were absorbed into Roman control. Macedon, under Philip V's son Perseus, attempted once more to assert itself, but another crushing defeat at the hands of the Roman legions at the Battle of Pydna (168) finally put an end to the Macedonian kingdom. Greece remained nominally independent, but a last attempt by the city-states to throw off Roman control ended in failure, the sack of Corinth (146) and the absorption of Greece into direct Roman control.

The Seleucid and Ptolemaic kingdoms struggled on into the first century, along with a new power, the Persian-Hellenistic kingdom of Pontus in northern Asia Minor under its king Mithridates VI. Pontus had a remarkable late surge of activity, taking advantage of discontent with Roman rule to, like Antiochus, launch an invasion of Greece, and like Antiochus, suffer a succession of defeats to Roman armies, most importantly at a second Battle of Chaeronea (86). The Seleucid kingdom, squeezed between Roman expansion and resurgent native populations, particularly the Parthians in the Persian heartland, did not last much longer, and finally Ptolemaic Egypt, under its most famous queen, Cleopatra VII, backed the wrong side in the Roman civil wars as rival Roman generals fought to establish their own power at the expense of the ailing Republic. Ptolemaic defeat to the future Emperor Augustus, in the naval Battle of Actium (31), spelled the end of an independent Egypt, and so the final end of the Hellenistic Age. A Macedonian phalanx (or a phalanx armed in the Macedonian fashion) had fought in every war and every major battle of the previous three centuries, and had underpinned Greco-Macedonian rule over Greece, the Near East and much of ancient Asia. But Roman arms were now triumphant, and Roman legions would now be the dominant military force from Britain to Syria. No Macedonian phalanx ever went to war again, though this was not quite the end of the story.

Creation of the phalanx

We have, courtesy of Diodorus, an account of the origin of the Macedonian phalanx. First, some context. Diodorus is describing events of the first year of the reign of Philip II (359–358). Macedon was in a period of crisis, having suffered a costly defeat at the hands of the neighbouring Illyrians, when Philip came to the throne. Philip himself was only 24 years old at the time of his accession, the youngest of three sons of a previous Macedonian king, Amyntas, and would never have expected to become king at all. Macedon was long subject to crises with invasions by neighbouring peoples – chiefly Thracians, Illyrians and Triballians – combined with chronic internal weakness, a lack of military development and political instability as monarchs fought against neighbouring tribes and claimants to their throne from other branches of the royal family or members of the great aristocratic families, and against interference by southern Greek states, particularly Athens (which envied the plentiful timber resources of the kingdom). Philip's brother, Perdiccas, had been a more successful ruler than some, and seems to have increased the size, if not necessarily the quality, of the army – though this may have been his downfall in the end, as it encouraged him to risk a battle against the Illyrian invaders, in which the king himself was killed along with a large proportion of the Macedonian army. Emboldened by the defeat, Macedon's other enemies were quick to take advantage, and invasions, rival claimants and foreign intervention were all waiting in the wings. It was at this point, with the fortunes of the kingdom at a low ebb, that Philip came to the throne. According to Diodorus' account:

'The Macedonians because of the disaster sustained in the battle and the magnitude of the dangers pressing upon them were in the greatest perplexity. Yet even so, with such fears and dangers threatening them, Philip was not panic-stricken by the magnitude of the expected perils, but, bringing together the Macedonians in a series of assemblies and exhorting them with eloquent speeches to be men, he built up their morale, and, having improved the organization of his forces and equipped the men suitably with weapons of war, he held constant manoeuvres of the men under arms and competitive drills. Indeed he devised the compact order and the equipment of the phalanx, imitating the "locked shields" of the warriors at Troy, and was the first to organize the Macedonian phalanx.' (Diodorus 16.3.1–2)

In this passage are a number of key themes that we will be returning to often in the course of this book. First of all, we see how this ostensibly military reform had a large political element to it – the Macedonians were brought together in numerous assemblies, which gave Philip a chance to present himself to them as their king and to inspire them with speeches and to achieve, to use a modern expression, their buy-in to his political and military projects. Then he improved both the organization and the equipment of his forces, the two being closely related. He trained the men in the use of their new equipment and the drills required to employ it effectively, which included fostering a spirit of competitiveness. Finally, in specifics of the form that this reorganization took, he introduced a compact formation, inspired by Homeric precedent. We will be returning to all of these elements in future chapters, but for now I will concentrate on the technical and tactical aspects of this reorganization.[6]

Philip II was not, however, the first Macedonian king to attempt to reform the Macedonian army. At the time of Xerxes' invasion of Greece (480), Macedon was a minor military power, and while it seems that there was a capable force of cavalry, the infantry were not well regarded. During the course of the fifth century (and indeed well into the fourth), Macedon was subject to repeated invasions from its barbarian neighbours to the north-west and north-east, and lacking a disciplined infantry, was ill-equipped to withstand these invasions. It is not clear exactly how Macedonian infantry of this period fought and was equipped. It is generally assumed that the mass of Macedonian infantry, such as it was, fought in a traditional fashion (similar, it is assumed, to the Thracians and Illyrians), using more or less open-order or irregular formations and equipped with javelins or perhaps spears, and that the purpose of the various attempts at reform was to create a force of native Macedonian heavy infantry in the same style as the Greek city-states to the south – that is, hoplites equipped with armour, large shields and spears, who would fight in a close-order phalanx. It has to be said that although this assumption is reasonable, there is little direct evidence for it, and it is never clearly stated that the purpose of any reform was to create such a force of hoplites (nor indeed is it ever made explicit that Macedon did not already have hoplites of its own).[7]

Thucydides describes the initial weakness of the Macedonians in the context of a massive Thracian invasion of Macedon in 429, during the Peloponnesian War, and also looks forward to an early set of reforms:

> 'These Macedonians, unable to take the field against so numerous an invader, shut themselves up in such strong places and fortresses as the country possessed. Of these there was no great number, most of those now found in the country having been erected subsequently by Archelaus, the son of Perdiccas [the king at the time of this invasion], on his accession, who also cut straight roads, and otherwise put the kingdom on a better footing as regards horses, arms, and other war material than had been done by all the eight kings that preceded him.' (Thucydides 2.100.1–2)

So this first 'reform' (or more accurately, set of improvements) was only very tangentially to do with the infantry – the rather enigmatic reference to 'arms [hopla] and other war material' can cover many things, though hopla at least is often used to refer to the equipment of heavy infantry (hence, hoplites). At the time of this Thracian invasion (before Archelaus' reforms), the Macedonian infantry were still reckoned inadequate, as Thucydides 2.100.5 describes the cavalry alone attacking the Thracians while the infantry stayed out of harm's way ('The Macedonians never even thought of meeting him [the Thracian king] with infantry'). One thing Thucydides' text does suggest, however, is that arms were manufactured and stockpiled centrally, by the king, rather than being provided by the men themselves, as was usual in Greek armies. There do seem to have been some Macedonian heavy infantry of some sort. Thucydides describes an intervention by the Spartan Brasidas in a Macedonian civil war against the claimant Arrhabaeus, whose forces included 'the forces of his Macedonian subjects, and a corps of hoplites composed of Hellenes domiciled in the country', but in the ensuing battle there was also a force of 'Lyncestian hoplites' (Thuc 4.124.1–3, Lyncestis being one of the Macedonian regions), so it seems that Greeks were not the only hoplites available, although the Lyncestians were rapidly defeated, so again quality was the problem.[8]

Details of the later state of the Macedonian infantry are almost wholly lacking, but we do find that Philip's immediate predecessor, his brother Perdiccas, dared to meet an Illyrian invasion on the field of battle with what must presumably have been a large – but evidently still qualitatively inadequate – force of infantry. In the defeat that followed, 4,000 Macedonians were killed, including the king himself (we do not know what proportion of these losses were from the infantry or the cavalry, but given the scale of the losses, and cavalry's greater ability to get away from a lost battle, it is quite likely that many were infantry). It was in these circumstances that Philip II came to the throne and set about his own – ultimately highly successful – attempt to create a strong Macedonian infantry force, as described by Diodorus.

But this is not the whole of the story. A fragment from a contemporary historian of Philip II's reign is preserved in a later (though still ancient) lexicon, which suggests that an Alexander may have been the creator of the phalanx, rather than Philip:

> 'Anaximenes, in the first book of the *Phillippika*, speaking about Alexander, states: "Next, after he accustomed those of the highest honour to ride on horseback [or 'to serve as cavalry'], he called them Companions [*hetairoi*], and after he had divided the majority of the infantry into companies [*lochoi*] and files [*dekads*] and other commands, he named them Foot Companions [*pezhetairoi*], so that each of the two classes, by participating in the royal companionship, might continue to be very loyal.' (Harpocration *Lexicon* s.v. *pezhetairoi*: Anaximenes, *FrGrHist* 72 F 4)

Now, under Alexander the Great, at least some of the infantry of the phalanx were called the Foot Companions (*pezhetairoi*), as we will see below. This has led some scholars to identify the creation of the Foot Companions with the creation of the Macedonian phalanx, and as this is said to have happened under 'Alexander', to doubt the role of Philip as father of the phalanx.

Unfortunately our source does not specify which Alexander is meant. The Greeks did not follow the modern practice of using regnal numbers – which make Alexander the Great, for example, Alexander III in modern parlance – and only sometimes narrowed down the candidates in the usual way, by giving the patronymic, by which reckoning Alexander III is Alexander Philippou, Alexander son of Philip. So in this case, with three King Alexanders to choose from in the fifth–fourth centuries BC, it is unclear which one is supposed to be the originator of this reform. Much effort has been expended on deciding between the competing Alexanders. Alexander I (ruled *c.* 498–454) is one possible candidate, but this would mean an effective Macedonian infantry force would have been created in the early fifth century, long before such a force appears in any of the historical accounts of the period, and long before the other reforms recounted above. Some of the same problems apply to identifying the reformer as Alexander II (ruled 371–369), and in addition this king ruled for less than two years, which seems too short a time to implement any wide-ranging and successful army reforms. This would leave Alexander III (the Great), but in this case the problems are that Alexander's rule is very well documented and there is no other mention of such reforms, that Philip had already been ruling and campaigning successfully for twenty-four years with a presumably reformed and effective army, and (most importantly) that the Foot Companions are already recorded as existing under Philip, in a speech by the great Athenian orator (and arch enemy of Philip), Demosthenes:

'As for his household forces and Foot Companions, they have indeed the name of admirable soldiers, well grounded in the science of war.' (Demosthenes, *Olynthiac* 2.17)

But these arguments may be misguided anyway, since there is no reason to equate the Foot Companions with the Macedonian phalanx in this way. It is certainly the case that the Foot Companions under Alexander are part of the phalanx (and equipped in the Macedonian fashion), but the name 'Foot Companions' could perfectly well have been applied in some earlier period to some other body of infantry, equipped and fighting in some different way (perhaps as hoplites). So Alexander I might have first organized the cavalry and infantry Companions, but it would still have been Philip who first organized and equipped them as a Macedonian phalanx.[9]

Furthermore, the passage of Anaximenes is very hard to take at face value anyway. It states that 'he accustomed those of the highest honour to ride on horseback', as if the Macedonian aristocracy would not already, by practice and inclination as noblemen in good horse-breeding country, have been horsemen and cavalry. The division of 'the majority of the infantry into companies [*lochoi*] and files [*dekads*] and other commands' sounds more plausible, except that, as we will see below, it is the creation of formal organization and units in this way that is central to the creation of an effective phalanx, so the problems of identifying this with either Alexander I or II, and the absence of any effective Macedonian infantry in the historical record, remain. Attempts to identify the Alexander in question as 'the Great', on the assumption that it was Alexander the Great who renamed the existing phalanx as Foot Companions (extending the title from an earlier more select body), require ignoring the description of this Alexander organizing the files and companies, since Philip must already have done this, whatever name he applied to his infantry.

In my view it is necessary to treat Anaximenes' testimony with caution, compared with the clear statement of Diodorus that Philip first organized the Macedonian phalanx. Yet we can still reconcile the two accounts. The fact that the fragment of Anaximenes comes from 'the first book of the *Phillippika*' suggests that this was a backward-looking reference (chronologically), which would rule out Alexander III as the Alexander in question (if he were not already ruled out for any other reason). This leaves Alexander I and II. If we discount Alexander II due to the shortness of his reign, and the lack of any other reason to connect him to an important military reform, this would leave Alexander I, who did at least rule for a long time, and would suggest that the institution of the Companions (infantry and cavalry) was well established early in Macedonian history, which seems quite possible. We need not take too literally the suggestion that Alexander taught the Macedonian aristocracy to serve as cavalry, nor perhaps that the 'majority of the infantry' (if by this is meant the majority of those available to serve as infantry – but it might rather have meant the majority of those actually serving on a regular basis) were enrolled in the Companionate. But it would mean that the joint institutions of the Companions and Foot Companions were invented early on, and that there was a body of formed and well-organized infantry, presumably small in number, and serving as the infantry guard of the king – not a large enough force to be militarily significant (faced by large barbarian invasions) or to warrant mention in historical accounts.[10]

There is some possible independent confirmation of this conclusion in the fact that Alexander organized the men into 'dekads' – literally 'tens'. More will be said about such matters in future chapters, but we should note that Greek armies usually formed up in files of eight men, or multiples of eight, so a formation based on tens is unusual in Greek organization, but is found among the Achaemenid Persians, who used multiples of five and ten in their military structures. Alexander was king at the time of the Persian invasion of Greece (480–479 BC), during which time Macedon was subject to the Persians, so it could be that this division into tens was copied from the Persian occupiers. I do not think this theory should be pushed too far, since ten is an obvious multiple to use and also (like the Companionate itself) has Homeric origins (for example *Iliad* 2.124–129, should 'we Achaeans be marshalled by tens, and choose, each company of us, a man of the Trojans to pour our wine, then would many tens lack a cup-bearer'), which could be more important than Achaemenid practice. Nevertheless, it is suggestive.[11]

It is more encouraging that under Philip II the Foot Companions seem to have served as the infantry guard, a small elite part of the infantry (and not necessarily themselves armed in the Macedonian fashion). We hear that 'Theopompus says that men, chosen as tallest and strongest, served as a bodyguard to the king and were called the Foot Companions' (Photius, Theopompus *FrGrHist* 115 F 348). Only under Alexander III did the name come to be applied to a large part (perhaps the whole) of the phalanx, which seems to be a feature of Macedonian military nomenclature, as unit names of small elite bodies over time get extended to larger formations, with new names then being applied to the original elite units. Thus a small guard unit known under Philip by the old Macedonian title, Foot Companions, were renamed as Hypaspists by Alexander (Hypaspists being previously the name of the inner circle bodyguard and attendants of the king), and the name Foot Companions was extended to the whole (or at least a large part) of the infantry.[12]

If this is all correct, then the picture we have is as follows. Alexander I, in the early to mid-fifth century, created the Companionate (cavalry and infantry), but these remained small bodies for many years – just the immediate entourage of the king and his infantry guard. Alexander gave his Foot Companions a regular organization of 'companies and tens', but their equipment is unknown; they might well have been (as a small force maintained by the king) equipped as hoplites and fought in a standard, though small, Greek phalanx. Over the next 100 or so years, the various attempted reforms of a succession of kings did not alter this picture greatly, although the numbers at least of infantry available increased steadily, so that Perdiccas could field an infantry force of many thousands, but these were probably mostly armed in traditional fashion, as javelinmen, rather than as hoplites. Philip II, upon his accession, took over this force, and his reforms are as described by Diodorus: he greatly improved the morale and motivation of all the infantry, he expanded their numbers (and those of the cavalry) using means which will be described in greater detail in the following chapters, and he organized and re-equipped the mass of the infantry (not just his guard) as a Macedonian phalanx. Perhaps he also extended the title of Foot Companions to the mass of the infantry at some point in his reign, or maybe this was done by his son Alexander.

At any rate, we need not doubt Diodorus' account of the origins of the phalanx under Philip, nor does Anaximenes' testimony suggest that the phalanx was invented before Philip's reign. It is also worth noting that, while the implication of Diodorus' description is that these reforms all took place immediately upon Philip's accession, it is likely that a complete retraining and re-equipping of the entire infantry would have taken a fair amount of time – certainly years – and would not all have been accomplished in one go. Holding assemblies and raising the morale of the men would have been an ongoing process, and similarly devising new equipment, manufacturing it and rolling it out to the army, along with the drill and training necessary to become adept in its use, must have been something that extended over a considerable period, and it is likely that rather than upgrading the entire available infantry at once, Philip will have started with the core of his army (his own guards), and then rolled out the upgrade to the rest of the army over time.

Antecedents

But what of the particular equipment of the phalanx – especially the distinctive long spear, the sarissa – that Diodorus implies (though does not explicitly state) that Philip also invented? An earlier origin for this equipment has also sometimes been proposed. To recap, the equipment of the Macedonian phalanx is generally understood to be a long spear, known by its Macedonian name sarissa (or *sarisa*), a rimless shield called a *pelte*, smaller and lighter than the hoplite shield (*aspis*), and reduced (or no) body armour (the details of the equipment of the phalanx will be examined in more detail in the following chapter). This equipment sounds very similar to that described by Diodorus in the context of the much-discussed 'reforms of Iphicrates'.

Iphicrates was an Athenian general active in the first half of the fourth century, who achieved fame when the force of mercenary peltasts (that is, lightly armed javelinmen carrying small shields) he commanded defeated and captured a force of Spartan hoplites – an event considered almost incredible at the time, the Spartans being the elite infantry of the Greek world, considered invincible. He went on to have a varied career as a mercenary commander, including a spell in Egypt fighting for the Persians. Amongst Iphicrates' other activities, Diodorus has this to say about a reform he carried out of infantry equipment:

'Hence we are told, after he had acquired his long experience of military operations in the Persian War, he devised many improvements in the tools of war, devoting himself especially to the matter of arms. For instance, the Greeks were using shields [*aspisi*] which were large and consequently difficult to handle; these he discarded and made suitably sized light shields [*peltas summetrous*], thus successfully achieving both objects, to furnish the body with adequate cover and to enable the user of the *pelte*, on account of its lightness, to be completely free in his movements. After a trial of the new shield its easy manipulation secured its adoption, and the infantry who had formerly been called "hoplites" because of their heavy shield [*aspidon*], then had their name changed to "peltasts" from the light shield [*pelte*] they carried. As regards spear and sword, he made changes in the contrary direction: namely, he increased the length of the spears by half, and made the swords almost twice as long. The actual use of these arms confirmed the initial test and from the success of the experiment won great fame for the inventive genius of the general.' (Diodorus 15.44.1–4)

This passage – which is confirmed in a slightly modified form by the Latin historian Cornelius Nepos in his *Life of Iphicrates* – has caused much discussion and debate and has generated a considerable literature of its own. One of the sources of controversy is the exact nature of the new shields he introduced. I have translated the important phrase '*peltas summetrous*' as 'suitably sized light shields', since the common translations in use may be misleading. The Loeb edition of Diodorus translates this as 'small oval' shields, but this is certainly incorrect as there is no reason to suppose the shields were oval; this seems to be inspired by the use of the word *summetrous* and understanding it to mean 'symmetrical', but all shields are symmetrical, round ones more so than oval, so 'oval' can be rejected as an error. But 'symmetrical' is itself an unusual meaning for this word, and more commonly it means either 'of the same size' (its literal meaning) or something like 'of suitable size'. If the first translation is correct – 'the same size' – then the shields Iphicrates introduced were not any smaller than the existing hoplite shields, but were just of a lighter construction, presumably thinner and (most importantly) lacking the distinctive rim of the hoplite *aspis* (which adds significantly to its weight). This is indeed one definition of *pelte* according to Aristotle: 'a *pelte* is a type of *aspis* without a rim' (Aristotle, Fragment 498 Rose). Alternatively, if the second explanation is correct, then Diodorus is not necessarily telling us anything specific about the size of the shields, just that they were lighter and 'of suitable size' (which might be smaller, but need not be). It is impossible to be certain which translation is correct. It would be nice if the shields were 'of the same size', since then we would know what size they were, but Diodorus' other uses of the word in passages close to this one in his *History* do not inspire confidence in such a translation. He uses *summetrous* to describe the height of city walls in comparison to their length (14.18.8), the size of a club (17.100.5) and the range at which a javelin was hurled (17.100.6), in all of which cases 'a suitable size (or distance)', or perhaps 'a moderate size', is obviously the correct translation. As such we can't say much about these new shields, except that they were lighter than the old hoplite shields.[13]

The nature of the shield is not the only controversial aspect of the reform. The length of the lengthened spear has also sparked some debate, not least because while Diodorus says that the spear was 'half as long again' as the traditional hoplite spear, Cornelius Nepos has it that it was twice as long. In this case I think we must simply reject Nepos' version in favour of the more detailed account in Diodorus. So Iphicrates probably did increase the spear length by half. However, there was of course no standardized length of hoplite spears – Greek hoplites provided their own equipment, and would have had spears of whatever length they felt comfortable with, generally reckoned (from depictions in art) to be about 2–2.5 metres. This would make the Iphicratid spears about 3 or 4 metres in length – long enough to still wield in one hand, though near the upper limit.[14]

More fundamentally, there is some reason to doubt whether this reform ever happened at all, or at least much doubt over whose equipment it was that was reformed. Xenophon, who wrote a detailed (if far from perfect) history of this period, has nothing to say about this reform, and there is no sign, either in the pages of Xenophon or in any other historical account, of hoplites having been replaced by (or renamed as) peltasts, as Diodorus suggests happened. Hoplites continue to appear in the historical record and seem, so far as we can tell, to be armed much as they always had been. There is also no archaeological or artistic record of such a reform (though it has to be said there is precious little such evidence for any military equipment in the fourth century). There had also always been peltasts – in the sense of lightly armed, usually javelin-wielding infantry such as those Iphicrates commanded in his victory over the Spartans at Lechaeum (391) – and so far as we can tell there continued to be such peltasts, although from the time of Alexander and throughout the Hellenistic period the name 'peltasts' seems to have been no longer applied to such infantry (who instead are simply called 'javelinmen', 'light armed' or some other similar term). Because of such doubts, while Diodorus clearly states that it was the heavy infantry, the hoplites, who were re-equipped as peltasts, many modern scholars instead conclude that the point of Iphicrates' reform was to re-equip peltasts, light-armed javelin-throwing infantry, as a sort of cut-price hoplite, making them better able to stand up against opposing heavy infantry on the battlefield while retaining some of their advantages of light equipment and manoeuvrability.[15]

The nature of the equipment developed in this reform – light shield (*pelte*) and long spear – combined with this suggested interpretation of the reform as a way of creating a cheap heavy infantry force out of javelin-armed light infantry, has led many to see a close parallel with Philip's invention of the Macedonian phalanx. The equipment of the Macedonian phalanx, it is commonly agreed, consisted of a long spear and light (perhaps smaller) shield, and Philip's problem at the start of his reign was how to create a battle-winning force of heavy infantry using the raw materials of the existing Macedonian infantry (who, we may surmise, were previously equipped as javelinmen). This has even led some scholars to suggest that it was not Philip who invented the Macedonian phalanx at all, but Iphicrates, and that Philip simply equipped his infantry as Iphicratean peltasts. This interpretation is obviously appealing in some ways, but it does mean ignoring Diodorus' statement that it was hoplites that Iphicrates re-equipped, and that the point was to lighten their equipment, not to increase it. It seems better, therefore, to accept that we don't really know which forces Iphicrates was reforming, and that while there may be a link between Iphicratean peltasts and Macedonian phalangites, the relationship is at any rate rather more indirect. Philip may well have been inspired by Iphicrates' innovations, but the Macedonian phalanx was not simply a phalanx of Iphicratean peltasts, not least because there is far more to the Macedonian phalanx than just its equipment. Philip's position as its inventor still seems secure.[16]

Another external influence on Philip's invention has often been pointed out. Philip spent some of his formative years as a political hostage in Thebes, and as such it is likely that he will have had contact with two great Theban generals, Pelopidas and Epaminondas. Epaminondas did not institute any reforms of hoplite or peltast equipment, so far as we know, but is regarded (and was regarded in antiquity) as a master tactician, whose grand tactical innovations brought about the overthrow of Spartan power at the Battle of Leuctra (371), where the Theban army and its Boeotian allies inflicted a crushing and unprecedented defeat on the Spartans. According to Plutarch, Philip 'was believed to have become a zealous follower of Epaminondas, perhaps because he comprehended his efficiency in wars and campaigns' (Plut. *Pelop*. 26.4). [17]

Despite the importance of his innovations, the exact nature of Epaminondas' tactics is not totally clear, not least because Xenophon, the historian who provides the main account of the period, was a great admirer of Sparta and preferred to pass over the events of Leuctra as swiftly as possible.

But the general picture seems to be that, rather than forming up his best troops on the right of his line of battle, in the position of honour long established in Greek military custom, Epaminondas formed them on his left, opposite the Spartan contingent (Spartans proper, the Spartiates and Lacedaimonians, always formed only a component of Spartan armies, the rest being padded out with allies or less well-regarded contingents). He also 'refused' his right wing and weaker allied forces, angling them backwards (an oblique deployment in military parlance) so that the battle would be decided by the clash of the best Theban and Spartan forces – a tactic Epaminondas referred to as 'crushing the head of the snake' – without the risk of the weaker tail of the Boeotian army being defeated and costing the battle. The tactic was spectacularly successful, the defeat of the Spartiates, with heavy losses, breaking Spartan power and their reputation for invincibility. There is clearly no direct link between this tactical innovation and the equipment and formation of the Macedonian phalanx, but the tactics of Philip, Alexander and the Hellenistic kingdoms were to show some debts to Epaminondas' new approach, as will be explored in later chapters.

But another Theban innovation may be more directly related to Philip's reforms. At Leuctra, Epaminondas' phalanx was said to have been 'at least fifty shields [that is, men] deep' (Xen. *Hell.* 6.4.12), an enormous depth when Greek phalanxes were typically formed up eight, or occasionally up to twelve, deep. The exact reasons for this greater depth, and the advantages it gave, are obscure and controversial, and will be the subject of further discussion in Chapter 8. However, this was not a radically new departure for Epaminondas, as Theban armies had a history of forming up in greater than usual depth (and in multiples of five, rather than of four or eight, which may or may not be significant). We might also note that Epaminondas may not be the true originator of either tactic: Herodotus reports that at the Battle of Plataea (479), where Thebans fought on the Persian side, 'seeing that the Persians by far outnumbered the Lacedaemonians, they were arrayed in deeper ranks and their line ran opposite the Tegeans also. In his [Mardonius, the Persian general] arraying of them he chose out the strongest part of the Persians to set it over against the Lacedaemonians, and posted the weaker of them facing the Tegeans; this he did being so informed and taught by the Thebans' (Hdt 9.31.2). Be that as it may, one of the distinctive features of the Macedonian phalanx, as noted above, was its greater 'weight'. Whatever exactly this means, one of the ways a formation could become 'heavier' was by forming up in greater depth, and it does appear that a typical depth for a Macedonian phalanx was sixteen men, double that of the usual hoplite phalanx.

Evidence for this greater depth at the time of Philip is, it has to be said, wholly lacking. We know that in Alexander's army, at least at the end of his reign, the file or '*dekas*' (literally 'ten') consisted of sixteen men, as Alexander proposed a reform that would see twelve Persian soldiers form the centre ranks of a file, topped and tailed by four Macedonians (Arr.*Anab.* 7.23.3–4). The later tacticians (writing about Hellenistic armies of undefined date) also assumed a phalanx depth of sixteen, and this is the depth recorded by Polybius (18.30.1). However, Polybius (12.19.6) also assumed that the phalanx at Issus was eight deep (rightly or wrongly – this complex problem will be examined further in Chapter 3). There is no direct evidence at all for how deep Philip's phalanx was formed up, and we are reduced to guessing. At any rate, given the extreme depths of the Theban phalanx, and that such depths were not copied by Macedonian phalanxes in battle (the deepest battlefield depth we know of is 32 ranks), there seems no reason to suppose that Philip took particular inspiration from his Theban hosts in this aspect at least of the development of the Macedonian phalanx, although the general concept of producing a heavier formation by making it deeper was no doubt familiar to him.[18]

A later invention?

A school of thought also exists that, far from the distinctive features of the Macedonian phalanx being invented by Philip II or possibly earlier (or at least that Philip was inspired by earlier developments), the Macedonian phalanx proper did not emerge until well after Philip's reign. According to some, it appeared in the course of the reign of Alexander, or possibly not until much later in the third century, perhaps as late as the end of that century. According to this line of thought, the phalanx of Philip and Alexander (at least at first) was basically a standard hoplite phalanx, although the spears it carried might, after the fashion of the Iphricatean peltast, have been longer, but still short enough to wield in one hand – and perhaps with lighter shields. Only in the course of the following century were the spears lengthened until they had to be wielded two-handed – becoming proper pikes (the English term I will use to refer to a spear held in two hands, when the distinction is important) – and only then were the distinctive features of the Macedonian phalanx (pike and small shield, but also the close-order 'locked shields' and the supposed great weight and unwieldiness of the formation) fully developed.[19]

This theory has something to recommend it, given that military reforms can tend to be gradual, evolving over time, rather than leaping fully formed onto the battlefield from the heads of their inventors. More will be said about aspects of this theory in the course of the following chapters, on particular matters of equipment and drill. I will just say at this point that I am unconvinced, and to me it seems more likely that when Diodorus says that Philip devised the Macedonian phalanx, what he has in mind is the Macedonian phalanx much as it appeared in the pages of Polybius at the beginning of the second century, although there would surely have been later developments of detail. It was certainly the assumption of ancient writers that the phalanx used by Philip and Alexander was the fully formed Macedonian phalanx. Aelian, for example, states of his *Tactics* that 'you will find, contained within, Alexander of Macedon's manner of marshalling his army' (Aelian, *Tactics* intro.). Polybius wrote that 'the Macedonian tactics' defeated by Rome were the same as those which had conquered Greece and Asia (Pol.18.28). Appian wrote of the Seleucid army at the Battle of Magnesia (190) that 'The total force of Antiochus was 70,000 and the strongest of these was the Macedonian phalanx of 16,000 men, still arrayed after the fashion of Alexander and Philip' (App.*Syr* 6.32). When the Roman Emperor Caracalla, who was an Alexander enthusiast, equipped a Macedonian phalanx in emulation of his hero, the equipment he gave them was that of the fully developed phalanx (Cassius Dio 78.7.1–2). When Polybius (Pol.12.19–22) describes the manoeuvres of the phalanx at the Battle of Issus in 333, where Alexander first defeated Darius, he does so in terms that are obviously very similar to those he applied to the phalanx of Philip V at Cynoscephalae in 197 (Pol.18.29–32). Rightly or wrongly, it certainly seems to have been the understanding of ancient writers that Philip and Alexander's phalanx was a fully developed Macedonian phalanx.[20]

The wars of the Successors of Alexander also provide numerous references to formations 'armed in the Macedonian fashion', with no indication that this meant something different at the end of the fourth century to what it would by the end of the next century. The 'late development' theory would also require that, while Diodorus ascribes the invention of the phalanx to Philip and numerous references refer to Philip and Alexander using it, it would in fact have had an anonymous inventor not recorded in any historical account. Given the gaping hole in our sources for the first three-quarters of the third century, this is certainly not impossible, but even so it would be odd if nobody thought to record who it was that actually invented the true Macedonian phalanx. Placing the invention of the phalanx after the foundation of the various Hellenistic kingdoms would also render it odd that, so far as we know, the phalanxes of all the kingdoms were armed and organized in a very similar way ('in the Macedonian fashion'). This makes perfect sense if each kingdom inherited its phalanx from the army of Philip and Alexander, but would otherwise require that all simultaneously went from long-speared hoplites to Macedonian phalangites proper at more or less the same time, straight after the invention of this new phalanx by person or persons unknown. Finally, too much of the case for Alexander in particular not using the fully developed phalanx revolves around arguments to the effect that his phalanx seems too capable and flexible, and does not match the image of the massive monolithic inflexible phalanx that we see in the confrontation between legion and phalanx in the late third and second centuries. I will have more to say on this topic in later chapters, and for now will just say that I think this is due to a misunderstanding of the real capabilities of the Macedonian phalanx. In short, I am not convinced by the arguments that whatever Philip invented, it was not a full Macedonian phalanx. While I'm sure there were developments over time, I think that the phalanx that faced the legions would have been instantly recognizable to Philip and Alexander.[21]

Much is obscure about the precise details of the invention of the Macedonian phalanx, and many of the uncertainties and controversies will be examined in more detail in the following chapters. However, the overall picture seems clear: Philip II was the first to organize the Macedonian phalanx and also devised its particular equipment, starting from the very beginning of his reign, though the process was likely to have been ongoing over a period of several years. He no doubt took inspiration from earlier precedents – Iphicrates' peltasts, Epaminondas' heavy formations and tactics – but there is no indication that a Macedonian phalanx (in the precise sense of a phalanx 'armed in the Macedonian fashion') preceded Philip's reign, and it is in my view unlikely that Philip and Alexander used some intermediate form of infantry, with the invention of the true Macedonian phalanx happening at some unknown place and time over the next century.

Many questions of detail remain, and we are far from finished with an examination of the phalanx under Philip. The following chapters, in digging deeper into the equipment, recruitment, organization and tactics of Macedonian phalanxes over the next three centuries, will revisit the details of Philip's reforms at every stage. But Philip's position as inventor of the phalanx seems secure.

Chapter 2

Arms and armour

So Philip II, as described by Diodorus, 'devised the compact order and the equipment of the phalanx' and 'equipped the men suitably with weapons of war'. But what was the nature of this equipment, and was this precise equipment then adopted by all other forces 'armed in the Macedonian fashion' for the next three centuries?

This second part of the question is important, and seems sometimes to be overlooked. Modern accounts of the army of Alexander the Great, for example, will often simply quote the evidence of Asclepiodotus for the size of the shield of the phalanx, though Asclepiodotus was writing more than 200 years after Alexander and describing (so far as we can tell) contemporary armies. It may be that there was complete continuity of equipment across the whole period, but it is something that needs to be established, or at least the reason for the assumption explained. As argued in the previous chapter, I think that there is good reason to believe that there was continuity in the basic nature of the Macedonian phalanx – that the organization and equipment under Philip II was likely similar to that in the first century when Asclepiodotus wrote – but this does not mean that every detail was the same. Phalanxes armed in the Macedonian fashion were active for a period of around 300 years, from the initial reforms of Philip around 358 until the defeat of Mithridates VI of Pontus at the hands of the Romans in the 60s. Following the breakup of Alexander's empire (and army), they served every major kingdom of this period, including those of the Ptolemies in Egypt, the Seleucids in Syria and the 'Upper Satrapies' (modern Iraq, Iran and Afghanistan) and of course Macedon itself, and this method of arming was also adopted throughout Greece. They marched to the borders of modern India under Alexander, and with Pyrrhus of Epirus to Italy, where they inflicted a string of defeats on the fledgling Roman Republic. The Macedonian phalanx saw a long period of service over a wide geographical area, and we must not expect all details of equipment, organization, drill and tactics to be identical across these expanses of space and time. Due to the patchy nature of our sources (as discussed in the Introduction above), we have good evidence only for a few isolated incidents or periods. So while there certainly was a single common way of arming and fighting that could be described as 'in the Macedonian fashion', we cannot assume that evidence from one time or place can be applied in detail to all. There must have been variation, development and change, sometimes due to changes in fashion as much as to improvements in technique.

This chapter will look at the evidence for equipment, offensive and defensive. Generally speaking, the evidence falls into three types: artistic (depictions of soldiers and their equipment, particularly in tomb paintings); archaeological (actual items of equipment); and literary (descriptions of equipment in written sources, chiefly the histories and the tactical manuals, but also some documents inscribed on stone). In recent years, the number of examples of the first two categories has increased dramatically due to ongoing archaeological investigations, in particular in northern Greece.

It is also worth repeating here that so far as we can tell, the equipment of Macedonian and Hellenistic armies was centrally supplied by the state (that is, usually, at the expense of the king), unlike classical Greek hoplite armies, where men were expected to provide their own equipment – and also unlike 'tribal' armies or contingents, where men would bring along their own traditional weapons. This means that we can expect a fair degree of regularity in the equipment of any particular army, if not between armies.[1]

Diodorus, as we have seen in the previous chapter, tells us that Philip 'equipped the men suitably with weapons of war' and 'devised … the equipment of the phalanx'. Diodorus does not, however, say what this equipment was, and for that we must look elsewhere. There are numerous scattered references to individual items of equipment, but most useful are four lists of phalanx equipment, at various points of time. I will set these out here, and then examine each of the items, along with the other scattered evidence, in turn.

The first list comes from the stratagem collection of the second-century AD Roman-Macedonian author Polyaenus, describing the training regime of Philip II (mid-fourth century):

> 'Philip accustomed the Macedonians to constant exercise, before they went to war: so that he would frequently make them march three hundred stades [about 54 km], carrying with them their helmets [*krane*], shields [*peltas*], greaves [*knemidas*], and spears [*sarisas*]; and, besides those arms, their provisions likewise, and utensils for common use.' (Polyaenus, *Strategemata* 4.2.10)

The second is a copy on stone of a decree from the reign of Philip V (early second century) setting out a series of army regulations concerning discipline, including fines for missing equipment:

> '[T]hose not bearing the weapons appropriate to them are to be fined according to the regulations: for the *kotthybos*, two obols, the same amount for the helmet [*konos*], three obols for the sarissa, the same for the sword [*makhaira*], for the greaves [*knemides*] two obols, for the shield [*aspis*] a drachma. In the case of officers, double for the arms mentioned, two drachmas for the cuirass [*thorax*], a drachma for the half-cuirass [*hemithorakion*]. The secretaries and the chief assistants shall exact the penalty, after indicating the transgressors to the King.'
> (*Meletemata* 22, Epig. App. 12 *SEG* 40.524 = Austin (1981), p.74)

I have left *kotthybos* untranslated above, as its meaning is uncertain (more on this below).

Next we have the description of the arms of the three components of the infantry (hoplites, peltasts, psiloi) found in the tacticians, taking Asclepiodotus as representative:

> 'The infantry is divided into the corps of hoplites, the corps of peltasts, and the corps of so called light infantry [*psiloi*]. Now the corps of hoplites, since it fights at close quarters, uses very heavy equipment – for the men are protected by shields [*aspisi*] of the largest size, cuirasses [*thoraxi*] and greaves [*knemesi*] – and long spears [*dorasi*] of the type that will here be called 'Macedonian'. The corps of the light infantry on the contrary uses the lightest equipment because it shoots from a distance, and is provided with neither greaves nor cuirasses … . The corps of the peltasts stands in a sense between these two, for the *pelte* is a kind of small light shield [*aspis*], and their spears are much shorter than those of the hoplites.' (Asclepiodotus, *Tactics* 1.2)

The final list is slightly more unusual, being an account of the formation at the start of the third century AD by the Roman Emperor Caracalla of an imitation Macedonian phalanx, and gives an idea of how the armament of the phalanx was understood in Roman times:

> 'He [Caracalla] organised a phalanx, composed entirely of Macedonians, 16,000 strong, named it "Alexander's phalanx", and equipped it

with the arms that warriors had used in his [Alexander's] day. These consisted of a helmet [*kranos*] of raw oxhide, a three-ply linen cuirass [*thorax*], a bronze shield [*aspis chalke*], long spear [*doru makron*], short spear [*aichme bracheia*], boots [*krepides*] and sword [*xiphos*].' (Cassius Dio 78.7.1–2)

As we can see, there are many similarities between these accounts, and also some differences. I will examine each item of equipment in turn, starting with perhaps the most distinctive feature, the spear of the phalanx, the mighty sarissa.

The sarissa

The word sarissa (or sarisa) is used throughout the Hellenistic period to refer to the Macedonian long spear which equipped the Macedonian phalanx. However, as is common for most Greek terms (or in this case, perhaps dialect Macedonian) it does not always carry a strict technical meaning, and it appears that 'sarissa' was originally just a word for a spear, without any strong implication as to the nature or length of that spear. The normal Greek word for a spear was *doru* (sometimes transliterated into English as *dory*), and this is what the spear of the Classical hoplite was called, though again this is not a technical term, and the spear of the Macedonian phalangite could also be called a *doru* – as in the quotes from Asclepiodotus and Cassius Dio above – without implying anything about the length or nature of the spear.[2]

But generally speaking when the word 'sarissa' is used in the literary sources, it is referring to the long Macedonian spear of the Macedonian phalanx (the spear of the Macedonian cavalry might also sometimes have been called a sarissa, although this was probably shorter than the infantry version and appears to have been carried in one hand). The distinguishing feature of the infantry sarissa is its great length, requiring it to be carried (so far as we know, in all cases) in two hands rather than one as the Greek *doru* was, and that is the sense in which the word will be used in this book.[3]

One of the immediate problems we are presented with when determining the exact length of the sarissa is the question of units of measurement (this applies to the size of Macedonian spears and shields, and also to the formations of the phalanx in the following chapter). The usual Greek measurement for shortish distances was the cubit, which was defined as the distance between a man's elbow and the tips of his outstretched fingers. As men's arms come in different lengths, this does not produce a consistent measurement, and as international trade and other areas of endeavour require some standardization, standard cubits were defined, with different standards being adopted in different regions. The precise length of the cubit in modern measurements, even where we think we know which cubit is meant, is not clearly defined, and much scholarly effort has been spent on attempting to define cubits, and which cubit is used, to the precise centimetre (or inch), even to the extent of proposing a short Macedonian cubit so as to make the length of the spear less spectacular. I find this effort, though undoubtedly admirable from an academic point of view, to be largely wasted in this context. Even when following a standard (like the Attic cubit) there must have been a lot of variation, and to attempt to give measurements accurate to the nearest centimetre seems absurd in the context of ancient formations and weapons. The cubit is a fairly approximate measure, access to standard lengths must have been variable, and in field conditions there must have been a lot of 'close enough', judgement by eye, and measuring off against existing known objects (not to mention field modifications – Early Modern pikemen often cut down their pikes to make them easier to carry). Therefore in this book I will give measurements in ancient units, along with a rough comparison in modern measures, which should not be taken to be anything other than an approximate equivalent. The measurements we will encounter are the cubit, which approximates to 50cm; the foot, which is around 30cm; and the palm, around 7.5cm. The relationships between the measures are: 1 cubit = 1.5ft; 1ft = 4 palms (so 50cm is a bit too long for a cubit, which strictly speaking should be 45cm using these ratios, but means that for example a 10 cubit sarissa translates to a 5 metre spear, which is a neater round number and close enough for these purposes). Throughout, bear in mind that the modern measures are meant only as approximations, and I also do not suppose that the ancient measures were anything other than approximate.[4]

As to the length of the sarissa, we must not expect to find a single defining measurement that would apply to all sarissas, nor any sort of orderly development of sarissa length applicable throughout the period and regions in which it was used. Different armies, different weapons workshops and perhaps different individuals would have specified sarissas of different lengths, and while for practical reasons it is likely that all the sarissas within any one phalanx would be the same length (especially if they were manufactured and distributed centrally), there is no reason to expect total consistency between different phalanxes. There was also no simple correlation between length and practicality, nor did any particular length prove consistently superior in battle, so far as we know. What we have, therefore, is a succession of snapshots, statements of sarissa length at different moments in history, and the reasons behind particular lengths (or even if there was any specific reason, rather than just experimentation, fashion or random variation) are lost to us.[5]

The length of the sarissa is defined in the following passages, arranged in chronological order of the period they describe (where known):

'The wood of the "male" [cornus] tree has no heart, but is hard throughout, like horn in closeness and strength; whereas that of the "female" tree has heart-wood and is softer and goes into holes; wherefore it is useless for javelins. The height of the "male" tree is at most twelve cubits, the length of the longest sarisa, the stem up to the point where it divides not being very tall.' (Theophrastus, *Enquiry into Plants* 3.12.1–2; writing in late fourth or early third century)

'At the siege of Edessa, when a breach was made in the walls, the sarissa-bearers, whose sarissas were sixteen cubits long, sallied out against the assailants.' (Polyaenus, *Stratagems* 2.29.2; writing in second century AD, describing events at start of third century BC)

'For as a man in close order of battle occupies a space of three feet; and as the length of the sarissas is sixteen cubits according to the original design, which has been reduced in practice to fourteen; and as of these fourteen four must be deducted, to allow for the distance between the two hands holding it, and to balance the weight in front; it follows clearly that each hoplite will have ten cubits of his sarissa projecting beyond his body, when he lowers it with both hands, as he advances against the enemy: hence, too, though the men of the second, third, and fourth rank will have their sarissa projecting farther beyond the front rank than the men of the fifth, yet even these last will have two cubits of their sarissae beyond the front rank … . And if my description is true and exact, it is clear that in front of each man of the front rank there will be five sarissae projecting to distances varying by a descending scale of two cubits.' (Polybius 18.29; writing in mid-second century, describing start of second century)

'... and their spear [*doru*], moreover, is not shorter than ten cubits, so that the part which projects in front of the rank is to be no less than eight cubits – in no case, however, is it longer than twelve cubits, so as to project ten cubits. Now when the Macedonian phalanx used such a spear in a compact formation it appeared to the enemy irresistible. For it is obvious that the spears of the first five ranks project beyond the front, since the soldiers in the second rank, being two cubits back, extend their spears eight cubits beyond the front, those in the third rank six cubits, those in the fourth rank four cubits, those in the fifth rank two cubits, and so five spears extend beyond the first rank.' (Asclepiodotus, *Tactics* 5.1; writing around start of first century)

'The size of the sarissa was sixteen feet. Of these four extended to the holder's hand and the rest of his body, but twelve projected in front of the bodies of each of the front row men. But those in the second row, standing back from the latter by two feet, have their sarissa extending ten feet in front of the front rank. Those in the third rank extend theirs eight feet beyond the front rank. And those in the fourth extend for six, those in the fifth four and those in the sixth for two. Hence there are six sarissas extending in front of each of the front rankers.' (Arrian, *Tactics* 12; writing in early second century AD)

'The spear [*doru*] should not be shorter than eight cubits and the longest should not exceed a length that allows a man to wield it effectively ... . Each soldier, when completely armed and arranged in close order, occupies a space of only two cubits. The length of the sarissas was sixteen cubits according to the original design which has been reduced in practice to fourteen. Two cubits of this length are taken up by the grip, being the distance between the hands, while the remaining twelve cubits project ahead of the body. Thus the weapons carried by the second rank, losing four cubits, project ten cubits beyond the front rank. The sarissas of the third rank therefore project eight cubits beyond the front, those of the fourth rank project six cubits, those of the fifth rank project four cubits, and those of the sixth rank project two cubits beyond the front.' (Aelian, *Tactics* 12 and 14; writing in early third century AD)

The earliest two accounts are those of Theophrastus and Polyaenus. Theophrastus' date is fixed by the fact that he died about 287, and Polyaenus' by the date of the siege he is describing (precise date unknown, perhaps 274 or 273). These are therefore chronologically the earliest. Polybius is talking about the phalanx at the time of the Battle of Cynoscephalae (197). The dates when the tacticians were alive are known (broadly), but not the period to which their works are referring, but given the close parallels to the text of Polybius, it seems safe to assume they are describing the phalanx as it was some time from the early second century to the first century.

The similarity between the account of Polybius and those of Asclepiodotus, Aelian and Arrian is obvious, and indicates that they shared a common source (or possibly that the source of the tacticians was a lost *Tactics* by Polybius, which

Polybius was paraphrasing in his *Histories*). The differences are interesting too. To take the most obvious, Arrian is unusual in using feet as his unit of measurement throughout, and talking of a sarissa of 16ft. This has led some modern scholars to suppose that Arrian is describing some early version of the sarissa that was 16ft long, but it is far more likely that Arrian (or some later copyist) simply got his measurements mixed up; the Greek for cubits (*pechesi*) is similar enough to that for feet (*posi*), especially if abbreviated, and the likelihood of Arrian's text being in error is greatly increased by his talking of a rank separation of 2ft, when every other source sets this at 2 cubits. Polybius may have sown confusion by starting talking about soldiers occupying a space of 3 ft, then switching to cubits for sarissa and rank spacing. So we can safely assume that Arrian meant to talk of a 16 cubit sarissa, the 'original' length described by Polybius.[6]

Taking Aelian's testimony next, he contradicts himself between Chapters 12 and 14 with lengths varying from 8 to an unspecified (but 'effective') number of cubits, and 14 to 16 cubits. The suggestion has been made, given the similarity in language between Aelian and Asclepiodotus, that a sentence has dropped out of Aelian's version ('the spear is not shorter than ten cubits, so that the part which projects in front of the rank is to be no less than eight cubits') and he meant to talk of a 10 cubit weapon which projects 8 cubits, not an 8 cubit weapon. This would still contradict his Chapter 14, however.[7]

Then we can see that the calculations for the projection of the sarissas are slightly different. Polybius has a 14 cubit sarissa, with 2 cubits occupied by the hands, 2 cubits sticking out behind the hands and 10 projecting forward, giving five ranks projecting in front of the formation (at a 2 cubit spacing of ranks). Asclepiodotus has a 12 cubit sarissa held by the rear end 2 cubits (with no projection backwards), also giving five ranks projecting. Aelian also has the sarissa held by the rear 2 cubits (no backward projection), but as his sarissas are 14 cubits long, he has six ranks projecting. Arrian, like Polybius, allows 4 'feet' (cubits) for hand and body (presumably two for the hands, two projecting backwards), but as his sarissas are 16 cubits, he too has six ranks projecting. We should note, incidentally, that Aelian (or rather his copyists) hedges his bets, since most manuscripts talk of the first five ranks only projecting, and the 'or six' is an uncertain addition.

What are we to make of these differences? Two ways of holding the sarissa are described: by the very end 2 cubits (Aelian and Asclepiodotus) or with a further 2 cubits projecting backwards (Polybius and Arrian). It may be that there were different ways of holding the sarissa at different times, and this in turn may have depended on the construction and point of balance of the weapon (since the point of the extra backward-projecting 2 cubits is presumably to help counterbalance the weight of the sarissa in front, although the balance of a two-handed weapon is less important than for one wielded in one hand). Or it may be that Asclepiodotus and Aelian just altered their descriptions to make their sums add up (Asclepiodotus to still allow his shorter 12 cubit sarissa to have five ranks projecting, Aelian to allow six ranks to project with the same 14 cubit sarissa as Polybius). It is to my mind unlikely that each author is describing a different practice at some particular point in history, given the close relationship between the text of all four – Aelian's language in describing the previous (16 cubits) and current (14 cubits) lengths of the sarissa, for example, is almost identical to Polybius' – and much more likely that some mixture of textual corruption, misunderstanding and working from memory has resulted in these slight differences. I do not think, therefore, that we can construct any chronology for the development of sarissa length from these accounts. All we can say is that sarissa lengths varied, and that ways of carrying the sarissa, and the number of ranks' spears projecting, may have varied too. I am also unconvinced by the suggestion found in the tacticians that the ranks sometimes carried sarissas of different lengths, so that they all projected the same distance; this would seem to me to pose enormous practical difficulties (particularly when 'doubling', as we will see in the next chapter, or when replacing casualties from the rear ranks).

So we can see that the sarissa is known to have varied between 10 and 16 cubits (5 and 8 metres). Longer or shorter sarissas may also have existed, but are just not recorded. It would be lucky if the measurements known equate exactly to the longest and shortest sarissa ever used, so the safest thing to say is just that the sarissa was generally around 6 or 7 metres in length, plus or minus a metre. I am not convinced that there is any point trying to establish any trends in increase or decrease in size of the sarissa, given the small number of data points, beyond the statement by Polybius that, while originally 16 cubits long, it was reduced to 14. Polybius doesn't say when it was originally 16 cubits, and we could look back hopefully to the 16 cubits of Polyaenus and conclude that the sarissa was 16 cubits long at the start of the third century and was reduced to 14 cubits some time at or before the start of the second century, but greater precision is impossible. We also do not know for sure when the 'longest' sarissa was 12 cubits (as described by Theophrastus), or when this went up to 16 cubits – perhaps the first figure was during the reign of Alexander (when the main enemies were classical hoplites or Persian infantry, both armed with short spears), the second during the wars of the Successors (when pike phalanx first fought pike phalanx, so that an advantage of length might have been sought). Also, such figures as we have apply probably to the phalanx of Macedon itself, and cannot with certainty be applied to the Seleucid or Ptolemaic phalanxes, or to any of the other armies that adopted the sarissa. It seems safest just to accept that sarissa length varied, between and around these known figures.

This is probably a sufficient length of spear to require that it was always wielded with two hands. It is in fact possible to wield surprisingly long spears in one hand (historical examples from other periods exist for spears of up to 5 metres being so wielded), but the balance of the spear when wielded one-handed is very different; it must be held much closer to or at the centre of balance, which means that its reach is much reduced compared with the two-handed hold. So far as we can tell, the Iphicratean peltast wielded his (slightly shorter) spear in one hand (at least, Diodorus and Nepos do not say that he didn't), and the cavalry spear (sometimes, probably erroneously, called a sarissa) was also held one-handed – but in this case we can see from artistic depictions that the spear was held quite a way along the shaft, so that a larger proportion projected out behind the bearer's hand. This would have been more practical for cavalry than for infantry, since the ranks in an infantry formation are much closer together, with consequent greater scope for fouling, tangling or accidental backward stabbing. It seems likely then that when Philip II devised the arms of the phalanx, he also devised the way of wielding the sarissa (in two hands), and that this remained fairly constant throughout the period.[8]

This way of wielding is best described by Polybius in the passage quoted above (Pol. 18.29.2). This is the clearest description of how the sarissa was held, and there is no reason not to accept it as accurate. There is (to my knowledge) only one depiction in art of a sarissa actually being wielded in action, in the form of a bronze plaque from Pergamon (fig. 2.1) showing Macedonian (style) phalangites facing cavalry and *thureophoroi* (that is *thureos*-carriers, the *thureos* being the long thin shield adopted in Greek and Hellenistic armies from the early third century in imitation of the Celts). The original of this plaque is sadly lost, and it is known only from a line drawing in the archaeological report, which may mean that some details of the original are lost or distorted. There are a couple of depictions of the cavalry spear in action (the Kinch Tomb painting and the Alexander Mosaic, which also contains the tops of what may be infantry sarissas, but does not show those holding them), but there are precious few depictions of Hellenistic infantry in combat at all, and the Pergamon plaque is the only depiction of the infantry sarissa in use. That this should be so is not too surprising, as a 5 metre spear is a difficult thing to illustrate effectively, especially in a battle scene which, in accordance with Greek artistic convention, would usually show combatants intermingled and intertwined in various action poses. [9]

There are more depictions of what may by sarissas in 'at ease' positions, but here in many cases either the length of the spear is too great for the frame of the picture (which is usually defined by the architecture, since these are invariably wall paintings), or else the spear is shown quite short, which may be because a short spear is depicted or because the artist has shortened the length of the spear to fit it into the frame. The best example of Macedonians carrying long spears is from the Agios Athanasios tomb, where two figures on the exterior wall are holding spears which are depicted (very unusually) full length, from butt to head. These spears have been estimated to be about 3.5 metres long, leading to suggestions that these may have been wielded in one hand, and so provide evidence for the late fourth century phalanx using such spears one-handed, rather than full pikes. I think there are two problems with this: we can't be sure that these men are members of the pike phalanx anyway, rather than, say, peltasts (on which more below), or cavalry, who we would expect to carry a shorter spear. Then, it is noticeable that the spears extend exactly from the ground to the bottom of the architrave of the tomb – if they were any longer the heads would extend out of the available 'frame' (the wall) of the picture. So perhaps the artist, rather than depicting spears precisely to scale with the figures at the correct length, simply painted spears as long as they could be while still fitting on the wall. As such it simply may not be valid to measure the length of spears in such contexts and draw any firm conclusions about them.[10]

In the case of the Pergamon plaque, the sarissa is being held broadly as Polybius describes it, although it appears that the butt end of the sarissa is nearer to the bearer's right hand than Polybius' 2 cubits (1 metre), but this may just be in order to fit the end of the weapon within the frame. A peculiarity of the grip depicted is that the sarissa appears to pass to the left of the shield, rather than to the right as we would expect, which seems impossible using any plausible way of holding the shield; this may just be an error on the part of the artist, or may indicate a possible use of the overhand grip, see below. The length of the sarissa is impossible to judge, since the end is missing or concealed by the enemy infantry depicted. The grip appears to be the standard low position – that is, the sarissa is held with the arms extended downwards, right arm toward the rear and left arm across the front of the body (see fig. 2.2). This is similar to the way that Xenophon recommends a boar spear be held:

'... the man must approach him [the boar] spear in hand, and grasp it [the spear] with the left in front and the right behind, since the left

Fig. 2.1. The 'Pergamon plaque'.

steadies while the right drives it. The left foot must follow the left hand forward, and the right foot the other hand. As he advances let him hold the spear before him, with his legs not much further apart than in wrestling, turning the left side towards the left hand.' (Xenophon, *On Hunting* 10.11–12)

Here we may perhaps see a trace of the origins of the infantry sarissa in a hunting spear. This is also the typical hold for pikes and long spears in Medieval European warfare, according to contemporary depictions. It is not known whether other ways of holding the sarissa were adopted. In the Renaissance, the shoulder-level hold for pikes became popular, with the pike held at the shoulder, the right arm straight out behind grasping the butt end and left arm pointing upwards. This grip continued in widespread use through the seventeenth century, up to the final demise of the pike in European warfare. So far as we know, this shoulder grip was not adopted by the Macedonian phalanx; which is not to say it might not have been, since there are advantages in this grip in terms of fitting the pikes and shields together in a tight formation (as we will see in the next chapter), although it is unclear how the shield would then have been held. A shoulder-level grip for long spears is depicted in Mycenaean art, which, combined with the supposed Homeric inspiration of the Macedonian phalanx,

Fig. 2.2. Phalangite demonstrating the underarm grip for the sarissa.

might provide a very (very) slight nudge in favour of use of the high grip. At any rate, there is no direct evidence that it was used, while there is evidence for the low grip in the Pergamon plaque.[11]

There are also two possible variations on the low grip. The usual assumption is that the sarissa was held with the right (rear) hand overhand, and the left (forward) hand underhand, which is the natural posture when holding a long pole (as in fig. 2.2). It is also possible that the 'pole vaulter's grip' was used, in which both hands are overhand (fig. 2.3). There is no direct evidence for this, but one point in favour of such a grip is that it allows the left elbow to protrude further forward, which may have made it easier to carry the shield – particularly the very dished shield sometimes depicted in art (see below). It also allows the sarissa to more easily be carried at various heights, which may have been necessary in order to allow the sarissas of ranks behind the first to pass over the sarissas and hands of the ranks in front. This is, however, only a possibility.

A spear needs a point, or head, of course, and most Greek spears also had a butt spike (usually called a *sauroter*) at the opposite end, which served as an emergency backup point if the spear broke, protected the wooden end of the spear (especially if it was stuck in the ground) and provided a counterweight, allowing the spear to be balanced nearer its rear end, thus allowing it to

Fig. 2.3. Phalangite demonstrating the 'pole vaulter' grip for the sarissa.

project further and be more handy to use. Many heads (mostly iron) and butts (often bronze) of hoplite spears have been discovered, though it is notable that while all are broadly of the same size, there is little uniformity and a wide range of different shapes and weights were used. For sarissa heads, the situation is more complicated. No certain examples of a sarissa head have been discovered, and it is not even known for sure if they had butts. In art there are few certain depictions of a sarissa, and none make it clear what size or shape the head might have been, or if they had a butt. Yet in the excavations at the old Macedonian capital of Aegae (modern Vergina), a large spear head and butt were discovered that were confidently identified as those of a sarissa, an identification that has been, perhaps surprisingly, widely accepted since. It is surprising since there is no particular reason to associate the head and butt with a sarissa, other than their being found in Macedonia, and they are of unusually large size and weight, which would be inappropriate for a weapon as long as a sarissa since a heavy head would make the weapon very tiring to hold and difficult to balance. The large butt might make more sense in terms of balance, but would still increase the overall weight considerably, and we should note that Medieval, Renaissance and Early Modern pikes never have metal butts of any sort. Even if the sarissa had a butt, there is no reason to suppose that this particular object is an example of one, and its unusual design (with large 'wings') suggests that it might possibly have been the foot of a pole for a standard or a ceremonial spear. Both butt and spear head might belong to the spear of a guardsman or bodyguard, or be the badge of office of a senior officer, or perhaps a hunting spear. The finding of these spear parts in the context of high-status tombs makes it unlikely that they are standard weapons of the mass of the infantry.[12]

So while many reconstructors and re-enactors have used these items to reconstruct a sarissa, and while their shape and weight have formed the basis for a number of calculations of the weight and balance of a sarissa, all this is based on extremely shaky ground and on the unsupported assumption that these are indeed parts of a sarissa. As such, all these experiments and calculations are in my view rendered void, or at best can give only indications of the theoretical maximum weight such a weapon could have, and tell us very little about the actual weapon.[13]

Even more controversially, another object discovered in the excavations was a metal tube or sleeve, with approximately the same internal diameter as the head and butt (in fact a little smaller). This was identified as a 'connecting tube', leading to the (on the face of it) remarkable suggestion that the sarissa was made in two parts, which would have been slotted together before going into action. While such a two-part weapon would certainly have been easier to carry on the march, it is surely significant that no other spear of any length in the whole of military history – even those Medieval, Renaissance and Early Modern pikes that reached comparable lengths to the sarissa – were ever made in two parts. There are also tremendous practical difficulties: a spear shaft in two parts with only a short metal connecting tube would surely be far too likely to break in two in combat (a common enough occurrence for shorter spears as it is), or even to be deliberately pulled apart by an opponent (as we will see in later chapters, those fighting a sarissa phalanx would try to knock aside the shafts or cut off the points). It would also not have been just a matter of simply slotting a sarissa together in its tube. It would surely have been necessary to fix the parts in place (presumably with pitch, as is assumed to have happened with heads and butts from the pitch traces found inside them). This means that the sarissas on the march would have been useless without a presumably lengthy process of heating, applying and setting the pitch, and this surely would have been impractical when it was not possible to be certain when the phalanx might be called into action. All such objections might be overcome if there was any evidence at all that the tube was used in this way, but there is not; it is simply an unidentified artefact, of which only a single example has ever been found, and without any compelling context relating it to a sarissa. We simply don't know what it was used for, but it is vastly unlikely, in my view, that it was used to connect together a two–part sarissa.[14]

Finally, there is the question of the wood from which the sarissa was constructed. The passage of Theophrastus quoted above has often been taken as evidence that the wood of the cornel tree (the Cornelian cherry, *cornus mas*), was used. However, this seems to be a misinterpretation of Theophrastus' words: he states that the cornel tree was as tall as the tallest sarissas, but also that the trunk was short and branched frequently. This would make it totally unsuitable for making into a long-shafted weapon of the same length as the tree is high (unless it was made in sections and slotted together, but the arguments against this notion still stand), and it is more likely that the same wood was used as was preferred for long spears and pikes in the Medieval and later periods; that is, ash. This grows tall and straight, and importantly is much lighter than cornel wood, making it more suitable for a large weapon. It should also be noted that on campaign, or in the various Hellenistic kingdoms spread throughout the Ancient Near East, it might not always have been possible to obtain ash, and we should expect there to have been sarissas made from whatever local wood was available, according to need. Ash would, however, probably have been preferred, and would presumably have been harvested by the kingdoms to form stockpiles, at least in time of peace.[15]

So, there is much to be said about one of the defining features of the Macedonian phalanx, the sarissa, and one of the most important points to make is that there was probably much variation in, and consequently now much uncertainty about, precise dimensions. This means that confident statements such as that 'the phalanx of Alexander the Great carried sarissas 14 cubits long' – or even worse, giving a precise metric measurement correct to the centimetre – are unfounded. All we can say is that broadly the sarissa was a two-handed weapon of great length, averaging around 6–7 metres.

Other spears and javelins

So much for the distinctive long Macedonian spear. Many writers, however, in accordance with the line of argument discussed in the previous chapter that Philip II was not in fact the inventor of the Hellenistic equipment of the phalanx, see evidence for the continued use by the phalanx – particularly under Alexander, and perhaps into the third century – of shorter spears or javelins. Such evidence takes two forms: firstly, the depiction in art (especially tomb paintings) of shorter spears; and secondly, references in sources to Macedonians using spears that seem from the context to be shorter than pikes, or which are specifically referred to as javelins.

In the case of tomb paintings, I think that as usual great caution is needed in taking technical measurements from such depictions. As noted above, a full-length sarissa is a very difficult object to depict, and artistic or architectural considerations are likely to be just as important as military ones in determining the size of a weapon depicted in a painting. So while the figures in the Agios Athanasios tomb, for example (both those on the front wall and on the frieze), all have shorter spears (approximately 2–3.5 metres), I don't think any strong conclusions can be drawn from this.

As to literary evidence, here again we have two groups of evidence. One is passing references to spears which seem from context to be shorter than a full-length sarissa. The classic example is the case of the murder by Alexander of his officer Cleitus, which took place at a banquet when (in one version of the story, Arr. *Anab.* 4.8.8–9) Alexander grabbed a sarissa from a guard and ran Cleitus through with it. It has been reasonably pointed out that this would have been difficult with a 5 metre pike. But then, the idea that a guard at an (indoor!) banquet would have been carrying a 5 metre pike is utterly ludicrous anyway. Surely, guards on banquet guard duty would carry an appropriate weapon, which might still be called a sarissa since, as we have seen, this may have been a generic Macedonian word for spear. This is without considering the fact that we don't know which military unit such guards would have been drawn from. They are surely more likely to be Hypaspists or bodyguards than members of the regular infantry, and as such we would expect them to have shorter spears anyway. So I do not believe that this evidence carries much weight either.[16]

The second set of literary evidence is, however, much more persuasive. The most important passage is the description in Diodorus (and Quintus Curtius) of a single combat between two members of Alexander's army, the Macedonian Coragus and the Greek Dioxippus:

> 'The Macedonians and Alexander backed Coragus because he was one of them, while the Greeks favoured Dioxippus. The two advanced to the field of honour, the Macedonian clad in his expensive armour but the Athenian naked, his body oiled, carrying a well-balanced club ... . As they approached each other, the Macedonian flung his javelin [*longche*] from a proper distance, but the other inclined his body slightly and avoided its impact. Then the Macedonian poised his sarissa and charged, but the Greek, when he came within reach, struck the sarissa with his club and shattered it.' (Diodorus 17.100.4–6)

So here we have a Macedonian armed with both sarissa and *longche* (the latter evidently being a javelin, or at least used as a javelin on this occasion – the word itself is used for various types of thrusting or throwing spears in other authors). Curtius, in his account of this event, records:

> 'The Macedonian had assumed his usual arms, holding in his left hand a bronze shield and a spear – they call it sarisa – in his right a lance [*lancea*], and girt with a sword.' (Quintus Curtius 9.7.19)

The Latin *lancea* – often confusingly translated 'lance' – can also be a javelin.

So if this story is anything to go by, the 'usual arms' of a Macedonian consisted of both a sarissa and a javelin. This is also reflected in the account of the phalanx created by the Roman Emperor Caracalla that was quoted at the start of the chapter, where the javelin was called an *aichme* – a very generic word that can be applied to just about any shafted weapon, or even just to the spearhead. So Caracalla's (or Cassius Dio's) understanding at least is that Alexander's men carried two spears. It is not clear, to say the least, how a sarissa and a javelin could both be carried at once. Curtius adds some details about switching from left to right hand, but as these details are not in Diodorus' version, they may be his invention.[17]

Then there are scattered accounts of men in Philip's and Alexander's army using missiles. For example at the siege of Halicarnassus, where two of Alexander's men (clearly phalangites, since Arrian calls them hoplites and they were in Perdiccas' *taxis*) fell to drunken boasting about their prowess, and decided to take on the city defenders singlehanded. When the defenders sallied out to meet them, 'they killed those who came up close and discharged missiles at the more distant enemies' (Arr. *Anab.* 1.21.1–2). That individual soldiers attacking a city at night would not be carrying 5 metre-plus pikes is not too surprising.

There is also the interesting case of the Battle of the Hydaspes (326), where Alexander's army faced an Indian army complete with elephants for the first time. Here, the Macedonians 'attacked the animals at their own judgement, giving way wherever they charged, but following close as they turned round, and shooting at them with javelins'. The Macedonians in question may be phalangites, or they may be javelin-armed skirmishers fighting in front of the phalanx (see further in Chapter 7); but if phalangites, then this is another example of javelin use.

We should also note that toward the end of his reign Alexander planned to incorporate Persians with bows and javelins into his phalanx (Arr. *Anab.* 7.23.3–4). Although this scheme was not carried through (so far as we know), it might provide some further indication that using javelins was not wholly alien to the phalanx.

What are we to make of these indications? I think it unlikely that the phalanx ever went into pitched battle with both sarissa and javelins (or javelin). The practical difficulties – even if the sarissa was much shorter than the full Hellenistic pike, which I doubt – seem too great, and there is no indication in any of the major battle accounts that the phalanx used javelins (except perhaps the Hydaspes). What I think is more likely is that the phalanx, at least up to the time of Alexander, retained its ability to fight with javelins when appropriate; that is, not in pitched battle but in all the other circumstances in which infantry are called upon to fight, such as sieges, forced marches, assaults over difficult terrain and the like. As discussed in the previous chapter, Macedonian infantry were probably initially javelin skirmishers, so while Philip retrained them to fight in the phalanx with the sarissa, it is easy to believe that they would have retained their ability to fight with javelins and in a looser order when necessary (a skill probably not quickly forgotten). If this is correct, then the phalangites of Alexander – who were after all originally almost all members of Philip's army – would have been able both to fight in close formation with the sarissa in pitched battle, and adopt a more skirmishing role with javelins when called upon to do so. As I will discuss below with regard to the 'lighter-armed' part of the phalanx, even if this did not apply to the entire phalanx, it might have applied to particular units. Thus Philip and Alexander's phalangites could have been dual-role infantry, able to fight in the phalanx and as javelineers. We might note also in this context that the training regimes for young soldiers that the Greek cities established from the late fourth century – the *ephebeia* or ephebate – always included training in the use of javelins and other missile weapons.[18]

After Alexander, this dual role appears to have been abandoned – at least, we do not encounter further examples of phalangites fighting with javelins, and the point of Polybius' (second-century) critique of the phalanx is that it was a one-use formation, good only at fighting pitched battles, while the equipment lists in Asclepiodotus mention only the sarissa as the weapon of the phalangite. We may speculate that there were two reasons for this. The larger armies of the Successors and Hellenistic kingdoms had access to vast numbers of light infantry from the native populations over which they ruled, allowing the Greco-Macedonian phalangites to specialize on their heavy infantry role. Then, during the wars of the Successors, the men of Philip's army were becoming elderly and would have retired or died, so that experience in fighting as light infantry might have died with them, with no need to train up new recruits in this style of fighting, since so many specialist light infantry were available.

We should also consider the case of the Peltasts. In the Classical period, the word 'peltasts' (*peltastai*) was used to refer to javelin-throwing light infantry (although perhaps slightly less light, and with more ability to stand and fight rather than just skirmish, compared to the pure light infantry, the *psiloi*). From the fourth century and into the Hellenistic period, this use of the word fell out of use, and instead we find 'peltasts' being used primarily for the elite infantry guard of the Antigonid army. These were clearly armed with the sarissa, as Plutarch's account of the Battle of Pydna makes clear (see Chapter 9 below). However, the tacticians also provide a definition of peltasts, as seen in the quote from Asclepiodotus 1.2 at the start of this chapter. I will say more on the shield below, but for now it is the spear that is of interest. If the description in Asclepiodotus ('The corps of the peltasts stands in a sense between these two [hoplites and *psiloi*], for the *pelte* is a kind of small light shield (*aspis*), and their spears are much shorter than those of the hoplites') is accurate, and if it can correctly be applied to the Antigonid Peltasts, then we should expect them to have smaller shields and shorter spears than the hoplites (phalangites, in our terminology) of the phalanx – which would indeed make them, in the terms that I discussed in the previous chapter, similar to Iphicratean peltasts. This is an appealing identification, although the difficulty is that many of the accounts of Antigonid Peltasts in action make it sound as if they are armed identically to, or at least very similarly to, the phalanx proper. It is possible that this shorter spear was still wielded in two hands and was still called in the Macedonian style the sarissa, even though it was shorter than the long weapon of the main phalanx. It is also possible that the elite Peltasts retained a dual armament role, bearing the shorter spears when they were called on to perform the duties of light infantry (scouting ahead of the army, seizing high ground or making rapid marches), but picking up full-sized sarissas to fight as part of the phalanx in pitched battle. It is also just possible that the tacticians' description of three types of infantry (alongside their three types of cavalry, three types of intervals for the phalanx, and so forth) is a bit too neat, and that they are oversimplifying a more complex set of real distinctions. I do not have any complete solution to these questions, though my suspicion is that the Hellenistic Peltast was a dual-role infantryman, able to fight with short spear in more open order or full-length sarissa in the phalanx. I will have more to say on this question shortly.[19]

There is also the possibility that the sarissa under Alexander (and presumably Philip) was itself much shorter than its later Hellenistic incarnation, and was a one-handed weapon much more similar to the traditional hoplite spear. I do not find this at all likely, for the reasons discussed already and because of the evident assumption in antiquity that the distinctive features of the phalanx were already established under Philip and Alexander, but will revisit this question in the course of discussing the shields of the phalanx, below.[20]

The Macedonian shield

'Of the shields [*aspidon*] of the phalanx the best is the Macedonian, bronze, eight palms, not too hollow.' (Asclepiodotus, *Tactics* 5.1)

Close variants of the above statement by Asclepiodotus, who was writing probably in the early first century, are found in the parallel texts of Aelian and Arrian. From this statement, rather as is the case for the sarissa, many modern authors feel able to confidently assert that the Macedonian phalanx at all times carried small shields called *peltai*, 60cm in diameter, with a flat profile. Several observations can be made about such assertions. Firstly, as with the sarissa, there is no reason to suppose that all Macedonian phalanxes throughout the period carried the same type of shield. For example, it is often stated that the phalanx of Alexander the Great carried such shields, and while perhaps they did, Asclepiodotus' statement is not good evidence for it. Asclepiodotus also uses the word 'aspis', not pelte, to describe the shield – more on this below. It is not clear whether he means that the best shield is the Macedonian one, a shield which is of bronze, eight palms in diameter and not too hollow, or that the best shield is of bronze, eight palms in diameter, not too hollow and of the Macedonian type – in other words, is the 'Macedonian-ness' of a shield separate from its material, size and profile? And again, Asclepiodotus is stating that in his, or his sources', view the best shield for the phalanx is of this type, and this tells us that other shields, less good perhaps (in his opinion), were available and used, and other opinions might have been available as to which was best and why.[21]

Most discussion of the shield of the phalanx has centred around attempts to reconcile this statement of Asclepiodotus with the available artistic and archaeological evidence. Such attempts have always been fraught with difficulty, and may be misguided from the outset, since we must expect shields of different design and specification to have been used at different times and places. As recently as forty years ago, the lack of surviving examples of Macedonian shields could lead a modern scholar to conclude that in art the '"Macedonian" shield and aspis [the Classical hoplite aspis] are shown as approximately the same size'. But in the past few decades a number of Macedonian shields have been discovered, in various states of disrepair, allowing an estimate of their size to be made that fits more closely to the eight palms of Asclepiodotus – eight palms is two Greek feet, so using the approximate measures I used for the sarissa, about 60cm. Surviving shields vary in size (as we should expect), but some are around 66cm, which is close enough to count as about eight palms, although eight palms would be right at the bottom end of the range of surviving sizes. So there is no longer any reason to doubt that shields of this size did exist; but that is not the end of the story.[22]

Although shields of this smaller size have been discovered, not all shields are this size, with existing examples, so far as can be determined given their state of preservation, going up to about 80cm in diameter. This figure might still loosely be considered about eight palms, and is at any rate smaller than the traditional hoplite shield, which is believed to have averaged about 1 metre in diameter. It is worth stressing here that, quite apart from any doubts about uniformity of sizes across the period, we should expect shields, even of the same pattern, to come in different sizes. Classical hoplites provided their own equipment, so that each shield would have been bespoke. Macedonian shields were probably manufactured and distributed centrally, but even so, different sized men must have carried at least slightly different sized shields, since the length of the forearm determines whether the shield can be used properly. Small variations, at least a 'small, medium or large' size, should therefore be expected, and this could easily account for variations of 10cm or so, which would cover almost all the extant examples, and seems too small a variation to allow such shields to be divided into two separate types.

There still remains the matter of depictions in art, which led to the original conclusion that the eight palm shield was not in fact standard. Here we come across further complexity around the question of what a Macedonian shield was like (and called). The traditional hoplite shield was about 1 metre in diameter, with a bowl-like shape but a fairly flat profile, the bowl shape being created by a steeply angled and thick side wall to the bowl, creating a wide flat bowl (see fig. 2.4). Around this bowl was a flat rim of around 5cm width. This classic shape – flat bowl with offset rim – remained remarkably consistent throughout the Classical era, with hoplite shields of this shape depicted in art from the seventh to the fourth centuries (and beyond). The shield was constructed from wood, with (usually) a bronze facing over the whole of the front and on the rim, and was carried using two attachments on the inside – a central rigid *porpax* or armband (often bronze), into which the forearm was inserted up to the elbow, and a flexible *antilabe* or handle (often of rope), near the rim, which was grasped with the hand. Shields of this appearance continue to be common in Hellenistic art (for example, the gods and heroes on the Great Altar from Pergamon bear such shields). However, there is some debate as to whether this is because such shields were still widely used, or because this was the traditional shape for a shield and thus carried a strong sense of 'Greekness', and so would be used particularly in art depicting mythological or heroic subjects or where symbolism was more important than military accuracy. This shield was called an *aspis*, which is the general Greek word for shields of any kind, or if more precision was required, sometimes an 'Argive *aspis*'.

The Macedonian shield seems to have differed in several ways, but the most important was that it did not have the offset rim, being instead a simple bowl shape (fig. 2.4). This seems to be the defining difference (aside from the decoration, on which more below). The shield would not, presumably (despite the implication in Asclepiodotus), have been made only of bronze, but of wood with a bronze outer surface, like the hoplite shield. A shield made from a single sheet of bronze without a wooden core would have been very weak. As we have seen, existing examples are all smaller than hoplite shields, if not quite so small as eight palms, so assuming that what have survived are a representative sample (not a totally secure assumption), then we can say that Macedonian shields were somewhat smaller in diameter than hoplite shields, if not dramatically so.

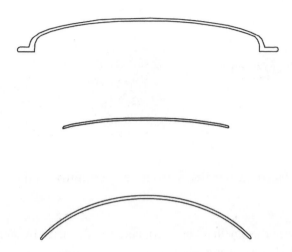

Fig. 2.4. Shield cross-sections: top, Argive aspis; middle, Macedonian *pelte*; bottom, Macedonian *aspis*.

Asclepiodotus' preference that they be 'not too hollow' – that is, presumably, that the bowl shape not be too concave – is interesting, since several depictions in art of Macedonian shields are very hollow indeed. The stand-out examples are the Pergamon bronze plaque examined above in the context of the sarissa (fig. 2.1) and the shields on the Aemilius Paullus monument constructed in Delphi to celebrate the Roman victory at Pydna (fig. 2.5). In the case of the latter monument, the shields depicted are assumed to be Macedonian given their surface decoration, but they are of a highly dished shape, and also appear just as large as a hoplite shield, so far as it is possible to tell from a depiction in art of this type. It is possible that the sculptor struggled to depict a flattish shield in a perspective view and this is the reason for the heavily dished shape. It is also possible that the sculptor was just depicting a generic shield and wasn't too careful about ensuring that it was precisely the right diameter and shape. Nevertheless, this does reinforce the suggestion that there were several, perhaps many, variations on the shape and size of Macedonian shields, and perhaps that those used by the Antigonids in Macedon itself were larger and more bowl-shaped than those in use in other kingdoms.[23]

Some corroboration of this is provided by another piece of physical evidence, a stone shield-mould from Ptolemaic Egypt. This object would presumably have been used to hammer the pattern into a sheet of bronze (which would then have been affixed to a wooden shield). It is around 70cm in diameter, again a bit large for 'eight palms', but it is possible that the outer surface might have

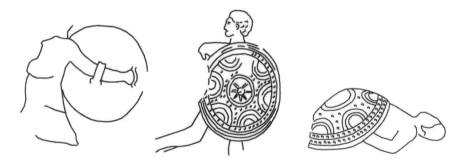

Fig. 2.5. Macedonian shields from the Aemilius Paullus monument in Delphi.

been bent over the wooden core, reducing the diameter by some centimetres. This mould also has a notably flat profile – not conclusive, since the mould might have been flat for the patterning, and the bronze then bent into shape over a curved core, but it is likely that this does match the finished shape of the shield. If so, we may be seeing evidence of regional variations: Antigonid (and based on the Pergamon plaque, Seleucid) shields might have been of a larger and more dished size and shape, while Ptolemaic shields were smaller and flatter. This idea is supported by the possibility, from internal evidence, that Asclepiodotus was describing the Ptolemaic army (the only army of the major kingdoms still in existence in more than skeleton form at the time he was likely writing). Certainty is impossible given the paucity of evidence, but it could well be that the words of Asclepiodotus are a specific description of one regional variation, the Ptolemaic Macedonian shield. However, it is not quite so simple as to suppose that the shields used in Macedon itself were larger, of course, since several of the surviving examples, with a smallish size, are from Greece and Macedon. So again there is no simple pattern of shield size, geographical or chronological.[24]

One more thing is worth noting about Asclepiodotus' testimony concerning hoplite and peltast shields (*Tactics* 1.2, as quoted at the start of this chapter). As is common for many ancient writers, Asclepiodotus uses 'hoplites' to mean heavy infantry generally (not in the semi-technical modern sense of Classical Greek heavy infantry), and the heavy infantry he is talking about are of course the phalangites of the phalanx. Now, if the phalangites' shields, at eight palms width, are really the largest, and the peltasts' shields are really smaller, as Asclepiodotus states, then peltast shields would have to be very small indeed. It is open to doubt whether such small shields would be useful, or indeed existed at all, and there is little artistic and no archaeological evidence for shields smaller than 60cm. This might suggest that the usual hoplite shields were larger than eight palms, and it was the peltast shields which were really more in the region of this size, and Asclepiodotus was conflating two sources, one on the different sizes of shields (where hoplite shields are large and peltast shields smaller), and a different source (perhaps Ptolemaic) for the Macedonian shield he describes. This is only a tentative suggestion, but it should be noted at least that there is a contradiction in Asclepiodotus here, and the assertion by many modern authors that the phalangites' shield was a small one, while avoiding the problem of the relative size of peltast shields, requires serious qualification.[25]

Mention of the peltasts brings up the question of the name of the Macedonian shield. To many modern authors, the situation is simple: the phalangite's shield was called a *pelte*, and this is what the eight palm shield is called. As usual, it is not that simple. Asclepiodotus says that of the shields (*aspidon*) of the phalanx, the best is the Macedonian, and does not refer to *peltai* being used by hoplites (phalangites) at all, but only by peltasts. Now, as noted in other contexts, we do not find the same strictly technical usage of words in Greek as we would hope to find in modern English, and there tends to be a fairly free and easy approach to the use even of what we would think of as technical terms. It may well be that Greek authors use the terms *aspis* and *pelte* pretty much interchangeably, or more according to the personal preference of the author than in line with any technical terminology. One definition of the word *pelte* does indicate the important difference. As noted before, Aristotle states that 'a *pelte* is a type of *aspis* without a rim', and this distinction makes perfect sense in the case of the rimless Macedonian shield. He does not say that a *pelte* is (necessarily) smaller or lighter than the Classical hoplite *aspis*, though lack of a heavy rim would certainly make the shield lighter (and compare with Asclepiodotus' definition above, 'for the *pelte* is a kind of small light *aspis*'). The simple assertion that the phalangite's shield was a *pelte* may therefore be sound inasmuch as the Macedonian shield was rimless, but this does not prevent many ancient authors – and indeed many ancient official documents – calling the shield simply an *aspis*.

Asclepiodotus, as we have noted, refers to the shield of the phalanx as an *aspis* throughout (as do the other tactical manuals in the same tradition). When, in the late third century, the Spartan army was rearmed 'in the Macedonian fashion' by Cleomenes, they are said by Plutarch (*Philop.*9.2) to have adopted the sarissa and to have changed the carrying arrangements of their shields – *aspisi* – but not the type of shield, which a later source (Pausanias 8.50) specifically calls an Argive *aspis* (that is, a traditional hoplite shield). Polybius describes a force of Megalopolitans being re-equipped 'in the Macedonian fashion' by the Macedonian king Antigonus Doson (Pol.2.65.3; 4.69.4–5; 5.91.7), and calls the shields with which they are issued *chalcaspides* (and they were confused with Macedonians because of these shields). The Macedonian military regulations in inscriptions from Amphipolis, including the one detailing fines for missing equipment quoted above, also call the shield an *aspis*. It is possible that such cases, particularly in literary sources, are all just using *aspis* in a loose sense to mean any kind of shield, including a *pelte*, but the Amphipolis regulations makes it certain that the Macedonians themselves called their shields *aspides*.[26]

We can also approach from the other direction and look at examples where Macedonian shields do seem to be called *peltai*. Here we find the curious fact that one writer, the biographer Plutarch, seems to refer to Macedonian shields exclusively as *peltai*, even though this terminology is rare in other authors. The most well-known example comes from his description of the Battle of Pydna:

> 'And when he [the Roman general Aemilius Paullus] saw that the rest of the Macedonian troops also were drawing their *peltai* from their shoulders round in front of them, and with sarissas set at one level.' (Plutarch, *Aemilius Paullus* 19.1)

This passage is quoted very frequently as evidence that the Macedonian shield was called, by all, a *pelte* (as well as for details on the carrying arrangements, as we shall see shortly). The Aemilius Paullus monument at Delphi, as discussed above, depicts large (albeit rimless) shields, so Plutarch may just be using the term to convey their shape rather than their size. It may be that Plutarch's understanding, from whatever source, was that Macedonian shields were *peltai*, but it does appear as if this might be a distinctively Plutarchian usage, and certainly among other authors the general word *aspis* is far more common (or appears exclusively). Another Plutarch passage from the Battle of Pydna is similarly widely quoted:

> 'Now that the Macedonians engaged man to man or in small detachments, they could only hack with their small daggers [*encheiridioi*] against the firm and long shields [*thureoi*] of the Romans, and oppose little peltai [*peltariois*] to their swords.' (Plutarch, *Aemilius Paullus* 20.5)

Again, this is usually taken to apply to the entire Macedonian phalanx, and note that here the Macedonians have not just *peltai*, but 'little peltai', using the diminutive *peltarion*, though we don't find this comment in other authors; neither Livy, whose account of Pydna, also based on that of Polybius, also survives, nor Polybius himself, who wrote a detailed comparison of the strengths and weaknesses of legion and phalanx. In this case I believe that these details in Plutarch are taken from a particular source, the account of Scipio Nasica, who was in overall command of the Paelignian cohort defeated by the Peltasts at the opening of the battle, and who likely took part in the final massacre of the Peltasts at the end. I think it likely that this detail of daggers and little *peltai* should therefore apply specifically to the Peltasts, who we would indeed expect to be the bearers of smaller shields (see further below).[27]

There is also inscriptional evidence for Macedonian *peltai*, in the form of four (fragmentary) dedications of captured equipment where *peltai* are mentioned, three from the late fourth century and one from the late third century. The first refers to 'Arms dedicated by Alexander son of Polyperchon. Fine full cuirass. Gilt pelta. Silvered bronze greaves', the second to a 'bronze Macedonian pelta' and another to a 'Macedonian pelta'. Perhaps the most interesting, that from the third century (reign of Philip V), refers to 'Ten peltai, ten sarisai, ten helmets, upon which is inscribed "King of the Macedonians, Philip son of King Demetrius, upon his victory over the Dardanians and Maidoi"' – this being a reminder (since dedications were of arms captured from the enemy) that Macedon's Balkan neighbours could also use *pelte* and sarissa.[28]

So what are we to make of these differences in terminology? I think at least that the simple statement, oft repeated (and generally quoting Plut. *Aem*.19.1), that the shield of the phalanx was called a *pelte*, needs qualification. It could be called a *pelte*, where the rimless Macedonian shield was meant. This was probably lighter, and could be smaller, than the traditional hoplite shield, but the name itself does not carry any strong implication of size or weight (but rather of form – lack of rim), and the two terms, *aspis* and *pelte*, could be used interchangeably. I think given the casual Greek approach to technical terminology that not too much can be read into the use of *pelte* or *aspis* in any given situation, although we can safely assume that while a rimless Macedonian shield could be called an *aspis*, a traditional rimmed hoplite shield could not be called a *pelte*. It seems likely, especially from the inscriptional evidence (the Amphipolis regulation in particular), that while the Macedonians themselves called their shield an *aspis* (as a familiar shield shape, it was simply 'what a shield looked like'), southern Greeks, with a tradition of large rimmed *aspides*, were more likely to call the Macedonian shield a *pelte*, perhaps to emphasize its 'otherness' and difference. This could be why we see *peltai* referred to more often in Athenian inscriptions and in the pages of Plutarch. On occasions where Macedonians do refer to *peltai* (as in the dedication mentioned above), then perhaps some specific smaller example was meant. In particular, they may be referring to the shields of the peltasts, not of the hoplites (phalangites) of the phalanx.

The existence of two names for shields, and the presence in art and archaeology of shields of different sizes, has led some to conclude that there were in fact two sizes of Macedonian shields, a larger and a smaller size, as we might expect from Asclepiodotus talking of the hoplites (phalangites) having the largest size of shield, and the peltasts having smaller shields (and shorter spears). This leads to problems when it is also then asserted that the phalangites' shield was the smaller shield, of eight palms' width, and called a *pelte*; for then we would have to look for a yet smaller shield for the peltasts to carry to match Asclepiodotus' account, and we would have to conclude that the hoplites (phalangites) carried small *peltai* while the peltasts carried even smaller *peltai*. (The diminutive *peltarion* of Plutarch, referenced above, might be suggestive in this case, but there is still no evidence for shields smaller than eight palms.) The name 'peltasts' itself is not necessarily conclusive as to what the name of the shield they carried would have been, but we might at least strongly suspect that peltasts carried *peltai*. This is the point of, for example, Diodorus' account of the reforms of Iphicrates, where hoplites are said to have re-equipped with *peltai* and thus become known as peltasts. If the Macedonian hoplites carried small *peltai*, then what did the peltasts carry? And more seriously, who would then carry the larger-sized shields that are also depicted and found in art and archaeology (shields up to, if not classical *aspis* size, at least nearer 70–80cm diameter).[29]

Allied to this question, there is another thorny problem, and that is the survival in art of shields of the classical type (large and rimmed) in a Macedonian context. There are several examples of this. The best known is the Alexander Sarcophagus (not in fact Alexander's Sarcophagus, but probably that of a client king). This large stone tomb is decorated with detailed depictions of Macedonian and Persian warriors in combat, infantry and cavalry. Although some of the Macedonians are depicted 'heroically nude' (nudity being the normal default in Greek art of mythological subjects), not all are, and those who are clothed are depicted with a high degree of technical accuracy, as can be seen by comparison with surviving artefacts such as helmets. The paintwork (now greatly faded, but surviving in late nineteenth-century AD copies) shows that technical details such as the colours of Macedonian cloaks and Persian tunics match those known from other sources. There is thus a good chance that the Sarcophagus depicts Macedonian infantry equipment accurately, and all the infantry are carrying shields which in size and shape appear identical to traditional hoplite *aspides*. The Sarcophagus itself is dated to the late fourth century and depicts Alexander in combat alongside his Macedonians, so it is generally supposed that this may be a depiction of the infantry of Alexander, or at least of a time only shortly after his death.[30]

There are a couple of other notable depictions of what appear to be classic rimmed *aspides* in Macedonian contexts. The first are the remains of a large monument at ancient Beroea (modern Veria), which may have been constructed for Pyrrhus of Epirus, and which depicts a combination of small, rimless shields (*peltai*, we may assume) with larger rimmed shields of classical *aspis* appearance. There are also similar rimmed shields depicted in wall carvings alongside armour at Dion (Dium), the Macedonian religious centre.[31]

The Sarcophagus (and these other monuments) pose a problem for those who want to assign eight-palm wide *peltai* to all Macedonian phalanxes at all periods: who are the infantry depicted on the Sarcophagus? We must assume they are Macedonians, not Greeks, since the point of the monument is to depict Alexander among Macedonians (and some scenes depict the execution of what are presumably Greek mercenaries), and they are clearly heavy infantry, from their equipment (those who are not naked). There are two Macedonian infantry contingents to choose from, the regular phalangites and the Hypaspists, the elite infantry force of the Macedonian army. The usual conclusion is that these infantry are Hypaspists, and that Hypaspists were therefore armed with the traditional *aspis* and a shorter spear, held in one hand, and fought either as traditional hoplites, or perhaps as some form of light hoplite, with hoplite equipment but operating in a more mobile role. This would mean that the bulk of the infantry, the (putatively) *pelte*-and-sarissa-carrying phalangites, are not depicted on the monument.

I have a number of reservations about this conclusion. More will be said in later chapters about the various royal guards of the kingdoms, but in the context of equipment, the following points should be made. First of all, the name 'Hypaspists' itself is not indicative of equipment carried. Greeks did often name infantry from their equipment – such as *sarissophoroi*, sarissa-carriers or phalangites, or *thureophoroi*, bearers of the large Gallic or Roman shield, and of course peltasts – but in the case of Hypaspists, although it means 'shield (*aspis*) carrier', it is not an equipment-derived name but an honorary title. A hypaspist (small 'h') is the shield bearer of a notable personage (often the king), in the sense of his squire or personal attendant. The Macedonian Hypaspists were originally the personal attendants of the king, a combination of his senior staff and bodyguards, and they can be seen in this role under Alexander and also, 150 years later, under Philip V and Perseus. As we have seen, Philip II seems to have called his infantry guard Foot Companions, and it is likely that Alexander, in extending this title to most or all of the infantry phalanx, needed a new honorary title for the infantry guard. They therefore became Hypaspists, extending the title of the inner staff (though these may have continued to be called Hypaspists alongside them). So they were the 'Shield Bearers of the King' (or possibly the 'Shield Bearers of the Companions'). As such, the name alone does not indicate that the shields they carried were Argive *aspides*. We should note, however, that later in Alexander's reign the Hypasists were renamed *Argyraspides* (Silver Shields), and in this case it is more likely that the name indicates the shield carried. It could be then that these re-equipped Hypaspists did carry larger shields, but equally it could be that the *aspis* part of the name in this case just means a generic shield without regard to type, especially if the Macedonians themselves did not usually call any of their shields *peltai*, as discussed. At any rate, this particular name (Hypaspists) is not conclusive either way.[32]

So there is no *a priori* reason to suppose that the Hypasists would have carried Argive shields. There are two, in my view compelling, arguments that they did not. One is that the successors of the Hypaspists in the later Antigonid army of Macedon (late in the third century) were the Peltasts whom we have already encountered above, and it is also possible to detect traces of Peltast royal guards, at least in the Seleucid army. It seems reasonable to suppose that Peltasts did carry *peltai*, since this is a specific shield-derived name (and the particular, *pelte*, overrides the generic, *aspis*). According to what we would expect from the name, and to the evidence of Asclepiodotus and others discussed above, peltasts carry *peltai* and hoplites do not. That the Guard Infantry of the later kingdoms were peltasts and carried *peltai* is not conclusive as to the shields carried by the Guards of Alexander, but Macedonian military conservatism, in which equipment and organization often remained broadly unchanged across a period of 200 years (despite many variations of detail), suggests to me that it is at least quite likely that the difference between the phalangites and the Peltasts of Philip V and Perseus reflects a similar difference between the phalangites and Hypaspists of Philip II and Alexander. As such, the phalangites are hoplites, the bearers of the largest type of shield, and the Hypaspists are peltasts, bearers of smaller, lighter shields (as Asclepiodotus says).

Confirmation for this conclusion comes from a second line of argument. The Hypaspists under Alexander, as has often been noted, functioned tactically as a lighter form of infantry than the phalangites of the main phalanx. They have often been said to form a link between the slower phalanx and the faster cavalry (although I do have doubts about this characterization, as I will discuss in Chapter 7), and also were used for a variety of special missions under Alexander where speed and lightness of equipment were important. The Peltasts of the Antigonid army acted in similar roles, as a special fast strike force of infantry. The Argive *aspis* was noted as being a particularly heavy and unwieldy piece of equipment. Hoplites so equipped were notoriously unsuited to operating at speed (to chase down enemy light infantry, say) or on difficult terrain, and the first act of any hoplite hoping to run away from battle to save his life was to discard his shield, even though it was his main form of protection. Its weight and unwieldiness outweighed its defensive uses, outside the close formation of the phalanx. This means that I find it unlikely that a fast strike force such as the Hypaspists would have been equipped with such shields, and it is surely more likely, if anyone is to be carrying a lighter, handier shield, that it would be the Hypaspists.

If this is correct, then we are left with the problem of which type of infantry is depicted on the Alexander Sarcophagus, and whose are the shields depicted at Beroea and Dion. The obvious conclusion is that these are the phalangites, the bearers of 'shields of the largest size', according to Asclepiodotus' later definition. Before reaching this conclusion too certainly, we should of course consider the possibility that neither the Sarcophagus nor the other monuments depict shields with strict technical accuracy. The Argive *aspis* was the quintessential Greek shield, and it could be that shields of this type were depicted in sculpture more to symbolize Greekness than because they are an accurate record of military equipment. I think this is quite possible – that the shields on the Sarcophagus should then be seen alongside the heroically nude infantry figures, rather than the accurately depicted helmets and clothing of the fully dressed figures. It is not an entirely satisfactory argument, however. There is precious little direct evidence for the arms and armour of Alexander's infantry, and it is unfortunate to explain away the one piece of evidence there is as artistic licence. It is also harder to make this argument for the Beroea and Dion monuments, particularly Beroea, where two types of shields are depicted together.

So if we are to accept the evidence from sculpture, and at the same time prefer to assign *peltai* to the lightly equipped Hypaspists (later Peltasts), then we are left with the conclusion that at least some of the phalangites under Alexander did not carry Macedonian shields (smaller rimless shields), but rather traditionally shaped and sized Argive shields. This should not be too shocking a conclusion since, as we have seen, Asclepiodotus only notes (200 years later) that 'of the shields of the phalanx the best is the Macedonian'. We must expect that different shields were used at different times, and therefore it is not too surprising if, at some time in the reigns of Philip or Alexander, at least some of the phalangites (perhaps all – we simply don't know) were equipped with Argive shields. However, many modern historians are highly resistant to this conclusion. Usually the opposition follows two strands: one is the evidence of Asclepiodotus about the eight-palmed Macedonian shield, but we have already seen that this cannot simply be applied as a blanket prescription for all phalangites, and the other is the supposed impossibility of carrying an Argive *aspis* while also wielding a sarissa in two hands.

The latter objection is a strong one that needs to be looked at in detail. Two possibilities need to be considered: that the evidence for use of Argive shields by Alexander's phalanx is itself evidence that they did not wield the sarissa in two hands; and that the prohibition on using an Argive shield with a two-handed sarissa is in fact in error.

The argument that Alexander's phalanx did not wield the sarissa in two hands – and that the sarissa of this period was in fact a long spear rather than, strictly speaking, a pike – has a long history, having been proposed by the late nineteenth-century historians of Alexander's army, and periodically proposed by a number of scholars since, in opposition to the orthodox view that his phalangites were all pikemen. It is a difficult point to prove or disprove either way since (rather surprisingly perhaps) the evidence for Alexander's phalanx is extremely sketchy, and most of the firm evidence for Macedonian equipment dates, as we have already seen, from later in the Hellenistic period. As discussed above, the nearest thing to contemporary evidence is Theophrastus' reference to the Macedonian sarissa of 12 cubits; as noted, a case can be made, through comparison with long Medieval spears, that even a spear of this length could be wielded one-handed. However, I think that the main objection to the idea that Alexander's phalangites were not pikemen is the more general one, as discussed in the previous chapter, that it was assumed in antiquity that the phalanx of Alexander was a pike phalanx, and that Philip devised the equipment and organization of the Macedonian phalanx. If this is not taken to mean a pikeman's equipment, then Philip is left having invented nothing new, and there would have to be some unknown inventor of the actual pike phalanx, perhaps some time in the third century, along with an unrecorded introduction of such equipment to the Hellenistic armies that went unnoticed by all ancient authors, who continued to believe that the phalanx equipment they were familiar with dated back to Philip and Alexander. I think that the balance of probability is greatly in favour of Alexander's phalanx, or at least a proportion of it, consisting of pikemen.

This leaves the second argument: is it really impossible to carry a sarissa in two hands with an Argive shield? Again there is a paucity of evidence, and this also seems as if it is a question of simple physical possibilities that could easily be resolved by experimental archaeology or re-enactment, though to my knowledge it has not (yet) been tried (perhaps because re-enactors seem completely committed to the idea that the shield of the phalanx was at all times an eight palm *pelte*). Two pieces of evidence suggest to me that it was in fact possible. One is that some of the figures on the Alexander Sarcophagus have their left hands free, and are using them to seize hold of Greek or Persian prisoners (fig.2.6). The sculptor does not depict how the shield is carried (and perhaps did not know), but if the left hand could be freed to this extent, it could presumably also grip the shaft of a sarissa. The second indication is that, as we have seen, when the Spartan king Cleomenes equipped his phalanx with the sarissa in the late third century, he is said to have changed the carrying arrangements of the shield (more on this shortly), but not to have issued new shields (and we can assume that previously Argive shields were carried as part of standard Classical hoplite equipment). I think, therefore, that the burden of proof rests with those who believe that an Argive shield could not be carried with a sarissa, and that in the present state of our knowledge, there is no reason to conclude that the infantry depicted on the Sarcophagus cannot be phalangites.

We could speculate further that some or all of the phalanx of Alexander were equipped with such shields in the course of his reign (or perhaps already under Philip), while other elements of the phalanx continued to use Macedonian shields. There might thus under Alexander have been two types of phalangites, with heavier (Argive shield) or lighter (Macedonian shield) equipment. We do indeed read in the Alexander historians, particularly Arrian, of the 'lighter equipped' part of the phalanx (e.g. Arr. *Anab.* 1.27.8, 'the lighter armed hoplites'; 3.23.3 'the Hypaspists and the lightest armed of the Macedonian phalanx'). This distinction has caused much debate, and we should note that Arrian also uses *kouphotatoi*, translated as 'lighter armed', for light infantry, archers and javelineers (e.g. 2.4.6; 3.18.5), so it is likely that a better translation would be 'more active' or 'more agile'. Even so, given the possibility that two types of spears were carried, there might also have been two types of shield: the 'more agile' parts of the phalanx could have carried a Macedonian shield and shorter spear or javelins, while the less agile

Fig. 2.6. Macedonians with prisoners, from the Alexander Sarcophagus.

parts carried an Argive shield and full sarissa, though we should expect both parts to be equipped with the full sarissa for pitched battles, since there is no indication of a different tactical role for different parts of the phalanx in battle. To engage in wilder speculation, this distinction might be reflected in the much-discussed term *asthetairoi* ('Kin', 'Best', 'Town' or 'Star Companions') which is applied to some parts of Alexander's phalanx – perhaps these were equipped with Argive shields and the *pezhetairoi* ('Foot Companions') with Macedonian shields, or vice versa (but this is only a very tentative suggestion). At any rate, I do not think there are grounds for ruling out the carrying of Argive shield and sarissa, and it may be that amongst all the variations in shield size, shield shape and sarissa length that have been discussed, this was just one of the available permutations.[33]

But this does bring up the question of how the shield was carried; not just a putative Argive phalangite's shield, but also the more widely recognized Macedonian shield. An idea has grown up among modern historians that, the hands and arms being fully occupied by the sarissa, the shield was suspended from a strap around the neck. This is a notion that has proved remarkably attractive to many, and even to those who accept that the shield must also have been attached to the left arm, the idea of an additional neck strap has proven irresistible. I am convinced that it is wrong.[34]

The actual evidence for this neck strap – often termed a *telamon*, using the Greek word – seems to come down entirely to a single passage in Plutarch, the description we encountered above of the reaction of the Roman general Aemilius Paullus to the sight of the Macedonian phalanx at the Battle of Pydna in 168:

> 'And when he saw that the rest of the Macedonian troops also were drawing their *peltai* from their shoulders round in front of them, and with sarissas set at one level were withstanding his shield-bearing troops [*thureophoroi*], and saw too the strength of their interlocked shields and the fierceness of their onset, amazement and fear took possession of him, and he felt that he had never seen a sight more fearful.' (Plutarch, *Aemilius Paullus* 19.1)

As we have seen, Plutarch, unusually, always uses *pelte* to describe the shields of the phalanx. The words translated 'drawing their *peltai* ['targets' in the original translation] from their shoulders round in front of them' can be translated literally as 'drawing [*perispanton*] *peltai* around from the shoulder' (or arm). *Perispanton* (*perispao*) is a word with a wide range of meanings, but a short time later in this same book (Plut. *Aem.* 23.1) Plutarch uses it to describe Perseus in flight from the battle drawing his cloak in front of himself to hide his identity, and it is likely to have a similar meaning here – simply moving the shield round in front of the bearer, ready for action. It is by no means clear to me that this carries any implication at all of a strap being used, just that when marching the shield was held to the side, and in action it was angled to the front. More bizarrely, some modern authors interpret this passage to mean that the phalangites drew their shields not round in front of them but *behind* them, that as they went into action they slung their shields round onto their backs. Now shields were sometimes carried slung across the back – especially in Homer – but this would surely not be how a shield was carried going into action, since it would of course be completely useless, and it would be better not to bother with a shield at all. We can reject this notion, for which there is no evidence whatever, out of hand. But Plutarch's words do not to me carry any meaning stronger than that the phalanx carried their shields on their shoulders when marching (and here we might note that the Argive shield is widely assumed to have been carried on the shoulder, and that one reason for the deep rim was to allow it to be rested on the shoulder), and that as they went into action they moved their shields into the 'ready' position in front of them. It is easy to imagine how impressive an entire phalanx doing this in unison on a word of command would have been.

As further evidence for the strap idea, some scholars use the account in Plutarch (discussed above) of Cleomenes arming a new contingent of the Spartan army in the late third century:

> '[Cleomenes] thus raised a body of four thousand hoplites, whom he taught to use a *sarisa*, held in both hands, instead of a spear, and to carry their shields [*aspides*] by an *ochane* instead of by a *porpax*.' (Plutarch, *Cleomenes* 11.2)

The words I have left untranslated are the crucial ones. The *porpax* is the bronze or leather armband in the centre of the traditional Argive aspis, through which the forearm was inserted. *Ochane* (or more usually, *ochanon*) means 'handle', without any very specific or technical meaning; but Herodotus (writing of events at the start of the fifth century) has this to say about the Carians of Asia Minor:

> 'They invented three things in which they were followed by the Greeks: it was the Carians who originated wearing crests on their helmets and devices on their shields, and who first made handles [*ochanes*] for their shields [*aspisi*]; until then all who used shields carried them without these handles, and guided them with leather straps [*telamosi*] which they slung round the neck and over the left shoulder.' (Herodotus 1.171)

So Herodotus specifically distinguishes between an *ochane* on the shield and a strap (*telamon*) around the neck. As such, the passage from Plutarch's Cleomenes, far from being evidence for use of a neck strap, directly contradicts it.

It is not clear to me precisely how a neck strap is supposed to help with carrying a shield. It is sometimes said that the strap was used to 'control' the shield, though a strap round the neck cannot be used to move a shield about, or that it took some of the weight of the shield, though this would be possible only if the strap was so short that the shield was fully supported in its ready position (raised in front), in which case the strap would be too short to allow the arm to be lowered when at rest. I think it perfectly possible that a strap was used to carry the shield on the march, and would still have been in place going into battle. But the shield must primarily, like any other shield, have been supported and positioned by the arm of the wearer – otherwise, any blow to the shield would just knock it out of the way, and the shield would have no solidity at all – and any strap can only have had at most a supplementary role.[35]

The only depiction in art of the carrying arrangements of a Macedonian shield (or at least a shield used by a Macedonian) seems to be the inside of a Macedonian shield on the Aemilius Paullus monument (fig. 2.6), which shows what looks like the standard arrangement of *porpax* and *antilabe*. But as the depiction is stylized and we can't tell what materials the handles are made from, no strong conclusions can be drawn from this. It could be that an *ochane* looked like a *porpax* but was made of different material. It could also be that the sculptor didn't know or much care how a Macedonian shield was carried, and did not depict it accurately on the monument. This hasn't stopped some modern historians from using this depiction to conclude that at least some Macedonians at Pydna were not armed as phalangites but as traditional hoplites, but this seems absurd given the plentiful literary evidence to the contrary.[36]

The only safe conclusion seems to be that we don't know exactly how the shield was carried (though various sensible suggestions have been made by re-enactors), but that the carrying arrangements of the Macedonian shield were probably not greatly different from those of the Argive shield, and that in any case it was possible (although again we don't know exactly how) to carry an Argive shield along with a sarissa. The *ochane* may simply have been a more flexible, probably leather, variant on the *porpax* (which was rigid, and could be made of bronze), which allowed the bearer to slide it above the elbow, which would have moved the hand out beyond the rim of the shield. This was probably combined with a rope handle or loop that would go around the wrist to keep the shield in place.

So various Macedonian phalanxes at various times will have carried shields of different sizes and different designs, as fashion and experimentation came and went, and there was no single design or size to fit all. Either way, the shield was carried on the left arm and held in front of the bearer, and wilder speculation such as shields slung on the back, or held by a neck strap, can be rejected.

To summarize the points discussed in this section, I do not think that there is any single phalangite's shield used across the whole period. Rather, there was a choice between two major classes of shields: Argive shields, large (up to 1 metre in diameter), with a shallow bowl profile, and rimmed, as carried for centuries by the Classical Greek hoplites; and Macedonian shields, smaller (up to around 80cm in diameter or more) and unrimmed. Of the Macedonian shields, sizes could vary between the largest, which are visually almost identical to Argive shields, and smaller versions, down to about 66cm in diameter. The larger Macedonian and Argive shields were carried by the phalangites of the main phalanx, while the smaller Macedonian shields were carried by the Hypaspists and, later, the Peltasts. Macedonian shields in turn could have two distinct shapes: a strongly domed or bowl-shaped profile (typical for the larger examples), or a much flatter profile (typical for the smaller kind). Macedonian shields were usually made from wood faced with a layer of bronze. Both types of shield were carried in a way that kept the left hand free to grip the sarissa, probably by using a flexible leather handle that could be slipped above the elbow rather than a rigid bronze armband, and a rope wrist loop rather than a rope handle inside the rim.

So much for the size and shape of the shield. For its decoration, we are on much firmer ground. The Macedonian shield carried a distinctive pattern of concentric bows or hoops that, while changing across the period, remained broadly consistent. This pattern was so distinctive that it came to stand, as a sort of badge, for Macedonians everywhere, especially in the settlements in Asia where there was a desire to keep alive the settlers' cultural identity, distinct from the native populations. I do not intend to describe the full range of these patterns, nor to chart their development over time, as there are other studies that do this. Fig. 2.7 shows some typical examples, and shields with this patterning are known from art (painted and sculptural), coinage and actual physical examples. This distinctive patterning was what was considered typically 'Macedonian' about the Macedonian shield (along with its shape, as discussed). Only rimless Macedonian shields carried this pattern, and there are no examples I know of Argive shields decorated this way. So the shield decoration of Alexander's phalanx, if indeed it used Argive shields, remains unknown, though the Alexander Sarcophagus depicts shields with painted heads – perhaps of Alexander – on them and it may be that a range of painted devices were used (as for Classical shields), or that the shields were left plain bronze. In the Hellenistic period, so far as we can tell, all phalangites' shields carried the Macedonian pattern in one of its forms.[37]

The central roundel of the shield would be more variable, and could carry various devices: the distinctive 'Macedonian star' or sunburst, well known from many contexts, particularly in examples from excavations at Vergina (it adorned the burial casket identified as that of Philip II, for example); the initials or cypher of the king (shields of Pyrrhus exist with a Pi-Upsilon-Rho cypher, the first three letters of Pyrrhus' name in Greek); or the face of the king (or of a mythological figure). Shields, in the surviving examples, though not in art, also tend to carry the name of the king, which again indicates that

Fig. 2.7. Macedonian shield patterns, clockwise from top left: tomb of Lyson and Kallikles; coin of Antigonus Gonatas; Ptolemaic shield mould in Allard Pierson Museum; Boscoreale wall painting.

they were centrally manufactured and issued by the kings to their army – the shield is then identified as the property of the king.

Though the patterning described above came to be thought of as distinctively Macedonian, it also occurs in other, earlier, non-Macedonian Balkan contexts, so it is likely that this style of shield decoration was common to the northern Greek and southern Balkan region. As such I think it likely that Philip's infantry carried shields with this pattern even before he organized the first Macedonian phalanx, and the pattern was taken with them thereafter by the infantry of Alexander and their descendants as they marched, fought and settled throughout Asia.[38]

Armour

It is not known what armour if any was worn by the phalanx as originally created by Philip II. The list of equipment given by Polyaenus for route marches quoted at the start of the chapter does not mention armour, so it may well be that at least initially the phalanx was entirely unarmoured. As discussed, the raw material of the phalanx, the native Macedonian infantry, was probably a force of skirmishing javelineers and presumably was not armoured. As they were not individually wealthy, it is likely that they could not afford their own armour, except in a few cases, so any armour would have been provided centrally by the royal government. The words put into Alexander's mouth by Arrian (*Anab.* 7.9.2) do not paint a flattering picture of the material wealth of Macedonian infantry at this stage: 'Philip took you over when you were helpless vagabonds, mostly clothed in skins.'

So it could well be that under Philip the phalanx was mostly unarmoured. By the time of, or at least during, Alexander's reign this had changed. There are references to armour in the course of the campaigns of Alexander, and of the figures depicted on the Alexander Sarcophagus – those who are not naked – most are wearing corselets of some soft material (softer, that is, than bronze). These might have been made of leather, but the usual assumption (and it seems a reasonable one) among modern authors is that these are examples of the 'linen cuirass' (sometimes called 'linothorax') which had become popular during the late fifth century. Such armour was made of multiple layers of linen cloth glued together, producing an armour with some flexibility and lightness while still offering decent protection, particularly, we may imagine, against missiles. The armour was generally made in a 'tube and yoke' style, with a cylindrical section which wrapped around the torso and two long flaps which were folded down over the shoulders. Depictions in vase paintings sometimes show hoplites dressing for action with these flaps untied, sticking vertically upwards, indicating the stiffness of the material. The bottom part of such armour was cut into a series of flaps or *pteruges* ('feathers'), which served to protect the groin while being flexible enough to allow free movement to the legs. These *pteruges* were often in an overlapped double row, and are familiar from depictions of Classical hoplites back to the fifth century.[39]

Armour of this type was perhaps worn by all members of Alexander's phalanx, though the front-rankers, who faced greater risk (and were also better paid), may have been equipped with heavier bronze armour. It may also be that the 'lighter' parts of the phalanx, as discussed above, may have worn either lighter armour or no armour at all. I think it quite likely that the Hypaspists, if they were indeed 'peltasts', may also have been unarmoured. There is no direct evidence for this, but comparison with the Peltasts of the Antigonid army, for whom there are some indications that they were unarmoured, does suggest that, presumably for lightness and speed, these specialist troops may not have worn armour at all. If this is so, it in turn may cast some light on the equipment list given by Polyaenus above. If Philip was here training not the entirety of the phalanx, but his peltasts (his Foot Companions at this stage, before the name was extended to the whole phalanx), then that would explain both the absence of armour and the presence of *peltai*.[40]

After Alexander, the opening up of the treasuries of the Persian Empire to the Successors and Hellenistic kingdoms meant that money was, if not no object, at least less of an obstacle to equipment procurement. There is, however, little evidence for the armour of any of the later phalanxes, with only scattered and unclear depictions in art and occasional references in literature. It seems reasonable to assume that the pattern established by Alexander continued and that the phalanx was generally equipped with linen (or other soft) armour, with possible bronze armour for officers or file leaders (fig 2.8).

In terms of direct evidence, there are some depictions of what can be assumed to be infantry (and presumably phalangite) armour, of which the clearest example is the pair of full-sized painted sets of armour in the 'Lyson and Kallikles' tomb, a third-century Macedonian tomb for two warriors

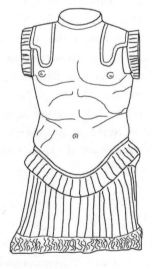

Fig. 2.8. Hellenistic armour from the Sanctuary of Athena at Pergamon: left, linen or leather armour; right, bronze 'muscle cuirass'.

(and their descendants), at least one of whom can be assumed to be a phalangite (presumably an officer) from the painted Macedonian-patterned shield also depicted on the tomb walls (the second occupant might possibly be a cavalryman). This armour looks to be a typical tube and yoke linen cuirass, though with particularly long *pteruges* (this may just be an effect of perspective, since the armour is painted high on the tomb walls and so as if viewed from underneath). The problem with all such depictions, of course, is the difficulty of connecting them with any particular army unit or any particular rank. The most that can be said is that this is the type of armour that was available for at least some infantry.[41]

As to written evidence, the Amphipolis regulations quoted at the start of the chapter prescribe fines for missing equipment, which among other expected items of equipment (spear, shield, helmet) mentions no armour (for other ranks), unless this is what is meant by the mysterious and otherwise unknown term *kotthybos*. This might have been some form of light linen or leather armour for the rank and file. The 'leaders' (whether this means file leaders or officers of higher rank is unclear) are fined more for lacking their cuirass or 'half-cuirass' (*hemithorakion*) – what exactly is meant by 'half' in this context is unknown, but this may be some form of partial bronze armour or perhaps a linen cuirass with bronze reinforcement. It is impossible to be more precise than this, but the usual assumption, which seems reasonable, is that the file leaders and higher-ranked officers would have had a *thorax* or *hemithorax* (full or half-armour), while the other ranks would have had lesser armour, perhaps also of linen. The 'three ply linen' armour of Caracalla's phalanx would fit this description (note that 'three ply' is not a certain translation, but something of this sort seems to be meant), and we can assume that the number of ranks who had at least this much armour would not have been fixed throughout the period (any more than the size and nature of sarissa and shield was fixed), but varied according to local circumstances, available funds, intended tactical task and the status and prestige of the unit involved. At any rate, a linen cuirass of classic design was probably the most common type of armour worn.[42]

Helmets

A helmet seems always to have been part of the equipment of the Macedonian phalangite – at least, Polyaenus includes them in his equipment list for Philip II. Such helmets were generally made of bronze; iron helmets are also a possibility, and according to some arguments are indicated by the blue colouring of helmets on the Alexander Sarcophagus, but the large majority of surviving examples of helmets from the period are bronze.[43]

A number of patterns were available (no fewer than fourteen have been identified, though many of these are minor variants on each other – see fig. 2.9), and as with the sarissa, shield and armour, there was considerable variability throughout the period and geographical range of the phalanx. There are several different designs of helmet depicted in art, of which the most common are the 'Phrygian' (or 'Thracian'), an open-faced helmet with a large bulbous forward-angled crest and usually equipped with cheek pieces to protect the face (sometimes elaborately decorated to represent a beard), and the *pilos* or later *konos*, a simple cone-shaped helmet initially without cheek pieces, apparently originally adopted by the Spartan army (and so also sometimes called Laconian). This latter type becomes increasingly common in art and archaeology from the reign of Philip II, and also features on issues of coinage from after the reign of Alexander, where coins frequently depict a *pilos* or *konos* helmet on one side and a Macedonian shield on the other; it has been argued that this represents the deliberate, centralized adoption of this type of helmet by the Macedonian army, as part of the state-led, unifom re-equipment of the Macedonian infantry. The *konos* helmet is also identified by name as the phalangite's helmet in the Amphipolis regulations.

Two other types of helmet are illustrated in the tomb of Lyson and Kallikles. One, a rounded version of the earlier Attic helmet, with a low crest, also appears in the Aemilius Paullus monument. The other is a much taller helmet, apparently a variant on the *pilos*, also with a rounded profile and in this particular case also bearing a crest and double feather plumes. Which of these helmets belong to infantry, and (if either) to ordinary phalangites rather than high-status officers, is uncertain, though the domed version does seem to be an infantry helmet (as its wearer has been identified as an officer of the *Chalcaspides*). A common feature of many Hellenistic helmets is the 'visor' (purely decorative and not in fact functioning as a visor, though no doubt it reinforced the front of the helmet) on the front above the brim. Later in the Hellenistic period a new helmet type becomes increasingly popular – this style has been termed the *morion*, from comparison with similar-shaped Renaissance helmets. This may possibly have been mainly an officer's helmet.[44]

A well-known helmet type from Alexander's reign in particular is the Boeotian helmet, a type which resembles a broad-brimmed hat reproduced in metal, and which is depicted on the Alexander Sarcophagus and the Alexander Mosaic. However, this appears to have been an exclusively cavalry helmet, not worn by infantry so far as we can tell.

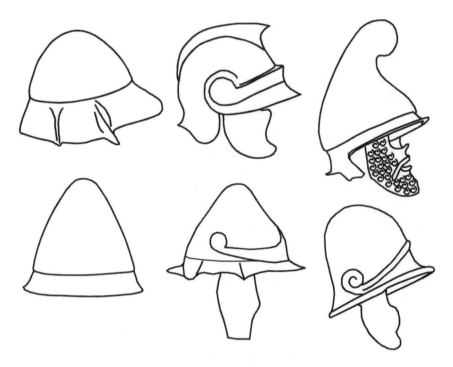

Fig. 2.9. Hellenistic helmet designs, clockwise from top left: Boeotian; Attic; Thracian (or Phrygian); bell (or rounded pilos); brimmed pilos; conical pilos.

It is also likely that the number or shape of the crests (if any) on such helmets was a mark of the rank of the wearer. There is only indirect evidence for this. An Aetolian officer has a triple-crested helmet in Plutarch, *Aratus* 32.1, and the helmets depicted on the common 'shield/helmet' coinage of the late fourth century have a transverse crest, like that worn by Roman centurions, which may, as for the Romans, be a badge of office, though which office is not clear – possibly the file leader or the commander of the *syntagma* (on which see the following chapter). Helmets of the rank and file were possibly plain, with no crest.[45]

The 'ox hide helmet' of Caracalla's phalanx is of interest. There is no hint that other helmets were of hide, rather than of metal, although it would be very difficult to tell purely from artistic depictions, as opposed to surviving examples. It is possible that what is meant in this case is not a helmet as such, but the other distinctively Macedonian piece of headgear, the *kausia*. This was the national hat of ancient Macedon, frequently depicted in art (examples include the guard figures from the Agios Athanasios tomb and a wall painting from Boscoreale, Italy), and appears to have resembled the modern Pakistani and Afghan *pakol* or *chitrali* hat, a flat beret-like hat now usually made from wool or felt. It is possible that the hats are related – either that Alexander's men adopted the hat in Afghanistan and brought it back home to Macedon with them, or that transmission was the other way around, Macedonian settlers introducing the hat to Afghanistan. Or it could just be a case of parallel development, with the similar appearance of the hats no more than a coincidence. At any rate, the *kausia* seems not to have been worn in battle, so far as we can tell, and would have been a campaign hat worn for warmth and comfort away from the battlefield, similar to the forage caps of more recent armies. Another type of hat is the *petasos* or sun hat, depicted for example in the lion hunt pebble mosaic from Pella, a traditional Greek broad-brimmed hat with small crown, worn with straps under the chin or the back of the head. A complicating factor is that the *kausia* could (like a modern beret) be worn in different configurations, resulting in a wider or smaller crown area, and it is difficult to be certain whether any given depiction (such as those on some coins) are of a broad *kausia* or a small *petasos* (resulting in the two often being confused: there may indeed have been much overlap). Note also that the *kausia* is often depicted worn by cavalry, or those who may be cavalry (such as the Agios Athanasios figures), and there are suggestions that it was a high-status garment (though this seems unlikely). See fig. 2.10 for some examples.[46]

Greaves

The final common piece of equipment are greaves or shin guards (fig 2.11). Again these were made of bronze, usually thin enough to be bent over the shin and held in place by the metal's own elasticity, though there may also have been a leather or fabric lining. Greaves were common amongst Classical hoplites, though so far as we can tell, they were on the way out during the fourth century as hoplite equipment generally was reduced in weight and encumbrance. The Iphicratean reform, if it was real, dispensed with greaves in favour of boots. It is rather surprising then, given the usual identification of Philip II's phalanx as a way to build a cheaper and more lightly equipped infantry, to find greaves listed in Polyaenus' equipment list, and continuing to be mentioned in all the other equipment lists. We might guess that, as with body armour, the file leaders were more heavily equipped than the rank and file, and they alone wore greaves, though if so there is no hint of this in any of the sources. We must also assume, as with other equipment, that whatever the

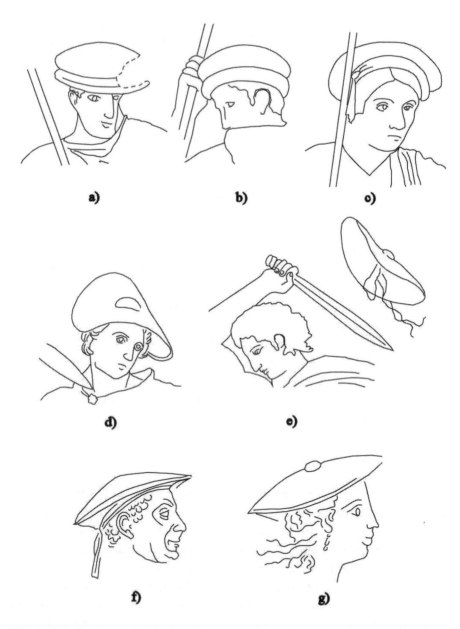

Fig. 2.10. *Kausia* and *petasos*: a) to c) show the *kausia*; a) and b) from the Agios Athanasios tomb; c) a Roman copy at Boscoreale of a Hellenistic painting; d) and e) show the petasos, from the hunt scenes at Pella; f) shows a coin of Antimachus (second-century king of the Bactrian kingdom) in broad *kausia* (?); g) is a second-century Aetolian coin, showing the *petasos*. Note the stylized crown of the *petasos*, and the tying cords.

Fig. 2.11. A pair of greaves, from the Sanctuary of Athena at Pergamon.

on-paper requirement to wear greaves, whether they were actually available in any particular campaign must have depended on circumstances.[47]

If greaves were more frequently used by the Macedonian phalanx than by contemporary hoplites, we may surmise a practical explanation for this. The hoplite spear was (probably) wielded overarm (or just possibly in a 'high underarm' or couched position), meaning that its obvious and most common striking point on an enemy in an opposing phalanx would have been the head, neck or upper body. The sarissa, in contrast, was probably held in a low hold, as depicted on the Pergamene plaque discussed above. This means that its likely striking point would be the lower body or legs of an opponent. As such, for front-rankers facing another sarissa-armed phalanx, protection for the legs would have been far more important than it was for Classical hoplites, which may account for why greaves were reintroduced by Philip II and remained popular (so far as we can tell) throughout the period.

Swords

As well as the sarissa, a phalangite seems to have normally carried a sword, though again all the usual caveats apply as to regional and temporal variation, as well as variations in rank, wealth and status. But swords are commonly depicted in art – again, good examples come from the Lyson and Kallikles tomb – and are of two main types: a straight-bladed sword (*xiphos*) with a cutting edge on both sides of the blade and a point for thrusting, not wholly dissimilar to the Spanish sword used by the Romans, and a curved sabre-like sword (*kopis* or *machaira*) with the cutting edge on the inside of the blade (fig. 2.12). It is likely that the curved sword was a cavalry weapon and the straight sword was the infantry weapon (Xen. *Horse.* 12.11). Classical hoplites had carried swords too, but they were weapons of last resort for when the spear had broken rather than being the weapon of first choice as they were for the Romans, and the same seems to have been true for phalangites – only more so of course, since the whole point of the sarissa was to hold off the enemy well out of sword reach (as I will explore in Chapter 8). So the sword was definitely a weapon of last resort in pitched battle, although it would also have been useful for the other types of combat, such as raids and sieges, in which the phalangite might have been required to take part.

Plutarch describes Macedonians at the Battle of Pydna, when their formation had been broken up by Roman attacks, fighting with 'daggers' (*encheiridioi*) (*Aem.* 20.5) against the firm shields of the Romans. The *encheiridion* is a smaller weapon popularized from the fourth century by the Spartans. We might take this to mean that phalangites carried only small or light swords (and so perhaps that the swords depicted in tombs are those of officers); or it could be that Plutarch is exaggerating the smallness of the swords to make a point, that he is referring to a specific unit (the Peltasts, see n. 27 above) or that he used the word *encheiridion* in a non-technical way, as he seems elsewhere to use it for any type of sword: for example Plut. *Alex.* 16.4, Alexander's sword in the fighting at the Granicus, which a sentence later at *Alex.* 16.5 is called a *xiphos*. As with *peltai* and *aspides*, Plutarch is not the best place to look for technical terminology, and the modern tendency to attribute small daggers to all phalangites based solely on Plut. *Aem.* 20.5 is unfortunate.[48]

Other clothing

Aside from the defensive equipment so far considered, phalangites would have worn the regular clothing common across much of Greece, with minor variations. This consisted of a simple (usually woollen) short-sleeved (or sleeveless) tunic or *chiton*, with one variant (the *exomis*) having an uncovered right shoulder, worn with a belt over which excess material was gathered to hang in loose folds. Another common variant (seen particularly for cavalry or high-status wearers, such as the Kinch tomb and the riders on the Alexander Sarcophagus and Alexander Mosaic) had long sleeves (perhaps borrowed from the Persians).

Fig. 2.12. Hellenistic swords – *xiphos* (first and third from top) and *kopis* or *machaira* (second and fourth), from the tomb of Lyson and Kallikles and Sanctuary of Athena at Pergamon.

Over this was worn a cloak, which for Macedonians would usually have been a *chlamys*, semi-circular in shape and clasped over the right shoulder so that it hung with two points. Another type of cloak was the Thessalian, rectangular in shape so that it hung with four points. Cloaks would probably not have been worn (by infantry) in combat, however. Feet are often depicted bare, which is possible in battle but unlikely on the march, when boots would have been worn, usually the traditional *krepis* (plural *krepides*), a lattice boot-sandal similar to (though extending higher up the leg than) the Roman *caliga*. As we saw in the previous chapter, Iphicrates also invented a type of boot, and these may be the solid boots depicted in some paintings (though these may also be *krepides* worn over socks, socks and sandals being a valid fashion choice in the Hellenistic period). This combination – *chiton*, *chlamys*, *krepides* and *kausia* – appears frequently in art, and though it is not always possible to identify those wearing it as infantry, still less as phalangites, it is likely that this was a common combination across all arms and classes. Fig. 2.13 illustrates some of these items.[49]

Fig. 2.13. Macedonian military clothing – *kausia, chiton, chlamys* and *krepides* – from the Agios Athanasios tomb (probably depicting cavalry).

Uniformity and colours

I have frequently mentioned in this discussion how much variation there was likely to have been in the details of equipment across the whole of the period in which the Macedonian phalanx was in use. But within restricted geographical areas and time periods, was there likely to have been uniformity, and would there have been uniformity of coloured clothing as is familiar from modern armies?

The first question – uniformity of equipment – is more easily answered. In terms of spear length, there must from a practical point of view have been uniformity, since spears of different lengths would not allow the phalanx to present a uniform hedge of spear points, as it evidently did, and Polybius' comments, for example (that the sarissa was formerly 16 cubits but now reduced to 14 cubits), implies uniformity also. Shields too were most likely uniform within given units, even though shields of more than one pattern – as we have seen with the shields of Alexander's phalanx – may have been used at the same time. Surviving examples of Macedonian shields have the name of the king inscribed on them, and this suggests that each king had a uniform design that would equip the whole phalanx during his reign (although in practice no doubt old equipment sometimes outlived its 'use by' date). Shield colour – and therefore presumably also shield pattern – was also used as an identifying feature of given units. The most well-known examples are the *Argyraspides* (Silver Shields) of Alexander and his Successors, with a unit bearing the same name also serving the Seleucid kingdom, and the *Chalcaspides* or Bronze Shields, which formed a central component of the Antigonid army, perhaps forming half of the full phalanx. What was distinctive about the shield of the Bronze Shields, since all shields were bronze, is not clear, though it does appear that many shields were painted – those depicted in Macedonian tomb paintings are often highly coloured and illustrated – so it may be that the Bronze Shields' shields were plain bronze, with just the classic Macedonian embossed patterning. These are the shields, presumably, depicted on the Aemilius Paullus monument. Units of Bronze Shields are also recorded in the Seleucid army at the great parade at Daphne (Pol. 30.25), and later in the army of Mithridates of Pontus (Plut. *Sull.* 19.2), the last army to use the Macedonian phalanx in anger. Alongside the Bronze Shields at Pydna were a unit of *Leucaspides*, White Shields – presumably with shields painted white – and at the Daphne parade the Seleucid army may also have had a unit of *Chrysaspides*, Gold Shields, though this name is not present in the original text and is a rather speculative emendation (Pol. 30.25).[50]

We have also seen that there are arguments that helmet design was standardized, with the *pilos* helmet being standard issue to the armies of Philip and Alexander, and given centralized weapon manufacture and distribution, this does indeed seem very likely. Greaves presumably would also have been issued, though there is no evidence that these were made uniform in any way.

What of clothing, particularly colours? We know that some items of clothing were centrally issued, mainly as prestige items or indications of status. Alexander issued his Companions with yellow cloaks with a purple border (Diod. 17.77.5), and such cloaks are depicted on the Alexander Sarcophagus and elsewhere in Hellenistic art. It is also likely that the Peltasts, the Guard infantry unit of the later Antigonid army, also had standard-issue red tunics (the actual colour, *phoinix*, is not known for certain, but it was some shade of red), and depictions of red tunics in Hellenistic art are common. Perhaps all guard units, from Philip's Foot Companions on, had uniform tunics of this kind, and perhaps all a uniform red (given the general slow pace of change in such matters).[51]

For the clothing of other units we are on less certain ground. Tomb paintings depict a number of different colour schemes, and it is possible with some imagination to assign such schemes to particular units. But the main problem in the tomb paintings is the very lack of uniformity. The Agios Athanasios tomb paintings, for example, show a number of different 'uniforms', all different, as does the Alexander Sarcophagus, though there are some common themes (such as purple armour). There do seem to be some elements of uniformity – in particular, purple cuirasses worn by figures on the Agios Athanasios tomb and the Alexander Sarcophagus, white cuirasses (often with red details) depicted in a number of paintings, crimson (*phoinix*) tunics worn by Antigonid Peltasts, blue helmets depicted on the Alexander Sarcophagus, yellow cloaks with purple borders worn by Companions, and plain bronze (but patterned) or white shields carried (presumably) by the *Chalcaspides* and *Leucaspides*. But tunic and cloak colours seem to vary considerably – common colours being red (most common), followed by white, blue, yellow and, less frequently, brown, pink, green, grey and purple – as do non-bronze shields (often blue and red). My own view is that uniformity of clothing was very likely for the elite and permanent units of the armies (such as Hypasists/Peltasts) but increasingly unlikely for the mass of infantry of the phalanx, who though equipped with arms and armour by the king were likely to have provided their own clothing. It has to be conceded that there is very little evidence either way.[52]

Summary

The above description and that in the previous chapter have provided an outline of the evidence for the equipment of the Macedonian phalanx, while highlighting the variety and high level of uncertainty about details. Here I would like to present a speculative overview combining the evidence for the equipment along with that for the origins of the phalanx discussed in the first chapter. Not every detail I will suggest here can be absolutely proven from the evidence, and there are of course other possibilities. But I hope that this will provide a plausible narrative that may well provide an account quite close to reality.

The Macedonian infantry before the reign of Philip II probably consisted largely of skirmishers armed with javelins and light rimless shields carrying the traditional Macedonian (and Balkan) decoration. They were probably mostly unarmoured and any helmets or other equipment would have been that provided by better-off individuals. From earlier times a royal guard of infantry had also existed, who would have been similarly armed but with a higher quality of equipment and more metal armour, who might possibly have been equipped like Greek hoplites, and who increasingly had equipment supplied centrally by the king, including standard helmets of Illyrian or later *pilos* design.

Philip II took the core of this infantry – the existing Foot Companions infantry guard – and first trained them to fight in the style of the new phalanx. They were equipped – at Philip's expense – with smaller, rimless bronze-faced shields and with a long sarissa (though not so long as it would eventually become), and trained and drilled to fight in close-order formations, holding the sarissa in two hands, with the points of the first few ranks extending beyond the front of the formation. Infantry armed this way were termed 'peltasts', because the shield they carried was generally called a *pelte*, in a similar way to that in which the earlier peltasts of Iphicrates, who carried similar equipment, had been named. Fig. 2.14 depicts a phalangite of this period.

From the start of his reign, Philip also began the process of training and arming the mass of the Macedonian infantry, those outside the Foot Companions, who were still fighting as javelinmen. Given the scale of the project (training and equipping up to 20,000 infantry), this was probably a process that was stretched out over several years. These infantry were also drilled to fight in a close-order formation, but they were equipped with heavier equipment, making a formation of hoplites rather than peltasts. Their sarissas were longer, up to 12 cubits, and their shields larger. Experiments may have been made with different sizes and patterns of shields, including variations on the classical Argive shield as well as rimless Macedonian shields, and variations of the equipment were employed simultaneously, perhaps in different named units of the phalanx. These hoplites were increasingly heavily equipped, with simple bronze *pilos* helmets and linen armour, or heavier bronze or partial bronze armour for front-rankers. Some of the phalanx units – perhaps those who had the smaller shields and lighter equipment, but perhaps all – would also have continued to use the javelin, not in pitched battle and while in close formation, but for all the other military tasks required of any infantry, such as guard duty, assaulting cities or traversing difficult terrain. Gradually the use of javelins became less important, especially as non-Macedonian auxiliaries were added to the army, and fighting in the close-order heavy formation would become the major role of these hoplites.

Under Alexander, the name of Foot Companions was extended to the whole of the phalanx infantry, with the old infantry guard now being renamed Hypaspists. Armament would have remained largely unchanged, with the new Foot Companions of the phalanx still equipped with larger shields and longer sarissas, while the Hypaspists continued to fight as peltasts (in the new sense of light phalangites, with smaller shields and shorter sarissas). Javelins were

Fig. 2.14. Phalangite equipment from the reign of Philip II.

still used in sieges and difficult marches, with such tasks falling mostly to the more mobile (younger, more lightly equipped) units of the phalanx and the Hypaspists.

After Alexander, the Successors continued with much the same sorts of equipment. Sarissas became progressively longer as phalanx fought phalanx and each general's Macedonians sought an advantage over the other, and more and better-quality bronze equipment was adopted with increasing availability and wealth. Each army would also have had its own unit of guard peltasts, able to fight as part of the phalanx in pitched battles or take on special duties in difficult terrain, sieges and forced marches. From this time the sarissa reached its maximum length of 16 cubits.

In the later Hellenistic kingdoms, the main theme is continuity. Sarissa length was reduced somewhat, back to 14 cubits for most of the heavy infantry, and shield size, shape and pattern went through various permutations. In Antigonid Macedon, the main part of the phalanx, the *Chalcaspides*, carried large but rimless Macedonian shields with a heavily dished shape, while in Ptolemaic Egypt, smaller, flatter shields, still of the Macedonian design (patterned and rimless), were preferred. Figs 2.2 and 2.3 show these later phalangites. Guard units still consisted of peltasts, with smaller shields and shorter (though still lengthy) spears. This pattern continued with few major, though perhaps many minor changes throughout the Hellenistic period, and it is phalanxes of this kind that were to be overcome by Rome – first the Antigonids, then the Seleucids and last of all the 'Macedonian revival' armies of Pontus (the phalanx of Ptolemaic Egypt was never put to the test against the Romans).

This narrative, I hope, ties together most of the strands of evidence that have been discussed above. So now we have considered the origins and the equipment of the phalanx, it is time to turn to its organization, drill and tactics.

Chapter 3

Organization and drill

The tacticians and Homer

Much of what we know about the internal organization and drill of the Macedonian phalanx is derived from the works of the tacticians, which have already been used several times in the preceding chapters. Because of the reliance we must place on these writers, and because their reliability has often been called into question, a brief digression is in order to consider whether they are really reliable witnesses to the sort of details we will be discussing here.

The earliest of the tactical writers whose works have survived is Asclepiodotus. This is to take 'tactical writers' in the slightly more limited Hellenistic sense of writers on the drill and organization specifically of Hellenistic armies, in particular of the sarissa-armed phalanx. There existed, at least during the fourth century, a tradition of Greek military writing of which we now have two examples – Xenophon (the historian), who wrote books on horsemanship and on the duties of a cavalry commander, and Aeneas (called 'The Tactician'), who wrote a series of books on military matters, of which just one, on how to defend against a siege, has survived. We must assume that there were other works from other writers covering similar topics. However, these are all rather different from the tradition of tactical manuals now represented by the works of Asclepiodotus, Aelian and Arrian. Aeneas' and Xenophon's works are highly practical manuals full of tips and good practice on a range of military topics. They have more in common with (though are still very different from) the later tradition of collecting 'Stratagems' (a tradition now represented by Polyaenus and Frontinus), though these collections of clever tricks were derived from a trawl through history rather than from practical experience, as Xenophon's and Aeneas' works seem to have been.

The tradition of the tacticians is rather different; they are closer to what we would think of now as a drill or organization manual, with little in the way of practical advice or real-life examples. This has been the basis on which many modern authors have criticized them: they have been condemned as dull, pedantic, theoretical, the works of philosophers rather than experienced military commanders. There is inevitably some justice in this, in that even Asclepiodotus, the earliest, wrote probably around the turn of the first century, when the phalanx was at best on the way out, while Aelian and Arrian wrote under the Roman Empire, when the phalanx was a matter of largely antiquarian interest. It does appear that Asclepiodotus at least was a philosopher not a general, and wrote at a time when the teaching of tactics had become part of the philosopher's repertoire (a philosopher in the Greek sense being a learned man, rather than the modern sense of a student of abstract knowledge, but still with an implication of lack of practical experience). But at the same time, these criticisms are still unfair. They are based partly on a misunderstanding of the genre – after all, an organization and drill manual is supposed to be dull and pedantic, it is never going to be a thrilling read. Furthermore, there is good reason to suppose that these surviving examples are part of a tradition of such manuals with some much less philosophical authors, and they were well regarded in antiquity and continued to be so for centuries, in fact right up to the Early Modern period.[1]

The earliest of the manuals we have, that of Asclepiodotus, contains no indication as to its sources, though the first to second-century AD versions of Aelian and Arrian – which are similar enough in many details to the text of Asclepiodotus to suggest that they had a common source – do contain lists of previous authors of such tactical manuals. These lists start with Homer (surprisingly enough – I will consider this aspect below), but the first 'real' author they name is Pyrrhus (presumably the famous King of Epirus). If there is a close similarity between the surviving manuals and the originals dating back to Pyrrhus, then far from being merely pedantic philosophers' works, these manuals may in fact have their origins in the writings of one of the great generals of the Hellenistic age. Furthermore, we know from other sources that Asclepiodotus was a pupil of the philosopher Poseidonius, and that Poseidonius in turn continued the historical writings of Polybius. We also know (because he tells us so himself, Pol. 9.20.4) that Polybius also wrote a tactical manual. Some of the wording in Asclepiodotus is very close to that of Polybius' well-known discussion of the strengths of the Macedonian phalanx (the relevant quotes were included in the previous chapter). So it is quite likely that Asclepiodotus' work is also closely based on one by Polybius.

As such, the sources of the surviving tacticians are excellent, and though we cannot tell how closely their works follow the originals, there is a good chance that they follow them quite closely. There is also reason to suppose that writers of tactics were not necessarily men of no practical experience. For example, Philostephanos, called 'the tactician' by Josephus (Jos. *Ant.* 13.340 {12.5}), directed the manoeuvre which won the Battle of Asophon in 103 (making him an approximate contemporary of Asclepiodotus), and their works were well regarded by contemporary generals – Plutarch tells us that the Achaean general Philopoemen was fond of the *Tactics* of Euangelus (Plut. *Phil.* 4.4). So there is every reason to suppose that the surviving works are quite similar to those that were used by practical commanders, not just philosophers, and that they do accurately reflect actual tactical theory of the time, for all that a certain philosophical pedantry may have crept in.[2]

The claimed origin in the work of Homer is of interest. There is of course no possibility that Homer actually produced a tactical manual, least of all one for the Macedonian phalanx (since he lived, if he lived at all, some 400 years before the phalanx was invented). But there was a tradition in Greek thought that saw Homer as the original military authority. Xenophon reports the claim of a would-be teacher:

> 'You know, doubtless, that the sage Homer has written about practically everything pertaining to man. Any one of you, therefore, who wishes to acquire the art of the householder, the political leader, or the general, or to become like Achilles or Ajax or Nestor or Odysseus, should seek my favour, for I understand all these things.' (Xenophon, *Symposium* 4.6)

This to some extent just reflects the seminal importance of Homer, whose writings were regarded in much the same as way the *Bible* and Shakespeare have been regarded in English-speaking cultures. But there is inevitably much military material in Homer, the *Iliad* in particular, which consists almost entirely of detailed descriptions of duels, skirmishes and battles. Homer was Alexander the Great's favourite author, and he is said to have carried a treasured copy of the *Iliad* with him throughout his campaigns. What's more, we have already encountered a supposed Homeric origin of the Macedonian phalanx in the first chapter, in the account of Diodorus, who claims that Philip II was 'imitating the "locked shields" of the warriors at Troy' (Diod. 16.3.2). The reference to the 'warriors at Troy' is of course to the *Iliad*. Similarly, when Polybius discusses the close order of the Macedonian phalanx, he adduces a Homeric parallel:

> 'if only the phalanx is properly formed and the men close up properly both flank and rear, like the description in Homer:
>
>> "So buckler pressed on buckler; helm on helm;
>> And man on man: and waving horse-hair plumes

> In polished head-piece mingled, as they swayed
> In order: in such serried rank they stood."'
> (Polybius 18.29, quoting Homer, *Iliad* 13.131)

Polybius repeats the Homeric allusion in his criticism of the Alexander historian Callisthenes:

> 'But the greatest blunder [by Callisthenes] is still to come. "As soon as Alexander," he says, "was within distance of the enemy he caused his men to take up order eight deep," which would have necessitated ground forty stades wide for the length of the line; and even had they, to use the poet's expression, "laid shield to shield and on each other leaned," still ground twenty stades wide would have been wanted, while he himself says that it was less than fourteen.' (Polybius 12.21)

'The poet' in this case means Homer, much as we might call Shakespeare 'the bard'.

So Homer was seen as in some sense the originator of tactical writing, and his descriptions of the warriors at Troy as the inspiration for the Macedonian phalanx. This cannot be taken literally. While there is much debate about how the Homeric warriors might have fought, it is unlikely that they formed a formal phalanx. But Homer's descriptions may well have inspired the development of the Macedonian phalanx, particularly its close order. This in turn opens up a new field for dispute, the question of the intervals of the files of the Macedonian phalanx.[3]

Ranks, files and intervals

A phalanx is (when used in its more technical sense, not when meaning just a line of battle) a close-order infantry formation. The infantry in such a formation, unlike those in looser, more open-order formations (such as those likely used by archers, javelineers and skirmishers), were organized into strictly ordered ranks and files. A file is a line of men standing one behind another, while a rank is a line of men standing side by side, so that the files run back to front of the formation and the ranks run side to side (frustratingly, as with weapon names, these terms are sometimes used with some inexactitude by modern historians).

It is not certain, and the subject of considerable debate, whether the earlier Classical Greek phalanx also had formal ranks and files (of course any body of men will have informal ranks and files in the sense that men will be standing behind and beside each other). Some armies – in particular the Spartan – did have a formal organization, which is described in some detail by Xenophon, although many obscurities remain. Many Classical Greek phalanxes, though, were made up of citizen militias with little or no formal training – indeed, training was regarded with some disdain by many Greeks, who thought it sufficient to be brave and stubborn. While there is evidence that every man was expected to know his place in the phalanx, it is not clear that this doesn't just mean to know where his comrades (his fellow demes-men) were standing, so that he could join them, and there was also (as we know from Xenophon) an understanding that the best men should be placed at the front and back of the formation – at the front to lead the formation and to perform most of the fighting, and at the back to keep those in the body of the phalanx moving forward and prevent them from running away (see Chapter 8).

An important consideration for any phalanx commander was how many ranks (often expressed as 'shields') deep to form his phalanx. Typically, eight shields was the preferred depth, though sometimes deeper formations were preferred, up to the remarkable fifty shield depth adopted by the Thebans in their victories over Spartan armies. I will have much more to say about formation depths and their purpose, but the general principle is that a deeper formation was stronger (less likely to be defeated in face-to-face fighting and more likely to defeat its opponent) but also narrower, and so more likely to be outflanked. There was thus a tension in choosing a preferred depth: too shallow, and the formation might be penetrated or simply collapse; too deep, and it might be outflanked and defeated before its greater depth could drive back the enemy. There are records of debates between the contingents of allied armies as to the preferred depth for a coming battle. A given depth in men ('shields') does imply formal rank (and therefore also file) organization, but does not absolutely require it, and other than the Spartans, it remains uncertain how much formal drill the classical phalanx was subject to.

For the Macedonian phalanx, on the other hand, there is no doubt. The Macedonian phalanx was a strictly drilled and organized formation, and the basic elements of this organization were the rank and the file. The file in effect formed the smallest subunit of the phalanx – the building block from which all the larger units were constructed, although it was not (in the way a modern infantry squad is) an independent tactical unit in its own right. A phalanx file could do nothing on its own, being entirely dependent on the neighbouring files for its combat effectiveness, and furthermore as the depth of the whole phalanx was increased or decreased, the file might have to be halved or quartered, or two or more files stacked up behind each other. The standard depth of the phalanx (and so size, in men, of the file) in Polybius and the tacticians was sixteen men. There are some indications that under Alexander the standard depth was eight men (as it had been for the Classical phalanx) – this is the depth that Polybius assumes Alexander's army to have used at Issus (Pol. 12.19). In Alexander's day, the file was called a 'dekad', or 'ten', which suggests that this may once have been the strength of the file and may perhaps be following Persian precedent (since the Persians used base units of ten men, and multiples of them). But already by the end of his reign, Alexander was planning a 'dekad' of sixteen men, mixed Macedonians and Persians (Arr. *Anab.* 7.23.3–4), so the word had already lost its literal meaning. In practice, the size of the file and so the depth of the phalanx in action must have varied according to the situation – for example, if the phalanx needed to cover a wider frontage to match the terrain or the size of an enemy force, it would have formed a shallower depth. But there must still have been a nominal size of the file, since the pay of the soldiers depended on their position in the file, with front and rear ranks receiving higher pay (Arr. *Anab.* 7.23.4). This depth after the reign of Alexander was doubtless sixteen men, and this, or sometimes a doubled phalanx thirty-two deep, was probably the standard depth of every phalanx (in pitched battle at least) throughout the period.[4]

So the depth of the phalanx could vary. But another variable affecting the space occupied by the phalanx was the spacing or interval between files. Here we enter some surprisingly controversial territory. According to the tacticians, there were three intervals available, and it is worth quoting Asclepiodotus' definition:

> 'The needs of warfare have brought forth three systems of intervals: the most open order, in which the men are spaced both in length and depth four cubits [2 metres] apart, the most compact, in which with locked shields each man is a cubit [50cm] distant on all sides from his comrades, and the intermediate, also called a compact formation, in which they are distant two cubits [1 metre] from one another on all sides.' (Asclepiodotus 4.1)

To be clear, these distances are not of the interval between men, but of the interval including the man, so that for example in open order the distance of 2 metres could be measured from right shoulder of one man to the right shoulder of the next, rather than there being a 2-metre gap between the men, as is apparent when calculations are made of the total space occupied by given numbers of men in given order (as in Pol. 12.19). This distinction assumes some importance when comparisons are made to the Roman formation below and in Chapter 9. 3.1, 3.2 and 3.3 depict these intervals schematically.

Some doubt has been cast on this division into three intervals, since Asclepiodotus is fond of categorizing things into threes, and Polybius seems never to refer to the most compact formation. His descriptions and calculations, as in his discussion of the phalanx and the legion at 18.29–30 and of the Battle of Issus at 12.21, are all based on the intermediate or open order (two cubits or 1 metre, and four cubits or 2 metres), and the word used for the most compact formation (in the passage quoted above translated 'locked shields' – as here the verb *synaspizo*, usually the noun *synaspismos*, although Polybius himself never uses the noun) seems to be used by Polybius and other authors as a general term for 'close order', rather than specifically for the one cubit interval. The same word is used to describe some close-order Classical Greek formations, where it is extremely unlikely (given the 1 metre diameter shield typically carried by hoplites) that a half-metre spacing is meant. Nevertheless, it seems to me to be preferable to allow Asclepiodotus' definitions here, since the existence of a very close formation is likely from other evidence, and these three spacings continued in use right into the seventeenth century AD in Early Modern pike armies.[5]

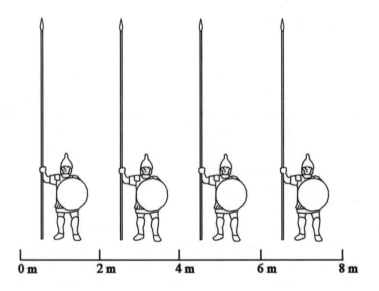

0 m   2 m   4 m   6 m   8 m

Fig. 3.1. Four-cubit interval.

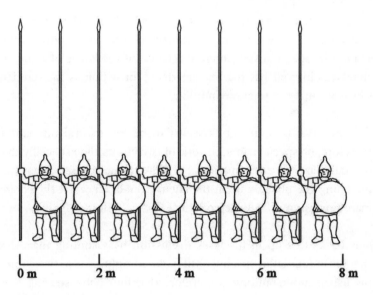

Fig. 3.2. Two-cubit interval.

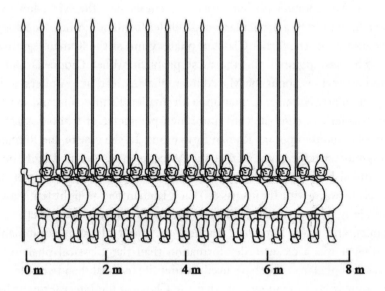

Fig. 3.3. One-cubit interval.

As we have seen, Diodorus reported that Philip II in inventing the phalanx was 'imitating the *synaspismos* of the warriors at Troy'. This might lead us to suppose that the most compact formation – *synaspismos* – was the normal formation of the Macedonian phalanx. Yet this poses three problems. Firstly,

Polybius, as noted above, thinks that 'Homeric close-order' refers to the two cubit spacing, as shown in his discussion of the comparative strengths of legion and phalanx, and Callisthenes' account of the Battle of Issus. Secondly, Asclepiodotus himself has the 'intermediate' formation as the standard close-order formation; again to quote in full:

> 'The interval of four cubits seems to be the natural one and has, therefore, no special name; the one of two cubits and especially that of one cubit are forced formations ... . The former is used when we are marching the phalanx upon the enemy, the latter when the enemy is marching upon us.' (Asclepiodotus 4.3)

Polybius backs this up in his Issus discussion by assuming that Alexander's phalanx was in four cubit spacing until it closed right up into two cubit spacing, and the usual understanding is therefore that four cubit spacing was 'march order' and two cubit spacing 'battle order', with one cubit spacing a special static defensive formation. The third problem is that if the standard interval of the Macedonian phalanx was two cubits, yet the Macedonian phalanx was thought to be a particularly close-order formation, what does this mean for the interval of the earlier Classical phalanx and of the Roman legions?

This last point is the thorniest problem. What Diodorus and Polybius (and others) say about the Macedonian phalanx lead us to understand that it is a particularly compact formation, with smaller file intervals, and so was denser, or 'heavier', in combat, with more men per metre of frontage than previous Greek or contemporary Roman formations. In the case of the Roman legions, Polybius' specific point is that the Macedonians occupied half the frontage occupied by Roman soldiers, so that (allowing for the five ranks that could reach forward with their sarissas) each Roman had to fight ten Macedonians. Similarly, if the standard file interval of the Macedonian phalanx was two cubits, and if (as Diodorus implies) the point of the Macedonian phalanx is that it was a closer-order formation than the Classical phalanx, then the Classical phalanx must have used a wider file interval than two cubits. We have no knowledge or evidence of what the Classical file interval might have been, but if it was, say, the four cubit open order of the Macedonians, then this seems, to many modern authors, a surprisingly open order for what was considered a close-order, heavy infantry formation. Similarly, if the standard Macedonian interval was two cubits and each front-rank Roman faced two Macedonians, as Polybius tells us, then Roman legionaries too must have used a four cubit interval, and again this seems too open for a heavy infantry formation.

This question of the standard file interval of the Classical Greek phalanx then gets tied up in a long-running debate about the nature and origins of the phalanx. To summarize and simplify, the orthodox view of the development of the phalanx is that it developed quite early in the Archaic/Classical period, perhaps some time around the seventh/sixth centuries, and was from the beginning a close-order formation of heavy infantry in its fully developed form, similar to that described by Thucydides and Xenophon (late fifth/early fourth centuries). While there is no direct evidence for Classical intervals, there is indirect evidence in the size of the hoplite shield (typically about two cubits, or 1 metre, in diameter) and in the fact that Thucydides describes how hoplites would keep as close as possible to their neighbour so as to benefit from the protection of their shield (5.71.1). This would suggest that an interval of no more than two cubits is likely. An alternative ('heretical') view of the Classical phalanx has been proposed, which sees the formation of the all-heavy infantry close-order phalanx we see in Thucydides and Xenophon as a very late development – perhaps as late as the Peloponnesian War (late fifth century). According to this theory, earlier phalanxes fought in a more open order, and may still have contained within their ranks skirmishers – archers, javelinmen, stone throwers – rather than these being relegated to separate units behind or to the sides of the phalanx. According to this view, the four cubit order might well have continued to be the standard formation of the Classical phalanx, and Philip's innovation was in closing this up to two cubits.[6]

For the file interval used by the Romans there is a similar degree of uncertainty. Polybius unhappily does not express himself quite as clearly as he might in the relevant passage. After detailing the 3ft file interval (and two cubit rank spacing – the two are the same) of the phalanx, he goes on:

'Now in the case of the Romans also each soldier with his arms occupies a space of three feet in breadth, but as in their mode of fighting each man must move separately, as he has to cover his person with his long shield, turning to meet each expected blow, and as he uses his sword both for cutting and thrusting it is obvious that a looser order is required, and each man must be at a distance of at least three feet from the man next him in the same rank and those in front of and behind him, if they are to be of proper use. The consequence will be that one Roman must stand opposite two men in the first rank of the phalanx, so that he has to face and encounter ten pikes. (Polybius 18.30.5–9)

So Polybius is saying that each Roman soldier occupies a space of 3ft, but that in addition (because of their more mobile method of fighting) they need a space of 3ft between each man, for a total of 6ft per man. While it is clear enough to me that he assigns the Romans a four cubit (6ft) interval, he does not do so explicitly, and he (or perhaps a corruption of his text) leaves just enough doubt for some to question this open order for Romans. We have almost no other evidence for Roman file intervals at any period. Rather astonishingly, perhaps, given the long period for which Roman legions dominated warfare, and the generally technical and sophisticated nature of the Roman military, there are no extant contemporary technical writings at all on Roman legionary organization, equipment, tactics or drill. The only tactical treatises to survive from the Roman era are Aelian's and Arrian's copies or adaptations of Hellenistic manuals. The only positive statement on the subject comes from Vegetius, writing in the late fourth century AD. Vegetius collected various works on the earlier legions to produce a somewhat confused and idealized account of the golden age of the legion (from which he hoped contemporaries could learn), and he assigns 3ft – two cubits – to each file (Veg. 3.14, 15). Thus we have Polybius, contemporary but rather unclear, apparently specifying intervals of 6ft (four cubits, 2 metres), and Vegetius, much later and often confused, clearly specifying 3ft (two cubits, 1 metre). Meanwhile, as with the Classical phalanx, many modern historians see the four cubit spacing as too wide for a heavy infantry formation, and find it more likely that Romans too usually fought with a two cubit (1 metre) frontage.[7]

This has led to various attempts to square the circle. For some, the four cubit spacing (particularly for Roman legionaries) just feels too wide for a heavy infantry formation. (We might question of course how a modern historian with no experience of massed close-order infantry formations would be able to form such a judgement, though doubts about this spacing go back at least to the late nineteenth-century German historians who considered this issue, and who had some familiarity with drill, if not with close-order hand-to-hand combat.) For these, the assumption is that Polybius is mistaken, or his text corrupt; Romans must have used a two cubit spacing, so Macedonians, to preserve Polybius' two against one testimony, must have habitually used the one cubit spacing (approximately 50cm). This is a neat solution inasmuch as it allows us to retain Vegetius' testimony, and also assume a similar two cubit spacing for the Classical phalanx. Philip II's innovation would then have been introducing the (Homerically inspired) one cubit spacing.

The problems with this solution are, however, also many. It requires rejecting not just Polybius' testimony, but also the statement of Asclepiodotus (*et al*) that the one cubit spacing was a defensive formation (used 'when the enemy is marching upon us'), and assuming instead that this was the standard Macedonian formation. It also impacts on the discussion of the length of the sarissa. It is clear, from Polybius and the tacticians, that formations are usually drawn up with the same spacing in breadth and depth; that is, with the same interval between ranks as between files. Asclepiodotus (4.2) indicates that intervals could be formed by rank (that is, the interval described is between the ranks), by file (where the interval is between the files) or by both rank and file, which Asclepiodotus calls '*kata parastaten kai epistaten*', very literally 'by stand-besider and stand-behinder'. It is evident that this latter is the normal arrangement, since it forms the basis of Polybius' discussion of the nature of the phalanx (18.29.5) where, after discussing the sarissa projections due to the two cubit rank interval, he refers to the phalanx being 'properly formed and the men close[d] up properly both flank and rear [*kat' epistaten kai kata parastaten*]', clearly the same term. So any closing up or loosening of the file intervals would ordinarily also involve closing or loosening the rank intervals. If the standard file spacing were to have been one cubit, then the rank spacing would also have been one cubit, but all the calculations of Polybius and the other tacticians about the length of the sarissa and the number of sarissa points that project beyond the front rank are based on a rank spacing of two cubits.

There are also practical considerations, as some have doubted it is possible for men with shields and sarissas to form up as close as one cubit, with spears projecting. This latter point cannot be pressed strongly, at present. It should be a matter of simple physical possibility, and be answerable by equipping a small group of volunteers with suitable reproduction weapons and shields and having them test the various intervals. This has been done a number of times, but unfortunately either the experiments have been badly designed or they have been inadequately documented. The first two attempts (some 100 years apart) found that forming and manoeuvring a phalanx with one cubit spacing was perfectly possible (though details about the experiments performed are sadly lacking or inadequate). The most recent attempt, however, concluded that it was impossible for phalangites to form on so tight a frontage (but, strangely, that Classical hoplites, despite their putatively larger shields, did do so, for which there is no evidence). This perhaps tells us more about the value of such experiments than it does about the reality of what happened in the past. I believe we must rely on the testimony of the ancient sources that such a formation was possible, at least on the defensive, even if we don't know exactly how it was done (presumably shields either overlapped or were held at an angle, and it is unclear how the sarissas projected past the shields). But we should then also respect their view that the usual, natural and most-used formations were those of four and two cubits.[8]

My own view is that the problem cannot be definitively resolved, given the state of the evidence, but that we may be misguided (and indeed so may Polybius) in attempting to find a single typical file interval and a solution that will fit every case. For all the mathematical precision with which the matter is sometimes discussed (for example, an interval of 48cm is sometimes proposed for the closest order), in the field there would have been no such precision, and even more so than for the size of spears and shields, we must expect variety and approximation rather than mathematical exactitude. Formations of infantry are not formed up using measuring sticks (even if such things existed in the ancient world with its lack of standardized measurements) – rather they are formed by eye, by approximation (what 'feels about right') or by using some body part as the measure. The usual way to take intervals in modern army drill is for each soldier to place an outstretched arm on the shoulder of the neighbour to his right or left (this gives a two cubit spacing), and some such similar method was no doubt used in antiquity. Ideal intervals may have been one, two or four cubits, but in practice this would either have been judged by eye (likely in comparison with the size of shield in use) or by some such human measurement as one cubit being packed as tightly as possible (shoulder to shoulder), two cubits at arm's length and four cubits at double arm's length. It is interesting to compare with a seventeenth-century AD Scottish pike drill manual on precisely this point, using the same intervals (inherited from Aelian's *Tactics*):

> 'Now the measure of those Distances cannot be taken justlie by the eye; but the Souldier to learne them must acompt the distance of sixe foote to bee betwixt file and file, when the Souldiers streatching out their airmes, toucheth one anothers hands: and betwixt Rankes, when the endes of their Pickes come well neare to the heelles of them that march before … . And the measure of the 3. foote betwixt the files, is when their Elbowes toucheth one another, betwixt Rankes, when they come up to touch one anothers Swords; The measure of a foote and an halfe betwixt files, is when they joyne shoulder to shoulder.' (Thomas Kellie, *Pallas Armata*)

Polybius, in making his point about legion and phalanx, chose to use the two cubit interval as typical for Macedonians. In his discussion of Issus, he seems to be using the four cubit interval as his yardstick, offering two cubit spacing only as a special argument – 'even had they, to use the poet's expression, "laid shield to shield"' (Pol. 12.21.3). In practice, the phalanx no doubt used different intervals in different circumstances depending on the tactical situation and problem that needed to be solved. The same, we may assume, would apply to Romans, and it may also be that Romans tended to prefer a more open order, as Polybius says, because of their individual style of fighting with sword and shield, and there are other hints to this effect, such as Julius Caesar's well-known order at the battle against the Nervii (57), 'he ordered them to loosen their order, that they might the more easily use their swords' (*B.G.* 2.25). It is also possible that Romans did not have formal file intervals and drill at all, but fought in more of a loose 'cloud' of fighters, standing apart at a distance that felt comfortable. If there was no formal Roman drill at the level of the individual soldier, this could explain why there is no trace of such drill in existing sources or any outstanding Roman drill manual. Or it could be that Romans had their own simple drill for changing intervals quickly: in a formation with 6ft intervals in rank and 3ft intervals in file, as described by Vegetius (3.14), if every alternate man in each rank took one step forward or back, the result would be a formation with one man every 6ft in each rank, but still with one man every 3ft when viewed from the front, with the men in *quincunx*, that is, arranged like the spots on the five on a dice (fig. 3.4). There is no evidence for such a manoeuvre, but while it is just a speculative suggestion, it seems to me to be quite likely. At any rate, we must assume that Romans also changed file intervals according to the tactical demands of the situation. As such, Polybius is being disingenuous in offering a simple comparison of file intervals in legion and phalanx. The actual number of men opposed in each formation would have depended greatly on circumstances, with no simple single ratio between the two that would apply in every case.

As for the Classical phalanx, we must remember again that most Classical hoplites were not closely drilled or trained, and as such probably simply did not have a standard file interval. A phalanx would have formed up using whatever formation looked or felt about right at the time, and judged by eye, arm or shield (all imperfect and inexact measures). Classical phalanxes might well have formed up with approximately two cubit (1 metre) intervals, if dictated by the size of the shield – this would have meant the edges of the shields touching. They might have spread themselves out a bit, if they wanted to cover more frontage, the ground was broken or uneven, or they felt they needed more room for spearplay. They might have huddled together more, overlapping their shields, if they felt threatened (for example by cavalry) or for

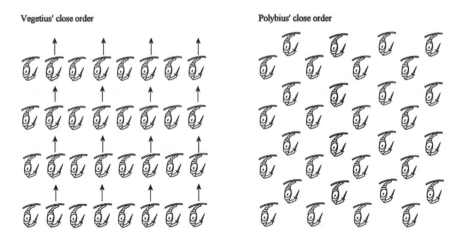

Fig. 3.4. Roman intervals: Vegetius' 3ft between files and 7ft between ranks (left), moving to Polybius' 3ft gap between men (right).

protection from missiles. Philip's innovation may have been to introduce (or perhaps copy from, for example, the Spartans) formal file intervals, and formal drills for transitioning between them, and the closest of these intervals (that of one cubit) was no doubt closer than anything that Classical hoplites, with their larger shields and need for room for individual spear fencing, could have adopted. So Classical hoplites probably used formations of about two cubit spacing, sometimes more; Philip formalized this into a two cubit spacing with the option, on the defensive, to close up to one cubit; and the Romans often used a more open order (four cubits) for swordplay, though they too could close up if they felt that doing so would benefit them. Polybius' assertion that one Roman faced two Macedonians (and ten sarissa points) would be true in some situations, but not in all, depending on the circumstances, while the Macedonian phalanx was a closer-order ('heavier') formation than the Classical in that it was well drilled in holding a tight interval and had the option in some circumstances to adopt a tighter one still, even if it did not always do so. So rather than try to assign a single interval in all cases, we should accept this variety. The Macedonian phalanx was a tighter, better-drilled formation than the Classical phalanx, and it had a range of file intervals that included tighter ones than would have been available to Classical Greeks or Romans, and that is all that can be said for certain.

It is worth in this context noting something that I will revisit in Chapter 8. The Roman formation, Polybius tells us, needed to be more open to allow the legionaries to wield their swords. Classical Greek phalanxes were also more open, in part because the hoplites needed room for individual fencing with their spears (we hear evidence of certain tricks and manoeuvres being taught by which spearmen could gain an advantage over their opponents). But part of the purpose of the sarissa in the Macedonian phalanx was that it did not need to be wielded by the individual, but just held firmly in advance of the formation, and that the effect of the phalanx lay in this assembled mass of projecting sarissa points, not in individual weapons play. This means that the men could be packed more closely together, since they needed only room to stand with sarissa advanced, not to fence, dodge or parry, or to aim or avoid blows. This allowed the phalanx to become heavier (in the sense of denser, with more men per metre of frontage) while protecting the men (against anything other than a similarly armed phalanx) from enemy weapons by holding them off at sarissa-length. It is this use of a two-handed pike, held firmly and statically forward, that allowed and was in turn made possible by the dense formation, since an individual with a sarissa would be hopelessly vulnerable one-to-one, as the duel of Dioxippus and Coragus described in the previous chapter makes clear. The Macedonian phalanx was therefore a more integrated formation, achieving its effect through mass, rather than simply a collection of individual soldiers at whatever spacing.

The question of how the phalanx switched between these different intervals is an important one, but first we need to look at the larger formations, those above the level of the file.

Larger formations

Aelian, in his introductory remarks on the art of war, has this to say about the organization of an army:

> 'It is the first duty of a commander to select the fittest men out of the general levy and to appoint each of these men to their proper place (that is, to arrange them into files and to form these into larger bodies) and to organise a total levy that will be suitable to conduct the war on the desired scale ... .Polybius calls it "a skill whereby a man can take a given number of men, arrange them into files and bodies that mutually support each other, and instruct them in all the matters pertaining to war".' (Aelian, *Tactics* 3)

We might compare this with the remark from Anaximenes on the first organization of Macedonian infantry under an Alexander, examined in Chapter 1, where Alexander 'divided the majority of the infantry into companies [*lochoi*] and files [*dekads*] and other commands'. There is also the example of the late third-century reform of the Achaean army (the Achaean League being one of the groups of Greek city-states that rose to prominence in the third century) to use Macedonian weapons and drill, where their commander Philopoemen pointed out that their existing army was weak because 'a division of line and formation into *speirai* was not customary with them' (Plut. *Philop.* 9.2). I will discuss the nature of the *speira* below.

So the first step in building an effective infantry (or any military) force is to divide it up into its constituent subunits. This may seem obvious, though it is open to doubt how thoroughly this was done for many Classical Greek phalanxes. The Spartans at least certainly had a high level of internal organization, but other less well-drilled armies might not have had any at all, and the Spartans were considered unusually well organized and drilled in that every man knew his proper place in the phalanx, and there was a hierarchy of officers at every level. Other phalanxes must at least have had subunits based on the groups by which the phalanx was recruited – recruitment by age group and/or tribe or deme (*demos*) being the norm in all cities – but likely did not have a full hierarchy of subunits or officers at every level.[9]

The purpose of such subunits and officers is two-fold. Firstly they allow the phalanx to form up rapidly and efficiently, with each man having and knowing his assigned place and able to take it without disorder or confusion (the mortal enemies of any close-order infantry formation). Secondly, they give the phalanx flexibility, the ability to move across varying terrain, to change facing, heading, depth and overall formation, and to detach subunits to perform specific tasks. Again these may seem obvious requirements, but it is striking how often Greek phalanxes (and other ancient formations generally) are, or appear to be, single monolithic masses without this sort of articulation and flexibility. In a typical hoplite battle, once the decision is taken which city contingent is to form up where in the line, and how many shields deep, there was little else to be done but advance to contact, fight for a while and for one side to run away. Spartans on occasion might attempt more complex tactical manoeuvres, but these did not always turn out well (see for example the failed manoeuvre at Mantinea, Thuc. 5.71.2–3). All of this indicates that a division into formal, independently commanded subunits was not normal practice for most of these armies. Creating such a level of organization was not an innovation of the Macedonian phalanx – Spartan armies already did so, and according to Anaximenes some Macedonian infantry had also done so from early times – but in the Macedonian phalanx it was carried through with great efficiency and thoroughness and formed an essential part of the effectiveness of the entire phalanx.

The smallest subunit was the file, though depending on the depth at which the phalanx would form, the file could itself be broken down. Asclepiodotus 2.2 refers to half-files, quarter-files and double-quarter-files – the latter, of twelve men, being presumably a three-quarter-file. The name Asclepiodotus gives the file – *lochos* – is unfortunately also the generic Greek name for a subunit of many and various sizes (see earlier comments on the lack of precise Greek technical terminology; the same can be said of the Romans, since the Latin word *ordo* was used for files, ranks and whole formations of any and every size, making it exceedingly tricky to understand exactly what is being referred to in many historical accounts). Asclepiodotus also gives alternative names for the file – *stichos*, *synomotia* and *dekania* – the last being a reminder that Macedonian files had (presumably) originally been of ten men, as Anaximenes suggests.

The tacticians go on to name all the various combinations of files. The following table shows the subunits of the phalanx, each unit formed by doubling the previous unit, two files (*lochoi*) to a *dilochia*, and so on. Where an author gives alternative unit names, they are listed together, or if they are older, previous names, these are listed in brackets.

Men	Asclepiodotus (Asclep. 2)	Aelian (Ael. 4–5; 9) Arrian (Arr. Tact. 5–6; 10)
4	*Enomotia*	*Enomotia*
8	*Hemilochion, dimoiria*	*Hemilochion, dimoiria*
16	*Lochos (stichos, synomotia, dekania)*	*Lochos, stichos, dekania*
32	*Dilochia*	*Dilochia*
64	*Tetrarchia*	*Tetrarchia*
128	*Taxis*	*Taxis*
256	*Syntagma, syntaxiarchia*	*Syntagma, xenagia*
512	*Pentakosiarchia*	*Pentakosiarchia*
1,024	*Chiliarchia*	*Chiliarchia*
2,048	*Merarchia (keras, telos)*	*Merarchia, telos*
4,096	*Phalangarchia, apotome keratos*	*Phalangarchia, strategia*
8,192	*Diphalangia, keras*	*Diphalangarchia*
16,384	*Phalanx*	*Tetraphalangarchia*

Note that the word *taxis* is commonly used in the literary historians such as Arrian to describe a much larger formation – as we will see, Alexander's phalanx was divided into six *taxeis* of 1,500 men or more – while Polybius seems to use *speira* instead of *syntagma* to describe the 256-man unit. Once again, terminology can be highly variable. While the various combinations of files were no doubt real, it is the *syntagma* that was really significant, as Asclepiodotus explains, and it is worth quoting his words in full, in what is a highly informative passage:

> 'The supernumeraries [*ektaktoi*] were formerly attached to the *taxis*, as their name indicates, because they were not included in the number of the *taxis*: a herald, a signaller, a bugler, an aide and a file closer ... . For when the file consisted of eight men, eight files constituted the square, which alone of all the detachments, by reason of the equal length of the sides of the formation could hear equally well the commands from every quarter and so was properly called a "command"; when however the file was later doubled, the *syntaxiarchia* constituted the square, and as a consequence, included the supernumeraries.' (Asclepiodotus 2.9)

Note also that Asclepiodotus is already using a different name (*syntaxiarchia*) for the *syntagma* than the one he used a paragraph earlier. Unfortunately it is not clear when it was that the file consisted of eight men, or when it was increased to sixteen. As we have seen, there is some reason to suppose that it was under Alexander that the file was increased from eight men (as at Issus) to sixteen (as in the proposed incorporation of Persians). So it may be that Philip, and Alexander at the start of his campaigns, used the shallower formation and the smaller unit, Asclepiodotus' *tetrarchia* of 64 men (then called a *taxis*), as the building block of the phalanx, and the depth was later doubled at the end of Alexander's reign, and the size of the basic unit quadrupled to the *syntagma*, to maintain a square number. It is perhaps rather surprising to find Asclepiodotus referring back in this way, given that he was writing 200 years later, though he may have been reproducing this comment from some earlier version of the work (as early as Pyrrhus perhaps, early third century). At any rate, this square formation, the *syntagma* (under various names), sixteen files of sixteen ranks, is the basic manoeuvre unit of the later phalanx; the unit on which the various manoeuvres were based, and so the smallest proper building block of the phalanx. It was also the smallest unit which could be commanded independently, as it had its own signaller and bugler.

There is then a corresponding list of the units above the *syntagma* in size; two *syntagmata* make a *pentakosiarchia* (512 men), two of these a *chiliarchia*

(1,024 men), two of these 'formerly' (when Asclepiodotus doesn't say) a wing (*keras*) or *telos*, later a *merarchia* (2,048 men). Two of these make a *phalangarchia* (4,000 men, to round the numbers); two of these a double-phalanx (*diphalangia*) or wing (*keras*) (8,000 men); and finally two of these make the full phalanx, of 16,000 men. Some of these units are reflected quite clearly in literary histories. In particular, the *chiliarchia* (unit of 1,000 men) is well known from the reign of Alexander, when units of this name start to be introduced in the cavalry as well as the infantry (the specific phalanx formation must already have existed of course, perhaps under a different name). Fig. 3.5 illustrates this progression of major unit sizes.

But few of the larger units are reflected in other sources (literary, epigraphic and papyrological), or if they are it is often under different names, which can make it difficult to be certain of the identification. For the Antigonid army, the *syntagma* of Asclepiodotus seems to correspond to the *speira* found in Polybius (for example at Sellasia, the *Chalcaspides* and Illyrians were drawn up in alternate *speirai*, Pol. 2.66.5, while at Philip V's siege of Palus, the Peltasts are drawn up in *speirai*, Pol. 5.4.9), and in Plutarch, where Philopoemen's reform of the Achaean army, as well as the changes of equipment discussed in previous chapters, involved forming the Achaean phalanx by *speirai* (presumably previously they had either used larger units or no formal division of subunits at all). We also see *speirarchs*, commanders of a *speira*, above *tetrarchs* and below *strategoi* (presumably commanders of a *strategia*, unless it is meant in a more informal sense) in the Amphipolis regulations. *Speira* is also used (with *tagma* and *semeia*) by Polybius (6.24.5) to translate the Latin *manipulus*, 'maniple', the smallest independent subunit of the Roman legion, around 120 men strong (so smaller than the 256-man Macedonian unit).[10]

The next level of organization that is evident in other sources is the *chiliarchia*, the unit of 1,024 men. A unit of approximately 1,000 men is an obvious subdivision for any larger force, and the *chiliarchia* probably has a long history even before the Macedonian phalanx, being perhaps a subdivision of the Persian army (1,000 being of course a multiple of ten). Such units are known in the Ptolemaic army, and the fact that many larger units always come in multiples of 1,000, such as the Hypaspists or Peltasts, typically 3,000 (as under Alexander) or 5,000 (at their largest under Perseus), suggests that they were formed into three or five *chiliarchiai*. The largest subunit traceable outside the tacticians is the *strategia*, equivalent to the *phalangarchia* of Asclepiodotus and around 4,000 men strong (unless of course Antigonid usage is again different; the *strategia* might have been a smaller unit, perhaps equivalent to the *chiliarchia*). This appears to have been the largest normal subunit of the phalanx. The full

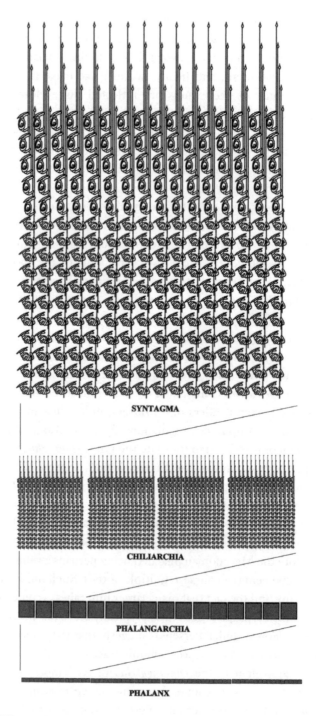

Fig. 3.5. The major subdivisions of the phalanx.

phalanx at Cynoscephalae was 16,000 men strong, which would correspond to four *strategiai*.

It is perfectly likely that the numerous interim unit sizes described in the tacticians did really exist as nominal organizational units in the various armies (perhaps under different names depending on date and army), but that these familiar units – *speira/syntagma, chiliarchia, strategia* – were the real organizational and tactical building blocks of the phalanx, which we might think of in modern terms as 'battalion', 'brigade' and 'division'. A phalangite would have known to which *speira* and *chiliarchia* (and perhaps *strategia*) he belonged, but the other various subdivisions might have been more like paper formations without particular tactical uses. This may be equivalent to, for example, battalion and regimental organization in the British Army of the Napoleonic period, where battalions were organized into regiments for administrative purposes, but the battalion was the actual battlefield unit, with battalions from the same regiment not necessarily fighting in the same campaign, or even on the same continent, at any given time.

The most important division of Alexander's phalanx, as already noted, was the *taxis* (in Arrian's telling), each under a named commander and recruited from a specific area of Macedon. There is some uncertainty over the size of this unit. Alexander is said to have taken 12,000 Macedonian infantry with him to Asia, of whom 3,000 were Hypaspists, leaving 9,000 in the phalanx. These were divided into six *taxeis*, which would therefore have contained 1,500 men each. This is a slightly awkward number, though, if the tacticians are to be followed, as there is no subunit of this number (or even approximately this number), so the *taxis* of Arrian would appear to consist of either three *pentakosiarchiai* or one *pentakosiarchia* and one *chiliarchia* (assuming these divisions, or their equivalents under different names, existed in Alexander's day). There is a possibility that the 3,000 Hypaspists (themselves, presumably, three *chiliarchiai*) should not be included in the 12,000 total; if this is correct then the phalanx proper was 12,000 strong and each *taxis* corresponds to a *keras* or *telos* of 2,000 men, which would certainly fit more neatly with the theoretical strengths. Units on this level are not readily apparent in the historians for the period after Alexander, for which we just don't have the detail in the battle accounts to discern any of the smaller units, the phalanx usually being referred to as a single monolithic whole (for all that we can be sure that it was in fact divided into smaller units). It seems reasonable to guess that the *chiliarchia*, well known under Alexander and an obvious round number of 1,000 men, may well have been the basic building block, or that the *merarchia* of 2,000 men, the *telos/keras/taxis* of Alexander's day, continued to be the basic unit. What we can say is that, although these figures and unit sizes are sometimes dismissed as being highly theoretical, and certainly the exact figures such as 1,024 men must have been paper strengths only – very rarely met in practice given all the contingencies of war – the figure of 16,000 men for a full phalanx does occur more than once in the histories. For example, Philip V had a 16,000-man phalanx at Cynoscephalae (196) and Antiochus III had 16,000 phalangites at Magnesia (189). So these numbers are not purely theoretical, and do seem to have formed the basis of phalanx organization and recruitment.[11]

We have seen in the previous chapter that larger units tended to be named after the shields they carried. What there is not strong evidence for in any of the Hellenistic armies is the systematic naming or numbering of army units, as was to become familiar from the Roman army (the Ninth Legion, and so forth) and in most organized armies since then. Whether this is an accident of survival of evidence or due to an actual absence of individual unit identification is uncertain, but I am inclined to think that units were probably named or numbered even though we only catch glimpses of this practice. For the army of Philip II, we have already seen that the *Pezhetairoi* (Foot Companions) are the only named unit known, and that this was probably the guard unit, which formed the core of the later expansion of the phalanx to include the whole of the Macedonian infantry. Under Alexander, the name *Pezhetairoi* was expanded to include half or perhaps all of the main phalanx, alongside the enigmatic *Asthetairoi*. Possibly these were names for two halves (each of two *strategiai* perhaps) of the phalanx, with the *Asthetairoi* being recruited from Upper Macedonia, the inland highland regions absorbed into the kingdom by Philip II, and the *Pezhetairoi* from the original lowland kingdom. Alongside them, the old *Pezhetairoi* of Philip were now renamed as Hypaspists, and were probably armed as peltasts (in the new sense – light phalangites) and organized in three *chiliarchiai*, of which one, the elite infantry unit of the army, was termed the *Agema* (the vanguard, as we might say). Arrian lists these units in his account of the mutinous Macedonians at Opis:

> 'But when they [the Macedonians] heard about … the Oriental [*barbarike*] forces being drafted into the units [*lochous*], and the Macedonian names – an agema called Persian, and Persian foot-companions [*pezhetairoi*] and *asthetairoi* too, and a Persian battalion [*taxis*] of silver shields [*arguraspidon*] … they could no longer contain themselves.' (Arrian, *Anabasis* 7.11.3)

All subsequent Hellenistic armies appear to have an Agema drawn from the ranks of the peltasts of the guard (and usually also a cavalry Agema, the elite cavalry unit).[12]

Below this level of organization, as we have seen, Alexander's phalanx was divided into *taxeis* which could be identified in two ways: by their region of recruitment or by the name of their commander. Both of these methods of naming were somewhat transient. Later in Alexander's reign, the practice of forming regional *taxeis* was abandoned, with new recruits being added to units regardless of where they were recruited, and depending on availability, sickness or death the named commander of a unit (its 'eponymous commander') might not actually command a unit on any given occasion. For example at Gaugamela, Alexander's phalanx consisted of:

> 'The battalions [*taxeis*] of Coenus son of Polemocrates, Perdiccas son of Orontes, Meleager son of Neoptolemus, Polyperchon son of Simmias and Amyntas son of Philip; this was led by Simmias, since Amyntas had been sent to Macedonia to collect troops. The left of the Macedonian phalanx was held by the battalion of Craterus son of Alexander.' (Arrian, *Anabasis* 3.11.9–10)

Under the Successors there is almost no trace of unit organization at this level, the only named unit being the *Argyraspides*, Silver Shields, as the Hypaspists started to be called from late in the reign of Alexander. The main phalanx of each Successor general was called simply the phalanx, the phalangites or 'those armed in the Macedonian fashion'.[13]

We have better evidence, though, for the Hellenistic kingdoms. As we have seen, the Antigonid army had its Peltasts (the guard peltasts, including an Agema – the spelling with a capital 'P' incidentally is a modern practice to distinguish this particular unit from generic peltasts; written Greek only used one letter case at this period). These were generally 3,000 strong, expanded to 5,000 for the Pydna campaign. The main phalanx consisted of the *Chalcaspides*, Bronze Shields, and also (probably) the *Leucaspides*, White Shields. The identification of the *Leucaspides* as a unit of the phalanx is not absolutely certain; they are referred to in the Antigonid army only twice, when Cleomenes before Sellasia recruited extra helots (serfs) 'as a counter-force to the *Leucaspides*' (Plut. *Cleom.* 23.1), and at Pydna, where the Roman First Legion faced the *Chalcaspides* and the Second Legion the *Leucaspides* (Liv. 44.41.2). These might possibly have been some non-phalanx (or even non-Macedonian) unit, but I think the nomenclature (units named from their shields) and context makes it most likely that a phalanx unit is meant. I am inclined to agree with the common view that the Antigonid phalanx consisted of these two units, each making up half of the phalanx (so of 8,000 men each), and that not all of either unit was necessarily called up at any time (so the arrival of a *merarchia* or *chiliarchia* or two of *Leucaspides* for the Sellasia campaign might have prompted Cleomenes to make his extra recruitment drive).[14]

For the Seleucid army we have evidence only of the basic division into a guard unit (probably peltasts) called the *Argyraspides* (ultimately, successors of Alexander's Hypaspists) and of the rest of the phalanx, which carried no special name (that we know of). As we saw in the last chapter, Bronze Shields and perhaps Gold Shields are also known (although the status and indeed existence of the latter is uncertain), and it may be that the bulk of the Seleucid phalanx was, like the Antigonid, called *Chalcaspides*, Bronze Shields. Unit division below this level, though it certainly existed, is unknown. I think it quite likely that phalanx units, like the early *taxeis* of Alexander, were named after the city or region of Syria where they were recruited (more on this in Chapter 5).

The Ptolemaic army also has its guard peltasts. The preparations for the Battle of Raphia provide the best account: 'Eurylochus of Magnesia commanded a body of about three thousand men known as the Royal Guard, Socrates the Boeotian had under him two thousand peltasts' (Pol. 5.65.1–2). This would make the organization similar to that of the Antigonid army, with a unit of 5,000 peltasts, of which 3,000 make up the Agema. The subunits of the phalanx itself, though, are not further identified: 'Phoxidas the Achaean, Ptolemy the son of Thraseas, and Andromachus of Aspendus exercised together in one body the phalanx and the Greek mercenaries, the phalanx twenty-five thousand strong being under the command of Andromachus and Ptolemy and the mercenaries, numbering eight thousand, under that of Phoxidas' (Pol. 5.65.3). The unusually large figure of 25,000 men for the phalanx is notable (Antiochus' phalanx was itself 20,000 strong), and was obtained by recruiting as many as 20,000 native Egyptians into the phalanx; the precise size of the Ptolemaic phalanx is disputed, and the subject of a long-running debate. There is no literary evidence for named subunits of the Ptolemaic army, though it may well have had its own *Chalcaspides*. A later reference to the Battle of Asophon (103) in Josephus states that 'those in the first rank of Ptolemy [IX]'s soldiers also had shields [*aspides*] covered with brass [bronze]' (Jos. *Ant.* 13.340 {12.5}), which unless it is simply a description of equipment (the opposing Jewish forces had bronze *thureoi*) might be an echo of the old unit name.

There is much more evidence from the numerous Egyptian papyri for unit organization at lower levels, though this does not tie in especially well with the high-level accounts in literary sources. What we do see is glimpses of numbered units (the 7th *chiliarchia* is mentioned, for example), ethnic units (particularly of cavalry) and the common occurrence of eponymous officers – that is, those who, as in Alexander's army, gave their own name to the units they commanded. It is not often possible to tell what size of unit is meant, but the likelihood is that Ptolemaic units at all levels, as for Alexander's army, were named after their current commander. This may well have been the practice in all the Hellenistic armies.[15]

Drill manoeuvres

The tacticians, naturally enough, contain comprehensive (if not always clear) details of the drill manoeuvres of the phalanx. There is not much trace of such drill in the literary battle descriptions to be found in the historians; there is a tendency for such literary descriptions to refer on a very large scale and with a broad brush to the movements of the phalanx, without much hint of the actual drill manoeuvres that must underlie such movements. This is much as we would expect; although some literary historians – in particular Polybius, as shown in his critique of Callisthenes' account of Issus – did have some knowledge and understanding of the drill that would be required to move and manoeuvre a phalanx, many historians did not, and at any rate all were writing much higher-level accounts of the events of a battle on the largest scale. This does not mean that the tactical manoeuvres in the tacticians did not take place and were not important, simply that the literary historians are focusing on a different scale. Underlying the simple descriptions of phalanx movements in the historians must be the detailed drills of the tacticians, and on occasion we can still see an echo of these drills, as will be explored further in this chapter and in Chapter 7 with an examination of some key battle accounts. Here my intention is just to discuss some of the most common or important manoeuvres, and the extent to which we can, using the tacticians, understand how they were performed. Their tactical usefulness will be considered further in Chapter 7. I will be using chiefly the *Tactics* of Asclepiodotus for this, as his is the earliest and therefore (putatively) the purest. Arrian's version contains a lot more Roman material, while Aelian will be introduced only where he adds something missing from Asclepiodotus.

So as discussed above, there were two key characteristics of the phalanx in how it was initially formed up and how it could be altered in battle: its density or file intervals (spacing between the files and ranks) and its depth (number of ranks). These two measures are clearly closely interrelated – Asclepiodotus uses the same word (*diplasiasmos*, doubling) to refer to changes in both, as he explains (perhaps without absolute crystal clarity):

> 'The term "doubling" is used in two ways: either of the place occupied by the phalanx, while the number of the men remains the same, or of the number of the men … doubling of men takes place by length when we interject or insert between the original files other files of equal strength, maintaining all the while the length of the phalanx, so that a compact order arises only from the doubling of the men … [doubling is also possible by depth, by interjecting ranks] … . Doubling of place occurs by length when we change the above mentioned compact formation by length into a loose formation, or when the interjected men countermarch by rank, either to prevent being outflanked by the enemy or when we wish to outflank the enemy … [likewise, doubling of place is possible by depth].' (Asclepiodotus, *Tactics* 10.17–18)

Doubling of men by length is illustrated in fig. 3.6, and doubling of place by length in fig. 3.7. So a phalanx that occupied, say, a front of 16 metres (one 256-man *syntagma* formed up sixteen deep with file intervals of two cubits, 1 metre) could double its men by inserting equal-strength files between the existing files. In this case, a second *syntagma* could march such that each of its files passed between the files of the first *syntagma* – there would then be 512 men in the same 16 metre frontage, with the file intervals now reduced to one cubit.

It is usually assumed that a similar manoeuvre could take place without involving a second *syntagma* in order to achieve a halved file interval. This is a reasonable assumption since it seems an obvious manoeuvre to use, though it is worth pointing out that it is not exactly what Asclepiodotus describes – his doublings are either of length (frontage of the whole phalanx) or of the number of men. Nevertheless, it is likely that such a manoeuvre was possible, and the description of Aelian 28 seems to describe this; that is, that a single *syntagma* would have the second, rearward, half of each file perform the 'interjection' described above, marching into the file intervals of the front half of each file. This would result in the same number of men, 256, occupying the same frontage, 16 metres, but now with half the file interval (one cubit) and half the depth (eight ranks). This manoeuvre is not explicitly described by Asclepiodotus and there are some problems with it, in that the rank of file

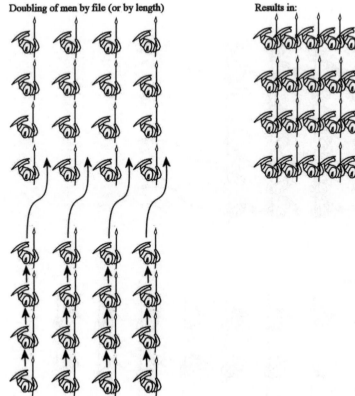

Fig. 3.6. Assuming compact formation 'doubling of men by length'.

leader, the man behind and the file closer were positions of special responsibility, as Asclepiodotus describes:

> 'We shall place the strongest in the front rank and behind them the most intelligent, and of the former the file-leaders shall be those who excel in size, strength and skill; because this line of file-leaders binds the phalanx together and is like the cutting edge of the sword ... . The second line must also be not much inferior to the first, so that when a file-leader falls his comrade behind may move forward and hold the line together; and the file closers, both those in the files and those attached to larger units, should be men who surpass the rest in presence of mind, the former to hold their own lines straight, the latter to keep the *syntagmata* in file and rank with one another.' (Asclepiodotus, *Tactics* 3.5–6)

Doubling of place by length

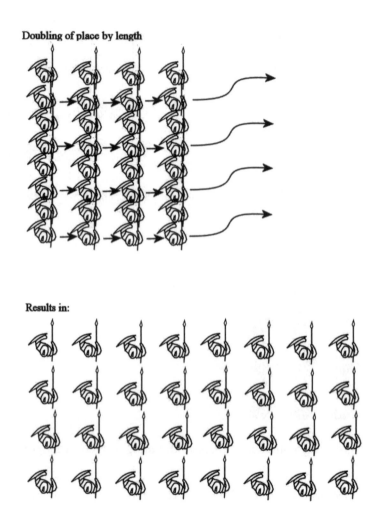

Fig. 3.7. Assuming open formation 'doubling of place by length'.

The file leader, his second and the file closer were higher ranks, and in the army of Alexander at least they received higher pay (Arr. *Anab.* 7.23.3–4). Any change of file interval that required interjecting half or quarter files between the files of the same *syntagma* would disrupt this arrangement, placing an ordinary (and presumably inferior in terms of experience, bravery or skill, and maybe armour) soldier into the front (and rear) rank. There were (as described by Asclep. 2.2 and Ael. 5) intermediate ranks of half file leader and quarter file leader to alleviate this problem (though these would certainly have been impossible in Alexander's proposed hybrid phalanx in which the middle ranks were missile-armed Persians), but at any rate we must be cautious in assuming that the usual way to change the intervals was to interject half files within the same formation, each time halving the depth in ranks. The standard depth in ranks (according to Asclepiodotus, originally eight, later increased to sixteen) was fixed by the structure and organization of the file, and could not be easily altered, at least in combat. It may be of course that when marching different intervals could be adopted in this way since it would matter less if the front rank consisted of fifty percent ordinary soldiers. The account of Aelian (*Tactics* 28) is also more suggestive of the insertion of men from the same formation (that is, presumably, the rear half files). Another possibility is that alternate men in a file would step forward to form the inserted file so that the new file would be led by the original second man of the original file. Unfortunately, the text of Aelian is very unclear on these points.[16]

To avoid these difficulties, there was a second way of changing the file intervals, which Asclepiodotus rather confusingly covers only in his description of the different commands to be used, rather than in the section on doublings (see fig. 3.9):

'If the phalanx must assume the compact formation by wing, we shall give the command, if on the right wing for the right file to hold its position and for the other files to right face, close up to the right, and then face to the front, and for the rear ranks to advance. Then if we wish to resume the original position, we shall command the rank of file-leaders to hold its position, the rear ranks to about face and advance, and then again to about face; after that, while the right file holds its position, let the other files left face and advance, until they have resumed their original intervals, when they face to the front.' (Asclepiodotus, *Tactics* 12.8)

Similar manoeuvres were used to close up on the left or on the centre. This, we may assume, was the usual way of changing the file intervals, since it retained the depth of the phalanx and did not interfere with the file structure – the file leaders and closers retained their correct places in the files – nor did it require the interjection of two separate units. It has one obvious difficulty, that the frontage of the phalanx would be halved (which depending on circumstances could mean the phalanx would be left open to outflanking), and if the manoeuvre was carried out with a large unit (such as a half phalanx or entire phalanx), there would be a long way for those at the extremities of the line to march to close up their intervals. For example, if a 16,000-man phalanx, sixteen

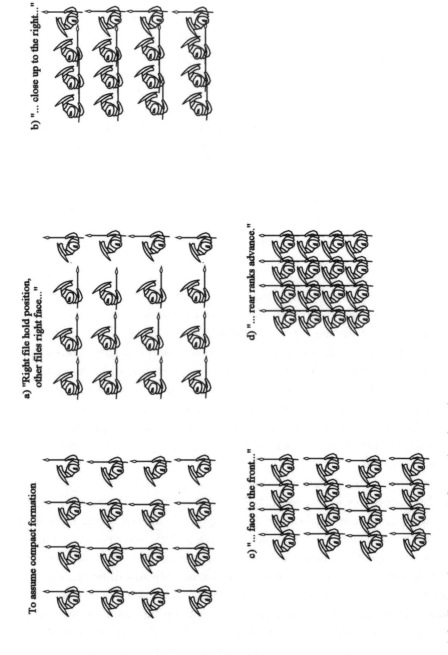

b) " ... close up to the right..."

a) "Right file hold position, other files right face..."

d) " ... rear ranks advance."

To assume compact formation

c) " ... face to the front..."

Fig. 3.8. Assuming compact formation by wing.

deep (so a frontage of 1,000 metres), were to perform this manoeuvre as one, then those on the flank would have to march 500 metres to reach their final positions – hardly possible in the face of the enemy. If the manoeuvre was carried out at the level of the individual *syntagma*, then gaps in the phalanx, each the width of a closed-up *syntagma*, would be left, and further marching would be required to close these gaps. Conversely, if this technique was used to open the order of the phalanx then the phalanx width would be doubled, which would likely cause problems given other units in the battleline, constricted terrain and so forth. Aelian (*Tactics* 11) spells out the different widths (frontage) of the phalanx in each interval, making it clear that he does not envisage any reduction in depth. So there are complexities around either technique for changing the file intervals (doubling by men or doubling by length), and part of the skill of the commander would have been in selecting and ordering the correct drills, which would require a high degree of experience and professionalism in the commander as well as in the men to carry it out.

These, then, are the manoeuvres available for altering the file intervals (and in the case of doubling by length, the frontage) of the phalanx. It is notable that the tacticians deal with the intervals and the frontage of the phalanx, rather than with changes to its depth, except when these arise as a consequence of one of the other manoeuvres (for example, in Aelian and Arrian's account, adopting open order involves having one file form up behind another). However, they also describe (Aelian 28, Arrian 25) a doubling of depth (in ranks) by the insertion of one file into another, so that the first man in one file becomes the second in the new deeper file, the second man becomes the fourth, and so on, interleaving the two files to create a combined file of double the number of men (and presumably the reverse of this manoeuvre would halve the number of ranks). This manoeuvre is not described by Asclepiodotus, although it is functionally equivalent to his doubling by marching interjected ranks (10.18), and it would also cause difficulties (though fewer) with the file structure and location of the file leader and closer as discussed above. It may be significant that doubling of ranks in seventeenth-century armies was usually carried out by alternate men in the file stepping forward into the rank ahead, or back into the file (see fig. 3.9). An army on the march would probably form in greater depth (in column, see below) not by altering the lengths of the files within units but by stacking up individual units – presumably, individual *syntagmata* – one behind another, and deployment into line, and hence reduction in depth, would have been carried out at this level rather than by adjusting the file depths and intervals. Once deployed for battle, the depth would be fixed and, as noted by Asclepiodotus (10.20, quoted below), not easily adjusted once the enemy were close.

Halving ranks and intervals   Results in:

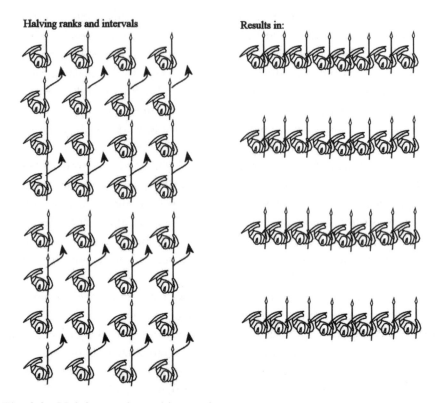

Fig. 3.9. Halving ranks and intervals.

As well as changing the intervals and depth, the other thing a phalanx would need to be able to do is turn, whether to follow a route through terrain, face an enemy in any direction other than straight ahead or perform one of the other larger-scale drill manoeuvres. There are two ways for a military unit to change its facing (face in a different direction): it can wheel or it can turn. A turn is carried out by the individual soldiers each turning in place, so that the formation as a whole retains its original position but the men within it are now all facing in a new direction. Such turns by individual men (*klisis*, Ascl. 10.2) are an essential part of the doublings discussed above, since for example to close up on the right, all files but the rightmost must turn to the right and advance toward the rightmost file (fig. 3.8). It was apparently not, however, preferred at the unit level – a *syntagma*, for example, would not turn to the right by having each individual man in the formation right face. While such a manoeuvre is extremely quick to carry out, it too would disrupt the file structure, leaving all the file leaders on the left flank and forming a new front rank out of ordinary soldiers from the middle of the file.

Rather, Asclepiodotus describes the procedure for wheeling a unit (*epistrophe*, Ascl. 10.4), pivoting it on its front left or right corners. Interestingly, this is combined with first closing the unit up into close (two cubit) order – assuming it is not already closed up – making the manoeuvre sound more complicated than it is:

'It is a quarter turn [*epistrophe*] when we close up the entire formation [*syntagma*] by file and rank in the compact formation [two cubits] and move it like the body of one man in such a manner that the entire force swings on the first file leader as on a pivot, if to the right on the right file leader, and if to the left on the left file leader.' (Asclepiodotus, *Tactics* 10.4)

Asclepiodotus gives the commands needed to carry out this manoeuvre at *Tactics* 12.2. Note that most of this description concerns forming close order, with only the pivot of the whole formation (and subsequent individual turn by the file leader, who has otherwise not moved) involving a change of facing. In such a manoeuvre, the phalanx would necessarily move from its original position (as shown in Asclepiodotus' diagrams) and so space would be needed to perform the turn. Also, while Asclepiodotus talks only of a quarter turn (90 degrees), it would be possible to wheel through any lesser angle so as to face in a precise desired direction. Note also that the unit of manoeuvre is specified as the *syntagma*. So for example a larger unit, such as a *chiliarchia* of 1,000 men, would presumably not wheel as a single block; rather, its constituent four *syntagmata* would each wheel and march independently, re-forming the continuous line at the desired new location and angle (fig. 3.10). Necessarily, the line would be broken somewhat during the manoeuvre, since the *syntagmata* would have different distances to travel.

If it was desired to face completely about, turning through 180 degrees, this could be accomplished by performing two quarter turns in succession, but this would require gaps in the line the size of each *syntagma* for them to wheel into. The alternative was to use one of the 'countermarches', which allowed the formation to face about in place. Note again that simply having each individual man face about would not be sufficient, as this would disrupt the file organization, leaving the file closer at the head of the file. Instead, one of three types of countermarch could be used: the Macedonian, where the file leaders remained in place and faced about, and the rest of the file marched past them, facing about themselves as they reached their new position; the Laconian, where it was the file closers who remained in place as the file marched past them; and

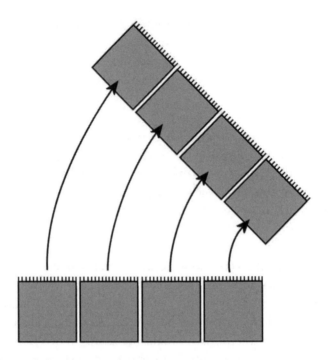

Fig. 3.10. Wheeling a *chiliarchia*.

the Cretan or Persian, which involved both file leader and closer (and those between) marching past each other to swap positions. These countermarches, incidentally, have a remarkably long history, appearing in almost identical form in European tactical manuals of the seventeenth century AD, having been transmitted via the pages of Aelian, and would have been familiar to pikemen fighting in the English Civil War.

Mention of the Laconian countermarch also reminds us that the Spartan army (Laconia being the region where Sparta lies), perhaps alone among the Greek city-state armies, also had a well-developed organization and drill, from which Macedonian drill naturally borrowed heavily (both being concerned with manoeuvres of the infantry phalanx, although the phalanxes were differently armed). In fact, for the next manoeuvre the evidence for the Spartan army is better than that for the Macedonian, since the tactical manuals are strangely silent on the issue. All armies on the march adopt some sort of column, a formation whose depth is greater than its width, as this allows the formation to follow roads and move through constricted and difficult terrain and is a much more efficient marching formation than the line, where width exceeds depth. The tacticians detail a number of marching formations: line and column, and

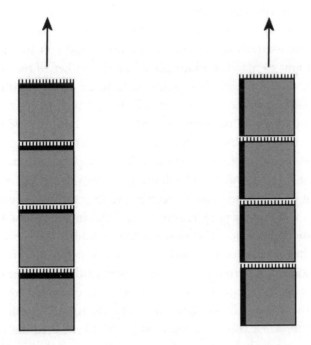

Fig. 3.11. Two types of column of a *chiliarchia* of four *syntagmata* - the dark line indicates the rank of file leaders, and the 'sarissas' show the direction of facing of the *syntagma*.

also crescent, half square, wedge and square formations in various permutations (we may wonder how useful such exotic formations actually were on the march, as the column would surely be the usual choice). Note, incidentally, that as the *syntagma* is the usual manoeuvre formation and is itself a square, a column could be formed by lining up *syntagmata* one behind another so that each individual one was in standard phalanx formation, while the larger unit of which it was a part would be in column (a *chiliarchia* of four *syntagmata*, for example, would be in a column sixteen men wide and sixty-four deep). Alternatively, a *chiliarchia* could form up facing, say, to the north, then have each man turn individually to the right, and march off in column to the east – the difference being that in the first case the file leaders are in their correct position (relative to the *syntagma*) but positioned throughout the column, while in the second they will be on the left flank of the column (see fig. 3.11).

On approaching an enemy, a column would need to deploy into line for combat, a manoeuvre which is not explicitly covered by the tacticians; it does, however, appear in literary battle accounts, and also in the drill 'manual' of the Spartan army (preserved in the *Constitution of the Lacedaemonians* by, probably, Xenophon). The manoeuvre could be carried out in one of two basic ways. Either the unit at the head of the column could halt (or slow down), allowing each unit to march up into place beside it either to the right or the left (fig. 3.12); or else the whole column could wheel to the right or left and march perpendicular to the previous line of advance, then when in the correct position, each unit would perform a quarter turn to face forward again (and if necessary, a countermarch might then be performed to ensure the file leaders were at the front of the formation) (fig. 3.13). It is obvious that which of these might be performed could depend in part on whether the column was formed of lined-up subunits, in which case they can more easily use the first method, or of a phalanx marching to its flank, in which case the second would be more appropriate. The first method is said to have been used by Alexander as he approached the battlefield at Issus, deploying his phalanx as the terrain widened out from the narrow coastal road he had been following into the wider coastal plain. The second method is described by Xenophon (*Lac.Pol.* 11.10, though the circumstances are slightly different, this being a deployment to face a threat on the flank), who likens it to the manoeuvre of a fleet of triremes. It is interesting to note that very similar manoeuvres would indeed be carried out by fleets, since ships too move in column ('line ahead', one ship behind another), but fight in line ('line abreast', ships lined up beside each other). Just as for land armies, it is often difficult to tell from a literary account of a battle whether a fleet is using the first method of deploying (each ship rowing up alongside the ship in front of it in the column) or the second (the whole column rowing parallel to the enemy, then individual ships performing a 90-degree turn together to face the enemy). Mostly we can only guess which manoeuvre was used, and assume that depending on circumstances there may have been benefits to one or the other. We will encounter these manoeuvres again in practice in Chapter 7.[17]

Another manoeuvre of great potential use in battle was that of outflanking the enemy phalanx so as to attack them from the flank. One technique for making this possible has already been considered above, as one of the forms of doubling – doubling of space – involved extending the width of the phalanx while decreasing its depth (in men) or increasing its intervals, by marching some of either files or ranks out to the right or left. Asclepiodotus describes the process:

'Doubling of place occurs by length when we change the above mentioned compact formation by length into a loose formation, or

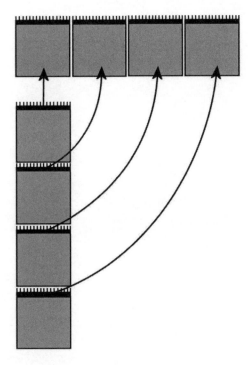

Fig. 3.12. From column to line by deploying to the right.

when the interjected men countermarch by rank, either to prevent being outflanked by the enemy or when we wish to outflank the enemy.' (Asclepiodotus, *Tactics* 10.18)

In other words, the frontage of the phalanx could be increased either by adopting open order (by marching the files out to the left or right) or by marching some ranks (the 'interjected men' Asclepiodotus refers to are those extra files inserted into the original formation as part of a 'doubling by men') to left or right, thus retaining the original intervals but decreasing the depth in men. As usual, this would tend to disrupt the proper structure of the file, unless whole files had already been interjected (in which case they could be countermarched as a whole) and so would probably be unwillingly undertaken, as Asclepiodotus says:

'Some condemn such doublings, especially when the enemy is near, and, by extending the light infantry and cavalry on both wings, give the appearance of the doubling without disturbing the phalanx.' (Asclepiodotus, *Tactics* 10.20)

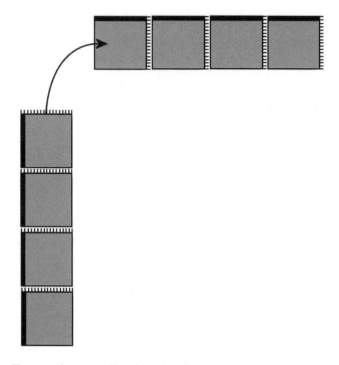

Fig. 3.13. From column to line by wheeling.

We can well imagine that this would be the case, and so while it is often tempting to think of the flanks of the phalanx as being especially vulnerable and outflanking as a correspondingly attractive tactic, the drill involved in outflanking an enemy was not straightforward. It would often be better, having established the depth and frontage of the phalanx, to stick with it and not risk disruption by attempting a flanking move. For comparison, the Spartan army at Mantinea (418) attempted a lateral move of some units, but the manoeuvre was badly executed and nearly resulted in disaster, only the Spartans' fighting ability saving the day as they, 'utterly worsted in respect of skill, showed themselves as superior in point of courage', as Thucydides (5.72.2) wryly observed.

When outflanking was carried out, either as a redeployment or as a result of an existing overlap, it often did not take the simple form that might be imagined. We might suppose that once overlapping an enemy formation, it was simply a matter of wheeling inwards, hinged on the extremity of the enemy line, in order to take the enemy in flank. But apparently this is not how it was done, perhaps because of the difficulty of wheeling a large formation. As discussed above, wheeling individual *syntagmata* may have been easy enough, but in order to re-form a continuous line there would be much marching adjustment, during which time the phalanx would be vulnerable. There are no clear examples in battles involving a Macedonian phalanx of this sort of manoeuvre, though Xenophon gives an account in his historical novel, the *Cyropaedia* ('Education of Cyrus'), of such a manoeuvre at the Battle of Thymbra by the Lydian army (7.1.5), which was probably inspired by his knowledge of Spartan drill. Here, the overlapping flanks of the larger Lydian army did not wheel inwards on the smaller Persian force (in the manner of a door swinging on a hinge), but instead made a 90-degree turn outwards in place, then marched toward the flank in column, wheeling at a given point to then advance and end up on the Persian flanks, forming as Xenophon states the shape of a gamma (Γ) (see fig. 3.14). A Roman army at the Battle of Ilipa performed a similar manoeuvre, as described by Polybius (11.23).

One final consideration is whether the Macedonian phalanx practised cadenced marching, or marching in step. There is no direct evidence that it did, although if it did it would certainly make the complex drill manoeuvres described easier and more precise. Earlier Greek armies had often marched to the sound of flutes, and the charge was accompanied by the *paean*, a battle hymn or battle cry. In the Macedonian army, the tradition was to shout the *alala* (or *alale*) upon attacking. These cries, however, were more about frightening the enemy while bolstering one's own morale rather than step marching. According to Polybius (4.20), the Arcadian young men 'practise military parades to the music of the flute and perfect themselves in dances and give annual performances in

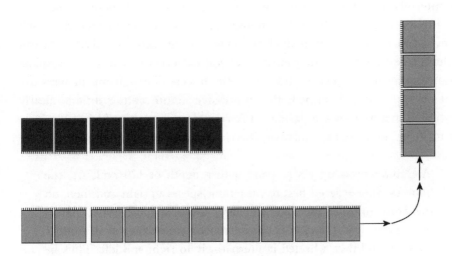

Fig. 3.14. Outflanking: the attacking phalanx would turn 90 degrees right, march in column to the right, wheel left and turn 90 degrees left.

the theatres, all under state supervision and at the public expense'. This might have been the case for Macedonian armies also, though even so we cannot be sure that marching to the flute meant marching in step.[18]

Conclusions

This has been a necessarily brief overview of the organization and drill of a phalanx armed in the Macedonian fashion. More detail – excruciatingly more detail – is available in the pages of the tacticians. But I hope that the overall picture is clear enough. A Macedonian phalanx, like the earlier Spartan phalanx and perhaps unlike most classical Greek armies, was divided into ever smaller subunits which could be marched and manoeuvred independently and which, by combining and moving in different ways, provided a high degree of flexibility to the phalanx. The normal unit of manoeuvre was the *syntagma* (or whatever name, such as *speira*, may have been applied to it at any given time), a square formation, sixteen men wide and sixteen deep (or earlier, eight by eight), with its own signallers and officers outside the ranks. This was the basic building block of the phalanx, and the unit by which all the larger-scale manoeuvres would have been carried out. Literary accounts of battles are necessarily high-level and broad brush in their descriptions, but when we hear of a given phalanx moving or manoeuvring in a certain way, we must picture the individual *syntagmata* carrying out manoeuvres of the sort discussed above: turns, wheels, countermarches, opening and closing of intervals. In Chapter 7 I will attempt to apply some of these manoeuvres to attested large-scale battlefield moves. For now we should note that such movements do not appear at all clearly in the literary accounts, though we can infer their existence, and they must have required a very high level of discipline and training of the phalangites and their officers. Though manoeuvres are not always clearly described, the impressive nature of the drill is clearly indicated in a well-known passage of Arrian, describing how Alexander, early in his reign, overawed a Taulantian (Illyrian) enemy by a display of drill:

> 'Alexander drew up his phalanx with a depth of 120 ranks ... the hoplites were ordered first to raise their spears upright and then, on the word, to lower them for a charge, swinging their serried points first to the right, then to the left; he moved the phalanx itself smartly forward, and then wheeled it alternatively to right and left. Thus he deployed and manoeuvred it in many difficult formations in a brief time, and then making a kind of wedge from his phalanx on the

left, he led it to the attack. The enemy, long bewildered both at the smartness and the discipline of the drill, did not await the approach of Alexander's troops, but abandoned the first hills.' (Arrian, *Anabasis of Alexander* 1.6.1–4)

A depth of 120 ranks is unusual, but may represent a column of fifteen units, each eight men deep – perhaps an eight by eight *taxis* as described by Asclepiodotus 2.9.

This high level of drill was retained by all the Hellenistic armies armed in the Macedonian fashion; to a greater or lesser extent, we must suppose, but it was a defining characteristic of a Macedonian phalanx. Philip II's invention of the phalanx is generally taken to be chiefly a matter of introducing new equipment, and it is in those terms that I have discussed the question in the preceding chapters. But just as important, more so perhaps, was the increase in discipline and professionalism required of the soldiers, and the constant training and practice that must have been required to maintain it. This would have been near impossible to achieve with a citizen militia such as most Greek city-states maintained, and was difficult even for the full-time but sometimes tactically conservative Spartans. Philip, as monarch and with a professional army at his disposal, at least as Macedonian wealth and power expanded in the course of his reign, was able to impose and make time for the high level of training required, and this, at least as much as the new equipment introduced, lay behind his army's remarkable success.

One other point is worth repeating. The Macedonian phalanx is often viewed as a highly inflexible, monolithic body, incapable of doing more than marching stolidly straight ahead. But I think that this view is wrong, as shown by the complex movements and high level of organization discussed above. The Macedonian phalanx was in fact considerably more flexible than the hoplite phalanx it replaced. Although the sarissa was more unwieldy and the equipment heavier from that point of view, the most important factor in determining the manoeuvrability of a formation is not the equipment carried but the drill available for carrying out manoeuvres. By this measure, the Macedonian phalanx far exceeded its predecessors and was capable of manoeuvres that would have been impossible for most hoplite phalanxes. As such we should not think of the Macedonian phalanx as being especially inflexible, even though the weapons carried were unwieldy on an individual level; it is part of the point of the phalanx that the weapons did not need to be handy in use since their effect derived from being a part of a larger formation, as Polybius recognized. Similarly, the phalanx is often imagined and depicted as a single mass, a great block stretching across the battlefield (as so often depicted in battle diagrams), but it was in fact made up of a number of smaller units, the *syntagmata*, which were individually quite manoeuvrable and capable of operating independently – at least to a certain extent. The degree to which this is true should not be overstated, especially in comparison with the Roman Army, as we will see in Chapter 9, but the phalanx at any rate was capable of more varied and subtle deployments and manoeuvres, as a result of its high level of discipline and drill. Conversely, the broad brush description of literary battle accounts can disguise the very high complexity involved in moving and manoeuvring any large body of men, not just a phalanx. Apparently simple matters such as marching in various directions, or changing formations, were underpinned by a complex series of small unit manoeuvres (mostly, presumably, at the level of the *syntagma*), and even an apparently simple movement such as outflanking a numerically inferior enemy would have required a complex series of drills, and could have gone badly wrong and resulted in hopeless disorder if not carried out effectively.

The requirements of such drills and manoeuvres therefore placed high demands on the individual soldiers, the phalangites, who made up the phalanx, and it is to them that we shall be turning next.

Chapter 4

The men in the phalanx

So far I have been looking at the phalanx as a strictly military institution, in terms of its equipment, organization and drill. But it was more than that. In the Classical period, the hoplite phalanxes of the Greek city-states represented the armed citizenry of each state, the politically entitled male (always male) inhabitants of a certain economic standing. The political organization of the Greek cities is a complex subject: each had its own constitution which determined the system of government of that city, and the involvement and degree of power available to full citizens (those who, by meeting the property or wealth requirements set by each city, were entitled to a say in the running of the government) and to non-citizen inhabitants (which included both those of a lower social and economic standing than the citizens, and 'foreigners', those originating from other city-states). These systems of government varied from democratic (where the citizen body was relatively large, and all had the right to vote on laws and policy in the assembly), through oligarchic (where the actual work of government was carried out by a smaller body usually of the wealthy, and citizens had no direct say) to monarchic (where all power lay in the hands of one or sometimes two usually hereditary rulers). Macedon itself was of course a monarchy, with a single hereditary king, and this is the type of government that was also established in all the Hellenistic kingdoms founded by Alexander's Successors. But there was still a concept of citizenship – of inhabitants of the kingdom who, by meeting certain wealth and property requirements, had a higher political standing. Just as the hoplites, the close-order heavy infantry of the Greek city-states, had been formed from the armed citizenry of those states, so in Macedon and the Hellenistic kingdoms the phalanx was drawn from its citizen body, even though they probably had no formal political role as they did in democratic or oligarchic states (although this point is disputed, as we will see below). The purpose of this chapter is to look at the role of these citizen soldiers of the phalanx in the context of the kingdoms in which they lived, at their social and economic status and their political role, but also at their lifestyle, training and motivation.

Soldiers and settlers

The hoplite armies of the Greek cities were made up of the citizens of each city, and their duty to provide military service was based on the understanding that, as citizens, they were required to serve and protect the city in which they had a personal financial stake. Inhabitants who did not meet the requirements of citizenship might still serve in the army, but would do so in a lesser role, often as light infantry fighting with bow, sling or javelin (and conversely, those with greater wealth than the average could be required to serve in the cavalry). There is both a practical and a political basis for this arrangement. The hoplite was expected to provide his own equipment, and a hoplite panoply could be expensive, so in practical terms a certain level of wealth was needed to meet the requirement of bronze armour, shield and spear. Because of the nature of the phalanx, where every man was dependent on his neighbours to maintain the formation, there could be no question of anyone in the phalanx being inadequately equipped, which could put everyone at risk. But this was also how the citizens justified their political dominance: because they were citizens, they were required to stand in the line of battle and fight to defend their home state, but also because they were heavy infantry, the battle-winning dominant arm on the Classical Greek battlefield, their dominant political position in the state was reinforced. There is some dispute about the degree to which Classical Greek battles were formalized and followed strict rules, but whether through rule or custom it is clear that Classical warfare was arranged in such a way as to make the clash of the heavy infantry the decisive factor, and to downplay the role both of light infantry and cavalry. This arrangement had a strong political dimension in maintaining the political dominance of the hoplite class. The exceptions to this prove the rule. Especially as we head into the fourth century it became increasingly common for hoplites to offer their services to foreign states as mercenaries, but the hiring of mercenaries broke the compact between the state and its citizens. A ruler who hired mercenaries was thought to be doing so to get around the need for the loyalty and support of the citizen body, and it became a definition of the tyrant that he relied on mercenary forces, while the legitimate ruler or king relied on the service of the citizens. (The word 'tyrant', incidentally, did not have quite the same negative connotations in Greek as it does in English. To the Greeks, a tyrant was simply an authoritarian ruler, often relying on the support of the mass of inhabitants to impose his will on the wealthy oligarchic or aristocratic faction. Here I am using the word more in its English sense of a despotic ruler.)

In the kingdom of Macedon, there was probably no tradition of a large, politically active citizen body. The system of government was monarchy, with a hereditary king exercising more or less total control over the state so far as he was able in the circumstances pertaining, supported (or otherwise) by a relatively small landed, and independently powerful, aristocracy. Below the aristocracy was the mass of the Macedonian population, who as we have seen had traditionally made up a militarily rather inadequate infantry. Yet even in Macedon there was a distinction between Macedonians proper and those of lower standing, which included, aside from the ubiquitous slaves (all of ancient Greece being a society entirely built on and dependent on institutionalized slavery, usually though not always of 'others' – non-Greeks or at least non-natives of each state), foreign inhabitants and those of the lowest social class, such as labourers and unskilled workmen. These Macedonian citizens, the *Makedones*, were the raw material from which Philip formed his first phalanx. For while it is often said (with some justice) that the phalanx was formed from the mass of the Macedonian peasantry, we should not imagine that this means it was created from the entire population down to the lowest social level (above slaves). Rather, those who formed the *Makedones* seem to have been peasants in the strict sense, for it appears that some ownership of land, or at least some minimum level of wealth, was required to be a *Makedon*, a full Macedonian. The evidence for this is largely from the later Antigonid kingdom, and it is not certain that the situation was the same under Philip II. As we have seen, part of Philip's reforms were to change the social and economic structure of the kingdom by promoting economic activity and, particularly, increasing urbanization, founding cities and settling inhabitants who presumably had previously been small-scale farmers in scattered rural settlements, but who in the new cities must have retained some land holdings (perhaps at the pleasure of the local aristocrats or the king, who would ultimately have been the true landowner) in order to support themselves and their families.[1]

So the Macedonians of the first Macedonian phalanx were not just the mass of the inhabitants of the kingdom. Still less were they mercenaries serving only for pay; they were also those of some minimum standing in the kingdom, with land to support them and to give them a stake in the success of the state. The Successors adrift in Asia with large armies of Macedonians at their command needed to set up some sort of similar system in their kingdoms, to create a class of 'citizen' soldiers (such men did not necessarily have the formal legal status and certainly not the same level of political power as true citizens of a city-state would have) who could then be drawn on to form the heavy infantry – the phalanx – that continued to form the core of the army. The way this was done varied according to local circumstances, particular to each kingdom, and probably varying also according to local arrangements in different regions within the kingdom.

In Ptolemaic Egypt, the Ptolemies established a system based on the traditional means by which Greek cities had planted overseas colonies on conquered or requisitioned land, and which also made use of long-standing Egyptian practice. Each soldier was granted a plot of land, a *kleros*, which he would either farm himself or let out to subtenants so that he could live on the proceeds – such settlers are usually referred to as cleruchs, using the Anglicized word (Greek *klerouchoi*), and the land plots as cleruchies. In Egypt, the amount of decent agricultural land was fairly limited (only land close to the Nile made viable farmland), and there was already a thriving and densely settled population of native Egyptians. We should not therefore see cleruchies as plots of virgin land granted to soldiers to expand agricultural use, though this might have been the case in some marginal areas, but as the change of ownership of already productive land from its previous owner to the soldier-settler, made possible by the king's position as ultimate owner of such land in the kingdom.[2]

One effect of this granting of land was to tie the soldier to the country, and in addition the possession of land itself was something that would be very much hoped for by soldiers at the end of the fourth century. Once established in the kingdom, there was a range of legal and economic privileges available to improve the standing of the soldiers. The land granted to the cleruchs in Egypt was originally reclaimed by the kings upon the death of the holder, and had been liable to confiscation on a number of other pretexts, and was apparently turned over to royal labourers while the soldier was on active service. In the course of the third century it became possible for the cleruch to rent out his land, although the king still monitored the arrangements. But by the late third century, the *kleros* was being handed on as a matter of course to the heir of the cleruch, and while the king still approved the hand-over the land is described as belonging to the cleruch. In the second century, the *kleros* seems to have become the private property of the holder, free from any royal control and able to be left to any heir, including women. It is not clear whether this slide into private ownership was policy on the part of the kings, allowing the cleruchs greater privileges as an attempt to win their favour, or was more an involuntary response to events. Nor is it known how this alteration in land holding procedures may relate to the decline of the Ptolemaic army before the Battle of Raphia (in 217, when there was a crisis of manpower which I will consider further below). Possibly the granting of greater land privileges was to compensate the cleruch for receiving poorer-quality lands, since by the second century lands granted are no longer first cultivated by royal labourers; the changing agricultural role of the cleruchs may therefore be behind these changes in land holding. In a perhaps similar arrangement, Eumenes II of Pergamon granted reductions of taxation and exemptions of payment to a settlement of Cardaces who were having difficulty making a living from their poor soil.[3]

In addition, in Egypt we see the frequent granting of financial privileges and amnesties, which may be equivalent in function to advances of pay and special gifts, intended to buy the affections of the soldiers in times of difficulty, although it also seems that cleruchs were as a matter of right granted a number of privileges. Under Ptolemy II (early third century), for example, the cleruchs, along with the land which required special irrigation, were to pay only one-tenth instead of one-sixth of their produce to the cult of Arsinoe. The second and first centuries, with their dynastic upheavals, saw many such privileges granted. Ptolemy VIII granted various privileges to the soldiers on Cyprus, and with Cleopatra released cleruchs from arrears of rent and rendered the *machimoi* (native Egyptian soldiers) exempt from confiscation, along with a long list of other benefactions. Soldiers were also granted billets in which to live, often the source of friction between them and the original inhabitants forced to share their homes. These billets could be made over by will from as early as the third century, and a soldier can be seen making over his horse and armour to his son, and his billet to his wife.[4]

In the Seleucid kingdom, arrangements were similar in some ways, but with some major differences. The Seleucid kingdom, though its land area rose and fell according to the success of the king in defeating usurpers, rebels, foreign invaders and native uprisings, was vastly larger than Egypt, and while most productive land was already inhabited, there would have been greater scope to make land available to soldier-settlers. There seem to have been two main forms of settlement. Soldiers could be settled into distinct settlements usually attached to an existing city, and granted plots of land to maintain them from that settlement's lands – these settlements were called *katoikiai* (I will have more to say about these in the following chapter). But most Seleucid settlers must have settled into the major new cities that were founded in the kingdom's Syrian heartland. Major city foundations, named after the kings or queens (Antiocheia, Seleucia, Apamea) or with traditional Macedonian names (Pella, Beroea), were established particularly around the Orontes River in northern Syria, and Macedonians originally from the army of Seleucus must have formed the bulk of their population. These men presumably also needed land to farm (or to be paid by others to farm, although the arrangements here are less clear than in Egypt). This would have allowed for the establishment of a large urban population that was available for service in the phalanx (or cavalry, as required), and who were able to maintain the standard of living required for soldier-citizens, as well as a land stake in the kingdom. As in Egypt, Seleucid settlers seem also to have been granted various financial privileges. An agreement between the cities of Smyrna and Magnesia in Asia Minor refers to the possession of land plots by the settlers in the fort of Old Magnesia which are to be free from the tithe, and the soldiers are to continue to enjoy their present exemption from taxation; in addition, the 'soldiers present in the fort, the phalanx men, the "Persians under Omanes" and the detachment from Smyrna' are all to be exempted from taxation. The nature of land holding in the Seleucid kingdom is more obscure than in Egypt, although it is possible that a gradual move towards greater control over the land by the holder gradually occurred as in Egypt.[5]

The establishment of these sorts of settlements at the end of the fourth and beginning of the third century had been intended to provide a population of Macedonians (which in practice would increasingly have included other Greeks) for service in the phalanx, though this was not the purpose of all military settlers. Later on, settlements could be established for the purposes of internal security, creating a pool of loyal settlers in the midst of, and to keep an eye on, a potentially restive native population. This was the purpose of the placement of Jewish settlers by Antiochus III recorded by the Jewish historian Josephus. These settlers were also granted various exemptions: exemption from taxation for the first ten years and the granting of corn until they produce their own food (Jos. *Ant*. xii. 151–2). It is likely that exemptions of this sort were a normal part of the procedure of settlement irrespective of the military status of those involved, so cannot necessarily be seen as attempts to win army loyalty as such. For example, after the destruction of Sardis by Antiochus III (Pol. 7.18.9), Antiochus refounded the city, granting seven years' exemption from taxation for those settling there.[6]

So the new kingdoms in Asia, lacking a native population of Macedonians from which they could draw their armies, used grants of land to create a class of soldier-settlers at first, who became soldier-citizens as their possession of the land became established by precedent and law, who would then form the core of the kingdom's armies, and in particular the phalanx. In this way the Asian kingdoms were able to reproduce, in a slightly different form, the arrangements available to Macedon with its native Macedonian population. In the next chapter I will look at the sources of these military settlers, and their numbers, and go into greater detail as to how the distribution of settlers and land was organized.

Citizen soldiers

We have seen that the phalanx of each kingdom, the heavy infantry of Greeks and Macedonians, was formed from a citizen class, whether native (in Macedon) or settled. It is this body of men – those who fought in the phalanx – who are generally referred to as 'the army' in the Hellenistic kingdoms, even though the full army in any given campaign would also contain other forces, native subject peoples, mercenaries and cavalry, who were separate from the phalanx, as we will see in the following chapter. A decree of Ilium giving the city's thanks to Antiochus I notes that he had 'advanced his interests and the kingdom to a more powerful and brilliant position, most of all through his own excellence, but also through the good will of Friends and military forces'. This formula – 'the king, his Friends and his military forces' – occurs frequently in Hellenistic texts and inscriptions. These three components are the three pillars of what we might call the Hellenistic state. The king's Friends (note that while the title is honorific and signifies all those who formed the court, officers and governors, hence the capital 'F' in English, the personal nature of Hellenistic kingship meant that often they would literally be the king's friends, as their predecessors in the Macedonian homeland, the Companions, had genuinely been the companions of the king) will be the subject of Chapter 6. Here we are concerned with the army and its role within the Hellenistic kingdoms.[7]

There has been a long debate among scholars as to whether the Macedonian army, in Macedon at least, formed a formal element of state, either in its own right or as a representative of the Macedonian people. The question can be broken down into several elements. Some maintain that there was an assembly of the Macedonian people which could make formal decisions. The king may also have been restricted by certain constitutional checks on his power; the Macedonians are said to have had a right of free speech before the king and the right of petition, and the assembly had the right to act as judge and jury in trials of capital offences, and the right of election or acclamation of a new king, amongst other more minor powers.[8]

It is clear that there was for at least part of this period a formal *koinon* of Macedonians (that is, a political union), at least from the time of Antigonus Doson and probably earlier in the third century and possibly to the time of Philip and Alexander, but it is unknown what formal powers, if any, the *koinon* possessed. During the period of the Successors in particular there are frequent references in the sources to meetings of an assembly (*ekklesia*), usually specifically of soldiers. Some scholars would see these assemblies as a formal institution with established powers, and as being representative of the *koinon* of Macedonians. But this seems to go beyond the evidence.

Whatever the position and powers of a national assembly of this sort might have been, it is at least clear that it cannot be assumed that the many assemblies of the army described in the sources can really represent the meetings of any such formal body. It is apparent, for example, that 'the Macedonians' referred to as taking decisions in trials and in other affairs of the Successors does not mean a formally constituted representative of the Macedonian people. In general the term rather means 'the Macedonian element in the army', and in particular 'those present on a particular occasion'. For example, at the trial of Philotas by Alexander, the 'Macedonians' who formed the jury are the 6,000 who were present at the time (Q.C. 6.8.23). It is impossible to identify such groups as a formal body unless it is assumed that the law allowed any one group of Macedonians to represent the whole. Rather, it is plain that when, for example, the Alexander historian Quintus Curtius states that it was the Macedonian custom to bring capital cases before 'the Macedonians', he does not mean before a regular legal body; he means 'in public', rather than conducting trials behind closed palace doors. The group of Macedonians involved could thus comprise whoever was present, or indeed whoever the organizer of the trial or meeting wished to be present. For example, Olympias (mother of Alexander) was initially tried in her absence by 'the general assembly of the Macedonians' (Diod. 19.51.1), yet she then declared her willingness to be tried before 'all the Macedonians' (19.51.4); presumably her intention was that a wider audience be present at her second trial. Similarly, the Peltasts requested Philip V 'not to try Leontius in their absence' (Pol. 5.27.5), wishing to be among those present at the trial; but Philip had Leontius condemned and executed immediately – presumably without a public trial at all. The term *ekklesia* was in normal use for such army meetings, without implying that a formal assembly is meant. The assemblies are therefore to be seen simply as mass meetings, although they may well still have exercised certain informal powers in practice. This is clearly the nature, for example, of Eumenes' thwarting of Antigonus' attempt to win over his Macedonians. Calling a meeting, he urged rejection of the overtures by telling the men the fable of the lion; 'while the crowd [*plēthos*] was shouting approval and saying "right" he dismissed the assembly [*ekklesia*]' (19.25.7). Similarly, Philip V, faced with the disaffection of his Peltasts, 'called a meeting of the Macedonians in the theatre and addressed them there, exhorting them all to resume discipline' (Pol. 5.25.5).[9]

The 'assembly' is therefore any mass meeting of those with a political role – referred to as often as *plēthos*, mass or crowd, as *ekklesia*, assembly – in which decisions can be taken, but which is also a forum for the king, or whoever is in control, to assert his authority in public. Assemblies of this kind are familiar from the passage of Diodorus quoted in the first chapter concerning the first creation of the phalanx by Philip II ('bringing together the Macedonians in a series of assemblies and exhorting them with eloquent speeches', Diod. 16.3.1–2).

Similarly, the freedom of speech exercised by the Macedonians need not be seen as a formal right of free speech, so much as an informal custom which defined what was expected of king and army, leader and led. A good example is the letter of the Peltasts to Philip V, threatening him with their displeasure over the arrest of their commander, Leontius:

> 'When the Peltasts heard what had happened from a messenger sent to them by Leontius, they despatched ambassadors to the king, begging him that, "if he had arrested Leontius on any other score, not to have him tried on the charges alleged against him without their presence: for otherwise they should consider themselves treated with signal contempt, and to be one and all involved in the condemnation." Such was the freedom of speech towards their king which the Macedonians always enjoyed. They added, that "if the arrest was on account of his bail for Megaleas, they would themselves pay the money by a common subscription." The king however was so enraged, that he put Leontius to death sooner than he had intended, owing to the zeal displayed by the Peltasts.' (Polybius 5.27.5)

This is an example of typically Macedonian blunt and forthright behaviour on the part of the Peltasts, in accordance with a Macedonian tradition of such conduct (as Polybius observes), rather than the exercise of a formal right of free expression. This tradition of forthright language, as well as possible royal responses to it, can also be seen when Demetrius Poliorcetes was king of Macedon:

> 'King Demetrius, after arresting all who habitually defamed him in the public assemblies and contentiously opposed him in all things, let them go unharmed, remarking that pardon is better than punishment.' (Diodorus 21.9)

There is no constitutional impediment to Demetrius arresting those who speak their minds, but because the Macedonians would sympathize with those who did so, he declines to punish them.

On the right of the assembly, or the army, specifically to try capital cases, there is conflicting evidence. On the one hand, Alexander, for example, holds trials at which the army clearly is acting as judge. On the other, Philip V disregarded any legal niceties, and the objections of part of his army, in his execution of Leontius, or of Apelles and his co-conspirators. Quintus Curtius comments on Alexander's trial of Philotas that:[10]

> 'in capital cases it was the Macedonian custom for the army – in peacetime it was the people – to judge and the king to examine, and the power of the king availed nothing unless his authority had previously been made efficacious.' (Quintus Curtius, 6.8.25)

There are numerous examples of trials from the period of the Successors where it is quite clear that the Macedonians in the army are acting as judge. For example, Cassander had the relatives of Olympias' victims 'accuse the aforesaid woman in the general assembly of the Macedonians [*koine ton Makedonon ekklesia*]' and 'the Macedonians condemned her to death' (Diod. 19.51.1–2). The followers of Perdiccas similarly had sentence of death passed upon them by the Macedonians (Diod. 18.37.2), meeting in assembly (*ekklesia*, 18.36.6). Seleucus stated that 'he would never consent to carrying out the orders of Eumenes, whom the Macedonians in assembly had condemned to death' (19.12.2; the condemnation is at 18.39.6), while Eumenes himself brought Sibyrtius to trial, who 'would have been condemned to death by the assembly [*plēthos*]' had he not escaped (19.23.4; clearly a different group of Macedonians are involved in this assembly). Philip V executed Leontius without trial, but his accomplice Ptolemaios he 'put on trial before a Macedonian court and executed' (5.29.6). Yet Curtius also relates (6.9.9.f.) a private meeting of Alexander and his closest friends in which they debate whether to torture Philotas or execute him immediately, and the decision is taken to torture him to obtain a confession to present to the next day's meeting. Clearly this is an arrangement which defies precise legal definition. Curtius is obviously correct to call the trial by the army a Macedonian custom, not a law, and indeed the whole account of the trial of Philotas in Curtius abounds with references to Macedonian custom: the question of the language in which Philotas is to address the meeting, for example, and of the execution of the relatives of the accused. As a matter purely of legality, the decision to execute or acquit the accused could evidently be taken by whoever had the greatest power and influence at the time, whether king, nobles or army – so there were trials also before the king's Friends, as of Megaleas and Crinon (Pol. 5.16.5). If the king was to behave in a way that was, in the terms of Macedonian tradition, 'illegal', no sanctions could be applied against him. However, if a king did for example pass judgement without recourse

to the customary procedures he was in danger of arousing the anger, and so
undermining the loyalty, of his subjects by ruling, in Arrian's formulation,
'by force and not in accordance with custom', or as Aristotle defined it, in the
manner of a tyrant rather than a true king (*Politics* 3.9.3). Curtius seems to
accurately express the nature of the situation after Philotas' confession under
torture and condemnation:

> 'Alexander had been freed from great danger, not indeed of death,
> but of hatred; for Parmenion and Philotas, the chief men among
> his friends, unless clearly shown to be guilty, could not have been
> condemned without exciting the indignation of the whole army. Thus
> the issue of the case was doubtful as long as he denied the crime.'
> (Quintus Curtius, 6.9.39–40)

Thus the army did not have a formal legal right to try cases, but it did need to
be convinced that the conviction was sound.

On the right of acclamation of a new king, there are many examples of kings
raised to the throne by Macedonians, and also cases where acceptance by the
army is important, but it is again impossible to identify any of these armies as
formal bodies. For example, the army of Alexander V 'proclaimed Demetrius
king of the Macedonians' (Plut. *Dem.* 37.2), but this army can only have been
a small proportion of the Macedonians, and indeed Plutarch goes on to say
that 'to the Macedonians at home the change [in kings] was not unwelcome'.
It is not necessary to imagine that acclamation by the Macedonians, meaning
by some body of Macedonians who are present at the time, represents a formal
procedure. Demetrius' mercenaries deserted him in Cyrrhestica and turned
to Seleucus I, and 'they all welcomed him, hailed him as king, and went over
to him' (Plut. *Dem.* 49.3), but this could not be taken as evidence that the
mercenaries had a right of acclamation of the king. The acclamation rather
represents a statement of present and future loyalty; no doubt it would be
possible for a pretender to declare himself king, but if there was no one willing
to support or accept him in his position his reign would be a short one. Pyrrhus
was made king of Macedon, but when Lysimachus demanded a share in the
kingdom he acquiesced, being unsure of the Macedonians' support (Plut.
Pyrr. 12). On the other hand, it is not necessary to postulate that the army
had no role and that only the support of the nobles was important; there are
occasions where kings, or prospective kings, seek the support of 'the first of
the Macedonians', and no doubt the opinion of the most powerful men could
be significant and, depending on circumstances, might be crucial. But whether

on the part of the army, the people or the nobles, what occurs is a statement of intent to support the candidate, by force if necessary, not a true election or acclamation.[11]

It is in fact clear throughout the period that the Macedonians retained tremendous loyalty to the hereditary principle, which is surprising perhaps when the power of the king was otherwise so personal. It took more than twenty years and the death of Alexander IV (Alexander the Great's posthumous son) before any of Alexander's Successors declared in public what had long been true in practice by becoming kings. Throughout the confusion of the early third century, a succession of weak hereditary rulers were able to take power in Macedon. The Successors could not count on being 'elected' king unless they first established a legitimate claim to win the approval of the Macedonians. So, for example, Perdiccas decided to marry Cleopatra, sister of Alexander, 'believing that he could use her to persuade the Macedonians to help him gain the supreme power' (Diod. 18.23.3), and in turn Cassander, Lysimachus, Antigonus and Ptolemy sought her hand, 'for each of them, hoping that the Macedonians would follow the lead of this marriage, was seeking alliance with the royal house in order to gain supreme power for himself' (20.37.4). Demetrius, with no real claim, was chosen king by the Macedonians 'owing to their hatred of Alexander [V], who was a matricide, and to their lack of a better man' (Plut. *Dem.* 37). It is apparent that when a hereditary heir was available he would ascend the throne without the need for army election, although a display of loyalty and support from the army might still be desirable. Only when the succession was for some reason in dispute, as when there was more than one candidate or no legitimate heir, is there any evidence for the direct role of the army or the nobles in supporting their chosen candidate. In the case of the assumption of the kingship by the Successors, it is not clear whether the army played an important role. According to Diodorus, Antigonus and Demetrius first declared themselves king, 'and in a similar fashion in rivalry with them the rest of the princes also called themselves kings' (20.53.2), although in Plutarch's version (*Dem.* 17) upon the news of the victory at Miletus reaching Antigonus, 'the multitude [*plēthos*] for the first time saluted Antigonus and Demetrius as kings', Antigonus was crowned by his Friends and the followers of Ptolemy made him king also; evidently what is important is not so much the political rights of the mass or assembly, as the desire of the kings to seem to be offered royal status and not just to be usurping it for themselves. But the army is still involved, if not in choosing then in approving a king. Before the Battle of Ipsus (301), Antigonus 'presented his son to the army [*plēthos*] and pronounced him his successor'

(Plut. *Dem*. 28.4), and later Seleucus I 'called an assembly of the entire people' and announced his intention to make Antiochus joint king (38.8).[12]

A strong king could do without the support of a decision of an assembly of the army, but traditionally the masses were consulted when it was expedient to do so, and it is easy to see why such consultations might have been more common for the Successors than for later members of the dynasty, or indeed for the earlier kings, supported as they were by a line of hereditary succession, a history of royal authority and the reflected glory of famous ancestors. As the importance of public acceptance by the people or by the army was more important for a king with no legitimate claim to the throne, or a claim that was disputed, so a head of the army who did not have the authority of king might have to ensure that he did not seem to be acting in a manner that exceeded his authority. Thus when Perdiccas decided to reject the 'last plans' of Alexander (whatever they might have been), 'that he might not appear to be arbitrarily detracting anything from the glory of Alexander, he laid these matters before the common assembly of the Macedonians for consideration' (Diod. 18.4.3). The difference in levels of authority of Eumenes and Antigonus is also clear: Eumenes wanted to hold the field of Battle of Paraitacene, but when his soldiers wanted to return to camp, he 'was forced to yield to the majority; for he was not able to punish the soldiers severely when there were many who disputed his right to command' (Diod. 19.31.3), while Antigonus, 'who firmly held the command without need of courting the popular [*plēthos*] favour, forced his army to make camp by the bodies' (31.4). Plutarch describes the result of the change in authority that occurred when the Successors did acquire royal status – 'they became harsher in their judicial verdicts and no longer concealed their power, which had often in the past made them more lenient and gentle with their subjects' (Plut. *Dem*. 18). In other words, their new royal authority freed them to some extent from dependence on the willing support of their army.

Equally, the general opinion of the army was expressed through these meetings, and any leader had to respect the power of public opinion, particularly again if he did not have strong royal authority. Cassander, for example, plotted against Polyperchon, but his actions were restricted because 'he perceived that the favour of the Macedonians inclined to Polyperchon' (Diod. 18.54.2). Antigonus, after his failed attempt on Egypt in 306, 'called together the army and its leaders and laid before them the question whether it was better to remain and continue the war or return for the present to Syria ... when all inclined towards the quickest possible withdrawal he commanded the soldiers to break camp' and retreated (Diod. 20.76.5). As Diodorus remarks, 'most leaders of armies, when confronted with serious reverses, follow the urgings of the mob rather than risk its opposition' (21.10). This favour could turn against a member of the royal family also, if they seemed not to be ruling according to the customary conventions; Olympias, mother of Alexander, was supported at first by the Macedonians who had previously supported Eurydice, but later behaved cruelly and 'was thereby losing favour with the Macedonians' (Diod. 19.11.5). In Epirus at the same time, Aiacides the king marched against Cassander but 'most of the Epirotes set out for Macedonia against their will and were mutinying in the camp'; when he sent the disaffected home, they 'rebelled against their absent king, condemned him to exile by a public decree, and made an alliance with Cassander' (Diod. 19.36.3–4). Meetings would then be a way to arouse and confirm popular support for a chosen course of action. It is this sort of meeting that Perseus held at Citium before the war with Rome; having determined on war in consultation with his Friends, he paraded the army and addressed them. Their shouts of approval led to a general outburst of enthusiasm for the war and support for Perseus, so he dismissed the assembly and gave orders to march (Liv. 42.50–53).[13]

This then seems to have been the political function of the Macedonian army, and those fragments of the Macedonian army which found themselves in Asia under the Successors, and these functions can be seen to have continued to some extent at least under the Antigonids. It is worth noting that it is quite specifically the Macedonians (the men of the phalanx, plus the Macedonian cavalry) who hold these powers, and there is no suggestion that any other element of the various armies expected to exercise equivalent political power. Throughout the examples given above it is frequently clearly stated that 'the Macedonians' alone are meant; thus Eumenes of Cardia 'was an alien [he was Greek], and hence was excluded from the power that belonged of right to the Macedonians' (Diod. 18.60.4). When there was dispute over who was to command Eumenes' army, Antigenes, commander of the *Argyraspides*, 'said that the right to make the selection ought to be granted to his Macedonians' (Diod. 19.15.1). On occasion other groups were involved, however. The army and 'the people' could both exercise the same influence in a mass meeting; thus Antigonus, in camp at Tyre, 'calling a general assembly of the soldiers and of the foreigners who were dwelling there laid charges against Cassander' (Diod. 19.61.1), and the decree passed by this assembly was termed 'what had been decreed by the Macedonians with Antigonus' (19.62.1).

But what we usually see is that under the Successors such political powers as the army (or civilians) possessed were restricted to the Macedonian citizens themselves; other elements of the army did not share in any of the decision making processes. If such powers were restricted to the Macedonians, it is unclear exactly which of these powers were inherited by what part of the armies that settled in Asia, which were made up only in part of Macedonians. Political rights in Greece traditionally had belonged to those bearing arms, and it might be expected that the political role played by the Macedonian citizens in the armies of the Successors would in time be adopted by all the soldier citizens of the new kingdoms. The citizen component of the army would then be politically aware and directly involved in the political life of the kingdom. Mercenary soldiers, on the other hand, would not normally be concerned with the kingdom's politics, having in most cases loyalties to their own home states and their fellow citizens, or being more prepared to offer loyalty to their paymaster. When the Ptolemaic minister Agathocles attempted to usurp power in Egypt, the steps he took are highly informative:

'He also sent Scopas, the Aetolian, to Greece to hire mercenaries, providing him with a large sum of money to advance to them. Two reasons underlay this plan; for in the first place, he wished to use the troops he hired for the war against Antiochus, and next to send away the existing force of mercenaries to the country forts in Egypt and to the foreign settlements, and then with these new arrivals to fill up and remodel the household troops and the guards of the court, and of the rest of the city, thinking that the men he himself had enlisted and whom he paid, as they had no political sympathies regarding past events of which they were ignorant, as they reposed their hopes of preservation and advancement on himself, would readily support him and join heartily in executing all his behests.' (Polybius, 15.25.16–18)

In general, it seems that the role of the army in Macedon endured throughout the Hellenistic period in some form, and in Asia political forms reminiscent of those of Macedon were continued, although the civil population at large is as often seen to be involved as the army specifically (especially in Egypt), and the actions of the masses are as often expressed through riotous scenes as formal assemblies. This is not surprising, since it seems that the Macedonian tradition was not of formal constitutional process but the informal interaction of the led with their leaders in the forum of the mass meeting. Survival of these political forms is to be expected in the Seleucid kingdom especially, where the Macedonian settlers clung tenaciously to their Macedonian identity and institutions. The pattern is slightly different in Egypt, as here the army was an exclusive element within the population and, being scattered in the country, had less opportunity to express itself *en masse*; participation in politics is thus limited to the guards, the mercenaries and the Alexandrian mob.[14]

In Alexandria, assemblies of the masses could still be held. In the second century, Eulaios and Lenaios, 'the regents of Ptolemy, having summoned the populace to an assembly, promised to bring the war [against Antiochus] to a speedy end' (Diod. 30.16). Meetings of people or army are involved in the acclamation of kings: the younger of the Ptolemy brother kings was proclaimed king by the masses (Pol. 39.23.4); Dionysios Petosarapis began his attempted coup by putting out word that Ptolemy VI was plotting against his co-ruler; 'the populace assembled in haste at the stadium' and were 'aroused to such a pitch that they were preparing to kill the older brother and entrust the kingdom to the younger'. A new king would be presented to the army: Agathocles and Sosibios 'summoned a meeting of the bodyguard and household troops as well as of the officers of the infantry and cavalry' and proclaimed Ptolemy V king. 'They begged the officers to remain well disposed and maintain the boy on his throne' (Pol. 15.25.3–5). Later, Agathocles 'summoned a meeting of the Macedonians and appeared together with Agathocleia and the young king' (Pol. 15.26.1). The Macedonians shouted down Agathocles, and 'the same kind of thing happened at the meetings of the other regiments'.

Similarly, although there is no evidence for the right of trial in Egypt, the masses took an interest in such matters and objected to improper procedure. Agathocles brought accusations against his rival Tlepolemos, 'with the object of working up the populace' against him (Pol. 15.25.36). He then arrested Moeragenes, but he escaped and fled to the Macedonians encamped near the palace (15.28.4), persuading them to rebel, 'as the people had long been disposed to revolt and required only some man of courage to appeal to them' (29.1). Under Ptolemy VIII, Timotheos arrested and tortured his opponents; 'as the populace from this point on was little by little becoming aware of the utter knavery of their leaders and was beginning to regard the hapless victims with pity, Timotheos and his associates, alarmed, put an end to their torture of the rest of the accused and had them done away with in private' (Diod. 31.20). After Timotheos was assassinated, 'the populace ... being disgusted at Alexandria with the king for his shameless treatment of his brother, stripped him of his royal retinue and sent to recall the elder Ptolemy from Cyprus' (Diod. 31.17c). The clearest indication of the goodness of Ptolemy VI was that 'he did not put to death any of his Friends on any of the charges brought against them' (Pol. 39.7.2–4). Whether assemblies of the army continued with the frequency they had under the Successors may be doubted, as there was now less need for them; but before any great crisis, in particular a pitched battle, the army would still be called together and addressed by the king, as at Raphia, where Ptolemy IV, his queen Arsinoe and his chief officers and Friends rode along the line and addressed the army, concentrating in particular on the phalanx (Pol. 5.83).

In Syria there are indications of similar proceedings. Popular support would be a factor in state murders – Antiochus III had Hermeias murdered, and in Syria the populace 'bestowed during his progress the most hearty applause of all on the removal of Hermeias' (Pol. 5.56). There may have been no right of acclamation, but for example when Achaeus took command of the army of Seleucus III in Asia Minor, 'he was eagerly urged by the troops to assume the diadem' (Pol.4.48.7; the diadem is a head band which functioned like a crown). At first he refused, but later he 'assumed the diadem and styled himself king' (4.48.12). Demetrius, in exile in Rome, was advised that if he was to go to Syria, 'the Syrians would at once transfer the crown to him, even if he appeared accompanied only by a single slave' (Pol. 31.12.4), and on his arrival Lysias and Antiochus V were seized and killed by the army (*I Macc.* 7.1). Ptolemy Philometor was proclaimed king by the Antiochians and their army (Jos. *Ant.* xiii. 113). Diodotus Tryphon was led to revolt against Demetrius II by 'the excitement of the masses', and he was joined by the First Agema cavalrymen of Larisa (Diod. 33.4a). The army declared Antiochus VI king (*I Macc.* 11.59), but Tryphon subsequently bribed the army to elect him king instead (Jos. *Ant.* 13.219). The soldiers and Syrians hostile to Demetrius II requested Ptolemy VIII to provide them with a king (Jos. *Ant.* 13.267). Andriscos, one of Demetrius' mercenaries, passed himself off as a son of Perseus and approached Demetrius, demanding aid in regaining his throne; 'the populace [*plēthos*] had gathered and many speakers declared that Demetrius should either restore Andriscos or, if he could not or would not play the king, abdicate' (Diod. 31.40a).

These scenes are strongly reminiscent of the political functions of the Macedonian people and army; assemblies of the mass to make demands and be placated by a personal appearance by the king, the removal or appointment of kings when the kingship is disputed, and disgust with those who kill their opponents without going through the proper channels. None of these episodes is evidence that there were any formal rights or constitutional limits on royal power, but they all show the army and populace taking an active part in the politics of the kingdom and expecting to be ruled in accordance with the old traditions, and this is probably the nature of these 'rights' in Macedon also. It was usually the mass of the population in Egyptian Alexandria which exercised these powers, since there the army was dispersed in the country; but in Syria at least the city populations were also those who made up the army. Such scenes may therefore be seen as the continuation of the political function of the Macedonian soldier citizens.

In contrast, the mercenaries did not usually participate in the political function of the true citizens; a tyrannical ruler could therefore use these men to suppress the citizens if his behaviour was such as to earn the citizens' contempt. Demetrius II brought in mercenaries which he used to suppress the citizens of Antioch, stripping them of their arms, confiscating their property and leaving them to wander about Syria (Diod. 33.4.2–3; *I Macc.* 11.38, 11.45). As we saw above, Agathocles' attempt to seize power in Alexandria in the same way involved the recruitment of a force of mercenaries (Pol. 15.25.17.f.). As Polybius remarks, 'the safety of despots depends on the affection and strength of their foreign soldiers [i.e. mercenaries]' (Pol. 11.13.8). Similar perhaps is the decision of Philip V to remove from the cities 'all men who took part in politics' and replace them with barbarians, 'whose fidelity to him would be surer' (Pol. 23.10.4). With the decline of the monarchies through the second century, the use of mercenaries in this way became more widespread, until eventually, as in Alexandria, the mercenaries, 'an overbearing, numerous and intractable crowd', who 'had learned to rule rather than to obey, by reason of the weakness of the kings' (Pol. 34.14.6), in effect held the true political power. The distinctions Polybius draws between mercenary and citizen armies (e.g. 11.13) applied not only in the Greek cities, but in the kingdoms as well, so long as the kings wished to be monarchs and not tyrants. The recurring theme is the willingness to obey orders; soldiers do not seem to have become slaves to the commands of their officers or kings, and soldiers' obedience to orders was never to be taken for granted, as it sprang from their conception of their status in the state and on the ability of their leaders to convince them of the rightness of the chosen course of action and to win their personal approval.[15]

The other side of the same coin is shown by the way that the arming of the native Egyptian population by Ptolemy IV before Raphia in effect conferred on that population the same political legitimacy as the Greco-Macedonian military class that had formerly held power. The result was that 'the [Egyptian] soldiers, highly proud of their victory at Raphia, were no longer disposed to obey orders, but were on the lookout for a leader and figurehead, thinking themselves well able to maintain themselves as an independent power' (Pol. 5.107.1–3). This episode clearly demonstrates why the Seleucids did not utilize the native populations of Syria as the heavily armed element in their armies, because the right to bear arms (or at least, the arms of heavy infantry) had to be restricted to the politically and socially dominant element of society if their special status was not to be undermined.

Loyalty and leadership

While kings and generals could be unpopular, as we have seen, it is apparent that the hereditary principle remained strong and that the Successors were able to take the throne themselves only after a considerable delay and with great regard for the feelings of their followers. After the Successor period, a new legitimacy was established with the creation of new dynasties, and from now on kings could benefit from the loyalty that went with their legitimate descent, while rebels had to contend with the disinclination of their followers to fight against their legitimate ruler. Dynastic religious cults exploited the incumbent king's position by glorifying his ancestors, so that the glory would be transferred to him and again provide a strong instance of a source of respect for the king based not on his personal achievements but on his birth. It is clear from the conflicts between Antiochus III and Ptolemy IV that the personal ability of the king was not the only factor that could legitimize his rule. Antiochus III was a young king with no experience, who must have been completely unknown to his subjects, yet when Achaeus, a commander of proven ability and success, marched towards Syria, 'his troops mutinied, the cause of their dissatisfaction being that, as it now appeared, the expedition was against their original and natural king', and Achaeus had to attempt to convince them that he had had no intention of invading Syria (Pol. 5.57.6). Similarly, Molon's men deserted at the very sight of Antiochus (Pol. 5.54.2), although they had already defeated a royal army in battle. Ptolemy IV was criticized by Polybius for his unroyal habits, yet when he appeared with his phalanx at Raphia he encouraged them sufficiently for them to defeat the Seleucid phalanx (Pol. 5.85.8). It is not the king as a man that is important here, but the king as an institution; the hereditary descent of the king from rulers of great prestige is what impresses the army, not necessarily his known qualities. As under the Successors, anyone who could claim even a tenuous link with the royal house could find himself accepted by the populace, in the absence of a better candidate. Alexander Balas, for example, was enabled to launch his attempt on the throne of Syria because of his physical resemblance to Antiochus V (Diod. 31.32a). Similarly, Andriscos, a mercenary of Demetrius, because he bore a close resemblance to Philip, son of Perseus, was able to make an attempt on the vacant Macedonian throne (31.40a); 'as he gained followers, he was soon asserting, on the ground of inheritance, a legal claim to the Macedonian throne' (32.15).

However, the armies owed other loyalties too, apart from those to their rulers or leaders. It is apparent that the soldiers' loyalty to their own families was a potent force. Under the Successors, with permanently mobilized armies campaigning, the soldiers' families formed part of the baggage train, or *aposkeue*. Eumenes, after Paraitacene, wished to occupy the battlefield, but 'the soldiers would not listen to him, insisting with shouts that they return to their own baggage train' (Diod. 19.31.3). After Gabiene, this baggage was lost to the enemy. While Eumenes and the satraps discussed what to do, 'the Macedonians ... refused to heed either party since their baggage had been taken', and by arresting Eumenes and turning him over to Antigonus they got back their baggage, along with 'their children, their wives and many other relatives' (Diod. 19.43.7–8). The lesson was obvious: so long as the army's families were with them on campaign, there was a danger that the soldiers would be more concerned with their fate than with that of their leaders. When the armies were settled, the families could be left behind on the land that had been granted, and soldiers' families ceased to follow the armies. Ptolemy I's army, captured on Cyprus, deserted from the army of Demetrius into which they had been enrolled and tried to return to Ptolemy, 'because their baggage had been left behind in Egypt' (Diod. 20.47.4). When Pyrrhus and Lysimachus invaded Macedon to oust Demetrius, Pyrrhus captured Beroia, and when the report of this reached Demetrius' army, 'his camp was full of lamentations and tears ... and the soldiers would not hold together but insisted on going away, ostensibly to their own homes but in reality to Lysimachus' (Plut. *Dem.* 44.3–4).

In Egypt the army's 'baggage', including their families, was left at home when the army was on campaign, and there are examples of laws relating to these families, in particular protecting them against interference or exploitation while the soldier was absent. Thus the soldier was firmly tied to his home territory, and at the same time was (in theory) freed from concern for the welfare of his dependants. Exemptions were granted to the soldiers stationed in Alexandria and to their families in the countryside from special cultivation requirements after the invasion of Antiochus IV. Ptolemaic soldiers in Syria also received special privileges if they married native wives, perhaps in an effort to link them closely to their lands. Alexander had granted special exemptions to the families of the fallen at Granicus (Arr. *Anab.* 1.16.5), and this too may have been a common practice.[16]

But as well as their natural loyalty to the legitimate king and to their own families, armies – not just mercenaries – would also be loyal to the source of their pay, and the support even of citizen soldiers could be won through gifts and bribes, in particular through the chance to collect plunder. In 306, when

Ptolemy offered a generous individual bounty to Antigonus' invasion army, 'an urge to change sides fell upon the mercenaries of Antigonus', which was checked only through the use of archers and catapults to shoot down deserters (Diod. 20.75.1). It is perhaps significant that only the mercenaries are said to have been tempted by the offer; Antigonus' Macedonians would have left their families behind in Antigoneia or one of the other settlements, and so been less inclined to abandon them. In general, mercenaries are particularly noted as being easily won over by money. Gallic mercenaries were used by Apollodoros, attempting to set himself up as tyrant in Cassandreia, and 'when he had conferred gifts upon them, found them loyal guardsmen and convenient tools', assuring the loyalty of a considerable force by 'an increase in the pay of his soldiers' (Diod. 22.5.2). Eumenes, 'having recruited a force of mercenary troops, not only gave all of them their pay, but honoured some with gifts and beguiled them all with promises, evoking their goodwill' (Diod. 31.14). The Achaeans, on the other hand, had difficulty raising a mercenary force in 219 because of their failure to pay off the mercenaries in full at the end of the war with Sparta (Pol. 4.60.2).

But pay was also given to the regular forces and its prompt distribution was obviously important to loyalty and discipline. The army of Antiochus III assembled at Apamea mutinied over outstanding pay (Pol. 5.50.1), and the courtier Hermeias was able to win their goodwill by paying off the arrears (5.50.7). Similarly, Agathocles and Sosibios 'granted three months' pay to the troops, feeling sure of taking the edge off their hatred by appealing to the soldiers' spirit of avarice' (Pol. 15.25.11). Demetrius II took the step of discontinuing payment to his men and dismissed them to their homes; 'for this reason he became very unpopular with the soldiers, to whom he no longer gave anything, although the previous kings had continued to pay them even in time of peace to ensure their loyalty when the need for them in war did arise' (Jos. *Ant.* 13.129 f.; cf. *I Macc.* 11.38). Evidently it was a Macedonian tradition for the soldiers to be unruly towards their kings when pay was in arrears: Philip II is recorded to have been abused by his soldiers for this reason (Polyaen. 4.2.6). Advances of pay were common before a major campaign or in a special attempt to win the soldiers' approval – Antigonus set out for the Ipsus campaign and at Tarsus gave the army three months' pay (Diod. 20.108.1). Eumenes of Cardia gave the *Argyraspides* six months' advance wages (Diod. 19.75.1). Sosibios gave the soldiers in Alexandria a two-month advance of pay (Pol. 15.25.11). Antiochus IV payed out a year's wages before departing for his expedition to the East (*I Macc.* 3.27). There is also some evidence for special awards granted for distinguished service – the Amphipolis code refers to 'those who have received crowns' (in the sense of a military medal or decoration), Alexander distributed crowns to some of his officers (Arr. *Anab.* 7.5.4–6) and an inscription from Gaza records crowns granted to officers in the garrison. It is evident at any rate that maintaining the loyalty of a large army could be an expensive business.[17]

The favour of the soldiers could be also be won by special gifts and the promise of plunder. Antigonus, after a difficult march, 'by giving horses to men who had lost their own and by distributing most of the pack animals as presents, regained the goodwill of the soldiers' (Diod. 19.19.4). Similarly, when Eumenes' army was in Persia, Peucestes gathered cattle 'and distributed them without stint to the soldiers, seeking their goodwill' (Diod. 19.21.3). When Craterus was preparing for battle with Eumenes, he 'summoned the whole army to an assembly and spurred them to battle with suitable words, saying that he would give them all the baggage of the enemy to plunder' (Diod. 18.30.2). Ptolemy campaigned in Syria in 313, and 'after sating his army with spoil, sailed back to Cyprus. His playing up to the soldiers in this way was designed to evoke enthusiasm in face of the encounters that were approaching' (Diod. 19.79.7). Demetrius in his speech before Gaza, 'after encouraging the crowd with words suitable to the occasion and promising to give gifts to them as they were deserved and to yield the booty to the soldiers, drew up his army for the battle' (Diod. 19.81.6). After the defeat at Ipsus, Demetrius plundered Lysimachus' territory in the Chersonese, 'thereby enriching and holding together his own forces, which were beginning to recover their spirit' (Plut. *Dem.* 31.2). The Macedonian Peltasts of Philip V were stirred to mutiny by the suggestion that 'they were in risk of losing all their privileges, that they were most unfairly treated, and did not get in full their customary plunder' (Pol. 5.25.1–2). When Achaeus feared a mutiny of his army, he pleased them with plunder by pillaging Pisidia (Pol. 5.57), while Molon won support from his men by the hopes of plunder he held out (Pol. 5.43.5). The Macedonian regulations on the division of spoils have survived in the Amphipolis regulations; here the plunder is to be collected in front of the camp and divided by the appointed officers (A 1 l. 10 f.). Any disputes are to be adjudicated by the Friends, and in addition a double share is to be given to those who have received a crown (A 3). In fact it is plain that the chief function of the seizure of plunder was to please the soldiers and gain their goodwill. As Polybius remarks, 'most men endure hardship and risk their lives for the sake of gain' (Pol. 10.17.1).[18]

Feasts and banquets could also be given to the army. While those given to the king's Friends served to emphasize the personal nature of the relationship between them and provide ties of personal acquaintance, banquets for the army were probably intended simply to win the soldiers' favour through the provision of plentiful food (and drink). There are several examples from the Successors. Peucestes feasted the entire army in Persia in an attempt to win its support (Diod. 19.22), although his hopes were foiled when a forged letter prepared by Eumenes led the army to believe that 'he [Eumenes] would be able by help of the kings to promote whoever he wished and to exact punishment from those who wronged him' (Diod. 19.23). Eumenes himself, marching against Antigonus, 'performed a sacrifice to the gods and entertained the army sumptuously' (Diod. 19.24.4). Ptolemy, meanwhile, addressed an assembly of Perdiccas' invasion army and distributed food to them (Diod. 18.36.6).

Splendid displays of wealth and power were an important part of the public display of the royal authority of the king. The great procession of Ptolemy II included a parade of 80,000 soldiers (Athen. 5.202 f.), and Antiochus IV held great games and a military parade at Daphne (Pol. 30.25 f.). Such games are often a prelude to or a celebration of a military victory: the Daphne games were either a celebration of the success of the campaign in Egypt or a preparation for the campaign against the eastern satrapies. Of a similar nature was the parade held by Perseus at Citium (Liv. 42.51–53), at which the army was assembled, performed some manoeuvres and was addressed by the king, preparatory to the war with Rome. In Macedon the army was paraded at ceremonial occasions. For example, the alliance of Perseus and Gentius was finalized at Dion in the presence of a column of cavalry; the king wished them to be present on the assumption that this would give a considerable boost to their morale (Liv. 44.23.8). We should also note that the newly reformed Achaean army, armed in the Macedonian fashion by Philopoemen, put on special drill displays:

'Moreover, we are told that at the celebration of the Nemean games, when he was general of the Achaeans for the second time and had recently won his victory at Mantineia, but was at leisure the while on account of the festival, Philopoemen in the first place displayed before the assembled Greeks his phalanx, with its splendid array, and performing its tactical evolutions, as it was wont to do, with speed and vigour.' (Plutarch, *Philopoemen* 11.1–2)

The army also had a role in religious festivals, and in general religious practice was one way in which the bonds between king and army could be formalized – an early example was the use by Eumenes of an Alexander cult to bolster his authority with the army (Diod. 18.60.4). Ruler cult was not just a device on the part of the rulers; the Athenian hymn to Demetrius (Athen. 6.253e), for example, expresses the sense of the need for a great figure to act as protector and saviour in times of difficulty and upheaval, but the dynastic cult established by the rulers also acted as a way of providing a suitable means of religious observance specially tailored to bureaucrats and soldiers. Religious belief, with the promise it offered of divine protection or (if that fell through) everlasting life, has always been of great importance to those involved in dangerous activities such as warfare. The religious role of the Macedonian king as chief priest of the kingdom, along with the growing practice of dynastic cults in the Hellenistic kingdoms, gave the king a special status, and the dramatic impact accorded to the appearance of Ptolemy at Raphia, for example, should be seen in this light.[19]

Formal relations probably consisted of an oath, although much evidence for this is from the time of the Successors, for example the oath to Eumenes (Plut. *Eum.* 12.2; Just. 14.1, 14.4), when other factors may have made such an oath desirable; but it was probably the old Macedonian custom. Sosthenes, having defeated the Gallic invaders of Macedon, refused the kingship and made the army take an oath to him not as king but as general (Just. 24.5). The army and population of Antioch are said to have taken an oath to Demetrius II and Alexander Balas (Just. 35.2). An oath was taken in Egypt – the would-be usurpers Agathocles and Sosibios, attempting to ensure the support of the soldiers, 'imposed on them the oath they were accustomed to take on the proclamation of a new king' (Pol. 15.25.11). Apart from formal oaths sworn by subjects to their king, soldiers could be bound by an oath in other circumstances. The Smyrna-Magnesia agreement required the 'settlers at Magnesia, the cavalry and infantry in the city and the soldiers in the camp', along with the other citizens, to swear that 'what I have received from King Seleucus I will preserve to the best of my ability and return to King Seleucus'.[20]

So there were a number of institutional ties between the army and the king, ranging from the king's status as ruler and heir to the glory of his ancestors, reinforced by dynastic cult, through displays of the power of the kings in processions, to the more mundane matters of the monetary rewards given to the soldiers in pay and special bonuses, and the land on which they lived or from which they drew their livelihood, together with tax exemptions to improve their economic status in the kingdom. In addition, there were more personal ties between the king in his role as leader of the army in time of war and the soldiers forming that army, and from these ties developed a range of ideal characteristics of the king connected to this style of leadership.

Alexander had held the loyalty of the army because he had campaigned as one of them and had fought at their head, taking the same risks (see Arr. *Anab.* 7.10 for the wounds he suffered), and the Successors naturally followed the same style of leadership, partly because it worked so well, but surely largely as it would not have occurred to them to do otherwise. The Macedonians in their armies expected this of them, and respected them for it, and the tradition lasted. The examples of good leadership in the Alexandrian style are especially frequent in the period of the Successors, although it is apparent that the traditions continued throughout the Hellenistic period. In battle, the king was to fight at the head of his men and lead by example. Each of the Successor generals fought in this way, and individual combats sometimes arose between them, as when Eumenes fought Neptolemos (Diod. 18.31.2). Pyrrhus similarly engaged Pantauchos, general of Demetrius, in single combat (Plut. *Dem.*41.). Later rulers engaged in the same type of leadership. Antigonos Doson was at least with the phalanx at Sellasia (Pol. 2.67f.), if not actually in the front rank, and died from overexertion in cheering on his men against the Illyrians (Pol. 2.70.6–8); Philip V, while usually not taking part personally in his city assaults, did for example lead a picked force in a rock-climbing attack on Alipheira, and was first to enter the citadel (Pol. 4.78.9–11). The Seleucids seem to have stuck even more firmly with personal leadership. Antiochus III was visible to the enemy when fighting Molon (Pol. 5.53), and planned to engage Ptolemy in single combat at Raphia (Pol.5.84), while the frequent deaths in battle of the kings after Antiochus IV testify to their position in the front rank (eg. Just. 35.1). As for the Ptolemies, Ptolemy IV was personally present at Raphia, but abandoned his left wing when it was routed in a way that Polybius would have criticized, had it not been for the fact that the result turned out in his favour. Very often the king would be fighting with his guard cavalry units, as Alexander had done at the head of his Companions, but there are also examples – such as Sellasia and Raphia – of the king fighting with (or at least being stationed close to) the phalanx.[21]

This style of personal leadership was effective for a number of reasons. Its technical results in pitched battle, and its wider implications, will be considered further in Chapter 7. Its result on the men's loyalty was to demonstrate to them that the king shared their hardships, inspire them to greater efforts by example, but also impress them with the physical prowess of the king. The need to share in the soldiers' hardships is demonstrated by the story of Demetrius who, when his army was suffering heavy losses in the siege of Thebes, 'wishing not to be thought reckless of other's lives only, but also to share the perils of battle', went forward himself and was wounded through the neck (Plut. *Dem.* 40.3). The admiration felt by the Macedonians for a warrior king is demonstrated by Pyrrhus, who after defeating Demetrius' army, 'was admired for making most of his conquests in person', and was compared by the Macedonians with Alexander for his victory (Plut. *Dem.* 41.3), for 'from of old they had been wont to consider the man who was mightiest in arms as also the most kingly' (Plut. *Dem.* 44.4).

Just as the effective leader shared in the dangers of combat, so he should share in the hardships of the soldiers' life. Eumenes, besieged in Nora, 'gave the same rations to all the soldiers, sharing in their simple food himself, and by his unchanging affability he gained great good will for himself and secured harmony among all his fellow refugees' (Diod. 18.42.5). Seleucus, in his march to Babylon, reassured his friends. 'but he also sought the favour of his fellow soldiers, and put himself on an equality with them all in such a way that each man respected him and willingly accepted the risk of the daring venture' (Diod. 19.90.5). Lysimachus, when his army was hard-pressed for food and he was advised by his friends to save himself, 'replied that it was not honourable to provide a disgraceful safety for himself by abandoning his army and his friends' (Diod. 21.12). This also meant that a simple lifestyle was expected of the king, at least in wartime; Demetrius was prone to drinking in peacetime but made up for this by his energy and efficiency in war (Plut. *Dem.* 19), but even so the Macedonians grew resentful of his extravagant style of living (Plut. *Dem.* 42.1, 44.6).[22]

A good leader also showed care for his soldiers' wellbeing and would not allow them to suffer unnecessarily. This is of course a simple practical requirement, but it also could increase the leader's prestige among his men. When Antigonus advanced against Eumenes through difficult country in 317, 'although he did everything in his power, he lost a large number of men because of the extreme heat' (Diod. 19.18.2). A further difficult march followed; 'the soldiers of Antigonus, however, because of the continuous misfortunes and their own extreme misery, became so critical of him that they let fall hostile remarks [cf. Plut. *Mor.* 182c] ... Nevertheless, by mingling with the soldiers on friendly terms and by making ready an abundant supply of all provisions, he restored the army from its miserable state' (Diod. 19.20.1). The campaigns of the Successors provide numerous examples of armies being rested after difficult marches or treated to abundant supplies after times of hardship. After Paraitacene, Antigonus, finding his men disheartened, withdrew 'to an unplundered country in which to refresh his soldiers' (Diod. 19.32.1). Cratesipolis, widow of the son of Polyperchon, 'succeeded to his power and held his army together, since she was most highly esteemed by the soldiers for her acts of kindness; for it was her habit to aid those who were in misfortune and to assist many of those who were without resources' (Diod. 19.67.1). Similarly, for example, Philip V in his Peloponnesian campaign rested his army for three days in Olympia (Pol. 4.73.3), and showed concern on his march to allow them to gather plentiful plunder and provisions.[23]

Care for the soldiers was demonstrated in other ways. The soldiers, for example, set great store by the prospect of a proper burial in the event of their death in battle. Eumenes, after Paraitacene, provided a magnificent burial for the dead (Diod. 19.32.3); Demetrius, after Gaza, was 'very anxious at any cost to honour those who had perished with the funeral that was their due'; Ptolemy 'gave a magnificent burial to those of his own men who had died in the battle' (Diod. 18.85.1–4); and during the siege of Rhodes, Demetrius devoted himself to the burial of the dead and the care of the wounded (Diod. 20.97.3).[24]

This care for the soldiers was extended to a general regard for fairness and the wellbeing of the subjects. Ptolemy I in particular is attributed such virtues: 'men, because of his graciousness and nobility of heart, came together eagerly from all sides to Alexandria and gladly enrolled for the campaign' against Perdiccas (Diod. 18.28.5). Philip V, according to Polybius, 'both by his behaviour to those with whom he was associated in the camp and by his ability and daring in the field, was winning a high reputation' (Pol. 4.77.1). Ptolemy VIII, on the other hand, acted in a tyrannical fashion; 'as these acts provoked dissatisfaction and resentment, he brought upon himself the wrath of the entire populace' (Diod. 33.6). This need for fair treatment also extended to acts of generosity to the defeated – Demetrius' army were attracted to Pyrrhus by, among other things, the fact that he treated his prisoners well (Plut. Dem. 44.4; a matter of great practical significance to those planning to desert). Antiochus IV spared the defeated Egyptian army, which contributed to the success of his campaign in Egypt (Diod. 30.14). Similarly, Antiochus III acted with magnanimity towards enemies such as Xerxes (Pol. 7.23), Arsaces (Pol. 10.27) and Euthydemus (Pol. 11.39); as Polybius says, 'all the inhabitants of the district ... considered that he had acted in a truly royal and magnanimous manner' and attached themselves to him (Pol. 7.23.5).

The way in which the king or commander communicated with his soldiers was often through addressing the mass meeting, or assembly, of the soldiers. At such meetings it was necessary to provide an impressive display of authority, as well as to promote the enthusiasm of the soldiers for a coming venture, typically by holding out promises and hopes of future gain. Eumenes addressed the Macedonians debating whether to side with Antigonus; he 'discussed many matters pertinent to the subject and ... gained greater favour with the crowd than before' (Diod. 18.63.5). Similarly, the generals of Ptolemy IV addressed frequent meetings of the troops before Raphia (Pol. 5.64.4), and in general before each battle the king would address the army before giving the signal to proceed. Demetrius addressed such a meeting before Gaza; 'when he had called together an assembly under arms and, anxious and agitated, had taken his position on a raised platform, the crowd shouted with a single voice, bidding him be of good courage' (Diod. 19.81.2). The reasons for their support were that as he was young he had as yet made no enemies, but also 'he was outstanding both in beauty and stature' and 'when clad in royal armour he had great distinction and struck men with awe' (Diod. 19.81.2; his stature, beauty and royal splendour are stressed again at 20.92.3). This splendid royal appearance was heightened by the wearing of special clothing: the Rhodians captured Demetrius' robes during the siege and sent them to Ptolemy, since they were purple and so suitable for a king (Diod. 20.93.4), while the brother Ptolemies donned their robes before appearing before the populace of Alexandria to assert their authority (Diod. 31.15a). Antiochus IV, on the other hand, although he held magnificent games at Daphne, was contemptible in his personal appearance and dress, and behaved without proper royal dignity at drinking parties (Diod. 31.16.2–4), and when the future Demetrius I met Ptolemy VI in Rome he was shocked by his shabby appearance and provided him with expensive clothes, a horse and a diadem (Diod. 31.18). Thus, while the traditional costume of the Ptolemies may have been Macedonian military dress (Plut. *Ant.* 54), it was obviously military dress modified by various splendid refinements, in particular by the use of purple in the clothing.

A general was also respected for his practical ability in the field: the Macedonians and Greek cities began to favour Cassander over Polyperchon, for 'Polyperchon seemed to lack both energy and wisdom in representing the king and his allies, but Cassander, who treated all fairly and was active in carrying out his affairs, was winning many supporters of his leadership' (Diod. 18.75.2). Failure could lead to a contempt for the commander's leadership, as when Perdiccas failed to get his army across the Nile; 'since more than 2,000 men were lost, among them some of the prominent commanders, the rank and file of the army became ill disposed toward Perdiccas' (Diod. 18.36.1). When he was deposed, Ptolemy, who had defeated him, addressed the army and was enthusiastically received, 'and was in a position to gain the guardianship of the kings through the favour of the rank and file' (Diod. 18.36.6). An interest and ability in military affairs was expected of the king; Antiochus IX was condemned for his unroyal interests, taking a delight in actors and puppets (Diod. 34/35.34). Hellenistic kings were brought up in the arts of war from birth, and studied them as a science – thus Pyrrhus had great knowledge of and ability in generalship, as was shown in his writings, and 'regarded it as the most kingly branch of knowledge; the rest he regarded as mere accomplishments and held them in no esteem' (Plut. *Pyrrh*. 8.2). Demetrius is said to have devoted his time not to trivia but to important matters like siege machines and ships (Plut. *Dem*. 20). The writing of handbooks and the existence of many other tactical writers, whose works might have been intended for the education of kings as well as of subordinates, demonstrates the need for technical skills, and their importance in battle is obvious.[25]

Victory was in itself, not surprisingly, a major factor in ensuring the support of the led. The Seleucid rebel leader Molon's troops, for example, after initial successes, 'were in high spirits, owing to their expectation of success having been so far fulfilled' (Pol. 5.45.2). Successful military action by the commander served three purposes: for the populace at large it guaranteed protection from enemy attack or invasion, while for the army it offered the opportunity for them to fulfil their hopes of plunder or of other gain, and of course protected them against the death that might ensue if they were to be defeated by the enemy. A leader therefore had to show himself able, by his personal abilities and skill, to provide victories for his followers. As Polybius notes with regard to Philip V's bungled first attempt to seize Phthiotic Thebes, by failure commanders 'create distrust and hatred of themselves ever afterwards and bid all men be on their guard against them' (Pol. 5.98.7). To this extent, those military characteristics and virtues which seemed to offer a guarantee of victory, such as technical skill, personal prowess, competence in handling affairs, quick thinking and inventiveness, would in turn excite the greatest confidence and so loyalty amongst the led. This means that a leader who could provide victory would be in a strong position as regards the favour of his army and so his own status. Achaeus, for instance, at first refused the suggestion of his army that he assume the kingship, but when he defeated Attalus he was elated, assumed the diadem and styled himself king (Pol. 4.48.10–12).

The example of Alcetas' attempts to win the support of the Pisidians in 319 provides a perfect summary of the way in which this style of leadership worked:

'[Alcetas] had decided to show kindness to the Pisidians, thinking that he would thus secure as allies men who were warlike and who possessed a country difficult to invade and well supplied with strongholds. For this reason during the campaigns he honoured them exceedingly above all the allies and distributed to them spoils from the hostile territory, assigning them half the booty. By employing the most

friendly language in his conversation with them, by each day inviting
the most important of them in turn to his table at banquets, and
finally by honouring many of them with gifts of considerable value,
he secured them as loyal supporters.' (Diodorus, 18.46)

Polybius includes in his narrative many assessments of the characters of
various kings, with observations as to whether or not they were worthy of royal
status. For example, he lists the virtues of Philip V, before the deterioration in
his character brought on by associating with the wrong type of friend, which
made him most suitable to hold power: 'he possessed a quick intelligence, a
retentive memory and great personal charm, as well as the presence and
authority that becomes a king, and above all ability and courage as a general.'
The Companions of Philip and Alexander 'defeated the enemy in many
marvellous battles, exposed themselves often to extraordinary toil, danger and
hardship', and despite gaining great wealth did not allow 'any impairment
of their physical powers' through overindulgence, and were 'kingly men by
virtue of their magnanimity, self-restraint and courage' (Pol. 8.10.9–10). Justin
(13.1) describes also how Alexander's friends were all royal in their powers of
mind and body and in their ability and authority, and Lysimachus, as well as
great physical strength, had great military skill (Just. 15.3). Pyrrhus too was
upright and just, and also had great military skill (Just. 25.5). Attalus I also
shows typical royal virtues, in particular 'the largesses and favours he conferred
on his friends', but also successes in war against the Gauls, virtuousness and
austerity, and his passing on the kingdom without dispute to his heirs (Pol.
18.41). Perseus also had royal qualities – 'in personal appearance he looked
capable, and was expert in all kinds of bodily exercise which are of real service';
he also had a gravity of demeanour and composure, and was moderate in his
personal tastes (Pol. 25.3). Antiochus IV was 'both energetic, daring in design
and worthy of the royal dignity' (Pol. 28.18), although this good impression
was let down by his excessive populism (Pol. 26.1) and his unkingly appearance
and manner of dress (Pol. 30.26). Eumenes II was particularly impressive for
having raised his kingdom from its low status to a position of great authority
and importance, all through 'his own acuteness, industry and energy', for his
generosity in making benefactions, and for maintaining his brothers in loyalty
to himself (Pol. 32.8). The importance to Polybius of liberality is shown by
his account of the great gifts given to Rhodes by former kings (Pol. 5.88–90).
Ptolemy IV, on the other hand, according to Polybius, 'abandoned entirely the
path of virtue and took to a life of dissipation', and late in his reign was forced
into a war in Egypt in which there were no pitched battles or anything worthy

of note (Pol. 14.12). Prusias of Bithynia, who comes in for especially harsh criticism, was 'a man by no means worthy of the royal dignity' as he was servile in his dress and behaviour (Pol. 30.18), but also because 'though possessed of fair reasoning power', he was 'but half a man as regards his appearance, and had no more military capacity than a woman; for not only was he a coward, but he was incapable of putting up with hardship and, to put it shortly, he was effeminate in body and mind', as well as 'most incontinent in satisfying his sensual appetites' (Pol. 36.15).

To be worthy of royal status meant to be endowed by nature with the sort of virtues required in a military leader in the Alexandrian Macedonian style; therefore, one who was able to meet these requirements would be by nature, and by virtue of his own character, suitable to be king.

Pay, rations and plunder

Pay has been mentioned several times above. The soldier settlers in the Asian kingdoms and the inhabitants of Macedon were probably not paid while they were not on active service (while they were living on the proceeds of their own lands or the lands they were granted). While there is mention of armies being paid in peacetime (such as the Seleucid army, Jos. *Ant.* 13.129), it is likely that it was the household forces, those kept on permanent service, who were paid, rather than the mass of the army (see further below). But while on active service, campaigning against the king's enemies – which could be for months or years at a time – the army would of course need to be paid, which represented both an important reward for the soldiers and a significant financial burden for the kings.[26]

Although there were local variations in terminology, payments were usually divided into two parts: pay, usually called *opsonion* or *misthos*, and ration money, under a variety of names (*sitos*, *sitometria*, *sitarchia* or *metrema*). The actual purchasing power of ration money could vary considerably, as the price of corn naturally varied with time and with changing circumstances, so rations were often paid in kind, as shown in the recruitment treaties specifying daily amounts of grain to be distributed to the soldiers. Various scraps of evidence in inscriptions and papyri, together with some literary evidence, indicate likely daily rates of pay for the army. On average, a typical rate of pay was probably around 6 obols (1 drachma) per day for a phalangite. Light infantry would receive half this, and officers and cavalry double or more. What the yearly amount of pay may be is difficult to determine, depending as it does on the length of the campaign year; ten months is the period given in Eumenes' agreement with his mercenaries, and might have been typical. An ideal phalanx of 16,000 men serving for ten months at one drachma a day (and ignoring additional costs for officers) would cost around 800 talents in pay alone (at 2.67 talents a day, 18.67 talents a week – a talent beng a measure of silver, equivalent to 6,000 drachmas).[27]

It is not clear what proportion of the army had to be paid in peacetime and in wartime. It is obvious that men engaged in active service would need to be paid grain rations before and during service and pay at least not too long afterwards (or as an advance). Mercenaries too would need to be paid throughout their period of service, however long that was. Most likely the military settlers, or the population from which the army was conscripted, were only paid while on active service. In the Smyrna-Magnesia treaty there are three groups of soldiers referred to: the garrison of the fort of Palaimagnesia, the infantry detached from the phalanx under Timon, and Omares' Persians, Menecles' men and the men from Smyrna. Of these it is apparently only the last who are to be 'given from the royal treasury the rations and pay and everything else which is normally given to them from the royal treasury'. The mercenaries (if that is what Omares' and Menecles' men are) and the phalanx men are therefore distinct from the settlers who hold *kleroi*. It would indeed be surprising if settlers on their own lands were sent food or pay from the royal treasuries. For comparison, Josephus (*Ant.* 12.147–53) recounts the arrangements between Antiochus III and Zeuxis for the settlement of Jewish settlers, who are to receive royal grain 'only until they gain produce from the soil'. In *I Macc.* 3.27, Antiochus IV 'gathered all the troops of the kingdom and opened his treasury and gave them a year's pay', which would suggest that they were not paid until he gathered them together. As we have seen, according to Josephus (*Ant.* 12.130), the predecessors of Demetrius II used to pay the army even in times of peace, but it is likely that only the guard units are meant, as the evidence suggests that the Seleucid army was levied from the population at the beginning of the campaign year according to need. For Egypt it appears that the active army (the guard units in Alexandria) and the mercenaries were paid at all times, but it is unlikely that cleruchs were usually paid while they were on their lands. Thus a considerable proportion of the armies of the Seleucid and Ptolemaic kingdoms were paid only in times of war, and the likelihood is that the situation in Macedon was similar.[28]

In time of war, grain could be bought (as Liv. 35.44) from the surrounding peoples or else requisitioned from the area passed through. In Egypt, pay and ration money were distributed through the royal banks, though corn was not apparently issued in this way. Grain from the royal granaries was also sold to the army in specially laid on markets, at a reduced price. In wartime or overseas this practice could not of course be followed. While an army was being amassed, grain had to be stockpiled to supply it (Pol. 5.63). Because of the difficulties of overland transport, however, such supplies could not be sent to the army except by sea (as was done by Antiochus III, Pol. 5.68). Thus royal grain stores could not always be used on campaign. There were two other options; either grain could be seized from the countryside, if in hostile territory, or it could be bought from local suppliers. Seizure of grain seems to have been the normal procedure for the Successors – Diodorus describes the supply problems of Antigonos and Eumenes, who solved any such difficulties by moving into an unplundered area, in great detail (e.g. 19.12, 32) – while Philip V also seized grain in the course of his campaigns in Greece (for example at Pol. 4.63, grain stocks are captured and distributed, at 5.8 Philip seizes grain and at 5.19 Laconia is stripped of its grain) and Polybius describes distributions of grain by Antiochus to his army in India (11.34). The treaty of Attalus I and Malla specifies that Attalus' men be given grain 'unless they are in enemy territory where they can seize provisions'. However, while this method was of course free of charge, it was possible only in enemy territory and must have antagonized the inhabitants. Antiochus III is described marching through Asia Minor 'as if through enemy territory', seizing rather than buying grain (Liv. 37.19) – and buying grain could be expensive; Philip V had to arrange for the Achaeans to supply him with grain free (Pol. 4.1); the pact between Philip V and Antiochus III included terms under which the satrap Zeuxis was to keep Philip supplied (Pol. 26.1); and Antiochus arranged with the Aetolians to sell him grain (Liv. 35.44). In 169, Polybius (in his role as a general of the Achaean League) was to be responsible for ensuring that the Achaean army find markets (*agoras*) in every city it marched to from which to buy provisions (Pol. 28.12.5). Even when grain was bought in this way it could place a great burden on those supplying it. Eumenes, for example, was worried that if his allies, the Romans, crossed to Asia they would use up his grain supplies (Liv. 37.19). Thus, having the army on campaign could pose problems even though it freed the home country from grain requirements.

From the soldiers' point of view, pay was one attraction of military service; another, as we saw above, was the chance to seize plunder. Polybius sometimes presents the hope of seizing plunder as a reason for going to war; for example, for the rapacious Aetolians (Pol. 4.3), or Philip V, tempted with plunder by the Achaeans (Pol. 4.64). There are three basic types of plunder: captured hoards of money, goods plundered from a town, and slaves. The value of movable property captured in the plundering of a town is difficult to determine, with one clear piece of evidence, the criticism by Polybius of Phylarchus' figures for the wealth of Megalopolis when seized by Cleomenes (Pol. 2.63). Polybius asserts that the maximum that the city could have held would be some 300 talents, and that there was probably at most 6,000 talents in the whole of the Peloponnese. For comparison, he points out that the total capital of Athens, including fixed and moveable property, was less than 6,000 talents in 378. The value of the plunder of Mantinea, including from the sale of captives, is given as 300 talents – counting the sale of captives as 225 talents, this leaves only 75 talents from property in Mantinea, with a population of perhaps 12,000. Although, for example, the account of Philip V's campaigns is full of occasions of towns being plundered, it should not always be assumed that the army was enriched by this; for example, only the most easily carried plunder could be taken away, and bulky objects might have to be destroyed (e.g. Pol. 5.8) to retain the army's manoeuvrability. If the army became overburdened with plunder, then it would have to be sold quickly (Pol.5.75, 77), and this would not always have been easy. Also, it is easy to confuse the plundering of a town or area with the seizure of grain from that area – in Diodorus (19.12), Eumenes avoids plundered country so that his men can obtain supplies. Philip V often seized grain as plunder (Pol.4.63, 5.8,19, 10.42, 16.24), and a country was sometimes devastated, meaning that the crops were destroyed, rather than goods being seized from it (Pol.4.67, 5.7; Plut. *Cleom.* 26). Also, some captured cities could not be handed over to the army to be plundered for political reasons – for example, those in Coele-Syria captured by Antiochus III (Pol. 5.62). When Demetrius ravaged Babylonia, held by Seleucus I, this was thought to indicate an admission that the country no longer belonged to his father Antigonus (Plut. *Dem.* 7.3).

Seizure of treasures may have brought more wealth. Ptolemy III is said to have taken 1,500 talents from Cilicia, and Antiochus IV to have seized an enormous plunder in Egypt in 168 (*I Macc.* 1.19), presumably including captured money as well as slaves and goods, and 1,800 talents from Jerusalem (*II Macc.* 5.21). Philip V plundered Thermum (Pol. 5.7–8), which was the treasury of the Aetolians. Plutarch lists the enormous treasures captured by Flamininus from Philip V (Plut. *Flam.* 14), although given Polybius' assertion that the Macedonian treasury contained only 6,000 talents, and Perseus' recovery (Liv. 45.40), it is likely that the Roman takings are exaggerated. Temples also held large sums and could be seized and plundered (e.g. Pol. 5.9, 21.9, 32.15). Antiochus III seized the treasures of Ecbatana, amounting to 4,000 talents, and coined them (Pol. 10.27), probably in order to pay the army. Similarly, Eumenes of Cardia had taken the treasures of Susa and used them to give a six-month advance of pay to his army (Diod. 19.15). The treasures taken by Ptolemy III in the Laodicean war are said to have amounted to 42,500 talents, but this too is surely an exaggeration: the Romans only demanded an indemnity of 12,000 talents over twelve years from Antiochus III (Liv. 38.38), and even this seems to have caused great difficulties, while Plutarch (*Aem.* 28.3) claims that the total tax revenue of Macedon was only a little over 200 talents. It is unlikely that the Seleucids possessed 42,500 talents, still less that they could have survived its loss.[29]

The sale of slaves might well have been the most lucrative aspect of plunder. War captives could be taken back and used in the home country, or even settled as military settlers, like the prisoners taken at Gaza. However, captives were normally sold as slaves. The most complete accounts of the seizure and sale of slaves are from the campaigns of Antigonos Doson and Philip V. That Antigonos raised 225 talents from Mantinea has already been mentioned. Philip V took 1,200 Aetolian captives (Pol. 5.68), who were sold at Corinth (4.69), and 5,000 Eleans at Thalamae, sold at Olympia (4.73, 75). His Achaean allies took and sold 2,000 prisoners (5.94, 95), and Philip at Pyrgos took 4,000 slaves (Liv. 27.32). There are other occasions where the figures are not known (for example, Pol. 5.99, 100, or the Achaean seizure of the Aetolian fleet, 5.94), or where captives were released, not sold (4.84). The income from these sales is (assuming a price of 150 drachmas per head), for Aetolian captives, 30 talents, for Eleans, 125 talents, 50 talents made by the Achaeans, and for Pyrgos, 100 talents.

Plutarch describes the disappointing proceeds from the Romans' coordinated and systematic plundering of the entire kingdom of Epirus:

> 'But when the appointed day came, at one and the same time these [the Roman forces] all set out to overrun and pillage the cities, so that in a single hour a hundred and fifty thousand persons were made slaves, and seventy cities were sacked; and yet from all this destruction and utter ruin each soldier received no more than eleven drachmas as his share, and all men shuddered at the issue of the war, when the division of a whole nation's substance resulted in so slight a gain and profit for each soldier.' (Plutarch, *Aemilius* 29.3)

Eleven drachmas would be very roughly two weeks' pay. Livy, however, has different sums for this same event, claiming that 'so great was the booty that a distribution was made of four hundred denarii apiece to the cavalry, and two hundred apiece to the infantry' (Liv. 45.34.5). Two hundred denarii is more like at least a year's pay. Given that the Roman army was apparently dissatisfied with this outcome, Plutarch's lower figure is perhaps more likely. But at any event, the asset-stripping of an entire country like this was a very rare event, and not something that would have been expected in any campaign by a Hellenistic king.

These sums were divided between the king and the army. The Macedonian regulations on the division of spoils have survived, though unfortunately the proportions are not mentioned. However, the king was limited by these regulations – Philip V was faced with a mutiny when his men suspected he was dividing the spoils unfairly (Pol. 5.25). Furthermore, even though captured grain was presumably distributed as rations, there is no reason to suppose that armies would accept plunder instead of, rather than in addition to, their regular pay, *opsonion*. The capture of plunder could provide an influx of cash to the kings, but the costs of paying an army of tens of thousands would greatly outweigh any of the figures discussed above, so it is unlikely that any king was able to turn a profit from a campaign by the seizure of plunder (though he might offset some loss). Rather, the capture of plunder was an event more likely to please the army than to enrich the king, and we have seen above that the distribution of plunder was a common method of winning the good will of the army.[30]

We should also keep in mind that the process of plundering a defeated city would have presented one of the grimmest aspects of warfare. As an example, Plutarch provides a sober account of the plundering of the Greek city of Pellene by the Aetolians:

'For as soon as they had entered the city, the common soldiers had scattered themselves among the houses, jostling and fighting with one another over the booty, while the leaders and captains were going about and seizing the wives and daughters of the Pellenians, on whose heads they put their own helmets, that no one else might seize them, but that the helmet might show to whom each woman belonged.' (Plutarch, *Aratus* 31.3)

More florid accounts of the sack of cities were a mainstay of Hellenistic historiography, but Hellenistic Greek practice was (as in other areas) restrained in comparison with that of the Romans, who exhibited utter brutality, often with the intention of terrorizing a populace rather than merely seizing material (or human) wealth, as famously described in Polybius' account of the Roman sack of New Carthage in Spain:

'When Scipio thought that a sufficient number of troops had entered he sent most of them, as is the Roman custom, against the inhabitants of the city with orders to kill all they encountered, sparing none, and not to start pillaging until the signal was given. They do this, I think, to inspire terror, so that when towns are taken by the Romans one may often see not only the corpses of human beings, but dogs cut in half, and the dismembered limbs of other animals, and on this occasion such scenes were very many owing to the numbers of those in the place.' (Polybius, 10.15.4–6)

Training, discipline and service

As discussed above, it is likely that only some proportion of the army was paid in peacetime, thus forming a full-time professional force with no occupation but military service. Probably only the guard units were mobilized permanently and so formed that part of the army which would have played the greatest part in the internal affairs of the kingdom, while other units may have been dispersed to their own lands; hence the difficulties experienced by Philip V with his Peltasts and their commanders, the importance of the Ptolemaic Macedonians in the usurpation of Agathocles, and very likely the disaffection of the Seleucid guard when their pay was stopped by Demetrius II. Command of the guard units, particularly the infantry guard, was also an important position of state, to be held by a powerful Friend.

It is possible that the Seleucid infantry guards, the *Argyraspides*, were drawn from the young men in the kingdom, the sons of the military settlers who were liable to serve in the main phalanx, and as such they may perhaps be seen as the means by which the settlers' loyalty and attachment to the kings was maintained. After a period of service in the guard units, the soldiers would be retired back to their lands, to be succeeded by the next age class, hence ensuring that the settlers, even if not mobilized, at least had their share of military experience and of proximity to the king. In Macedon, the Peltasts were recruited from the more wealthy element of the population, and from the age groups up to 45 (for the Agema) or 35 (for the rest of the Peltasts), so regular Peltasts at least could conceivably also be sons of still-active phalangites. The Ptolemies too have similar guard units – the *Therapeia* (Household) in Alexandria. These guard units, along with the mercenaries in Alexandria, appear to have been the only permanently mobilized soldiers in Egypt, although it is interesting that they seem to play no part in the affair of Cleomenes; Polybius states that the only soldiers in Alexandria were the mercenaries (Pol. 5.36).[31]

For the bulk of the phalanx, military service was probably a more occasional (though potentially long-term) requirement. Only in Macedon do we have details, thanks to the survival of conscription regulations setting out the rules for conscription and service. These reveal a remarkably complex and well-developed bureaucracy which kept track of the age (and so date, or at least year, of birth) and status of every potential recruit, with rules for how each household was to supply recruits. Conscription was determined by household rather than applying on an individual level, presumably so as to ensure that men remained at home to carry out agricultural or other essential tasks even when the army was fully mustered. Whether such rules were also applied in the other kingdoms – and indeed whether these conscription rules applied for the whole period or were a product of the manpower shortages experienced at the start of the second century under Philip V – is unclear. The conscription rules do appear to be fairly generous to the populace in terms of requiring only one man per household, so do not give the impression of emergency measures in times of great manpower shortage.[32]

So conscription was levied at the level of the household, and two ways of grouping the recruits were important – their age class and their location (home city or region). As we have seen, Alexander's phalanx was levied by region and, although later in his reign the formation of region-specific *taxeis* appears to have been discontinued, it seems likely that conscription would still have been on a regional basis, if only because it would obviously be most effective to centre recruitment and its administration around the major population centres (the cities), as would have been true also for the Seleucids, especially in Syria. Age classes were the means by which the size of the muster was determined, by calling up all recruits of a given age range (this had also been the common practice in many Greek cities). Before the Cynoscephalae campaign, Philip V, finding himself short of recruits, was forced to extend the conscription age range: 'Mere youths, therefore, from the age of sixteen, were enlisted; and even those who had served out their time, provided they had any remains of strength, were recalled to their standards' (Liv. 33.3.4–5).

The division into age classes was also important for the purposes of military training. It appears that there were three youth age classes: boys or *paides* of 14–18 years old, *ephebes* of 18–20 and *neoi* or *neaniskoi* of 20–30. The *ephebes* (as in some Greek cities) were required to undertake training at city *gymnasia*, following a state curriculum that covered all sorts of physical training including weapons handling – with the weapons in question including bows and javelins, a reminder that the men of the phalanx may also have been capable of fighting outside the ranks of the phalanx. There was a Greek precedent for this, the philosopher Plato having recommended such training in his ideal city:

> 'We are establishing gymnasia and all physical exercises connected with military training – the use of the bow and all kinds of missiles, light skirmishing and heavy-armed fighting of every description, tactical evolutions, company-marching, camp-formations, and all the details of cavalry training. In all these subjects there should be public instructors, paid by the State; and their pupils should be not only the boys and men in the State, but also the girls and women who understand all these matters.' (Plato, *Laws* 7.813–4)

Plato was of course describing a Utopian ideal rather than actual practice in any Greek city, and there is no indication that Macedon or any of the Hellenistic kingdoms (or Greek states) took Plato's advice to train girls too.[33]

In slightly unusual circumstances late in his reign, Alexander applied this training regime to the native inhabitants of his new empire:

> 'Now there came to Susa at this time a body of thirty thousand Persians, all very young and selected for their bodily grace and strength. They had been enrolled in compliance with the king's orders and had been under supervisors and teachers of the arts of war for as long as necessary. They were splendidly equipped with the full Macedonian armament and encamped before the city, where they were warmly commended by the king after demonstrating their skill and discipline in the use of their weapons ... . Alexander had formed this unit from a single age-group of the Persians which was capable of serving as a counter-balance [*antitagma*] to the Macedonian phalanx.' (Diodorus, 17.108.103)

Arrian (*Anab.* 7.6.1) tells us that this force was called *Epigoni* (Successors); their arrival caused considerable ill-will among the Macedonians (though Diodorus puts it the other way around in saying that they were intended as a counter to already ill-willed Macedonians). As we have seen, arming the native population in this way was an unusual step, and there is no evidence that the practice was continued under the Successors or other kingdoms until the Egyptian mobilization before Raphia, though these men may appear as the otherwise mysterious *pantodapoi*, 'all sorts', who formed part of the phalanx of some

Successor armies. The point here is the central organization and recruitment, enrolment by age class (and at a young age – these were perhaps *neoi*, having been trained as *ephebes*), state training under teachers and trainers, and centralized supply of equipment, which all reflect the normal Macedonian practice, though on a very large scale.

So physical fitness, weapons use and drill would have been taught to all young men, but it was also necessary to keep up this training in later years, and to train specifically as part of a formed unit. Refresher training was also necessary at the start of a major campaign, as some recruits might not have actually served for several years if there had been no need for a full muster. As we have seen, Philip II's initial invention of the phalanx contained a strong element of drill and training: 'he held constant manoeuvres of the men under arms and competitive drills' (Diod. 16.13.1). Note the competitive nature of the drills, as competition was central to Greek and Macedonian education, with awards and prizes for those who excelled in each subject or at the various special parades and ceremonies. Diodorus comments that Alexander on his accession continued these practices: 'He busied his soldiers with constant training in the use of their weapons and with tactical exercises, and established discipline in the army' (Diod. 17.2.3; it would be better to say that he maintained discipline rather than established it, as there is no reason to suppose discipline had declined under Philip). The preparations for the Battle of Raphia involved the reshaping of the Ptolemaic army by Ptolemy IV's ministers:

'First of all they divided them [the recruits] according to their ages and nationalities, and provided them in each case with suitable arms and accoutrements, paying no attention to the manner in which they had previously been armed; in the next place they organized them as the necessities of the present situation required, breaking up the old regiments and abolishing the existing paymasters' lists, and having effected this, they drilled them, accustoming them not only to the word of command, but to the correct manipulation of their weapons.' (Polybius, 5.64.1)

Mock battles could also form part of the training programme. Livy describes the military parade held by Philip V late in his reign, in which the army was first purified by marching between the two halves of a dog (a curious practice):

'It was the custom when the ceremony of purification was finished to manoeuvre the army and dividing it into battle-lines to clash in a sham battle. The princes [Philip's sons] were assigned as commanders for this mock engagement: yet it was not the imitation of a battle, but they came together just as if it were a struggle for the throne, and many wounds were dealt by the un-pointed weapons, nor was anything but iron wanting to make it look like a regular battle.' (Livy, 40.6.5–6)

Presumably wooden weapons without metal parts were used for such encounters.

When Philopoemen reformed the Achaean army after the Macedonian fashion, this involved, as well as a change of equipment, the introduction of a similar programme of drill and training, and the fostering of a competitive spirit:

'After he had thus arrayed and adorned the young men, Philopoemen exercised and drilled them, and they eagerly and emulously obeyed his instructions. For the new order of battle pleased them wonderfully, since it seemed to secure a close array that could not be broken; and the armour which they used became light and manageable for them, since they wore or grasped it with delight because of its beauty and splendour, and wished to get into action with it and fight a decisive battle with their enemies as soon as possible.' (Plutarch, *Philopoemen* 9.7–8)

A similar training regime had also knocked the Achaean cavalry into shape:

'He [Philopoemen] went round to the different cities and roused the spirit of ambition in each young man individually, punished those who needed compulsion, introduced drills, parades, and competitive contests in places where there would be large bodies of spectators and thus in a short time inspired them all with an astonishing vigour and zeal.' (Plutarch, *Philopoemen* 7.4)

Before the Pydna campaign, Perseus held a similar review of his army at Citium:

'The array of the review was set briefly in motion (not however in a regular manoeuvre), so that they might not seem to have merely stood under arms; the king summoned them, in arms as they were, to an assembly. He himself stood on a platform, having about him his two sons ... [Perseus then described the Roman forces] ... let them consider their own army, how much it excelled in numbers and in type of soldiers, how much they, trained in the arts of warfare from boyhood, disciplined and hardened in so many wars, excelled these [Roman] recruits hastily enrolled for this war.' (Livy, 42.51.4–10)

This point is important too, as for all the importance given to training and the effort expended on it, the best training for war was experience of war itself, as Livy comments:

'The twenty-sixth year was passing, since peace had been granted to Philip [V] at his request; throughout all that time unmolested Macedonia had both produced offspring, a large number of whom were of military age, and yet, in minor wars with her Thracian neighbours, of a sort to give training rather than to produce weariness, had been unremittingly in arms.' (Livy, 42.52.1–2)

Minor wars with Thracian neighbours were considered the ideal way to maintain military excellence, and while no individual soldier would have been 'unremittingly in arms' through this period, some portion at least of the army was, and this allowed experience to be shared across the whole of the population. The lack of such constant practical experience perhaps accounts for the decline of the Ptolemaic army before Raphia, where the country's isolated position meant that more regular service was entrusted to mercenaries, allowing the men of the phalanx too much leisure.

It is also worth noting here that, as in the comments earlier about the phalangites' ability to take part in siegecraft or other operations, they were also able to take to sea. Philip V decided to man a fleet for his campaign against the Spartans and their allies:

'Having resolved on this he collected at the Lechaeum the Achaean ships and his own, and by constant practice trained the soldiers of the phalanx to row. The Macedonians obeyed his orders in this respect with the utmost alacrity, for they are not only most intrepid in regular battles on land, but very ready to undertake temporary service at sea, and also industrious in digging trenches, just as Hesiod represents the sons of Achaeus to be "joying in war as if it were a feast".' (Polybius, 5.2.4–6)

We have seen that the soldiers (and citizens generally) had an expectation of being allowed a certain frankness of speech before their king (and direct access to him to vent their grievances), and that they played a political role in the kingdom. We have also seen occasions where soldiers became mutinous, or at least unruly, often due to disputes over pay. But as soldiers on active duty, they were also subject to military discipline. Classical Greek armies did not have a strong tradition of military discipline in the way we would now understand it, that is the unquestioning and immediate following of orders, with harsh punishments for rules transgressions of any kind. Being (except the Lacedaemonians) citizen militias with a more egalitarian ethos, a lack of defined officer structure and rotating or elected commanders, Greek army discipline appears to have been based more on peer pressure and shared interests and values. The Macedonian monarchy could expect a higher level of obedience from its subjects, and it does seem to have been a central part of Philip's reform to instill military discipline in his new army, in particular with regard to the rapid and efficient execution of drill in response to the orders of officers at every level, without which the Macedonian phalanx would have been unable to function effectively (and which in turn made the Macedonian phalanx more flexible and easier to control than most Classical Greek phalanxes). The exhortation of Alexander before Gaugamela quoted by Arrian (*Anab.* 3.9.8) – the officers 'were to urge each man ... to attend to his own place in the line ... to keep perfect silence when that was necessary ... to obey orders sharply and to pass them on sharply to their *taxeis*' – well illustrates what was expected of the soldiers of the phalanx, but note also that the reason for such obedience was that 'every man should recall that neglect of his own duty brought the cause into common danger while energetic attention to orders contributed to the common success'. I think this is a telling combination: quick obedience to orders was the way to further the common good, not to avoid punishment. Where in many Early Modern armies (particularly of the gunpowder era), drill and obedience were enforced by harsh punishment, in the Macedonian phalanx they seem to have been accepted for the common good. This is to be expected given the combination of the political role of the soldiers, and the tradition of freedom of speech with their kings.[34]

There certainly were harsh – usually capital – punishments meted out by the kings (particularly Alexander), but these were usually for high-ranking officers or officials, and for offences such as rebellion or plotting against the king's life rather than for infringements of military discipline. While flogging was known, it does not seem to have been a common punishment. Curtius (8.6.5) claims that flogging could only be administered by the king, though this might depend on who was being flogged – Aelian records that Philip II flogged one and executed another son of Macedonian nobles, presumably royal pages, for breaches of discipline (Ael. *Varia Historia* 14.48). Uniquely for the later Antigonid army we have a code of military discipline (the Amphipolis regulations) which sets out a number of fines for various infringements, chiefly concerning failure to have the proper equipment, as well as rules for the collection and distribution of plunder and posting of sentries. It is difficult to tell how typical these rules may be for Hellenistic armies generally (they may be a special response to wars with Rome and the Peltasts' grievances over plunder), but assuming they are typical, what is striking is that even what we would think might be quite serious offences (such as failing to have a shield or sarissa, absolutely essential for every phalangite, or falling asleep on sentry duty) were punished with a modest fine (a day's pay or less). The use of fines as punishments for infringements for military discipline contrasts markedly with European armies in recent centuries (where corporal punishments were the norm) and particularly with Roman armies, where capital punishment was common for many offences (e.g. Pol. 6.37 for sentries). The Macedonian phalanx appears to have been a very highly drilled formation, but one with relatively benign (though not slack) discipline. The emphasis was on leadership, inspiration and consent, not on coercion and punishment.[35]

Attitudes to war

The Hellenistic phalangite was usually a farmer or landowner of moderate means, likely living on land granted by the king and liable to be called up for service in times of war. How would he have felt on receiving his call-up? It is notoriously difficult to discover popular attitudes to war in the ancient world, but it is at least likely that to some elements in society war had many attractions. As we have seen, the function of plunder was probably largely to please the armed forces, so it may well be that there would be popular enthusiasm for war in order to make available opportunities for such enrichment. There were several groups outside the regular armies who sought plunder particularly actively: at the siege of Rhodes, Demetrius was joined by 'about 1,000 privately owned ships, which belonged to those who were engaged in trade; for since the land of the Rhodians had been unplundered for many years, there had gathered together from all quarters a host of those who were accustomed to consider the misfortunes of men at war a means of enriching themselves', (Diod. 20.82.5). Similar are the Aetolians and the Illyrians: the Aetolians, for example, being annoyed at a general peace with all the Greeks as it cut off their normal sources of plunder (Pol. 5.107.5–7). That Polybius singles out these peoples for criticism, however, implies that their attitude was the exception not the norm – and later the Aetolians are said to have been in debt through constant war and their extravagant way of life (Pol. 13.1). Although plunder could enrich the common soldiers, it is also important not to overestimate its monetary value, as it is likely that only upon the capture of a major city or treasury would significant wealth be available, as we have seen. There were also elements in society – in particular the professional or mercenary soldiers – to whom war was necessary in order to make a living. In Athens there was support for the Lamian War from 'those who preferred war and were accustomed to make their living from paid military service ... these were the men of whom Philip once said that war was peace and peace was war for them' (Diod. 18.10.1). The implication of this passage is that the other elements of society would not desire war. A military career could be attractive in the third century, however, even for the relatively well off, if the propaganda view of the poet Theocritus (whose works extol the virtues of military service in the Ptolemaic army) is accurate, and it is likely, as we will see in Chapter 5, that many mercenaries in the Hellenistic period were not of the class Diodorus describes but were citizen contingents from allied cities. The remaining professional mercenaries could expect to find long-term employment in the various kingdoms' garrisons irrespective of a state of war or peace.

Aside from such special groups, the political awareness and involvement of the regular armies should not be underestimated. The soldiers did not of course have any say in the formulation of foreign policy, but as we have seen above, they were at least interested in the affairs of the kingdom and it was important to win popular support for a war as much as for any other aspect of royal policy. Such support clearly was normally gained by the standard combination of gifts and promises, but armies were also interested in wider aspects of policy, particularly if their own homeland was threatened. The address to his army by Perseus at Citium (as recounted by Livy) provides a clear demonstration of the motivations of the mass of the soldiers, or at least of the way a king could play upon them, with a combination of an outraged sense of fair play, confidence in themselves, their leaders and arrangements for the war, and patriotic support for their own country:[36]

'[Perseus] cheered the soldiers on to the war; he recited the wrongs done by the Roman people to his father and himself; the former had been driven by all sorts of outrages to fight back ... . [The soldiers] must have, too, the spirit which their ancestors had possessed, who, having subdued all Europe, had crossed to Asia and opened up with their arms a whole world unknown even to rumour, and had not ceased their conquests, until, within the barrier of the Indian Ocean, there was nothing left for them to conquer. But now, by Hercules, fortune had proclaimed a contest, not for the furthermost shores of India, but for the possession of Macedonia itself. When the Romans had been waging war with his father, they had held out the plausible pretext of the freedom of Greece; now openly they sought to enslave Macedonia, that there might be no king neighbouring the Roman empire, that no people famed in war might keep its arms. All these things they must surrender to haughty masters, along with their king and kingdom, if they wished to cease waging war and do the bidding of others. Although throughout all the speech there had been often enough outbursts of applause, at that moment indeed such an outcry arose from those who were at once enraged and threatening, while some of them bade the king be of good cheer, that he put an end to his speech, merely ordering them to prepare for a march.' (Livy, 42.52–3)

As to wider attitudes to the relative desirability of war or peace, Polybius at least often bewails the evils that result from war, but he shows throughout his narrative great enthusiasm for those who wage war within the confines of his own rules. The poet Theocritus' *Idyll* 16 is in part an account of the joys of peace – 'grant that towns which the hands of foes have wasted utterly be peopled again by their ancient masters … may spiders spin their delicate webs over armour, and the cry of onset be no more even named' (ll. 85 f.). However, this is peace only after the defeat of the enemy in war – 'grant that ill constraints may drive our enemies from the island over the Sardinian sea with tidings of the death of dear ones to children and wives'. Diodorus describes the scenes in Antioch on the news of the annihilation of the army of Antiochus VII – 'not only did the city go into public mourning, but every private house as well was dejected and filled with lamentation. Above all, the wailing of the women inflamed their grief … . Some were mourning the loss of brothers, some of husbands, and some of sons, while many girls and boys, left orphaned, wept for their own bereavement' (Diod. 34/35.17). Such scenes would, however, be associated not with war but with defeat, and the greatest danger facing the inhabitants of a city was that it fall to an enemy army, the result of which could well be the massacre or enslavement of the entire population. Successful war would be a means by which this fate could be avoided, or inflicted on the people's enemies, so there would be no opposition to the concept of war as such, provided it was waged successfully.[37]

Ptolemaic Egypt, with its documents on papyri, provides some rare examples of letters from ordinary soldiers; these tend to reveal a matter-of-fact attitude, along with attempts to reassure families left at home. For example, a soldier named Esthladas, involved in the mid-second-century dynastic conflicts in Egypt, wrote home to his father, the cavalry officer Dryton (we can't tell for sure what unit or even arm Esthladas served with):

'Esthladas to his father and mother, greeting and good health. As I keep writing to you to keep up your courage and take care of yourself until things settle down, once again please encourage yourself and our people. For news has come that Paos [the king's general] is sailing up in the month of Tybi with abundant forces to subdue the mobs in Hermonthis, and to deal with them as rebels. Greet my sisters also and Pelops and Stachys and Senathyris. Farewell.' (Bagnall and Derow, 2004, p.53)

Evidently there was no censorship of letters in Ptolemaic Egypt, and no concept that 'careless talk costs lives'.

An idea of the pride in military service felt by many soldiers (not necessarily, strictly speaking, phalangites) can be gained from the painted and inscribed tombs and tombstones depicting the deceased in their military attire, fully armed, or recounting their heroic exploits in battle. An example is the epigram of the Bithynian officer (*hegemon*) Menas:

'Although a long tomb contains my bones, stranger, I did not shrink back in view of the heavy weight of the enemies. Although I fought on foot I stood my ground in front of riders among those who fought in the first line [*promachoi*], when we battled in the plain of Kouros. After I had hit a Thracian in his armour and a Mysian, I died because of my great bravery. For this, may someone praise the swift Menas, son of Bioeris, the Bithynian, an excellent officer.' (SGO I 09/05/16)

A second epigram records that Menas died 'for my fatherland and for my parents'. It is likely that such attitudes represent general Hellenistic values.[38]

So the combination of a strong Macedonian military tradition, admiration for martial virtues, the possibilities of enrichment and adventure through war, a professional military class who saw soldiering as a way of life and the importance of protecting one's homeland from enemy invasion mean that attitudes toward war were probably highly favourable amongst the men who made up the phalanx. Morale for any given battle or campaign may not always have been high, depending on leadership and immediate prospects, but in general war was regarded not just as a necessary evil but often as a desirable state. How this translated into performance on the battlefield, along with other considerations relating to battlefield morale, will form part of the subject of Chapter 8.

Chapter 5

Manpower and recruitment

We have seen how the Macedonian phalanx was equipped and organized, and have examined the role of the phalangites within the kingdom they served. In this chapter I will be looking at the wider picture, and the arrangements made within each kingdom to ensure a supply of men to serve in the phalanx.

Macedonians, Greeks and others

The kings of the Hellenistic kingdoms in Asia ruled over considerable numbers of native peoples; yet despite this, as we have seen, they wanted to establish a pool of Greco-Macedonian manpower from which they could draw their phalanxes. It was a commonly held view in this period that Greeks (including Macedonians) were militarily inherently superior to non-Greeks. So, for example, Polybius could comment on the Alexandrian population that they were 'superior to the mercenaries [in Alexandria] because, although they were a mixed lot they were of Greek origin and had not forgotten their common Greek way of life' (Pol. 34.14.6). In Greek military thought, ethnic distinctions were important, and armies were frequently built up around units of uniform ethnic groups, often with distinctive national equipment. Certain nationalities were thought of as particularly skilled at certain types of fighting. Polybius (himself an Achaean) comments that:

'the Cretans both by land and sea are irresistible in ambuscades, forays, tricks played on the enemy, night attacks, and all petty operations which require fraud, but they are cowardly and down-hearted in the massed face-to-face charge of an open battle. It is just the reverse with the Achaeans and Macedonians.' (Polybius, 4.8.12)

There were also ethnic weapon specializations, so that if a particular type of soldier was required – archers or slingers, for example – then a unit of the nationality that specialized in that armament – Cretan archers, or Rhodian slingers – would be raised. In certain cases, perhaps where demand outstripped supply or when political considerations prevented the recruitment of a given group, the national equipment desired could be issued to another group. There were, for example, units of Carians and Cilicians armed in the Cretan manner in the Seleucid army (Liv. 33.3.10, 37.40.13, 42.55.10). In some cases it may well be that the ethnic designation applied to a particular unit was based not on the true ancestral origins of the individuals in the unit but on the armament carried; in particular, the Macedonian phalanx of the Seleucid army (described as Macedonian at Pol. 30.25.5) is usually supposed to have consisted in reality of a mixture of (originally Greek) ethnic groups armed in the Macedonian fashion. Other units certainly bear a military 'pseudo-ethnicity' of this sort, such as the Tarentine cavalry, whose connection, if any, with the Italian city of Tarentum is unclear. In Ptolemaic Egypt, military pseudo-ethnics became increasingly common, with enrolment in a given unit or, later, admission to a *politeuma* (a sort of military-political club open to soldiers) involving a corresponding change in ethnic designation. However, while it is clear that such 'fake' units did exist, and no doubt became increasingly common during the second century (when there was no access to fresh recruits from Greece), more often when a unit of a particular ethnicity or specialization was required it was obtained from individuals of that type.[1]

This could be done in one of two ways: a unit or individuals could be obtained from the supplying state, whether as mercenaries, allies or subject auxiliaries, or alternatively immigrants of the desired type could be attracted (or brought) to the kingdom and granted plots of land on which they would settle. Such settlers would not always retain their national armament; the vast majority of settlers in the Ptolemaic, Seleucid and Attalid kingdoms were an assortment of Greeks and Macedonians armed in the Macedonian fashion and fighting in the phalanx. Other units did retain their national arms, however; Thracians and Gauls from settlements in Egypt fought at Raphia, in units separate from the phalanx and so presumably with their original weapons (Pol. 5.65.10), and at Paraitacene there were 500 Thracian cavalry from colonies in the Upper Satrapies (Diod. 19.27.5). However, the core of all the armies were the 'Macedonian' units. It was clearly highly important that these units be considered Macedonian, whatever their true origins. The settlers in Seleucid Asia Minor are always termed Macedonians in inscriptions, even into the Roman period. The Romans for their part claimed in their propaganda that the Seleucid phalanx was composed not of true Macedonians but of Syrians, for it was the Macedonians who were considered the experts at phalanx warfare and who were most to be feared as opponents. The Roman general Glabrio, before Thermopylae in 191, is supposed to have said in a speech to his army that in an earlier engagement the enemy had been:

'superior in the quality of the soldiers. There, as you well know, they were Macedonians, Thracians and Illyrians – all very warlike races; here you have Syrians and Asiatic Greeks, the most worthless types of men, born for slavery.' (Livy, 36.17.5)

Livy also claimed that the settlers in Asia were no longer true Macedonians:

'The Macedonians who hold Alexandria in Egypt, who dwell in Seleucia and Babylonia and in other colonies scattered throughout the world, have degenerated into Syrians, Parthians, Egyptians.' (Livy, 38.17)

The availability of Macedonians to the various kingdoms and the origin of those forces that made up the bulk of their armies was therefore of great importance.

Only in Macedon itself was a supply of native Macedonians available. It is often thought that the population of Macedon was considerably reduced by the campaigns of Alexander and their aftermath, leading to the relative enfeeblement of Macedon compared to the other Hellenistic kingdoms, although there is an alternative view that Alexander's campaigns in fact had little long-term impact. Since the armies of the kingdoms in Asia were made up at least in some proportion of Macedonians, there can be little doubt that there was a considerable movement of the population of Macedon into the newly opened-up East, and, as we will see, most of the military settlers were drawn from the Greeks and Macedonians of the Successor armies. In the period of the Successors, true Macedonians were regarded as a valuable resource, and each general eagerly tried to obtain some whenever they were available, through enrolling the defeated army of an opponent or by diplomatic agreement with the possessor of a supply. Thus, for example, Eumenes, having defeated the army of Neoptolemus, 'increased his own power … by having acquired a large number of Macedonians, (Diod. 18.29.5), and after defeating Craterus he invited his Macedonians to join him, although they later deserted (18.32). Lysimachus, upon defeating an army of Antigonus, ransomed some of the captives and enrolled others in his own army (Diod. 19.73.10), and Asander, satrap of Caria, agreed to transfer his soldiers to Antigonus (Diod. 19.75.1). Antigonus distributed Ptolemaic captives in 316 among his own ranks (Diod. 18.39.2). Ptolemy sent the captives from Gaza to be distributed around Egypt (Diod. 19.85.4), and in 309 captured and distributed in his own army the soldiers of another army of Antigonus (Diod. 20.27.3). By the agreement between Polyperchon and Cassander, in which Polyperchon killed his candidate for the Macedonian throne, Polyperchon received in return 4,000 Macedonians (Diod. 20.28.3). Demetrius captured a Ptolemaic army on Cyprus and 'distributed them among the units of his own soldiers'; when they attempted to desert he sent them off instead to Antigonus, who at that time was founding Antigoneia in Syria (Diod. 20.47.4–5).[2]

However, whether Macedon itself really suffered from severe long-term manpower shortages, at least up to the early third century, is doubtful. Firstly, impressive armies continued to be raised from Macedon by the Successors. Diodorus (18.12.2) does state that Macedon under Antipater was 'short of citizen soldiers because of the number of those who had been sent to Asia as replacements for the army [of Alexander]', but this is in the context of a passage describing Antipater mustering 13,000 Macedonians and leaving Sippas with 'a sufficient army' in Macedon, so still a sizeable force. The army of Antipater at the end of the Lamian War consisted of 40,000 infantry, 3,000 light troops and 5,000 cavalry (Diod. 18.16.5). Cassander raised a force of 29,000 infantry and 2,000 cavalry (Diod. 20.110.4); considering that other forces were in Asia with Lysimachus (Diod. 20.107.1) and that Demetrius had an army of 56,000 at the time which included 8,000 Macedonians – 6,000 of whom were defectors from Cassander (Plut. *Dem.* 23.2) – this is not an unimpressive total (it is larger than that used by Antigonus Doson at Sellasia, with 13,300 Macedonians in an army of 29,200; Pol. 2.65.1). Other impressive armies with at least a Macedonian core abound: Demetrius in 288 raised an army of 98,000 infantry and 12,000 cavalry, according to Plutarch (*Dem.* 43.2), an army 'the like of which no man had possessed since Alexander' (44.1). While fighting Pyrrhus, Demetrius has 10,000 infantry and 1,000 cavalry in Thessaly in addition to an army large enough to besiege Thebes (Plut. *Dem.* 40.1–2). There were frequent recruitment campaigns in Macedon – by Sippas, Leonnatus, Craterus and Perdiccas, for example. While it is impossible to establish the exact Macedonian element in such armies, it is at least clear that the Macedonians remained militarily vigorous into the early third century at least.[3]

Secondly, even though Macedon was weaker under the Antigonids than under Philip II and Alexander, it is doubtful whether there was a great difference between Macedon and the other Hellenistic kingdoms. Philip V could gather, for the crisis of Cynoscephalae, 16,000 Macedonians of the phalanx, plus 2,000 Peltasts and 2,000 cavalry. This figure compares reasonably well with the contemporary Ptolemaic and Seleucid Macedonian forces: for Ptolemy at Raphia, either 5,000 or 25,000 in the phalanx, plus 6,000 guards and cavalry; for Antiochus, 20,000 in the phalanx and up to 16,000 cavalry and *Argyraspides* at Raphia, and at Magnesia 16,000 in the phalanx plus perhaps 6,000 cavalry and *Argyraspides*. (The size of the Ptolemaic phalanx at Raphia is uncertain due to difficulties with Polybius' account, which I will consider further below). The phalanxes of the three kingdoms are comparable, around 20,000 strong (including peltasts), and this even though the Ptolemies and Seleucids included many non-Macedonians in their phalanxes, while the Antigonids, so far as we know, still raised their phalanx solely from Macedonians. Thus in terms of numbers of Macedonians, Antigonid Macedon was at least as strong as and very likely stronger than the other Hellenistic kingdoms (unsurprisingly). Some estimate of the number of Macedonians in the Ptolemaic army may be arrived at from the percentage of Macedonian cleruchs attested in Egypt; 23.6 per cent of cleruchs with an ethnic designation are Macedonians, which means we might expect, if the Ptolemaic non-Egyptian phalanx was 25,000 strong, and including the 6,000 cavalry and guard, some 7,500 Macedonians in total. The figure for the Seleucids was no doubt comparable, though there is insufficient data for it to be computed. This figure is small in comparison with any period of Antigonid history.[4]

It is then unsafe to assume that the campaigns of Alexander alone drained Macedon of its manpower in the long term. Certainly, other factors will have adversely affected Macedonian manpower, in particular the incessant warfare between rival claimants to the throne up to the accession of Antigonus Gonatas and the damaging Gallic invasion of the early third century, in which Macedonian losses must have been high.

It is often supposed in addition that there was a process of steady emigration from Macedon, and indeed from the whole of Greece, to the new kingdoms of Asia. The common view is that mercenary service, or the attractions of a new life overseas, attracted emigrants from the Greek mainland to the Asian kingdoms at least until the end of the third century. However, we will see that the sources for the original military settlers, at least of the Seleucid and Ptolemaic kingdoms, were the armies of Ptolemy I, Antigonus Monophthalmos and Seleucus I, and that these original settlers were supplemented by individual emigration into the third century only to a limited degree.[5]

In Ptolemaic Egypt, the origins of the soldier settlers can be studied through the ethnic designations used in the official records recorded on papyrus. There are considerable difficulties with the use of these 'ethnics', as papyrologists call them, since it is clear that ethnics acquired an increasingly technical, fictitious meaning throughout the period, and that by the second century an ethnic is no longer a reliable indication of a soldier's true ethnic origin. We must also keep in mind that the usable sample of names is tiny in comparison with the total number of men who passed through the ranks of the army, and it is by no means certain in every case which papyri can be taken to refer to soldiers. An ethnic designation of some sort was a legal requirement in all official documents at least from the time of Ptolemy II, and exactly how an individual came by a given ethnic is not clear. By the second century, ethnic designations seem to have become entirely technical and bear no relation to a person's true ancestry. For example, documents reveal that one Dionysios, son of Kephalas, was classified first as Persian, then as Macedonian, and his brother as Libyan. Such designations in this period can therefore tell us nothing about patterns of immigration. The consensus appears to be, however, that in the third century at least the ethnic still provides a reliable indication of origin. There have been attempts to identify changes in the use of certain ethnic groups through time on the basis of this information, and in general it is assumed that there was a steady process of immigration into Egypt throughout the third century at least, and that the cleruchs were constantly augmented by these new arrivals. Only in the second century is it supposed that this flow of manpower ceased, so causing the decline in the cleruchic army. However, this view may well be incorrect.[6]

Firstly, it is apparent that the ethnics attested for soldiers at any given date cannot be taken as evidence of immigration at that date. In other words if, for example, an Athenian is attested in Egypt at the end of the third century, we cannot assume that he is himself an immigrant; he may merely be a descendant of an Athenian who emigrated at the end of the fourth century. This is so because there is no known designation for Greeks living in Egypt, other than the simple ethnic, that could indicate that they are themselves immigrants; the ethnic 'Athenian' must cover all those Greeks in Egypt who are Athenian or of Athenian descent. The term that might be thought to be an indication of descent from immigrant status, *tes epigones* (literally 'of the descent'), is the subject of much controversy as to its precise meaning (for example, some evidence suggests that it refers to civilian foreigners in Egypt with no official army position). The most likely explanation of the meaning of *tes epigones* is that it applies to the sons of cleruchs who have not yet succeeded to their father's position in the army. Objections have been raised to this theory, though not very strong ones perhaps. Although there are indeed cases of very old members of *tes epigones*, or those whose fathers are known to be dead, who might be expected to have succeeded to their fathers' *kleroi*, it is not impossible to offer explanations for these cases, which are anyway very much a minority. For example, the individual concerned may be physically unfit for military service and so never advance beyond the status of *tes epigones*. It is therefore possible that *tes epigones* does (or did originally) indeed mean 'son of a cleruch'. Nevertheless, the important point here is that even if those who are *tes epigones* are the sons of cleruchs, the status designation would be lost on succeeding to the cleruchy and so we are again in the position that all cleruchs, whether first-generation immigrants or distant descendants of immigrants, would be designated only by the simple ethnic. It is therefore not possible to make a certain identification of any cleruch as a first-generation immigrant, so even if immigration was an ongoing process it is impossible to reliably identify new periods of overseas recruitment through the ethnic designations of the cleruchs.[7]

Secondly, a study of the known ethnic origins of the cleruchs supports the suggestion that the majority were drawn from the original army of Ptolemy I and that there were no large-scale additions to their numbers after this. By examining the relative frequency of the ethnics in the papyri, it has been shown that most of the cleruchs are drawn from areas outside Ptolemaic influence in the third century, where we would not expect the Ptolemies to be able to recruit, while most mercenaries come from areas within the Ptolemaic area or sphere of influence, leading to the conclusion that most of the cleruchs, among whom there is a preponderance of Macedonians, were drawn from the army of Ptolemy I, along with forces acquired during the wars of the Successors. The only occasions when Ptolemy could have acquired Macedonians in large numbers after his arrival in Egypt were when he defeated the armies of Perdiccas (Diod. 18.19–21, 33–36), Antigonus Monophthalmos (20.37.1, 75.1, 76.7) and Demetrius. Additions to the cleruchic system after this period have often been postulated (for example, that mercenaries could become cleruchs), but for the third century at least this goes against the evidence of the ethnics in the papyri, at least if it were to have happened on a large scale. So it seems that the bulk of the cleruchs were formed from the original army of Ptolemy I.[8]

Seleucid settlers cannot be studied as individuals as they can in Egypt, and ethnic origins are not attested in the same way. However, it is clear at least that the scale of settlement in the late fourth century was very great, and it is likely that in terms of population the settlement of Seleucid Asia was largely complete by the beginning of the third century. For example, of the great cities of northern Syria and their attendant towns, Antioch on the Orontes was a refoundation by Seleucus of Antigoneia, founded by Monophthalmos in 307 (Diod. 20.47.5–6;

Strabo 16.2.4). The population originally contained 5,300 Macedonians and Athenians (Malalas 201.12–16), and it is likely that arrangements were made for the transfer of a large body of Athenians in 307. Demetrius established friendship and alliance with Athens, and the Athenians sent an embassy to Antigonos (Diod. 20.46.1, 46.4), who at that time 'was tarrying in upper Syria, founding a city on the Orontes river, which he called Antigoneia after himself' (47.5). Similarly, Seleucus' Apamea was a refoundation of a settlement of Macedonians; 'it used to be called Pella by the first Macedonian settlers because most of the Macedonian troops lived there' (Str. 16.2.10). Strabo adds that the city was to become the military headquarters of the Seleucid Empire. Seleucia in Pieria was also a refoundation of an earlier settlement called Hydatos Potamoi (Str. 16.2.8; cf. Diod. 19.79.6), the establishment of which may be attributed to Antigonus. Other towns bearing Macedonian names, such as Cyrrhos or Beroia, may similarly be identified as settlements of Macedonians from before the kingship was claimed by Seleucus, after which time new foundations tended to be named after the king or his family. The foundation of several other important Asian cities can be dated to the reign of Antigonus. Carrhai was settled by Macedonians by 311, when it was acquired by Seleucus (Diod. 19.91.1). Antiochus I founded Apamea Kibotos using the population of nearby Kelainai, which was probably also established by Antigonus (Str. 12.577–8). Four new cities in Media, foundations apparently of Seleucus (Rhagai-Europos, Heraclea, Apameia and Laodiceia), may have drawn on soldiers settled there by Antigonos, who is known to have distributed men in the region for the winter of 317/6 (Diod. 19.44.4, 46.1–5). Antigonus' and Eumenes' armies both contained Thracians from settlements in the Upper Satrapies (Diod. 19.27.27). Europos and possibly Nisibis were founded by a Nicanor, possibly Antigonos' satrap of Media. Settlements in Asia Minor must have been made at a later date if they are to be attributed to the Seleucids, since the area did not fall to the Seleucids until after the defeat of Lysimachus. However, it is important to also consider where the Seleucids will have obtained the Macedonians for such settlements; it is most likely that they are soldiers from the army, in which case they will have been drawn from Syria, from soldiers already settled or serving there.[9]

Many of the cities in existence under Seleucus I therefore at least made use of populations already in place by the end of the fourth century, and many of these settlers must themselves have been soldiers, who would in turn, with their descendants, serve in the Seleucid phalanx. Indeed, the strongly Macedonian character of many Seleucid settlements, if it is to be taken as evidence of at least a high proportion of true Macedonians, demonstrates that the settlement must have taken place in the fourth century or using soldiers already in Asia at that time, for Antigonus or Seleucus I would no more have been able to recruit in Macedon itself than would Ptolemy I.

The process of settlement of the Successor armies in the Seleucid and Ptolemaic kingdoms is illuminated by a number of examples. When Ptolemy I took 8,000 prisoners at Gaza, he 'sent the captured soldiers off into Egypt, ordering them to be distributed among the *nomes* [administrative regions]' (Diod. 19.85.5), presumably as cleruchs. A number of inscriptions show the settlement of mercenaries taking place in this period. In the agreement between Eupolemos, ruler of Caria, and Theangela for example, around 315, Eupolemos agrees to pay off or take into service the mercenary garrison, and permits those who so desire to settle in the nearby villages of Pentachora. Similar perhaps is the agreement between Ptolemy I and Iasos of 309, in which the garrison, having been paid off by the Iasians, may either leave the city or settle there as resident non-citizens. In the confrontation between Antigonos and Eumenes, Antigonos promised 'that to some of the Macedonians [under Eumenes] he would give a large gift of land, [and] would send back others to their homes with honours and gifts' (Diod. 19.23.3). At the end of the fourth century there was apparently a widespread desire among the soldiers in Asia to gain land – although we must of course remember that not all colonists were entirely willing, from the Greeks settled by Alexander in the Upper Satrapies, who 'longed for the Greek customs and manners of life and were cast away in the most distant part of the kingdom' (Diod. 18.7.1), to the *Argyraspides* captured by Antigonos and settled in 'secure and out of the way places' to keep them out of mischief (Polyaen. 4.6.15), or the plan of Antipater and Antigonos to move the Aetolians 'to the most distant desert of Asia' in punishment for their role in the Lamian War (Diod. 18.25.5).[10]

In general, then, the settlement of Asia was carried out largely during the final years of the fourth and beginning of the third century, and primarily using soldiers from the Successor armies. Large numbers of these soldiers were of course Macedonians, but the effect of this movement on Macedon was probably not that lasting, at least as regards Macedon's standing alongside the new kingdoms, and there was no continuous drain of Macedonian manpower to Asia. Those Macedonians who were to settle in the East had already left Macedon by the end of the fourth century. To this body of original settlers there would of course have been some additions, new immigrants (whether soldiers or civilians) and settled mercenaries, although on a scale lower (judging by the evidence for Egypt) than is sometimes thought.

In addition to newly settled soldiers, there were also large native populations which could be mobilized for military purposes. Clearly, considerable manpower resources were available, as some impressive numbers are mentioned; 8,000 Pisidians and 4,000 Aspendians, for example, fought in Asia Minor at the end of the third century (Pol. 5.73.3), while Ariarathes of Cappadocia could raise 30,000 infantry, natives and mercenaries in the late fourth century (Diod. 18.16.1). Antiochus III faced large forces in the East – Artabazanes' people were 'numerous and warlike and especially strong in cavalry' (Pol. 5.55), and Euthydemus' Bactrian kingdom raised 10,000 cavalry (Pol. 10.49.1). Under the Successors there were several units of indigenous peoples. Alcetas, for example, is said to have raised 6,000 Pisidians among a force of 17,000 men (Diod. 18.16.1), and Eumenes was joined in the Upper Satrapies by the satraps each with their satrapal army, consisting largely of natives. Peucestas raised 20,000 archers from Persis, the population of which was said to be very warlike, and the land densely populated (Diod. 19.21.3). Antigonus Monophthalmos made use of several units of natives: at Paraitacene, for example (Diod. 19.29.1–7), he has 3,000 Lycian and Pamphylian infantry – who appear again with Demetrius in Syria in 313 (19.69.1) – and at Gaza (19.82.4) 1,000 Lydian and Phrygian cavalry and 2,000 Median cavalry. Whether such forces fought as mercenaries is of course impossible to tell, as in practice there was no real difference between mercenaries and other forces in the Successor period. All soldiers must have been paid in some way, and until the armies started to settle on the land and in the new cities, there were no 'national' contingents. However, importantly, none of these contingents were armed in the Macedonian fashion or incorporated into the phalanx.

It is sometimes suggested that native forces may have been incorporated into some of the phalanxes, as for example the 'soldiers of all kinds [pantodapoi] armed in the Macedonian style' (Diod. 19.29.3) in the army of Antigonus at Paraitacene; these may be troops levied by the generals in their capacity as governors of the provinces. Peucestas joined Eumenes with large numbers of Persian archers and 3,000 pantodapoi armed in the Macedonian style (Diod. 19.14.5), who appear with Eumenes at Paraitacene 5,000 strong (19.27.6), and they may also have been formed from the 30,000 Epigoni recruited by Alexander, whom we met in the previous chapter. However, it is also possible that these were not native peoples. It is just as likely that they are a mixture of Greeks, perhaps the Greek mercenaries of Alexander, which would make their arming in Macedonian style more understandable.

In addition, not all settlers were Greco-Macedonians, and settlers were drawn from indigenous peoples living on the boundaries of the kingdom, for example the Mysian settlers in Seleucid Asia Minor (Pol. 5.77.7), who after the treaty of Apamea came under the control of Pergamon. In Egypt, Thracians and Gauls were introduced as settlers: Polybius (5.65.10) refers to a force at Raphia of Thracians and Galatians, 'some of them from the military settlers and their descendants, numbering about 4,000'. However, it seems that only in Egypt were indigenous peoples ever admitted to the phalanx itself.

Research into the question of the role of Egyptians in the Ptolemaic army is dogged by some basic uncertainties in the interpretation of the evidence. It is still not clearly decided how it is possible to identify a given individual as Egyptian, particularly in the later second century. For example, the wife of the 'Cretan' soldier Dryton, Apollonia Senmonthis, has been variously identified as a Hellenized Egyptian or as an Egyptianized Greek. It appears that by the second century it was possible for a soldier to have a Greek name and status as a result of his position within the army, but for him to be by descent an Egyptian, and to bear an Egyptian name in the context of local village affairs. Nevertheless, the use of Egyptians in the army can be studied on name evidence despite such problematical cases.[11]

There had in fact been some use of Egyptians before the second century, principally under Ptolemy I, the clearest example being the Battle of Gaza, where of the Ptolemaic army 'some were Macedonians and some were mercenaries [xenoi], but a great number were Egyptians, of whom some carried the missiles and the other baggage but some were armed and serviceable for battle'. These Egyptians were probably the traditional Egyptian warrior class, the machimoi, who, though they were armed for battle, had a status below that of the rest of the army until the time of Raphia, and did not form part of the phalanx (it is uncertain exactly how they were armed). Egyptians are said also to have taken part in the Chremonidean War (Paus. 3.6.5), although it is possible that here 'Egyptian' means 'Ptolemaic'. At the higher levels, there were figures such as Amphionis, 'Chief of the Army', or Nectanebo, 'Commander in Chief of the King's Army'; it is likely that these ranks were a survival from the Pharaonic period and that their holders retained their positions during Ptolemy's gradual acquisition of power. During most of the third century there is no evidence for high-ranking native Egyptians, but they occur again by the second half of the second century, including notable figures such as Dionysius Petosarapis, and several other Egyptians are known to have carried high honorary titles. Officers of lower rank within the army structure show the same contrast between the third and second centuries. There are no known Egyptian 'eponymous officers' (that is officers who gave their name to the unit they commanded; 'the men under Antigenes', for example) during the third century, and only seven out of 119 in the second and first centuries are known to have been Egyptian, and there are for example only two known Egyptian *hipparchs* (cavalry commanders) in the second century. Thus, although the officer class was not entirely closed to non-Greeks, access was very much restricted.[12]

In the other ranks of the army, Egyptians had originally formed the *machimoi* and been excluded from the other parts of the army, but this was to change by the second century. The greatest change in the use of Egyptians occurred before the Battle of Raphia; as part of the preparations to restore the kingdom to military readiness, a phalanx of 20,000 Egyptians was raised and armed in the Macedonian fashion (Pol. 5.65.9, 5.107.1–3). Exactly what this meant for the Egyptian *machimoi* is not clear; were the *machimoi* armed as Macedonians and enrolled in the main phalanx, or were Egyptians who were not previously soldiers recruited and armed? Whatever the procedure, the result was that henceforth Egyptians could become phalangites and cleruchs. At the same time, the originally strict ethnic divisions between the different parts of the army broke down. With the introduction of Egyptians into the cleruchic system, it has been suggested that the Greek cleruchs became designated as *katoikoi* (compare the similar use of this term in the Seleucid kingdom), but in fact it seems that there were also Egyptian *katoikoi*. Conversely, Greeks also appear in the *machimoi*, unless it is just that these are Egyptians who have taken Greek names.[13]

On the whole, then, there was little use made of the indigenous manpower of the kingdoms until the crisis of Raphia in Egypt, and when non-Greek manpower was used it was most often in the form of peoples from the outlying regions of the empire serving as auxiliaries. The reasons for this are partly to do with internal security and partly with the need to exclude some elements of the population from military functions. But in addition, some peoples were conceived, rightly or wrongly, as poor soldier (or at least, poor phalangite) material.

Non-Macedonian Greeks

So far we have been considering the populations of Macedonians and Greeks who could form the phalanx of the Hellenistic kingdoms. But the city-states of Greece continued to be independent (at least nominally) throughout this period, and continued to field citizen armies of quite considerable size. Aside from Sparta, most city-states grouped themselves into various leagues in this period, to pool their strength, and so we see the emergence of league, as opposed to just city, armies. The most important leagues were the Aetolians in west-central Greece, the Boeotians in east-central Greece and the Achaeans in the northern Peloponnese. These leagues would all have fielded hoplite armies in the Classical style during the fourth century (with the possible exception of the Aetolians, who specialized in cavalry and light infantry and were known more for raiding and irregular actions than for pitched battles). Their military arrangements in the third century are obscure, but it appears that some at least re-equipped their heavy infantry as *thureophoroi*, that is '*thureos*-carriers', the *thureos* being the rectangular or oval shield introduced into Greece by the Gallic invaders of the early third century. This may in some sense have been a development of the Iphicratean reform discussed in Chapter 1, where hoplites were equipped with light shields and longer spears in order to lighten their equipment. Perhaps the experience of the Gallic invasion persuaded some Greeks that lighter infantry of this sort were more useful than traditional hoplites – at least the account of the Achaean reforms (discussed below) suggests that such infantry were intended more for skirmishing than for close-order hand-to-hand fighting (although so far as we know they carried spears, not javelins). At the same time, some cities, particularly Sparta, seem to have continued to use traditional hoplites, so far as we can tell (there is in fact very little evidence either way). What is perhaps surprising, given the defeat of the Greek armies at the hands of the Macedonian phalanx at Chaeronea in the fourth century, and the spectacular success of the Macedonian phalanx in Asia under Alexander and the Successors (and its continued successes over Greek armies in, for example, the Lamian War), is that Greek cities did not earlier adopt Macedonian armament. It would be easy to put this down to military conservatism and the preservation of traditional forms of fighting, if it were not for the fact that *thureophoros* equipment was apparently adopted to replace traditional hoplite equipment.

At any rate, it is not until the late third century that we see Greek armies adopting Macedonian organization and equipment. The first to do so may have been the Boeotians, though here the picture is a little obscure. We know a lot about the Boeotian army thanks to numerous inscriptions detailing matters of recruitment and organization, which show Boeotian *thureophoroi* in the later third century being re-equipped as *peltophoroi* (*pelte*-carriers). As we have seen, *pelte* is one possible name for a rimless Macedonian shield, so this may be evidence for the adoption of Macedonian equipment; but we have also seen that the bulk of the Macedonian phalanx possibly used larger shields, perhaps rimmed, and later Greek reforms did not adopt a different kind of shield, so there is no simple relationship between *peltophoroi* and Macedonian phalangites. It is possible that the Boeotians were equipped as peltasts, in the Hellenistic sense of light phalangites (like the guard Peltasts of the kingdoms).[14]

The first certain cases of arming in the Macedonian fashion are the Spartans, and a Megalopolitan (Achaean) contingent gifted Macedonian equipment by Antigonus Doson. The Spartan rearmament took place under the revolutionary king Cleomenes, who undertook a series of reforms aiming to restore Sparta to its old power and conducted an ultimately unsuccessful war with the Achaeans and Antigonus' Macedon. We have already encountered this reform in the context of the discussion of equipment, but to reiterate:

> 'Then he filled up the body of citizens with the most promising of the free provincials [*perioikoi*], and thus raised a body of four thousand hoplites, whom he taught to use a sarissa, held in both hands, instead of a spear, and to carry their shields by a handle instead of by an armband.' (Plutarch, *Cleomenes* 11.2)

This force was later increased:

> 'Cleomenes … set free those of the Helots who could pay down five Attic minas (thereby raising a sum of five hundred talents), armed two thousand of them in Macedonian fashion as an offset to the White Shields of Antigonus.' (Plutarch, *Cleomenes* 23.1)

As discussed earlier, these appear to have been using the traditional shield with the sarissa. What is significant here is the way in which social and economic reforms are intimately tied up with the formation of a Spartan Macedonian-style phalanx. In order to raise the men necessary, Cleomenes extended the military franchise to *perioikoi* and helots (the Spartan serf class), an act similar in some ways to the Ptolemaic recruitment of native Egyptians into their phalanx before Raphia (although in this case the differences were social, not ethnic).

The Achaeans, for their part, shortly afterwards formed a Macedonian phalanx at the urging of their general Philopoemen:

> 'In the first place, however, he changed the faulty practice of the Achaeans in drawing up and arming their soldiers. For they used *thureoi* which were easily carried because they were so light, and yet were too narrow to protect the body; and spears which were much shorter than the Macedonian sarissa. For this reason they were effective in fighting at a long distance, because they were so lightly armed, but when they came to close quarters with the enemy they were at a disadvantage. Moreover, a division of line and formation into *speirai*

was not customary with them, and since they employed a solid phalanx without either levelled line of spears [*probole*] or wall of interlocking shields [*synaspismos*] such as the Macedonian phalanx presented, they were easily dislodged and scattered. Philopoemen showed them all this, and persuaded them to adopt sarissa and *aspis* instead of spear and *thureos*, to protect their bodies with helmets and breastplates and greaves, and to practise stationary and steadfast fighting instead of the nimble movements of light-armed troops [*peltastikes*].' (Plutarch, *Philopoemen* 9.1–2)

This appears to be a transition from *thureophoroi* to heavy phalangites, and did not in this case involve any social reforms but was purely a question of equipment, organization and training (which Plutarch goes on to detail). This Achaean phalanx was to later defeat the Spartans at the Battle of Mantinea, as the Macedonians had defeated the Spartans also at Sellasia.[15]

We should also remember Plutarch's comments on the effects of this reform on the self-confidence of the Achaean citizens, quoted in the previous chapter. We can imagine the effect of such an increase in self-confidence on a socially and economically disadvantaged class such as Egyptians or Helots.

Whether other Greek states also adopted Macedonian armament at this time is unknown. The kingdom of Pergamon in Asia Minor, which rose to prominence at the start of the second century, may have done so, but information on their army is sadly lacking, and later the Greek-Asian kingdom of Pontus did have a Macedonian phalanx (which we will encounter in Chapter 9). We can only say that Macedonian armament was adopted outside the Hellenistic (Macedonian-derived) kingdoms, but apparently not universally, and only after a considerable lapse of time and when driven by a forceful leader prepared to push through the necessary changes in organization and training, which may well have been more significant in the adoption of this armament than the simple difference of equipment.

Settlers and mercenaries

We have seen that the central elements of the armies of the Successor kingdoms (that is, broadly, their Macedonian-armed phalanxes) were drawn from settlers in cities, cleruchies or *katoikiai* in the new kingdoms, or from the indigenous Macedonian population of Macedon. But the Hellenistic age is also noted for another feature: the prevalence of mercenary recruitment and service.[16]

At the end of the fifth and during the fourth centuries, social and economic changes in Greece led to the creation of a class of impoverished, landless men who wandered through Greece and overseas and accepted work as mercenary soldiers from whoever was willing to employ them. This at least is the picture painted by the orator Isocrates in speeches pointing out the dangers inherent in these roving mercenary bands, and suggesting as a solution the conquest of the Persian Empire (or some part of it) and settlement of the landless in new cities in Asia. Isocrates claims that men 'are wandering with their women and children in foreign countries and many, compelled through lack of the daily necessities of life to enlist as mercenary soldiers, perish fighting for their enemies against their friends' (Isoc. *Paneg.* 168). Isocrates characterizes the 10,000 of Cyrus' expedition, immortalized in Xenophon's account of their travails in the *Anabasis*, as 'not picked troops selected on account of their good qualities but men who, owing to poor circumstances in their own cities, were not able to live there' (*Paneg.* 146). This view of the nature of fourth-century mercenary life is to some extent supported by Xenophon, who states that some of Clearchus' men served 'from want of resources or under the compulsion of any other necessity' (Xen. *Anab.* 2.6.13). But Xenophon, perhaps for reasons of his own, also stresses a different type of mercenary, one who serves not through hardship but by choice, in the hope not of subsistence but of enrichment; 'most of the soldiers had sailed out for this mercenary service not because their means were scanty but because they heard of Cyrus' noble character, some also bringing men, others having even spent money in addition, while some of them had left their fathers and mothers and others had left behind children with the idea of making money for them and returning home' (Xen. *Anab.* 6.4.8). Xenophon refers to another distinction between groups of Clearchus' men; 'those who served under his command either by order of a city or from want of resources' (Xen. *Anab.* 2.6.13). So in addition to the nomadic mercenaries, wandering and engaging in mercenary service permanently and accompanied by their families, there are those who leave their families at home and intend to serve only for a short period before returning, and those who are sent out by their home city as some sort of official contingent.[17]

The hope of Isocrates was that this first group, the wandering mercenaries, who posed a threat to the settled life of Greece by their very existence, could be disposed of by the conquest of the Persian Empire. He urges Philip II:

'to employ men of this sort in a campaign against the barbarians, to strip from their empire as much land as I mentioned a moment ago [ie from "Cilicia to Sinope", Asia Minor], to deliver the men who are

living as mercenaries from the miseries by which they are themselves
afflicted and which they inflict upon others, to found cities by settling
them together, to fix with these cities the boundaries of Greece, and to
protect us all.' (Isocrates, *Philippus* 120–2)

This was of course broadly what Alexander and his Successors were to do,
conquering an even greater expanse of the Persian Empire and settling in
new cities there large numbers of Greco-Macedonians, many of whom were
soldiers and at least some of whom must have been mercenaries.

In the fourth century, the 'poor' mercenaries were apparently peasant
farmers of the hoplite class driven into service by economic hardship. Where
studies have been made of the social status of third-century mercenaries,
similar conclusions have been reached: Cretan mercenaries, for example,
are thought to be often members of previously land-holding families,
impoverished by the concentration of land into fewer, larger holdings and
seeking service abroad to fill their leisure time as well as to provide an income
(although Cretans can be seen to be among those least likely to settle). Other
studies have considered the social status of mercenaries and other soldiers,
using evidence of rates of pay and standard of living. In the fourth century,
wages seem to have been sufficiently low that service could only have been
accepted in desperation, by the poor, and there are cases of hardship among
Successor mercenaries. Polyperchon's mercenaries, for instance, were loyal to
his son's widow because she 'assisted the unfortunate and succoured the many
in poverty' (Diod. 19.47). But from the third century it appears that there
was hope of enrichment abroad, and evidence from, for example, funerary
stelai has been taken to show a fairly high standard of living, among some
classes at least. Any such calculations are, however, complicated by a number
of factors; where rates of pay are given they may be for citizen soldiers, long-
term professionals or short-term auxiliaries, for fully equipped hoplites or for
light forces, all of whom may have been paid at different rates, and the value
of money itself is also often in doubt.[18]

That many of the mercenaries fighting for and against Alexander and his
generals were also political exiles is highly likely, and Alexander's 'exiles decree'
(Diod. 17.111.1) was apparently intended to secure the return home of these
men after his disbandment of the satrapal armies had left them wandering
through Asia. Any of these mercenaries who did return home were very likely
re-enlisted in one of the Successor armies, and as such they were to form a
proportion of the settlers of the new kingdoms in Asia, and so provide the
raw material for their phalanxes.

However, there is good reason to suppose that this sort of landless or exiled independent mercenary was no longer a major factor into the third century (though of course there are exceptions). The settlement of large numbers of Cretan mercenaries by Magnesia at Myous in the 220s provides a detailed list of mercenaries that may indicate a basic distinction in types. The first settlement, of 228/7, was of a large group, probably several hundred, of Drerian and Milatian men with their families. Such a large number of men from two small Cretan cities is surprising, and it may well be that these men were a body of mercenaries serving in Caria who became stranded in Asia Minor – perhaps because of the destruction of their home cities in war with Lyttos (Str. 10.4.14) – and who turned to Miletus for help because of kinship between the cities (Str. 14.1.6). The second group of settlers were a more diverse group from a number of cities within Crete. The families of this group of individuals seem to have a low proportion of female children, which may be taken as evidence that they live a migratory existence in which girls, considered a burden, would have been abandoned at birth (infanticide by exposure being commonplace in Ancient Greece). This seems again to indicate the difference between official city contingents, who in this case are accompanied by their families only because of exceptional circumstances, and the mixed units of individuals on more permanent service. Soldiers travelling with an *aposkeue* ('baggage', but including all the soldier's possessions including his family) had been a common feature in the fourth century, but are far less so in the third. The exceptions are themselves revealing – for example, Galatians (Celts), whether serving for Gonatas (Polyaen. 4.6.17) or Attalus I (Pol. 5.78), who are clearly in search of land, which they eventually receive, their baggage having become such a hindrance to the rest of the (presumably lightly equipped) army. The Autoriatae settled by Cassander in Macedon were also travelling with their women and children (Diod. 20.19.1).[19]

The question of whether mercenaries wanted to be given land is obviously important in identifying the types of men who served, since the comfortably-off soldier seeking a living in service abroad and planning to return home with his earnings would probably not be hoping to settle overseas. At the end of the fourth century there is evidence for mercenaries settling and indeed for this being one of their main hopes, due perhaps to the social and economic disruption in Greece. Diodorus describes the motives of one group of emigrants: '[C]onditions throughout Greece on account of the continuous wars and the mutual rivalries of the princes [the Successors] had become unstable and straitened, and they expected not only to gain many advantages but also to rid themselves of their present evils' (Diod. 20.40.7). Therefore when Ophellas came to Athens seeking recruits for a campaign in Libya, 'many of the Athenians eagerly enlisted for the campaign. Not a few of the other Greeks hastened to join in the undertaking, since they hoped to parcel out the most fertile part of Libya and to plunder the wealth of Carthage' (Diod. 20.40.6). Over 10,000 soldiers joined Ophellas, and 'many of these brought their children and wives and other possessions, so that the army was like a colonizing expedition' (Diod. 20.41.1). In the treaty between Eupolemos and Theangela mentioned above, the mercenaries in Theangela could depart when the city surrendered or take up service with Eupolemos and be settled. In Sicily there were a number of cases of mercenaries, presumably without home or *aposkeue* of their own, massacring the male population of a city and settling there themselves, taking over the wives and children of their victims (e.g. Diod. 21.18.1, 22.1).

It is often assumed that mercenaries in the third and second centuries would also settle and that there was a flexible boundary between mercenary and settler, but as we have seen it is doubtful whether such opportunities really existed on a large scale beyond the fourth century and whether there were significant additions to the body of settlers after the initial establishment of the settlement system. This does not mean that Greeks would not be enticed to the new kingdoms. The poet Theocritus presents the propagandist image of Ptolemy II's Egypt:

'if you really mean to emigrate, Ptolemy is the free man's paymaster, the best there is ... if you are ready to clasp the military cloak on your right shoulder, if you have the courage to plant your legs firmly to withstand the attack of a bold warrior, get you quickly to Egypt.' (Theocritus, *Idyll* 14.58–68)

But it is not clear that settlement is the objective rather than mercenary service followed by a return home. Where mercenary soldiers are granted land there are often special circumstances, such as them being exiles – such as the Cretans at Myous, as when in 201/200 Magnesia, into whose possession Myous had then fallen, asked Knossos and Gortyn to accept these settlers back to Crete, they firmly refused, and the settlers' goods were confiscated and they were treated as enemies. The Cretans, Boeotians and Aetolians settled by Antiochus III at Antioch are also most likely to be allied survivors from his army, exiled after the Roman victory brought about the return to power of the pro-Roman factions, their political enemies, in their home cities. Similar perhaps are the group from Entella in Sicily, resettled after the destruction of their home city. It is likely that, after the fourth century, only those mercenaries without a home for some reason, usually exiles from their home cities, hoped to be granted land and to settle, and it is likely that such exiled mercenaries no longer formed the majority of mercenary recruitment after the fourth century.[20]

There is, however, evidence of another type of mercenary who might be living abroad with a family: mercenaries hired as individuals could apparently serve overseas for long periods and even in some cases over several generations, as professional paid soldiers who are not ever given land and incorporated into the main army and population of the kingdom. The clearest examples of this type of mercenary come from the garrison of Demetrias in Thessaly, where there are many foreigners, male and female. There are also tombstones here from several members of the same family from Tylissos in Crete. There is also the example of the Cretan Eraton on Cyprus, who married on the island, and families and *epigonoi* of soldiers on Cyprus are known. In Egypt there seems to be a class of non-cleruch professionals serving inside the country. There may have been many such professional soldiers living their entire lives in service, and perhaps succeeded by their sons. Where garrisons did serve over long periods in one town, mercenaries hired only for a limited period would have been of little value, and the permanent units of *misthophoroi* in the various armies may represent professionals serving on a permanent basis without ever acquiring citizenship in the employing state, or ever being recruited into the phalanx.[21]

The suggestion that mercenaries from the third century on were mostly, except in special cases such as political exiles, either long service professionals or aiming to return home after a limited period of service, rather than hoping to settle, is reinforced by looking at the way in which mercenaries were most often recruited. When Rome imposed a treaty on Aetolia in 191, one of the terms was that 'in the first place none of you must cross to Asia [i.e. to Antiochus III], neither individually nor by decree of the League' (Pol. 20.10.4). This illustrates two classes of mercenary: those serving as individual volunteers and those serving by order of a city, state or league. The first class can be further subdivided, as suggested above, into those who serve permanently, as a career, and those who enlist for a particular campaign, intending to return home or to serve further elsewhere. This difference results in a basic distinction in the types of mercenary units found in inscriptional and literary evidence. Polybius, for example, is careful to give the ethnic composition of most units in an army, but he will then for some units use the general terms *xenoi* (foreigners) or *misthophoroi* (mercenaries) – such units are presumably not ethnically uniform. This seems to be the case for mercenary garrison forces, and many such garrisons are known; for example the Lilaia garrison, with a unit of Mysians, of

Pergamenes and of mixed mercenaries, or a Ptolemaic mercenary unit in Syria, a mix of mainland Greeks, islanders, Thracians and Anatolians. Sidon stelai show Ptolemaic (or Seleucid) mercenaries as a mixture of Cretans, Greeks, Carians and other Asia Minor peoples. The garrison on Samos is of mixed Greeks, and that in Tralles is a mixture of fifty-four different ethnic groups. Garrison lists from Athens show similar ethnically mixed groups. While such mixes of types may be due to the inclusion of individuals from different units in the same inscription, most garrisons are too small for there to be a large number of different units, and where formal, ethnically uniform, units are used in garrisons they are identified as such.[22]

Such units of mixed mercenaries must by nature be different from the homogeneous units mentioned in literary accounts. This is especially true where different nationalities have their own national weapons, as a military unit could not function if it was made up of men with a wide variety of arms and equipment. It seems reasonable to suppose that these groups of individuals are in general made up of the professionals, recruited as individuals and organized not into ethnic units but into pre-existing army units. In other words, the garrisons, and the mixed units in battle, were enrolled in permanent units on the establishment of the royal army whose members were recruited from individual volunteers, and they are different in kind from the ethnically uniform units which were apparently taken into service ready-formed by agreement with the supplying state. These individuals were obtained through recruiting officers sent out by the recruiting power, although it was also possible for individual volunteers to go abroad to offer their services. Eumenes of Cardia, for instance, sent out his friends with money to recruit, and 'many reported of their own free will even from the cities of Greece and were enrolled for the campaign' (Diod. 18.61.4).

The other type of unit, the ethnically uniform mercenaries, were hired usually for short periods of service. Although such units are variously identified (by modern historians) as 'subject', 'allied', 'mercenary' or 'auxiliary', it is apparent that in practice they were often paid as mercenaries but hired through political agreement with the supplying power. The literary sources are not always clear on this point, so it is impossible to be certain that, just because a unit is not defined as 'allied' it is not serving in accordance with the terms of a recruitment treaty. It is also worth noting that individual recruitment would often take place as the result of a treaty, and the mercenaries so recruited may not be classed as allies. Similarly, the ethnically uniform units found in army lists may well be mercenaries by the modern definition, but it is likely that, given their probable method of recruitment, they could also be classed as allies.

There are a number of examples of units likely recruited through alliance which are not classed in the sources as allies. For example, the Achaeans provided 300 archers for Philip V (Pol. 4.61.2) who are certainly allies (recruited under the terms of the alliance Philip concluded with the Achaean League). The Aetolians fought in many foreign wars and were widely regarded as typical 'pirate' mercenaries, with total freedom to fight overseas, and units of pirates or individual mercenaries are identifiable (such as Pol. 4.9.2, 4.6.18). The 1,000 Aetolians who helped Knossos against Gortyn, though, were sent on the basis of a reciprocal treaty (Pol. 4.53.8, 55.5). A force of 3,200 Aetolians joined their ally Antiochus III before Thermopylae (Liv. 36.10.5) under an Aetolian general. In Perseus' army before Pydna, there were 500 Aetolians and Boeotians, described by Livy as *'socii et amici'* (allies and friends) of Perseus (Liv. 42.12.7), but as they are serving under an Achaean officer, Lycon, it is less likely that they are a formal Aetolian ally contingent, so may well be individuals recruited under the terms of a recruitment alliance. Units of Thracians helping Antiochus II were under their own kings and so are taken to be allies (Pol. 4.16). Thracians who served in the army of Philip V might be expected to be allies, and Perseus' army included 3,000 independent Thracians under their own rulers and 2,000 Odrysians given by their king, Kotys (Liv. 42.51). Perseus attempted also to negotiate the support of 20,000 Bastarnae, but in the event he failed because he was unwilling or unable to afford their pay (Liv. 44.26.f.). Thracian and Trallian units are found in the Attalid armies after the 211 alliance with the Thracian kings (Liv. 36.24.9). Antiochus Hierax established treaties with various tribes in Asia Minor (Eusebius *Chron.* I 251); Justin (27.2.10) calls them simply 'mercenaries'. Antiochus III formed an alliance with Galatians (App. *Syr.* 6) and spent the winter of 190 'summoning his allies from all parts' (Liv. 37.8), yet the 4,000 Gauls who ravaged Pergamene territory are described as mercenaries by Livy (37.18). Illyrians are known to have served as allies of Antigonos Doson at Sellasia (Pol. 2.65.4), but the Illyrians earlier used by Demetrius II to relieve Medeon (Pol. 2.2.4–5) have been described as definitely mercenaries rather than allies, on the basis of Polybius' remark that their leader, Agron, was paid for his services; however, it would equally be possible to see Agron as a paid ally, serving under the terms of the same alliance as was in force at the time of Sellasia.

These are typical examples of a large number of units, indicating that even when a unit is not actually defined as allied, and may even be called mercenary, it could still be hired as the result of an alliance and perhaps a recruitment treaty. Although the number of such treaties surviving on stone is fairly small, and limited mostly to Crete, it is likely that they were really far more widespread. A similar example is the agreement between Jonathan and Demetrius, by which 30,000 Jews were to be recruited and employed in garrisons (*I Macc.* 10.22 f.). These treaties commonly make arrangements for the dispatch of allied contingents by either side at need, to be paid by the employer, but there are also clauses covering the enlisting of voluntary mercenary forces and restrictions on the service of either side's mercenaries with enemies of the signatories. The treaty between Antigonus and Eleutherna, for example, specifies that if Antigonus needs auxiliaries they will be sent by the Eleuthernians and paid by Antigonus one drachma and (?) three obols, while the Rhodes-Hierapytna treaty includes similar terms for the sending of allied contingents (ll.15–30), but then includes provision for Rhodian mercenary recruiting in Hierapytna and the prevention of recruiting by anyone else (ll. 40–49) and terms preventing Rhodians serving against Hierapytna (ll. 78–79). The treaty also specifies that half of the allied force sent must be Hierapytnians (ll. 20). If this means that the other half may be foreign mercenaries, then this shows clearly the similarity between mercenary and allied units. The treaty of Attalus I with Malla lays out similar terms for the sending of a contingent of 300 men by Attalus, who will provide transport for the men while the Mallaioi will pay them and give them provisions. The Aetolians were considered unusual in that, as Livy reports Philip V complaining, 'they themselves have long observed this custom as an established practice, of allowing their own young men to fight against their allies, official sanction being merely withheld, and opposing battle-lines will very often both contain Aetolian auxiliaries' (Liv. 32.34.5). These treaties demonstrate that while there were two basic types of recruitment – of allied contingents and of individual volunteers – both could be made through official alliance with the supplier and the actual terms of service would be very similar.[23]

Whether the recruitment treaties were a new development at the end of the third century, replacing an earlier, freer system, is not certain, but the widespread examples of mercenary allies make it unlikely. Recruiting conditions in the third century had changed since the fourth-century heyday of the independent mercenaries. There was, for example, no 'mercenary market' equivalent to Cape Taenarum, which is often described as a gathering place for those looking for independent mercenary service. But it is likely that the recruiting function of Taenarum is overstated; it was probably never more than a convenient assembly point rather than a permanent market, and Spartan authorization was needed to recruit in Laconia – 'Of the generals who had been sent out by Antigonus, Aristodemus sailed to Laconia and, on receiving permission from the Spartans to recruit mercenaries, enrolled eight thousand soldiers from the Peloponnesus' (Diod. 19.60.1). While it is sometimes asserted that other places, for example Ephesus, could serve a similar function, this is unlikely, if only because when Ephesus was under the political control of the Ptolemies or Seleucids they would be unlikely to allow their rivals to recruit there. The most that can be said is that the Ptolemies or Seleucids may have maintained an army base there which would engage in recruiting. Thus while mercenaries could be enrolled as individual volunteers rather than as official city contingents, it is likely that the method of recruitment was identical, requiring a treaty or at least agreement with a supplying power.[24]

Once mercenaries were hired, treaties could be drawn up between units of mercenaries and the employer; these have been seen as an equivalent to agreements between kings and cities, and indicative of the political independence of mercenary bands. Such treaties are indeed equivalent to those treaties with cities that include terms for service by allies, and in fact would be unnecessary in the existence of such a treaty, which would lay down in precise terms the arrangements for length of service, payment and other details such as arrangements for transportation to the theatre of war. Both sorts of treaties (with the mercenaries themselves and with cities) constitute in effect a formal contract of employment, and it is clear that agreements of this sort were prevalent before the Hellenistic period: Cyrus' 10,000, for example, had at least informal agreements on what the campaign was to involve, and changes in the terms had to be supported by extra pay from Cyrus and a new agreement. In the Hellenistic period, these agreements were reached in advance with the supplier, and (we may imagine) needed to be restated with the mercenaries themselves only when there was some change in circumstances, such as after the mutiny of Eumenes' mercenaries. In the case of recruitment treaties with cities, the terms of the agreement were reciprocal and the kings were required to send aid to the city on demand, in return for recruiting there. Such treaties also allowed the supplying city to use allies/mercenaries as an extension of its foreign policy, favouring powers it supported and banning recruitment by hostile powers.

The important point for our purposes is that all such mercenary or allied forces were quite distinct from the 'citizen' forces settled in the kingdoms that made up the Macedonian-armed phalanxes. Rather, mercenaries provided specialists (such as archers and slingers) or auxiliary forces (armed with their national weapons, or else, judging by depictions on grave stelai, as *thureophoroi*), and above all for garrisons, which then freed up the settlers (or native Macedonians) for service in the field army.

Garrisons themselves were not, however, totally separate from the field armies, and garrisons might have to be withdrawn for service in the army for a major campaign. Livy 31.25 is a good example: Philip V tells the Achaeans that if he is to campaign against Sparta, 'it is only right that my defence of your possessions by my arms should not entail the stripping of protection from my own possessions. Therefore if you approve the suggestion I ask you to equip a force sufficient to safeguard Oreus, Chalcis and Corinth so that I may make war on Nabis and the Spartans in the confidence that my possessions in the rear are safe.' Livy presents this as a ruse by Philip, but it was at least a believable ruse.

Also, although many scholars suppose that large permanent garrison forces of mercenaries were maintained at all times, this may be a misunderstanding of the way garrisons worked. While there certainly were garrisons controlling towns away from a war zone, a lot of the known garrisons in literary sources are clearly, or can be inferred to be, part of the field army detached to carry out the specific defence of a town for the purposes of a given campaign, and to be withdrawn and concentrated in the main army when a battle was imminent. It was common, especially in the defensive wars in northern Greece against the Romans, to station the army in a central location and send out garrisons from it to important towns as and when they came under attack. In some cases garrisons of this sort were of Macedonians, clearly members of the phalanx, and not mercenaries at all. For example, Philip V in Thessaly in 198 established his camp in Tempe, 'from where he sent out supporting detachments as occasion arose, when particular places were in danger of enemy attack' (Liv. 32.15). Carystus was reinforced by a garrison 'hastily sent from Chalcis', and Eretria was encouraged to resist by promises from Chalcis that reinforcements would be sent (Liv. 32.16). Atrax was defended by a 'numerous body of picked men', the Peltasts, who defended a breach in the wall with their sarissas – these, being the Antigonid guard, were certainly not a permanent garrison (Liv. 32.17). Perseus similarly sent out garrisons in 168: 2,000 Peltasts were sent to protect Thessalonica against Roman amphibious raids, 1,000 cavalry were sent to Aenea to guard the coastal district and 5,000 Macedonians were sent to defend Pythous and Petra. Some 3,000 more 'picked troops' were sent to raise the siege of Meliboea, and went on to help defend Demetrias (Liv. 44.13). None of these garrisons could possibly be permanent – they were often Macedonians detached from the phalanx and sent to meet the requirements of the campaign. Even the 2,000 Thracians in Amphipolis may be seen as a rearguard sent to reinforce the town before the battle; certainly the city commander did not know or trust them, and got them out of the city by a trick at the first opportunity.[25]

In Egypt also, garrisons seem to have been recalled to the army in times of need. Ptolemy I set out for Gaza 'after collecting his forces from everywhere' (Diod. 19.80.4), which perhaps reflects this. For Raphia also, the overseas garrisons were recalled and added to the army (Pol. 5.63.8–9). Of the main body of 8,000 mercenaries at Raphia, it is not known how many were specially recruited, but given the emergency recruitment programme undertaken it may be that half or more were. The total of mercenaries who may have been in service before the Raphia campaign is therefore around 10,000, plus the residual garrisons. That mercenaries were recruited by the Ptolemies usually to meet specific emergencies is clear, such as the 4,000 Gauls recruited to counter the revolt of Magas (Paus. 1.7.2) or Scopas' recruitment drive before Panion (Pol. 15.25.16 f.).

To summarize this highly complex picture, mercenaries were of two main types: allied contingents sent on an official basis by the supplying power, often as the result of a treaty or at least an informal agreement, and mixed units of individual volunteers, who may themselves very often have been recruited from a supplier under the terms of an alliance. Because mercenaries were often official city contingents, it is unlikely that many would have wished to settle, and the type of mercenary most likely to be given land and settle – the impoverished, landless men – were far less common in the third century and after (with the exception of some political exiles or refugees), replaced by the professional mercenary on permanent or long-term service in garrisons or in army units of mixed mercenaries. A number of such mercenaries will have been retained on the permanent establishment of the royal armies to serve in garrisons, but this number was not very large. Far more often, mercenaries were hired as allies, through diplomacy and as needed, before a particular campaign. At any rate, such garrisons, and allied and auxiliary units in the army, were separate from the phalanx proper, and the Macedonian phalanxes of the kingdoms were certainly not themselves made up of mercenaries.

Manpower management

We have seen then that the military settlers who were to form the regular forces of the Seleucid and Ptolemaic kingdoms were largely drawn from soldiers of the armies that fought in Asia under the Successors and their descendants, together with some use of indigenous populations by the end of the third century in Egypt. In each of the kingdoms, the kings (and central government generally) carefully managed their manpower resources, whether by the introduction of new settlers or the manipulation of existing populations.

As stated above, Antigonid Macedon's 'regular' forces were small in comparison with those of the other kingdoms only because they were formed exclusively of true Macedonians, and there was no immigration of

Greeks who could be settled onto the land and then be made available for the
army. The reasons for this are clear enough: with a large pre-existing pool
of Macedonians, there was no need to artificially create a source of Greco-
Macedonian manpower, but in addition the Antigonids did not have vast tracts
of spear-won territory to offer to settlers. However, the Antigonids are known
to have been willing and able to move their existing population resources
for military purposes. Philip II and Alexander had moved populations onto
the frontier to aid defence, and Philip especially was noted for the way he
transferred populations freely; it is this tradition that was continued by the
Antigonids. There is little evidence for the late fourth to early third centuries,
although Cassander undertook some projects of settlement and city foundation
– for example, he founded the city of Cassandreia, 'uniting with it as one city
the cities of the peninsula [Chalcidice], Potidea and a considerable number of
the neighbouring towns. He also settled in this city those of the Olynthians
who survived [the sack of their city]' (Diod. 19.52.2–3). In a similar fashion,
outside the borders of Macedon he refounded the city of Thebes (Diod.
19.53.2.f.) and persuaded the Acarnanians to leave their villages and settle
in cities for their mutual defence (Diod. 19.67.4–5). He also settled 20,000
Autoriatae on the Macedonian-Thracian border (Diod. 20.19.1). Demetrius,
for his part, transferred the city of Sicyon to a better defensive position in
303 (Diod. 20.102.2) and founded Demetrias as a union of the villages
about Iolcos (Plut. *Dem.* 53.3).

Evidence of manpower management is clearer from the late third century.
Philip V, for example, captured Phthiotic Thebes, sold the inhabitants into
slavery and planted a Macedonian colony there (Pol. 5.100.8). However, after
the crushing defeat at Cynoscephalae, Macedon faced a crisis of manpower and
Philip took steps to tackle the problem – 'to restore the country's previously
flourishing population, which had been depleted in the disasters of the war,
besides seeking to increase the birthrate by compelling all to have children
and to bring them up, he had even settled a large number of Thracians in
Macedon' (Liv. 39.24.3) – the reference to 'bringing them up' again reflecting
the widespread Greek practice of infanticide. Philip also decided 'to deport
with their whole families from the principal cities on the coast all men who
took part in politics and transfer them to the country now called Emathia
and formerly Paeonia, filling the cities with Thracians and barbarians whose
fidelity to him would be surer' (Pol. 23.10.4–5). Philip had also, in the course
of the war with Rome, taken the populations of the Thessalian towns with
him when the towns were abandoned to the Romans (Liv. 32.12.8.f.); in the
same way, Perseus took the population of Dion with him on his retreat to

Pydna (Diod. 30.11), and this was evidently an accepted strategy – part of Illyria was deliberately depopulated to make it difficult for the Dardanians to invade (Pol. 28.8.3). Philip's direct intervention in the population levels of Thessalian towns is also revealed in his letter to Larisa of 217, requiring the city to enrol resident Greeks and Thessalians as citizens, on the grounds that 'because of the wars your city needs more inhabitants' (ll. 5). However, it is important not to overstress the military function of all these changes. In the case of Larisa, for instance, an improvement in agriculture was the stated purpose for the increase in the citizen body (ll. 9, 16), while Livy describes the settled barbarians in Macedon as 'a large population of Gauls and Illyrians, who are energetic farmers' (Liv. 45.29), and the numbers of soldiers made available by the new settlements are small – the Thracian settlers formed only part of a unit of 3,000 in Perseus' army before Pydna (Liv. 42.51).[26]

For Egypt we have already seen that the cleruchs were probably little augmented by further settlement after the beginning of the third century. In the second century there may have been an increase in new internally recruited cleruchs and the use as cleruchs of soldiers who apparently were not originally of that class. For example, Dionysius, son of Kephalas, was a 'son of a *misthophoros*' (in this context perhaps better translated as 'professional' rather than 'mercenary') who then became *Perses tes epigones* ('Persian of the descent', the designation 'Persian' being one of the fictitious or pseudo-ethnics that developed during the second century) and finally a 'Macedonian'; and Dionysius, son of Apollonius, after serving in the infantry becomes a cleruch and a 'Macedonian'. In the early second century there is evidence for large-scale grants of cleruchic land, generally occurring after periods of warfare (so that, for example, there is a break in new settlement from 180–151 during the upheavals of Antiochus IV's invasion and the rebellion of Dionysius Petosarapis), which suggest that at this time soldiers who were not cleruchs could, after a period of active service, be granted cleruchic status. It is unlikely that all of these grants can be relocations of existing cleruchs, although some probably were. In addition to such new cleruchs, forces were raised in the second century from the civil inhabitants of Egypt – native and non-native – for use presumably in internal security roles within Egypt, particularly in the Thebaid. There is some reason to suppose too that mercenaries could sometimes be enrolled as settlers (despite the caveats above): Polybius (15.25.15) states that the mercenaries in Alexandria were distributed between the garrisons and the *katoikiai*, although he may be using the term in some non-technical sense, and may mean only that they were established in internal garrisons. All such measures, however, may represent emergency sources of recruitment after the failure of the cleruchic system before Raphia.[27]

In the Seleucid kingdom there is again a lack of the sort of direct evidence available for Egypt, but there are only a handful of known examples of Greek reinforcements being sent to Seleucid cities, and they follow a familiar pattern. A decree of Antioch in Persis in favour of Magnesia on the Maeander records that 'when Antiochos Soter [Antiochos I] was eager to increase our city, as it was called after him, and sent (an embassy) to them about (the sending of) a colony, they passed an honourable and glorious decree, offered a sacrifice and sent a sufficient number of men of great personal excellence, as they were anxious to help in increasing the people of Antioch'. Antiochos III, for his part, is said by Libanius (*Orat.* 11.119) to have introduced Cretan, Aetolian and Euboian settlers into Antioch on the Orontes; probably supporters of his campaign in Europe exiled from their cities after the Roman victory. There are some indications that the populations of the cities remained at a similar level over a long period: Malalas 201 describes the contingent of 5,300 settlers in Antigoneia, and Polybius mentions, under Antiochus III, 6,000 Cyrrhestai and 6,000 citizens in Seleucia (Pol. 5.50.7–8, 61.1). It is likely that examples of new settlements being established represent the installation of soldiers or other settlers from some other part of the kingdom, as the standard Seleucid means of maintaining order and internal security was to establish (soldier) settlers. Hence the Smyrna-Magnesia agreement includes provision for the settlement of soldiers who were placed there for strategic reasons, a large population of Jewish settlers were transferred to Lydia and Phrygia to help suppress a revolt (Jos. *Ant.* 12.47–53) and there were reportedly plans to divide up the land of Jerusalem into lots and settle foreigners there (*I Macc.* 3.36). None of these new settlements would actually involve immigrants or an increase in total manpower. The pattern is therefore similar to that in Macedon, with the kings organizing increases in city population on a grand scale when required. Internal population transfers also occurred, like those known in Macedon – Antiochus III, for example, upon withdrawing from Europe in 190 is said to have brought the population of Lysimachia with him and ordered the inhabitants 'to find residence in the cities of Asia' (Diod. 29.5). Lysimachia had itself been refounded by Antiochus gathering together the original inhabitants (Pol. 18.51.7–8).[28]

The Attalid (Pergamene) army, belonging to a kingdom which only became established later in the third century, follows a pattern slightly different from that of the armies of the other major kingdoms. The army used by the first Attalids was probably largely mercenary, but by the First Macedonian

War more regular forces were in use. An inscription honouring a Pergamene garrison in Lilaia shows soldiers drawn from Pergamene citizens, Macedonians and Mysians, as well as soldiers (mercenaries?) from Greek Asia Minor, Thrace and the mainland. The Mysians are known to have lived in *katoikiai*, and the presence of so many Mysians at Lilaia suggests that they were especially liable to recruitment. There is some evidence for similar soldier settlements near Pergamon – ephebic lists designate individuals as *apo* or *ek* (of or from) a named place, generally a settlement near to Pergamon, including, frequently, those from Masdue. Masduenoi are among the soldiers listed in a document granting citizenship, after the death of Attalus III, to a number of classes of soldiers – 'the soldiers settled in the city and in the country, the Macedonians and Mysians, those enrolled in the garrison and settled in the old city … and the royal guards'. These classes are difficult to interpret, but suggest that alongside the citizen soldiers there were numbers of settled non–citizen soldiers, perhaps originally mercenaries or of course ex-Seleucid settlers. Other settlements occurred, such as the Gallic soldiers of Attalus I who were settled onto lands in Asia Minor after a campaign (Pol. 5.78.1–5). It is possible too that Attalus II's foundation of Eumeneia included a contingent of Achaian settlers, perhaps mercenaries of Eumenes II. The Pergamene population itself also provided a source of settlers, with the establishment of a settlement on the coast by Attalus II, for instance. There is little information on the origins of Pergamene settlers, but there are at any rate few examples of the introduction of new colonists from Greece.[29]

Systems of recruitment

We have seen that the core of the armies – the phalanx – was made up from settled Greco-Macedonians (or the indigenous Macedonian population in the case of Macedon), but how were the men actually recruited for the phalanx?

The kingdom of Macedon might well be expected to provide the model on which the recruitment systems of the other kingdoms were based, though the evidence is unfortunately rather limited. The literary evidence for the reign of Alexander is good, but it is primarily concerned with events in Asia and provides only a few clues concerning arrangements within Macedon itself. There is good inscriptional evidence in the form of actual recruitment regulations for the Antigonid army (the 'conscription diagramma' from the reign of Philip V), though it is not absolutely certain that this represents typical arrangements throughout the period, rather than special measures (Philip was facing a manpower crisis) or possible Roman influence.[30]

Nevertheless, some points are reasonably clear. The backbone of all the armies of the kings of the Macedonians were the phalanx, the guard and the royal cavalry, formed from the Macedonians proper of the kingdom (the *Makedones*). When an army was required, it was levied from the population (from that part of the population that was liable for service), as when Cassander in 316 'enrolled those of the Macedonians who were fit for military service' preparatory to making a campaign into the Peloponnese (Diod. 18.52.5). Such enrolments were apparently generally made at the beginning of each campaign year – 'while wintering in Macedonia Philip [V] spent his time diligently levying troops for the coming campaign' (Pol. 4.29.1). The Macedonians are generally seen as farmers, levied at need but returned to the land as quickly as possible after a campaign. However, the army of Alexander was able to operate away from home for many years, and under the Successors many of these Macedonians remained in Asia fighting as professional soldiers. The passages in Polybius often quoted as evidence that the Macedonian army needed to be returned to the land at the end of the year may in fact represent the normal practice of sending a large army into winter quarters to ease supply problems. It was evidently usual to return the Macedonian army for the winter in this way – Doson, for example, returned the army to Macedonia in 222 (Pol. 2.54.14), and Philip V does so also (Pol. 4.87, 5.29.5, etc.). The only time it is said that the army was dismissed for agricultural reasons is Pol. 4.66, where Philip marched back to Pella to face a feared Dardanian invasion; finding the invasion did not materialize, he 'sent home all his Macedonians to gather in the harvest' and himself spent the summer in Larisa – clearly the harvest was gathered in the summer, not at the end of the campaign year. The Seleucid army also was often returned home for the winter (for example Pol. 5.66.3–6).

The army of Alexander was recruited on a regional basis, with *taxeis* of the phalanx and units of cavalry, designated as being from specific regions of Macedon. This practice was most likely continued by the Antigonids, with the army being conscripted on a regional basis from the towns. Polybius (5.97.3–4) mentions how Philip 'dispatched Chrysogonus [a Friend] with all speed to collect the levies of Upper Macedonia and he himself with those of Bottia and Amphaxites arrived at Edessa'. The population was also divided into age categories, as we have seen. The elite Peltasts in Perseus' army were 'selected for their strength and the vigour of their youth' (Livy 42.51.4), and Polybius calls the Peltasts of Philip V the 'young men' (*neaniskoi*, Pol. 5.25.1), so these guard units were drawn from the younger of the age classes as we saw in the previous chapter. As the Peltasts and the guard cavalry were probably the only permanently levied parts of the army, the wider levy being called up only at need, it is tempting to see the Peltasts as the men performing their military service after ephebic training. The system would then seem to be one of conscription on a regional and age basis, with particular age classes and regions providing men for particular units, and with a standing army of the young men augmented by a full levy in times of need.

In the Seleucid kingdom, as in the Antigonid, there are certain core units of the army (the phalanx, the guard units and the cavalry) who are drawn from the military settlers of the kingdom. There is, however, considerable uncertainty, given the scanty nature of the evidence, as to exactly how the army was recruited. A common view is that the Seleucid army was drawn from a specific element of the population who are to be found living in *katoikiai*, rural settlements without the status of cities, largely in Asia Minor. In addition, settlements where the population identifies itself as Macedonian are also classified as military settlements, presumably equivalent to *katoikiai*, and settlements with a similar function occur in a number of specific areas of the Seleucid kingdom, such as Media (or indeed Ptolemaic Palestine).[31]

However, it is doubtful whether it is really correct to talk of Seleucid military settlers in this way, as if the population from which the army was drawn is distinct from the general population of the kingdom. Given the evidence set out above for the bulk of settlers being Macedonians or Greeks of the armies of Antigonus or Seleucus, then most settlers are soldiers and most could be called 'military settlers', and it is apparent from several examples that the city populations also served in the army: Demetrius II disarmed the citizens of Antioch (Diod. 33.4.2; Jos. *Ant.* 13.135); every Antiochene household suffered from the disaster of Antiochus VII's campaign (Diod. 34/35.17), and the cities of Syria were said to be empty of fighting men as a result of this expedition (Jos. *Ant.* 13.254); Strabo (16.2) notes that the Seleucids kept 'the larger part of their army in Apamea'; Apollonius, governor of Coele-Syria, claimed to have the best men of each city in his army (Jos. *Ant.* 13.89); some soldiers of the army of Demetrius captured by the Parthians were citizens of Antioch (Jos. *Ant.* 13.385–6); and *politikoi hippeis* at Daphne also show city forces being used (Pol. 30.25.3). These city forces are sometimes described as the militias of the cities, distinct from the true army, but such a view seems to be unfounded. The soldiers fighting the war between Apamea and Larisa (Athen. 176b), for example, who 'grasped daggers and lances covered with rust and dirt' are not ramshackle city militia, for the Larisans served in the regular cavalry Agema (Diod. 33.4a).[32]

Some scholars see the Seleucid system as essentially similar to the Ptolemaic, with soldiers granted *kleroi* in return for military service, and farming such *kleroi* while living in their settlements in time of peace. But the exact function of the settlements called *katoikiai* is unclear; it is certainly likely that the inhabitants could and did serve in the army, just as the inhabitants of other Seleucid settlements did, but the evidence for a system similar in nature to that in Ptolemaic Egypt is not great. The inscription from Thyatira recording 'the officers and soldiers of the Macedonians at Thyatira' is taken as evidence of a system of soldiers settled as a complete unit, but it is equally possible that these soldiers are present as a garrison or are simply posted in the town. Similarly, the soldier at Susa described as from 'the cavalry of Alexander', or the grouping of 'Leon and the officers and soldiers under him', may be from a garrison. Neither is there clear evidence of a system of land-holding based on rank and arm of military service as in Egypt. The Seleucid army was most likely drawn from the mass of the population settled throughout the kingdom, but in particular in the cities of Syria, in a manner similar to that in Macedon, except that in Asia the Greco-Macedonian population employed was of course formed of immigrants or their descendants. The description of 'soldiers and citizens' in Seleucia meeting Ptolemy III's arrival (*FGrH* 160 l. 25) does not imply that the two formed separate classes; though the army can be drawn from the entire population, there will still be real distinctions between those who are currently mobilized on active service and those who are merely available when needed. The *katoikiai* should perhaps be seen as settled garrisons or as postings, more or less permanent, of soldiers serving in the army, to areas in need of policing for internal or external security. The evidence of the Smyrna–Magnesia treaty supports this view: here there is a body of settlers living at Magnesia, termed *katoikoi*, and classed as infantry and cavalry, both in the town and in the open, presumably in a camp; to this body of settlers are added a unit 'detached from the phalanx' and a body of Persians. If the function of the *katoikiai* is to provide a pool of manpower from which the phalanx is to be drawn, it is difficult to see why such men should be distinguished from the men of the phalanx, nor why men of the phalanx are settled in amongst them. What is apparently happening at Magnesia is that a settlement of soldiers already in place is augmented by the settlement of a further group of soldiers formerly serving as a garrison. The purpose of such settlements is therefore not to provide a manpower pool for the phalanx, but to allow permanent settled garrisons, drawn from those who are already soldiers and who are recruited apparently from the general settled population of the kingdom. Of course, more than one motivation for such settlements is possible. Compare (for the fifth century) Pericles' purpose in establishing Athenian cleruchies abroad; 'all this he did by way of lightening the city of its mob of lazy and idle people, rectifying the embarrassments of the poorer people, and giving the allies for neighbours an imposing garrison which should prevent rebellion' (Plut. *Peric.* 11.5). Philip II's population management in Macedon was intended both to make up citizen numbers in the cities and also to defend the frontiers of the kingdom (Just. 8.5.7–6.2). The settlers used are naturally soldiers, but as the settlement of Jewish settlers shows, other sources of men might also be used.[33]

For the recruitment of the Seleucid army itself, a system of regional recruitment seems likely. The inhabitants of Cyrrhos seem to mutiny against Antiochus III as a single body (Pol. 5.50.8), and the units at Thyatira, Susa or Seleucia may be identified as the levies of those particular regions. The settlers at Larisa in Syria were Thessalians who served in the first agema of the cavalry under Seleucus and his successors (Diod. 33.4a). A division of the population into age classes is also likely, and it is possible, as discussed, that the guard units of infantry and of cavalry were formed from the youngest age classes as in Macedon – the evidence is not conclusive, but there are some indications that this was the case. For example, the daughter of Diophantos, a Macedonian settler at Abae in Arabia, upon turning into a man shortly after her marriage (an unusual case of spontaneous gender realignment, according to Diodorus), was enrolled in the cavalry that accompanied Alexander Balas on his retreat; presumably his guard cavalry (Diod. 32.10) and the unit armed in Roman style at Daphne, which may be a rearmed contingent of the *Argyraspides*, are described as picked men in the prime of life (Pol. 33.25.3) – compare with the Antigonid Peltasts. It is clear also from the campaigns of Antiochus III that the army could remain on active service for long periods; between 221 and 189 at least some units of the army are active, launching successive invasions of Coele-Syria, then campaigning in the Upper Satrapies and suppressing the revolt of Achaeus, before marching into Europe and confronting the Romans. These events also demonstrate that the Asia Minor settlements were not needed to provide forces for the regular army. Certainly they could be used, as the rebel Achaeus raised 6,000 men there, who regarded Antiochus as their natural king (Pol. 5.76.6), and Molon, who rebelled in the Upper Satrapies, had soldiers under his command who, after his defeat, were sent back to Media (Pol. 5.54.8). However, the forces of Syria alone were sufficient to confront Ptolemaic Egypt – in the terms of the Smyrna-Magnesia treaty, perhaps Achaeus used the *katoikoi* but the Syrian forces formed the 'men of the phalanx'. It is likely that in normal circumstances the army was levied and concentrated in the Syrian heart of the kingdom at the beginning of the campaign year, just as it was in Macedon. Antiochus III levied his army at the beginning of each year at Apameia (e.g. Pol. 5.45.7). Antiochus agreed to an armistice in the war over Coele-Syria 'as he was anxious ... to winter with his army in Seleucia' (Pol. 5.66.3), and the following spring he gathered his army together again (68.1), while the march against Achaeus was preceded by winter preparations levying troops (5.107.4). Alexander Balas gathered his army from mercenaries and the soldiers of Syria (Jos. *Ant.* 13.58). For each mobilization it is either clearly stated, or at least very likely, that the soldiers are levied from Syria alone, and there is no evidence that settlers from Asia Minor or the East were drawn on for these armies. In the case of the Daphne parade (Pol. 30.25 f.), the army could only be drawn from Syria as the western and eastern parts of the empire were no longer available.[34]

So the Seleucid system, so far as it is possible to tell from the limited evidence, seems to be akin to that of Macedon, with an army conscripted from the population, divided by cities or regions, but with the possibility of settled garrisons being established in strategic locations. It is likely that there was a permanent standing army of some size, probably the guard infantry and cavalry rather than the whole phalanx. The bulk of the army would be mobilized only at times of need.

For the Ptolemaic kingdom there is, by contrast, a wealth of information and the recruitment system can be traced with some clarity, and as far as we can tell there were few changes in the cleruchic system until the end of the third century. However, although the mass of surviving papyri provides far more information than for any of the other kingdoms, it also raises problems of its own, largely due to the fact that the papyri deal with soldiers as individuals rather than with military units as a whole. One difficulty lies in the small size of the sample in comparison with the total number of soldiers in the army. The evidence is also restricted geographically to those areas where the climatic conditions are suitable for the preservation of papyrus – thus there is disproportionately little evidence for Alexandria itself (or for much of the Nile Delta). Furthermore, papyri tend to be discovered in archives, which means that clusters of evidence occur, disrupting attempts at statistical analysis.[35]

Despite such problems, the basic mechanics of the cleruchic system seem clearly enough established. Cleruchs were soldiers who were granted plots of land in the Egyptian countryside and were then available to perform military service in times of need. The cleruch was expected to serve on active duty, and was not merely a settled veteran granted land as a reward for long service (in the Roman style); but neither was he always on active duty and he was probably not paid in peacetime. At the same time, the cleruch was not a civilian merely liable for service; he was a permanent soldier who spent his life in the army, and whose social and economic status was based entirely on his army rank. Any comparison with the situation in Macedon, where the army was levied from the mass of the population, is therefore not strictly accurate. The army was permanently levied and organized, it was merely not always on active duty. The cleruchs thus formed a distinct class in Ptolemaic society, separate from the civilian population. It was also possible for citizens of Alexandria to serve in the army, although this was apparently not the normal practice, and alongside the cleruchs there was a population in Egypt of those of Greek descent, in Alexandria and in the country, who were connected neither with the army nor the official bureaucracy. Also, while it is sometimes said that the cleruch owed military service in return for his land, it would be better to say that the cleruchs owed military service in their role as soldiers, members of the army, and land was merely one of the benefits of the job, one form of payment. The size of *kleros* granted was determined by the arm in which the soldier served (cavalry, infantry or one of the police groups, when they were included in the cleruchic system), the seniority of his unit (the guard, or the numbered or ethnic hipparchies, for example) and on the soldier's rank.[36]

It is likely that the cleruchic system in this form was confined to Egypt itself. There is, however, some evidence for Ptolemaic settlers outside Egypt; *katoikoi* and cleruchs are mentioned in Ptolemaic Phoenicia, perhaps utilizing native forces. Some of the overseas garrisons may also have been settled – there are *epigonoi* on Cyprus and soldiers' families in the countryside. Such forces are inherently unlikely to have provided men for the main army, if only because of their relative isolation from Egypt. They should also, as for the Seleucids, be seen as settled garrisons. Perhaps of the same sort was the body of men originally stationed by Antigonus Monophthalmos in Iasos who fell under Ptolemaic control at the end of the fourth century and were permitted to settle in Iasos as non-citizens; they are then settled by Ptolemy, but not as cleruchs. Garrisons of this sort were equally necessary inside Egypt in the second century to suppress the many revolts; soldiers, whether cleruchs or not, were transferred to the Thebaid and there settled as permanent garrisons.[37]

Divisions by age and the role of, for example, the sons of the cleruchs are more difficult to determine, complicated by the confusion surrounding the *tes epigones* and the *epigonoi*, discussed earlier. There is also second-century evidence for soldiers entering service under a commander of recruits before being assigned to a formal army unit and, later, becoming cleruchs. An alternative explanation for the *tes epigones* is that they are sons of soldiers themselves, liable for active (paid) service in Egypt in army units and later enrolled as cleruchs, presumably on the death of their father, or beforehand if new land is available to give to them. It would be in general surprising if only the cleruch, who can be an old man, was liable for service and the sons in their prime of life passed over. Whether soldiers ever retired in Ptolemaic Egypt, like Philip V's time-expired veterans, is not known, unless that is the meaning of the soldiers *exo taxeon* ('outside the ranks') that are seen in some papyri.[38]

This, then, is the system established in Egypt by the early third century; the army of Ptolemy I, together with such additions as became available through warfare or immigration, was granted land in Egypt to farm, while still being enrolled in army units and available for army service at such time as they were required. These cleruchs formed a distinct class in Egyptian society, and their descendants continued to form the central components of the army up to the end of the third century. They were socially and economically superior to the Egyptian *machimoi*, who, while used in various paramilitary roles, held smaller plots of land and formed in effect the non-citizen class. The cleruch did not usually farm his own lands, and more often can be seen leasing them to Egyptian peasants while he himself lives in one of the nearby towns, while the *machimos* more often had to work his own lands. The cleruch was a comfortably off landlord rather than a subsistence farmer (as the *machimos* might have been), with land plots ranging from the generous (25 *arouras* being typical for an infantryman of the phalanx, one *aroura* measuring about 0.27 hectares, about a quarter of a football field) to the substantial (100 *arouras* for the cavalry and officers).[39]

However, by the last quarter of the third century this system had in some way been seriously degraded militarily, so that before the Battle of Raphia the Ptolemaic authorities were forced to take emergency steps to remedy the situation. The problem here is that we cannot be sure in what way the cleruchic army was inadequate before Raphia, because Polybius' account is unclear. It may be that the cleruchs could produce only 5,000 men, which was increased to 25,000 with the addition of Egyptians. It is also possible that there were 25,000 cleruchs, to which an additional 20,000 Egyptians were added. If the cleruchs could really only produce 5,000 men then this is indeed a dramatic decline, while if 25,000 men could be raised, that is a very healthy number indeed, and adding a further 20,000 Egyptians would produce a phalanx more than twice – and more like three times – the size of any other phalanx throughout the Hellenistic period. If the failure was of quality or training, then it is not clear why enrolling untrained Egyptians remedied the situation. I am inclined to think that the problem must have been one of numbers (although doubtless training was lacking as well), and that only 5,000 cleruch phalangites could be mustered, because a phalanx of 45,000 men is so disproportionate to other armies of the time, but the fact is we will never know for sure. Whatever the nature of the problem, however, it is clear that the solution adopted was to admit Egyptians into the phalanx for the first time. This involved not just a change in ethnic practice but also a dislocation of the social structure, as the lower classes were elevated to a position of military equality not matched by their economic status. The second-century native revolts inside Egypt can therefore be seen as being as much socially as ethnically motivated. This also led to wide-ranging but poorly understood reforms in the Ptolemaic army, perhaps directed partially towards retaining the exclusivity of the Greek military element; for example, the *politeumata* seem to have been introduced at this time as a means of providing the increasingly ethnically dislocated army with a stronger sense of national characteristics, and these *politeumata* possessed a number of political forms, though no real powers. Unlike in the Seleucid kingdom, there is evidence in this period of a higher level of ethnic mixing, for example in mixed marriages, although these may have been relatively unusual.[40]

So each of the kingdoms recruited its phalanx from a more or less exclusive citizen population. In Syria this population lived in the midst of, and was considered socially, politically and militarily superior to, the mass of natives in and around the cities. In Egypt they lived among the native Egyptians as an exclusive element of the population, afforded land to farm, distinguished from the civilians and most of the citizens of Alexandria and other cities, and handing on service in turn to their sons. In Macedon and Syria the army was drawn by conscription from the mass of the (Greco-Macedonian) population. The non-citizen (and non-Greco-Macedonian) elements in the kingdoms were excluded from military service in the regular units of the phalanx and the infantry and cavalry guards, at least until, in Egypt, the reforms before Raphia, while mercenaries were recruited mostly to supply the long-term permanent garrisons, or for specialist or supplementary units before a major battle or campaign.

Chapter 6

Command and control

Having examined the equipment, organization and recruitment of the phalanx, in this chapter I will be turning to the question of how the phalanx was commanded, in times of peace and war.

Friends and officers

'The King, his Friends and his military forces' is a formula that occurs more than once in Hellenistic inscriptions. There are a number of studies of the Friends themselves, and of the officers of the army, which have tended to concentrate on establishing institutions and precise terminology. This is rendered difficult given the nature of the evidence. For the Ptolemies there is abundant papyrological evidence for different men and different ranks, but despite the greatest efforts it remains confused and contradictory. For the Seleucids and Antigonids there is largely only literary evidence, in which technical terms are used loosely. Rank and authority therefore remain difficult to identify with precision. Nevertheless, some conclusions have been reached – for example, that the king drew on the army to supply his governors and administrators. Such an arrangement suggests that the administrators were primarily related to the army, and that it was through army personnel that the king controlled his kingdom. Yet the use of the formula 'King, Friends and military forces' casts doubt on this kind of interpretation, for it suggests not only that the Friends were distinguished from the king, but also that they were distinguished from the army; that they were an intermediary level, not a part of the army structure as such.[1]

In general, the Hellenistic institutions of Friends and army developed out of those under Philip and Alexander, although there are also Achaemenid precedents for the Friends in particular. The officer structure and the role of Companions, the precursors of the Friends, of Alexander's army may be summarized as follows. There was a hierarchical division of officers' ranks equating to the hierarchy of units detailed in Chapter 3, starting from, at the lowest level, 'double-pay men' and 'leaders of ten (*decadarchai*)' (Arr. *Anab.*

7.23.3) – NCOs in modern terms – up to the commanders of the *taxeis* that formed the largest subdivisions of the phalanx. Above the level of the *taxis* (and the *hipparchia* in the cavalry), which are the largest units attested for Alexander, there is no evidence for formal division, and if the allied forces – those outside the regular phalanx and Macedonian cavalry – had a similar formal structure there is little trace of it; units are identified by the officer commanding them, and subdivisions are called simply, for example, 'half the Agrianians' (Arr. *Anab.* 3.11.8). Furthermore, it seems apparent that an officer's command was not dependent on his rank: that is, the rank, for instance, of taxiarch did not carry with it a definite, prescribed authority; an officer could be called a *taxiarch* (as at Arr. *Anab.* 2.16.7), but this meant that he had personal command of a *taxis*, not that this was all that he could command, nor that he was therefore equal in rank to all other *taxiarchs*. This is why alongside the ranks of *taxiarch*, *hipparch* and *chiliarch* we also see the vaguer term *strategos*, 'general', which is used to cover a wide variety of commanders, irrespective of the unit they command, if any. It is used of, for example, Andromachos, commander of mercenary cavalry at Gaugamela (Arr. *Anab.* 4.3.7), and of Menedemos, with no known command (Arr. *Anab.* 4.3.7). A *taxiarch*, as well as his *taxis*, could also command other units: Coenus in Bactria commanded his own and Meleager's *taxeis*, Companion cavalry and *hippokontistai* (Arr. *Anab.* 4.17.3), yet clearly Coenus commands these units not in his position of *taxiarch*, but as a *strategos, a* general in an informal sense. Being a *taxiarch*, or whatever rank, did not even imply command of one's own unit – in 328, Antiochus and Nearchus were *chiliarchs* of the hypaspists, yet on one occasion (Arr. *Anab.* 4.30.5) Antiochus commanded all three *chiliarchies* while Nearchos led the Agrianians and light infantry. Only in pitched battle is each officer stationed exclusively with his own unit (for example at Gaugamela, Arr. *Anab.* 3.11.8.f.). So it is that the lesser *taxiarchs*, like Meleager and Amyntas, while nominally holding the same rank as the important officers such as Craterus and Coenus, hardly ever exercise independent commands. So also most of the *ilarchs* of the Companion cavalry are insignificant figures, except Cleitus, commander of the royal squadron, who in 330 commanded 6,000 Macedonians and the treasure (Arr. *Anab* .3.19.7); yet the *hipparchs* who commanded the cavalry after Alexander's army reforms were men of great authority, in some cases former *taxiarchs* – Perdiccas, Craterus, Coenus and Hephaistion, for example, who hold a succession of independent commands, although again there is considerable variation between *hipparchs*, from the important commands of Hephaistion (e.g. Arr. *Anab.* 4.16.2, 4.22.7, 5.21.5, 6.17.4) to White Cleitus, who never commanded more than his own *hipparchy*. Thus an officer's named rank did not specify which units he could command nor his authority relative to other officers. It was therefore possible for Ptolemy, with the rank of bodyguard, to command in 329 three *hipparchies*, a *taxis* and a *chiliarchy* (Arr. *Anab.* 3.29.7), while most of the bodyguards (Aristonous, Arybbas, Demetrius) are non-entities. Officers were clearly assigned units which they would command in battle and whose affairs they presumably were to manage, but their actual authority was not defined or limited by their rank but rather was at the discretion of the king. This meant that the pool of available officers was defined not so much by the number of serving officers in the army as by the circle of Friends and, on a wider scale, Companions of Alexander; satrapies, for example, were frequently allocated to otherwise unknown Companions, such as Tlepolemos (Arr. *Anab.* 3.22.1), Mazaros (3.16.9), Panegoros (1.12.7) and many others. Thus, authority in the army was dependent not on rank but on personal preferment from the king (although in practice the king would often have been limited in choice by factors other than his personal preference), so that strange appointments were possible, such as the interpreter Pharnuches, who had command over three *strategoi* (Arr. *Anab.* 4.3.7).[2]

When officers were in command of specific units, their close association with that unit could threaten the loyalty owed by the soldiers to the king. Such was the case with the Lyncestian Alexander, as 'the Companions held that [Alexander the king] had originally acted unwisely in committing the best of the cavalry to an untrustworthy officer, and that he should now get rid of him as soon as possible, before he became more popular with the Thessalians and secured their help for a rebellion' (Arr. *Anab.* 1.25.5). After the execution of Philotas, Alexander was unwilling to trust the Companions to one man, and the murder of Parmenion was apparently motivated by the fear that he would encourage his troops to rebel (Arr. *Anab.* 3.26.4). It is likely that the new arrangements of the army after this episode, with *hipparchs* replacing *taxiarchs* as the more important men, was intended to overcome this danger, since the *hipparchs* commanded a more widely varied number of units than the *taxiarchs* had done, and so seem to have been less closely tied to any one specific unit and thus even more dependent on the king for their authority. The development in importance of the men who served as *hipparchs* and as bodyguards should then be seen as a deliberate move by Alexander to replace the powerful unit commanders, mainly *taxiarchs* of the phalanx, with men with no such unit affiliations, who were exclusively his personal friends.

In the Hellenistic armies, a complex hierarchy of junior commands can be discerned, junior officers being those up to the rank of officers of units that formed a single large tactical entity in battle, the equivalent of the *taxiarch* under Alexander or the *chiliarch* in later armies. In the papyri, which give for the Ptolemaic army the most complete information on army command, the highest-ranking officers within the army are the *chiliarches*, *hegemon* and *hipparchos*. The evidence for the ranks provided by documentary evidence can also be compared with that of Asclepiodotus, who provides a detailed breakdown of rank structure, although it is not known to which army he refers, if indeed to any real army at all. In the Ptolemaic army, the hierarchy of officers approximates to that of Asclepiodotus; for the infantry, the hierarchy of ranks below the *chiliarch* is clearly attested. Most revealing is the rank of *taxiarch* (a lower rank, note, than the *taxiarchs* of Alexander). According to Asclepiodotus (2.8), the *taxiarch* 'is nowadays called *hecatontarches*', and in Egypt two *taxiarchs* are known from the third century and several *hecatontarchs* from the second or first century, which suggests both that Asclepiodotus had the Ptolemaic army in mind and that the account he gives of ranks is fairly close to reality. The only major problem is that of the 'eponymous commanders', those officers whose name is used to identify a given body of men. This is a well-attested practice in Ptolemaic Egypt, and also for the Seleucids, as in the Smyrna-Magnesia agreement, where there is a unit referred to as 'the men under Timon'. Various attempts have been made to establish a precise rank for these officers, but such attempts appear too formalistic. It is not necessary to suppose that any one rank is specified by an eponymous commander, rather that in some circumstances, just as it was correct to group all officers together as *hegemones* (generic 'officers' – but note that the same word is also used for file leaders), so it would be possible to refer not to a named unit (for example, the 'third *hipparchy*'), but to the men under a particular officer. It is easy to imagine occasions when this would be necessary: for instance if men from different units were grouped under the same commander, or if a detachment did not correspond exactly to one of the formal divisions. It would also occur simply on less formal occasions or when the writer was ignorant of or not interested in the correct rank. Thus in the Smyrna-Magnesia agreement it is easy to imagine that it would be simpler for the garrison to be referred to by the name of the commander than to list precise ranks and unit designations. This would explain why the eponymous commanders do not easily fit into one slot in the command structure.[3]

Inscriptions provide evidence for the Seleucids for only two levels, *hegemones* and *stratiotai* (officers and enlisted men). This might conceivably mean that these were the only ranks in existence, that all officers were grouped together under one rank. In the recruitment treaties, pay is specified for Cretan and Attalid armies and there are only two classes, soldiers and officers, with all officers apparently receiving the same amount of pay. However, the Seleucid army, like the Ptolemaic, developed out of that of Alexander, and is therefore likely to have had a similar command structure. It is more likely that the nature of the evidence obscures the true organization of the Seleucid army. In Egypt there are technical documents relating to army administration which therefore use the correct terminology, but for the Seleucids many of the inscriptions are concerned with matters external to the army, where technical terminology was not necessary. Administrative positions are also attested, chiefly the *strategoi* who governed provinces and the *oikonomoi* (financial officers) who assisted them.[4]

The organization of the Antigonid army is illuminated by a small body of documentary evidence, and seems only to approximate to the structure given by Asclepiodotus. The *protolochoi* of the manual, for example, which should be the four front-rank men of the *lochos*, is shown by the Greia land grant to be a larger unit containing at least six men, unless more than one *protolochos* is there referred to. The Amphipolis code shows a succession of units from *lochos* (file), through *tetrarchia* (presumably four files), *speira/syntagma* (sixteen files) and *chiliarchia* (1,000 men, sixty-four files). Polybius, as we have already seen, calls the *syntagma*-sized unit a *speira* (Pol. 11.11.6). The Chalcis code draws attention to the other military and administrative posts, such as *phrourarch* (garrison commander) and *oikonomos*, which are not mentioned in Asclepiodotus, and the administrative structure of the army, with *grammateis* (secretaries) collecting fines and *archyperetai* (chief adjutants) supervising them, and taking part in other activities such as the distribution of plunder. We see throughout the existence of an administrative hierarchy working alongside and checking on the actions of the military officers. Asclepiodotus does list a vaguely similar body of supernumeraries (2.9), including signallers and *hyperetes* (adjutants), though these are more concerned with battlefield command than with administration.[5]

The structure of ranks up to the level of the *chiliarchy* can therefore be defined quite accurately in the Antigonid and Ptolemaic armies at least. It would be interesting to trace the interaction of these ranks, paths of promotion or spheres of authority, but this is unfortunately virtually impossible given the available evidence. What can be said is that these are permanent ranks, not just descriptions of office, for it was possible to have officers without a current appointment who nevertheless retained their rank. Such officers are therefore part of the formal army structure. Also, officers often have their sons associated with them in their commands, which suggests that such commands might have been hereditary, at least to some extent. This seems especially likely if the officers were themselves cleruchs, as if the land was inherited then presumably the rank must have been also, as the amount of land held varied according to rank. What the prospects were of promotion from the ranks, and whether a normal career involved steady advancement up a ladder of ranks, is unclear, but if rank was hereditary then this suggests rigid divisions between ranks with little movement, and correspondingly small chance of talent being rewarded by promotion. This is only speculation, however.[6]

Senior officers are those above the level of the largest tactical unit, who might command two or more *hipparchies* or *chiliarchies*. Asclepiodotus (2.10 for infantry) gives a very full listing of such ranks (two *chiliarchies* under a *telarches* or *merarches*, four under a *phalangarches*, eight under a *kerarches* and sixteen under a *strategos*). His arrangement is very neat and formal, and some have suspected that it is pure theory, bearing no relation to any real organization, but it would be strange if Asclepiodotus provided an account of ranks up to the level of the *chiliarch* that is reasonably close to reality, and then simply invented levels above this. Furthermore, his language suggests that he is quoting historical examples – for instance, 'two chiliarchies were formerly called a *keras* and a *telos*, but later it was called a *merarchia*'. Yet there are no examples of these higher ranks in the papyri, inscriptions or literary texts. This would not be so serious if only the precise terms used were absent, as names in practice might differ from those known to Asclepiodotus, but there is no evidence for formal division or for ranks above the level of *chiliarch* at all. Asclepiodotus' testimony can be saved if we assume that for these positions it is not rank but office that is described. It has been noted, for example, that the Seleucids were very flexible in their appointment of officers, and that the same man could command widely different sizes of units at different times; this suggests that an officer of given rank could hold different levels of office. We may thus speculate that the army in peacetime (for which there is most evidence) was divided up by the units known – in Egypt, the 'third *chiliarchy*' and so on – and commanded by officers of corresponding rank. But whenever, for example, two or more *chiliarchs* operated together, the officer over them would be temporarily designated by one of the titles given by Asclepiodotus for higher officers, or its equivalent. Thus an officer whose rank was *chiliarch* might, on a given occasion, be called *merarch* or *telarch*. In papyri he would still appear as a *chiliarch*, as that would remain his permanent rank. It is impossible to prove that this theory is correct, but some such distinction between rank and office on this level seems likely. For comparison, the Mysarch of *I Macc.* 1.20 might have had a certain rank, but, while commanding a unit of Mysians, his office is Mysarch. Asclepiodotus would thus be describing a hierarchy that was real but which we would not expect to find reflected in documentary evidence.[7]

The most senior commanders of the army were the *strategoi*. There is a considerable difference between the word *strategos* as used in inscriptions, and its use in literary sources. Generally, in the period of the Successors, a *strategos* was any man who commanded a military force, but the word also acquired a technical meaning and became associated with the command of a particular geographical region. In this way *strategos* came to designate not so much a general of the army as a particular administrative post: *strategos* of Syria and Phoenicia, for example. In literary sources, the term *strategos* retained its original meaning, however, and could be applied to any commander of a military force. In the Antigonid army, on the other hand, *strategoi* appear in the Amphipolis regulations as (presumably) commanders of the *strategiai*, equivalent therefore to the *taxiarchs* of Alexander's army. They appear to be strictly military figures, grouped with their juniors (*speirarchs* and *tetrarchs*) in such tasks as the distribution of plunder.

The status of the *strategoi* and the meaning of the term have been studied in considerable detail, and the administrative institution need not be described here. Yet it is clear that the *strategoi*, in the sense of the officials appointed to command various regions within the kingdom, were not necessarily the same men who would command the army in action. For example, at the Battle of Raphia the Egyptian army was commanded by 'mercenary' generals (Pol. 5.63) who indeed could later become *strategoi* of regions, and the Seleucid by a variety of figures ranging from court officials to deserters from Ptolemy (Pol. 5.79). These Ptolemaic new arrivals were given commands presumably over the heads of the existing officers. These men, who actually commanded the army, are not known to have had any official rank, other than the loose and generic term *strategos*. The appointment of such men to command the army in war implies that the *strategoi* of *nomes* or regions, and the Seleucid regional governors, while they did have authority over the forces stationed in their regions in peacetime, did not generally command them on campaign. The officials would also of course command units in operations within the confines of their regions – the Egyptian *strategos* of the Thebaid and *epistrategos* were created as posts apparently with the purpose of suppressing the revolts of Upper Egypt, and in general regional commanders led their men in internal security operations, as we will see below. But even when *strategoi* have command over the troops in their areas, this does not make them officers of those units, nor does it make them members of the army themselves.[8]

Similarly, the commanders of units at the level of the *chiliarchy* do not themselves appear to be important men. In literary descriptions of the deployment of armies for battles, the commanders of individual units within the phalanx are never named (after the time of Alexander); only the commander of the phalanx as a whole may be given, and it is often clear that he is not formally speaking an officer in the army, but is appointed specifically for that battle. Thus, important figures in the kingdom can be given command over units: in Antiochus III's battle against Molon, the left wing was given to Zeuxis and Hermeias, Hermeias' actual office being 'Chief Secretary' (Pol. 5.52.6); in the Ptolemaic army before Raphia, commands were handed out to the various 'mercenary' officers, as well as to the courtier Sosibios (Pol. 5.65.1); and in the Seleucid army command of the phalanx went to Nicarchos and Theodotos Hemiolios (Pol. 5.79), who had held senior commands at the siege of Rabbatamana (5.71.6) and the attack on the Porphyrion pass (5.68.9), and Theodotos with Xenon had commanded the first expedition against Molon (5.42.5). Hippolochos, deserting from Ptolemy with 400 cavalry, received command of all the Greek mercenaries (5.79), and the elephants are under Myiscos, a royal page (5.82.12). The variations in the size of the commands held by these figures have been taken to show that there was no formal hierarchy of ranks, and conversely explanations have been offered for these cases that would permit a formal rank structure. However, the most obvious conclusion is that these commanders do not have a rank at all, and are appointed at need. Those officers who do carry a formal hierarchical rank, the permanent officers of the units, *chiliarchs* or its equivalent, whoever they might have been, would be passed over. No doubt in the same way, court figures such as Apelles could be given commands over units for short periods, over the heads of the permanent commanders attached to the unit, who were themselves relatively unimportant figures.[9]

It thus appears that commands over the army in war were handed out by the king not to ranking officers attached to those units, or even necessarily to their peacetime commanders, but to members of some less formal body of men. Such men could of course on occasion be the *strategoi*, governors or satraps, as for example Didas, governor of Paeonia, commanding Agrianians, Thracians and Paeonians in the Macedonian army before Pydna (Liv. 42.51), but they could equally be men with no formal connection to the army. The posts that would in general be made available to subordinates are defined as commands in the army and control of territory; thus Antigonus, after the death of Antipater, 'assigned satrapies to some of the more important Friends and military commands to others' (Diod. 18.50.5), and Attalus III feared his father's Friends, 'those who had been appointed to commands in the army or as governors of cities' (Diod. 34/35.3). But it is apparent that 'commands in the army' does not mean actual army ranks, but the control of given army units. Under Alexander, the most important positions had been the highest-ranking army posts – *taxiarch* at first, then *hipparch*. Command of a satrapy had generally been left to lesser men. Yet clearly in the later period it is command of satrapies or regions and of overseas possessions that is most highly prized, or at least that falls to the well-known figures of the period, rather than military rank. Of the true army ranks, only that of commander of the guard was a position of any importance. After the death of Alexander there were numerous distributions of the satrapies between the competing generals as each sought to obtain his own piece of territory, and after one such distribution Perdiccas 'placed Seleucus in command of the cavalry of the Companions, a most distinguished office' (Diod. 18.3.4); command of these guard cavalry is the only army appointment mentioned. The most important men in Macedon upon the death of Doson were Apelles, the guardian, Megeleas, chief secretary, Taurion, responsible for the Peloponnese, Alexander, in command of the bodyguard and Leontius, commander of the Peltasts (Pol. 4.87.7). Leontius was evidently an important political figure, one of those Philip was engaged in manoeuvres to try to overthrow. None of the other unit commanders appear as of any political importance. Theodotos, distinguished commander of Ptolemy IV, deserted to Antiochus III and was appointed commander of the *Argyraspides* (Pol. 5.79.4), a post he still apparently held at the siege of Sardis (Pol. 7.16.2). In contrast, the other commanders from Raphia held different commands.

While appointment to the command of a region of the kingdom would bring with it opportunities for gain and personal power, there also seem to have been a group of officials attached closely to the king who would follow him on his campaigns; such men must of necessity have been those who made up the councils and who were given commands over the army in battle. Although there was a formal hierarchy of 'Friends', and the term came to imply a formal rank, it is clear that there was also an inner circle of friends about the king, who do not hold regional commands and would in practice have great political power. Apelles tried to get Taurion removed as the official responsible for the Peloponnese by 'saying that he was a most proper person to be attached to the king's person in the camp' (Pol. 4.87, commenting on the perversity of Apelles' methods of removing his opponents by having them promoted; 'kicked upstairs', as we might say). Agathocles, wishing to usurp power in Alexandria, appointed to overseas commands or sent on embassies several officials, his object being 'to remove all men of distinction from Egypt'; he then 'filled up the vacant places of the royal friends by appointing from the body servants and other attendants those most remarkable for their effrontery and recklessness' (Pol. 15.25.). Philip V earned a high reputation 'both by his behaviour to those with whom he was associated in the camp' and by his ability as a general (Pol. 4.77.1). Apelles, when he fell from favour with Philip, was still invited to banquets, 'but took no part in councils and was not admitted to the king's intimacy' (Pol. 5.26.15). These Friends in close attendance on the king would be those to whom army commands would be distributed in battle.

The Friends themselves were a disparate group of men who might have attracted the attention of the king for a number of reasons. Philosophers, actors and musicians were included as well as military commanders or politicians – the historian Hegesianax, for example, was appointed Friend by Antiochus III after a recitation of his works (Athen. 155b), and was sent on a diplomatic mission to the Romans (Pol. 18.47.4), while the philosopher Persaios held Corinth for Gonatas (Athen. 4.162d). The position of Friend was originally an indication of personal closeness to the king rather than a formal rank, although, as with *strategoi*, there was a steady development in the formality of the position throughout the period, until by the second century there was an elaborate hierarchy of 'Friend', 'First Friend', 'First and Honoured Friend' and so on. Nevertheless, it is likely that the title of Friend still indicated a degree of personal closeness to the king, and furthermore this title seems to have been held independent of any offices occupied. Thus, although there was a hierarchy of court titles and also of administrative posts, the real power lay not in the offices themselves but in the personal power of those who held them, and this power was still largely dependent on a personal relationship with the king. The occurrence of Friends in the army is also of interest; there are only a handful of examples of a Friend of the rank of *hipparch* or below, although a very high proportion of the *strategoi* are known to have been Friends. It would be useful to know whether lower-ranking officers were promoted to higher status and simultaneously received the rank of Friend, but this is difficult to see, given the nature of the evidence. Nevertheless, what is known of the origins of the Friends suggests that they had not at any time held a ranking position in the army. They seem rather to be drawn from a body of important men in or outside the kingdom, whether appointed to administrative positions or associated with the king, according to their talents. Because the office of regional commander is called *strategos*, and because *strategoi* were, or became, military as well as civil officials, this has given the impression that figures appointed to such an office are themselves army officers, but such an impression is surely false. Their rank is defined in terms of their personal proximity to the king (in however stylized a form it may be expressed), and *strategos* is only an office they hold. Army figures with army ranks do not receive such appointments.[10]

What, then, gave the important men in the kingdom their status – was political and military power entirely in the hands of the king, to be handed out at will to his personal adherents, or were there men within the kingdom with independent power? In the period of the Successors it is clear that the important men, those who could expect power for themselves and appointments from those who were establishing themselves as kings, were the commanders who had served under and been promoted by Alexander. After the death of Alexander, those who were to decide events were 'the most influential of the friends and of the bodyguards' (Diod. 18.2). Respect was shown to such men as Attalus, who 'excelled in daring and dexterity, thanks to their service with Alexander' (Diod. 19.16.1), or Damis, who helped defend Megalopolis against Antipater and had served with Alexander (Diod. 18.71.2), or Aristonous, who 'was respected because of the preferment he had received from Alexander' (Diod. 19.51.1). Antigonus was accused of wishing to remove all those whose power he felt might be a threat to his position; in particular he wished 'to remove from their satrapies all who were men of rank and in particular those who had served under Alexander' (Diod. 19.56.1), but the advisors Antigonus appointed for Demetrius in 314 were 'men advanced in years who had accompanied Alexander on his whole campaign' (Diod. 19.69.1). The friends of Seleucus who accompanied him on his dash to Babylon were 'men who had campaigned with Alexander and had been advanced by him because of their prowess' (Diod. 19.90.3).

The importance of having been one of Alexander's commanders was perhaps that military expertise and experience were highly sought after, and experts could supersede existing commanders. Eumenes of Cardia, at the low point of his fortunes besieged in Nora, hoped 'that many would have need of him because of his judgement and experience in warfare' (Diod. 18.42.2). This is a theme which is stressed by Polybius; the reason for Ptolemy's use of outsiders at Raphia was that they were men who had gained practical experience under Antigonus (Pol. 5.63.13). Whether all military commanders received training it is impossible to tell, although it is likely. At any rate, there were drill experts and trainers in Apamea (Str. 16.2.10), and according to Polybius there were three methods of acquiring skill in generalship: through studying histories, through systematic instruction and through practical experience (Pol. 11.8.1–3). Tactical treatises were composed by men of real military experience – Philostephanos, writer of a *Tactics*, commanded the army of Ptolemy IX (Jos. *Ant.* 13.339), and as we have seen there are many examples of books on 'Tactics' or 'Generalship', some composed by kings or generals and presumably used for the instruction of their subordinates; Pyrrhos wrote on tactics (Plut. *Pyrr.* 8), and Demetrios of Phaleron wrote a *Strategica* (D.L. 5.80). But clearly it is practical experience that is valued before Raphia. The status of these 'imported' officers is uncertain. Later in their careers they became established into the standard framework, for instance Polycrates of Argos (Pol. 5.64.4), who became governor of Cyprus (Pol. 18.55.6) and was involved in the fall of Scopas (Pol. 18.54.1, 55.4–6), and his son became a First Friend. On their first arrival, however, they are often classed (by modern writers) as mercenaries, but this seems to be unfounded; they are rather individual immigrants seeking service abroad. While it is likely that such immigration did not occur on a large scale among the ordinary citizens, it is clear that an experienced general could be sought after throughout the Hellenistic world. Antiochus III, for example, setting out against Molon, 'was anxious for Epigenes to accompany him on the campaign owing to his military capacity' (Pol. 5.50.4). The defence of Coele-Syria against Antiochus was entrusted to Nicolaos, 'in military experience and martial courage excelled by none of the officers in Ptolemy's service' (Pol. 5.68.2). A lack of experienced subordinates was damaging – Eulaios and Lenaios 'were completely without experience of warfare and battles, and they lacked even a single competent advisor or capable commander' (Diod. 30.15). Ptolemy Physcon was inexperienced in war but he had as a general Hierax, 'being a man of extraordinary talent in the arts of war' (Diod. 33.22). While the Ptolemaic officers at Raphia had previously served with Antigonus, it is important not to be too quick to designate any foreign-born commander in the service of a king as a mercenary (or as a *condottiere*, as some do). Because of the use of ethnics over many generations, just because a commander has a given ethnic this does not mean that he was not born in the kingdom, and even if he was not he may not be a mercenary as such; Alexander's commanders Nearchus the Cretan and Eumenes of Cardia would not be called mercenaries.[11]

As for whether Friends and officers could have independent means and be wealthy independent of their proximity to the king, under the Successors, satraps could use their territories to establish an independent power base. In the distribution of satrapies of 316, for example, Oxyartes was left in command of his satrapy 'since he could not be removed without a long campaign and a strong army' (Diod. 19.48.1). In Macedon, whether any of the Friends could be independently powerful is dependent on the question of the nobility in the kingdom, and so on the difficult question of land-holding; it is likely that all land within the kingdom was in the gift of the king, and that subordinates held lands only as a result of a grant from the king that would be subject to review.

It is therefore likely that the landed men in the kingdom would be largely those selected by the king, his personal choice of Friends. There were, however, independently important men in Macedon – Polyperchon, for example, called together a council of 'all the commanders and the most important of the other Macedonians' (Diod. 18.55.1). Whatever the source of land, it is evident that important Macedonians were wealthy: Theopompus states that 800 of Philip II's Companions had as much revenue from the lands granted to them by Philip as 10,000 Greek estate owners. The same is true of the Friends in the other kingdoms. Land was granted by the king on a revocable basis to his Friends, and became irrevocable in the Seleucid kingdom only if attached to a city. Again, whatever the source of land, great wealth was possible. Scopas, when in Egypt, was paid by the king (Pol. 13.2), but this must be unusual as in many other cases the important men obviously have considerable personal wealth – such as Hermeias, who offered to pay off Antiochus III's debts to his army, presumably from his own private funds (Pol. 5.50.1), or Hierax, general of Ptolemy VIII, who ended a rebellious movement among the soldiers over arrears of pay 'by providing for the army from his private purse' (Diod. 33.22). Governors of regions or satrapies could presumably hope to raise money from the regions they controlled, as for example Polycrates, governor of Cyprus, who raised considerable sums for the government but also amassed a fortune for himself (Pol. 18.55.). The private fortunes of these men evidently rivalled the available wealth of the king. A story is told of Ptolemy V, that when asked by some courtiers where he would find sufficient money for a campaign to seize Coele-Syria, he 'pointed to his Friends and said "There, walking about, are my money bags"' (Diod. 29.29). Antiochus IV's procession at Daphne was paid for partly from the spoils of Egypt, partly from 'contributions from his Friends' (Pol. 30.26.9). 'Mercenary' officers perhaps received bonuses only until they were established in the kingdom.[12]

It is also clear that there were families with a tradition of authority in the Ptolemaic kingdom at least, and that members of these families might expect high office in their turn. This is clear from the *strategoi* of Cyprus, where often the fathers or children are known to have held high rank. High-level posts never became hereditary and were always in the gift of the king, but there were families with a long history of service, and corresponding stability of loyalty, and the sons of important men within the kingdom themselves often rose to important positions, sush as Philon, *strategos* of Cyrene, whose father was a friend of Ptolemy III, or Theodoros, son of a *strategos* of Cyprus who himself also became *strategos*. Tlepolemos, who played an instrumental role in the overthrow of Agathocles, was himself from a family with a long history of important service. Philip V ordered the sons of the opponents he had executed to be imprisoned, for 'as most of these young people were notable owing to the high stations their fathers had held, their misfortune too became notable and excited the pity of all' (Pol. 23.10.8–10). It is therefore likely that a major contribution to the importance and standing of any figure in the kingdom was the status of his father.

So there could certainly be men described as important in the kingdom, but it is still apparent that the favour and personal attachment of the king was what brought real power. Diodotos Tryphon, for example, was important because 'he stood high in esteem among the king's Friends' (Diod. 23.4a). Galaistes was son of the ex-king of the Athamanians and so came to be a Friend of Ptolemy VI and commander of his forces, but when the king 'showed himself ill disposed towards him' and stripped him of his estates he fled to Greece (Diod. 33.20). Apelles was 'unable either to keep Philip under his influence or to endure the diminishment of his power that resulted from the king's disregard' (Pol. 5.2.8), so he returned to Chalcis, 'all yielding him obedience owing to his former credit at court' (5.2.10). The ultimately total dependence on the king of such court officials is made clear by Polybius: Apelles returned from Chalcis to visit Philip V, accompanied by a crowd of soldiers, but Philip refused to see him, 'upon which his followers at once began to drop away quite openly' (Pol. 5.26.7). Polybius remarks that courtiers are like counters on a reckoning board, 'for those at the will of the reckoner are now worth a copper and now worth a talent, and courtiers at the nod of the king are at one moment universally envied and at the next universally pitied' (5.26.13). Polybius' observation is commonplace enough, but it is apparent that it is also true; the personal approval of Philip really was vital in determining the standing of Apelles. Courtiers, those attached to the king, might have been able to exercise the greatest influence on the affairs of the kingdom, but without the independent power base that lands and armed forces gave, as were available in the command of a satrapy for example, they were entirely dependent on the good will of the king and also of those other Friends and soldiers around them. The whole episode of the conspiracy of Apelles can be seen as an attempt by Philip to shake off his predecessor's advisors. If this is the case, then what Philip had to overcome to remove Apelles and the others was not their personal power or status, but the relative approval felt towards them and himself by the army and the others around him.

Council meetings had occurred under Alexander and they were continued by his Successors, involving Friends and military commanders. For instance, Perdiccas, wondering whether to march against Macedon or against Ptolemy, 'gathering his Friends and generals, referred to them for consideration of the question' (Diod. 18.25.6). Antigonus called a council of his Friends at which he informed them of his plans for imperial power (Diod. 18.50.5), while Polyperchon, pondering the problem of Cassander, 'since he had made up his mind to do nothing without the advice of his Friends, called together all the commanders and the most important of the other Macedonians' (Diod. 18.55.1). Ptolemy in Syria in 312 'called together his leaders and Friends and took counsel with them' (Diod. 19.93.5). Similarly, the kings discussed matters in council – 'the council was called to discuss the revolt of Molon, and the king [Antiochus III] ordered everyone to state his opinion as to how the rebellion should be dealt with' (Pol. 5.41.6; with a further meeting to discuss the same issue at 5.49.1), and Antiochus VII was advised by his Friends to wipe out the Jews, although he declined to do so (Diod. 34/35.1), and his Friends tried to persuade him not to engage in his final battle with the Parthians (34/35.16). Antiochus III also decided on his settlement of Jewish colonists after consulting with his Friends (Jos. *Ant.* 12.147). Philip V held a succession of councils: to decide to prosecute the war against Aetolia at sea (Pol. 5.2.1), to lay plans against Sparta (Pol. 5.22.8) and to discuss peace with Aetolia (Pol. 5.102.2). Perseus in council discussed peace terms with Rome (Pol. 28.8). A council of Ptolemy V tried Scopas for treason (Pol. 18.54), while Ptolemy VI and his advisors 'decided to draw up a list of councillors' from the most distinguished commanders (Pol. 28.19.1), which dispatched envoys to Antiochus IV. It is not necessary to suppose that such councils any more formed a formal element of state than did the army assemblies; clearly they are informal meetings, attendance at which is in the gift of the king, on the basis of personal choice. Thus, for example, an Alexander, who 'reached the degree of friendship with Philip V where he took part in private councils' (Liv. 30.18.1), although of course the king would not always have had a completely free choice. The meetings of the king's council were frequent, and it is clear that they were more than just a rubber stamp. Particularly if the king was young or of inactive character, the king's ministers could exercise considerable power. According to Polybius, it was Antiochus III's council which decided that the king should take the field against Molon (5.49.6). But the council meetings had no formal powers and served only as an opportunity for the exchange of ideas, which the king was free to accept or reject. Too great a role in affairs on the part of one of the Friends would be avoided – Antiochus III was suspicious of Hannibal (who after his exile from Carthage joined Antiochus' court), feeling that there should be only one leader (Liv. 33.42).[13]

As under Alexander, so for the Hellenistic kings: there were ways in which the king could stress the personal attachment his subordinates owed to him. It is likely, as mentioned above, that the high officials and officers did not usually receive military pay, but it is clear that the wealth to be had from plunder or, more frequently, from possession of lands and management of taxation was considerable, and it is fair to suppose that this was an important consideration. Certainly, the loyalty of subordinates could be bought, with the usual combination of gifts and promises, as well as earned by more personal means. Perdiccas, facing Ptolemy, 'called the commanders together, and by gifts to some, by great promises to others, and by friendly intercourse with all, won them over to his service and inspired them to meet the coming dangers' (Diod. 18.33.5). Eumenes obtained the support of Peucestes 'with kind words and great promises', although he also took loans from the other satraps as hostages for their loyalty (Diod. 19.24.1–3). Antigonus tried to win over the commanders of the *Argyraspides* by promising them 'great gifts and greater satrapies', although he failed, as they calculated that if Antigonus became more powerful he 'would take away their satrapies and set up some of his Friends in their places' (Diod. 18.62.4). Eurydice in Macedon, 'by plying the most active of the Macedonians with gifts and promises, was trying to make them personally loyal to herself' (Diod. 19.11.1). When Polycleitos defeated a fleet of Antigonus, 'Ptolemy praised him, honoured him with great gifts, and gave him much greater preferment' (Diod. 19.64.8). Scopas in Alexandria received pay from Ptolemy and also 'the profit from field operations', meaning perhaps plunder (Pol. 13.2.3). Reward could of course be in the form of promotion as well as of gifts. Ptolemaios, nephew of Antigonus, rebelled against him because 'he was not being honoured according to his deserts' (Pol. 20.19.2). Agathocles and Sosibios in Alexandria 'were compelled to conciliate the whole court, holding out hopes of favour to everyone if things fell out as they wished' (Pol. 5.36.2).

There were also many reasons why a subordinate's loyalty could be undermined; commonly a king could be despised for his weakness or apparent lack of authority. Molon and his associate Alexander 'despised the king [Antiochus III] on account of his youth' (Pol. 5.41.1). Demetrius I attained the Syrian throne, but without the support of the Romans; as a result 'not only the other kings but even some of the satraps subject to him regarded his kingship with scant respect', including Timarchos, who rebelled against him (Diod. 31.27a).

However, the relationship between the king and his subordinates remained essentially personal, and it is personal factors that are often stressed as the reason for loyalty to a king. Ptolemy I in particular appears in Diodorus as especially personally amenable – upon his arrival in Egypt, Ptolemy collected mercenaries, and 'a multitude of Friends also gathered about him on account of his fairness' (Diod. 18.14.1). In contrast, Perdiccas 'was a man of blood, one who usurped the authority of the other commanders and in general wished to rule all by force; but Ptolemy on the contrary was generous and fair' (Diod. 18.33.3). Ptolemy again 'had, as a rule, the advantage in his undertakings, since he had many persons who were well disposed to him and ready to undergo danger gladly for his sake' (Diod. 18.33.4), and he 'was exceptionally gentle and forgiving and inclined towards deeds of kindness. It was this very thing that most increased his power and made many men desire to share his friendship' (Diod. 19.86.3). The king's personal leadership and willingness to share in the dangers faced by his men could also encourage his subordinates. Ptolemy, resisting the invasion of Perdiccas, 'who had the best soldiers near himself and wished to encourage the other commanders and Friends to face the dangers', took a sarissa and fought in the forefront (Diod. 18.34.2). Pyrrhus was 'kind towards his familiar friends' (Plut. *Pyrr.* 50.4). Ptolemy IV, on the other hand, failed in this regard; Theodotos had performed great services for his kingdom, 'but in return for them he had not only received no thanks, but had been in danger for his life' (Pol. 5.61.4), and as a result Theodotos was disgusted with the king (5.61.5). Ceraias, another of Ptolemy's officers, deserted to Antiochus, 'and by his [Antiochus'] distinguished treatment of him he turned the heads of many of the enemy's commanders' (Pol. 5.70.10). Of Philip V, during his early morally upright period, Polybius comments that 'it would be impossible to speak in adequate terms of the affection and devotion to him of Alexander, Chrysogonos and his other Friends' (Pol. 7.11.6).

The holding of frequent banquets of the king with his Friends and officers also served to underline this personal relationship. Ptolemy, after defeating Antigonus' 306 invasion, 'entertained his Friends lavishly' (Diod. 20.76.6). Philip V, after his successful invasion of Aetolia, 'invited all his commanding officers to a banquet' (Pol. 5.14.8). Such banquets were special occasions laid on for what was obviously a wider circle than the king's personal acquaintances – in Philip V's case, the officers of the army are included; on a more regular basis, the king also dined with a more intimate circle of friends that would include philosophers as well as military figures.[14]

The function of the Friends as counsellors and the expected personal affability of the king meant that Friends might hope to be allowed a certain freedom of expression, equivalent in Macedonian custom to the freedom of speech enjoyed by the army. Ptolemy 'granted to all the commanders the right to speak frankly' (Diod. 18.33.3), and Pyrrhus pardoned those who had abused him while drunk (Plut. *Dem.* 50.5). Philip V, on the other hand, executed one of his Friends, and so 'none of his Friends any longer dared speak their minds and rebuke the king's folly for fear of his impetuous temper' (Pol. 28.2). Similarly, Ptolemy V 'came to hate Aristomenes', his guardian, 'for his frankness of speech, and finally compelled him to end his life' (Pol. 28.14), and Ptolemy VIII executed some Cyreneans for 'certain frank and honest statements' (Pol. 33.13). Perseus was inclined to offer concessions to Rome to end the war, but 'most of his Friends found fault with him and told him that now he was victorious he was acting as if he were unsuccessful and indeed utterly defeated' (Pol. 27.8.14).

There also developed a genuine sense of duty and of obedience to orders among subordinates. Nicanor, commanding the garrison in Athens, told the Athenians that 'as a garrison commander appointed by Cassander he himself had no power of independent action' (Diod. 18.64.6). Aristonous refused to surrender Amphipolis to Cassander until directly ordered to do so by Olympias, who had appointed him (Diod. 19.50.7–8). Andronicos, commander of Tyre for Antigonus, when summoned to surrender by Ptolemy after Gaza, 'said that he would in no wise betray the trust that had been placed in him by Antigonus and Demetrius'. When Ptolemy later captured him he was specially rewarded for this loyalty (Diod.19.86.2). When Lysimachus captured Ephesus in 302, 'Philip, one of the Friends of Antigonus, who was guarding the citadel, held firm his loyalty toward the man who had placed trust in him' (Diod. 20.107.5). The commander of Perge in Pamphylia refused to evacuate in accordance with the treaty of Apamea until he received a direct order from the king to do so (Pol. 21.44.1). Garrisons were likely all under oath not to give up their positions without authority from the king.[15]

As I argued above, there do not seem to have been independently powerful army commanders as such; but the important men within the kingdom, who would be grouped as Friends around the king, were also holders of military authority, whether directly, as commanders of the Peltasts or *strategos* of a region of the kingdom, or indirectly as they accompanied the king and army on campaign. These figures could also sometimes command personal loyalty from the army units under their command. The clearest example is that of Leontius, commander of the Peltasts. Upon his arrest by Philip V, the Peltasts wrote to Philip in characteristically blunt language, expressing the view that any harm done to Leontius would be regarded as a slight to themselves. 'This warm support of Leontius by the Peltasts served only to exasperate the king' (and no doubt to frighten him), and Philip had Leontius executed (Pol. 5.27). In the event they gave no trouble, but they had already shown that they were an unruly group, becoming mutinous over alleged irregularities in the distribution of plunder. Subordinate figures could win over the loyalty of men posted under them by the same methods – promises and gifts – as were used by the kings to secure the loyalty of their subordinates. Antigonus learned that Pithon 'was winning the support of many of the soldiers in the winter quarters by promises and gifts and that he planned to revolt' (Diod. 19.46.1). Ptolemaios, a general of Antigonus, joined Ptolemy, but 'on discovering that he had become presumptuous and was trying to win over the leaders to himself by conversing with them and giving them gifts', Ptolemy had him killed (Diod. 20.27.3), this in spite of Ptolemy's reputation for kindness. Hermeias paid off the arrears of the army of Antiochus III and the soldiers 'grew well disposed to the man who had procured payment of their pay' (Pol. 5.50.7).

If a general was to revolt against the king, he first needed the support of some military forces; this was a simple necessity, and it is clear from Polybius that it was the support of the army that could tempt a general into open rebellion, as was the case with Achaeus (Pol. 4.48). No doubt kings were aware of this danger, and some aspects of administrative organization may have been directed towards lessening the possibility of the army siding with their general. Alexander, governor of Corinth for Antigonus Gonatas, was able to rebel, presumably with the support of the garrison of Corinth, and maintain himself independently for some years. The majority of his forces must have been mercenaries, however, so the loyalty of the mass of Macedonians was not in question. Ptolemaios, governor of Ephesus in the third century, was also able to revolt with the aid of his Thracian mercenaries, although in the end they mutinied against him. Molon gained the support of the troops for his revolt by a mix of gifts and threats – 'having worked upon the troops in his own satrapy till they were ready for anything, by the hopes of booty he held out and the fear which he instilled into their officers by producing forged letters from the king couched in threatening terms' (Pol. 5.43.5). Similarly, Hermeias had 'subjugated to his will the councillors by fear and the troops by doing them a service' (Pol. 5.50.9). Dionysios Petosarapis scorned the brother Ptolemies 'because of their youth and inexperience', and 'sending messages to the soldiers who were ripe for rebellion he sought to persuade them to share his hopes' (Pol. 31.15a). Foreigners might have particular connections with mercenary troops, as was the case with Cleomenes and the Peloponnesian troops in Alexandria (Pol. 5.36), where 'the thought of Cleomenes' daring and popularity with the mercenaries kept on haunting' Sosibios (Pol. 5.36.7), or with some of the defectors to Antiochus III (Pol. 5.61 f.), for example Hippolochos, who took with him 400 cavalry, presumably his own contingent, but it is the Friends rather than the army officers as such who are likely to rebel against the king. Generally the permanent officers of units were too insignificant to consider rebellion themselves.

Equally important was an ability to deal with the masses. Molon, after initial successes, 'carefully refreshed his troops and after addressing them started again to pursue his further projects' (Pol. 5.48.16), but even so, his men were said to be 'exceedingly well disposed to the king' (Pol. 5.46.7). Ptolemy VIII's general Hierax inspired devotion, 'having a gift for dealing with crowds, besides being open hearted' (Pol. 33.22), while Epigenes, who brought back the army of Seleucus III from Asia Minor, 'was capable both as a speaker and a man of action, and enjoyed great popularity with the soldiers' (Pol. 5.41.4). The generals of the Egyptian army before Raphia inspired the men with frequent reviews and addresses (Pol. 5.64.4, 64.7). Tlepolemos, opposing the growing power of Agathocles, 'collected his forces round him' and provided himself with money, hoping that 'both the troops under his own command and those in Alexandria placed in him their hopes of overthrowing' Agathocles, but he also, 'as he was desirous of attaching to himself the commanders [*hegemones*], taxiarchs, and inferior officers, entertained them sedulously at banquets' (Pol. 15.25.26.f.), and he was naturally courageous and got on easily with the soldiers (Pol. 16.21.3).

The moral qualities required of the ideal official in Egypt were similar to those of the king. The importance of the courage of the commander is reflected in the fact that the lesser commanders shared with the kings the practice of leading from the front, inspiring their men with their own example and sharing their dangers. A failed escalade at the siege of Rhodes led to the capture of part of the attacking force, 'among whom were some of the most distinguished leaders' (Diod. 20.87.3), and Pyrrhus fought a single combat with Pantauchos, general of Demetrius in Aetolia (Plut. *Dem.* 41.2; *Pyrr.* 7.4). In battles the subordinates seem always to be leading from the front, and this was also true in local operations – Nicanor, *strategos* of Judaea and formerly *elephantarch*, was the first to fall in battle with the Jewish rebels (*I Macc.* 7.44).

Apparently the primary military function of the subordinate commanders holding independent authority was to suppress rebels, while the task of leading expeditions against foreign enemies would fall to the king alone. This is most clear in the case of the revolt of Molon, where Hermeias sent Xenoitas against Molon, 'saying that to fight against rebels was the business of generals, but that against kings the king himself should plan the operations and command in the decisive battles' (Pol. 5.45.6). The best examples of activities of this sort appear in *I Maccabees*, where there is a succession of local campaigns by figures of apparently low standing, whose job is evidently to maintain the peace in their own regions. These begin with Apollonius, governor of Samaria (Jos. *Ant.* 12.261), who mustered the soldiers from Samaria (*I Macc.* 3.10.12), followed by Seron, 'commander of the army', who hoped to win renown for himself by actions which evidently were not authorized by his superiors (*I Macc.* 3.13–26), and culminating in the involvement of Ptolemy, *strategos* of Coele-Syria (*I Macc.* 3.38) and former general of Ptolemy IV (Pol. 5.65.3) and, when the revolt was still not under control, finally that of the king. The king might have to be consulted by his juniors on points of politics, but there clearly was scope for some military glory at the lower levels. Such regional commanders might also act to maintain order in areas outside their strict jurisdiction. Hippomedon, Ptolemaic strategos of Thrace, sent troops to aid Samothrace, and a decree from Athens records the aid to the city of Kallias, who brought a contingent of mercenaries from Andros to help the city in its revolt against Demetrius Poliorcetes, and was wounded while leading the resistance to the garrison forces. The duties of such regional commanders in maintaining order within their areas provide an exception to the observation that regional commanders do not normally lead their men in battle. When the forces of a region are involved in the suppression of revolt within the province, the regional commander clearly does lead the men, often in person. In this case, however, it is again clear that the regional commander, usually a Friend and high-ranking official, holds the command and not the unit commanders, who again are unimportant, and there is no evidence for the existence of independent satrapal armies in the style of the Achaemenids or the satraps of Alexander. The soldiers used are settlers, regulars of the royal army or mercenaries, but mercenaries hired by the king, not privately by the subordinates. Where units do have their own officers, they are usually ally mercenaries, and the officers are independent nobles or dynasts, not royal Friends or officers.[16]

In conclusion, the commanders of the army were not always or necessarily the same figures as the administrators of the kingdom, even where those administrators had elements of the army under their command in peacetime. Similarly, the administrators were not themselves drawn from the army; rather, the king's personal friends and attendants could serve as army commanders or regional administrators, or both, as circumstances and their special abilities demanded. These figures were distinguished from the professional officers of the army whom they commanded by special titles, proximity to the king and flexibility in terms of service. The army for its part showed no great tendency to support its commanders above the king, as the only figures with which the army had close contact were the professional officers, with little influence in the kingdom. Independent power could, however, be gained by those who controlled large territories and the soldiers in them. The main division was therefore not between the king on one side and the army with its officers on the other, but between the king and his Friends, and the army. This did not always mean that army or Friends were loyal to the king, of course, but after Alexander the phenomenon of officers important in the kingdom and holding personal commands over army units had been replaced by commanders dependent for their authority entirely on the king.

Battlefield command

We have seen that there was a formal hierarchy of officers at least up to the level of the largest subunits (the Alexandrian *taxis*, or later *chiliarchia* or *merarchia* or its equivalent), and perhaps a more informal level of command above this level; and that overall command of larger units, or of groups of several units, in the army was entrusted not to army officers, but to Friends of the king. There remained a distinction between the army commanders who were themselves part of the army or phalanx, and the senior commanders placed over the whole phalanx or large sections of it. But the ultimate purpose of the phalanx was of course to win battles, so now we must turn to the question of how the phalanx was commanded in combat.[17]

The basis of the command system as described by Asclepiodotus is worth quoting again:

> 'The supernumeraries [*ektaktoi*] were formerly attached to the company [*taxis*], as their name indicates, because they were not included in the number of the company: an army-herald, a signalman, a bugler, an aide, and a file-closer. The first was to pass on the command by a spoken order, the second by a signal, in case the order could not be heard because of the uproar, the third by the bugle, whenever the signal could not be seen for the dust; the aide was there to fetch whatever was needed, while the supernumerary file-closer was to bring up the straggler to his position in the company.' (Asclepiodotus, *Tactics* 2.9)

So these supernumeraries, 'formerly' (Asclepiodotus doesn't say when) attached to the *taxis* (a formation of eight files of eight men, not the larger 1,500-man unit of Alexander's army), were, when the file was increased to sixteen men, then attached to the *speira* or *syntagma* (or *syntaxiarchia*, as Asclepiodotus throws in another name for the formation as this point), the formation of sixteen files of sixteen men, since 'the square, by reason of the equal length of the sides of the formation could hear equally well the commands from every quarter' (*Tactics* 2.9).

So the supernumeraries are those who are not counted among the number of the formation, and so do not form up in its ranks and files – these men literally stood outside the formation, whether to its front, flanks or rear we don't know (except in the case of the file-closer, of course). One thing to note is the obvious omission of the *syntagmatarches*, the commander of the *syntagma*, which raises the interesting question of where the phalanx officers stood. It is sometimes supposed that the officers themselves stood in the ranks of the phalanx, usually (it is assumed) at the head of the rightmost file (the position of honour). This may well have been true for the junior officers below the level of the *syntagmatarch*, but it cannot have been true for the *syntagmatarch* himself, since he must have stood beside his herald, signaller, bugler and aide in order to tell them the orders he wanted them to transmit. So we should assume that officers from this rank upwards were not themselves physically part of the phalanx, but stationed themselves outside the ranks and files – presumably in front of the phalanx in normal circumstances, so that they could see what was going on, though when the phalanx came into action it must have been necessary to take shelter in, beside or behind the ranks.

Armies of this period had a very strong tradition of personal leadership, where the officers right up to the highest level, including the kings themselves, wishing to display their qualities of leadership and set an example to the men, fought in the front rank (or at least near the front rank, since they fought among their bodyguards and senior officers). But where the senior officers of the phalanx might have stationed themselves in combat remains unknown. The tradition of personal leadership, and the fact that senior officers were sometimes killed or wounded in battle, suggests they would have been in or near the front of the formation, but, as with the *syntagmatarches*, the requirements of command and communication with the supernumeraries must have meant that they did not simply form part of the front rank. At the top level of command (the commanders of the *taxeis* of Alexander's army, the *chiliarchiai* or *merarchiai* of Asclepiodotus), it is also possible that the officers were on horseback (as this would give them a bit of extra height to see what was going on, and speed to get to a point of crisis when needed), but how then they would have positioned themselves – behind the line for a good view, but a most unheroic place to stand, or somehow in the front among the pikes – remains unknown. Asclepiodotus also has nothing to say about any supernumeraries above the level of the *syntagma*, but they must surely have existed. Officers at each level would have required a similar number (at least the trio of herald, signaller and bugler to pass on orders, and an aide) and could not have simply used those of the *syntagmata*, who would have been busy with their own tasks. So presumably there were similar functionaries for each of the higher levels of command, though not every interim level would necessarily have needed them. We might guess that the *chiliarchia*, the unit of around 1,000 men, four *syntagmata*, would have had its own supernumeraries, as would the *taxis/merarchia*. In the accounts of Alexander's battles, the *taxeis* appear to operate largely independently, so it is likely that a separate command structure above this level was not needed, but the overall phalanx commander, or quite likely the commanders of the left and right wings of the phalanx, might have had their own aides and staff. At Gaugamela, for example, 'Parmenion sent a despatch rider to Alexander to report with all haste that his troops were in distress and needed help' (Arr. *Anab.* 3.15.1), although Parmenion was stationed with cavalry on this occasion, and the Greek is not explicit that it was a rider, though in order to catch Alexander it is a fair assumption. Again we can only guess where commanders would have positioned themselves in the phalanx, but very likely they were not simply incorporated on foot into the front rank.[18]

As to the mechanics of transmitting orders, Asclepiodotus goes into great detail, but we should note that he is again specifically talking about orders at the level of the *syntagma*:

> 'We shall furthermore train the army to distinguish sharply the commands given sometimes by the voice, sometimes by visible signals, and sometimes by the bugle. The most distinct commands are those given by the voice, but they may not carry at all times because of the clash of arms or heavy gusts of wind; less affected by uproar are the commands given by signals; but even these may be interfered with now and then by the sun's glare, thick fog and dust, or heavy rain. One cannot, therefore, find signals, to which the phalanx has become accustomed, suitable for every circumstance that arises, but now and then new signals must be found to meet the situation.' (Asclepiodotus, *Tactics* 12.10)

Asclepiodotus goes on to list some of the voice commands used, which like modern drill commands, have the particular command before the general – so not 'face right', but rather 'right face' – and for the same reason (so that nobody anticipates the order and turns the wrong way). The other commands he lists are immediately familiar to anyone who has ever been subjected to any military drill: 'Attention! ... Shoulder arms! ... Dress ranks! ... Right face! ... Forward march! ... Halt!' and so forth. He does not list a command which we know from battle accounts was also given – 'Lower sarissas!' for bringing the sarissas down level prior to going into action (e.g. Pol. 2.69.7 for Sellasia, and 18.24.9 for Cynoscephalae).[19]

Given the comments on signals and bugles, there must have been signal and bugle equivalents for some or all of these verbal orders, at least for the most important of them. The form the signal would have taken is not clear, though we can assume a standard of some sort, perhaps a small flag suspended from a pole. Such a standard is visible on the depiction of the phalanx in action shown in fig 2.1, Chapter 2, and a similar one (though highly fragmentary) appears to be held by a Persian cavalryman in the Alexander Mosaic. So it may be that this type of standard, swung or dipped in various ways, would have been used to transmit the orders (the signaller would then of course have had to be at the front of the formation, in order to be seen by the men). Presumably a bugler would have various combinations of brief phrases, similar to those of more modern military buglers, which would have functioned in a similar way; there is no direct evidence for such advanced commands (the trumpet signals we hear of in literary sources being considerably more rudimentary), but I think their existence is implied, at least to some extent, by Asclepiodotus' account. It does appear that the Spartan army, however, relied on word of mouth for transmitting signals – 'orders to wheel from column into line of battle are given verbally by the *enomotarch* acting as a herald' (Xen. *Const.Lac.* 11.6).[20]

So we get a fairly clear picture of the mechanics of command at the level of the *syntagma*. The commanding officer would have made his wishes known to the herald, who would have shouted the order to the men. A *syntagma* in standard formation would have made a sixteen metre square, so a man with the voice of a typical sergeant-major should have had no difficulty making himself heard in normal circumstances, and if circumstances were not normal (or perhaps anyway to be sure) the signaller and/or bugler would also transmit the command. As Asclepiodotus makes clear, commands issued were at a low level of granularity. For example, the officer would not simply say 'form close order to the right', but would break the command down into constituent components, as we saw in Chapter 3 – 'right file hold position, other files right face, close up to the right, face the front, rear ranks advance'. It is admittedly hard to see how all this could be transmitted by signal, so perhaps the signaller was used only for the simpler orders (halt, advance and so on).

What Asclepiodotus does not tell us, and for which there is no good evidence elsewhere, is how command worked at levels above the *syntagma*.

For example, if a whole phalanx, taking as an example Alexander's phalanx in his major battles, of some 9,000 men, needed to manoeuvre together, this would require coordinating the movements of each of the major subdivisions (six *taxeis* in Alexander's case), each of which was in turn made up of six *syntagmata* (taking the standard interpretation of 1,500-man *taxeis*), giving the overall phalanx thirty-six separate subunits to be commanded and moved individually. Presumably a *taxis* could be manoeuvred by issuing appropriate orders to its constituent *syntagmata*, though the senior commander (*taxiarch*) could hardly have issued orders of the very fine level of granularity described above. Rather it was probably the practice, if anything more complex than a forward advance in current formation was required, to control the movement of the rightmost or lead *syntagma*, and rely on the commanders of the other *syntagmata* to take formation on the lead unit, issuing appropriate commands to make this so. In wheels and deployments from line, for instance, a lead unit would have had to march to its required destination while leaving space for the other units to form up, something that must have required considerable expertise and judgement (recall the great importance attached to officers and commanders having practical experience in the field).

Because of the complexity and difficulty of manoeuvring in this way in any direction other than straight ahead, it was probably usual practice to march and wheel in column with turns in place into line (as we will see in the following chapter), rather than wheeling whole lines. Although it is common, and tempting, to imagine the neatly drawn blocks usually to be found on modern battle maps as wheeling and manoeuvring at will, executing a wheel in any sort of extended line would have been exceptionally difficult, with plentiful opportunity for error and disorder. A march in column simply required each *syntagma* to follow its leader, marching where it marched and turning at the same point it did, in much the same way as a formation of ships in line ahead could be easily manoeuvred. This is why outflanking manoeuvres, for example, seem to have been conducted by forming a column perpendicular to the line of advance, with a turn in column to the desired heading, then a turn in place to form line (examples of which we will see in the next chapter), a much more controllable manoeuvre. This was not a feature unique to the Macedonian phalanx – all linear formations would have been subject to similar problems of manoeuvre, and although there is a tendency to imagine manoeuvres in line, in fact anything more than a straight-ahead advance would probably have required the formation of a column first to execute efficiently. Sadly, none of the tacticians take an interest in manoeuvre at this intermediate level, and we are left to infer it from the sometimes vague battle accounts in literary authors.

A *syntagma* itself is a very compact formation: just 16 metres on each side in normal spacing. But a line of four *syntagmata* making up a *chiliarchia*, even assuming no gaps between units, will already occupy 64 metres, and either orders to coordinate the movements of the four constituent parts need to be transmitted to each *syntagma* separately and then relayed to the individual phalangites, or else there needs to be a separate set of orders for the *chiliarchia* as a whole, with predetermined drills for the individual *syntagmata*. For example, if the *chiliarchia* was to be deployed from column into line to the right, would it be necessary to send low-level orders to each individual *syntagma* – 'march x paces, halt, face right, march y paces, halt', and so forth – or would it be sufficient to order the whole *chiliarchia* to 'deploy to the right' and rely on the officers of the *syntagmata* to apply set drills to achieve the desired result? And what is true at this level is true also at each higher level: would separate orders and drills be required for each *merarchia* (2,000 men), each *keras* (8,000 men) and so forth?

Here we can only speculate, as the tactical manuals describe some high-level formations and manoeuvres (such as found in Asclepiodotus 11, where various marching formations are defined), but give no details of the drills or commands needed to adopt or switch between such formations. All the details of drill and commands in the tacticians are at the lowest level, orders that would be transmitted at the level of the *syntagma*. I think it is inconceivable that the larger-level formations could have been commanded only with these very granular, low-level orders. For comparison, the tactical manuals of other eras, particularly the seventeenth to nineteenth centuries (AD), where formed masses of men were still manoeuvred on the battlefield, contain considerable detail on higher-level manoeuvres and formations (those of battalion, regiment and brigade, at the least, bodies of hundreds up to several thousands of men), with details of the manoeuvres required by the subunits to achieve the desired outcome. I imagine that, although they are not recorded by the tacticians, such set drills also existed for higher-level units in the Macedonian phalanx, at least for the more common manoeuvres. While the basic unit of manoeuvre was the *syntagma*, the unit of command (the level at which individual commanders would issue orders more or less independently) would have been either the *chiliarchia* (1,000 men) or *merarchia* (2,000), or sometimes an intermediate size. The *taxis* commanders of Alexander's army seem to have formed the basic unit of command (to which Alexander himself, for example, could transmit independent orders), and there would have been set drills for the constituent *syntagmata* of these units (four, six or eight in number) to achieve the overall manoeuvre required. Above this level, there may also have been drills for half-phalanx (*keras*, 8,000 men) and whole phalanx, or at this level it might have been necessary to issue individual commands to the *chiliarchia/merarchia* or to rely on their commander's initiative. I will examine some practical examples of what was involved in the following chapter.

As usual in sophisticated military structures, the overall picture was of delegated hierarchical command, with the low-level commanders handling the low-level drill and tactics required to move and manoeuvre the phalanx, while higher-level commanders (and the king or commanding general himself) concerned themselves more with the 'big picture'. The usual rule of thumb in military command is that officers at each level should only have to concern themselves with the next two levels of command down from their own, so an overall phalanx commander might send orders to half-phalanx commanders (units of 8,000) and to merarchs (units of 2,000), but not below. Arrian's account of Alexander's address to his officers before Gaugamela gives a good idea of what was expected:

> '[H]e required each of them [the officers] to encourage his own men; the *lochagoi* their *lochoi*, the *ilarchs* their *ilai*, the *taxiarchs* their *taxeis*, and the *hegemones* of the infantry the phalanx of which each was placed in charge... . They were to urge each man in the moment of danger to attend in his own place in the line to the requirements of order, to keep perfect silence when that was necessary in the advance, and by contrast to give a ringing shout when it was right to shout ... they themselves were to obey orders sharply and to pass them on sharply to their *taxeis*, and every man should recall that neglect of his own duty brought the whole cause into common danger.' (Arrian, *Anabasis* 3.9.6 f.)

To repeat a point made earlier, because of this command and order structure and the practised drills, the Macedonian phalanx was certainly much more flexible and manoeuvrable than the Classical phalanx that preceded it, or than most other heavy infantry formations of the time, though less so than the Roman legion, as we will see in Chapter 9.[21]

Higher-level command

At the higher level, the army commander (the king in major battles) would need to decide on a plan, communicate his intentions to his subordinates and then coordinate their actions. Evidently the formulation and communication of the plan could take place in council meetings – similar to those held by the king to decide matters of higher policy and discussed above – at which the commanders would be present. Alexander's council before Gaugamela again provides a good example:

> '[Upon sighting the Persians, Alexander] stopped his phalanx there, and again summoned the companions, *strategoi*, *ilarchs* and *hegemones* of the allies and foreign mercenary troops, and put the question whether he should advance his phalanx at once from this point, as most of them urged, or as Parmenion thought best, camp there for the time being [and reconnoitre]. Parmenion's advice prevailed, and they camped there, in the order in which they were to engage in battle.'
> (Arrian, *Anabasis* 3.9.3–4)

In this case, the 'companions' are the king's Friends (to use the later terminology – and not, of course, the Companion cavalry), the *ilarchs* are the commanders of the cavalry, and the *strategoi* presumably the *taxiarchs* of the phalanx. For Alexander's battles generally, we often see such councils of war in which possibilities are discussed. The ultimate decision would of course lie with the king. Such councils would also be used to pass on the orders (particularly the order of battle – that is, the position in which each unit was to form up) and any instruction on particular tactics to be employed. This would have been done verbally at such councils, though there may also have been written orders. Arrian tells us, quoting Alexander's general and biographer Aristobolus, that the Persian order of battle for Gaugamela was captured after the battle (Arr. *Anab.* 3.11.3).

Just before battle would also have been the time at which the king made a speech (or more likely a series of speeches) to inspire his army. These pre-battle speeches have a special place in ancient historiography. Historians from Thucydides onward included pre-battle speeches in their accounts, although needless to say there are serious doubts whether the actual words of any such speeches were ever recorded, or how it would have been possible to deliver a long formal speech to an army tens of thousands strong. For ancient historians, such speeches were an exercise in rhetoric; but this is not to say that their contents were entirely imaginary, as a historian would want to set out the sorts of things that he expected would have been said on such an occasion, even if he could not quote the actual words. For the Hellenistic era we have many rhetorical speeches of this nature, but also indications of what would more likely have been the usual practice. There are records of longer, more formal speeches given in camp or on parade (we have already seen such speeches outside the context of pitched battle in previous chapters), but also that the general would pass down the line once the army was drawn up for battle, addressing short encouraging remarks to each unit as he passed. Such exhortations followed a familiar pattern, emphasizing reasons for confidence, along with 'why we fight' arguments, and restating the need for discipline and responsiveness to orders. The best example comes from Polybius' account of the Battle of Raphia:

> 'The armies having been drawn up in this fashion, both the kings rode along the line accompanied by their officers and friends, and addressed their soldiers. As they relied chiefly on the phalanx, it was to these troops that they made the most earnest appeal, Ptolemy being supported by Andromachus, Sosibius and his sister Arsinoë and Antiochus by Theodotus and Nicarchus, these being the commanders of the phalanx on either side. The substance of the addresses was on both sides very similar. For neither king could cite any glorious and generally recognized achievement of his own, so that it was by reminding the troops of the glorious deeds of their ancestors that they attempted to inspire them with spirit and courage. They laid the greatest stress, however, on the rewards which they might be expected to bestow in the future, and urged and exhorted both the leaders in particular and all those who were about to be engaged in general to bear themselves therefore like gallant men in the coming battle. So with these or similar words spoken either by themselves or by their interpreters they rode along the line.' (Polybius, 5.83)

The interpreters were presumably needed for the Egyptian phalanx, none of the Ptolemies before the last Cleopatra taking the trouble to learn Egyptian.

To encourage the men to a peak of fighting spirit was not enough, however; orders had to be issued and tactics decided upon. It is often tempting to see a general's dispositions as a response to the array of the enemy, but in many cases the dispositions must have been decided well beforehand. This was especially necessary when the two camps were near; impossible confusion would have resulted if the dispositions were decided on at the spur of the moment. If one army obliged by being drawn up already, or if the approach march was made over a long distance, then last-minute adjustments could be made. At Issus, Alexander had altered the position of the Thessalians and made other minor adjustments (Arr. *Anab.* 2.9); at Paraitacene, Antigonus, on drawing up his battle line, 'seeing that the right wing of the enemy had been strengthened with the elephants and the strongest of the cavalry, arranged against it the lightest of his horsemen' (Diod. 19.26); and at Gaza, Ptolemy and Seleucus at first strengthened their left, but 'when they learned from scouts the formation [Demetrius] had adopted, they quickly reformed their army' (Diod. 19.83). At Sellasia, Antigonus could base his dispositions on several days' reconnaissance, but at Magnesia and Raphia the armies deployed simultaneously and so in accordance with a set plan. At Cynoscephalae similarly, where the armies deployed out of sight of each other, a set deployment must have been followed, as also when Lycurgus left Sparta before an engagement with Philip V, 'leaving directions with his officers and friends as to the coming engagement … in order that whenever he raised the signal they might draw their troops from the town at several points at once and draw them up facing the Eurotas' (Pol. 5.21).

We must anyway suppose that the intelligence that could be gathered about an opposing army was limited. Xenophon, describing the Persian army approaching the Battle of Cunaxa (401), gives an idea of what could be discerned of a large army at a distance:

> '[I]n the early afternoon dust appeared, like a white cloud, and after some time a sort of blackness extending some way over the plain. When they got nearer then suddenly there were flashes of bronze, and the spear points and the enemy formations became visible. There were cavalry with white armour on the enemy's left, and Tissaphernes was said to be in command of them. Next to them were soldiers with wicker shields, and then came hoplites with wooden shields reaching to their feet. These were said to be Egyptians. Then there were more cavalry and archers. In front of them, and at considerable distances apart from each other, were what they call the scythed chariots.' (Xenophon, *Anabasis* 1.8)

Shields were often a distinguishing feature: at Stymphalus, the Eleans mistook the approaching Macedonians for Megalopolitans because of their bronze shields, similar to those issued to the Megalopolitans by Antigonus Doson at Sellasia (Pol. 4.69). Evidently only information of the most general nature could be extracted from such observations; furthermore, these were made at a distance of only a few hundred yards, by which time it might be too late to make changes. Also, dust would make the picture more obscure and, in the absence of any high ground, only the forces in the front of the line would be visible – any drawn up behind them would be obscured. This perhaps was in part the purpose of the front line of skirmishers present in most battles.

The disposition then was largely determined well before battle commenced. General orders to the officers must similarly have been discussed beforehand, although it often appears in the accounts that instructions were sent out as the army was drawn up. On occasion specific orders were issued to senior commanders – at Issus, 'Craterus had been put in command of the infantry of the left and Parmenion of the entire left wing, with orders not to edge away from the sea' (Arr. *Anab.* 2.9). At Gaugamela, Alexander posted a reserve line and 'the commanders of this force had instructions to face about ... if they saw their own forces being surrounded by the Persian army' (Arr. *Anab.* 3.12). At the Hydaspes, 'Coenus was sent ... and ordered to close on the barbarians from behind' (Arr. *Anab.* 5.16). At Paraitacene, Antigonus 'arranged [on his left wing] the lightest of his horsemen, who, drawn up in open order, were to avoid a frontal action but maintain a battle of wheeling tactics' (Diod. 19.29). At Gabiene, Eumenes drew up his right wing under Philip, 'whom he had ordered to avoid battle and to observe the outcome on the other wing' (Diod. 19.40.4). At Sellasia, arrangements were made for different flag signals to begin the attacks (Pol. 2.66). It is of course possible that the sources give only an incomplete idea of the sort of orders issued – we usually hear of orders to only a few officers, although all must have received them. However, the sources find such orders credible, although they appear rudimentary. Two points can be made about them. Firstly, large numbers of units are usually grouped together under a single officer, and orders issued to this officer; the king does not usually concern himself with the individual actions of separate units. Secondly, the orders only specify who, when or where to attack, or how, in general terms, to fight (for example, 'a battle of wheeling tactics'). Of course, these examples cover the whole battleline, not just the phalanx, but we can assume that orders to the phalanx commanders would be similar.

The one order that was clearly given in all battles was the signal to begin the fight. If there had been skirmishes before the lines, as for example at Sellasia and Mantinea (Pol. 2.66, 11.13), then a trumpet signal would recall the skirmishers and a further trumpet signal would be the sign for the battle formally to begin. On occasions specific signals might be arranged for particular units, as at Sellasia, where 'it was arranged that the Illyrians were to begin their assault ... when they saw a flag of linen raised from the direction of Olympus; and that the Megalopolitans should do the same when the king raised a scarlet flag' (Pol. 2.66). There is no evidence for a complex system of trumpet signals at this level of command – only the recall and attack signals are mentioned in battle accounts in literary sources. Sometimes the attack signal would apply to the whole line, but modified by orders to some parts of the line to delay. For example, Eumenes' officer Philip, ordered to observe the outcome on the other wing, or Echecrates on Ptolemy's right wing at Raphia, who 'waited at first to see the result of the struggle between the other wings of the two armies' (Pol. 5.85). At Paraitacene, Antigonus advanced with his right wing forward 'as he had most confidence [in it] and determined to avoid battle with the one and decide the contest with the other' (Diod. 19.29.7), and at Gaza Demetrius intended to fight on the left while the commander of the right 'was ordered to hold his line back and avoid fighting, awaiting the outcome of the conflict fought by Demetrius' (Diod. 19.82). In other words, the battle was often to be fought in stages: first one wing, then the other, then the centre, each stage being delayed to await the result of the previous one, although this was of course not always the pattern. Sometimes the first attack would go to the auxiliary forces, generally chariots or elephants, posted in front of the line, as at Raphia, where the kings 'gave the signal for battle and opened the fight by a charge of elephants' (Pol. 5.84). Livy explains that chariots had to be stationed in front of the line – otherwise they would have to be driven through their own men to reach the enemy (Liv. 37.41). Such advanced forces would then fight, as at Magnesia, before the main lines came into action.

The order of deployment having been drawn up, orders given to the officers and the signal for battle given, what could king or generals do to affect the outcome of the battle? There are obvious physical restrictions in communication, even by mounted dispatch riders, in a battle between lines a few hundred metres apart but a kilometre or two long. It would be quicker to attack and drive away the enemy opposite than to send a message to the other end of the line. Visibility must also have been limited – at Gaugamela, we are told that Alexander turned back to help his left wing, only to find on arrival that it had prevailed without his help (Arr. *Anab.* 3.15.1). At Raphia, Antiochus discovered that his left and centre were defeated only when he saw a cloud of dust moving toward his own camp (Pol. 5.85). At Cynoscephalae, Philip V had to leave the line of battle and make for a hill, from where he could see whether he had won or lost, before retreating (Pol. 18.26). At Caphyae, Aratus had 'an imperfect view of what was going on, and made a bad conjecture of what would happen next' (Pol. 4.12). A general was therefore likely not to know exactly what was happening in a battle, and if he did know, would be restricted in his ability to do anything about it. Orders could be sent out in the course of battle, but only to units near to the general. At Gaugamela, Alexander sent orders to Menidas and to the Paeonians, units alongside the Companions in the line (Arr. *Anab.* 3.13.3). Antigonus, stationed with his phalanx at Sellasia, was able to order it to adopt close order (Pol. 2.69.9), though the nature of any order issued is unclear, as we will see in Chapter 7. On many other occasions generals were able to give orders to or lead units they were with, and to lead them exactly where they were needed. Antiochus at Raphia wheeled his men past the elephants and charged; Eumenes at Paraitacene summoned his light cavalry and outflanked the enemy; while Antigonus for his part attacked Eumenes' forces also on the flank. Such personal leadership could of course inspire the men, but it was also the only practical way to control these units and send them to the exact point, at the precise time, required.

There are few examples of commanders sending detailed orders to units further away in the line; rather, it is clear that other parts of the line, beyond the immediate reach of the general's orders, had to be entrusted entirely to other officers. These would have general instructions from the king, but would in turn issue commands to their junior officers, according to these orders or their own estimation of the situation. At Raphia, 'Echecrates, the commander of the right wing ... when he saw the dust coming his way ... ordered Phoxidas to charge the enemy, while he made a flank movement with the cavalry' (Pol. 5.85). At Paraitacene, 'Pithon's cavalry ... did not consider it safe to make a frontal attack against elephants but went round the wing' (Diod. 19.29). Eumenes at Magnesia, when he attacked the chariots (Liv. 37.41), seems to have been acting on his own initiative. Such initiative on the part of these commanders was expected – hence Antigonus' anger with his cavalry commanders at Sellasia, who stuck too rigidly to their orders (Pol. 2.68). At every level of command, leadership was personal: an officer could order adjacent junior officers but was largely dependent on taking the troops where needed himself. Kings are often criticized for becoming involved in the fighting and so 'losing control of the battle', but it is clear that often only by being in the front line could they have any control at all. Polybius criticized the notion that the commander should ride out in front of his men (Pol. 10.24), but his comments obviously apply largely to manoeuvres outside of battle, and he ignores the undoubted moral advantage of a force led by its commander. For example, Philip V rode far in advance of his army in attacking Athens, motivated – according to Livy – by the desire for personal glory, but in addition 'he pressed into the thick of the enemy, instilling unbounded enthusiasm in his own men and corresponding panic in the enemy' (Liv. 31.24). Control in a battle was therefore limited to the commander's immediate vicinity, while other officers had to be entrusted to fight their own, separate battles on their own initiative.

The most important tactic was always for the king to try to win the battle by his own activities, by leading his best forces to a weak point in the enemy line, such as an exposed flank. The king's presence could inspire the men even where he had no particular personal qualities, as happened at Raphia, where 'Ptolemy, who had retired behind his phalanx, now came forward in the centre, and showing himself in the view of both armies struck terror in the hearts of the enemy, but inspired great spirit and enthusiasm in his own men' (Pol. 5.85).

Given that pursuit made a battle decisive, it was often tempting to press on regardless of what was happening elsewhere. Antiochus III twice lost battles (Raphia and Magnesia) because he pursued too vigorously. However, there were reasons for this, quite apart from the fact that possession of the enemy's baggage could be a major constituent of a victory. No general could assume that he would have time to cross from one flank to the other, or even necessarily to the centre, and it was rarely if ever done in Hellenistic battles. Alexander turned back at Gaugamela, but even here he was too late as Parmenion had won his battle without him. Also, a general simply could not tell whether the rest of his line was winning or losing, and would not want to abandon his pursuit only to find it was unnecessary to do so; as in the conduct of the rest of the battle, he would simply have to trust to the abilities of his officers.[22]

So the command and control capabilities of the phalanx were considerable at the low level of individual drill and the manoeuvres of individual units; but the ability of a general to control the course of a battle on the grand tactical scale would be quite limited, due to limitations of visibility, communication and high-level drill, and much reliance was placed on a preconceived plan and the initiative of subordinates. How the phalanx actually performed in battle will be the subject of the next chapter.

Chapter 7

Battles and tactics

In Chapter 3 I looked at the formations and drill which were available to the Macedonian phalanx, and in Chapter 6 at the mechanics of battlefield command. Here, I want to look at the ways in which a general and his officers could command a phalanx in battle, and the sort of manoeuvres of which the phalanx was capable. This will lead to some discussion of the battles in which the phalanx fought, its manoeuvres and what they tell us about its capabilities. I will not examine every battle in which a phalanx fought (there are quite a few, and they are well described in other publications), but will instead pull out representative or important examples. I will also concentrate chiefly on the great pitched battles rather than the numerous minor operations in which phalanxes, or subunits of a phalanx, were involved. Mostly this is due to restrictions of time and space, but should not blind us to the fact that (despite Polybius' analysis of the phalanx as fit only for one type of fighting), phalanx units were involved in a much wider range of actions than just the formal pitched battles, and we have good details of such actions, particularly for the reign of Alexander.[1]

Deployment

There are two main circumstances in which armies can meet for battle. The first is a formal engagement, where two armies camp near to each other (sometimes very near – just a few hundred metres), then usually through mutual agreement both deploy into line of battle facing each other. They then advance in line (whether as a whole, or sending some contingents in advance) and engage. The alternative is where two armies meet while one or both are on the march: a meeting engagement. In this case the armies must deploy from column of march into battle line (if they have time) and then engage. There are variations on both these possibilities, and other situations might also arise, but formal engagements and meeting engagements make up the vast majority of the battles of the Macedonian phalanx.

It is worth stressing that phalanxes and armies would indeed march in column on their approach to the battlefield. The reasons for doing so are obvious: varied terrain, especially roads or trackways and narrow passes or defiles, would require a column to pass through or along them, while a line, covering a much larger extent of country, would encounter and so be slowed and disordered by a much larger number and variety of terrain features. The tacticians, though not very informative on battlefield deployments, contain a lot of detail on marching formations, which are mostly variations on a column (e.g. Asclep. *Tact.* 11), although other variations (squares, half-squares, wedges) are also described; but the column must have been much the most common in practice. Polybius well expresses the reasons for this when discussing Alexander's approach march to the Battle of Issus, where he criticizes what he sees as flaws in the account (now lost) of Callisthenes:

> 'After this he [Callisthenes] says that Alexander led on his army in an extended line, being then at a distance of about forty stades [about 7.2km] from the enemy. It is difficult to conceive anything more absurd than this. Where, especially in Cilicia, could one find an extent of ground where a phalanx with its sarissai could advance for forty stades in a line twenty stades long? The obstacles indeed to such a formation and such a movement are so many that it would be difficult to enumerate them all [...] But, it may be said, Alexander wished to be prepared for the appearance of the enemy. And what can be less prepared than a phalanx advancing in line but broken and disunited? How much easier indeed it would have been to develop from proper marching-order into order of battle than to straighten out and prepare for action on thickly wooded and fissured ground a broken line with numerous gaps in it. It would, therefore, have been considerably better to form a proper double [*diphalangia*] or quadruple [*tetraphalangia*] phalanx, for which it was not impossible to find marching room and which it would have been quite easy to get into order of battle expeditiously enough, as he was enabled through his scouts to receive in good time warning of the approach of the enemy.' (Polybius, 12.20)

A 'double or quadruple phalanx' is not necessarily what we would think of as a column of march, which would have a very narrow front and be very deep (and is what is apparently described in Asclepiodotus 11). A double phalanx is formed at double depth and half total frontage, as at Sellasia (Pol. 2.66.9): 'Putting the mercenaries in front, he [Antigonus] drew up the Macedonians behind them in double phalanx with no interval between [*diphalangian epellelon*], the narrowness of the space rendering this necessary.' A slightly different definition is found in Aelian (*Tactics* 35), where the *diphalangia* and *tetraphalangia* (and *triphalangia*) – not qualified as *epallelon*, 'one after another' – are double- to quadruple-fronted formations, that is an open or closed square, designed to face an attack from multiple directions, whereas Polybius apparently has in mind (at Sellasia) a phalanx drawn up in double depth not by doubling the depth of the files within each formation, but by forming half of the units (*syntagmata*, presumably) immediately behind the other half. I think that Polybius is just muddying the waters by bringing in the double or quadruple phalanx in the case of Issus, since even such a formation would be much wider than it was deep, and not truly a column in the usual sense of the word, and would still require a considerable extent of ground to deploy effectively.

The usual words used for marching in column (*epi keros*) mean literally 'to the wing', and indicate that the line advanced towards its flank, its narrow edge, rather than on a broad front. As described by Aelian (*Tactics* 35), there seem to be two ways of marching a column. The first option is the *paragoge*, where the whole formation marches towards its flank, so that the file leaders (usually forming the front of the phalanx) would form a single very long file, either on the left or the right of the phalanx, or both (double phalanx), depending where a threat was anticipated. In such a column, ordering the column to halt and then for each man to make a quarter turn left or right would result in a phalanx already fully formed up and facing at 90 degrees to the original direction of march. This would clearly be a very rapid manoeuvre to make, and would be ideal for confronting a sudden threat from the flank. In order to deploy such a column into a phalanx facing forward (in the original direction of march), it would be necessary to wheel the column perpendicular to the direction of march – a much longer, slower and riskier procedure.

The alternative form of column was *epagoge*, where, as Aelian describes it (35), 'the *epagogia* is correctly where unit [*tagma*] follows unit, so if a *xenagia* leads, then the others follow, or if a *tetrarchia* leads, the remaining *tetrarchiai* follow, unit after unit'. So this is a column in which individual subunits (of whatever size, depending on circumstances) are stacked up one behind the other, each marching to their front, so that the file leaders will be at the front of each unit, but distributed throughout the column. See fig. 3.11 in Chapter 3 for these types of column. Clearly such a column cannot be so rapidly deployed into line by a single turn; in order to form a line facing the front, units would need to march up to the front of the column (to left or right), presumably while the column was halted.

This latter version appears to be what is described by Arrian in his account of the approach to Issus:

> 'As long as the defile enclosed on every side remained narrow, he led the army in column [*epi keros*], but when it grew broader, he deployed his column continuously into a phalanx, bringing up [*paragon*] one after another *taxis* of hoplites on the right up to the ridge, and on the left up to the sea.' (Arrian, *Anabasis* 2.8.2)

In this case Arrian is doubtless using '*taxis*' as a generic term for a unit, not meaning specifically the 1,500- (or 2,000-) man *taxeis* of the Alexandrian phalanx.

There remains considerable uncertainty about the precise details of how this manoeuvre was performed, and we are unlikely ever to know the exact details. At any rate this would have been a slow manoeuvre to perform while continuing to advance. The usual practice when deploying from column to line in this way would be to halt the column and deploy in one go, but in this case Alexander needed to keep marching forward toward the Persians. So whether the whole column halted while each unit deployed, or at least greatly slowed its advance, at any rate it would have been a time-consuming business but would have allowed Alexander to extend his column into the increasingly wide plain without ever leaving a large gap on either flank (into which, in theory, Persian cavalry or light troops might have penetrated). By this means Alexander was able to advance while extending the frontage not just of the phalanx but of the whole army, until ultimately they extended across the whole plain and were in position to engage the Persian army. Fig 7.1 illustrates one possible version of this manoeuvre (compare with fig. 3.12 in Chapter 3).[2]

A rather different sort of meeting engagement was the Battle of Cynoscephalae, between Philip V's Macedonians and the Romans. Here, the two armies were unaware of each other's presence, being separated by a range of hills in poor visibility, and advanced scouting forces from each side met on the summit of the intervening ridge, bringing on a general engagement as Philip brought up his phalanx. Philip was not expecting a pitched battle, but ordered his phalanx to deploy when he received favourable reports from his advance forces. The Romans, on the other hand, did deploy fully from their camp and were in line of battle. Polybius provides a detailed account:

> 'Philip at this time, now that he saw the greater part of his army drawn up outside the entrenchment, advanced with the Peltasts and the right

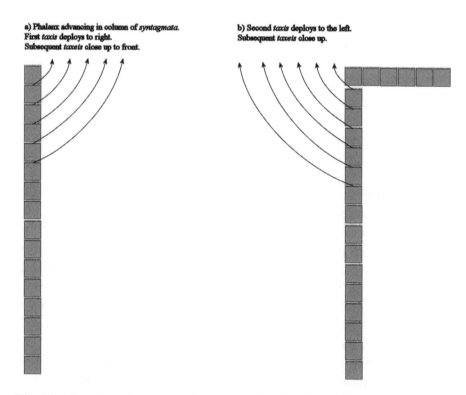

a) Phalanx advancing in column of *syntagmata*. First *taxis* deploys to right. Subsequent *taxeis* close up to front.

b) Second *taxis* deploys to the left. Subsequent *taxeis* close up.

Fig. 7.1. Possible phalanx deployment at the Battle of Issus.

wing of the phalanx, ascending energetically the slope that led to the hills and giving orders to Nicanor, who was nicknamed the Elephant, to see that the rest of his army followed him at once. When the leading ranks reached the top of the pass, he wheeled to the left, and occupied the summits above it; for, as the Macedonian advanced force had pressed the Romans for a considerable distance down the opposite side of the hills, he found these summits abandoned.' (Polybius, 18.24.1–3)

Note that Philip himself pressed ahead with the Peltasts and the 'right wing' of the phalanx, which we can take to be one half of the total, the wing (*keras*) being the largest of the subunits listed by Asclepiodotus (2.10), made up ideally of thirty-two *syntagmata*, 8,000 men. The rest of the phalanx was slower to form up because some men had been sent out foraging and would have had to be recalled.

Philip's deployment manoeuvre has been variously translated. The Loeb edition translation is given above, an alternative being, 'As soon as his first files reached the summit, he deployed his men into line by the left, and occupied the range of high ground.' So, is this a deployment by wheeling a column followed by a turn or by marching up successive units to the left, as for Alexander at Issus? Although the translations seem full of detail (some conflicting: 'the leading ranks' or 'the first files', very different things), Polybius' Greek is much more terse and lacking in precision – literally 'as soon as the first attained the ridge he straight away deployed them to the shield [i.e. to the left]', the word for 'deploy' (*paremballo*) being used by Polybius for any sort of deployment of a formation. However, this seems to me most likely to be a deployment of successive subunits to the left of the column. Polybius goes on:

> 'Receiving therefore the men who had been already engaged, he massed them all upon his right wing, both infantry and cavalry; while he ordered the Peltasts and heavy armed to double their depth and close up to the right.' (Polybius, 18.24.8)

The words used are *diplasiazein to bathos* for 'double the depth' and *puknoun epi to dexion* for 'close up to the right'. Asclepiodotus gives a definition of a similar, presumably equivalent, phrase:

> 'Doubling of place is performed by depth [*kata bathos de ginetai topou diplasiasmos*] when we change the above mentioned compact formation by depth into a loose formation, or when the interjected men counter-march by file.' (Asclepiodotus, 10.19)

So what seems to be happening here is that Philip's column arrived on the ridge, over to the right (the left of the opposing Roman line), the head of the column halted and subsequent units adopted their place to the left of the leading units (whether the units in question are *syntagmata*, as seems most likely, we can't be sure). Then Philip decided he wanted a deeper, narrower, formation, so gave the order that would cause alternate files, or alternate men within the files, to countermarch to the rear of their neighbours, hence doubling the number of ranks and halving the number of files, while still occupying the same frontage (so now in open order). Polybius does not tell us how many ranks were involved at each stage – we might assume that the initial deployment left the phalanx sixteen ranks deep and with intermediate (1 metre) intervals. Philip's first order would have doubled the depth to thirty-two ranks and left the phalanx in open order, 2-metre intervals. So the phalanx then closed up to the right (the sequence of right face, march, left face discussed in Chapter 3, fig. 3.8), leaving it thirty-two ranks deep and now back in intermediate,

1-metre order. This is just one possibility of course, since the phalanx might instead have deployed eight deep then redeployed to sixteen deep. The precise details may elude us, but at any rate the manoeuvre left the phalanx properly deployed and able to drive the Romans back from the ridge. Fig. 7.2 illustrates one interpretation.

Nicanor's *keras*, arriving late on the field, was less fortunate:

> 'The Macedonians now, having no one to give them orders and being unable to adopt the formation proper to the phalanx, in part owing to the difficulty of the ground and in part because they were trying to reach the combatants and were still in marching order and not in line, did not even wait until they were at close quarters with the Romans, but gave way thrown into confusion and broken up by the elephants alone.' (Polybius, 18.25.6–7)

It is not explicit what 'marching order' is (Asclepiodotus titles his Chapter 11 '*Peri poreion*', 'About marching', using the same word as Polybius does here, and describing a wide range of formations), but the contrast with 'line', *parataxis* – literally 'drawn up beside', used by Asclepiodotus (2.5) to describe all the front-rankers of the phalanx drawn up together – makes it certain that a column is meant. So the left wing, like the right, arrived on the ridge in column, but unlike the right had no time to deploy into 'side by side' formation, the 'formation proper to the phalanx', and so was quickly defeated (the implication is they broke without even engaging, just running from the elephants). It is a very clear illustration of the dangers of meeting the enemy while still in column, and of the time that would be required to deploy into line, time that was not available with the Romans already deployed. However, it is not clear why Nicanor was unable to issue any orders, nor why nobody else took any initiative, as if only Philip himself could give such a basic order as to deploy into line, which is hardly likely.[3]

The approach and deployment of the Spartan army at the Battle of Mantinea (one of several battles at Mantinea, this being that of 207 against the Achaeans, after both sides had adopted Macedonian armament and drill) offers another example of a meeting engagement:

> 'Machanidas at first looked as if he were about to attack the enemy's right with his phalanx in column, but on approaching, when he found himself at the proper distance he wheeled to the right, and deploying into line made his own right wing equal in extent to the Achaean left.' (Polybius, 11.12.4)

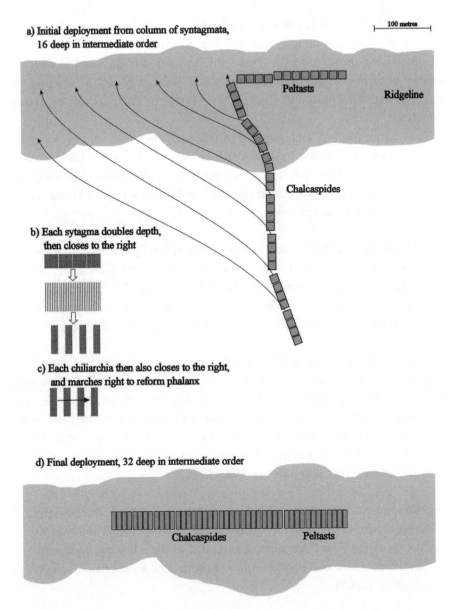

a) Initial deployment from column of syntagmata, 16 deep in intermediate order

100 metres

Peltasts

Ridgeline

Chalcaspides

b) Each sytagma doubles depth, then closes to the right

c) Each chiliarchia then also closes to the right, and marches right to reform phalanx

d) Final deployment, 32 deep in intermediate order

Chalcaspides   Peltasts

Fig. 7.2. Possible phalanx deployment at the Battle of Cynoscephalae.

The words Polybius uses, here translated as 'wheeled to the right', *periekla epi doru*, do not exactly match any manoeuvre in the tacticians, but is the same expression Polybius uses to describe the Romans army's manoeuvres at the Battle of Ilipa against the Carthaginians, where Roman flanking forces wheeled into column in order to outflank the Carthaginian army, so it is likely that at

Mantinea too Polybius has in mind a wheel from column into line, the second form of deployment discussed earlier. Whether the Spartan army marched with individual units facing the front (which would have then had to wheel 90 degrees to form a proper line after the wheel was complete), or whether the army was marching toward its flank, is not revealed by Polybius, so we can only speculate.[4]

Aside from meeting engagements of this sort, the second major way for a phalanx (and whole army) to deploy was from a nearby camp. The formality of the camp might have varied, from a ditch or palisade around a camping area to a more formal camp similar to the familiar Roman army marching camps. Before Gaugamela, for example:

> 'Alexander was about thirty stades [5,400 metres] away and his army was already descending these hills when he sighted the enemy; he stopped his phalanx there [and asked for the advice of his generals] ... Parmenion's advice prevailed, and they camped there, in the order in which they were to engage in battle.' (Arrian, *Anabasis* 3.9.3–4)

Camping in battle order is an unusual arrangement, though we should not imagine a full battle line with a palisade thrown round it; rather, Arrian probably just means that the positioning of the units in camp mirrored the positions they were to occupy in the line. This is further evidence that the battle order was decided well in advance, and perhaps in contrast to the apparently normal Macedonian practice of rotating the order of the units of the phalanx daily, as described in an earlier encounter in Asia Minor:

> 'Alexander deployed the Macedonian phalanx as follows: on the right wing, where he stationed himself, he had the Hypaspists, and next to the them the Foot Companions, extended to the left wing, each *taxis* under the commanders in the order of preference for the day.' (Arrian, *Anabasis* 1.28.3)

More often, an army would be encamped in what was presumably a more compact fashion (accepting that we know very little about Greek or Macedonian military camps), and the phalanx would deploy by marching out of the gates, or possibly over a torn-down palisade, as the Spartan phalanx did at Sellasia:[5]

> 'But when Cleomenes saw that his brother's division was retreating, and that the cavalry in the low ground were on the point of doing the

same, alarmed at the prospect of an attack at all points at once, he was compelled to demolish the palisade in his front, and to lead out his whole force in line by one side of his position.' (Polybius, 2.69)

This was more of a fortified position blocking a pass than a simple camp, however. Usually the camp was retained as a defensive strongpoint in case of reverse in the battle, so the palisades must have been retained. Some battle accounts reference this process of exiting camp more or less in passing, though they make what must have been a highly complex and time-consuming set of manoeuvres sound far simpler. At Mantinea, the Achaean army was in the city rather than in camp, and deployed through three separate gates:

'Meanwhile Philopoemen too had arranged his army in three divisions, and was leading them out of Mantinea, the Illyrians and the men with body armour by the gate leading to the temple of Poseidon, and with them all the rest of the foreign contingent and light armed troops; by the next gate, toward the west, the phalanx; and by the next the Achaean cavalry.' (Polybius, 11.11.4)

Using a number of different gates in this way must have been common practice to speed the process of exiting a camp or city (a gate being an obvious chokepoint). At Pydna, the Macedonian army was in camp when the skirmish that precipitated the battle took place, and deployed rapidly:

'As these [Thracians and Peltasts] took their places in the line they were illumined by the phalanx of the Chalcaspides, issuing from the camp behind them and filling the plain with the gleam of iron and the glitter of bronze, and the hills with the tumultuous shouts of their cheering. And with such boldness and swiftness did they advance that the first to be slain fell only two stades [360 metres] from the Roman camp.' (Plutarch, *Aemilius Paullus* 18.3–4)

It is often suggested that the Macedonian army at Pydna deployed fully from the camp before the main fighting began, and that the battle was therefore a formal engagement between two fully deployed armies. However, I think that the account of Plutarch and the details of the fighting that follow (on which I will have more to say in Chapter 9) make it clear that the Macedonian army did not fully deploy before advancing: the Peltasts clearly attacked immediately in support of the skirmishers, while the *Chalcaspides* were still deploying from camp. The *Chalcaspides* for their part also advanced rapidly, probably without waiting for the right flank of the phalanx (probably the *Leucaspides*, 'White Shields') to deploy. Pydna was therefore more of a meeting engagement than a formal battle, but with the armies meeting as they deployed from camp.[6]

More usually, each army would deploy in front of its camp and only advance into contact once fully deployed. The Battle of Magnesia between the Seleucid army and the Romans provides an example. Here, both sides remained in their camps for several days before the battle, the Romans 'offering battle' by deploying each day in front of their camp, an offer which the Seleucids declined by forming their own battle line close to their camp rather than advancing into the intervening space (an alternative was simply to remain in camp and not deploy at all). This rather formal offering and acceptance of battle is a common feature of many battles across the period – not just between Greek or Hellenistic armies, so it is not purely a cultural phenomenon. As camps were rather close, and it must have taken some time to deploy from camp, we might expect one or other side to seek an advantage by attacking before the other was fully deployed (as happened perhaps accidentally at Pydna), but rather each side would politely allow the other to complete its deployment before battle commenced. There may have been sound tactical reasons for this (the confusion of a battle starting too soon without formal preparation would have tended to harm both sides, and would therefore tend to have disadvantaged the stronger, more capable army), and there may also have been a desire to engage in 'fair and open battle' to ensure that the outcome was truly decisive and could not be explained away by the loser as down to foul play. We can compare the reported exchange between Parmenion and Alexander before Gaugamela, where Parmenion urged a night attack, which Alexander refused on the grounds that it was 'dishonourable to steal the victory' (Arr. *Anab.* 3.10.2). Arrian is of the view that this was a cover for the real reason, which was that:

> 'at night, whether forces are adequately or deficiently prepared for battle, things have so often turned out contrary to rational expectation that the stronger side has been foiled and victory gone to the weaker.' (Arrian, *Anabasis* 3.10.3)

What is true of a night attack could also be true of a surprise attack on a deploying army. Probably there was a combination of considerations: 'fair play', the desire for a decisive victory that could not be explained away and the wish to avoid a confused battle which might leave the result too much to chance. Whatever the reasons, the deployment, offering and acceptance of battle were a common feature, with failure to accept battle for too long being damaging to an army's morale, as Livy described events at Magnesia:

> 'After the consul perceived that the enemy declined to fight, he called a council the next day, to consider what they should do if Antiochus would not give them an opportunity for a battle. The cry from all sides was that he should immediately lead them out and take advantage of the enthusiasm of the soldiers, who … were ready to attack the camp over ditch, over wall, if the enemy would not come out to fight … . On the third day [after] the standards were advanced to the centre of the space and the battle-line began to form. Nor did Antiochus think that he should remain longer on the defensive, lest he both diminish the courage of his own men by declining battle and increase the hopes of the enemy, and he too led out his forces, advancing so far from the camp that it was clear that he meant to engage.' (Livy, 37.38–39)

So here we see all elements of the offer and acceptance of battle from camp, and the formality of the arrangement – the camps at this stage were only some 2,500 metres apart, and the Seleucid battle line probably at least a couple of kilometres long (although the phalanx itself occupied only a small part of this frontage). Once they had advanced from their camps, the battle lines would therefore have been much closer to each other than the flanks of each army were to their own opposite flank, and deployment into this advanced position from camp (presumably using one of the column to line manoeuvres discussed above) must have taken some time, during which the opposing army simply went about its own deployment without offering any interference to the enemy. Livy unfortunately gives no details as to how the deployment was accomplished in this case.[7]

The Battle of Raphia offers a similar example, with less reluctance shown by either side, but with similar mind games concerning the placement of the camps. Polybius describes how Ptolemy arrived on the scene first and camped near Raphia:

> '[Antiochus] passed Raphia and encamped about ten stades [about 1,800 metres] from the enemy. For a while the two armies preserved this distance, and remained encamped opposite each other. But after some few days, wishing to remove to more advantageous ground and to inspire confidence in his troops, Antiochus pushed forward his

camp so much nearer Ptolemy, that the palisades of the two camps were not more than five stades [about 900 metres] from each other ... . After being encamped opposite each other for five days, the two kings resolved to bring matters to the decision of battle. And upon Ptolemy beginning to move his army outside its camp, Antiochus hastened to do the same.' (Polybius, 5.80–82)

The armies were camped astonishingly close, and must have deployed just a few hundred metres apart at most.[8]

Depth and intervals

Once a phalanx was deployed into the proper formation for battle (itself often just called a 'phalanx' by the sources), the next decision would be the depth and the intervals to be adopted. As we have already seen at Issus and Cynoscephalae, this decision was naturally enough integral to the deployment of the phalanx, although adjustments were possible, as at Cynoscephalae, after the phalanx was in place, using one of the 'doubling' drills.

The standard depth for the Macedonian phalanx was probably sixteen ranks (as described by Polybius, and see Chapter 3), though it is possible that Alexander's phalanx commonly drew up eight ranks deep. Polybius' account of the approach of Alexander's army to Issus assumes that the phalanx was formed eight deep, while in his comparison of legion and phalanx (18.29 f.) he assumes sixteen ranks, the standard depth given by the tacticians. There was a trade-off between greater depth and greater frontage – a deeper formation was considered stronger in battle (the reason why this might have been so will be considered in Chapter 8), but was also more easily outflanked, as it had a narrower front. A numerically inferior army could compensate for its lack of numbers by deploying at a shallower depth, thereby expanding its front to equal that of the more numerous enemy. We have seen above how at Mantinea, the Spartan Machanidas, 'deploying into line made his own right wing equal in extent to the Achaean left' (Pol. 11.12.4), and one of the ways this could be done, if numbers were not equal, was by adjusting the depth. At Cynoscephalae, Philip may initially have deployed his phalanx with eight ranks, and doubled this to sixteen. Livy (33.8.14) provides an explanation as to why: 'To prevent his line from being quickly broken he halved the front and gave twice the depth to the files.' This reasoning is not in Polybius, and Livy's understanding of phalanx drill is not great, but it seems a perfectly reasonable explanation, Philip presumably calculating that a greater depth would allow him to overwhelm the Romans to his front before those on the right flank could come to their aid (a calculation which proved faulty in the event). [9]

Alexander's phalanx was faced chiefly by hoplite phalanxes that were presumably deployed with a typical eight ranks, or by more numerous Persian armies where it was important to prevent, or at least to hinder, outflanking moves, which may account for why eight ranks was considered sufficient. In the wars of the Successors, Macedonian phalanxes fought each other, so we may well expect that greater depth was tried as a way to overcome a similarly armed and motivated enemy, with sixteen ranks becoming standardized as the best compromise of depth and frontage. Because of the way the file structure and numbers of officers were determined by the number of men in the file, as discussed in Chapter 3, it must have been relatively hard to alter the depth of the phalanx without suffering downsides in terms of file structure and cohesion (such as the proper position of file leaders and file closers). For most battles the depth of the phalanx is not specified, and we are left to assume sixteen ranks. One exception is Magnesia, as Livy describes the Seleucid deployment:

'There were sixteen thousand infantry armed in the Macedonian fashion, who are called *phalangitae*. They formed the centre of the line, and their frontage was divided into ten sections; these sections were separated by intervals in which two elephants each were placed; from the front the formation extended thirty-two ranks in depth.' (Livy, 37.40.6–7)

The placement of the elephants will be further discussed below. The unusual depth of the phalanx – double normal depth – is of interest. Livy does not give any explanation, but it is possible that, outnumbering the Romans as the Seleucids probably did, and with the recent defeat by the Romans of the Macedonian army at Cynoscephalae and of his own army at Thermopylae, Antiochus reckoned that a greater depth would give the phalanx greater stability, while his large forces of light infantry and cavalry would protect its flanks (in the event, the positioning of the elephants among the phalanx was to prove a fatal error).

The depth of a phalanx is closely related to its intervals, the width of each file. As we have already seen, the standard interval for a phalanx was that of two cubits (1 metre), with double this in open (marching) order and half for the 'locked shields' defensive formation. In the vast majority of battles, intervals for the phalanx are not specified. One exception again comes from Polybius' analysis of Issus, where his calculations are based on the open order (four cubits), though he also considers the possibility that the phalanx closed up to two-cubit order; neither here nor in his comparison of legion and phalanx does Polybius ever mention the one-cubit order. There is no absolutely clear example in literary sources of a phalanx forming the one-cubit order in battle, as the occurrence of the word *synaspismos* or a similar variant in literary sources sometimes refers just to close order (two cubits) or to a close but unspecified order for the less precisely drilled hoplite armies, and cannot automatically be taken to mean one cubit in the strict technical sense of the tacticians.[10]

One occasion where use of the closest order has been suggested is the Battle of Sellasia, between the Macedonian and Spartan armies. Here, Antigonus formed his Peltasts and the rest of his Macedonian phalanx on his left wing opposite the similarly armed Spartans. Polybius gives the details:

> 'Putting the mercenaries in front, he [Antigonus] drew up the Macedonians behind them in double phalanx with no interval between, the narrowness of the space rendering this necessary ... . Each side now recalled by bugle their light-armed troops from the space between them, and shouting their war-cry and lowering their sarissas, the two phalanxes met. A stubborn struggle followed. At one time the Macedonians gradually fell back facing the enemy, giving way for a long distance before the courage of the Lacedaemonians, at another the latter were pushed from their ground by the weight of the Macedonian phalanx, until, on Antigonus ordering the Macedonians to close up in the peculiar formation of the double phalanx with its serried line of sarissas, they delivered a charge which finally forced the Lacedaemonians from their stronghold.' (Polybius, 2.66, 2.69)

Polybius' account is not totally clear. He first describes the Macedonians initially deploying in double phalanx, '*diphalangia epallelon*' ('two phalanxes' in the original translation), this last word meaning 'one close after another' and used by Polybius to qualify *diphalangia* (double phalanx) here, or *triphalangia* (triple phalanx) in his discussion of Issus, where he claims that to fit in the available space Alexander's cavalry would have had to deploy *triphalangia epallelon* (note the rather surprising use of 'phalanx' to describe a cavalry formation), as discussed above. While the Loeb translation given above, 'on Antigonus ordering the Macedonians to close up in the peculiar formation of the double phalanx with its serried line of sarissas', gives the sense, it is a little too free. More literally, 'at last those around Antigonus crowding together their sarissas [*sumphraxantes tas sarisas*] and utilising the nature of the double phalanx [*epallelou phalangos*]' suggests that there was no change of depth (the phalanx had already deployed in 'double phalanx') though there may have been a change of intervals ('crowding together their sarissas'). This may imply adopting a closer order, though the crowding or 'fencing together' of the sarissas uses the verb *phrasso*, which is the word used by Homer to describe the Achaeans 'fencing spear with spear' (that is, 'making a fence of', not in the sense of sword fencing) in the very same passage (*Iliad* 13.130) that Polybius quotes (at 18.29) to illustrate the close formation of the phalanx, when referring to the formation at two-cubit intervals (and the tacticians each also use the same word in their version of the passage). This Homeric parallel would certainly have been in Polybius' mind. It might be assumed that what Polybius is describing is a closing up of the phalanx from thirty-two ranks deep and two-cubit intervals, to the '*synaspismos*' of the tacticians at sixteen ranks and one cubit, achieved by interjecting the files of the rearward half of the double phalanx between those of the front half (a 'doubling by men'). This may well be, and does seem to make sense, but we have to keep in mind that it is not clearly what Polybius describes. So while this is probably an example of the use of the one-cubit interval, the case is not certain.[11]

Special formations

So far we have considered deployment, depth and intervals, but into what formations might a phalanx deploy? The standard formation is of course the line – often called simply 'phalanx'. For all that this formation is so familiar – both as the standard deployment of the Macedonian phalanx and also that of the Classical hoplite phalanx that preceded it – it is striking that we don't really know exactly how it worked in detail. The basics are straightforward: a phalanx is a continuous line a set small number of ranks deep and a much larger number of files wide. A 16,000-strong standard Macedonian phalanx would typically have 1,000 files, and therefore would cover (at standard intervals) 1,000 metres in frontage and 16 metres in depth.

Yet there are uncertainties even around this basic model – most importantly, what gaps if any were there between the subunits that made up the phalanx? The calculations of, for example, Polybius in his comments on the Battle of Issus (12.19) imply that he expects the entire formation to form up without any gaps at all, a continuous solid line of men (he specifically contrasts the cavalry, who would have gaps between units, 12.18), and it is often stated (by modern historians) that any sort of gaps would be anathema to a phalanx (hoplite or Macedonian). Yet infantry formations of other, better-documented, eras certainly did have gaps in them – even pike formations very similar to the Macedonian phalanx such as the pike blocks of Medieval and Early Modern European warfare, where each block (of a few hundred men) would form up with a considerable gap between it and its neighbour (as shown in numerous illustrations of battles of the period). These gaps would often be filled with musketeers, but while there certainly were skirmishers with a similar role in Hellenistic armies, these skirmishers seem to have formed up in front of the phalanx, not within its gaps. However, the Macedonian phalanx, as we have seen, was built up from numerous smaller building blocks, and in order for these blocks (and the larger units of which they were components) to operate independently we would certainly expect them to have maintained some separation from their neighbours. Indeed, infantry formations of later periods maintained such gaps largely because it was practically impossible to manoeuvre a large continuous formation over any sort of terrain while maintaining a continuous line – obstacles, irregularities of ground, and the natural surge and drift of large bodies of men moving together would have produced gaps and crowdings or condensations of men unless gaps were left to soak up or make room for these natural variations.

Polybius comments on the difficulty of moving a phalanx over any sort of terrain:

'No one denies that for its employment it is indispensable to have a country flat, bare, and without such impediments as ditches, cavities, depressions, steep banks, or beds of rivers: for all such obstacles are sufficient to hinder and dislocate this particular formation. And that it is, I may say, impossible, or at any rate exceedingly rare to find a piece of country of twenty stades [about 3,600 metres] or sometimes of even greater extent, without any such obstacles, every one will also admit.' (Polybius, 18.31)

The importance of terrain to the phalanx will be considered further below, and we might also note that the ground Polybius requires for his phalanx (as at Issus) is exceedingly generous: at standard intervals and sixteen deep, 20 stades should be room enough for some 58,000 men, with no gaps. But taking the general point for now, Polybius' position is that sufficient ground without obstacles would be extremely difficult to find – yet Macedonian phalanxes operated successfully on such terrain for several hundred years. This suggests firstly that Polybius may be overstating his case for rhetorical effect, but also that the phalanx found a way to cope with such difficulties, at least if they were not too severe, and the most obvious way to do so would be to leave gaps, even if only small ones, between units to make the phalanx more flexible and articulated.

Practical considerations might also lead us to this conclusion. As well as the difficulty of marching, it would be very hard to coordinate perfectly the movement (advancing, halting) of a single solid block of men a kilometre wide, and as we have seen, drill was controlled at the level of quite small subunits. This means that the phalanx must have lost some cohesion naturally as units started or stopped marching at slightly different times. We see at Issus that in order to maintain good order a phalanx might have to halt several times in the course of an advance to reform (Arr. *Anab.* 2.10.1). It is likely then that a phalanx marched in its constituent subunits rather than as a massive solid block, even though they might have re-formed and closed-up in closer contact immediately before contact with the enemy. Note also that there was a 'file closer' for each *syntagma* whose job was to keep the *syntagmata* aligned (Asclep. 3.6, which illustrates the need, and also that a response was found for it).

The accounts of battles in which larger units operated independently also suggests that there must have been some separation between such units. This is true also for the earlier hoplite phalanx – often hoplite armies were made up of numerous allied city contingents, sometimes formed at different depths, so it is unlikely that they formed a continuous solid block. Also such contingents often broke and ran as whole units, while their neighbours continued fighting – it is hard to see how this would be possible if they formed a single block (a man would hardly stand and fight while his neighbour ran just because they were from different cities). In the accounts of Hellenistic battles, the phalanx is often referred to as a single monolithic whole, but we know that it was made up of smaller units – even if only on the scale of the *taxeis* of Alexander's army – that were capable of operating independently, even if the sources do not often record them doing so. Gaugamela provides a clear example of this happening; as Alexander's charge broke the Persian left, the phalanx attacked alongside him:

> 'But Simmias and his *taxis* were no longer able to join Alexander in the pursuit, but had halted their phalanx and were fighting where they stood, since the Macedonian left was reported to be in difficulties.'
> (Arrian, *Anabasis* 3.14.4)

This is not just the phalanx tearing roughly apart as one section is unable to keep up, but a deliberate, ordered halt by one *taxis* (and presumably also the one to its left). This shows that even if the *taxeis* did form very close together, the phalanx at any rate did not operate as a single mass. There must have been clear enough divisions between the units to allow the officers to monitor and control, and issue orders to, their own men as distinct from those of neighbouring units.

Indeed, there are a good number of occasions where a phalanx is known to have formed a 'gappy' line, sometimes with units of other contingents formed in the gaps. For example, at Mantinea the Achaean phalanx was 'drawn up in companies [*speirai*], with an interval between each' (Pol 11.11.6 – *speira* being Polybius' word for *syntagma*). At Sellasia, Antigonus 'drew up the Macedonian *Chalcaspides* and the Illyrians in alternate *speirai*' (Pol. 2.66.5 in my translation; the Loeb translation reads 'in alternate lines', but Polybius' words are '*kata speiras enallax tetagmenous*', literally 'by *speiras* alternately drawn up'). Such an 'articulated phalanx' had been used much earlier by Pyrrhus in Italy. According to Polybius, "Pyrrhus, again, availed himself not only of the arms, but also of the troops of Italy, placing a maniple [*semeia*] of Italians and a company [*speira*] of his own phalanx alternately [*enallax*], in his battles against the Romans' (Pol. 18.28.10). This is often seen as a special response to the Roman manipular formation or to the broken ground encountered by Pyrrhus in his battles, but as Sellasia shows, the formation was not used only against Romans. At Magnesia, the phalanx was similarly divided: 'their frontage was divided into ten sections; these sections were separated by intervals in which two elephants each were placed' (Liv. 37.40). Doubt has been cast on this formation by modern historians, but we can see it as a variant on a tradition stretching back a hundred years, using elephants in this case in place of Italians or Illyrians. At any rate, it seems that the phalanx did not have to maintain a single continuous front in order to operate effectively.

Another use for separated units – in particular separated columns – is to avoid disordering the line on rough terrain, and I will have more to say about this scenario in the section on terrain below.

The most common other special formation mentioned is the 'oblique line' (*loxos*), in which rather than the phalanx forming parallel to the enemy line and perpendicular to the line of advance, it is formed at an angle, with one wing pushed forward and the other held back. The intention, broadly, was thus to bring one wing (the stronger one) into action sooner than the other with the hope of deciding the battle before the weaker wing could be overcome. As we have seen, this formation traces its origins to the innovations of Epaminondas in the Theban army, who seems to have been the first to deliberately lead with one wing (that containing the best Theban troops and the elite Sacred Band), angling the weaker allied contingents back to keep them out of action. In the tacticians (e.g. Asclepiodotus, 10.1, 11.1), the oblique formation appears as one of the possible formations for marching. Others include the hollow square, half-square, crescent and wedge – but the benefit of these formations are not made clear, nor is there any evidence that I am aware of that these peculiar formations were ever actually used on the march. The oblique formation, however, certainly was used in battle, though often the whole army was arranged obliquely (with one wing 'refused', in military parlance, so as to keep it out of the action for longer), rather than just the phalanx. Even so, as the phalanx formed a large component of any infantry battle line, we can assume that if the army is deployed obliquely, the phalanx is also.

Although this formation is well known and often taken to be typical of Macedonian tactics, actual examples of it in use are relatively hard to come by. Reconstructions of the Battle of Gaugamela often suggest that the Macedonian army (and phalanx) formed an oblique line, but this is not clearly stated in the sources: Arrian (*Anab.* 3.11–12), for instance, has Alexander form a double-fronted phalanx, as we will see, and Alexander advances toward the right, but there is no indication that the phalanx was deployed obliquely.[12]

One clear example is the Battle of Paraitacene. Diodorus describes how Antigonus deployed his army, then:

> 'When he had drawn up the army in this fashion, he advanced down the hill against the enemy keeping an oblique front, for he thrust forward the right wing, in which he had most confidence, and held the left back, having determined to avoid battle with the one and to decide the contest with the other.' (Diodorus, 19.29.7)

The whole army was deployed obliquely (*loxen*), so presumably the phalanx, which formed the centre (made up partly of Macedonian-armed and partly of unspecified heavy infantry), was also, though oddly it was the refused flank that actually engaged the enemy first. There is also no mention of the effect of this oblique deployment in Diodorus' extremely terse account of the phalanx battle ('it so happened that the infantry for a considerable time had been engaged in a battle of phalanxes', Diod. 19.30.5). At any rate, at this battle the oblique formation does not seem to have made much difference to the outcome.[13]

Assuming that Antigonus' phalanx was indeed deployed obliquely, it is worth considering exactly how this would be accomplished. The simple high-level view is that the line would be an angled block (such a block is depicted in the manuscripts of Asclepiodotus), but looked at in more detail, a phalanx could not actually deploy as an angled block in this way unless the men were to face at an angle to the line of deployment, or to walk crabwise when advancing (not likely). I think it is more likely, though sadly no such details are provided by the tacticians or any other writer, that in an oblique phalanx the individual subunits would each be deployed facing forward in the standard way, parallel to the enemy, but that units would be stepped back to produce the overall oblique line. Which size of subunit would be used to achieve this deployment is open to speculation – probably the *syntagma*, since that is the usual manoeuvre unit. An oblique line would then be not a single angled line but a stepped line of individual units, each facing forward. The flanks of each unit would have some degree of exposure to the enemy, but would be covered by the next unit back in line, as the degree of refusal of each unit from the next need not have been great. To take as an example a standard 16,000-man phalanx, sixteen deep with 1-metre rank intervals, made up of sixty-four *syntagmata*, if each *syntagma* was stepped back 5 metres (about the reach of the front rank's sarissas), then the left wing would be 320 metres behind the front. Whether this would have been enough to achieve the desired result of 'avoiding battle with one wing and deciding the contest with the other' depends on how long the contest might take, among many other factors, which is one of the great unknowns of ancient combat. If the *syntagmata* were stepped such that the front rank of each was in line with the rear rank of its neighbour, then the phalanx would slant back 1 kilometre, which would certainly be a more significant distance tactically, though this would mean the flanks of each unit would be more unprotected. Unfortunately, we can really only guess what the arrangement might have been. Fig. 7.3 illustrates one possibility.

As for the other more exotic formations, the only traces in any battle accounts are of a possible phalanx wedge at Gaugamela and a phalanx square at Gabiene and Magnesia.

Taking the wedge first, Arrian's account of Gaugamela states that Alexander saw a gap opening in the front of the Persian army:

> 'He wheeled towards the gap, and making a wedge [*embolon*] of the Companion cavalry and the part of the phalanx stationed there led them on at the double with a loud battle cry straight at Darius.'
> (Arrian, *Anabasis* 3.14.2)

There is, however, good reason to doubt that the phalanx formed a wedge here. For one thing, the word *embolon* can mean a wedge – both in the form of the cavalry formations used by many Macedonian and Hellenistic cavalry, and

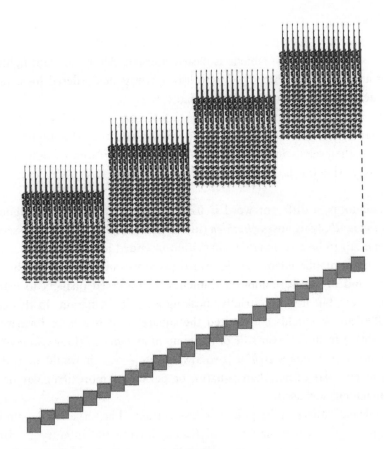

Fig. 7.3. Oblique deployment of phalanx.

as an infantry marching formation as detailed by Asclepiodotus (11.5) – but can also be used in a looser sense to mean just a dense attacking formation (it is apparently in this sense that the word is used for the Theban formation at the Battle of Leuctra). The word is used for the ram of a ship, and in this loose sense it can convey an idea of a massed attacking force (and note that Arrian qualifies the word with 'like an *embolon*', though 'like' is missed out of the translation above), so it is likely that at Leuctra and Gaugamela the sense is more of 'attacking like the ram of a ship' than 'attacking in a wedge formation' (yet again, the imprecision of the language used by literary historians stymies attempts at greater tactical precision). At any rate, while the Companion cavalry at Gaugamela were doubtless already deployed in wedge formation, I think it highly unlikely that the phalanx stopped to perform the complex evolutions necessary to adopt a wedge before launching the crucial attack. Note also that while a cavalry wedge is a formation of a small subunit (the cavalry *ile* or squadron), the infantry wedge of Asclepiodotus is a formation for the whole phalanx, not its individual units.[14]

As for squares, that at Gabiene is clearly attested. After the main fighting was over and Eumenes' forces had withdrawn, Antigonus ordered his cavalry commander Pithon to harry Eumenes' infantry:

> 'When Pithon promptly carried out his orders, the Macedonians formed themselves into a square [*plinthion*] and withdrew safely to the river.' (Diodorus, 19.43.5)

In Asclepiodotus, a different word is used for a square (*tetragonos*), though Arrian (*Tactics* 29.8) also uses *plinthion* (literally, a brick). At any rate this seems clearly enough to be a rectangular formation intended for all-around defence against a more mobile enemy, as described (as a marching formation) by the tacticians, and in this case allowed Eumenes' beleaguered phalanx to march off to the river, but it is not strictly speaking a battle formation. In this case some 3,000 Silver Shields constituted the square, so it is a large formation, perhaps with a front and rear side of made up of *chiliarchiai* (four *syntagmata*) and the sides of *pentakosiarchiai* (two *syntagmata* – which would of course make it rectangular rather than square), or perhaps a more irregular or ad hoc arrangement was used.

The alleged square at Magnesia is less certain. The situation is similar. Antiochus' cavalry wings had been defeated, leaving the infantry phalanx, 16,000 strong, isolated among Roman and allied cavalry and light infantry. However, of the two accounts of Magnesia that survive, that of Livy makes no mention of a square, and only Appian (who is not, generally speaking, wholly reliable) mentions one (App. *Syr.* 35), calling it a *tetragonos*. Livy has the phalanx deployed thirty-two deep and presumably in a line (with interspersed elephants), and I do not think it likely, given the rapidity of the defeat of the cavalry wings, that the phalanx would have had time to redeploy into a formal square (or rectangle). I think it more likely that the outer files would simply have faced 90 degrees left or right and the rearmost ranks faced about, resulting in an all-around defensive formation, though not quite like the hollow squares of the tacticians. If the rear half of the phalanx (assuming Antiochus' thirty-two-deep phalanx was a double phalanx like Antigonus' at Sellasia) was made of separate subunits, rather than by stacking up the files of units one behind the other, then this would have facilitated the formation of a square, since the rearward *syntagmata* could have been ordered to countermarch to face the rear. In this formation the phalanx was able to hold off the Romans until eventually missile fire overcame them, and particularly caused the elephants to panic and disorder the whole formation.

Advance and contact

Once the phalanx was deployed, its next task was to advance into contact with the enemy, unless its role was to stand on the defensive. The latter, though, is very uncommon in battles of the period, so far as we can tell, despite the occasional claims by modern historians that the phalanx was primarily a defensive formation. There are examples of phalanxes acting defensively – whether in specific circumstances, like the Peltasts who defended a breach in the city walls of Atrax (Liv. 32.17), or in pitched battle simply holding a defensive position, like the Spartan phalanx at Sellasia (Pol. 2.66). Even in the latter case, when the Spartan king Cleomenes saw his left flank was being defeated, he brought his phalanx out from behind its defences to engage actively rather than standing waiting to be attacked. The Seleucid phalanx at Magnesia ended up not advancing to the attack and holding off its opponents in place, but this was due to the unusual circumstances of the rapid defeat (or pursuit off the field) of its flanking forces. In most cases, in pitched battle at least, the phalanx advanced to the attack, whether it was facing another phalanx similarly armed or different sorts of opponents. Part of the reason for this may be entirely practical: as for Cleomenes at Sellasia, remaining on the defensive surrendered the initiative and allowed the enemy to defeat parts of the army piecemeal, or to attack from different directions. Part was also moral (or cultural), in that standing on the defensive indicated an unwillingness to come to open battle, and so a lack of confidence – it was better in most circumstances to boost the men's morale by a confident advance. Arrian's comments on the Battle of Issus nicely illustrate this point: 'Once the barbarians had taken up their first positions, Darius made no further advance; … . This made it plain to Alexander and his staff that Darius was in spirit a beaten man' (Arr. *Anab.* 2.10.1).

Not much information is available on the nature of this advance. In Arrian's account of the advance to Issus, Alexander proceeded at a leisurely pace, 'to avoid any part of the phalanx fluctuating in a more rapid advance and so breaking apart' (Arr. *Anab.* 2.10.3). As we have seen, it would be exceedingly difficult to have any long linear formation march any distance over any sort of terrain while retaining a continuous front, and the subunits of the phalanx would naturally have moved at slightly different speeds, resulting in significant breaks and gaps if the line was not halted and dressed frequently. In most pitched battles where armies deployed out of nearby camps this may not have been too great an issue, though as we have seen, in encounter battles the longer marches involved and lack of preparation could result in broken, disordered or not properly formed phalanxes, as also could an uneven advance due to varying fortunes in the fighting itself. Polybius makes this the chief weakness of the phalanx compared with the Roman legion, in his comparison of the two:

> 'Now, whether the phalanx in its charge drives its opponents from their ground, or is itself driven back, in either case its peculiar order is dislocated; for whether in following the retiring, or flying from the advancing enemy, they quit the rest of their forces: and when this takes place, the enemy's reserves can occupy the space thus left, and the ground which the phalanx had just before been holding, and so no longer charge them face to face, but fall upon them on their flank and rear.' (Polybius, 18.32.4)

This is broadly what happened at Pydna, where three major divisions of the phalanx, the Peltasts, the *Chalcaspides* (Bronze Shields) and the *Leucaspides* (White Shields), advanced at varying rates, the Peltasts rapidly driving back the Latin allied outposts, the *Chalcaspides* and *Leucaspides* following behind more slowly against the main Roman legions, allowing the Romans to insert their more flexible forces into the large gaps that appeared (Liv. 44.40–2; Plut. *Aem.* 16–22). In this case, the gaps were large – between whole, several thousand-strong subunits of the phalanx – while in other cases (as at Issus) gaps were probably on a more local scale, between or within individual *syntagmata*. I argued above that the phalanx was probably not as monolithic or inflexible as it is sometimes (perhaps for rhetorical effect) made out to be, but even so any formation will suffer from gaps and dislocations in its line, and the phalanx was relatively more greatly disadvantaged by such gaps than the Romans (as we will see in Chapter 9).[15]

The phalanx therefore probably usually advanced at a relatively slow pace and with pauses to redress the ranks where possible. We should not imagine a phalanx running to the attack, and the 'charge' of the phalanx referred to in the sources was probably an 'advance to contact' at a steady walk, rather than a 'hell for leather' charge, which given the closeness of the formation and the encumbrance of the sarissas would probably have been impractical. Hoplite phalanxes are said to have advanced at the run since Marathon, but hoplites had less encumbrance from the spears and, possibly, from the tightness of the formation, and the disciplined Spartans were a famous exception, advancing at a walk to the sound of flutes.[16]

One special type of advance that might have occurred, however, is the 'oblique advance' (in modern terminology). Unlike the oblique phalanx, where the line is angled with one wing held back, an oblique advance is a forward movement at an angle to the direction of facing of the unit, so that it moves both forward and to one side. According to a well-known passage of Thucydides, an inadvertent oblique advance was a common feature of all hoplite phalanxes:

'All armies are alike in this: on going into action they get forced out rather on their right wing, and one and the other overlap with this their adversary's left; because fear makes each man do his best to shelter his unarmed side with the shield of the man next him on the right, thinking that the closer the shields are locked together the better will he be protected. The man primarily responsible for this is the first upon the right wing, who is always striving to withdraw from the enemy his unarmed side; and the same apprehension makes the rest follow him.' (Thucydides, 5.71.1)

Whether this was true also of the Macedonian phalanx is not known for sure. On the one hand, we might expect a similar phenomenon, since the Macedonian phalanx was similar to the hoplite phalanx in many ways and relied on the mutual support of the phalangites and their shields. On the other hand, Macedonian phalanx was generally better and more rigorously drilled and disciplined, and also had the protection of the projecting pikes, both of which factors should have made any such drift less likely to occur. At any rate, such a drift is never mentioned and seems never to have had any effect in battle.

On at least one occasion there may have been a deliberate oblique advance. At Gaugamela, Alexander's entire army (including the phalanx in the centre) marched towards its right so as to avoid encirclement by the large Persian army, and to threaten to move off the specially levelled ground the Persians had prepared for their scythed chariots. There is some doubt, however, as to whether this actually constituted an oblique advance in the strict sense. Arrian's account is not totally clear:

'But Alexander moved his men rather in the direction of his right ... . The Scythian cavalry, riding along Alexander's line, were already in contact with the troops posted in front of it; but Alexander still continued steadily his march towards his right ... . [Darius] ordered the troops in advance of his left wing to ride round the Macedonian

right, where Alexander was leading, so that they might not prolong
their wing any farther.' (Arrian, *Anabasis* 3.13)

Clearly, Alexander's army as a whole is moving to the right, but is this an
oblique advance proper? As Arrian expresses it, the army appears to be marching
directly to its right, and he uses three different expressions to describe the
movement: 'as if toward the right', 'leading to the spear' (a common way of
expressing the right, since the spear is held in the right hand) and 'leading out
the wing'. It is possible – especially since marching 'toward the wing' is the
usual expression for marching in column, as we have seen – that rather than
advancing obliquely, the army was marching in column to its right (or an angle
between forward and right), and I am inclined to think that this is what is meant
rather than the traditional view of a diagonal advance, which is not described
in any of the tacticians either. It may be then that an oblique advance in that
sense was never actually used by the phalanx.

It is also worth noting here a phrase that is sometimes applied to the tactics
of Hellenistic armies: 'hammer and anvil'. According to this conception, the
heavy cavalry on the wings formed the main striking force (the hammer), and
the role of the phalanx was more passive, to 'fix' the enemy in place (the anvil)
while the cavalry delivered the decisive below. I do not find this analysis of
Hellenistic tactics particularly convincing. Certainly, in Alexander's battles
the charge of the Companion cavalry is given great importance in the written
accounts, in large part in order to magnify the exploits of Alexander, but the
phalanx attacked alongside it even if its exploits are relatively less well recorded:
at Issus the phalanx launched a costly but successful attack across the river
(Arr. *Anab.* 2.10.5), while at Gaugamela the phalanx presumably engaged the
mercenary hoplites, who were stationed in the Persian centre specifically to
oppose them (Arr. *Anab.* 3.11.7). Far from being a defensive or passive force,
Alexander's phalanx attacked aggressively, alongside his cavalry, in all his
battles. Later battles follow a different pattern, in part because the relative
proportions of cavalry to infantry, especially in the Antigonid army, altered in
favour of the infantry, but also because in battles where both armies fielded a
phalanx, cavalry would have been unable to launch a decisive charge against the
enemy centre as Alexander liked to do against Persian infantry and cavalry, who
were less able to defend themselves. Hellenistic battles tended to take the form
of two-phase battles, where the cavalry and light troops would engage first on
the wings, then the phalanxes would engage in the centre. The simple reason
for this was that only a phalanx could successfully oppose an enemy phalanx,

and even so the phalanxes would advance and engage, not stand defensively. We might expect that victorious cavalry would assist by attacking the enemy phalanx from behind, but this is in fact not clearly attested.[17]

Another modern concept that I think is not helpful in aiding understanding is that Alexander's Hypaspists formed a 'flexible link' between the cavalry and the phalanx, a claim that is repeated very frequently in the modern literature but which makes very little sense to me. Given that the Hypaspists were themselves almost certainly armed similarly to the phalanx (or else as hoplites, if some modern interpretations are favoured), it is hard to see in what sense they would have been more flexible than the rest of the phalanx. Nor is it apparent how any heavy infantry force was to form a link between two disparate bodies on each side. If the cavalry advanced at full speed they would outpace any infantry, and it is not clear either how the Hypaspists would keep pace to prevent this happening (although some at least may have acted as *hamippoi*, infantry who run alongside cavalry, but the whole unit of 3,000 could hardly have done this) or how they could redeploy on a wider frontage, as presumably would be required, in order to maintain a 'link'. The position of the Hypaspists was determined by the status conferred by position in the battle line, with the Macedonians invariably forming the elite cavalry (Companions) on the right, then the elite infantry (Hypaspists), then the regular infantry (the phalanx), and it is this ordering by status that governed deployment, not any concept of forming a link.[18]

Terrain and obstacles

So far we have considered a phalanx moving over clear and open terrain. Polybius, however, in his comparison of the Roman and Macedonian systems, asserts that such flat ground would be very difficult for a phalanx to find in practice. Polybius makes similar assertions about the inability of the phalanx to operate on any sort of broken ground in his criticism of Callisthenes' account of the Battle of Issus:

> 'Again, how could a phalanx mount to the edge of the river bank, when it was precipitous and covered with brushwood? Such a piece of bad generalship must not be attributed to Alexander, because he is acknowledged by all to have been a skilful strategist and to have studied the subject from childhood: we must rather attribute it to the historian's want of ability to discern between what is or is not practicable in such movements.' (Polybius, 12.22)

For Polybius, terrain is paramount (see also his comments at 5.21), and the inability of the phalanx to operate effectively on broken ground is an essential feature of his argument for the superiority of the Roman system. However, we must suspect that Polybius is guilty of some rhetorical exaggeration in order to make his point. For one thing, despite his claim that it is 'impossible, or at any rate exceedingly rare' to find a suitable extent of ground (and as we have seen, Polybius exaggerates the extent of ground that would be required), nevertheless phalanxes did operate successfully for centuries in precisely such terrain. Similarly, while the riverbank at Issus may not have been quite as difficult to cross as Callisthenes made out, still we can be sure that the phalanx did fight its way across the river, as described by Arrian, for all that it found the task difficult:

> 'The Macedonian centre did not set to with equal impetus, and finding the river banks precipitous in many places, were unable to maintain their front in unbroken line; and the Greeks attacked where they saw that the phalanx had been particularly torn apart.' (Arrian, *Anabasis* 2.10.6)

The phalanx was in difficulties, suffered relatively heavy losses (including one of the *taxis* commanders) and was saved only by a flanking attack (on which more below). Yet the attack across the river was attempted and was ultimately successful, despite Polybius' doubts. Of course, a hoplite phalanx was not much better suited to broken terrain than a Macedonian phalanx, so in part it is the nature of the opposition that counts, as much as the nature of the ground. Against Romans the difference could be more disadvantageous, as we will see.[19]

In the wrong circumstances, terrain could certainly be very harmful to a phalanx. At Mantinea, the Spartan phalanx advanced precipitately against the Achaeans drawn up with a ditch or dyke to their front:

> 'Thereupon the Lacedaemonians ... without waiting for the word of command, brought their sarissae to the charge and rushed upon the enemy. But when in the course of their advance they reached the edge of the dyke, being unable at that point to change their purpose and retreat when at such close quarters with the enemy, and partly because they did not consider the dyke a serious obstacle, as the slope down to it was very gradual, and it was entirely without water or underwood growing in it, they continued their advance through it without

stopping to think. The opportunity for attack which Philopoemen had long foreseen had now arrived. He at once ordered the phalanx to bring their sarissae to the charge and advance. The men obeyed with enthusiasm, and accompanied their charge with a ringing cheer. The ranks of the Lacedaemonians had been disorganised by the passage of the dyke, and as they ascended the opposite bank they found the enemy above them. They lost courage and tried to fly; but the greater number of them were killed in the ditch itself, partly by the Achaeans, and partly by trampling on each other.' (Polybius, 11.15–16)

As Polybius explains, Philopoemen had drawn up his phalanx on the edge of the dyke (with intervals between the units, perhaps to increase their ability to exploit gaps that presented themselves) with this outcome in mind. In this case, though, the obstacle itself was not that challenging, as Polybius points out, and so it is not a simple case of the ditch disordering the Spartan phalanx and leading to its defeat. Rather it is a combination of disorder, the higher ground of the Achaean phalanx, the shout and vigour of their attack, and perhaps a lack of training and practice in this type of fighting on the part of the Spartans (who unlike the Macedonians at this time did not have a long history of fighting in a sarissa-armed phalanx). So an obstacle like this certainly could be harmful to a phalanx that was not prepared for it, but this does not mean that a phalanx could not attack across such an obstacle.

Several other of the battles in Greece fought by the Macedonian phalanx did not take place on flat or even terrain. Sellasia and Cynoscephalae both took place over hills. The Macedonians at Sellasia successfully attacked uphill – those on the right wing were (like the Achaeans at Mantinea) in a phalanx with gaps (the gaps being filled in this case with Illyrians), and though they were troubled at first by flanking attacks from Spartan light infantry, once the cavalry had removed this threat, they successfully drove the Spartans from their position. The Macedonian right had a long fight against the Spartan phalanx, which rather than defending the stockade behind which they were deployed, marched out in front of it – fearing in this case encirclement following the defeat of their right.

This brings us back to the use of separated columns as a way of avoiding the disordering effects of rough ground. This never (so far as we can tell) happened in the context of a major pitched battle, but several minor engagements show the use of such columns. The first good example comes from before the invention of the Macedonian phalanx and applies to the Greek hoplite phalanx of Xenophon's Ten Thousand, a passage which is so revealing and informative it is worth quoting at length:

> 'At this place was a great mountain, and upon this mountain the Colchians were drawn up in line of battle. At first the Greeks formed an opposing line of battle [*phalanga*], with the intention of advancing in this way upon the mountain, but afterwards the generals decided to gather together and take counsel as to how they could best make the contest. Xenophon accordingly said that in his opinion they should give up the line of battle [*phalanga*] and form the companies in column [*lochous orthious*]. "For the line," he continued, "will be broken up at once; for we shall find the mountain hard to traverse at some points and easy at others; and the immediate result will be discouragement, when men who are formed in line of battle see the line broken up. Furthermore, if we advance upon them formed in a line many ranks deep, the enemy will outflank us, and will use their outflanking wing for whatever purpose they please; on the other hand, if we are formed in a line a few ranks deep, it would be nothing surprising if our line should be cut through by a multitude both of missiles and men falling upon us in a mass; and if this happens at any point, it will be bad for the whole line. But it seems to me we should form the companies in column and, by leaving spaces between them, cover enough ground so that the outermost companies should get beyond the enemy's wings; in this way not only shall we outflank the enemy's line, but advancing in column our best men will be in the van of the attack, and wherever it is good going, there each captain will lead forward his men. And it will not be easy for the enemy to push into the space between the columns when there are companies on this side and that, and not any easier for him to cut through a company that is advancing in column. Again, if any one of the companies is hard pressed, its neighbour will come to its aid; and if one single company can somehow climb to the summit, not a man of the enemy will stand any longer." .... . When the officers had got to their several positions and had formed their companies in column, the result was about eighty companies of hoplites with each company numbering close upon one hundred; the peltasts and the bowmen, on the other hand, they formed in three divisions, one beyond the left wing of the hoplites, the second beyond the right, and the third in the centre, each division numbering about six hundred men.' (Xenophon, *Anabasis* 4.8.9–15)

This is a revealing passage in many ways (it also shows a degree of small unit organization in a non-Spartan army) and bears also on the discussion of gaps in the line above. Xenophon's view is that gaps appearing inadvertently in a phalanx would be dangerous as they would demoralize the men, while a line formed with intentional gaps would not suffer from this, and would have the benefits of ease of movement in column. Such columns are reminiscent of the separate pike blocks of Early Modern armies, or the independent maniples of the Romans (see Chapter 9). We see other examples of this use of columns to attack difficult terrain in Xenophon, and also in some of the minor actions of Alexander's army in Asia. For example, Alexander's general Ptolemy was ordered to lead a mixed force of Hypaspists, phalangites and light infantry against an Indian force:

> 'Ptolemy's troops marshalled themselves on uneven ground, but as the barbarians were holding a hill, they formed into columns [*orthious poiesantas*], and Ptolemy led them up to the point where the hill seemed most open to assault.' (Arrian, *Anabasis* 4.25.2)

The attack was a success, after a hard fight. We cannot tell for certain what role the light infantry played in this case (perhaps they deployed between the phalanx columns), but the use of columns for assaults on difficult positions of this sort seems to have been an established tactic.

Returning to pitched battles, at Cynoscephalae the Macedonian right was already on the top of the hills and the downhill attack helped in their defeat of the Roman left. The Macedonian left, as we have seen, was defeated not so much by the terrain as by the fact that they were not properly deployed. At this battle, the terrain appears not to have had a great impact on proceedings, other than by hiding the two armies from each other. Pydna is a battle where, according to modern commentators, terrain played a greater part; it is sometimes asserted that the Roman army deliberately withdrew onto rough ground, drawing the Macedonians on, until the nature of the ground broke up the phalanx and the Romans were able to exploit the gaps. I think, however, that this is a misinterpretation of the battle; far from deliberately withdrawing, it is clear from Plutarch's account (Plut. *Aem.* 20.3) that the Roman withdrawal was involuntary and caused the Roman commander much anxiety. The phalanx certainly developed gaps, partly perhaps due to terrain (Plut. *Aem.* 20.4), but due mostly to the rapidity of its advance (the Peltasts in particular pushing on well ahead of the *Chalcaspides* on their flank) and the uneven resistance encountered. As subunits (perhaps at the level of the *syntagma*, as in previous examples) encountered Roman maniples offering greater or lesser resistance, they would have become separated from each other (something that could have been avoided only by having the whole phalanx constantly stop and redress its lines, which in turn would have required a degree of command and coordination that was clearly lacking in this case) and the flexible Roman maniples were able to take advantage. I will have more to say on this battle in Chapter 9, but at any rate it is clear that this was not a battle where the terrain had much impact.

Overall I think we can safely conclude that the Macedonian phalanx certainly could be disordered and discomfited by broken ground or obstacles, but that this was not certain doom for the phalanx, and that other factors – such as training and experience – could overcome the situation. The phalanx was not well suited to fighting on broken ground, but nor was it incapable of doing so.

Outflanking

I have mentioned outflanking manoeuvres several times in the above discussion. The trade-off in any type of phalanx warfare is between the depth of the formation, which gives it greater strength, and its width, which allows it to outflank the enemy or prevents the enemy from outflanking it. Asclepiodotus provides a definition:

> 'By "outflanking" [*hyperkerasai*] is understood the throwing of one wing about the wing of the enemy – and this is done sometimes even when a wing is numerically inferior to that of the enemy – as when both wings are used in a flanking movement, it is called a double outflanking [*hyperphalangein*].' (Asclepiodotus, *Tactics* 10.18)

In fact, examples of phalanxes outflanking one another are rare – whether because it did not often occur, or because the battle accounts we have are often too vague and lacking in detail on the precise manoeuvres of the phalanx. If outflanking did not often occur, the reasons are easy enough to surmise: doubling manoeuvres and variations in depth and intervals were available to protect against outflanking; phalanxes generally had light or auxiliary infantry and cavalry on their flanks, so that their flanks were protected; and it was probably more efficacious to defeat a phalanx frontally (perhaps using greater depth or density) than it was to carry out complex outflanking manoeuvres. As Asclepiodotus notes, 'some condemn such doublings, especially when the enemy is near, and by extending the light infantry and cavalry on both wings give the appearance of the doubling without disturbing the phalanx' (Asclep. 10.20).[20]

One clear example of a successful outflanking manoeuvre is Alexander's phalanx at Issus, as Arrian describes it. The bulk of the Macedonian phalanx was encountering difficulties as they tried to fight their way across the river in the face of the Greek (hoplite) phalanx:

> 'At this point the *taxeis* on the right wing, seeing that the Persians opposed to them were already routed, bent round towards Darius' foreign mercenaries, where their own centre was hard pressed, drove them from the river, and then overlapping [*hyperphalangesantes*] the now broken part of the Persian army, attacked in the flank and in a trice were cutting down the mercenaries.' (Arrian, *Anabasis* 2.11.1)

The details of the manoeuvre are unclear, but the general thrust is plain enough: the flanking *taxeis* (Arrian does not say how many – perhaps two) performing the outflanking manoeuvre (which Arrian calls *hyperphalangein*, though it does not here mean the double outflanking of Asclepiodotus) to take the Greek mercenaries in the flank. Behind this high-level description must lie complex and highly skilled drill manoeuvres, the details of which are hidden from us. The mercenary hoplite line was probably eight ranks deep, covering about 8 metres in depth. A *taxis* of Alexander's phalanx, assuming around 1,500 men eight deep, with 1 metre intervals, would have a frontage of around 190 metres. If two *taxeis* had simply wheeled left while maintaining their original formation, they would have covered at least 380 metres of front (assuming no gaps between units), of which only 8 metres would have been in contact with the flank of the Greeks. Perhaps this is what happened, but I think it likely that more complex manoeuvres would have taken place at the low level, with individual *syntagmata* wheeling left and marching independently toward the Greek flank rather than wheeling the whole line, or (as appears to have been the norm) marching the outflanking *taxeis* in column to the right and wheeling left, before advancing in line. We will never know precisely how the manoeuvre was carried out, but should keep in mind that a few words in a description of high-level army manoeuvres, or a few blocks positioned on a battle map, hide a multitude of details of what must have been taking place on the ground. Fig. 7.4 illustrates some possibilities (note the use of the earlier sixty-four-man *taxis* as the manoeuvre unit, and see also fig. 3.14 in Chapter 3).

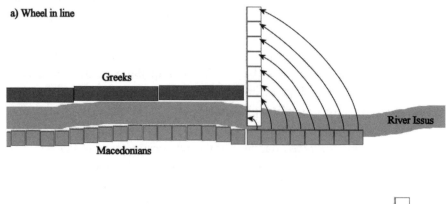

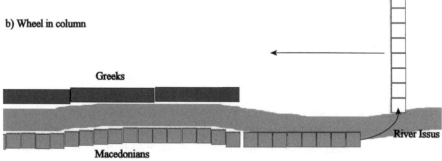

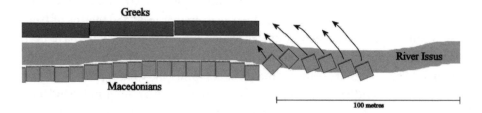

Fig. 7.4. Outflanking manoeuvres at Issus.

Withdrawals and reversals

Either while in contact with the enemy, or before contact took place, a phalanx might sometimes want, or be required, to withdraw to some extent. The tacticians provide copious details of the various countermarches available to a phalanx; that is, ways of changing facing through 180 degrees while retaining the proper file structure. The quickest way to turn 180 degrees would be to have every man turn around in place, but this would put the file leaders at the back of the phalanx, so instead countermarches were developed to allow the files to switch facing while maintaining their order, as we saw in Chapter 3. These countermarches were a component of many other drill manoeuvres, as we have seen, as the wheeling or turning of a unit might leave it needing to switch its facing to face the enemy. But they could also be an end in themselves, as they allowed a phalanx which was, for example, threatened unexpectedly in the rear, to about face and resist the new threat. In practice such manoeuvres are again rare, either because we do not hear of them in the high-level battle accounts we have or because a phalanx threatened in the rear was more likely to break and run than to countermarch to face the threat (as happened to the Macedonian right at Cynoscephalae). One example was the second phalanx Alexander employed at Gaugamela (though this was, presumably, a phalanx of allied hoplites rather than Macedonian-armed):

> '[Alexander] also posted a second line, so that the phalanx faced both ways. The commanders of this reserve had instructions to face about and receive the barbarian attack, if they saw their own forces being surrounded by the Persian army.' (Arrian, *Anabasis* 3.12.1)

In the event, Persian cavalry broke through a gap in the front line:

> '[T]he commanders of the troops that formed the reserve to the first phalanx quickly learned what had happened, turned about face, according to previous orders, appeared in the rear of the Persians, and killed large numbers of them.' (Arrian, *Anabasis* 3.14.6)

This account is not without its problems. For one, the translation 'faced both ways' is not a good one, since both phalanxes would have faced forward (or the direction they were marching, which is not necessarily the same); rather, the phalanx was 'double-fronted' (a double phalanx, in which the two components could face in different directions). It is also not clear what the second phalanx was doing when the Persians broke through the first. Why did the Persians not then encounter the second line face-to-face, unless the second line too had developed a gap – which is quite possible if the second line was closely attached to the first rather than being widely separated, as usually understood, so that in effect each *taxis* (of Macedonians) had a second *taxis* (of hoplites) positioned immediately behind it (a double phalanx similar to that at Sellasia).

When the Macedonian left flank *taxeis* halted, the second line would have done so too, so that the gap affected both phalanxes. At any rate, the second line then performed a countermarch of some sort (the translator says 'face about' and 'turned about face', translating *epistrepho* and *metaballo*, general words for turn around, so we can only guess precisely what manoeuvre was used) and marched to attack the Persians. This is a rare example of this sort of thing happening in battle, and again demonstrates the high level of drill that would be required, although obscured by the vague literary accounts.[21]

What of withdrawals in the face of the enemy? There is only one example of this that I am aware of in pitched battle: the withdrawal of the Macedonian right wing at Chaeronea (Philip II's decisive victory against the Greeks). There is, however, also an interesting example from one of Alexander's minor actions in India:

> 'Alexander, who had seen that the battle would be near the city, wished to entice them out further … as soon as he saw the barbarians sallying out, he ordered the Macedonians to turn right about and withdraw towards a hill, just about seven stades [1,200 metres] away from the place where he had decided to camp. Emboldened by the belief that the Macedonians had already given way, the enemy rushed on them at full speed and in disorder. When the arrows were just reaching his troops, Alexander wheeled [*epistrepsas*] his phalanx towards them at a signal and led them on at the double.' (Arrian, *Anabasis* 4.26.2–3)

The Indians were quickly defeated. Note that 'wheeled' is apparently a fair translation, since Asclepiodotus (10.4) and Aelian (31) define *epistrophe* as a wheeling quarter-turn, but we might expect a countermarch (such as the Macedonian) to be better suited to the occasion. At any rate, this is a deliberate withdrawal in the face of the enemy, but note that the enemy are at a considerable distance, the turn being executed at long bowshot (about 100 metres or more).

For Chaeronea, the story of the withdrawal is preserved in Polyaenus' collection of stratagems:

> 'Engaging the Athenians at Chaeronea, Philip made a sham retreat: and Stratocles, the Athenian general, ordered his men to push forwards, crying out, "We will pursue them to the heart of Macedonia." Philip observed, "The Athenians know not how to conquer" and ordered his phalanx to keep close and firm, and to retreat slowly, covering themselves with their shields from the attacks of the enemy. As soon

as he had by the manoeuvre drawn them from their advantageous ground, and gained an eminence, he halted; and encouraging his troops to a vigorous assault, he attacked the Athenians and won a brilliant victory.' (Polyaenus, 4.2.2)

This is a clear enough account, on the face of it, but it is not uncontroversial. For one thing, Polyaenus shortly after gives a slightly different version:

'Philip, at Chaeronea, knowing the Athenians were impetuous and inexperienced, and the Macedonians inured to fatigues and exercise, contrived to prolong the action: and reserving his principal attack to the latter end of the engagement, the enemy weak and exhausted were unable to sustain the charge.' (Polyaenus, 4.2.7)

This second version is also recorded in Frontinus' strategem collection, in similar (though Latin) words. It is not clear if they both describe the same thing. The only other account of Chaeronea we have, that of Diodorus (16.86), is hopelessly vague and unclear and makes no mention of this incident. A deliberate sham withdrawal by a phalanx in the face of the enemy is unknown in any other battle (Polybius, 11.16, talking of Mantinea, points out the danger and difficulty of withdrawing in the face of the enemy), and this seems to be a different case from Alexander's withdrawal with the enemy still at long range. Quite how the manoeuvre would be performed is not clear. If the phalanx were to countermarch and march away from the Athenians, then they would be presenting their unprotected backs, not 'covering themselves with their shields', and would surely be in great danger (assuming the Athenians were closer than in Alexander's ruse). Yet it is very hard to believe they could have walked backwards, as this would surely be even more hazardous, since it would be very hard to maintain order and avoid trips and stumbles, fatal to those in the front rank, while walking backwards for any distance. It is perhaps better to adopt one of two possibilities. The withdrawal at Chaeronea might have been similar to Alexander's tactic, performed with the Athenians still at long range and with a pair of countermarches, so that Polyaenus' 'covering themselves with their shields' is an error. Or else we could merge the two incidents from Polyaenus, and assume that the Macedonian phalanx was initially involuntarily pushed back by the Athenians, for a presumably short distance, but as the Athenians lost momentum the Macedonians were then able to reverse the pressure and direction of movement, and break the Athenian phalanx. Read this way, the incident would be very similar to what happened at Sellasia between the Macedonian and Spartan phalanxes, and indeed there is a similarity in vocabulary: at Sellasia, the Macedonian phalanx 'gradually fell back facing the enemy [*epi poda ... anachoresin*]' (Pol. 2.69.8), while at Chaeronea it was ordered to 'retreat slowly [*epi poda anachorei*]' (Polyaen. 4.2.2). So rather than a deliberate sham retreat at Chaeronea, we may see a similar to and fro as at Sellasia, with the superior training and endurance of the Macedonians allowing them to win out in the long fight against the Athenians as they did against the Spartans at Sellasia. The account of Sellasia to be found in Plutarch, which has the Macedonian phalanx pushed back 900 metres by the Spartans, offers a warning not to take too literally every story to be found in, especially, the less reliable sources.[22]

Reserves

The *amphistomos* (double-fronted) phalanx at Gaugamela is referred to in the translations above as a reserve, though the tacticians do not discuss such a concept, and it is generally accepted that one of the peculiarities of Greek and Macedonian warfare was the failure to adopt the use of reserves, unlike the Romans. In the Roman system, reserve formations – as much as two-thirds of the whole infantry force – were stationed behind the front line, and could support or take over from the front-line forces if the fight was going against them, or reinforce points under particular pressure. In traditional Greek hoplite battles, such reserve forces are wholly lacking. The possible reasons for this are various. It may be a cultural artefact of the desire to place the strongest and bravest men in the front rank, where they could prove their worth as well as deciding the combat; or there may be technical reasons, since in a close-quarters clash of heavy infantry, a break in the main line was likely to lead to a catastrophic collapse and rout of the formation, and it may have been felt that reserves would be unable to rectify such a break, so the manpower was better spent fighting in the first line. The Romans, with a more open order and style of fighting, were better able to give ground gradually under pressure rather than breaking. Whatever the reasons, Macedonian phalanxes largely followed in the same tradition, with the whole manpower available forming a single continuous line and no reserves held back to reinforce success or failure.

However, we have already seen above that a double phalanx could be formed, as at Gaugamela – the intent was rather to prevent encirclement than to provide a reserve, but the outcome was similar. The double phalanx at Sellasia was formed because space did not allow the phalanx to deploy at normal width, but even so the outcome was also similar to a reserve, in that the greater depth of the phalanx was able, in the end, to overcome strong Spartan resistance, though again this is really a single deep formation rather than two formations with one in reserve. On occasion, other forces (such as cavalry or light infantry) might be held back behind the phalanx, like Alexander's flank guards of cavalry and light infantry at Gaugamela or the reserve of cavalry that Pyrrhus held back behind his phalanx at Asculum (D.H. 20.1). Alexander also may have regularly used his Greek allied or mercenary forces to form a double phalanx, with the Macedonians in the front. On the approach to the Granicus, Alexander is said by Arrian to have drawn up his hoplites in a double phalanx (Arr. *Anab.* 1.13.1), though only the Macedonian *taxeis* are named, while at Issus, 'the foreign mercenaries were drawn up in support of the whole line' (Arr. *Anab.* 2.9.3). But I am not aware of any case of units of the phalanx itself being held back to form a proper reserve. The reasons may be similar to those for the Greek phalanx, or it may be that the idea had simply not yet occurred to anyone (this seems unlikely, given the high state of the tactical art in Hellenistic times). At any rate, we can imagine how useful a reserve might have been at battles such as Cynoscephalae, where the Roman right-wing reserve was able to attack the unprotected rear of the Macedonian right, or Pydna, where gaps in the phalanx were exploited unopposed by the Romans. One of the drawbacks of the Macedonian phalanx was that being a dense, deep, close-order formation, its manpower was not spread across a very wide front relative to other infantry formations, and there would always have been a danger of outflanking. It may be then that the need to extend the phalanx sufficiently to match or exceed the frontage of an enemy made it impossible to spare any significant manpower for a reserve; the manpower demands would have been great, since a small, relatively slow-moving phalanx positioned to the rear in the wrong place would have been useless, so that only a large reserve (or many small ones) had any chance of being effective. I think it more likely that Macedonian military theorists considered the pros and cons of a reserve and decided against using one, than that the concept simply eluded them. At any rate, the result was that the phalanx was a one-shot weapon, unable to survive a serious setback or sustain a prolonged fight. Victory must be won quickly, and the line of the phalanx maintained at all times, or defeat would follow.[23]

Combined arms

A point that has already been made a number of times throughout this book is that the Macedonian phalanx itself formed only a part of a Macedonian or Hellenistic army, and in some cases only a small part. Alexander's army at Gaugamela, for example, had a phalanx 12,000 strong (or 15,000 if the Hypaspists are counted separately) out of a total force of 40,000 infantry and 7,000 cavalry. The proportion of phalanx to army was higher for the later Antigonid armies, but even so the army at Cynoscephalae, for instance, as well as a phalanx of 18,000 (including Peltasts) had 5,500 other infantry and 2,000 cavalry. The phalanx ratio in Seleucid armies was more like Alexander's: at Magnesia the phalanx was 16,000 men (plus an unknown number of Argyraspides) out of a total of 60,000 infantry and 12,000 cavalry.

Classical Greek armies, which had always consisted chiefly of hoplites, had also included (sometimes very large) numbers of light infantry as well as cavalry whose roles expanded in the course of the fourth century, but the importance of the hoplites as the battle-winning force meant that the phalanx remained tactically dominant, even when it was not the only element of any army. Hellenistic armies, in contrast, were true combined-arms armies with a balanced mixture of heavy and light infantry and cavalry (as well as possible speciality units like chariots and elephants). This allowed specialist forces for operations (sieges, rapid marches, attacks over difficult terrain) outside of pitched battle, but in battle armies also relied on the cooperation of all arms to secure victory, not just the heavy infantry. The phalanx remained the primary battle-winning force, as no other arm was able to threaten the phalanx to its front, but other arms had important roles to play. In Alexander's battles against an enemy lacking a steady heavy infantry, cavalry were able to operate as the main strike force, delivering a decisive charge toward the centre of the enemy line, though as we have seen, the phalanx accompanied these attacks and did not play a passive role. Hellenistic armies could not use cavalry in quite the same way, since cavalry (see below) would be unable to attack the phalanx frontally, but instead battles were broken down into phases, with (speaking generally) light forces engaging first in skirmishing between the battle lines, followed by engagements on the wings as cavalry and medium infantry engaged to strip the enemy phalanx of its flank guards, and finally the decisive clash of phalanxes. The importance of cavalry and its ability to strip the enemy flanks and then envelop the centre, as demonstrated in Hannibal's victory over the Romans at Cannae, led Polybius to conclude that this was 'a lesson to posterity that in actual war it is better to have half the number of infantry, and the superiority in cavalry, than to engage your enemy with an equality in both' (Pol. 3.117.5). This conclusion seems not to apply strongly to Hellenistic battles, where there are no examples of envelopment quite equivalent to that achieved by Hannibal, but even so a phalanx that lost its flank guards would be desperately vulnerable, as shown by the Seleucid defeat at Magnesia, so it was important at any rate to maintain equality in cavalry and light forces. Combined arms also allowed the matching of particular troop types against particular opponents against whom they would have an advantage; this was particularly true for elephants and chariots, which could be most effectively opposed by missiles, and elephants in particular were generally assigned their own escorts of light infantry to keep enemy light infantry away.[24]

Phalanx versus ...

Another factor to consider is the range of opponents faced by the phalanx on the battlefield. The first major test of the Macedonian phalanx was at Chaeronea under Philip II, where it faced and defeated the phalanx of Athenian hoplites, in circumstances which are not totally clear, but suggest at any rate that it was not simply a matter of the phalanx rolling forward and driving the Athenians before them (perhaps in part because of disadvantageous terrain). In the first two of Alexander's major battles, the phalanx faced hoplites again: at the Granicus, the hapless Greek mercenaries, abandoned by the Persian cavalry, were attacked frontally by the phalanx and from all sides by the Macedonian cavalry, so would have been unable to put up much organized resistance. At Issus, as we have seen, the tables were turned, as the phalanx had to fight its way across a river opposed by hoplites, and was roughly handled until Macedonian flanking forces turned the tide. Honours in these battles seem to have been surprisingly even, provided the hoplites had some terrain to offset the Macedonians' advantage, and perhaps explains why Greek cities did not themselves adopt Macedonian armament for another hundred years. At Gaugamela, the phalanx attacked with Alexander, but whom they fought is unrecorded, since the accounts concentrate entirely on Alexander's attack at the head of his cavalry and Darius' flight.[25]

Alexander's last major battle, the Hydaspes, saw the first (and possibly last) time that the phalanx was matched against elephants. The Indians had formed up with elephants forward of and covering the gaps between the units of infantry (a formation reminiscent of that adopted by Antiochus at Magnesia), and Arrian describes the subsequent encounter:

'At this point the drivers of the elephants brought up their animals against the cavalry, and the Macedonian phalanx for its part boldly advanced to meet the elephants, hurling javelins at their drivers, and forming a ring round the animals, volleyed upon them from all sides ...

the beasts charged into the line of infantry and, whichever way they turned, began to devastate the Macedonian phalanx, dense though it was … . The elephants were now crowded into a narrow space … . The Macedonians however had plenty of room, and attacked the animals at their own judgement, giving way wherever they charged, but following close as they turned round, and shooting at them with javelins … . Alexander … then gave a signal for the infantry to lock shields, concentrate into the most compact mass possible, and advance the phalanx.' (Arrian, *Anabasis* 5.17)

This is a typical ancient battle description, a maddening mix of precision and vagueness, and has caused considerable controversy and uncertainty (though less so than the account of the cavalry engagement at Hydaspes, which I can happily pass over here). Taking 'the Macedonian phalanx' in Arrian's account literally, we would have to conclude that the phalanx – there were three phalanx units present: the Hypaspists and two *taxeis* of the phalanx (Arr. *Anab.* 5.12.2) – fought with javelins and at least partly in open order (able to encircle the elephants and to retire before them). It is possible that the phalanx units brought their javelins with them on this occasion and left behind their sarissas, which would after all have been difficult to handle on the river crossing that preceded the battle. But alternatively, the Macedonian infantry included units of archers and Agrianian javelinmen (5.12.2), so perhaps Arrian is using 'phalanx' here in the sense of 'battleline', so that it was the Agrianians, formed up in front of the phalanx proper, who shot javelins at the elephants, and the phalanx itself became engaged only at the end when it closed up for the final advance. I am inclined to think the latter is most likely, and also that one reason for the hopeless confusion of the accounts of this battle is that the situation on the ground was hopelessly confused, with units mixed together more than would have been the case in a straightforward battle against infantry. Arrian's reference to the phalanx locking shields (*xunaspisantas*) in closest order (*puknotaten*) might be taken as a reference to the *synaspismos* of the tacticians, the one cubit spacing; but as we have seen, these terms when used in literary accounts do not necessarily carry their technical meaning. On this occasion we might consider two possibilities: that the phalanx was initially in open order and javelin-armed, and was involved in skirmishing with the elephants, and closed up to normal close order for the final advance; or that the Agrianians skirmished with the elephants ahead of a close-order phalanx, which closed up to one-cubit order for the advance. I think the latter is again a little more likely, but unfortunately given the uncertainties not too much can be made of this.

At any rate, the performance of the elephants was sufficiently impressive to ensure that every Hellenistic army to follow did its best to obtain an elephant contingent, but they were always subsequently used against each other or against light infantry, to screen cavalry, or else their exploits in battle (if any) are simply ignored.[26]

The wars of the Successors and the Hellenistic kingdoms saw Macedonian phalanx matched against Macedonian phalanx, and indeed this was almost exclusively the type of fighting in which the phalanx engaged. There were further battles against Greek hoplites, but too little detail survives of such encounters to make anything of them. The battle accounts of these phalanx-versus-phalanx battles tend to be exceptionally terse and give almost no information on how such a battle was fought (I will look further at this question in Chapter 8). At Paraitacene the cavalry on the wings engaged first:

> 'At the same time that this was going on, it so happened that the infantry for a considerable time had been engaged in a battle of phalanxes, but finally, after many had fallen on both sides, Eumenes' men were victorious because of the valour of the Macedonian Silver Shields.' (Diodorus, 19.30.5)

The Silver Shields' success was put down by Diodorus to their 'hardihood and skill', they being elderly veterans of Philip and Alexander's armies. At Gabiene shortly afterwards, the Silver Shields again distinguished themselves:

> 'As for the infantry, the Silver Shields in close order fell heavily upon their adversaries, killing some of them in hand to hand fighting and forcing others to flee. They were not to be checked in their charge and engaged the entire opposing phalanx, showing themselves so superior in skill and strength that of their own men they lost not one, but of those who opposed them they slew over five thousand and routed the entire force of foot soldiers, whose numbers were many times their own.' (Diodorus, 19.43.1)

Such disproportionate numbers and casualties are hard to believe, yet given that the majority of casualties were suffered in the pursuit, are possible if the opposing forces gave way without putting up much resistance. The one noteworthy snippet of information from this account is the observation that they were 'in close order' – the word used is *sumphraxantes*, the same word we encountered above at Sellasia, and also used by Polybius of the Peltasts forming close order to resist cavalry (Pol. 4.64.7) and of Roman legionaries forming a 'tortoise' to attack a gate (Pol. 10.14.12). The vocabulary used is in fact very similar to that used by Polybius at Sellasia (Diodorus – *'sumphraxantes kai biaioteron ... epipesontes'*; Polybius – *'sumphraxantes tas sarissas kai ... biai prospesontes'*; 'closing up (their sarissas) and forcibly attacking'). So this might be another example of the one-cubit spacing being used. There were also elephants deployed in front of the phalanxes in both these battles, but what if anything they did, and how or whether they got out of the way to allow the infantry to fight, our sources do not reveal.[27]

Most of the later battles of phalanx against phalanx (chiefly Sellasia, Mantineia and Raphia) we have already encountered above and do not provide much more information. At Raphia, Polybius describes the cavalry and elephant engagements in some detail, but the phalanx battle is reduced to a few words:

> 'Lowering their sarissas, therefore, the phalanx under Andromachus and Sosibius advanced to the charge. For a short time the picked Syrian troops resisted, but those under Nicarchus quickly turned and fled.' (Polybius, 5.85.9–10)

Note again the 'lowering of sarissas', and that 'advanced to the charge' translates the generic word *epegon*, so isn't any evidence of the speed or character of the advance. Polybius attributes the poor showing of the Syrian (Seleucid) forces to the inspirational presence of Ptolemy, though if the Ptolemaic phalanx was really 45,000 strong (which, however, I doubt), the Seleucids would have been heavily outnumbered – the Ptolemaic phalanx would then have been able to form in greater depth (perhaps twenty-four or thirty-two ranks), which could account for their success.

The encounters between the phalanx and its ultimate nemesis, the Roman legions, are of sufficient importance to merit a chapter of their own. Here I will briefly consider the opposition of three last groups: chariots, other mounted forces and missile-armed light infantry.

The Macedonian phalanx first faced scythed chariots at Gaugamela (hoplite phalanxes had already had similar encounters). Famously, Alexander's men opened gaps in their lines through which the chariots (less manoeuvrable than cavalry) passed relatively harmlessly, at least according to Diodorus' account:

> 'Against the threat of the scythed chariots, he [Alexander] ordered the infantry of the phalanx to join shields as soon as these went into

action against them and to beat the shields with their spears, creating such a din as to frighten the horses into bolting to the rear, or, if they persevered, to open gaps in the ranks such that they might ride through harmlessly … . First the scythed chariots swung into action at full gallop and created great alarm and terror among the Macedonians … . As the phalanx joined shields, however, all beat upon their shields with their spears as the king had commanded and a great din arose. As the horses shied off, most of the chariots were turned about and bore hard with irresistible impact against their own ranks. Others continued on against the Macedonian lines, but as the soldiers opened wide gaps in their ranks the chariots were channelled through these.' (Diodorus, 17.57.6, 58.2–4)

Diodorus adds some lurid details of what happened to a few Macedonians who were unable to get out of the way. The information on the manoeuvre that Diodorus includes is intriguing – the order to 'join shields' (*sunaspizo*) may again represent the forming of the closest, one-cubit order, or may not be used in a strict technical sense. It is impossible to be sure how it was combined with the opening of gaps, for which there is no drill in the tacticians. Gaps large enough for a chariot to pass through would have to be quite wide, so a speculative reconstruction of the manoeuvre might go like this: the phalanx was formed sixteen deep in standard (two-cubit) order; on the chariots approaching, the phalanx was 'doubled by men', interjecting the rear halves of the files to form one-cubit order, eight deep. On the chariots continuing to close, alternate *syntagmata* were ordered to countermarch to the rear, face left or right and march across to take up position behind their neighbour, thus leaving 16-metre gaps through which chariots could pass. It is perhaps a test of the reader's belief in battlefield discipline and control whether such a manoeuvre in the face of onrushing chariots seems plausible. A simpler alternative is to assume Diodorus was wrong to separate the closing of intervals and creation of gaps, and that each *syntagma* was ordered to close up to its left or right while remaining in place, which would have meant there was no change of depth, and that gaps of 8 metres would be opened in the line. This seems more likely to me. A third alternative is that the chariots did not charge the phalanx at all, since Arrian's account implies that it was the Companion cavalry that was the target of the charge (Arr. *Anab.* 3.13.5–6).[28]

Attacks by regular cavalry on a phalanx are, not surprisingly, exceedingly rare. A phalanx of serried pikes would have every reason to consider itself invulnerable to cavalry attack since the horses would be unable to force their way through the pike points, and the riders' reach was much shorter than the length of the pikes. It is a curious fact that while in many ways a pike formation is ideally suited for opposing cavalry (and this was a large part of the reason for the adoption of the pike in Medieval Europe, where pike formations were a way for infantry, the socially inferior class, to level the odds against knightly cavalry), in this period, cavalry seem simply not to have attempted to attack a phalanx, at least not frontally. We must assume that in battles where the cavalry wings engaged first, before the infantry, then victorious cavalry would have tried to tilt the odds in favour of their infantry by harrying the enemy phalanx's rear, as happened at Cretopolis (Diod. 18.45) or Panion (Pol. 16.19). One incident, outside of pitched battle, that illustrates several of the points already discussed in this chapter is the river crossing carried out by Philip V's Peltasts in the face of Aetolian cavalry. Philip was advancing on an Aetolian-held town:

> 'When a body of Aetolian cavalry ventured to meet him, at the ford of the river which runs in front of the town at a distance of about twenty stades from it, trusting either to prevent his passage entirely or to inflict considerable damage on the Macedonians as they were crossing, the king, perceiving their design, ordered his Peltasts to enter the river first and land on the other bank in close order shield to shield and company to company. His orders were obeyed, and as soon as the first company had passed, the Aetolian cavalry, after a feeble attack on it, finding that it stood firm with shields interlocked and that the second and third companies as they landed closed up with it, were unable to effect anything, and seeing that they were getting into difficulties made off for the town.' (Polybius, 4.64.5–7)

The word translated as 'company' is *tagma*, a generic word for a military unit, without a definition in the tacticians, but we might guess that a *syntagma* is meant (at 6.24 Polybius uses the same word for the Roman maniple, offering *semeia* or *speira* as synonyms). 'In close order' is *sunaspizo*, the same word as discussed above, and would make sense in this context as the one–cubit order to provide maximum deterrence to the cavalry while holding a defensive position on the river bank. The cavalry, for their part, did not, we must assume, charge the phalanx, but would have threatened it in the hope of frightening men into breaking ranks. When this did not happen, the cavalry had no choice but to make off. Cavalry in general would have been powerless against a formed and facing phalanx that held its ground.

Finally, regarding skirmishers and missile-armed troops, Polybius notes the function of the raised sarissas of the rear ranks:

'They therefore do not severally level their sarissas, but hold them slanting up in the air over the shoulders of those in front of them, so as to protect the whole formation from above, keeping off by this serried mass of sarissas all missiles which, passing over the heads of the first ranks, might fall on those immediately in front of and behind them.' (Polybius, 18.30.3)

This may have been a desirable side-effect of the raised sarissas rather than an intended function, since after all they would have to be held up if they could not reach the enemy when levelled, but does indicate that defence against missiles was considered of some importance. In no battle account that we have, however, does missile fire against a phalanx have any recorded impact, with the notable exceptions of Magnesia, where it was the effect on the elephants in the formation that was most important, and Second Chaeronea, both of which battles will be examined in Chapter 9. Alexander's proposed phalanx with ranks of Persian javelinmen and archers was presumably intended to combine the strength of the sarissa-armed front ranks with a hail of missiles from behind, but was never put into practice. In general we can say that missiles, even Roman heavy *pila*, seem not to have had a significant effect on any phalanx (see Chapter 9), due no doubt to a combination of the protective sarissas overhead, decent shield and armour protection, a rapid and aggressive advance that minimized the time under fire, and the training and discipline of the phalangites which allowed them to dress the ranks and close up to replace casualties. In addition (and perhaps most importantly), Hellenistic armies were combined-arms forces with their own light infantry and cavalry able to keep enemy light infantry away from the phalanx, so that defeats of isolated heavy infantry by skirmishers – such as the noted defeats of Spartan hoplites at Sphacteria or Lechaion – were not a feature of Hellenistic warfare.

Other forms of fighting

Finally, we must consider those occasions where the phalanx fought outside of a pitched battle. This chapter has considered only pitched battle manoeuvres and formations, since the pitched battle was the natural home of the phalanx and the phalanx was conceived as a battle-winning force, as Polybius' discussion of the requirement of the phalanx for unbroken terrain makes clear:

'However, let us suppose that such a district has been found. If the enemy decline to come down into it, but traverse the country sacking the towns and territories of the allies, what use will the phalanx be? For if it remains on the ground suited to itself, it will not only fail to benefit its friends, but will be incapable even of preserving itself; for the carriage of provisions will be easily stopped by the enemy, seeing that they are in undisputed possession of the country: while if it quits its proper ground, from the wish to strike a blow, it will be an easy prey to the enemy.' (Polybius, 18.31)

While ostensibly talking about level terrain, Polybius' point is really that if an enemy declines pitched battle and concentrates on attacks on towns, disrupting supply lines and holding strategic locations, then the phalanx will be useless. As in other parts of this discussion, Polybius is overstating his case in order to make a rhetorical point. All Macedonian and Hellenistic armies supplemented their phalanx with auxiliary forces of light or medium infantry and cavalry – sometimes outnumbering the phalanx itself or at least in equal numbers – whose role was precisely the non-battle forms of combat Polybius has in mind. Light infantry were perfectly suited to holding strategic positions (such as hills and passes), and cavalry to harrying enemy supply convoys, and we see them employed in this way in numerous campaigns. Alexander, for example, usually formed mobile strike forces from the Companion cavalry and Agrianian javelinmen, which he would use for any rapid advances or operations in difficult terrain, sometimes joined by the more mobile of the phalangites and/or the Hypaspists. The fact that the phalanx itself was not well suited to such operations is therefore arguably not a major drawback, since Hellenistic armies were balanced forces in which specialists carried out particular roles – light infantry skirmishing and operating on rough ground, cavalry scouting and performing rapid attacks, and the phalanx providing the battle-winning force in pitched battle. This may be compared with Demosthenes' view of the army of Philip II:

'[Y]ou hear of Philip marching unchecked, not because he leads a phalanx of heavy infantry, but because he is accompanied by skirmishers, cavalry, archers, mercenaries, and similar troops.' (Demosthenes, *Philippic* 9.49)

The phalanx did not need to be effective in all roles, since other forces were available. Only those armies, such as the later Antigonid armies that faced the

Romans, where the proportion of phalanx to light infantry and cavalry was out of balance, would have been seriously disadvantaged in the way Polybius describes.

When it came to attacking and defending towns, the phalanx would still have been the most important force. This was demonstrated particularly by the Peltasts who held a breach in the walls of Atrax against Roman attackers, simply making a human wall to replace that of stone that the Romans had destroyed (Liv. 32.17). But in all sieges where Macedonian forces were attacking, the bulk of the workforce for all the operations of mining, building and assaulting that sieges required must usually have been phalangites (light infantry would have been valuable for using their missiles to clear the walls of defenders, while cavalry can have had only a very limited role). In such circumstances the phalangites, as we have seen, probably did not carry their cumbrous sarissas and reverted instead to javelins, at least in the early years. In this way the phalanx, even when not deployed with its characteristic formation and armament, was still a valuable and essential part of any army. As we have seen in Chapter 5, the phalanx could also provide men for garrisons, though it was probably mercenaries that provided the permanent garrisons as opposed to temporary forces stationed in strategic towns.

The decisive battle

The fact remains that while sieges, raids and the defence of passes were often important, the sources frequently describe the desire of the combatants to 'decide the issue by battle', that is to march against one another with their armies, without the benefit of defensive lines or fortifications, and engage in pitched battle on an open field. The concept of the decisive battle as the means to an ultimate decision in war remained paramount throughout the period. A defender could, if he felt his chances of success were too small perhaps, remain inside defensive positions – as when Alexander, son of Polyperchon, failed to come out of his defences to face Cassander in 316 (Diod. 19.54.4) or when Lysimachus, awaiting the arrival of his allies before Ipsus, remained in his fortified camp and refused to fight Antigonus (Diod. 20.108.5). Such a failure to fight, however, was taken as an indication of weakness – as in Livy's version of the consul's speech before Thermopylae, pointing out that Antiochus III had withdrawn deep into the pass, 'and how does this differ, as a demonstration of fear, from shutting himself up in the walls of a city' (Liv. 36.17). Most often the war would be decided by battle, with the consent of both sides. Ptolemy was spurred on by Seleucus in 312 'to make a campaign into Coele-Syria and take the field against the army of Demetrius' (Diod. 19.80.3). This campaign led to the victory at Gaza, but when Antigonus arrived with reinforcements, Ptolemy took counsel with his friends 'whether it was better to remain and reach a final decision in Syria or to withdraw to Egypt and carry on the war from there, as he had formerly done against Perdiccas' (Diod. 19.93.5). In the Ipsus campaign, Lysimachus' original refusal to fight Antigonus was due to the fact that he 'was taking every precaution not to be forced to decide the whole war in battle before the army in Europe came to join him' (Diod. 20.109.5). Ipsus was clearly regarded as a deliberate attempt to end the war in one encounter. Demetrius was facing Cassander in Thessaly, but 'neither came forward into battle since each was awaiting the decision of the whole matter that would take place in Asia' (Diod. 20.110.5), as Antigonus 'had definitely made up his mind to bring to an end by force of arms the war which had set in' (20.111.2). Nearly a century later, in 217, 'Antiochus and Ptolemy had completed their preparations and were determined on deciding the fate of the Syrian expedition by a battle' (Pol. 5.79.1). Antiochus had needed three years of campaigning to take the cities of Coele-Syria, during which time he thought that Ptolemy would not venture to fight a battle, but after his defeat the cities all reverted immediately to Ptolemy. Antigonus in Greece tried to force Cleomenes of Sparta to fight a pitched battle by harassing him with skirmishes (Pol. 2.54), and at Sellasia 'the kings agreed to try issues in a battle' (Pol. 2.66.4). Polybius remarks that 'wars in Greece and Asia are as a rule decided by one battle, or more rarely by two' (Pol. 35.1), and Diodorus remarks of Philip V and Antiochus III that both 'found themselves compelled by the outcome of a single battle to do the bidding of others' (Diod. 28.3).[29]

The reason such a battle could be decisive for the result of the war is that the losses on the defeated side would be vastly greater than those among the victors, and would represent a significant proportion of the total military manpower of the kingdom. After such a battle the loser would no longer be in a position to dispute the issue with the victor. These are the practical reasons why the decisive battle played such an important part in Hellenistic warfare. Underlying this there is, however, the question of the whole conception of the means and ends of warfare. The decisive battle, bringing together the two armies of the opposing sides in their entirety to decide the issue of the war in a single clash, was of course the most striking feature of Archaic and Classical hoplite warfare – as Herodotus describes it, 'as soon as they [the Greeks] declare war on each other, they seek out the fairest and most level ground and then go down there to do battle on it' (Hdt. 7.9.2). The Hellenistic conception of the decisive battle does not seem to be different in any important respect from this type of warfare, although it has been complicated by the capabilities in siege warfare which made possible the permanent conquest of territory. Furthermore, the decision achieved by battle validated the right of conquest of the victor, allowing him to consider the territory spear-won, and this was a genuinely important concept in international affairs. The legitimacy conferred by victory in battle is an extension of the Greek tradition of deciding an issue by hoplite battle on fair terrain and equal terms, and the two most essential contributors to victory in pitched battle – a specialist Greco-Macedonian heavy infantry phalanx optimized for fair and open battle, led by a king or general with the technical, tactical and leadership skills needed to bring about victory – in turn reinforced the political dominance of the Greco-Macedonian population over the native peoples, and of the king over his subjects.

Chapter 8

Fighting in the phalanx

The 'Face of Battle'

So far we have examined the armament and equipment of the phalanx, how the phalanx was recruited and organized, and how it was commanded and used in battle. One important question remains: how did the phalanx actually fight? There is a related question to this: what was it like to fight in the phalanx? This latter question itself has an interesting – and relatively brief – history. The idea that the experience of battle – the 'what it was like' to fight in battle – was a valid subject for historical research arose only quite recently. For the ancient historians themselves, it was taken for granted that their readers would understand what a phalanx battle was like and how it worked at the lowest, individual level. The historians, being citizens of Greek or Roman cities, had a strong likelihood of having experienced battle themselves (Xenophon certainly did, Thucydides and Polybius most likely did), or even if they did not have direct experience, they would have been closely acquainted with those who did, warfare being more common, and involving a higher proportion of the population, than has been the case since the first half of the twentieth century. Modern historians do not have this acquaintance with the realities of fighting, and though many aspects of warfare certainly formed a part of the historian's field of enquiry, it was only with the rise of the 'face of battle' approach in the 1970s that the experience of battle for the ordinary soldier was pushed to the forefront of military historical research. Key to this new approach was the recognition that most modern accounts or reconstructions of ancient, and more recent, battles are based on highly stylized narratives which emphasize the plans and tactics of generals (often 'great' generals), whose armies then become faceless automata performing the general's will. The new approach argued that real battles were probably never as controllable and predictable as these sorts of accounts suggest, and that the soldiers themselves remained individuals with minds of their own, however well drilled and trained they might have been. The alternative was to try to understand what actually happened on the battlefield, at the level of the individual soldier, and how military forces really functioned by breaking battles down into interactions between infantry and infantry, or infantry and cavalry, looking beyond the high-level narratives – where such a cavalry force charges such an infantry force and routs them – and asking what this would actually have involved, how charges were carried out, what it meant to rout an opposing force, and so on, at the level of the individuals taking part.[1]

While not everyone agrees with all of the detailed findings, the influence of this new methodology on military history has been enormous. In the field of ancient military history it took a little longer to really become embedded in mainstream historians' approach to the subject, but for the past twenty-five years or so at least, the 'face of battle' has become widespread, with hoplite warfare in particular being analyzed using these techniques. The 'face of battle' approach has itself formed two intertwined but discernibly separate strands. One, which could be termed the 'experience of battle', is chiefly concerned with the experience, motivation and psychology of the individual soldier – the 'what it was like' of warfare. The experience of battle is an important part of this approach, but so is the nature of medical care or treatment of the dead, the role of fear and training and group cohesion, and all such human factors in the waging of war. The second strand, slightly more technical, is the 'mechanics of battle', which seeks to understand the way in which bodies of men actually moved on the battlefield, how (or if) they were controlled, how they fought, and how and why one side won and the other lost. These two threads are highly interrelated in their techniques, but different in their emphasis: the 'experience' approach seeking to understand 'what battle was like' as an end in itself, the 'mechanics' approach trying to use these techniques to define and explain the course and outcome of ancient wars and battles. Much modern writing on ancient battle also concentrates on the extreme unpleasantness of the experience, which is no doubt true, though by modern standards many aspects of life in the ancient world were also extremely unpleasant. I will focus here on the mechanics, although aspects of the experience will arise naturally from this.[2]

In the field of ancient history, one aspect in particular of the 'mechanics of battle' has a rather longer history. The earliest scholars of ancient history in the modern style, from the late nineteenth century, were content to view hoplite battles much as historians had always viewed battle – they reproduced, while trying to elucidate and explain, the accounts of earlier historians, and concentrated on the large-scale, high-level movements of large armies, or at least large components of armies, in the rather stylized way that was to be criticized by 'face of battle' adherents. From the early twentieth century, however, Classical hoplite battles in particular came to be subject to a more 'mechanics of battle' approach, particularly from British scholars. Taking the ancient battle accounts of Herodotus, Thucydides and Xenophon, and drawing inspiration from a more familiar (and no doubt congenial) metaphor, the game of rugby, historians came to understand hoplite warfare as a giant, armed version of the rugby scrum, in which the two sides attempted, by bodily force, to literally shove each other off the field of battle (note, incidentally, that it is specifically the rugby scrum – a formal, controlled shove in a special formation – that was envisaged in this metaphor, not the more informal use of the word 'scrum' to mean an unruly free-for-all). This notion rapidly established itself as the orthodox view of hoplite battle among English-speaking ancient historians, and its more recent challenge by those who raise serious doubts whether battles were ever really fought in this way (I will examine this subject in greater detail below) led to the great and currently unresolved '*othismos* controversy' – *othismos* being the Greek word for 'pushing' or 'the push', which historians have adopted to describe this proposed style of fighting. So hoplite warfare has long been subject to a 'face of battle', or at least a 'mechanics of battle' approach, one which, strangely perhaps, was never extended to the closely related combat of the Macedonian phalanx, nor indeed to any of the other combat formations of the ancient world, not even the Roman legion – most surprisingly, given the central place that the legion holds in the popular conception of ancient warfare.[3]

Sources of information

Part of the reason for this is the question of available evidence. Herodotus, Thucydides and Xenophon never explicitly spell out the nature of hoplite battle, but their combat accounts preserve enough detail to make educated conjectures about the nature of hoplite fighting possible. The only contemporary historian for the battles of the Macedonian phalanx is Polybius, who certainly does preserve valuable material (which has already been used throughout this book, and which I will explore further below), but even so the available body of material is smaller than for the earlier Classical phalanx (plus, it has to be said, the Macedonian phalanx, and the Hellenistic period generally, have always been less fashionable). This explanation hardly applies to the Roman legion, since there are more historical accounts by writers familiar with the Roman way of war (including, in Julius Caesar, one of its most successful practitioners), and there have been efforts to apply a 'face of battle' approach to Roman warfare, though compared with the *othismos* debate, the volume of work produced (and level of controversy) is small.

To attempt a 'face of battle' account of the Macedonian phalanx there is certainly relatively little source material to work with, but I think there are two equally valid ways around this: one is to use material from the earlier Classical period, since while there certainly were (as we have seen throughout this book) important differences between the Greek and Macedonian phalanxes, there were also important similarities, and one was in effect a more highly developed form of the other. As such, material relevant to the Classical Greek phalanx can be used, with care. The second solution is to make use of the fact that close-order bodies of infantry armed with the pike were to survive into the Medieval period, and indeed to experience a late flowering – perhaps the height of their ubiquity and effectiveness – in the Early Modern period, the sixteenth to seventeenth centuries, before finally being supplanted by gunpowder weapons. This is a period with a larger range of histories and writings to draw on, including, importantly, a precious few written from the point of view of the soldier in the ranks (or at least, with a view to instructing such soldiers). The Early Modern pike block is not identical to the Macedonian phalanx, and it is important to be cautious in applying lessons from one to the other, but at the same time, military theorists of the Early Modern period certainly felt that they were continuing the Macedonian tradition, and the basic physical realities of using a two-handed pike in a close-order infantry formation cannot have changed that greatly. As such, I think it is valid to draw on Early Modern evidence to help us to understand the way in which the phalanx fought.

The hoplite phalanx – order and *othismos*

To begin first with the material for the Classical Greek hoplite phalanx, we have already touched on some aspects of the nature of hoplite fighting in earlier chapters, in particular the question of the depth in ranks of the formation (and some of the reasons for the depths chosen), the intervals between files and the weapons carried. To recap briefly, the hoplite phalanx was formed typically eight ranks deep, though other depths are attested, up to (unusually) twenty-five or fifty ranks deep. File intervals are unknown, but were probably fairly small, and it is reasonable to suppose that the ideal close-order formation had shields touching, so approximately two cubits (1 metre) per file, though it is likely that there were no formal file intervals in most city phalanxes (the more disciplined Spartans may have been an exception). The hoplite fought with a spear, around 2 metres in length, held in one hand around the point of balance and probably thrust overarm, with a sword to fall back on if the spear broke in combat. The Macedonian phalangite, for his part, fought in a phalanx perhaps at first eight but later typically sixteen ranks deep, and unusually up to thirty-two ranks; file intervals were firmly established and maintained by careful drill, and were essential for effective manoeuvres and use of the pike, while the closest formation (perhaps only used on the defensive) allowed just one cubit (half a metre) per file. The sarissa, typically 6 or 7 metres long, was wielded probably underarm in two hands, and held near the rear end so that most of the length of the weapon extended in front of the formation.

First let us briefly consider the evidence for the way in which hoplites fought. The usual view before the invention of the 'rugby scrum *othismos*' theory was that hoplites fought much as all other close-order infantry formations throughout history fought (or are thought to have fought, since first-hand evidence for any period is so scanty): they marched (or walked or ran) up to each other until the front ranks were within weapon reach, where they stopped and proceeded to fence with their spears, thrusting and jabbing in an attempt to kill or wound an opponent. The front two ranks at most would have been able to actually reach the enemy with their spears, and the ranks behind were thought to have been intended to step forward to replace losses and to provide moral and physical support to those in the front rank (though precisely what they were there for was not clear, as we will see).

The 'scrum *othismos*' theory of combat changed this picture (for Classical hoplite combat, since so far as I know no proponents of the scrum theory have ever suggested that any other formation in the whole history of warfare used the techniques they propose). According to the theory, hoplite lines did not halt in spear range and fence, but ran or walked into direct physical contact with each other, setting shield against shield (whether this happened immediately, right at the start of any combat, or whether there was an initial period of spear fencing that was later followed by a second-phase scrum, is one of the sub-controversies of the *othismos* debate, and opinion remains divided). Once in contact, the rear ranks of each phalanx closed right up on the ranks ahead and pushed their comrades in the back with their shields, so that phalanxes on each side were pressed hard up against each other. A shoving match would then ensue, with the objective, as in the rugby scrum, of physically shoving the opposition backwards. If this shove were successful and the enemy phalanx gave ground, then it might be able to hold together for some time as it was forced back, but very likely it would break apart as the rear ranks realized they were outmatched and broke off to run away – which would in turn decrease the support for the front ranks and lead to rapid collapse and the end of effective resistance. The defeated phalanx would then flee the field.

This theory gained considerable ground from the middle years of the twentieth century and probably still represents the orthodox view in academic circles. There have been dissenting voices, who doubt that hoplite battles were really shoving matches and believe that hoplites fought each other with weapons. The question of the interval of files in the hoplite phalanx has become tied up with this alternative view, with scrum-dissenters often proposing that the hoplite phalanx was a more open-order formation, allowing individuals a fair degree of freedom of movement to fence, dodge and parry, and also, at least up to early Classical times, allowing light infantry to fight from within the ranks of the phalanx, sheltering behind the hoplites' shields.[4]

I count myself on the side of the dissenters, as I am profoundly unconvinced by the scrum *othismos* theory of hoplite combat. The matter is not strictly relevant to the present work, but the Macedonian phalanx was a natural successor to the Greek, there was much continuity between them and some of the evidence adduced (by both sides) for hoplite warfare is in fact evidence for the Macedonian phalanx (it is alarming how often the tacticians such as Asclepiodotus are cited as evidence for the Classical hoplite phalanx). In order to understand how the Macedonian phalanx fought, and to highlight differences from the hoplite phalanx, it is worth considering at least in outline the evidence for the hoplite phalanx and the reason for objections to the scrum *othismos* theory.

First of all there is the question of terminology. In modern works, the debate is called the '*othismos* debate', and modern scholars will often talk about '*othismos*' as if this was the Greek word for the combat of two phalanxes (however the fighting may have taken place). But the word *othismos* is actually used to describe a battle of two hoplite phalanxes only once in the whole of Herodotus, Thucydides and Xenophon (the major contemporary sources for hoplite battle), and there it is qualified as *othismos aspidon* – an '*othismos* of shields' (Thuc. 4.96.2, describing the Battle of Delium – I will return to what *othismos* probably means in this context below). Herodotus uses *othismos* twice to describe fights involving Greek phalanxes (at Thermopylae, 7.225, and Plataea, 9.62), but in both cases they are fighting against Persian infantry, who are said (at Plataea) to have 'run out in small groups' so certainly don't seem to be taking part in a scrum, and scrum *othismos* proponents always claim that this style of fighting was unique to the Greek phalanx. It takes two to *othismos* in this sense, since unless both sides are pushing there will be nothing to push against, and no scrum will develop, so either Persians also engaged in the scrum or else *othismos* in this context does not mean a scrum.

The word is used more times by Herodotus in a metaphorical sense, to describe an argument or 'war of words' as we would say in English. Later authors make sparing use of the word, and very rarely in the context of infantry or phalanx combat (and sometimes, as Arr. *Anab*. 1.15.2 and 3.14.3, of cavalry, or Arr. *Anab*. 5.17.5, elephants). A common usage (occurring for example in Pol. 4.58.9, D.H. 7.35.5 and Plut. *Caesar* 64, amongst others) is for the movement and constriction of crowds – for example crowds passing through a gate or around a theatre entrance, or a politician or general in a riot. In these uses, some sort of pushing can well be supposed to have taken place, but not the concerted scrum-like shoving that is proposed for hoplite warfare. Rather, it would be the sort of thing that is expressed in English as 'pushing and shoving', the close-quarters interactions of crowds with some physical contact involved. The most profligate user of the word *othismos* is the sixth-century AD Byzantine historian Procopius, who amasses more uses of the word than all other historians put together, and who uses it to describe all sorts of contemporary combat – involving both infantry and cavalry (e.g. *De Bellis* 5.18.13, 8.29.18 and 8.32.17) – as well as general scenes of crowding (such as on a ramp during a siege, *De Bellis* 1.7.27). It is clear that to Procopius, *othismos* is a general word for what we might call in (French-derived) English 'melee', the close-quarters fighting, pushing and shoving of massed formations, often but not exclusively infantry, the sort of thing that in the Medieval and Early Modern period was called the 'press' or 'push of pike' (more on this below). There is no indication at all that any mass shoving is involved.

Scrum *othismos* proponents have recognized the limited use of the word *othismos* itself, and so call as evidence in support of their theory all other uses of the root word, *otheo* (to push), along with its common compounds (such as *exotheo*, to push out). Such words do indeed often appear in descriptions of hoplite combat in Herodotus, Thucydides and Xenophon. However, there is no reason to take the word to mean literal pushing (in the sense of massed, scrum-like shoving) when applied to hoplites, rather than, according to context, individual pushing and shoving by individual men in the close confines of a hoplite battle, or when applied to whole phalanxes, a metaphorical sense of pushing familiar to all military writing across all periods in English, where the word 'push' (and particularly 'push back') is used to describe all sorts of military setbacks without any implication of physical contact at all. That the word has this general, non-literal meaning is reinforced by the fact that writers in antiquity used *otheo* or its compounds to describe combats between heavy infantry, light infantry, cavalry, elephants and ships, where there is no question of massed physical shoving being involved. There is no reason to suppose that usage for hoplites carries any different meaning than usage for these other troop types.[5]

This is not to say that the pushing was never literal, on the individual level, the most well-known and much-discussed example being Xenophon's terse description of the hoplite fighting at the Battle of Coronea – 'they pushed, they fought, they killed, they died' (Xen. *Hell.* 4.3.19). In this case we can well imagine hoplites pushing hoplites, but this does not mean that phalanxes pushed phalanxes. What we should picture instead is the clashing of shields in the course of individual combat, as frequently depicted in vase paintings, and it is no doubt this that Thucydides had in mind with his *othismos aspidon*, 'pushing of shields' (Thuc. 4.96.2). Xenophon at Coronea also refers to the clashing together of shields (Xen. *Hell.* 4.3.19), which is even more clearly a matter of shield-bashing in combat, not static shoving. Clashing shields in this way is a general feature of much infantry fighting – it is common in descriptions of Roman battles where the legionaries use their large shield bosses to push or punch the enemy back (e.g. Liv. 30.34, for Zama), and nobody has ever suggested that Romans utilized a scrum tactic, Polybius being explicit that they did not, as we will see. I think that the linguistic evidence taken as a whole is clear that such pushing as occured was not massed scrumming, and that in the majority of cases the pushing of one formation by another, while containing some element of crowding or 'pushing and shoving', is meant in a more general sense, like the English 'push back', to describe being outmatched, overcome and forced to retreat in combat, with no reason to suppose that the meaning was any different solely in the context of hoplite combat.[6]

But there are other arguments against the scrum *othismos* theory, centring on the physical practicality of the idea. There is some confusion among adherents of the scrum theory about the stance the hoplites would adopt. Some have argued that hoplites in a scrum would retain a sideways stance, but this would be impossible, as even if they started out sideways on, the force of the rear ranks pushing would immediately force them into a face-on stance as the phalanxes squashed together. On the other hand, a common objection to the scrum is that if phalanxes pushed in this way, the forces generated would be sufficient to crush to death those in the front ranks (in the way that crowd crushes today often prove fatal). Recent research has demonstrated that this objection is invalid, as the pressure of files of eight men pushing, though considerable, is not sufficient to kill those in the front ranks, while additional ranks beyond the first eight do not add greatly to the force applied. It has also been proposed that the bowl shape of the hoplite shield, together with its thick rim, would ensure that each hoplite could retain breathing space for his chest, making such a crush survivable for hoplites even if it was not for infantry with different equipment. This finding is interesting so far as it goes – it is useful to be able to dismiss the argument that such a push was physically impossible. However, it leaves many loose ends unanswered. Why did not other infantry copy the shield shape, if it was so essential to this way of fighting, and if such fighting was so effective? And why, if the force of ranks behind the first eight do not add greatly to the force of the push, did Greek formations sometimes form twenty-five or even fifty ranks deep (after all, one of the main justifications for the scrum theory is that it provides an explanation for the use of deep hoplite formations)? Why, above all, is there clear evidence for pushing by non-hoplites, using non-hoplite shields? This evidence comes chiefly from Xenophon's *Cyropaedia*, a historical novel which Xenophon used to expound his ideas about tactics and military leadership. At the Battle of Thymbra (a real battle, of which Xenophon provides a highly imaginative account, but one which does represent his understanding of warfare at the time), it is Egyptians who push Persians, in a passage which is worth quoting in full:[7]

> 'Here, then, was a dreadful conflict with spears and lances and swords. The Egyptians, however, had the advantage both in numbers and in weapons; for the spears that they use even unto this day are long and powerful, and their shields cover their bodies much more effectually than corselets and targets [*gerrai*], and as they rest against the shoulder they are a help in pushing. So, locking their shields together [*sungkleisantes tas aspidas*], they advanced and pushed. And because the Persians had to hold out their little shields clutched in their hands, they were unable to hold the line, but were forced back foot by foot, giving and taking blows, until they came up under cover of the moving towers.' (Xenophon, *Cyropaedia* 7.1.33 f.)

So here we have pushing which is quite explicitly physical, not metaphorical, where hoplites are not involved. But here the Egyptians are said to have been formed up 100 ranks deep, and the Persians just two. If the Egyptians had pushed in the style of a scrum, even if the ranks beyond the first eight had not contributed much to the force applied, they would surely have brushed aside the two ranks of Persians. But Xenophon is explicit that the Egyptians did not take part in a mass shove by the whole formation – as he says, 'drawn up a hundred deep, it is clear that they will hinder one another from fighting – all except a few' (Xen. *Cyr*. 6.4.17) – while the Persians (two deep) are forced back by the Egyptians because their light hand-held shields were not suitable for pushing, not because the pressure of 100 men overwhelmed the resistance of two. Xenophon has Cyrus make the same point earlier:

> "'And do you think, Cyrus," said one of the generals, "that drawn up with lines so shallow we shall be a match for so deep a phalanx?"
>
> "When phalanxes are too deep to reach the enemy with weapons," answered Cyrus, "how do you think they can either hurt their enemy or help their friends?'" (Xenophon, *Cyropaedia* 6.3.22)

Here we have a case where a deep infantry formation, with shields well suited for pushing, do indeed push back a shallower formation; yet (as Xenophon envisaged it) there is no mass push or scrum involved, and it is clear that the pushing is being done by the front ranks only, not by the whole mass. As such, the burden of proof is firmly on those who claim that when similar (though far less explicit) terminology is applied to hoplite phalanxes, it must mean that there was a massed shove. The type of pushing Xenophon describes at Thymbra – the front ranks pushing with their shoulders and shields, to force back more lightly equipped enemies – fits well with descriptions of other heavy infantry combat (such as Romans) and also with the accounts of hoplite battles, including those such as Coronea where an element of pushing with the shield clearly was involved. There seems no need to invent a new and unique style of warfare, the 'scrum *othismos*', discovered only by hoplite armies and forgotten, never to be revived, once Classical Greek hoplites ceased to feature on the battlefield. It is far more likely that the type of pushing that took place in hoplite battles was not wholly metaphorical, but was of the same kind as that in other heavy infantry combat throughout history, being on the individual level and involving men pushing men, not whole formations scrumming with each other.

Pushing in the Macedonian phalanx

However, the story does not entirely end there, as there is a further strand of evidence that the rear ranks were involved in pushing in some way, and here the discussion becomes more directly relevant to the Macedonian phalanx. This strand begins with a discussion of the role of the rear ranks in a hoplite phalanx, again from Xenophon (writing here in more philosophical guise, but still expounding his own theories of tactics):

> "'It is well to understand tactics too; for there is a wide difference between right and wrong disposition of the troops, just as stones,

bricks, timber and tiles flung together anyhow are useless, whereas
when the materials that neither rot nor decay, that is, the stones and
tiles, are placed at the bottom and the top, and the bricks and timber
are put together in the middle, as in building, the result is something
of great value, a house, in fact." "Your analogy is perfect, Socrates,"
said the youth; "for in war one must put the best men in the van
and the rear, and the worst in the centre, that they may be led by the
one and driven forward [*othontai, otheo*] by the other.'" (Xenophon,
Memorabilia 3.1.7–8)

Here we have evidence for the rear rank at least (if not the intervening ranks)
being involved in pushing forward the ranks in front of them. We must be
cautious, however, and not immediately claim this as evidence for a scrum.
For one thing, while *otheo* can and often does refer to individual physical
pushing, it can also be used in a more metaphorical sense to mean (broadly
speaking) 'encourage'. The Loeb edition translation given above, 'driven
forward', has a similar ambiguity between physical and metaphorical force in
English (one can 'drive' men, or cattle, other than by leaning against them and
pushing). This sense is common in Xenophon – for example, this is how Cyrus
instructs the rear ranks of his formations:

'As you are behind, you can observe those who are valiant and by
exhorting them make them still more valiant; and if any one should
be inclined to hang back and you should see it, you would not permit
it … . And if those in front call to you and bid you follow, obey them
and see that you be not outdone by them even in this respect but give
them a counter cheer to lead on faster against the enemy.' (Xenophon,
Cyropaedia 3.3.41–2)

But let us grant that the pushing in Socrates' case is physical. We must now,
however, move to the evidence for the Macedonian phalanx.

First of all, there is the evidence of Polybius, from the comparison of legion
and phalanx which has already been quoted a number of times before:

'Of these sixteen ranks, all above the fifth are unable to reach with
their sarissas far enough to take actual part in the fighting … . These
rear ranks, however, during an advance, press forward [*piezountes,
piezo*] those in front by the weight of their bodies [*toi tou somatous
barei*]; and thus make the charge very forcible [*biaian men poiousi ten*

ephodon], and at the same time render it impossible for the front ranks to face about.' (Polybius, 18.30.1–4)

There are similar descriptions in the tacticians (deriving no doubt from a common source). This is what Asclepiodotus says on the subject:

'[W]hile the men in the lines behind the fifth, though they cannot extend their spears beyond the front of the phalanx, nevertheless bear forward with their bodies [*tois ge somasin epibrithontes*] at all events and deprive their comrades in the front ranks of any hope of flight.' (Asclepiodotus, *Tactics* 5.2)

Aelian and Arrian express the same concept in similar words:

'Additionally, those who form the ranks behind the sixth, although they cannot bring their sarissas to bear against an enemy, by pressing forward with the weight of their bodies [*toi barei ton somaton epibrithontes*], increase the momentum [*ten dunamin*] of the phalanx and leave no possibility of seeking safety in flight to those in the forward ranks.' (Aelian, *Tactics* 14)

'Those standing in the sixth row press on with the weight of their bodies [*barei ton somaton xunephreidon*], if not with their sarissas, so that the phalanx's attack [*embolen*] against the enemy is hard to endure, and flight is difficult for the front row men.' (Arrian, *Tactics* 12.10)

There is a parallel thread of evidence in the tacticians, which mirrors Xenophon's discussion of the role of the rear ranks in the hoplite phalanx:

'[T]he file-closers [*ouragoi*], both those in the files and those attached to the larger units, should be men who surpass the rest in presence of mind, the former to hold their own files straight, the latter to keep the *syntagmata* in file and rank with one another besides bringing back to position any who may leave their places through fear, and forcing them to close up in case they lock shields [*en tois sunaspismois sunedruein anangkazoien*].' (Asclepiodotus, *Tactics* 3.6)

'Furthermore, the supernumerary file closer of every *syntagma* should be a man of intelligence. He should see to it that every man in his line holds their position in both rank and file, and he should compel any man who is quitting his post, either from cowardice or on any other account, to resume it again. When a close-order formation [*sunaspismois*] is called for the file closer should ensure that his men lock up as close together as possible, for it is this that gives stability to the whole formation and is of great consequence.' (Aelian, *Tactics* 14)

'File closers must not be chosen for strength, but for intelligence and experience of martial matters so as to control the file's advance and not allow deserters to run away from the formation. When they adopt close order [*sunaspismou*], he generally gathers those deployed in front of him into [proper] density which provides full strength to this formation.' (Arrian, *Tactics* 12.11)

Here we see the file closers, whether those of the individual files (that is, the last rank as a whole) or the *syntagma* file closers (officers stationed behind the ranks), being involved in 'encouraging' (no doubt the encouragement often took a very physical form) the men in the ranks to remain in formation and to keep properly closed up, and to prevent anyone from running away. But this is not evidence that the whole formation took part in a massed push.

The Hellenistic tactical manuals, as we have already seen, had a long history and formed the basis of the numerous Byzantine (late Roman) military manuals that have come down to us. It is uncertain to what extent the Byzantines simply quoted Hellenistic practice wholesale, or adapted it to match the realities of battle in their day. Byzantine warfare was dominated by cavalry, and their manuals mainly deal with cavalry drill and tactics, on which the Hellenistic manuals have less to say, so it may be that the cavalry sections were written from scratch, while the infantry material was adopted more or less unchanged from the Hellenistic originals (referred to by the Byzantines as 'the ancients'). Whatever the case, we see a similar role for the rear ranks in these Byzantine manuals, for example:[8]

'The file closers should possess no less courage and physical strength than the men stationed in the second rank. They should also be notably superior to other troops in experience and good sense, for they are responsible for forming and keeping the men in their place in line. In action moreover they must keep the men ahead of them in close order so that the phalanx may maintain its compact formation and present a stronger and more formidable front to the enemy.' (Anonymous Byzantine, *On Strategy* 15)

'They tighten up or close ranks when the line gets to about two or three bow shots from the enemy's line and they are getting set to charge. The command is: "Close ranks". Joining together, they close in toward the centre, both to each side and to front and back, until the shields of the men in the front rank are touching each other and those lined up behind them are almost glued to one another. The manoeuvre may be executed either while the army is marching or while it is standing still. The file closers should order those in the rear to close in forcefully on those to the front and to keep the line straight, if necessary, to prevent some from hesitating and even holding back.'

'The depth of our own files should not exceed sixteen men, nor should it be less than four. More than sixteen is useless, and less than four is weak. The middle ranks consist of eight heavily armed infantry. Absolute silence must be observed in the army. The file closers of each file should be instructed that if they hear so much as a whisper from one of their men, they should prod him with the butt of their lance. In combat, also, they should push forward the men in front of them, so that none of the soldiers will become hesitant and hold back.'
(Maurice {Maurikios}, *Strategikon* 12 B 16, 17)

Finally, there is a third thread of evidence which also runs from the Hellenistic tacticians to the Byzantines, concerning the difference between infantry and cavalry in combat (and where we see a late occurrence of the word *othismos*):

'The Persians, Sicilians and Greeks regularly used the square formation since it can hold the squadrons in both rank and file ... the depth of the cavalry unit, provided it is enough to hold the squadron firm and in line, does not have the same importance as in the infantry, rather it may work more havoc than the enemy themselves, for when the riders run afoul of one another they frighten the horses.' (Asclepiodotus, 7.4)

'The Persians, the Sicilians and, generally speaking, the Greeks used square formations, being of the opinion that they were more easily formed and better suited to the easy preservation of the formation and general use ... . Those following in the rear ranks in no way support the leaders as happens in infantry formations. The rear ranks do not contribute to how well an enemy charge is resisted, nor do they increase the momentum [*epothousin*] of those before them, nor close up with them, nor, holding on to each other, make a solid mass. If the leading ranks are pressed forward from the rear, the horses become annoyed, create disorder and are more likely to do harm to themselves than to the enemy.' (Aelian, *Tactics* 18)

'The Persians especially use square formations, the barbarians in Sicily, and nearly all the most skillful horsemen of the Greeks ... . Since it is necessary not to ignore the fact that horsemen deployed by depth do not provide the same usefulness as depth among infantry. For horsemen neither push [*epothousi*] those in front of them, not being able to press [*epereidein*] horse upon horse, as the pushings [*enereiseis*] of foot soldiers along shoulders and ribs happen. Nor, becoming continuous with those deployed in front of them, do they achieve the single weight of the entire throng. Rather, if they were to press together [*xunereidoien*] and densify, they more likely will upset the horses.' (Arrian, *Tactics* 16.10–14)

'The cavalry phalanx, however, does differ from the infantry one. The latter is closed up very tightly, which gives it an irresistible weight as the men crowd together and push one another forward upon the enemy.' (Anonymous Byzantine, *On Strategy* 17)

'As far as the depth of the [cavalry] line is concerned, the ancient authorities wrote that it had formerly been regarded as sufficient to form the ranks four deep in each *tagma*, greater depth being viewed as useless and serving no purpose. For there can be no pressure [*othismos*] from the rear up through the ranks, as happens with an infantry formation, which may force the men in front to push forward against their will. Horses cannot use their heads to push people in front of them evenly, as can infantry.' (Maurice, *Strategikon* 2.6)

It is interesting that Maurice's text contains the word *othismos* (translated as 'pressure'). As we can see from the texts of Polybius through to Arrian quoted above, Maurice likely did not find this word in his sources, so it is unlikely to be a reflection of Classical Greek usage. Rather, this reflects the Byzantine understanding of the term, and as we have seen, the Byzantine historian Procopius was a prolific user of the word, and it is apparent that for Procopius the word is a general term for a vigorous close-quarters fight, as well as for crowding, pushing and shoving in a more general sense. We might also, however, note the similarities between Procopius' and Classical usage: Procopius (8.29.18) provides the only other occurrence besides Thucydides (4.96) of an *othismos aspidon*, 'othismos of shields' (in this case, of infantry fighting cavalry). Such similarities were deliberate, and Procopius' battle narratives intentionally echoed the Classical past.

We should also note, however, that Arrian does use the word *othismos*, in the plural, in a slightly different context:

'The second rank man must be second to the file leader in valour. For their spear [*doru*] reaches to the enemy, and they support the thrusts [*othismous*] of those deployed in front of them. Indeed someone of the opposite line with a sword [*machaira*] could reach the man deployed in front delivering the blow from above. With the file leader fallen or wounded so as to be unfit to fight, the second man, having leapt forward, stands in the place and role of the file leader and provides an entire unbroken phalanx.' (Arrian, *Tactics* 12.3)

The equivalent sentences in Asclepiodotus and Aelian make similar points but without using the word *othismos*:

'The second line must also be not much inferior to the first, so that when a file leader falls his comrade behind may move forward and hold the line together.' (Asclepiodotus, 3.6)

'Similarly, attention must be paid to those in the second rank, for the spears [*doru*] of those within it are projected forward together with those of the front rank, and being positioned immediately behind the latter, are of great use in emergencies. For, in the case the the file leader should fall or receive a wound, the man directly behind him, stepping into his place, closes the gap in the line and preserves its integrity.' (Aelian, *Tactics* 13)

Obviously, with varying degrees of clarity, all three passages are making the same point, that the second man can replace the first if he falls, and also (Aelian and Arrian) that the second man's spear will be able to strike the enemy (with normal rank spacing its point will be 1 metre behind the leading man's). In this context, Arrian's addition of *othismous* (plural) must mean thrusts (of the sarissa), not pushings (of men against men – the opposing lines are still separated by a sarissa's length), and may anyway just be his own interpolation, along with the strange and somewhat incomprehensible reference to reaching with a sword (I am not confident either of the translation or the meaning of this sentence, which clearly does not occur in either of the other two versions). Arrian uses *othismos* three times in the *Anabasis* to refer to to the pushing of horses (Arr. *Anab*. 1.15.2), the thrusting of spears or horses (Arr. *Anab*. 3.14.3) and the trampling of elephants (Arr. *Anab*. 5.17.5), the last two cases also being in the plural, and clearly having nothing to do with the supposed *othismos* of the hoplite phalanx.

Yet the Hellenistic manuals, and Byzantine manuals continuing the Hellenistic tradition, do speak quite clearly of closing, tightening and pushing in an infantry phalanx. As such, the evidence for a Hellenistic (and/or Byzantine) scrum seems to be much stronger than is that for a Classical scrum. Polybius, Asclepiodotus, Aelian and Arrian certainly, and the Byzantine writers probably to a large extent (depending how much they were simply echoing their sources, and how much they adapted to fit contemporary realities), were describing a phalanx armed in the Macedonian fashion, with the sarissa. It is notable from the passages quoted above that Aelian and Arrian expand considerably on the rather sparse descriptions of Polybius and Asclepiodotus, making references to pushing of the whole mass much more explicit. It is an open question whether this is because they had access to additional sources, they were adding information from their own contemporary experience or they were freely extrapolating from what was in their sources – a question which cannot now be answered, but it is important to keep in mind that Aelian and Arrian (writing in the second century AD) are a long way from providing contemporary evidence for a Macedonian phalanx.

That said, all sources together are quite explicit in their evidence for some sort of pushing or pressure within a Macedonian phalanx. All talk of the rear ranks (and not just the last rank of file closers) 'pressing forward with their bodies', the Byzantine authors expand considerably on pressing the phalanx into a compact formation, and the comparison with cavalry makes an explicit distinction between cavalry, who are not able to push in formation, and infantry, who are. All of this adds up to a very clear description of a Macedonian massed push of some sort.[9]

However, I would be hesitant to interpret this as evidence for a Macedonian scrum in combat, in the style of the supposed hoplite scrum. One of the chief objections to the scrum theory for Classical hoplites is the practical difficulty that would be involved in large bodies of men shoving each other. In the case of the Macedonian phalanx, I believe these practical difficulties are even greater. The standard view of the Classical hoplite scrum is of the opposing lines placing their shields together and pushing with them (and with their bodies pressed against their shields). But it is clearly impossible for a sarissa-equipped phalanx to push any opponent shield to shield, as a phalanx with sarissas levelled must have embedded the points of their sarissas (or those of the front rank at any rate) in the shields, armour or bodies of their opponents if they were to push at all. Their opponents, if similarly equipped, would have done the same back to them – or else (if they had no sarissas) they would have been held off at sarissa length, unable to reach their opponents with their weapons or shields (as famously described for the Roman forces at Pydna, see Chapter 9). So a Macedonian scrum would have had to have transmitted the entire force of a massed push down the shaft of the sarissa – that is, the total pushing power of (typically) sixteen men (on each side, if phalanx fought phalanx). It would take some experimental archaeology (which has never to my knowledge been carried out) to confirm, and at present I can only go with my hunch, which is that this sort of pressure on a sarissa would instantly snap the weapon, rendering it useless (or at least a lot shorter: the broken end would still have some value, but if used again for pushing, it would presumably just snap again). Modern reconstructions of sarissas invariably bend somewhat under their own weight, and any large pushing force on such a weapon would inevitably cause this bending to accelerate rapidly to a break. Furthermore, two such phalanxes facing each other, with spears embedded in shield, armour or body, would just mutually impale each other with any spears which did not break. Once a front-ranker had an enemy spear point in his shield or body, the pressure of fifteen men behind him and sixteen in front, pushing him inexorably onto the point, would serve simply to impale him rather than to drive back the opposition, given the attested ability of the sarissa to pierce shields and armour ('neither shield nor breastplate could resist the force of the Macedonian sarissa', Plut. *Aem.* 20.2). In order to push back an enemy formation, the pressure generated would have to be greater than that required to move a block of sixteen men, but less than that required to allow a sarissa point to pass through a shield, armour or unprotected body. Carefully designed experiments could quantify and test these numbers, but on the face of it I think it is clear that it would not be possible.[10]

We must also bear in mind that hoplites are supposed to have been pushing against each other with their shields braced by their shoulders or bodies, while men with sarissas would have been pushing with a sarissa held in their hands. Thus not only would the pushing of thirty-two men have had to be sustained by the shaft of the sarissa, it would also have had to be transmitted to the shaft, or absorbed from the shaft, by the grip of the man's two hands. Again, testing would be required to see how practical this is, but it seems hard to envisage. Surely the sarissa would just be forced to slip through the holder's grasp long before the pressure was sufficient to drive back a file of sixteen men.

Such a scrum would also make a nonsense of Polybius' account (18.29) of the intervals between ranks and files and the extent to which the sarissa extended beyond the front rank. Whatever controversies there may be about the size of the normal interval between files, there has been no dispute over Polybius' figure of 3 feet (two cubits) per rank, and the resulting projection of the spears of the first five ranks in front of the formation. But if the phalanx closed up in physical contact in a scrum there would be considerably less than 3 feet per rank, the sarissas would extend considerably further and more than just the first five ranks would be able to reach beyond the front of the phalanx. Polybius' description would then be irrelevant to how the phalanx actually fought, and I think that would be a major problem: Polybius' account has formed the basis of all analyses of phalanx combat, but must be rejected if we believe in a phalanx scrum.

Unless some solution to these problems can be proposed, I do not see how a Macedonian scrum could have worked without either a mass breaking of the spears or a mass impalement of the front-rankers (and of such of those behind them who came in the way of the points), or both. Standing the most experienced men in the front rank and then using the weight of fifteen men behind to impale them on the spears of the enemy does not seem to me a practicable or sustainable tactic.

A related consideration is that the tacticians all present, in slightly different words, the metaphor of the front rank as the cutting edge of a sword:

'We shall place the strongest in the front rank and behind them the most intelligent, and of the former the file leaders shall be those who excel in size, strength and skill; because this line of file leaders binds the phalanx together and is like the cutting edge of the sword.' (Asclepiodotus, 3.5)

'It is proper that the file leaders, who are the commanders of all the files throughout the entire phalanx, should be the best soldiers in the army, excelling all others in stature, strength and military skill, for this front rank keeps the entire phalanx intact; and this is of the utmost importance. Just as a sword presents the effect of its edge, increased by the stroke and the weight of the iron towards its back, so the rank of file leaders may be considered the edge of the phalanx, receiving its power and momentum from the mass of men that presses forward from the rear.' (Aelian, *Tactics* 13.1–2)

'Another good point to mention is that the file leaders are the tallest and strongest soldiers, and the most experienced in matters of war; for this element makes up the first rank, holds together the whole phalanx, and brings it forward in battles just as the cutting edge to an iron blade; since whatever it does the whole blade does the same.' (Arrian, *Tactics* 12.1–2)

Aelian's version seems to lend support to the idea of the rear ranks as adding literal weight to the attack of the first, though the other two writers do not make quite the same point. But there are two major caveats. One is that there would be no point or benefit in having the strongest, most skillful men in the front rank if their only function was to be pressed helplessly up against the shields or spear points of the enemy by the massed ranks behind, The other is that this metaphor of the cutting edge of a sword goes back to Xenophon:

> 'You should, to begin with, appoint file leaders after consulting each
> of the *phylarchs*, choosing sturdy men, who are bent on winning fame
> by some brilliant deed. These should form the front rank. Next you
> should choose an equal number of the oldest and most sensible to
> form the rear rank. To use an illustration, steel has most power to cut
> through steel when its edge is keen and its back reliable.' (Xenophon,
> *On the Cavalry Commander* 2.2–3)

Xenophon of course is talking about cavalry, where as we have seen there is, explicitly, no question of pushing. So the metaphor of the edge and weight of a sword could be applied to the phalanx, but it does not imply that the phalanx fought by pushing against its opponents.[11]

If these objections carry force, as I believe they do, then the Macedonian push of Polybius and the tacticians cannot be referring to a combat scrum. So what might they have meant instead, if we are to take them at their word (as we should) that the rear ranks had a pushing function?

Reading all the passages quoted above together, it is clear that there is physical pushing, but it is not clear that its objective is to push back the enemy. Polybius and the tacticians make one purpose very clear: the rear ranks push forward in order to make it impossible for the front ranks to flee. The objective is to keep the front ranks advancing, or in place and fighting, and to stop the formation from disintegrating. This is the only role attributed to the rear ranks by Asclepiodotus, though others add the effect, in varied wording, of making the attack more forcible. The Byzantine writers echo this theme – the formation closes up from the rear in order to prevent any holding back or hesitation. All of these cases are not to do with pushing the enemy, but with compacting the formation, keeping it moving forward, preventing hesitation and flight. Macedonians are not pushing their enemies, they are pushing each other.

We might note particularly in this context the Anonymous Byzantine's comment on the importance of 'the leaders of half files, who help in maintaining order in the files and who keep the men in front of them in close order, just as the file closers, who, by themselves, cannot tighten up the ranks of the whole phalanx'. This is an interesting observation, since it appears that pushing pressure from the rear rank alone would not be transmitted all the way up through the phalanx – it must be augmented by more closing of the ranks midway. It is also noteworthy that the Byzantines considered more than sixteen ranks to be useless, which suggests that the known very deep (Classical) formations were not intended to help with pushing.

Also, all of this would seem to apply not to the period of combat itself, but to the approach to contact, as is made explicit in Maurice ('They tighten up or close ranks when the line gets to about two or three bow shots from the enemy's line'). The pushing by the rear ranks starts well before there is any enemy to push against, with the objective not of shoving back the enemy but of tightening the formation and maintaining its forward momentum.

But would the pushing have stopped once in contact with the enemy? We must keep in mind that the transition from charge to fighting is one of the most debated and little understood aspects of mass combat. Did infantry, or cavalry, who charged at the run literally crash into their opponents, or did they pull up at the last moment? Was the point of the charge to hit the enemy at speed, or to prevent morale (and formation) collapse during the approach? Is 'momentum' to be understood as momentum with which to strike the enemy, or momentum to maintain the advance? There is varied and conflicting evidence, but the general view is that in other periods infantry at least would stop and fight with weapons, not just crash together (though of course there will have been exceptions). It is therefore likely that the pressure that was maintained during an advance would not be maintained in contact. It might well have been necessary, in order to allow the front ranks to fight effectively, not to keep pushing them into the enemy (those at the front of crowds or masses generally do not appreciate this sort of pressure in dangerous situations – see more on this point below). Polybius, for instance, says the 'charge' (*ephodos* – 'approach' or 'attack') was made very forcible, not that any part of the fighting was made forcible, and this is also reflected in the language of the later authors. The purpose of the dense formation seems to have been not so much to force the enemy back, as to prevent one's own formation being forced back – it is a supporting, bracing pressure, rather than a shoving, pushing pressure. So we can conclude that *othismos* could be used (as by Maurice) to describe a real phenomenon that did involve the rear ranks pushing forward the front ranks, but that it is not a description of a method of fighting (the pushing is not on the enemy) and it is not valid to take other occurrences of *othismos*, and (even less so) related words derived from *otheo*, as evidence for such combat-pushing every time they occur.[12]

All this being said, there is an important distinction between fighting in a pike phalanx and fighting in some other formation – a hoplite phalanx (with short spear) or legion (with sword), say – and to see this difference and how it affects our understanding of pushing in combat, we need to turn to the question of fighting with a pike.

Fighting with a pike

The evidence for the nature of sarissa fighting in the Macedonian phalanx is quite limited, but there is more material available for the pike formations of the Renaissance and Early Modern periods. We must be cautious in using such material, since there are clearly differences between the Macedonian phalanx and later pike formations (most significantly, later pikemen did not carry shields and co-existed with gunpowder weapons) but there are also similarities, and most importantly for our purposes, the later pike formations were consciously modelled on the Macedonian phalanx, with adapted translations of the *Tactics* of Aelian forming the basis of most drill manuals. We also have a very close analogy for the *othismos* of the ancient phalanx in the 'push of pike' so often referred to in contemporary English accounts of battles of the later period. Just as for the ancient 'scrum *othismos*', the push of pike poses some difficulties of interpretation. Many modern re-enactment groups of the English Civil War interpret the push of pike as a scrum very similar to the scrum theory of *othismos*, and in their battle re-enactments they engage in mass shoves, both sides crushed helplessly up against each other and trying to push the other back by bodily force. But because they are armed with pikes, which as argued above cannot easily be used in such a scrum (especially not in a re-enactment where health and safety are rather more of an issue than they would be in a real battle), the pikes are held vertically, safely out of harm's way. Now we know that real pike formations did not hold their pikes vertically this way – partly through numerous artistic depictions that show the pikes levelled horizontally as ancient pikes were, but also from contemporary accounts of pike fighting that make it clear they were levelled and used to thrust and stab, and because carrying a pike and not using it in battle is evidently absurd: there would be no point having such a long unwieldy weapon if it could not actually be used in combat. So we can be confident that the re-enactors' non-violent push of pike is not how pike formations actually fought; but at the same time, the nature of these scrum pushes reveals more problems with the scrum theory of ancient hoplite combat. One point is that re-enactors, despite not carrying specially shaped shields, and while not always or often engaging eight ranks or more deep, are certainly not crushed to death in the course of a push of pike. But this type of 'fighting' is very unstable, with the pressures involved causing people to pop out of the sides of the formation, and any individual who stumbles (or in real life, falls due to injury) causes the formation to rapidly disintegrate, sometimes into a mass of struggling men on the ground (like a collapsed maul in rugby). This bears little relation to the descriptions of pike or phalanx battles that we have, and surely two lines, perhaps thousands of men long, could not have engaged in such an unstable form of combat for any length of time without collapsing in chaos. I find it hard to envisage such an inefficient and chaotic method of fighting when reading the drill and combat descriptions of the Greek and Macedonian phalanxes.[13]

Yet Early Modern evidence does provide some insights into the use of the pike in combat. First-hand accounts of pike fighting (at least in English; I am not familiar with the literature in other European languages) are rare, since the regular soldiers did not, on the whole, write battle accounts, and those who did were, as in all periods, more concerned with the decisions of generals and the movements of whole bodies of troops than with the experience at the sharp end. Perhaps the most useful author for our purposes is Sir John Smythe, who in the late sixteenth century wrote a tactical manual and polemic, arguing for what he saw as improvements in the drill and training of infantry. Because Smythe was trying to prove a point, we must be cautious in accepting his views too unquestioningly, but even so his assumptions and descriptions shed valuable light on the nature of pike fighting in his day, and are worth quoting at some length:

'[T]he Sergeant Major or Captains would have their piquers to charge or to receave a charge of another square of piquers their Enemies, then are they to say to the first ranks of piquers. "Straighten and close your ranks, couch your piques and charge": which being pronounced, all the piquers of the first ranke must joine and close themselves in frunt, letting fall the points of their piques and carying them close breast high with both their hands steadilie and firmely, the points full in the faces of their Enemies: And the second ranke likewise straightening and closing themselves by flanke and frunt, and joyning themselves to the backe of the first ranke, and following them steppe with steppe carrying their piques above-hand over the shoulders of the first ranke the points of their piques likewise towards the faces of their Enemies.

And the third ranke closing and straightening themselves in flanke and frunt, and joyning themselves to the back of the second ranke; And the fourth ranke likewise straightening and closing themselves to the backes and shoulders of the third ranke, and carrying their piques firmlie with both their hands over ye sholdiers of all the ranks before them, the points of their piques likewise towards the faces of their enemies approaching. And all the rest of the ranks of piquers following step with step each one at the heeles of the other must carry their piques still upright in the palmes of their handes, and in boults of their armes as above said, but yet bending the pointes of them somewhat towards their enemies, that they may be seen ready in an instant to let fall the points of their piques towards their enemies, and to succor the ranke before them upon any necessitie ... .

'But in this place I thinke good further to notefie unto the Readers of these mine instructions that in the yeare, 1588, I did heare some two or three of our Nation of principall officers and charge militarie hold an opinion, that when two squadrons of Enemies all piquers should come to incounter and confrount the one with the other, that then the formost ranks of them should lie at the push of the pique and so should annoie the one the other, with thrusts and foines (as they terme it) at all the length of their Armes and piques, according to the use of single Combattes either in sport or earnest betwixt piquer and piquer by which kinde of fighting of squadrons at the push of the piques, I say, that none of the ranks can fight but only the first ranke, because that if they observe their proportionate distance according to order and discipline, the piques of the second ranke are too short to reach with their points the first rank of their enemies squadron likewise standing still joining at all length of their Armes and piques, as they vainlie imagine: Thea although to the trouble and disorder of the first ranke before them they do thrust and joine over their shoulders; During which time of the pushing and foyning of the two first rankes of the two squadrons of enemies, all the rest of the rankes of both the squadrons must by such an unskilfull kind of fighting stand still and looke on and cry aime, untill the first ranke of each squadron hath fought their bellies full, or untill they can fight no longer: which is a very scorne and mockerie mylitarie to be either spoken or thought of by any men of warre that doo pretend to have seene any action effectuallie performed betwixt any great numbers of piquers reduced into form of squadrons in the field. For in troth according to all reason and true experience, such a squadron as should thinke it their greatest advantage to fight in that sort, must (contrarie to discipline) inlarge themselves in their ranks and distances both in front and by flankes, to the intent that they may have elbow roome enough without an impediment by the nearness of the ranks behind them, to pul backe their armes, and to thrust at their enemies approaching them at all the length they can of their armes and piques, and again with dexteritie to pull backe, and retire them to give new thrusts: which opening and enlargement of ranks being perceived by the contrarie squadron (who if they be skilful men of warre) doe come closed in their rankes both in front and by flankes, as close as they can possiblie march pace with pace and step with step, as if they were one entire body, carrying their piques with both their hands breast high, all the points of the piques of the first rank of one evennesse and equality not any one preceeding the other: And so likewise the points of all the piques of the second, third and fourth ranks, carrying the like equalitie and evennesse; but yet the points of everie ranke of piques, shorter and further distant almost by a yard from their enemies faces, then the pointes of the ranke that do preceed them; And all those fower ranks marching or moving forward together pace with pace and step with step, carrying their piques firmly with both their hands brest high as aforesaid their points full in their enemies faces, they doe altogether give a puissant thrust, the points of the first ranke of piques, first lighting upon the faces of the first rank or rankes of their enemies; and the points of the second, third and fourth rankes, subsequently in a manner all in an instant, doe all one after another in such terrible sort light upon the faces, breasts and bodies of the formost rankes of the enemies that do stand still pushing and foining with their piques in their ranks opened and inlarged, that they never give them any leysure and waies to pull backe and recover the use of their piques to give any new thrustes, nor yet to close their ranks inlarged, but do overthrow, disorder and brake them with a great facilitie, as if they were but a flocke of geese; as all men of right consideration and judgement may easilie consider and see.

'But after all this it may be, that some very curious and not skilfull in actions of Armes, may demand what the foremost rankes of this well ordered and practised squadron before mentioned shall doo after they have given their aforesaid puissant blows and thrusts with their piques in case that they doo not at first incountre overthrow and

break the contrary squadron of their enemies: therunto I say, that the
foremost rankes of the squadron having with the points of their piques
lighted upon the bare faces of the formost ranks of their enemies,
or upon their Collers, pouldrons, quirasses, tasses, or disarmed
parts of their thighes; by which blowes given they have either slaine,
overthrown, or wounded those that they have lighted upon, or that
the point of their piques lighting upon their armours have glanced
off, and beyond them; in such sort as by the nearness of the formost
ranks of their enemies before them, they have not space enough againe
to thrust; nor that by the nearness of their fellowes ranks next behind
them, they have any convenient elbow roome to pull backe their
piques to give a new thrust; by meanes wherof they have utterly loste
the use of their piques, they therefore must either presentlie let them
fall to the ground as unprofitable; or else may with both their hands
dart, and throw them as farre forward into and amongst the ranks of
their enemies as they can, to intent by the length of them to trouble
their ranks, and presently in the twinkling of an eye or instant, must
draw their short arming swordes and daggers, and give a blow and
thrust (termed a halfe reverse, and thrust) all at, and in one time at
their faces: And therewithall must presentlie in an instant, with their
daggers in their left hands, thrust at the bottome of their enemies
bellies under the lammes of their Cuyrasses, or at any other disarmed
parts. In such sort as then all the ranks of the whole squadron one
at the heeles of the other pressing in order forward, doo with short
weapons, and with the force of their ranks closed, seeke to wound,
open, or beare over the rankes of their enemies to thier utter ruine ... .
By all which particularities before alleaged and declared, I thinke
it may be apparant to all such as are not obstinatelie ignorant, that
battles and squadrons of piques in the field when they do incounter
and charge one another, are not by reason or experience mylitarie to
stand all day thrusting, pushing, and foining one at another, as some
do most vainlie imagine, but ought according to all experiance with
one puissant charge and thrust to enter and disorder, wound, open,
and break the one the other, as is before at large declared.' (Sir John
Smythe, *Instructions, Observations and orders Mylitarie*, 1591)

There are some obvious similarities between this account of pike fighting
and the ancient practice, but some obvious differences. The references to
the formation 'straightening and closing themselves by flanke and frunt'

are strongly reminiscent of Polybius' description of the phalanx ('if only the phalanx is properly formed and the men close up properly both flank and rear'), while the role of the ranks behind the first – 'the second ranke likewise … joyning themselves to the backe of the first ranke, and following them steppe with steppe', and so on for subsequent ranks – reminds us of Polybius' (and the tacticians') role for the rear ranks ('These rear ranks, however, during an advance, press forward those in front by the weight of their bodies; and thus make the charge very forcible.')

There are also obvious differences. Smythe's pikemen hold their pikes at shoulder level, while as we have seen in Chapter 2, such little evidence as we have suggests the Macedonian sarissa was held underarm at waist height. Smythe gives no role for the pikes of the rear ranks in deflecting missiles (unsurprisingly, since a pike could offer little protection against a low trajectory musket ball). His pikemen do not have shields, so all blows are struck against the faces or bodies (or armour) of their targets, and he does not explicitly give the rear ranks the role of preventing the front ranks from facing about (though it is I think implicit in his account of the forceful advance).

Yet despite the differences, I think that Smythe's account provides valuable insights into the way a Macedonian phalanx actually fought. Clearly in Smythe's preferred way of fighting there is physical closing up and pushing of a sort, but this is not a 'scrum *othismos*', not least because pikes are indeed levelled and used as weapons, and because even though his ranks are 'as close as they can possiblie march pace with pace and step with step' they are still spaced a yard apart (with pike points 'shorter and further distant almost by a yard from their enemies faces', the same as Polybius and the tacticians). We also see the benefit of a tightly closed-up formation (by rank and by file) against a more open one which is hoping to give itself room to 'fence and foin' with their pikes. Note also that for Smythe, 'push of the piques' means fencing at the length of the pike, not closing in to push man to man (or even pike to man). Smythe was arguing for a particular style of fighting, the close-order massed thrust by the whole formation, which is strongly reminiscent of the descriptions, particularly, of the Byzantine tacticians, but it is clear (from his need to make this argument) that the other style, the rather more open-order 'fencing and foining' – stabbing and parrying with the pike, as with a rapier – was also considered a valid method of pike-fighting in his time. There are also some unclear aspects, in particular what would happen if two such close-order formations encountered each other or if the initial thrust was not immediately successful in breaking the enemy. Smythe's advice is that the front ranks, as their pikes would now be useless at such close quarters, should throw their pikes forward and take to their swords (there is no suggestion of simply shoving the enemy), and throughout the Early Modern period there were numerous experiments in ways to break pike formations at close range, using men equipped with halberds, heavy swords or sword and buckler (small shield), such as the sixteenth-century AD Spanish *rodeleros*. I personally think it unlikely that a Macedonian phalanx fought this way (and unless Smythe's advice was taken up more widely than we have reason to suppose it was, it is unlikely that dropping or throwing the pike and taking to the sword was often done by Early Modern pikemen either). The Macedonian pikeman's sword seems to have been a weapon of last resort, although there is no direct evidence either way on this point. We may imagine rather that if an initial 'puissant thrust' did not break the enemy (perhaps because they are just as closely formed), the attacking momentum would be lost and a period of 'fencing and foining', whether with pikes or swords, albeit at very close quarters, would naturally ensue.

That the style of fighting described by Smythe accurately depicts pike fighting (or at least one form of it) of the era can be deduced from other similar accounts. Sir Thomas Kellie, writing in 1627, reflects the same argument which so exercised Smythe:

'When Battelles commeth to push of picke, good Commanders sayeth, that your picke-men must not push by aduanceing and retireing their Arme as commonlie is done; but onelie goe joyntlie on together in a Rout without moueing their Armes.' (Sir Thomas Kellie, *Pallas Armata*, 1627)

Note 'as commonlie is done', suggesting that Smythe's arguments had not won the day by this time. Another good example (originally in French) is from the memoirs of Blaise de Monluc, who fought in a pike formation at the Battle of Cerisoles (1544). Again, his account is worth quoting at length:

'I began to cry out aloud, "Gentlemen, it may be there are not many here who have ever been in a Battel before, and therefore let me tell you that if we take our Pikes by the hinder end, and fight at the length of the Pike, we shall be defeated; for the Germans are more dextrous at this kind of fight than we are: but you must take your Pikes by the middle as the Swisse do, and run head-long to force and penetrate into the midst of them, and you shall see how confounded they will be."

'… The Germans march'd at a great rate directly towards us, and I ran to put myself before the Battail, where I alighted from my horse; for I ever had a Lacquey at the head of the Battaillon ready with my Pike … . I then call'd to Captain la Burre, who was Serjeant Major, that he should always be stirring about the Battaillon when we came to grapple, and that he and the Serjeants behind and on the sides should never cease crying, "put home, Soldiers, put home", to the end that they might push on one another.

'The Germans came up to us at a very round rate, insomuch that their Battail being very great, they could not possibly follow; so that we saw great windows in their body, and several Ensigns a good way behind, and all on a suddain rush'd in among them, a good many of us at least, for as well on their side as ours all the first Ranks, either with push of Pikes or the Shock at the encounter, were overturn'd; neither is it possible amongst Foot to see a greater fury: the second Rank and the third were the cause of our victory; for the last so pushed them on that they fell in upon the heels of one another, and as ours press'd in, the Enemy was still driven back: I was never in my life so active and light as that day, and it stood me upon so to be; for above three times I was beaten down to my knees.' (Blaise de Monluc, *Commentaires*, 1592, in the 1674 English translation)

Here we see the distinction between the pike held at the 'hinder end' and used to thrust and parry – the 'fencing and foining' of Smythe – opposed to the more direct approach, holding the pike nearer the centre and getting stuck in, as advocated by Smythe. The Macedonian pike, we know from Polybius and the tacticians, was held in the German fashion at or near the 'hinder end', but I do not think this means that it was necessarily used for fencing, since in theory it should still be possible to press forward with the pike held this way. As with Smythe and the ancient authors, Monluc's account shows literal physical pushing of the ranks in front by those behind, without (so far as we can tell) there being any sort of massed scrum by both sides – rather, the rear ranks are pushing the forward ranks onward, following on the heels of one another as they press forward, keeping up the forward momentum, even though Monluc tells us that most of the front rank were 'overturned' (that is, presumably, knocked over). Evidently, they had time and space enough to get back to their feet (as Monluc himself did three times), so there can be no question of their being crushed immobile in a scrum. Literal pushing there undoubtedly is, yet it is not a massed scrum.

Other descriptions of Medieval or Early Modern pike formations present a similar picture. For example, the English officer William Patten provides a description of the Scottish pike formation at the Battle of Pinkie (1547):

'In their array towards the joining with the enemy, they cling and thrust so near in the fore rank, shoulder to shoulder together with their pikes in both hands straight afore them; and their followers in that order so hard at their backs, laying their pikes over their foregoers shoulders that they do assail undissevered, no force can withstand them. Standing at the defence, they thrust their shoulders likewise so nigh together; the fore rank so well nigh to kneeling, stoop low before their fellows behind holding their pikes in both hands and therewith on their left arms their bucklers, the one end of the pike against their right foot, the other against the enemy breast high, their followers crossing their pike points with them forward; and thus each with the other so nigh as place and space will suffer, through the whole Ward so thick that easily should a bare finger pierce through the skin of an angry hedgehog, as any encounter the front of their pikes.' (William Patten, *The Expedicion into Scotlande*)

But the 'German' style of individual fighting still had its adherents. A sixteenth-century commander opposed the idea that formations should be deep, or that there should be pressure from the rear, 'for the foremost men, who are supposed to do the work, do not wish to be too closely pressed; they must be left room for freely jabbing', otherwise they would be pushed into the enemy 'as one pushes people into a ditch'.[14]

It is difficult for any modern author to understand or imagine exactly what is being described in such accounts, or to precisely define the mechanics involved. Nobody alive today, or for the past couple of centuries at least, has been involved in such close-quarters mass combat, and the best we have to go on are literary accounts by authors who took for granted a certain level of knowledge among their readers, together with what can be gleaned from reconstructions (whether from re-enactment groups, film or television, or computer games and simulations), or roughly equivalent situations such as riots or riot police drills, all of which are fraught with difficulties (not least, the lack of lethal force). Yet I think the sixteenth and seventeenth-century accounts fit well with what is described by the ancient authors, and suggest a model of combat in which there was pushing and shoving in a very close formation, but also weapons play, and in which the mass effects of ranks following closely on each other could be combined with standing off at the length of a pike and maintaining a gap between ranks, not simply crushing up into a scrum.

Whether the Macedonian phalanx chiefly practised the 'German' individual fencing style or the 'Swiss' massed advance style is open to question; but I think that the description of the role of the rear ranks in Polybius, and the importance of the strength and weight of the attack and of the closeness and tightness of the formation, particularly in *synaspismos*, make it likely that the 'Swiss' style was preferred. But across the several hundred years that the phalanx was in use, and with phalanxes of varying degrees of experience and training, and facing different opponents in different circumstances, we need not doubt that different techniques were used on different occasions (and as reflected in the polemic of Smythe, there could well have been ongoing debate about which was superior). It may be that the *synaspismos* of the tacticians, the closest order with half a metre per man in rank and file, represents the Swiss style of mass fighting, while a phalanx fighting in more open order (1 metre per man in rank and file) was using the German fencing technique (as Smythe says, pikemen using this technique must 'inlarge themselves in their ranks and distances both in front and by flankes, to the intent that they may have elbow roome enough'). Which interval was used, and which style of fighting, could have varied from case to case and depending on a wide range of circumstances and considerations not now known to us (not least of which might have been custom or habit), and this is why we do not see clear indications in battle accounts of which order was being used, or of the advantages or disadvantages of either. The matter was perhaps still open to dispute, and the thinking of the commanders on the ground unknown to any of the ancient historians on whose accounts we rely.

But at any rate, we see now the difference between the individual fighting of Classical Greeks or Romans (and other forms of heavy infantry) and the mass fighting of the Macedonians. The Greek hoplite fought as an individual with spear and shield, as did the Roman with sword and shield. This individual fighting might include clashing, punching or pushing with the shield, but it also involved individual weapons use, stabbing, cutting, parrying and dodging, as if in single combat (as Smythe says). For this, a certain amount of elbow room was required, as shown in Polybius' thoughts on the greater room needed by Roman soldiers ('in their mode of fighting each man must move separately, as he has to cover his person with his long shield, turning to meet each expected blow, and as he uses his sword both for cutting and thrusting it is obvious that a looser order is required', Pol. 18.30.7). Polybius formalized this difference into different drill intervals of files and ranks, which is no doubt true up to a point, but we might also see the difference as more like that described by Smythe, that Greeks and Romans 'inlarge themselves in their ranks and distances', while Macedonians could 'come closed in their rankes both in front and by flankes, as close as they can possiblie march'. This was possible because the Macedonian did not need to 'fence and foine' with his sarissa, thrusting and withdrawing it in the German style, but rather, as in the Swiss style, had to simply hold it firmly advanced in front of him and press forward, which needed less elbow room and allowed a tighter formation (by rank and file), and which indeed depended on this tight formation to give it its force. This is the great difference between a Macedonian phalanx and a Greek phalanx: a Greek phalanx was still a formation of individual fighters, however closely massed, whereas in a Macedonian phalanx, while individual fighting was one possibility, the greatest strength of the phalanx lay in the mass effect of rigidly held sarissas and the relentless advance of the mass of men behind them.[15]

Probole and *synaspismos*

Hopefully this detour through Classical Greek and Early Modern practice has demonstrated that the '*othismos* debate' about the hoplite phalanx is based on false premises, and that while we cannot be certain how the Macedonian phalanx fought, it is likely from comparative material that it could fight in at least two different ways: by individual fencing, but usually by a massed advance with sarissas levelled and held rigidly forward, in a tight formation in which the men were pushed on by those behind, but which did not squash up against the enemy and drive them back by bodily force.

The two great advantages of the Macedonian phalanx over non–pike–armed opponents, which recur a number of times in the ancient accounts (particularly Plutarch), were the *probole*, the projecting spears in front of the formation, and the *synaspismos*, the close-order formation itself. The effect of the *probole* was to hold off opponents at pike's length, unable, if their own weapons were shorter, to reach the phalangites at all. Most of the accounts of such asymmetric encounters concern battles of the phalanx against Roman swordsmen, and will form the subject of the next chapter. Faced by such a hedge of pikes, the enemy would have to try to force the pikes aside to penetrate the fence of serried points. Plutarch describes the encounter at Pydna: 'Aemilius found that the Macedonian battalions had already planted the tips of their sarissas in the shields of the Romans, who were thus prevented from reaching them with their swords' (Plut. *Aem.* 19.1). Clearly, provided the sarissas were held firmly enough, and there were enough of them, those facing a sarissa phalanx would be unable even to come to close quarters with the phalangites; the Romans at Pydna 'tried to thrust aside the sarissas of their enemies with their swords, or to crowd them back with their shields, or to seize them and put them aside with their very hands' but they 'were unable to force a passage' (Plut. *Aem.* 20). Polyaenus (2.29.2) recounts a stratagem of Cleonymus of Sparta, who left his front-rank men unarmed and ordered them to seize the spears of the enemy in their hands while those behind them attacked with their spears. We might doubt if this ever really happened, but at any rate it indicates another attempt to get through the hedge of sarissa points (we are left to wonder how grabbing the leading sarissas helped if there were four more ranks following up behind). Polybius remarks (18.30.10) that the Roman rear ranks can be of no help in 'forcing the pikes away'. Livy comments (31.39.10; see also 36.18) that 'the Macedonian phalanx with long pikes places a *vallum* [rampart, stockade] in front of the shields', and Plutarch (*Aem.* 20.3) that the phalanx presented 'a dense barricade of long spears, and was everywhere unassailable'. So against non-sarissa-armed opponents, the *probole* of spears simply presented an impenetrable hedge of spear points that would prevent spearmen or swordsmen even reaching the phalangites – they would have to either fall back, or try to knock or parry the sarissas aside to force a passage into the hedge of spears, and this evidently was very hard to do. Where it might become possible is when terrain obstacles or casualties (for example from missiles) caused a gap in the fence of spears, which could allow individuals to force a way through to the phalangites, but this must in general have been uncommon, as we have seen. Alternatively, opponents could operate against the flanks of individual phalanx units, where the varying fortunes of battle caused these units to lose close contact and so not to present an unbroken hedge of spears (as happened at Pydna).

So the *probole* was this hedge of spears, and the *synaspismos* was not necessarily, in this context, the precise one-cubit spacing of the tacticians, but rather the closing up of the files and ranks to perform the mass advance (which in practice might well have meant a one-cubit spacing, though I am certain it was never formally measured off). The Greek hoplite and Roman legionary, requiring room to fight as individuals, could not perform and more importantly would not benefit from this sort of *synaspismos* – they needed room to handle their weapons and fight effectively as individuals. We should note, though, that the word *synaspismos*, or one of its variants, is sometimes applied to a hoplite phalanx; we need not doubt that a hoplite phalanx could form a more or less close or open order according to circumstances and the desire and intention of the hoplites (or their commanders). Sometimes this might have involved hoplites closing up more tightly together, but they still had the basic requirement of fighting as individuals and could not, lacking the *probole* of sarissas, abandon this requirement and crowd up into a single mass. If they had done so, a more mobile opponent, not prevented by any *probole* from reaching them with weapons, would have been able to pick them off in the ranks with little fear of effective response, like the Roman legionaries at Trasimene and Cannae (Pol. 3.84, 3.116).

If both sides had sarissas, then the two options discussed above – fencing or a mass advance – would still apply, though here we lack even the anecdotal accounts of the fighting we have for Romans versus phalanx (assuming Cleonymus' stratagem was not a common tactic, and I doubt it would have been). Although phalanx frequently fought phalanx in the wars of the Successors and of the Hellenistic kingdoms, there is a sad lack of any detailed descriptions of the fighting, just the most vague and high-level description of a fight and an eventual winner or loser. We may guess that sometimes (perhaps between unenthusiastic or poorly motivated phalanxes) the fighting took the form of 'fencing and foining', of more or less half-hearted thrusting and stabbing, at sarissas' length. Where a veteran or determined phalanx was involved, it was likely to close up in the mass advance, and if the opponents did not do likewise would probably, in Smythe's words, 'enter and disorder, wound, open, and break' them. This may be what lies behind the description of the fighting at Selassia: an initial to-and-fro combat without decisive result, followed by a closing up and determined attack (mass advance) by Antigonus' men that broke the Spartan formation. It may also account for the Argyraspides' remarkable success at Paraitacene, if they performed a mass advance against a less willing opponent. If both sides employed the mass advance then we can imagine sarissa points being embedded in shields or the armour of opponents, and both sides attempting by force to drive their opponents back or find an opening through which their sarissa could penetrate, but this would not take the form of a massed scrum of the whole formation, which would have resulted only in broken sarissas and impaled file leaders.

Medieval and Early Modern pike formations sought numerous ways to break the deadlock of two equally determined pike formations, using differently armed men within the ranks such as the *Doppelsöldner* (double-pay men) or *rodeleros*, but none of these measures appear to have been decisively successful. They also grappled with the problem that in the 'press' the front ranks could become too closely packed to use their pikes, as we saw above, and would recommend either pikemen taking to the sword or using specialist swordsmen, but we see no trace of this in the Hellenistic phalanx – which of course is not to say that it did not occur. Perhaps the forward momentum of the advance to contact eased off when resistance was encountered, leaving the two sides in a dangerous but not mutually suicidal attempt to spear or knock down opposing front-rankers, to step forward and force the opponent to step back, open gaps in the enemy fence of spears and generally gain any advantage that might have broken the formation of the enemy and forced them to flee. The causes and nature of this transition from fighting to fleeing will be examined further below. Perhaps the projecting row of spears, the *probole*, was more effective in the Hellenistic phalanx at keeping the two sides apart (as certainly seems to have been the case when facing Romans), so that the close press of the later pike blocks did not develop. The tacticians' reference to the second ranks supporting the thrusts of the first rank and stepping forward to take their place if they fall strongly suggests to me a standoff, thrusting at pike length, rather than Smythe's closing to contact; but as for later pikes, so for the Hellenistic phalanx, both forms of fighting may have been tried.

It is this ability to form a close and solid mass of men that constitutes the 'weight' of a formation, and distinguishes a 'heavy' formation from a 'lighter' one. Polybius refers to various forces, such as Illyrians, as being 'heavy' or displaying particular 'weight', but it is the Macedonian phalanx in particular that was considered heaviest. This does not mean weight of armour (though no doubt some phalanxes did wear heavy armour, at least in some ranks), and it does not mean 'weight of pushing' in the 'scrum' sense. Rather, I think it reflects the extent to which the men could and did close up into a tight formation in rank and file (not necessarily just in the tacticians' sense of a particular drill) and drive forward against the enemy in a determined mass advance. Romans could be 'heavy' in this sense, as at Zama or Cannae, where legionaries seem to have concentrated on pushing and punching with their shields and stabbing with their swords (rather than engaging in individual swordplay as Polybius describes). Greek hoplites (or Illyrians) could be 'heavy' if they tightened their formation and concentrated on a determined advance rather than spearplay (as presumably happened at Coronea), but the Macedonians were the heavy formation *par excellence*, as the *probole* of spears freed them from the need to engage in individual weapons play, especially against non-sarissa opponents, and allowed them to employ their *synaspismos* to advance as a solid mass.

The rear ranks

It is worth recapping the function of the rear ranks in the Macedonian formation of sixteen or sometimes more ranks deep. There are three possibilities usually proposed for the role of these ranks: that they pushed forward those in front, that they prevented those in front from running away, or that they replaced casualties amongst those in front. Of these possibilities, the last can be rejected immediately (for ranks beyond the second or third), since in no case would either side suffer enough casualties, before fleeing, to make even a fourth rank necessary, if the casualty figures given in all the sources are of any value at all. Casualties in hoplite battles have been reckoned to average 5 per cent on the winning side and 14 per cent on the losing. For a formation eight ranks deep, this represents the loss of between one-third and half of the winners' front rank and just over all of the loser's front rank – but the losing side would suffer most of its casualties in the pursuit, after the ranks were broken up, and these statistics anyway probably overstate the winners' losses, since total battle casualties often include contingents on both sides that broke and fled.

Of the other possibilities, pushing forward those in front is the role I have described above. I am sure this was a primary function of the rear ranks, and we should envisage this not as a mass scrum but rather as Monluc describes, that the rear ranks 'so pushed them on that they fell in upon the heels of one another'. The rear ranks in this way gave the formation its weight, as they kept it moving forward. This does not mean that the third option, that the rear ranks prevented those in front from fleeing, was not also highly important, and indeed the two are clearly very closely related. As the Early Modern examples quoted above make clear, essential keys to success in a combat with pikes were maintaining forward momentum and a vigorous advance, right up to and (metaphorically) over and through the enemy formation (to 'overthrow, disorder and brake them with a great facilitie, as if they were but a flocke of geese'). The presence of the rear ranks (as in Monluc's account) would be a great aid in this by firmly following up the leaders and keeping them moving forward, and the deeper the formation, the greater the momentum there would be in such an advance – not so much because of the actual physical shoving of the men behind, but because the men at the rear, far removed from the immediate danger of the combat and probably unaware even of what exactly was happening at the front, would naturally tend to keep moving forward, 'encouraged' by the file closers and officers at the rear. A deep formation would thus tend to generate its own greater momentum, without shoving as a mass, and this alone could well be sufficient to overcome an enemy. If it was not, and the enemy stood their ground, then forward momentum could well peter out, but if it did, then the rear ranks would tend to make it difficult for the front ranks, not just to run away, but also to give ground, to fall back before the blows, or feared blows, of their opponents. After all, it would be difficult or impossible for a front-ranker to fall back, to take a step back, if there was a solid line of men with shields immediately behind him ('on his heels'). In order for a front-ranker to step back, the second rank would have to step back also, and the same applies to the second and third rank, and so on back through the formation. Ultimately, for a front-ranker to give ground in a tightly closed-up formation, the whole file would need to step back, and we can well imagine that the deeper the formation, the harder it would be for this chain reaction effect of recoils to be transmitted back through the ranks. In a very deep formation, those in the rearward ranks would be largely unaware of what was happening at the front of the formation, would not feel in any immediate danger from their front and would be more guided by the encouragement of the file-closer behind them than by fear of the more distant enemy in front. With more ranks there is also more opportunity for any backward movement to be absorbed by the gaps between ranks rather than being transmitted backwards through bodies in contact, so that any backward force would tend not to be transmitted all the way to the rear in a deep formation (the same phenomenon in reverse as the Byzantine comment on the role of half-files mentioned above). With a formation, say, four ranks deep, in contrast, it would not take much for the whole file of just four men to take a step back; any backward movement would not be absorbed by the mass, and the rear ranks would be much more immediately affected by what was happening at the front. Once the men at the back gave ground, the forward pressure that gave the formation its strength would be dissipated, and the effect of rear ranks in preventing flight by those in front would be removed. The enemy would also be encouraged and able to start pressing forward again, so that a positive feedback loop could become established where the more the formation stepped back, the greater forward momentum the enemy would generate.

This would give a deep phalanx greater solidity and make it harder to force it back; and if maintaining forward momentum was key to the success of a phalanx in battle, then denying such forward momentum to an enemy was equally important in avoiding defeat. Xenophon's imaginary combat at Thymbra has two ranks of Persians falling back before the blows of Egyptians 100 deep. Xenophon likes to imagine that falling back like this wouldn't matter too much, and perhaps in that case it wouldn't, as there were archers and towers to the Persians' rear, and friendly cavalry to attack the Egyptians' flanks, but in most cases without such aids, a formation that found itself driven back this way could expect to be beaten. It would take tremendous discipline (as shown perhaps by Philip's phalanx at Chaeronea or that of Antigonus at Sellasia) for backward movement not to lead rapidly to the collapse and rout of the formation.

Winners and losers

What then caused one side to be defeated by the other? It is not enough to think of one 'fighting better' than the other, if by this is meant actual hand-to-hand combat, because it is almost certain that it was not numbers of dead which led to flight. For Hellenistic battles, detailed casualty information is scarce, but if we keep in mind that most casualties were suffered in the pursuit rather than in the fighting, and that the victor's casualties are very light, then even if we assume that the losing side suffered three or four times heavier casualties in the fighting, the losses would still be small as a proportion of the whole. There are also clear anomalies of casualties: at the Granicus the lead group of Companions lost just twenty-five men, yet was thrown back (Arr. *Anab.* 1.15.3, 16.4), while at Gaugamela the Macedonian cavalry suffered heavier losses than their opponents, yet resisted them (Arr. *Anab.* 3.13). At Issus, the phalanx of 12,000 men was regarded as having been in difficulties, yet lost only 120 men (Arr. *Anab.* 2.10).

Two other factors were of more importance than numbers of dead: maintenance of order and high morale. Order could be lost by the irregularities of the ground, as for the Spartans at Mantinea, where 'the ranks of the Lacedaemonians had been disorganised by the passage of the dyke, and as they ascended the opposite bank they found the enemy above them. They lost courage and tried to fly' (Pol. 11.16). Speaking of cavalry, Polybius (10.23) notes that 'nothing is more dangerous and unserviceable than cavalry that have broken up their squadrons and attempt to engage in this state'. A unit could also be thrown into confusion by the flight of other troops, especially elephants or chariots, past or through them, as happened at Magnesia, where 'the auxiliaries in support who were stationed nearest to the chariots were terrified by their panic and confusion, and they also turned and fled' (Liv. 37.42). Morale could suffer from the loss of leaders – as when the commander of the Eleans surprised by the Macedonians above Stymphalus abandoned them and 'the rest of the Eleans being thus deserted by their leader and panic struck at what had happened, remained stationary on the road, not knowing what to do or which way to turn' (Pol. 4.69) – or the appearance of the enemy leader (such as at Raphia), the rout of nearby friends or any number of other causes. A well-disciplined and determined advance by the enemy could in itself be a terrifying spectacle, enough to unnerve unsteady troops. At Caphyae, 'taught by experience what to do, the Aetolians followed behind [the Achaeans] with round after round of loud and boisterous shouts' (Pol. 4.12) to keep them on the run. A particularly fearsome enemy (like the Argyraspides at Paraitacene) might be enough to make men flee, as in the case of the Eleans who believed the Macedonians facing them were Achaeans, but 'as soon as the Macedonians had advanced close up to them, grasping the true state of the case, they threw down their shields and fled' (Pol. 4.69). In the same way, Antiochus III's men at Thermopylae believed the Romans approaching their rear were Aetolians, 'but as soon as the standards and arms were close enough to be recognised and these revealed their mistake, such sudden terror grasped them all that they threw away their arms and fled' (Liv. 36.19), while at the Aous pass a Roman force got behind the Macedonians and 'this drove the king's men out of their wits with sudden panic' (Liv. 32.12). A unit could also very commonly be broken by an attack in flank or rear. Polybius (18.26.4) describes this at Cynoscephalae – 'as it is impossible for the phalanx to turn right about face or to fight man to man', the Roman tribune 'pressed his attack home, killing those he found in his way'. But it must have been unusual for men on the edge of a formation to have been unable to face round, and having done so they would fight as well, as individuals, as they would while facing forward. The effect of a flank attack was primarily moral. Since a formation runs away not from the front but from the rear, it is when the men in the rear are suddenly and unexpectedly put in fear for their lives that the risk is greatest, and the unit likely to disintegrate without even fighting.[16]

Because of all these factors, occasions of prolonged fights between opposing bodies of infantry are in fact quite rare. Cavalry or light troops could fight for a long time because their type of combat, at a distance with missile weapons, would not cause an opposing unit to flee, but close-quarter fights would generally be brief and often would not occur at all. There are examples of long fights between equally matched forces in similar circumstances, for example at Sellasia between the Macedonian and Spartan phalanxes. More often the fighting was brief, as at Raphia, or else one of the factors mentioned above was enough to cause a unit to flee when combined with only the threat of close combat. A good example of such flight occurred at Caphyae, where the Aetolians defeated the Achaean cavalry and light forces, 'whose flight involved that of the heavy armed troops also which were coming to their relief. For the latter were advancing in separate detachments in loose order and, either in dismay at what was happening or upon meeting their flying comrades on their retreat, were compelled to follow their example' (Pol. 4.12). At Magnesia, the entire Seleucid left wing was defeated by the panic of their own chariots. At Raphia, Ptolemy's left was defeated when its own elephants fell back upon it, and Antiochus' left by one flanking charge. Formations of thousands of men could be swept aside by the activities of a handful, as Polybius (4.12) says of Caphyae, 'whereas the number of them actually defeated on the field was less than 500, the number that fled was more than 2,000'. Numbers were therefore not of great significance, except that a longer line was harder to outflank.

Obviously, where units flee without even waiting to fight, their flight occurs very quickly – they delay only as long as it would take the enemy to charge towards them over a distance of, perhaps 100 yards or so. When whole wings were defeated by a single attack, then the time taken would be no more than for a single unit. Equal fights would go on longer, but where we have the opportunity to compare a fight on one wing with flight on the other it is clear that the difference is not great. Common sense demands that men in full armour could not stand giving and receiving blows for periods of hours; any degree of competence with weapons would mean that after an hour's fighting the two sides would have virtually annihilated each other, and any survivors would die of exhaustion. As battles were fought in single lines, as a general rule, the time taken for the first combat to be decided would also be the duration for that battle as a whole, and this would often be measured in tens of minutes, at most, except of course where one wing fought first and the other stood back to observe the result.

If it came to a face-to-face fight between two formations, particularly two phalanxes, the victorious side in such a fight might be that in which the fighters were more skilled, such as Eumenes' Argyraspides at Paraitacene, 'because of the great number of battles they had fought they were outstanding in hardihood and skill, so that no one confronting them was able to withstand their might' (Diod. 19.30.6). However, at Raphia 'the picked Syrian troops stood their ground only for a short time and the division of Nicarchus quickly broke and fled' (Pol. 5.85) when faced by the newly recruited Egyptian phalanx. In this case, Polybius tells us, it was the appearance of Ptolemy that made the difference: 'Ptolemy ... struck terror in the hearts of the enemy, but inspired great spirit and enthusiasm in his own men' (Pol. 5.85). Ptolemy was no Alexander and had no great reputation as warrior or commander, yet his presence is supposed to have made the crucial difference.

We cannot of course identify any one single factor that applies in all cases. There were many factors at play in the outcome of any combat, including the training, morale and motivation of the men, their organization and formation, effects of terrain, fighting skill, experience, leadership and no doubt many other factors. An ancient historian might have picked out one or more of these factors as being crucial in any given case, and he may well be right, but this does not mean it was the only factor in play or that the same factor would apply in all cases. There could be many reasons for defeat, but the crucial factor that keeps recurring is confidence, and its opposite, fear (in Greek, *phobos*). A formation which lost confidence would start to break apart and lose formation as the men at the rear stopped bearing forward and tried to back off or even run away. This would lead to a positive feedback loop in which the loss of formation and of physical support caused more men to lose heart, and so the effect, which might begin only at a single point in the line, would quickly be transmitted to neighbouring men and units, until a whole formation gave way. Polybus blandly describes how the Seleucid phalanx at Raphia, some 16,000 strong, 'quickly broke and fled'. But a formation hundreds of metres wide cannot simply run away spontaneously and simultaneously. Rather, we must imagine that in one or two places, perhaps due to slightly varying fortunes in fighting or degrees of anxiety among the men – or even to trivial terrain features too small to be recorded – a part of the phalanx would lose order, the men would lose confidence and they would back off, retreat, then turn and run. This having begun at one point, fear would be contagious and a whole formation could unzip from one point, as men, suddenly aware that their neighbours were no longer supporting them, would lose confidence too and join in the flight. This is, I think, how we have to understand that uninformative expression 'turned to flight' when applied to formations of thousands of men: a progressive loss of confidence that could have started even before fighting began, increasing at one or a few points until order began to break down and men to back off, and transmitted and increased throughout the formation in a cumulative collapse.

Aftermath

It was in the pursuit that the losers suffered their heaviest losses, hence the disproportionate casualties between winner and loser that are recorded for many battles. The forces most suited to pursuit were the fastest – that is, the cavalry and light troops – so it was they who were responsible for cutting down the fleeing enemy. The phalanx itself was wholly unsuited to pursuit, since those fleeing would abandon their spears and shields while the victors could not do so, and would prefer to remain in formation in case another enemy force presented itself, so that those fleeing could run much faster than a formed victorious phalanx. At Raphia, Ptolemy 'secured the final victory by his phalanx, and killed large numbers of the enemy in the pursuit by means of his cavalry and mercenaries on his right wing' (Pol. 5.86). The phalanx could be regarded as a battle-winning force, invincible according to Polybius, in the right circumstances, but inflicting little damage on the enemy army. Lasting damage, that is, large numbers of men killed, was achieved by the light forces and cavalry.

There is relatively little information in the sources on the fate of the dead and wounded after a battle. Alexander had set a precedent of good treatment of the wounded, including a mobile army hospital, and of honours to the dead. The victor of a battle would be in a position to take his wounded with him. Antigonos, after Paraitacene, 'sent the wounded men and the heaviest part of the baggage ahead to one of the neighbouring cities' (Diod. 19.32.1). The sources do not record the fate of the wounded of the losing side, if they were not able to get themselves away from the battlefield; presumably either death from loss of blood, exposure or dehydration, or if they were lucky, a *coup de grace* from one of the many looters and scavengers who no doubt frequented a battlefield.[17]

Control of the dead was in Greek tradition an important indication of victory. After Paraitacene, 'Eumenes undertook to march back to the dead, desiring to control the disposal of the bodies and put his claim to victory beyond dispute' (Diod. 19.31.3). The victor would bury his own dead, but disposal of those of the enemy required an admission of defeat. After Raphia, Antiochus, 'having sent an embassy to obtain leave to pick up his dead, obtained a truce for performing their obsequies' (Pol. 5.86.4). In terms of numbers of dead we are on difficult ground, since this is an area much prone to exaggeration, while the number of dead on the winning side might be correspondingly scaled down. However, if we assume most casualty figures to be at least to the correct order of magnitude, the disproportion between the losses of the winner and loser is obvious. At Paraitacene, for example, Antigonos lost 3,754 dead, Eumenes 540 (Diod. 19.31); while at Gabiene the Argyraspides supposedly killed 5,000 with no loss to themselves (Diod. 19.43). At Raphia, Antiochus lost 14,300 dead or prisoners, Ptolemy 2,200 (Pol. 5.86), at Thermopylae he escaped with only 500 out of his army, to Roman losses of 150 (Liv. 36.19), and at Magnesia he supposedly lost 53,000 to 300 Roman dead (Liv. 37.42). There are very many similar examples. While defeat could be disastrous to the losing side, victory was generally very cheaply won. Defeated armies typically lost 25 per cent or more of their strength and victorious armies only 2 or 3 per cent.[18]

Morale and motivation

We have seen that the Macedonian phalanx was a formation which depended on the maintenance of good order, and on drill and discipline, for its particular effectiveness, but also on the confidence and (to use the rather vague and all-encompassing term) morale of the men. What if anything can we say about the psychology of those serving within the phalanx, and what motivated them in battle? Needless to say there is little or no direct evidence, since no ordinary ranker of the period wrote any memoirs equivalent to those, still scant, resources available for later pike formations. We can only make some more general observations.[19]

One is that experience, training and also a strong cultural warlike tradition were of tremendous importance in the success of the phalanx on the battlefield. Philip II developed the phalanx more or less from scratch from raw material that was not thought to make good infantry, but the years he devoted to training and drill, together with the string of successful battles against Greek and barbarian opponents, succeeded in instilling a tremendous self-belief in the men of the phalanx. The Macedonians were generally regarded as a naturally warlike people, for all that lack of organization, equipment and leadership had previously rendered their infantry relatively ineffective. Once Philip provided those three essential elements, the Macedonian infantry were regarded as the best in the known world at the time, and were certainly fully aware of (and agreed with) that assessment. The Macedonian element of the Hellenistic armies, and in particular the native Macedonians of the Antigonid armies, were regarded as highly skillful and effective; even the later Seleucid army, which Livy denigrates as inferior Syrians, is described at Magnesia as a veteran force full of self-belief. Subunits of the phalanx could also be first among equals. As we have seen, all the kingdoms formed elite guard units of peltasts with particularly high *esprit de corps*: the Antigonid Peltasts at Pydna stood their ground when the army broke around them and were cut down to the last man. The most conspicuous example of such elite units was of course the Argyraspides of Alexander, who dominated the battlefields of the wars of the Successors (until their self-interest and lack of loyalty to lesser commanders led to Antigonus packing them off to garrison duty in the interior). This combination of professional pride and a warlike tradition would have been the primary motivating factor for most of the men of the phalanx. Compared with the hoplite militias of most of the Greek city-states, which had a strong sense of civic duty but little professionalism, training or self-belief (aside from the Spartans and the various 'picked men' that other cities began to field in the fourth century), Macedonian phalangites had an immediate advantage even before any considerations of equipment or tactics come into play.[20]

An ancient battlefield was undoubtedly a dangerous and brutal place, but in many ways far less so than any battlefield since the invention of firearms, where death is random, inescapable and delivered anonymously at a distance. The ancient warrior could on the whole see his enemy, and was usually in a position both to defend himself and to strike back. Casualty rates for the victorious side were also quite low – as we have seen, most deaths occurred in the pursuit after the battle was decided, and the chances of death in battle were relatively small, provided one was on the winning side. This compares with, say, the battlefields of the Napoleonic Wars, where even the victors routinely suffered around 30 per cent casualties, and where in any one campaign there would likely be several major battles. In an ancient battle, the victor's losses could be very light, and one victory had a good chance of deciding the war, perhaps for a generation. This meant that a phalangite did not have to endure the constant drain on morale of continuous service and lengthy exposure to death or wounding, and often could expect to be sent home, or at least to relatively comfortable winter quarters, at the end of each campaigning season (there are exceptions of course, such as the continuous campaigns of Alexander, and these did indeed eventually break the spirit of the Macedonians, leading to the mutinies on the Hyphasis and at Opis). The key to survival and to enjoyment of the benefits of a military career was therefore victory in pitched battle, and it was largely thought to be up to the skill and ability of the king or general to provide this. If the commanding general was able to deliver victory, then a military career could be quite a safe one.

We have seen in earlier chapters that a military career could also be desirable, both as a source of steady income and presenting opportunities for adventure, enrichment (through plunder) and state and culturally sanctioned sex and violence, that could well appeal to many young (or not so young) men, especially where the alternatives were economically uncertain and unfulfilling labour in field or workshop. There was no strong sense that warfare was in any way undesirable in itself, and a greater threat than death in battle would be death at the hands of hostile barbarian or foreign neighbours; a successful campaign to defeat such neighbours offered not only rewards of its own, but also a promise of safety from the neighbours. For the men of the phalanx we can imagine (although largely only imagine) that the soldier's life was a source of professional pride, along with the camaraderie fostered by belonging to a large military unit, and a source of potential enrichment and some measure of personal fulfilment, offering safety for the soldier and his family from a dangerous world full of threats, real and imagined.

We must also remember that, for at least some proportion of the men in the Macedonian phalanx, war was fun. We have already seen Macedonians described as 'joying in war as if it were a feast' (Pol. 5.2.6), and this was no doubt literally true for many. The modern idea of the 'universal soldier', that military experience and the individual's reaction to it is universal across history, and that the strongly negative experience of modern industrialized war can be applied also to the past, does not always bear scrutiny, at least in the ancient world. Undoubtedly fear played its part, and there could be a dread of battle beforehand, but there was also joy in victory, in successful fighting and in killing one's enemies. Direct evidence for this is lacking for the Macedonian phalanx, but more plentiful for Classical Greece, and is implicit in the pride shown by soldiers in their profession, discussed in Chapter 4. Xenophon expresses this clearly:

> 'For, you know, when states defeat their foes in a battle, words fail one to describe the joy they feel in the rout of the enemy, in the pursuit, in the slaughter of the enemy. What transports of triumphant pride! What a halo of glory about them! What comfort to think that they have exalted their city! Everyone is crying: "I had a share in the plan, I killed most"; and it's hard to find where they don't revel in falsehood, claiming to have killed more than all that were really slain. So glorious it seems to them to have won a great victory!' (Xenophon, *Hiero* 2.15–16)

Defeat and death could be dreaded, but victory and killing actively enjoyed (and of course, as the latter served to avoid the former, the two are closely linked).[21]

As noted above, an important aspect for the phalanx in particular was the pride and *esprit de corps* arising from being part of an elite and highly effective military unit. The evidence for this is largely indirect, in the examples we have already seen for the Macedonian enthusiasm for war and in the way that Macedonian and Hellenistic armies used unit names and special designations and symbology to promote *esprit de corps*, together with the competitive angle that was introduced into drill and training. We have seen how the extension of the title 'Foot Companions' – specifically noted by Anaximenes as being intended to promote loyalty to the king – was used. Macedonian armies generally made much use of such elite unit designations: Foot Companions for the heavy infantry (distinguishing them from lesser allied or mercenary forces, who would not be the king's companions), Hypaspists or Peltasts for the elite (richest, youngest, strongest) of the infantry and Agema for the elite of the elite, the vanguard units. Uniform equipment – particularly shields with distinctive materials, colours or patterns, or specially coloured clothing – emphasized such special status. When units were recruited territorially or from the same city, there would also have been a sense of civic solidarity and familiarity (something that had long been exploited by Greek armies), with men serving together who would be familiar to each other socially, down to the level of the smallest unit, the file, which would have consisted of men serving together long term and probably sharing a tent on campaign, as well as drilling and training together. All of this would ensure the mutual confidence and respect essential for small-unit cohesion, so crucial to the effective operation of a formation like the phalanx.[22]

Another aspect of the Macedonian military life that has received little attention is the role of homosexuality in maintaining group cohesion and encouraging battlefield performance. Part of the reason for this is the absence of direct evidence for the Macedonian rank and file specifically: such homosexual relationships as are known are generally those involving the king himself or the pages – for example, Philip II's assassin, Pausanias, was a spurned lover (Diod. 16.93.3–6), while the page Hermolaus conceived a plot with his lover Sostratus to kill Alexander after being humiliated by the king on a hunt (Arr. *Anab.* 4.13). There was a strong Greek tradition of homsexuality in a military context, particularly in Thebes, Sparta and Crete, although it is unclear how much this fitted into the pattern of Greek pederasty (relationships between adult men and adolescent, or pre-adolescent, boys) or involved relations between age peers. At any rate there was a school of thought that such relationships were beneficial to morale and *esprit de corps* in a military unit, most famously exemplified by the Theban elite infantry unit, the Sacred Band, composed, according to Plutarch (*Pelop.* 18), of 150 pairs of *erastai* and *eromenoi* (older and younger partners – although presumably members of such a unit would have both been of military age). Such views existed alongside a school of thought that saw an element of disgrace in such relationships, at least for the younger (presumed to be submissive) partner. Polybius (8.9.10–12) reports disapprovingly that the writer Theopompus could joke of Philip's Companions that 'we would be justified in calling them not courtiers [Companions, *hetairoi*] but courtesans [*hetairai*] and not soldiers but strumpets. For being by nature man-slayers they became by their practices man-whores.' At any rate, there is evidence that homosexual relationships were thought to be beneficial to military discipline and performance, but no direct evidence for their existence in the specific context of the Macedonian phalanx.[23]

Yet when it came to the ultimate test of battle, all of the training, faith in the commander, *esprit de corps* and sense of self-belief still had to overcome that enemy of formed bodies of men on any battlefield: fear. Greek historians, unlike many of their modern counterparts in more recent centuries, were honest about the role of fear on the battlefield, hence the emphasis on rear ranks preventing flight and forcing those ahead to advance, perhaps against their will. We have already seen above how often a sudden panic, sufficient to break apart a phalanx or an army, could be induced by apparently fairly trivial events. Hope and fear were the competing forces on the ancient battlefield just as much as were the opposing phalanxes, as Polybius (5.85) describes at Raphia: '[T]he phalanxes, left without the support of either wing, remained intact in the centre of the plain, in a state of alternate hope and fear for the result.'

Training, organization, drill and tactics were all directed toward the triumph of hope over fear (for one's own forces), and some aspects of the phalanx, such as its serried pikes, depth and close order, were specifically designed to sow fear among the enemy (as evidenced by the emotions experienced by the Roman commander at Pydna, as we will see in the next chapter). The extent to which they did so successfully varied from case to case, but this was the ultimate objective of all military organization, and while it is easy to get caught up in the technical details of the length of sarissas or the intervals of files, we must not forget that ultimately it is not the equipment but the men using it that are most important in determining victory or defeat.

Chapter 9

Legion and phalanx

W e have seen in the preceding chapters how the Macedonian phalanx came into being, and how and why it was so successful on the battlefields of the Hellenistic world. Yet, although the phalanx had a run of success of some 200 years, in the end it was to be defeated and ultimately replaced by the Roman legion. That this was so was considered remarkable at the time, and the desire to explain the ultimate triumph of Rome formed a central motivation for Polybius in writing his *History*, with special emphasis on the technical factors that allowed the legion to win:

'For since in former times the Macedonian tactics proved them-selves by experience capable of conquering those of Asia and Greece; while the Roman tactics sufficed to conquer the nations of Africa and all those of Western Europe; and since in our own day there have been numerous opportunities of comparing the men as well as their tactics, it will be, I think, a useful and worthy task to investigate their differences, and discover why it is that the Romans conquer and carry off the palm from their enemies in the operations of war: that we may not put it all down to Fortune, and congratulate them on their good luck, as the thoughtless of mankind do; but, from a knowledge of the true causes, may give their leaders the tribute of praise and admiration which they deserve.' (Polybius, 18.28)

As he says of his conclusions:

'I thought it necessary to discuss this subject at some length, because at the actual time of the occurrence many Greeks supposed when the Macedonians were beaten that it was incredible; and many will afterwards be at a loss to account for the inferiority of the phalanx to the Roman system of arming.' (Polybius, 18.32)

I have made use of Polybius' analysis many times already in this book, so it does not need to be repeated in full again here. Instead, I will summarize Polybius' key points, then consider to what extent they tell the whole story, and are sufficient as an explanation for the eventual triumph of the Roman legions.[1]

The analysis of Polybius

For Polybius, the differences between legion and phalanx are of a technical, tactical nature, to do with drill, equipment and fighting methods. Key for Polybius is the relatively open order of the Roman formation compared with the Macedonian, which meant that each individual Roman soldier faced two Macedonians in the front rank, and the pike points of a further eight behind. This made the Macedonian formation superior in a face-to-face, fair fight in ideal conditions (that is on level and unbroken ground), and in circumstances where the phalanx retained an unbroken formation. But the more open order of the Romans, together with their equipment of sword and easily manipulated shield (the Roman shield was large but held in one hand, so that it could be manoeuvred to face incoming blows), made the Roman legionaries more flexible, better able to fight on broken ground and to fight effectively in whatever tactical situation they found themselves, even in less than ideal conditions. For Polybius, the Romans could defeat the phalanx in two ways; firstly by refusing to fight on its own terms, that is on level open ground:

> 'If the enemy finds it possible, and even easy, to avoid [the phalanx's] attack, what becomes of its formidable character? Again, no one denies that for its employment it is indispensable to have a country flat, bare, and without such impediments as ditches, cavities, depressions, steep banks, or beds of rivers: for all such obstacles are sufficient to hinder and dislocate this particular formation.... If the enemy decline to come down into [such terrain], but traverse the country sacking the towns and territories of the allies, what use will the phalanx be? For if it remains on the ground suited to itself, it will not only fail to benefit its friends, but will be incapable even of preserving itself ... while if it quits its proper ground, from the wish to strike a blow, it will be an easy prey to the enemy.' (Polybius, 18.31)

Secondly, if they did accept an offer of battle and fight a pitched battle against the phalanx, they could still win by denying the phalanx its single perfect method of engagement:

'The Romans do not, then, attempt to extend their front to equal that of a phalanx, and then charge directly upon it with their whole force: but some of their divisions are kept in reserve, while others join battle with the enemy at close quarters. Now, whether the phalanx in its charge drives its opponents from their ground, or is itself driven back, in either case its peculiar order is dislocated; for whether in following the retiring, or flying from the advancing enemy, they quit the rest of their forces: and when this takes place, the enemy's reserves can occupy the space thus left, and the ground which the phalanx had just before been holding, and so no longer charge them face to face, but fall upon them on their flank and rear. (Polybius, 18.32)

It is worth stressing that these are two complementary but different ways of opposing the phalanx. In the first case, Polybius' point is not so much that the legion will defeat the phalanx on broken terrain (as is often stressed by modern historians), but rather that the Romans can simply refuse to fight a pitched battle on good terrain, and instead engage in a war of manoeuvre, the interdiction of supplies and assaults on fortified locations. As we have seen, the inability of the phalanx to fight on broken ground has probably been overstated. The phalanx was not incapable of fighting on less than perfect ground, whatever Polybius implies, but it was at a disadvantage doing so, especially against a more flexible opponent like the Romans. But Polybius' point is that the Romans could simply avoid this type of engagement altogether, refusing not just to fight the phalanx on its own terms, but to allow a war to be decided by a pitched battle at all, as was part of the traditional way of war in the Greek and Hellenistic world.

Polybius' second point is more subtle, and as it fits less well with the tactical analysis of equipment which preceded it, and is expressed in rather vague language, it tends to be relatively overlooked. This is that the phalanx fought as a single continuous line, depended to a large extent on holding this single line and relied on winning a single decisive combat that would determine the outcome of the battle. As we have seen, the concept of reserves, in the particular form of a second line or *amphistomos* phalanx, was not unknown to Hellenistic tacticians, but it was employed as a defence against outflanking by more numerous or mobile forces, rather than as a standard part of the tactical deployment. Usually, the phalanx did fight as a single line (even though made up of separate subunits), and in a fight of phalanx against phalanx, whichever side first broke the enemy line would likely roll up the rest of their line and win the battle. The Roman formation was fundamentally different in a way which Polybius understood but never fully articulated in his works.

The Roman legions always drew up in three lines, with not just the men themselves within the subunits (maniples) in more open order, but also with large gaps between the maniples in each line. The exact nature of the Roman formation is controversial and is never clearly spelled out by any ancient historian (astonishingly enough, given the number and otherwise generally high quality of the accounts of the battles of the Roman army, and the fact that we have, for the later Republic at least, first-hand accounts by the greatest generals such as Julius Caesar). The best description is to be found in Livy, talking of an earlier period of Roman history but probably describing (broadly) the legions of the mid-Republic, the time of the Punic and Macedonian wars.

> 'The first line, or *hastati*, comprised fifteen maniples, stationed a short distance apart; ... this front line in the battle contained the flower of the young men who were growing ripe for service. Behind these came a line of the same number of maniples, made up of men of a more stalwart age; these were called the *principes*; they carried oblong shields and were the most showily armed of all... . When an army had been marshalled in this fashion, the *hastati* were the first of all to engage. If the *hastati* were unable to defeat the enemy, they retreated slowly and were received into the intervals between the companies of the *principes*. The *principes* then took up the fighting and the *hastati* followed them. The *triarii* knelt beneath their banners, with the left leg advanced, having their shields leaning against their shoulders and their spears thrust into the ground and pointing obliquely upwards, as if their battle-line were fortified with a bristling palisade. If the *principes*, too, were unsuccessful in their fight, they fell back slowly from the battle-line on the *triarii*. From this arose the adage, "to have come to the *triarii*", when things are going badly.' (Livy, 8.8.5–14)

This triple Roman battle-line (*hastati*, *principes*, *triarii*) was the standard Roman deployment throughout the period when the Romans faced the Macedonian phalanx (in addition, each legion contained a large force of *velites*, the youngest men, equipped as skirmishers, who fought in front of and in the gaps between the main lines). The precise details of how the 'line relief' as described by Livy was executed in practice have been the subject of much discussion, and fall outside the scope of the current book, though my own view is that the various schemes proposed are far too formal and the drill required (of what was most of the time a militia infantry with little formal training) would have been far too complex. Rather than seeing 'line relief' as a complex series of formal drill movements, I am inclined to think that the point was simply to hold back double lines of reserves, which could be committed to bolster or replace a wavering battle-line or to reinforce success as whole units, taking advantage of the open order and 'gappy' line in which the Romans deployed. In most descriptions of Roman battles we see little trace of this system in action, and there is a tendency to talk of the Roman battle-line as if it were a single phalanx, or as if the *hastati* alone carried out all the fighting. But it is this triple line deployment that Polybius must have in mind when he talks of the Romans keeping some of their units in reserve, and using these reserves to exploit the gaps that inevitably opened in a single-line phalanx. So although Polybius lays great stress on the deployment of individual soldiers and their equipment, and though he emphasizes the role of terrain, it is this latter point, the grand tactical flexibility of the Roman formation with its independent subunits and reserves, which seems to have been of most importance in the major battles.

That this is so is emphasized by the fact that, for all Polybius' claims that the Macedonian phalanx would be invincible on its chosen terrain and that the Romans' best bet was to avoid pitched battle on level terrain, the Romans did fight a succession of pitched battles against the phalanx on relatively level terrain (chiefly Cynoscephalae, Magnesia and Pydna) and won them all, even though terrain probably played very little part in any of these encounters. But long before these decisive encounters in the first half of the second century, the Romans had already encountered a Macedonian phalanx, that led by Pyrrhus of Epirus in his invasion of Italy early in the third century, and the battles fought during this campaign provide our first comparison of the two tactical systems.

First encounters – Pyrrhus

Pyrrhus, King of Epirus and at one time also of Macedon, was a military adventurer who led a Greek-Epirote-Macedonian army – with a Macedonian-armed phalanx at its core – on an extended expedition to Italy between 280 and 275. The campaign saw three major clashes between Pyrrhus' army and the Romans, at Heraclea, Asculum and Beneventum – battles in which Pyrrhus' army came out victorious twice and was defeated once (so far as we can tell, as the results are disputed), but sustained such heavy losses that a 'Pyrrhic victory' became proverbial. The difficulty from our point of view is that the events of these battles are not well recorded, the only accounts being those of Dionysius of Halicarnassus, whose account is incomplete and not always reliable, and Plutarch, who was writing short literary biographies rather than detailed military history. As a result, only the broadest outlines of the course of the battles can be discerned and few detailed lessons can be drawn from them.[2]

At Heraclea, Pyrrhus' army faced the Romans across a river (the Siris), but the Romans crossed the river before Pyrrhus was ready to oppose them, driving back his advance forces. Pyrrhus' attempt to halt the Roman advance with his cavalry was unsuccessful:

> '[S]eeing that his cavalry were giving way, he called up his phalanx and put it in array, ... for a long time the issue of the battle remained undecided; it is said that there were seven turns of fortune, as each side either fled back or pursued ... . At last, when the Romans were more than ever crowded back by the elephants, and their horses, before they got near the animals, were terrified and ran away with their riders, Pyrrhus brought his Thessalian cavalry upon them while they were in confusion and routed them with great slaughter.' (Plutarch, *Pyrrhus* 17.1–4)

Not much tactical detail can be gleaned from this account (Plutarch adds a colourful story about how Pyrrhus swapped clothes with one of his generals, having been subject to an attempted assassination earlier in the battle, and had to reveal his presence to reassure his men when his stand-in was killed). At any rate, the phalanx was certainly able to stand up against the Romans, even if the ultimate victory was ascribed to the attack of the elephants and cavalry, presumably on the Roman flanks. Not much can be made either of the 'seven turns of fortune', although we might surmise that behind this vague statement lies that essential feature of the Roman formation, its ability to fall back under pressure and commit reserves to steady the line. The phalanx once broken anywhere was, in all probability, lost, but individual Roman maniples could be driven back while the line as a whole remained intact.

For the Battle of Asculum, we have a much more detailed account from Dionysius, who gives detailed orders of battle for each side and a more continuous narrative (though it is still hard work making sense of it). Pyrrhus had been joined by a large force of Italian allies, including an enigmatic 'white-shielded phalanx' of Tarentines; it is tempting to compare these with the 'White Shields' later found in the Antigonid army, though there is no reason to suppose that these Tarentines were armed in the Macedonian fashion. The Romans for their part, chastened by their experience with Pyrrhus' elephants at Heraclea, had equipped themselves with a force of anti-elephant wagons, which were to prove as ineffective in battle as such improvised devices usually do. Dionysius details the deployment and course of action:

'Having agreed through heralds upon the time when they would join in battle, they descended from their camps and took up their positions as follows: King Pyrrhus gave the Macedonian phalanx the first place on the right wing and placed next to it the Italiote mercenaries from Tarentum; then the troops from Ambracia.'

Greek and Italian allies and mercenaries formed the rest of Pyrrhus' line. Dionysius continues:

'The [Roman] consuls arrayed on their left wing the legion called the first, facing the Macedonian and Ambraciot phalanx and the Tarentine mercenaries ... . The right wing of each army was the stronger one, the left being weaker. Nevertheless, neither side turned its back ignominiously to the foe, but both maintained good order, remaining with the standards and protecting themselves with their shields while gradually falling back. Those who distinguished themselves for valour were, on the king's side, the Macedonians, who repulsed the first Roman legion and the Latins arrayed with it; and, on the Roman side, those who constituted the second legion and were opposed to the Molossians, Thesprotians and Chaonians.' (Dionysius, 20.2–3)

At this point the battle, and Dionysius' account of it, dissolve into confusion. Pyrrhus' army was victorious on the right where the Macedonians were, but was defeated elsewhere. An attempt to use the victorious right wing to defeat the Romans' victorious right was foiled by an unexpected attack on Pyrrhus' camp and by the retirement of the Roman force to a wooded height, on which they were engaged by Pyrrhus' light infantry and cavalry, until sunset brought the battle to a close. The Roman historian Cassius Dio presents a vaguely similar account of the battle, but has the Romans victorious (Dionysius is not explicit as to which side should be considered the victors, though Pyrrhus is generally supposed to have been). Plutarch, meanwhile, gives an account which is almost wholly useless as regards details of the events of the battle (which he has taking place over two days), although he appears to draw his account from the history of Hieronymus, who had access to the memoirs of Pyrrhus himself, and as such, his general view of the nature of the fighting is worth quoting. Plutarch's account has the first day's fighting as an indecisive skirmish in wooded terrain:

> 'But on the next day, designing to fight the battle on level ground, and to bring his elephants to bear upon the ranks of the enemy, Pyrrhus occupied betimes the unfavourable parts of the field with a detachment of his troops; then he put great numbers of slingers and archers in the spaces between the elephants and led his forces to the attack in dense array and with a mighty impetus. So the Romans, having no opportunity for sidelong shifts and counter-movements, as on the previous day, were obliged to engage on level ground and front to front; and being anxious to repulse the enemy's hoplites before their elephants came up, they fought fiercely with their swords against the Macedonian sarissas, reckless of their lives and thinking only of wounding and slaying, while caring naught for what they suffered. After a long time, however, as we are told, they began to be driven back at the point where Pyrrhus himself was pressing hard upon his opponents; but the greatest havoc was wrought by the furious strength of the elephants.' (Plutarch, *Pyrrhus* 21.6–7)

I don't think any sort of reconstruction of the events of the battle is worth attempting from these broken and confused accounts, but we can draw some general observations. The Romans accepted battle on relatively open and level ground, but were defeated by the phalanx, aided and abetted perhaps by the elephants. Plutarch's account of the Roman attempts to oppose the phalanx are strongly reminiscent of his description of the defeat of the Paelignians at Pydna (as we will see shortly), and convey a sense of the attempt – futile as it turned out – of Roman swordsmen to cut their way into the serried pikes of the phalanx. Behind his reference to 'sidelong shifts and counter-movements' may lie the ability of the small independent units of the Roman formation to engage individually, on their own initiative and piecemeal, rather than forming a continuous phalanx and fighting front to front, as they were forced to do on the second day. I think that this is key – we must not imagine the Roman formation as being simply a sword-armed phalanx, but as something fundamentally different, a collection of small independent units capable of engaging, fighting and disengaging repeatedly and independently. Figure 9.1 provides a representation of a confrontation of legion and phalanx, which may help in visualizing the differences between the formations (though the Roman reserve lines are probably far too close to the enemy).

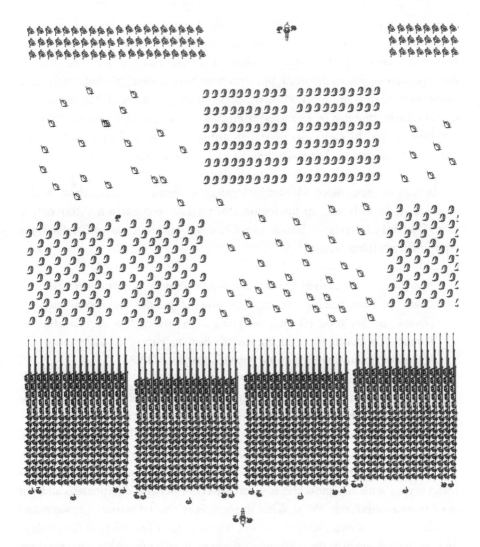

Fig. 9.1. A visualization of a phalanx (one *chiliarchia*) facing a legion (a maniple each of *hastati*, *principes* and *triarii*, plus *velites*).

The final battle of Pyrrhus against the Romans was at Beneventum (or Maleventum as it was still called at the time, the Romans later changing the name), but unfortunately this battle is so poorly documented that no use can be made of it, despite some bold efforts by modern historians to offer complete reconstructions. All we know is that Pyrrhus attempted a night attack on the Roman camp, which, as is often the way with such assaults, went wrong when the attacking force took longer than planned to reach their objectives. There followed a battle in the open in which the accounts we have (three sentences from Plutarch, and one each from Dionysius and Cassius Dio) place most emphasis on the exploits of the elephants, and record that the Romans were in places defeated, but the camp guards were able to turn the tide (something to bear in mind when we come to the accounts of Magnesia). No useful information can be extracted from this account, except to note that as in previous battles the elephants played an important role, and parts of Pyrrhus' army were successful, but parts less so (we can speculate that the successful parts may have been the Macedonian phalanx).

As well as these three admittedly inadequate battle accounts, there is also a comment by Polybius, in his legion and phalanx comparison. After noting that Hannibal preferred and made use of Roman arms over native Carthaginian equipment, Polybius adds:

> 'Pyrrhus, again, availed himself not only of the arms, but also of the troops of Italy, placing a maniple [*semeia*] of Italians and a company [*speira*] of his own phalanx alternately, in his battles against the Romans. Yet even this did not enable him to win; the battles were somehow or another always indecisive.' (Polybius, 18.28)

This is an interesting observation, though there is no trace of this deployment in such battle accounts as we have, but it is easy to imagine that Plutarch or Dionysius, in their brief to the point of incomprehensible accounts, would not have mentioned it. Perhaps this is how Pyrrhus deployed at Beneventum, at least. This deployment is similar to that at Sellasia, where the phalanx was interspersed with Illyrians, and is a further reminder that the phalanx did not need to be a monolithic block. What the benefit of this formation was supposed to have been is not clear, but presumably it gave greater flexibility to the phalanx and protected against the natural development of gaps, which as Polybius comments would be particularly harmful to a phalanx. Like Xenophon's attacking columns from Chapter 7, separate units with deliberate gaps, filled with lighter infantry, could be preferable to a solid phalanx which developed gaps inadvertently.

The best summary of the battles of Pyrrhus comes from Plutarch's report of Pyrrhus' own famous observation after Asculum, 'If we are victorious in one more battle with the Romans, we shall be utterly ruined' (Plut. *Pyrr.* 21.9), for though the losses to Pyrrhus' army were less than those of the Romans, Pyrrhus had difficulty in making up his losses (partly because he was far from his home bases, but also because he failed to win over his Italian allies to his cause, and the underlying manpower resources of Epirus and even Macedon were already strained). This observation is perhaps the most important, as Pyrrhus' ambassador to the Roman Senate, Cineas, commented:

'[A]s for the [Roman] people, he was afraid it might prove to be a Lernaean hydra for them to fight against, since the consul already had twice as many soldiers collected as those who faced their enemies before, and there were many times as many Romans still who were capable of bearing arms.' (Plutarch, *Pyrrhus* 19.5)

Pyrrhus won two major battles against Rome, but still had to fight a third (which he lost). As Hannibal was to find sixty years later, the combination of Roman stubbornness (or courage in adversity) and vast manpower reserves made them a difficult enemy to defeat. Polybius (2.24) enumerates the huge armies which Rome was able to field, calculating a total of 700,000 foot and 70,000 horse available for service at the time of the war with Hannibal, though of course these numbers could never have been called up in a single army given logistic and practical constraints. I will return below to some reasons why the Romans were able to draw on larger manpower reserves. So far as tactical differences go, the phalanx of Pyrrhus proved well able to defeat Roman armies in open battle, and was at least not greatly inconvenienced by broken terrain, aided in this by the fact that Pyrrhus had a combined-arms army with large contingents of light forces, cavalry, Italian allied infantry and above all elephants, so was not totally reliant on the success of the phalanx. Asculum showed that the phalanx was the superior tactical system in pitched battle, yet victory in battle was not enough to bring victory in war, and eventually the obscure events of Beneventum (where perhaps it was the allied forces that were defeated) forced Pyrrhus to withdraw his forces from Italy.[3]

Rome versus Macedon

The first encounters of legion and phalanx thus went in favour of the phalanx, but a number of features were established. The phalanx benefitted from being part of a combined-arms force, maybe to the extent, as Polybius claims, of having non-pike-armed units integrated into the formation. Its weakness compared with the Romans remained that it was a one-shot weapon, unable, unlike the Romans with their triple line (and fortified camps), to turn defeat into victory, and committed all in one go to a single hopefully decisive attack. Above all, Roman manpower reserves meant that they could afford to suffer defeat in battle without having to abandon the war. What does not seem to have been particularly significant is terrain – the Romans accepted battle on relatively open ground, and were defeated there, or if they retired to wooded hills, Pyrrhus' light forces and cavalry could take up the engagement.

For the next seventy years or so, the Romans were wholly absorbed with their wars against Carthage, culminating in the final defeat of Hannibal's army at Zama in 202. Only then did Rome turn its attention against Macedon again, Philip V's ill-judged intervention in the Second Punic War on Hannibal's side having earned Rome's resentment. The Second Macedonian War that followed (the First being in effect a sideshow of the Second Punic War) was characterized by Roman efforts to threaten Macedon and its Greek allies, while Philip attempted to defend his frontiers, and culminated in the Battle of Cynoscephalae, the key points of which we have already examined in previous chapters.[4]

The salient features for current purposes were that Philip's right-wing phalanx, properly deployed and commanded, and with the benefit of a downhill slope, was easily able to defeat the Roman legions facing it; but the battle was a meeting engagement in which Philip did not have time to fully deploy his army. His left flank met the Romans while still in marching column, and was quickly defeated (with help from elephants, this time fighting on the Roman side), not even waiting for the Romans to make contact. Polybius summarizes the situation on the Macedonian right:

> 'Philip's right wing acquitted themselves splendidly in the battle, as they were charging from higher ground and were superior in the weight of their formation, the nature of their arms also giving them a decided advantage on the present occasion.' (Polybius, 18.25)

The 'weight' of the phalanx – which as we seen does not mean its literal weight but refers to the deep and dense formation, which allowed the phalanx to advance and drive back its opponents – was too much for the Romans (the hill may have helped a little, but there is no reason to suppose it was decisive, especially since modern attempts to identify the site of the battle suggest the slopes involved were rather gentle). Macedonian arms were superior on the occasion – that is, the occasion of a straight fight, front to front. The Roman left was unable to resist the phalanx:

> 'Flamininus, seeing that his men could not sustain the charge of the phalanx, but that since his left was being forced back, some of them

having already perished and others retreating slowly, his only hope of safety lay in his right, hastened to place himself in command there.' (Polybius, 18.25)

But the Romans were able to retire while maintaining order rather than running away in headlong flight, this being (as Polybius points out at 2.33.7) a characteristic feature of Roman tactics. At this point, with each side victorious on one wing, the key Roman advantage – their multiple line system with units held in reserve – was what turned the tide:

'[O]ne of the tribunes with them [the Roman right], taking not more than twenty maniples and judging on the spur of the moment what ought to be done, contributed much to the total victory. For noticing that the Macedonians under Philip had advanced a long way in front of the rest, and were by their weight forcing back the Roman left, he quitted those on the right, who were now clearly victorious, and wheeling his force in the direction of the scene of combat and thus getting behind the Macedonians, he fell upon them in the rear.' (Polybius, 18.26)

The Macedonian right could perform no such manoeuvre, as there were no reserves and the phalanx fought in a single line, which was already engaged in pressing back the Roman left. The Romans had unengaged, independently mobile units (as well as junior commanders with the initiative to use them), and so were able to detach these and attack the Macedonian right from behind. Polybius elaborates on the effectiveness of a rear attack:

'As it is impossible for the phalanx to turn right about face or to fight man to man, he [the tribune] now pressed his attack home, killing those he found in his way, who were incapable of protecting themselves, until the whole Macedonian force were compelled to throw away their shields and take to flight.' (Polybius, 18.26)

This cannot be taken too literally; it most certainly is possible for the phalanx to face about, as we have seen, either using one of the countermarches or by a simple turn in place. But with the phalanx already engaged to its front, a countermarch of the whole phalanx would have been impossible, and while individual phalangites could certainly face about, they would lose the mass effect of the *probole*, the palisade of spears, and be forced to fight more as individuals, for which the sarissa was not at all suitable. But more to the point, an attack from the rear had a tremendous morale impact, as we saw in the previous chapter, and exacerbated a formation's natural tendency to run away from the rear. The Macedonians threw down their shields (and presumably their sarissas too) and fled (we should understand that the Romans did not form a solid perimeter, and the Macedonians could try to flee past or around them), rather than being defeated in combat. As the Roman maniples attacked, the shock to morale of the unexpected attack on their rear alone was probably enough to break the phalanx, which would then no longer have been able to offer coordinated resistance.

The aftermath of the battle is just as significant as its events. According to Polybius, 'the total Macedonian loss amounted to about eight thousand killed and not fewer than five thousand captured'. What proportion of these were phalangites, cavalry or light infantry is not recorded, but given that most of the action involved the phalanx (which was some 16,000 strong), it is likely that at least half of the phalangites were killed or captured. Philip was then completely unable to raise a new army or continue the war, and had to sue for peace and accept Rome's terms. What is more, it was a generation before Macedon was able to field another army of similar size, and that only after Philip had taken special measures to bolster the kingdom's manpower. Rome, suffering such a defeat (and the defeat at Cannae was far worse, an entire army twice the size of Philip's being destroyed), was able simply to raise a new army and try again (or at least keep fighting without risking a pitched battle). But the Macedonian army, like the Macedonian phalanx, was a one-shot weapon – either it prevailed or it was defeated for a generation.

Rome versus Seleucids

The Macedonian War was quickly followed by the next set of encounters of legion and phalanx. Antiochus III, king of the Seleucid kingdom and a long-term rival to Macedon, decided to take advantage of the power vacuum left in Greece by the Roman withdrawal after Philip's defeat, and of the disgruntlement of Rome's erstwhile allies, the Aetolians, who felt aggrieved by the peace terms, and invaded Greece with a modest expeditionary force.[5]

If Antiochus was hoping Greece would rise to support him, he was disappointed. The arrival of another large Roman army left him on the defensive, taking up a position at Thermopylae, in the same narrows where the 300 Spartans had held off the might of Persia nearly three centuries before.

Livy provides a description of Antiochus' dispositions and the nature of the fighting:

> 'Part of his light-armed troops he placed before the rampart in the front line, then he drew up the main body of the Macedonians, whom they call sarisophori [sarissa-carriers], as a bulwark around the fortification itself ... . The Macedonians standing in front of the rampart at first easily held off the Romans, who were trying the approaches from every direction, with much assistance from those who from the higher ground were hurling a veritable cloud of missiles from their slings as well as javelins and arrows at the same time; then, as a greater and more irresistible pressure was placed upon them by the enemy, driven from their places they gradually withdrew their ranks and fell back inside the fortifications; thence from the rampart they almost made another rampart of the spears held out in front of them. And the height of the rampart was so moderate that it both offered its defenders higher ground from which to fight and held the enemy within thrusting-distance below them on account of the length of the spears. Many who rashly drew near the rampart were run through; and either they would have withdrawn with their task unaccomplished or more would have perished had not Marcus Porcius, having dislodged the Aetolians from the heights of Callidromum and killed a large part of them – for he had caught them off their guard and many of them asleep – shown himself on the hill which overlooked the camp.' (Livy, 36.18)

The Romans turned the position in much the same way as the Persians had earlier, taking paths through the mountains which had been inadequately guarded. Until that happened, the key points are that the Seleucid phalangites ('Macedonians') were able to hold the Romans off, assisted by light infantry, until forced back by greater numbers, and that the sarissas formed their usual 'sort of palisade', aided in this case by the actual palisade across the narrows. In this case, the narrow space meant that the Romans were unable to carry out any small-scale manoeuvres or exploit gaps, and so were simply unable to penetrate the phalanx.

Exactly which part of the Seleucid phalanx Antiochus had with him at this battle is open to debate – possibly it was the 10,000-strong Argyraspides, successors of the Hypaspists of Alexander. If so, their feat is similar to that of the Macedonian Peltasts (the Hypaspist equivalents in the Antigonid army), who before Cynoscephalae, during the war between Rome and Philip, held a breach in the wall of the town of Atrax against an attacking Roman force. The details of that encounter bear quoting:

> 'For the Macedonians who formed the garrison, numerous and picked men, thinking that it would be a most noble exploit to defend the city with arms and valour rather than with walls, in close array, strengthening their formation by increasing the number of ranks within it, when they saw the Romans scaling the ruins, thrust them out over ground that was rough and admitted no easy retreat. The consul [Flamininus] was enraged ... and sent out cohorts, one after the other, under their standards, to pierce, if possible, with their attack the formation of the Macedonians – they themselves call it the phalanx. But in addition to the limits of space, only a little of the wall having been destroyed, the enemy had the advantage in character of weapons and in tactics. When the Macedonians in close order held before them spears of great length, and when the Romans, hurling their javelins to no purpose, had drawn their swords against this sort of *testudo*, closely-fashioned with shields, they could neither approach near enough to engage hand to hand nor cut off the ends of the spears, and if they did cut off or break any of them, the spear shaft, the broken part being itself sharp, helped, along with the points of the undamaged pikes, to make a sort of wall [*vallum*]. Moreover, the parts of the rampart that still stood protected the two flanks, nor was it possible either to retire or to charge from a distance, a manoeuvre which usually throws the ranks into disorder.' (Livy, 32.17)

A clearer description of the relative invulnerability of a formed phalanx could not be desired. Note particularly that while some modern commentators speculate that the Roman *pila* – heavy javelins carried by the legionaries – would have been highly effective in breaking up the phalanx, there is no evidence for this in any of these accounts (and 'hurling their javelins to no purpose' is explicit that they were not effective in this case). Of course, the phalanx was not invulnerable to missiles (as we will shortly see), but the use of *pila* alone by the Romans did not offer them any particular advantage against the phalanx. Rather, the Romans had to resort to their swords, and against a formed phalanx, assailed from the front, swordsmen were ineffective, because they were unable to penetrate the barricade of sarissa points (the *probole*) while the *testudo* of shields held the formation firm (this being Livy's analogy for *synaspismos*, the *testudo* or tortoise being the Roman formation of interlocked shields often used for protection from missiles in siege warfare).

Expelled from Greece after his defeat at Thermopylae, Antiochus withdrew to Asia and called up the full army of the kingdom to oppose the inevitable full-strength Roman invasion. The result – after some campaigning and battles at sea – was the Battle of Magnesia. Here the full Seleucid army met and was defeated by a Roman army in a pitched battle on favourable (flat, open) terrain, with none of the usual excuses of a meeting engagement or broken ground. What went wrong this time?

The first point is that the phalanx component of the Seleucid army, more like that of Alexander's army and unlike the very phalanx-heavy Antigonid army, was only a relatively small portion of the total army size, some 16,000–26,000 men, depending exactly which contingents were present, out of a total of 60,000–70,000. This could cut both ways. On the one hand, the auxiliary forces of cavalry and light infantry were essential to compensate for the unsuitability of a phalanx for all the types of fighting, other than pitched battle, involved in a full campaign (this is the point made by Polybius, that the phalanx was a specialist pitched battle-winning force and less useful for all the marching, foraging, raiding and besieging that war involved). On the other hand, light infantry and even cavalry could be a liability in pitched battle. The Roman and allied legions, in contrast, were good in battle and also useful for all the other aspects of warfare (particularly engineering and siege works). The Romans were jacks of all trades, perhaps, but still useful in battle, if the right circumstances presented themselves (as so far they always had).

Livy provides the best account of the Seleucid deployment at Magnesia:

> 'There were sixteen thousand infantry armed in the Macedonian fashion, who are called *phalangitae*. They formed the centre of the line, and their frontage was divided into ten sections; these sections were separated by intervals in which two elephants each were placed; from the front the formation extended thirty-two ranks in depth. This was the main strength of the king's army, and it caused great terror, not only from its general appearance, but by reason of the elephants, standing out especially conspicuously among the soldiers.'
> (Livy, 37.40)

Assuming the ten sections were evenly sized, they would be 1,600 men strong – making three *merarchiai* each, or six *syntagmata*, using the terminology of Asclepiodotus, and reminiscent perhaps of the 1,500-strong *taxeis* of

Alexander's phalanx. Why units of this size, rather than the more regular *chiliarchiai* of 1,000 men each, would have been used, we can only guess. There are a few points to note. One is this division into separate units with elephants in the gaps, an arrangement which has produced some incredulity among modern historians, who argue that as a continuous unbroken front was essential to a phalanx, this arrangement must be apocryphal. But we have already seen other occasions where the phalanx was formed into separate units alternating with (usually) lighter infantry, so I think there are no good grounds to doubt Livy's testimony on this occasion. Certainly, using elephants in the gaps was experimental and the experiment did not go well, but much in warfare is experimental, and new ideas must at some point be put to the trial of battle; if they turn out badly, there is often no second chance. Antiochus was an experienced general, and was also advised on this occasion by Hannibal, considered the greatest general of his age, and with plenty of experience in the use of elephants. This formation must have seemed a good idea at the time, and indeed it succeeded in what may have been its primary purpose, as it 'caused great terror' among the Romans. Antiochus was deploying *phobos* (fear) on his side, and if all went to plan, this might mean that any tactical niceties or differences of equipment would be moot. Also, we need not assume that gaps were left from front to back of the phalanx; rather the phalanx could have adopted something similar to the formation described in Asclepiodotus 11.7 (as a march formation), where units form up touching at the corners in a chequerboard formation, something that might possibly have been inspired by the Roman example. Elephants could then have been placed in the spaces in the front line, but the phalanx as a whole would have formed a complete line.

Finally, note that the phalanx was deployed especially deep (a point noted also in Appian's account), at thirty-two ranks. Again we can only guess what the intention was, but a deep deployment (as at Atrax or Sellasia) where the ground was limited had proved effective and also limited the frontage across which the phalanx had to fight, so reducing the number of places in which gaps could be opened up (unintentional gaps not filled with elephants, that is) or the extent to which different degrees of success could cause the phalanx to split up into separate, vulnerable parts. At this battle Antiochus need not fear outflanking, since he outnumbered the Romans (particularly in more mobile cavalry), and he may have calculated that a deep, dense and terrifying block of men breaking the Roman centre provided a better chance of victory than a longer, thinner line that might be subject to penetration at more points along its length. The calculation was a perfectly reasonable one.

The total size of the Seleucid phalanx at Magnesia is complicated by the case of the Argyraspides, the elite unit of the phalanx, often 10,000 strong. At Magnesia, Livy places these on the Seleucid right:

> 'On this side, the flank being advanced a little, was the royal bodyguard; they were called Argyraspides, from the character of their equipment; then the Dahae, mounted archers, to the number of twelve hundred; then the light infantry.' (Livy, 37.40)

Unusually, the Argyraspides are placed, not alongside the phalanx as we might expect, but beyond the Gallic and cavalry forces which formed the Seleucid right-centre. Also unusually, Livy does not give the strength of the contingent. It is possible that they were 10,000 strong, since the totals Livy gives for all other units, when added up, fall some 10,000 short of the total strength he gives for the army ('sixty thousand infantry and more than twelve thousand cavalry, Liv. 37.37) – but this difference might at least partly be accounted for by the camp guard and assorted losses, garrisons or desertions. It may also be that all 10,000 Argyraspides, if they formed the phalanx that fought at Thermopylae, were lost in Greece, since Antiochus is said to have returned from that campaign with just 500 men – though even if the unit had been wiped out (itself a remarkable occurrence), it would surely have been reconstituted from fresh recruits when the army was formed for Magnesia. My view is that we simply can't tell for certain how strong this unit was, or exactly where it was positioned. Livy's description of the deployment at Magnesia is highly problematic anyway, since he places the light infantry on the extreme flanks, where they would extend uselessly for hundreds or thousands of metres beyond the scene of the action. It is far more likely that the light forces were placed in front of the main line – as implied by Appian, *Syr.* 32 (166–7) – as an advanced skirmish force. I think it likely that there is some similar misunderstanding underlying Livy's description of the Seleucid right, hinted at perhaps by the opaque 'the flank being advanced a little', and that the Argyraspides might have had a more conventional deployment alongside the phalanx on its right, though they may well have been considerably weaker than 10,000 strong, but there is no point trying to guess a strength for them. We can at any rate discount Appian's claim that they were cavalry, since no cavalry unit called Argyraspides is known in any army, and the two Seleucid cavalry guards (the Agema and the Companions) are already accounted for; there is no need for a third.[6]

The course of the battle is clear enough, though Livy does his best to obfuscate events on the Roman left. Here, the Roman line was deployed alongside a river, and consequently had only a tiny cavalry force to protect its flank. Antiochus charged this flank with his cavalry and cataphracts (heavily armoured cavalry) and broke through the main Roman line. Livy implies only the cavalry flank guards were defeated, but clearly, not least given that Antiochus attacked with several thousand heavy cavalry (and possibly the mysterious Argyraspides), the main line infantry – at least a Latin *ala*, and perhaps the neighbouring Roman legion – were broken too. But on the Seleucid left, fortunes were reversed. Antiochus attempted the use of scythed chariots to break up the Roman line, but they proved as worthless as they usually did, were scattered by showers of missiles from the Romans' Pergamene allies, and their flight took the Seleucid flanking cavalry forces with them. This left the phalanx unsupported in the centre, the Seleucid right flank hotly pursuing the Roman fugitives back to their camp and their left flank chased off the field by the Pergamenes.

Whatever the advantages of a phalanx over the legions in a frontal contest, there is no denying its weakness when its flanks are unprotected, and now Antiochus' impetuosity, and the failure of the Seleucid left, meant that the phalanx had both flanks exposed. Livy and Appian offer slightly different accounts of what happened next, the former recording:

'The whole [Seleucid] left flank then wavered, and when the auxiliaries were broken, who were between the cavalry and those who were called the *phalangitae*, the panic spread as far as the centre. There, as soon as the ranks were thrown into disorder and the use of the very long spears – the Macedonians call them *sarisae* – was prevented by their own friends rushing among them, the Roman legions advanced and hurled their javelins into the disorganized mass. Not even the elephants posted in the intervals deterred the Roman soldiers, accustomed already by the wars in Africa both to avoid the charges of the beasts and either to assail them with spears from the side or, if they could approach closer, to hamstring them with their swords. By now almost the entire centre was being beaten back from the front and the auxiliaries flanking them were being cut down in the rear.' (Livy, 37.42)

At this point Antiochus' pursuit reached the Roman camp, where the camp guards rallied the fugitives and, with reinforcements from the main line, halted Antiochus in his tracks, in a manner reminiscent (so far as we can tell) of the intervention of the camp guards at Beneventum a century earlier.

Appian gives a different version of events:

'The Macedonian phalanx, which had been stationed between the two bodies of horse in a narrow space in the form of a square, when denuded of cavalry on either side, had opened to receive the light-armed troops, who had been skirmishing in front, and closed again. Thus crowded together, Domitius easily enclosed them with his numerous light cavalry. Having no opportunity to charge or even to deploy their dense mass, they began to suffer severely; and they were indignant that military experience availed them nothing, exposed as they were on all sides to the weapons of the enemy. Nevertheless, they presented their thick-set pikes on all four sides. They challenged the Romans to close combat and preserved at all times the appearance of being about to charge. Yet they did not advance, because they were foot-soldiers and heavily armed, and saw that the enemy were mounted. Most of all they feared to relax their close formation lest they might not readily bring it together again. The Romans did not come to close quarters nor approach them because they feared the discipline, the solidity, and the desperation of this veteran corps; but circled around them and assailed them with javelins and arrows, none of which missed their mark in the dense mass, who could neither turn the missiles aside nor dodge them. After suffering severely in this way they yielded to necessity and fell back step by step, but with a bold front, in perfect order and still formidable to the Romans. The latter kept their distance and continued to circle around and wound them, until the elephants inside the Macedonian phalanx became excited and unmanageable. Then the phalanx broke into disorderly flight.' (Appian, *Syrian War* 6.35)

Appian has the phalanx in a square (*tetragon*), though he doesn't say if he thinks they formed square when they saw their flanks defeated or were already in square. As discussed in Chapter 7, I am inclined to think it unlikely that they would have had time to form a formal square (as described by Asclepiodotus, 11.6), and more likely that Appian is talking loosely of the deep formation, though if the flanking units (perhaps whole *merarchiai*) wheeled to left and right, and if the phalanx was *amphistomos* – like Alexander's at Gaugamela – then the rear half of the phalanx could have countermarched to their rear and formed a square (strictly, a rectangle) this way in a relatively short time. Livy has the phalanx already disordered by fugitives, while Appian has them receiving the light armed among them, though this did lead to overcrowding. Finally, Livy has the Romans boldly assail the phalanx hand-to-hand, while Appian has them stand off and shoot. Appian is not usually to be preferred, but in this case Livy's attempt to gloss over the defeat of the Roman left already makes his account suspect, and based on what we know from other encounters of legion and phalanx, I suspect that Appian may be closer to the truth. The Romans would not have sought out a close-quarters encounter with the phalanx (and if they had, they would have come off badly), and it is more plausible, given that there was no hurry, that they would have avoided close combat, kept a safe distance, made use of their greater mobility and showered the phalanx with missiles (which could have included the *pila* of the legionaries as well as the arrows and javelins of the cavalry, which Appian describes). Even then, Appian tells us, the phalanx was withdrawing in good order (which implies that the surrounding Romans fell back before it), but the elephant experiment then proved its downfall – elephants being notorious for becoming unruly when annoyed by missiles – and the combination of an attempted withdrawal, the crowding of light infantry fugitives and the panic of the elephants would all have been enough to break up the formation. *Phobos* in the event did intervene, but in favour of the Romans, and the phalanx broke and fled. Its defensive formation lost, it would have been easy prey to the pursuing Romans.

In this battle, conditions of terrain and deployment were all in favour of the phalanx, and (discounting Livy) the Roman infantry were indeed unable to make any headway against it. But the phalanx was only a part of the army, and the defeat of the Seleucid flanking forces – and their impetuous pursuit off the field – left the phalanx surrounded, outnumbered and subject to missile attack. The presence of the elephants then proved unfortunate, and yet again the phalanx fell apart without really being put to the test.

Rome versus Macedon again

With the Seleucids and Antigonids both defeated, a period of relative peace ensued, but the Romans were never happy with the idea of strong independent neighbours who could even in principle offer any resistance to their authority, so another war with Macedon was inevitable. It came during the rule of Philip V's son, Perseus. As we have seen, Philip put in place measures to restore the manpower of the Macedonian kingdom, and this succeeded so well that Perseus, at the grand parade he held at the outset of the campaign, was able to field a phalanx 20,000 men strong (Liv. 42.51.3–11), with an additional 5,000

Peltasts, by some margin the largest single phalanx ever fielded by Macedon. As before, there was a period of manoeuvre in which Perseus attempted to defend the frontiers of the country, but eventually matters came to a head and a decisive pitched battle at Pydna. [7]

Pydna is a rather unusual battle in many ways. There are two good literary accounts of it, but both with their own problems. Livy's account, taken from Polybius, has a large gap just at the crucial point where the engagement began. That of Plutarch is complete, but discursive, anecdotal and vague. As a result, I believe the battle has often been misunderstood. It is frequently viewed as a set-piece pitched battle between two fully deployed armies, but I think it is clear that in fact it was more of a meeting engagement, like Cynoscephalae, except that here the armies met as they deployed from camp, rather than on the march.

The armies had been encamped in close proximity to each other before the battle, sharing water from shallow streams running across the intervening space. As usual, skirmishes took place over the water, and on the day of the battle, one of these skirmishes (rather like those that opened the Battle of Cynoscephalae) turned into a general engagement as each side committed reinforcements. On the Roman side, the first main-line units to engage were some cohorts of Italian allies (Marrucinians and Paelignians) who had been stationed in advance, while on the Macedonian side, the Peltasts hurried to assist their Thracian skirmishers. Plutarch describes what happened (though he presents it in his muddled account as if it was part of the general engagement between the main lines):

'The Romans when they attacked the phalanx were unable to force a passage and Salvius, the commander of the Paelignians, snatched their standard and hurled it in amongst the enemy. Then the Paelignians, since among the Italians it is an unnatural and flagrant thing to abandon a standard, rushed on towards the place where it was, and dreadful losses were inflicted and suffered on both sides. For the Romans tried to thrust aside the sarissas with their swords, or to crowd them back with their shields, or to push them aside with their hands, while the Macedonians, holding them fiercely advanced with both hands and piercing those who fell upon them arms and all, since neither shield nor armour could withstand the force of the sarissa, hurled headlong back the Paelignians and the Marrucinians, who with no consideration but with animal fury rushed upon the strokes that met them and a certain death.' (Plutarch, *Aemilius* 20.1–2)

Again we see the same pattern as before: in a frontal encounter, Romans (so far as we know, Rome's Italian allies were armed identically to the Romans themselves, so it is simplest to refer to them all as Romans) could try to push aside or cut a way through the fence of sarissas, but such attempts were doomed to failure and just led to heavy losses among the Roman forces. Livy (after the gap in his narrative) refers back to the same incident:

> 'If they [the Romans] had attacked frontally in solid line against an orderly phalanx, as happened to the Paelignians who at the beginning of the battle recklessly met the *caetrati* [Peltasts], the Romans would have spitted themselves on the spears and would not have withstood the solid line.' (Livy, 44.41.9)

As the Peltasts were attacking the Roman outposts, the main Macedonian phalanx, and all the Roman army, were hurriedly deploying from their camps:

> 'As these [the Peltasts and others] took their places in the line they were illumined by the phalanx of the Bronze Shields [Chalcaspides], issuing from the camp behind them and filling the plain with the gleam of iron and the glitter of bronze, and the hills with the tumultuous shouts of their cheering. And with such boldness and swiftness did they advance that the first to be slain fell only two stades [360 metres] from the Roman camp.' (Plutarch, *Aemilius* 18.4)

There is no suggestion that the Macedonians halted their advance to wait for the full army to deploy; on the contrary, the Peltasts are said to have advanced very swiftly. So I believe that the Macedonian phalanx – consisting of the Chalcaspides on the left and (probably) the Leucaspides (White Shields) on the right – deployed hastily to support the already advancing Peltasts, and the Macedonian cavalry (who are not mentioned in either account of the battle) might not have deployed at all. The Roman legions also deployed from their camp and encountered the phalanx, but they did not attempt to engage it face-to-face, as Livy makes clear ('*if* they had attacked frontally in solid line', Liv. 41.9), and only the Peltasts engaged frontally, as Plutarch states ('those in the Macedonian *agemata* [that is, the Peltasts] had already planted the points of their sarissas in the shields of the Romans, who were thus prevented from reaching them with their swords', Plut. *Aem.* 19.1). Rather, the Romans avoided contact:

> 'When the foremost units [the Paelignian and Marrucinian cohorts] had thus been cut to pieces, and those arrayed behind them were beaten back; and though there was no flight still they retired towards the hill called Olocros, so that even Aemilius, as Poseidonios tells us, when he saw it rent his garments, for this part of his army was retreating, and the other Romans were turning aside from the phalanx, which gave them no access to it, but confronted them with dense sarissas like a barricade and was everywhere unassailable.' (Plutarch, *Aemilius* 20.3)

Plutarch also quotes Polybius on Aemilius' fear at the sight of the phalanx:

> 'And when he saw the other Macedonians [that is, the main phalanx] drawing round their shields from their shoulders and with sarissas set at one level withstanding his shield bearers, and when he saw the strength of their locked shields [*synaspismos*] and the sharpness of their projecting spears [*probole*], amazement and fear took possession of him, and he felt that he had never seen a sight more fearful. Often in after times he used to speak of his emotions at that time and of what he saw.' (Plutarch, *Aemilius* 19.1)

Polybius' own account is lost, though a fragment recounting the same survives:

> 'Aemilius the consul, who had never seen a phalanx until this occasion in the war with Perseus, often confessed afterwards to certain persons in Rome that he had never seen anything more terrible and dreadful than a Macedonian phalanx, and this although he had witnessed and directed as many battles as any man.' (Polybius, 29.17)

So *phobos* was playing its part again, on the Macedonian side for now, and the phalanx, unassailable and terrifying, advanced unhindered as the Romans fell back before it.

But now three things happened that turned the tide of the battle. Firstly, the Macedonian extreme left (those forces including Thracians which had started the battle) gave way before the Roman right, supported by elephants (this time it was the Romans again who had elephants on their side). Then the Peltasts advanced so far and so fast that they lost contact with the Chalcaspides, leaving a large gap in the Macedonian line, into which the more manoeuvrable Romans marched:

> 'The legion filled the gap between the Peltasts and the phalanx and broke the enemy line. In the rear were the Peltasts; the consul faced *clupeati* – these were called Chalcaspides.' (Livy, 44.41.1–2)

The Peltasts were in the rear of the legion (we know they weren't in the rear of the Macedonian line, since we know they advanced rapidly and were the leading Macedonian unit). The word Livy uses to describe the Chalcaspides, *clupeati* or *clipeati*, distinguishes them by their larger shields from the Peltasts – which Livy calls, in Latin, *caetrati*; note the same grouping of *caetrati* (peltasts) and *clipeati* (hoplites, phalangites) in the Achaean army in 197 (Liv. 43.15.10). Presumably, Aemilius went on to attack the Chalcaspides in the flank (and eventually the Peltasts in the rear), though Livy does not stop to describe these events. Instead, he goes on to the rest of the Macedonian line: 'L. Albinus the ex-consul was ordered to lead the second legion against the Leucaspides phalanx; this was the centre of the enemy line' (Liv.44.41.2). He continues: 'In the centre the charge of the second legion scattered the phalanx' (Liv. 44.41.6). Figure 9.2 schematically illustrates the situation.

Both Livy and Plutarch provide some further ruminations on this contest of the second legion and the Leucaspides:

> 'No reason for this victory was more obvious than the fact that there were many scattered engagements which first threw into confusion and then broke up the wavering phalanx, which when closed up and bristling with spears extended is irresistible; but if by attacks at several points you compel them to swing their spears about, unwieldy because of their length and weight, they become tangled in a haphazard mass, and if indeed some sort of uproar is heard on a flank or from the rear they are involved in utter confusion. Such was the case when the phalanx was compelled to meet the Romans attacking in groups while the Macedonian line was broken at many points and the Romans, wherever gaps presented themselves, kept infiltrating their lines.' (Livy, 44.41.6–7)

> 'But the ground was uneven, and because of the length of the line of battle they could not maintain their locked shields [*synaspismos*];

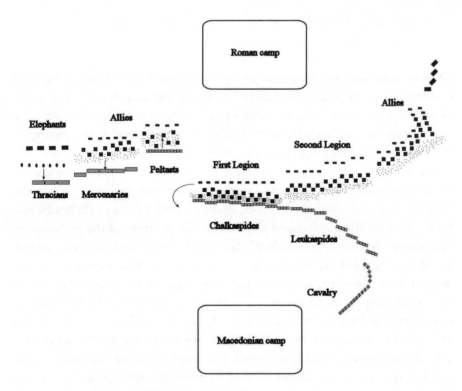

Fig. 9.2. The Battle of Pydna.

and he [Aemilius] saw the phalanx of the Macedonians getting many breaks and gaps in it, as is natural when armies are large and the efforts of the combatants are diversified; portions of it were hard pressed, and other portions were advancing. Thereupon he came up swiftly, and dividing up his maniples ordered them to plunge quickly into the gaps and spaces in the enemy line and so come to close quarters, not fighting a single battle against them all, but many separate and successive battles. These instructions being given by Aemilius to his officers, and by his officers to the soldiers, as soon as they got between the enemy and separated them they attacked some of them in the flank where their arms did not shield them, and cut off others by falling upon their rear, and the strength and efficiency of the phalanx was lost when it was thus broken up; and now that the Macedonians fought man to man or in small detachments, they could only hack with their small daggers against the firm shields of the Romans, and oppose little *peltai* to their swords which, such was their weight and momentum, penetrated through all their arms to their bodies. They therefore made a poor resistance and at last were routed.' (Plutarch, *Aemilius* 20.4–5)

The evidence here for Macedonian equipment we have already considered in earlier chapters. The important points are the reasons given for the defeat of the phalanx. Only Plutarch mentions that 'the ground was uneven', and more significant is clearly the scattered nature of the engagement. Inasmuch as these observations apply to the fight of the first legion against the Chalcaspides as they do to the second legion against the Leucaspides, the often large gaps that had opened in the Macedonian line were due to the uncontrolled, uncoordinated and excessively rapid nature of their advance. So we see a similar pattern as at Cynoscephalae: portions of the Macedonian line became detached, so that the phalanx had internal flanks exposed, as well as the two flanks at extreme left and right, and into these gaps the Romans were able to penetrate, while the scattered fighting by small units, rather than solid continuous phalanxes on both sides, meant that the Macedonian line inevitably became further disjointed, just as Polybius describes in his analysis. The small, mobile, independent and better-led Roman units were able to take advantage of this, attack the inner flanks of the phalanx and break it apart. It is sometimes claimed by modern writers that the Romans deliberately withdrew to tempt the Macedonians forward onto rough ground, but this is clearly not so. It is unlikely that terrain was at all significant in this battle, and even if it was, the Roman retreat was clearly involuntary and a source of great distress to Aemilius, caused by their inability to tackle the phalanx frontally while it maintained its order.

A meeting engagement of this sort makes better sense of the accounts of the battle, and makes Pydna similar in many ways to Cynoscephalae. It also explains the failure of the Macedonian cavalry to make any intervention – they may simply not yet have fully deployed from the camp by the time the phalanx was defeated – and the disputed role of Perseus himself. Polybius, relentlessly hostile to the Macedonian kings, accused Perseus of running away and abandoning the phalanx to its fate, but it may be rather that he was not even present when the order was given for the phalanx to deploy. If Perseus was absent from camp (performing religious ceremonies in nearby Pydna, according to one account), then it could have been subordinate commanders who gave the order for a general engagement. This may be surprising, but a similar thing had nearly happened earlier in the campaign when after the primarily cavalry victory over the Romans at Callinicus, Hippias and Leonnatus, commanders of the phalanx and the Agema (Peltasts), 'had brought the phalanx up swiftly on their own initiative in order not to fail the bold beginning, after they had received a report that the cavalry had won their battle' (Liv. 42.59.7). A full engagement was avoided on that occasion only because Perseus was persuaded to step in and hold the phalanx back. As always, having subordinates willing to act on their own initiative can be a two-edged sword.

So Pydna can be seen to fit in well with the other battles of legion against phalanx: the phalanx (especially the Peltasts) was totally successful in driving back the Romans in a face-to-face encounter, but the long line and lack of reserves, and the varied fortunes of different parts of the line across the battlefield, meant that parts of the phalanx became detached from each other, and into the resulting gaps the Romans were able to penetrate with their small, manoeuvrable, independent maniples, causing the phalanx to collapse. Terrain was not decisive or even especially important at Pydna, and conditions were highly favourable for the phalanx, but the inherent weakness of a single continuous line proved to be the Macedonians' undoing, as Polybus correctly identified.

Finally, the Romans put their other great advantage – that of greater manpower reserves – to effect after Pydna as after Cynoscephalae and Magnesia, with the systematic slaughter of the fleeing Macedonians, including those who tried to surrender. It had taken twenty years for Macedonian manpower to recover after Philip V's defeat, and it was never to recover after Pydna. So Pydna spelled the end of the Macedonian kingdom, but it was not quite the end for the Macedonian phalanx.

The last Macedonian phalanxes

With the Antigonid kingdom defeated, Macedon itself did not field another phalanx – or at least, not one for which we have any detail. A failed Macedonian uprising under the pretender Andriscus (or 'Pseudophilip', since he claimed to be Perseus' son Philip) led to an initial victory over a Roman army followed by a final defeat. A Macedonian phalanx may well have fought in these battles, but we have no information about either battle or army. The Achaeans – presumably still armed in Macedonian fashion – also tried their luck alone against Rome in 146, and met a similar (and similarly badly documented) fate. But the phalanx remained the core of the Seleucid and (so far as we can tell – there is very little detailed information) Ptolemaic armies, and also of such minor armies as served the independent or semi-independent kingdoms of Western Asia through the rest of the second and first centuries.

For the Seleucids, we have one detailed description of the army after Magnesia, that of the parade at Daphne held by Antiochus IV and described by Polybius. Here there were, among other forces, 'twenty thousand Macedonians of whom ten thousand bore golden shields, five thousand bronze shields and the rest silver shields' (Pol. 30.25). (As noted before, the text of this passage is corrupt and 'golden shields' is a most uncertain reading.)[8]

Also at the parade were 'five thousand men in the prime of life armed after the Roman fashion' (Pol. 30.25), evidence of an attempt by the Seleucids to adopt, at least to some extent, the weapons of the Romans who had defeated them. How far this rearmament went is very uncertain – there is no strong evidence for Roman-armed forces in either the Seleucid or Ptolemaic armies. Such evidence as there is consists of some depictions of chainmail-equipped infantry (in tomb paintings and also in literary accounts, particularly of the long Seleucid attempt to subdue rebellious Judaea after the Maccabean revolt) and in some similarities between unit names found in the tacticians (chiefly Asclepiodotus) and documentary sources, and the Roman centuries and maniples, together with the use of standards and standard bearers attested by the tacticians. So far as the latter points go, I think it is far from certain that naming a unit a 'hundred' (a 'century') is evidence of copying Roman practice, since number-based unit names, especially the *chiliarchia* or 'thousand', had long been a feature of Macedonian and Hellenistic practice. I also do not believe that standard bearers were copying Roman practice, since there are earlier depictions of standards in Hellenistic art, and all of the officers, including standard bearers, described by the tacticians are very clearly a part of a Macedonian-armed phalanx, as discussed in Chapter 3. As to the former point, chain mail was certainly a feature of Roman equipment but it was also widely used by Gallic infantry (and cavalry), and Greece, Macedon and Asia Minor were subject to Gallic invasions in the early third century, with Gallic settlers becoming permanently established in Asia Minor and forming regular contingents in Seleucid and Ptolemaic armies. I therefore think it just as likely that descriptions and depictions of chain mail had a Gallic inspiration as a Roman one, and chain mail may simply have become more widely adopted by Hellenistic armies as its advantages became apparent.[9]

So while there may have been experiments with adopting Roman equipment, I do not believe they were ever on a large scale, and most importantly, there is little evidence that they also involved adopting Roman organization or tactics at the army level. It is most likely that the phalanx remained the mainstay of all Hellenistic armies, such as they were, into the first century.

But the importance of such armies declined precipitously as a combination of native revolts against foreign rule, incessant civil wars and infighting among the Hellenistic royal families and ruling classes, and the rise of the Parthian kingdom in the old Persian heartlands drained the surviving kingdoms of their strength, while Roman attention (and hence, detailed literary accounts) was elsewhere, in their own relentless march toward civil war.

The last Macedonian phalanx we hear of to take the field – once more, facing the Roman legions – was that of the kingdom of Pontus in Asia Minor, one of the initially small kingdoms to fill the vacuum left by Seleucid withdrawal and temporary Roman lack of interest. Under its ambitious and not exactly likable king Mithridates VI (a ruler of a kingdom and army with strong Hellenistic traditions, successfully combined with Persian heritage), Pontus was to gain power over most of Asia Minor and, like Antiochus III, launch an ill-fated invasion of Greece in an attempt to take advantage of Greek resentment at Roman rule. The campaign that followed led to the final pitched battle between Macedonian phalanx and Roman legion, and fittingly it was to be fought at Chaeronea, near to the scene of the first great victory of the Macedonian phalanx, the defeat of the Athenians and Thebans by Philip II nearly three centuries earlier, at the dawn of the phalanx's period of dominance.[10]

Details of the Pontic army and the course of the battle are scarce, as we are forced to rely on the typically inadequate account of Plutarch (who himself had a good source in the memoirs of Sulla, the Roman commander, but Sulla's estimates of Pontic strength and of his own importance are no more to be trusted than Plutarch's). At any rate, the Pontic army included 'fifteen thousand slaves, whom the king's generals had set free by proclamation in the cities and enrolled among the hoplites' (Plut. *Sull.* 18.5). The cities in question were presumably the Greek cities of Asia Minor. Romans were totally confident in their inherent superiority to slaves, who were conceived of as effectively inferior beings, but a modern audience might be more inclined to expect men fighting for their own new-found freedom to do so with special determination, and this indeed was to prove the case. Plutarch describes events:

> 'Thereupon the infantry forces engaged, the Barbarians holding their sarissas before them at full length, and endeavouring, by locking their shields together, to keep their line of battle intact; while the Romans threw down their javelins, drew their swords, and sought to dash the pikes aside, that they might get at their enemies as soon as possible, in the fury that possessed them.' (Plutarch, *Sulla* 18.4)

In Plutarch's Greek we see again the two characteristic features of the phalanx, the *probole* (projection) of spears and the *synaspismos* (locked shields), and the encounter takes the familiar form already seen in previous battles, with the Romans attempting (unsuccessfully) to cut a way through the fence of pike points. Whether the Romans really 'threw down' their javelins (*pila*), rather than this being Plutarch's misunderstanding of the Romans throwing them at the enemy, is open to doubt. At any rate, at this stage the javelins had no discernible effect:

> 'These men, however [the phalangites], owing to the depth and density of their array, and the unnatural courage with which they held their ground, were only slowly repulsed by the Roman hoplites.' (Plutarch, *Sulla* 18.6)

The Romans may have regarded courage among ex-slaves as unnatural, but a newly recruited slave army must have lacked those features most essential to the successful conduct of phalanx fighting, that is discipline, training and experience, and it is no doubt this, rather than any tactical or equipment differences, that allowed the Romans eventually to prevail, combined with one more curious feature:

> '[A]t last the sling stones and the javelins which the Romans in the rear ranks plied unsparingly, threw them [the phalangites] into confusion and drove them back.' (Plutarch, *Sulla* 18.6)

In this case the 'sling stones' are mistranslated in the Loeb translation as 'fiery bolts' (due to an apparent misidentification of the word Plutarch uses on this occasion, *belosphendonai*, literally 'sling missiles', with the *phalarica*, a heavy javelin or catapult bolt that could be set alight for use in sieges). The javelins are *grosphoi*, used by the Roman light infantry or *velites*, distinct from the *hussoi*, or *pila*, that the Roman legionaries had earlier 'thrown down'. So on this occasion, unusually, missile weapons did play an important part in the defeat of the phalanx, though comparison with the events of Magnesia suggest that this was due more to the inexperience of the phalangites than to any inherent vulnerability of the phalanx.

This might not have been quite the end for the Pontic phalanx, since Plutarch also refers to a unit of Pontic 'bronze shields' at the same battle (Plut. *Sull.* 19.2), but exactly who they were and what they did, or how they were defeated, remains obscured by Plutarch's vague account of the battle. Presumably this was the main Pontic phalanx of regulars.

So the second Battle of Chaeronea (86) was to be the last appearance of the Macedonian phalanx on an ancient battlefield, or at least on one about which we have sufficient information to draw any conclusions. In later battles of the Mithridatic wars (which dragged on for another decade as a succession of Roman generals sought personal glory in victories against a succession of implausibly vast Pontic armies or their allies), the Pontic infantry may have been rearmed in Roman style. Appian states that they adopted Roman organization:

> '[Mithridates] selected the bravest to the number of about 70,000 foot and half that number of horse and dismissed the rest. He divided them into companies [*ilas*] and cohorts [*speiras*] as nearly as possible according to the Italian system, and turned them over to Pontic officers to be trained.' (Appian, *Mithridates* 87)

This would make little sense if they continued to carry their original arms, so these are generally taken to be 'imitation legionaries', that is Greek or native infantry armed in the Roman (rather than Macedonian) fashion, like those in the Seleucid army parade at Daphne or the possible Ptolemaic reformed infantry. Naturally enough, with no experience of fighting in this fashion and no cultural tradition for it, these legionaries did not prove a success.

This was not quite the last outing for a Macedonian phalanx, as over 200 years later, Caracalla, the eccentric Roman Emperor and Alexander the Great enthusiast, was to form a Macedonian phalanx of his own, but this was long after the end of the phalanx's dominance of the ancient battlefield, and there is no evidence that Caracalla's phalanx ever saw action. The Roman legion had proven triumphant time and again, and it was the legion that was to dominate European battlefields, and the imagination of European historians, for the next several centuries.

Legion and phalanx

So the legion was victorious over the phalanx on almost every occasion where they met after the reign of Pyrrhus. Yet we cannot conclude that the legion was the superior weapon system, since in terms of the direct face-to-face encounter, the phalanx was always dominant. While the decline and eventual collapse of the Hellenistic kingdoms and the end of any semblance of Greek independence meant that there were a declining number of armies with any tradition of fighting this way, even so the phalanx remained the mainstay of Hellenistic armies for a century after the defeat at Pydna. It was the political decline of the kingdoms and their eventual absorption by Rome that saw the phalanx finally disappear from the battlefield, rather than adoption of Roman weapons and tactics. Despite the string of defeats, the phalanx remained central to military thought in the East until Roman domination became complete.

Returning to Polybius' analysis, I think that his emphasis on the need for flat, open, unimpeded terrain was overstated, and it was easier for a phalanx to find suitable terrain on which to fight than he claims. Yet even when it did so, the phalanx still lost. The reasons for this are primarily due to the second part of Polybius' argument, that the Romans had a flexible deployment of small units with large parts of the army held in reserve, and this allowed them, both on the local and grand tactical level, to exploit gaps in the phalanx which occurred naturally in the course of a large and often chaotic battle. The phalanx too was divided into small units, but they were not intended for independent action, and all their drill and manoeuvres were directed toward maintaining a strict formation. The use by the legions of independent units and reserves was what made the real difference – and of course, the weakness of the phalanx on its open flanks was due to the method of armament and drill, which placed a barricade of pike points to the front but was ill-suited to fighting in different or unexpected directions. Polybius' further point, that the phalanx was a specialist battle-winning force while the Roman legionaries were generalists better able to cope with all the varied circumstances of war, is also very valid. However, Hellenistic armies were usually able to overcome this drawback by using large numbers of light infantry and cavalry alongside the phalanx. The drawback here is that, as at Magnesia, such forces could become a liability, while an army like that of Perseus with a very high proportion of phalangites was a one-shot weapon, dependent on a single initial success in pitched battle.

So this tactical, technical explanation does have considerable explanatory force as to why the legion was able to prevail over the phalanx. But it is not the only explanation. An alternative (or rather complementary) explanation we have already seen, that the Romans were able to put larger armies into the field, and were able to keep producing new armies to make up losses even after catastrophic defeats. The reasons why Rome was able to draw upon such large reserves of manpower are varied, and beyond the scope of this book, but we can note some general features. One is that the Macedonians too were demographically strong in the early years, producing an army large enough to conquer Greece under Philip II, and under Alexander to conquer and settle the whole of the Persian Empire while still holding sway over Greece against a series of major revolts. The period of the Successors saw huge armies with at least a Macedonian core campaigning throughout Asia, and large numbers of Macedonians and other Greeks settling permanently in the new kingdoms. The period ended with a damaging Gallic invasion that overran Macedon itself. Inevitably all of this must have drained Macedonian manpower, and though opinions are divided as to exactly how damaging to overall Macedonian strength this sequence of events must have been, it did at least mean that the manpower base on which the later Antigonid kings could draw to oppose Rome was smaller than it could have been, while the Seleucid and Ptolemaic kings drew their armies (at least the heavy infantry components) from the relatively thin layer of Greco-Macedonian settlers holding down a much larger, and militarily largely excluded, native population.

This point is perhaps of greatest importance. The Romans had a large manpower reserve from Latium itself, the Roman heartland, but this they supplemented with the populations of the allies. Every Roman army was 50 per cent Romans proper and 50 per cent allies, armed and fighting, so far as we can tell, in the same way and acting as a combined and homogeneous whole. But the Hellenistic kingdoms always drew their heavy infantry forces strictly from the Macedonian populations, or in the case of the Asian kingdoms their Greco-Macedonian settlers (or their descendants). Although the Antigonid kings were politically dominant in Greece, and Greek armies such as the Achaeans and Spartans eventually adopted Macedonian armament, no Macedonian king ever incorporated Greeks into the Macedonian phalanx proper, or even had them fighting alongside the phalanx on equal terms. Allied or mercenary forces were used as auxiliaries, specialist light infantry or for garrisons, but the phalanx remained exclusively ethnically Macedonian (for the Antigonids), or drawn from the Greco-Macedonian settlers (for the Asian kingdoms). The pattern established by Alexander – where the Macedonian phalanx was the key battle-winning infantry force and the allied hoplites played a role so subordinate that they are barely even mentioned by the Alexander historians – was continued by all the Hellenistic kings. There was no attempt to set up in Greece a system equivalent to that of the Roman allies, while the Asian kingdoms did not draw on their reserves of native manpower until forced to do so, in the case of the Ptolemies before Raphia, with serious consequences in terms of internal stability. This feature of the Hellenistic kingdoms – the way that, for internal political reasons, they reserved service in the heavy infantry as a privilege for a special class of citizens – differs markedly from the Roman practice of absorbing neighbouring peoples into their armies as (more or less) equals, and is the primary underlying reason why the Hellenistic kings could usually only draw on one army at a time, and when that army was defeated, the war was lost.

So there were two major factors giving legion-based armies a crucial advantage over phalanx-based ones: the tactical one, where the greater flexibility and resilience of the legion proved superior to the powerful but brittle phalanx, and the demographic and political one, in which large popular armies faced an ethnically and economically distinct, and therefore small, military class.

One more technical aspect should be considered – the generalship of the opposing Roman and Macedonian (and Seleucid and Pontic) commanders. We have already seen in Chapter 6 the importance of the technical, tactical skill both of junior commanders, to carry out the complex drills required for the effective operation of the phalanx, and senior commanders, up to the level of the king (Pyrrhus, Philip V, Perseus, Antiochus III) or commanding general (Archelaus, for Mithridates), to coordinate the grand tactical manoeuvres of the phalanx and its accompanying combined-arms forces. Could it be that the Romans had an advantage in this area, and that inferior generalship was to blame for the ultimate defeat of the phalanx?

I do not believe there is any evidence that there was a lack of experience or skill at the level of the junior commanders. The importance of tactical training has already been touched upon, and gave rise to the tradition of tactical writing (albeit in a somewhat stylized form) that influenced warfare right up to the seventeenth century AD. Junior phalanx commanders in armies that saw little action (such as the Ptolemaic army, perhaps) might have lost some of their edge, particularly if command became more or less hereditary, but the Macedonian and Seleucid armies at least saw long-term service and officers had ample opportunity to perfect and practise their skills. It might be more relevant that the simple drills (possibly non-existent, if we reject the complex 'line relief' manoeuvres proposed by modern authors) of the Roman army placed fewer demands on Roman junior officers, and provided less that could go wrong. The key characteristics of Roman junior commanders in the later Republic, the famed and feared centurions, were aggression, stubbornness and devotion to duty, rather than any tactical skills. The Roman army generally was suited more to a soldier's battle, where the fighting skills of the individual legionaries were paramount, than a general's battle, where tactical ploys could decide the outcome. This Roman emphasis on straightforward tactics and fighting skills is reflected in the way that the phalanx could collapse when its drills and manoeuvres failed to maintain a coherent formation, while the Roman army was better able to win the day through hard fighting.

At the level of the commanding general, the picture is more complex. Roman consuls, the commanders of Roman armies, were originally political appointees, often with little practical experience and correspondingly limited technical and tactical skill. Only in the course of the Second Punic War, after a succession of defeats at the hands of Hannibal (himself considered, in antiquity, to be a master tactician), did the Romans seek to improve the professionalism of their commanders and to make appointments accordingly. The consuls who fought and defeated the Macedonian phalanx from the second century (so not including those who faced Pyrrhus) were specially selected for their leadership and generalship abilities (though political and familial connections still helped, of course). On the side of the phalanx, Alexander the Great himself was of course considered in antiquity to be one of the greatest, if not *the* greatest, generals of all, while Philip II was also very highly regarded, especially for his organizational and political skills. But the generals who faced the Romans are often thought of, particularly by modern authors, as of inferior calibre, lacking that mysterious quality – so easy to identify in a successful commander, but so hard to pin down in terms of actual skill sets – of 'military genius'. So it is tempting to see the crucial difference between the successes of Alexander and the failures of Philip V, Perseus and Antiochus III as down to a failure of generalship (leading to much speculation, among ancients and moderns alike, as to what would have happened if Alexander had commanded an army against the Romans).

I am not convinced, however, that this explanation is sufficient. In terms of leadership, Philip V and Perseus were able to inspire great enthusiasm among their men, as we saw in previous chapters, and Antiochus was so successful in his campaigns to reconquer the detached parts of his kingdom that he became known in antiquity, like Alexander, as 'the Great'. Archelaus, for his part, was Mithridates' favourite general and had a long and distinguished career. It is far from certain that any of these figures were really inferior generals (inferior to the average, at least), in terms either of leadership or tactical skill. Certainly Alexander possessed the charisma, quick thinking, decisiveness, coolness under pressure and inventiveness required of a great (and successful) general, but when it comes to the actual showdown, in pitched battle, of phalanx against legion, it is not clear that the later commanders lacked any of the required skills or abilities to ensure success or avoid failure with any degree of certainty. Alexander was successful in his battles against Persians and Greeks, but how much this was due to his abilities, and how much to the fact that the Persians and Greeks had inferior equipment and tactical systems, is difficult to quantify. It is tempting to consider a victorious general a genius and a defeated general a fool, but in terms of actual battlefield command and tactics, it is not always easy to define the difference. Certainly the later generals committed errors: Philip V and

Perseus in engaging before their phalanxes were fully deployed, Antiochus in pursuing the fleeing enemy rather than exploiting his success. But Alexander at Gaugamela also pursued the fleeing Persians and relied on the ability of his subordinate (Parmenion) and the fighting qualities of his men. Meanwhile, Polybius criticizes the very notion that Alexander would have been so rash as to have committed his phalanx at Issus across a river, although this does seem to be what happened, and the phalanx may have come close to defeat, being saved only by the outflanking manoeuvre discussed in Chapter 7. If the phalanx had not survived its dislocation at Gaugamela or the river crossing at Issus, we might find grounds to blame Alexander's actions, as we do Philip's at Cynoscephalae or Antiochus' at Magnesia, and the extent to which the phalanx's success under Alexander was due to his abilities rather than the qualities of the rank and file and their junior commanders is disputed, and was disputed in antiquity, forming, we are told, one of the roots of the fatal argument between Alexander and his general Cleitus (Arr. *Anab.* 4.8). Certainly the commanding general could make a difference to the outcome of a battle, and (what can be seen with hindsight to be) mistakes could be made that would contribute to defeat, but I don't think it is clear that the defeat of the phalanx at the hands of the legion was due primarily to command failure at the senior level.

But alongside these technical explanations (manpower, tactics, weapons, generalship), favoured by historians in the Greek tradition such as Polybius, there is another strand of explanation, one favoured by historians in the Latin tradition, exemplified by Livy, and while we might not give this explanation too much credence, it should be considered. This is that the Romans were, on the individual level, better men than the Greeks, Macedonians and their Asian-settled descendents – that they were braver, stronger, more warlike and determined, that they were imbued with greater *virtus*, to use the Latin term, a word carrying meanings of manliness (literally, from *vir*, man) as well as the sense of its modern derivation, virtue.

To the ancients, it was taken for granted that some ethnic groups were militarily superior to others (or at least, better in certain specific types of fighting). Ethnic stereotypes of this kind are found throughout the literature, and a most important distinction was those who were most able to stand and fight face-to-face in pitched battle, as opposed to those who preferred to fight at a distance. As we have already seen, the Macedonians had a high reputation in this regard – at least from the time of Philip II. We might now be less inclined to see these as ethnic differences, and more cultural, though this is not a distinction that an ancient writer would have made. It was also the case that the military prowess of peoples was expected to rise and fall over time, and it was thought that the Macedonians, from their high point under Philip and Alexander, had declined by the time of their confrontations with Rome. This was particularly true of the Greco-Macedonians settled in Asia, who were regarded (by the Romans) as having become spoiled by Eastern decadence (to use the widespread stereotype of the time) and therefore making inferior soldiers.

Of course some caution is necessary in considering views of this sort, and we find this attitude expressed most often in pre-battle speeches put in the mouths of generals by later historians. Great care must be taken when using such speeches, and besides, a speech to an army about to go into battle is more likely to be intended to boost the men's morale than to give a fair assessment of historical reality. Even so, they can tell us something about Roman attitudes to their enemies. An example is Flamininus' exhortation to his army at Cynoscephalae – he reminded his men of recent successes against the Macedonians (in forcing the passes they had been defending to keep the Romans out of eastern Greece) and observed that 'the Macedonian kingdom rested on reputation and not on strength, and that even this reputation had at last wholly faded away' (Liv. 33.8.5).

This was said of the Macedonians, for whose martial history the Romans did have some respect. But in the case of the Seleucid army, the Romans preferred to ignore their Greco-Macedonian descent anyway, as the story Flamininus told of how the Seleucid army was like a cleverly disguised dinner using variously seasoned pork in place of a variety of game:

> 'This, he said, could be well applied to the forces of the king, about which there had been so much bragging a little while ago; the different kinds of weapons, the many names of unheard-of peoples, Dahae and Medes and Cadusians and Elymaeans – these were all Syrians, far better fitted to be slaves, on account of their servile dispositions, than to be a race of warriors.' (Livy, 35.49)

Plutarch tells a variant of the story:

> '"And so in your case," said he, "men of Achaia, do not be astonished when you hear of the Spear-bearers [*longchephoroi*] and Lance-bearers [*xustophoroi*] and Foot-companions [*pezhetairoi*] in the army of

Antiochus; for they are all Syrians and differ only in the way they are armed.'" (Plutarch, *Flamininus* 17.5)

The consul Acilius Glabrio contrasted Antiochus' army with that of Philip:

'[T]he hostile army [of Philip] was more numerous and made up of far better soldiery; there were in that army Macedonians, Thracians and Illyrians, all very warlike tribes; here there are Syrians and Asiatic Greeks, the meanest of mankind, and born only for slavery.' (Livy, 36.17)

The Roman view was that they, the Romans, were the better men, with greater *virtus*, and also we should note, that they had manifest destiny on their side, that Rome was predestined to dominate the known world. We might also note that Roman culture was unusually violent and brutal (the preferred forms of mass entertainment in Greece were drama and athletics; in Rome, gladiatorial combat and the execution of prisoners). Romans were also subject to iron, and violent, discipline (recall that a Macedonian sentry asleep on duty was fined a day's pay; a Roman was beaten to death by his comrades). The 'fury' of Roman armies and their enthusiasm to fight, often with disregard for their own lives, comes out in a number of the battle accounts quoted above, and we should remember that often, particularly in military contexts, 'better' men means more aggressive and violent. Even so, such ethnic stereotypes are not wholly convincing. Greeks or Macedonians did have a strong martial tradition, particularly for face-to-face, close-quarters fighting, but it is doubtful whether this was as all-important as it might seem – the phalanx of Egyptians at Raphia, after all, defeated the Seleucid phalanx of Greco-Macedonians (and if they had any tactical or technical advantages in their favour, we are not told what they were). Even so, the ancient world saw a succession of strongly martial cultures rise and ultimately fall. The Greeks defeated the Persians (who themselves were considered fine soldiers and had established a large empire on the ruins of the Assyrian and Babylonian empires); the Spartans dominated the Greeks, until supplanted by the Thebans (as a result of the individual genius of the Theban generals Epaminondas and Pelopidas, according to the usual accounts, though the Thebans themselves thought their own abilities had something to do with it too); the Thebans and Persians alike then fell before the Macedonians; and the Macedonians in their turn were overcome by the Romans (once the Romans had recovered from their defeats at the hands of the Carthaginians). It is tempting (indeed, it is the role of the historian) to seek explanations for these rises and falls, and in this tradition Polybius' technical, tactical explanations or Livy's emphasis on greater individual worth compete with modern explanations centring on manpower and socio–economic factors.[11]

But perhaps it is not possible to isolate any one cause, and we should not try to do so. In the vast complexity of war and politics, many factors come into play, and the ones that are noticed and recorded by historians may not be the only ones that were important. No doubt all of the factors proposed above played their part, and maybe others too that have not been considered. But we should also not exclude simple contingency, the chance outcome of events that might, on the day, have taken a different turn. If Nicanor's column at Cynoscephalae had completed its march and begun to deploy a few minutes sooner, or Antiochus at Magnesia had kept his cavalry in hand and turned the Roman flank rather than pursuing to the camp, or Perseus at Pydna had cancelled the order to deploy the phalanx until he was sure it was really the right moment to engage, then this chapter might have been examining a string of Macedonian victories and considering how much superior the Macedonian way of fighting was to the Roman. Perhaps Macedonian arms would never have overcome Rome itself, as Carthaginian arms had been unable to do despite a string of battlefield victories; but even so, a succession of Macedonian victories, and a few statesman kings able to conduct effective diplomacy against the Romans and to persuade the Greeks or other kingdoms to make common cause, might at least have persuaded the Romans to confine their interests to Italy and the Western Mediterranean. Polybius cautions against assigning Roman success to Fortune (*Tyche*), and the warning is a fair one, but even so, just as *Phobos* played so great a role on the battlefield, so *Tyche* did also. Perhaps structural differences meant Roman domination was more likely, but (at the risk of including myself among 'the thoughtless of mankind') I do not think it was ever inevitable. The Macedonian phalanx was still a highly effective fighting system, and the Macedonians (and Greeks, Syrians and Egyptians) who fought in it were still brave and highly capable soldiers, and perhaps events could have turned out other than they did.

Epilogue

In the first chapter, I outlined the particular features of the Macedonian phalanx as they are generally conceived by modern authors. It seems appropriate now to produce a new list of features – in some cases confirming the original list, in others modifying or adding to it – based on the evidence and arguments that have been set out in the course of this book. So I believe that the Macedonian phalanx is distinctive for:

- Fighting in a particularly close order, using a formation and weapons which did not require individual weapons play but instead depended on the mass effect of the whole formation, making this type of phalanx particularly 'heavy'.
- Using a long pike (the sarissa) held in both hands at or near the rear end, with the pike points of the first (usually) five ranks of the formation projecting beyond the front rank. The length of the sarissa varied across time and place, but was usually in the 5–8 metres range. Peltasts, the younger and elite element of the phalanx, used shorter spears, while the early phalanxes of Philip and Alexander could also fight with javelins, at least outside of pitched battle.
- Using various types of shields, originally probably relatively small, rimless shields of Macedonian design, though at other times large shields in the style of Classical hoplites, large rimless shields with a strong curvature or bowl shape and smaller, flatter shields were all used. Peltasts carried the smallest size of shields, probably rimless and flat in profile.
- Having, like later pike formations, two basic ways of fighting; a more tentative fencing with the pike in more open order, or a very close-order mass advance. When the 'locked shields' and 'projecting spears' are particularly referenced in battle accounts, it is this second method of fighting that should be understood.
- Possessing a particularly high standard of drill, necessary in order to operate effectively in close formation with long spears, and subject to

constant training, together with a command structure of experienced officers at the unit level, able to oversee the complex drill manoeuvres required. Higher-level command fell to the personal associates of the king rather than to army officers.

- As a result of this drill and training, having a higher degree of flexibility and manoeuvrability than most of the earlier Greek phalanxes or contemporary infantry, and being able to alter formation and have its larger constituent parts act independently on the battlefield. But as a result of the 'heavy' formation, it was not ideally suited to broken ground, and subject to developing gaps which could be exploited by the small, independent and open-order formations of the Romans.

- Being recruited from the citizen population of the major kingdoms (or city-states), who in the Asian kingdoms were ethnically, socially and economically distinct from the native populations, and also distinct from the mercenaries who were employed either for long-term garrison duty or to bulk out the army with specialists for a particular campaign.

- Being politically engaged with the affairs of the kingdom, able to speak their minds according to Macedonian tradition and meeting in assemblies to express their views, while expecting to be persuaded and led, rather than merely commanded.

- Being regarded as the battle-winning force that (like the hoplite phalanx before it) reinforced the political dominance of the citizen body; but supplemented by specialist light and mounted forces to increase its military effectiveness.

We have now followed the rise, the heyday and the ultimate fall of the Macedonian phalanx. We have seen how it was armed, recruited, organized and utilized, and explored some of the reasons why it ultimately failed. But the defeat of the last Macedonian phalanx on the battlefield – the end coming with the defeat of the Pontic armies – is not quite the end of the story.

As we have seen, Roman arms were already admired and copied, with the Seleucid and Pontic armies certainly, and the Ptolemaic army possibly, forming their own units of 'imitation legionaries' (I dislike this phrase, incidentally, since these Hellenistic legionaries were in no sense 'imitation' – they were simply armed in the Roman fashion without being ethnically Roman or Italian, just as many peoples had been armed in the Macedonian fashion). The defeat of the last Hellenistic kingdoms (last to fall, in 31, was the Ptolemaic kingdom under Cleopatra VII, who allied with both Julius Caesar and Mark Antony but was defeated by the future Emperor Augustus) meant Roman armies could concentrate on fighting each other in a succession of civil wars, although wars of expansion continued against their surviving neighbours – particularly the Parthians in Persia, Numidians in Africa, and Spanish and Gauls in Europe. The Roman method of armament and organization was refined over the following century or so but not greatly altered, and the Roman army remained one of heavily armed infantry who did not usually fight in a heavy (deep, tightly packed) formation, which emphasized individual fighting with sword and shield over massed spears, and which used multiple lines of small, independent units under aggressive junior commanders (the famed Roman centurions) to achieve both tactical flexibility and staying power, as they had in the Punic, Macedonian, Syrian and Pontic wars.

Yet the Romans seem never to have developed a written tradition of organization and drill – the 'tactics' of the Hellenistic theorists – whether because there was no equivalent low-level drill in the more loosely organized Roman formations or perhaps because oral traditions were strong enough to ensure continuity of practice. This means that when Roman authors wrote about tactics, they did so (as in the case of Aelian and Arrian) by copying and adapting Hellenistic manuals from the same tradition as Asclepiodotus, and it was not until the late fourth century AD that we have a Roman equivalent manual (at least one that has survived), that of Vegetius, which was as much a work of antiquarianism as were Aelian's and Arrian's works. But the enemies faced by the Romans also changed with time and circumstances, and there is reason to think that, particularly where Roman armies faced primarily cavalry armies – as in the East – a deep, closely packed infantry formation with projecting spears was found to be superior to the traditional Roman way of fighting, and the Romans turned, to some extent (and the extent is uncertain and disputed), back to the phalanx. The Roman governor Arrian, as well as a biography of Alexander and the manual of Hellenistic tactics we have already encountered, wrote an account of his special formation to counter the heavy cavalry of the Alani or Alans (a steppe people at that time raiding Rome's eastern provinces), and not surprisingly given his interests, this formation has many similarities to the Macedonian phalanx. The later Roman armies in the eastern half of the Empire – to become known as the Byzantine Empire – also faced primarily mounted enemies, and the Byzantines continued the tradition of using Hellenistic organization and drill if not necessarily armament – they seem not to have adopted the sarissa – and wrote tactical manuals which combined contemporary cavalry operations with the wisdom of the ancients (which included Aelian and Arrian) on the use of infantry. The Byzantines perhaps did not use a pike phalanx of their own, but the DNA of the Macedonian phalanx can still be clearly discerned in Byzantine infantry, at least as it is depicted in their tactical manuals.[1]

Yet the fall of the Western Roman Empire, and the isolation and long-drawn-out decline of the Byzantine Empire, meant that phalanx-based armies did disappear for a while from European and Asian battlefields – whether for tactical reasons or socio-economic ones, since a phalanx requires a settled population of infantry fighters on which to call and the central organization and control to arm, drill, train and command them. The 'barbarian' armies that supplanted the Romans in Europe had their own strong military traditions, centring on the use of heavy cavalry and of infantry fighting perhaps more as individuals with sword, spear or axe, and without any tradition of pike use (though barbarian infantry were not all disorganized mobs, the Germans in particular often being described as forming deep, dense masses of infantry that are reminiscent of the phalanx).

For several centuries, heavy cavalry – transformed eventually into the armoured knight – dominated European and Near Eastern battlefields; and it was not until the later Middle Ages that the pike phalanx made its long-delayed return. At first, pikes were adopted wherever infantry forces – often of city-dwellers of middling social standing, as opposed to the peasants of the general levies or the mounted warrior knights of the elite – needed to hold off a mounted enemy. The Scottish schiltron and the Italian and Swiss pike block were all attempts to find a military answer to the dominance of small numbers of elite heavy cavalry. Once pikes were adopted and found to be successful again, then every army found it needed them, and pike blocks would find their chief opponents to be, not cavalry, but each other, as they had in Hellenistic times. The Macedonian phalanx thus had its own Renaissance, as the pike became the principal weapon of infantry, and with the Renaissance rediscovery of the literature of the ancients, the Hellenistic manuals were rediscovered also, with Aelian's version in particular being copied, translated, adapted and expanded upon, to form the basis of military theory and practice right into the seventeenth century AD. Theorists of this era had two traditions to work from, of course, and the Roman army loomed large in military thinking as a model, but perhaps because of the lack of Roman manuals – and certainly because of the similarity of armament – it was the Hellenistic tradition that was followed most closely, with drill manuals for the armies of the English Civil War, for example, being in places almost word-for-word copies of the writings of Aelian.[2]

This is not to say that Early Modern pike blocks were identical to the Macedonian phalanx. There were, of course, differences. For one, modern pike blocks almost never carried shields (there were a few experiments with shields, but they seem never to have been followed through, perhaps because superior or more widespread iron armour construction made them unnecessary). Modern pike blocks also formed less deep, four or six ranks being often found adequate (though the earlier Swiss pike blocks in particular had formed very deep indeed). Also, the resurrection of the phalanx coincided with the rise of its ultimate nemesis, gunpowder weapons. This meant that only a part of the infantry were equipped with pikes, the rest being musketeers. Theory regarded these musketeers as equivalent to the *velites* of the Roman legions, and armies were formed with widely spaced blocks of pikes in multiple lines, surrounded by swarms of musketeer skirmishers, in direct emulation of the Roman manipular deployment. Armies of this period were therefore armed like Macedonians, but organized on the grand tactical scale like Romans, able to combine the best of both worlds, and perhaps reminiscent of the experiments with interspersed phalanx and lighter forces that we saw with Pyrrhus, or Antigonus at Sellasia. This, then, was the ultimate legacy of the contest of legion and phalanx, in the use for several centuries of a method of fighting that combined the best features of both. But not even this hybrid could last forever, and in the end it was technological change that (for the first time) was to prove crucial, as increases in the range, accuracy, rate of fire and ease of manufacture of the musket – along with the invention of the bayonet, which turned a musket into a spear – reached the point where, by the start of the eighteenth century, the pike phalanx was finally rendered obsolete and disappeared, this time forever, from the battlefields of the world.[3]

For nearly 300 years the Macedonian phalanx had dominated the battlefields of Greece and the Near East. It was instrumental in (though by no means the only factor permitting) the astonishing era of Macedonian expansion under Philip II and Alexander. The Hellenistic Age that these campaigns of conquest ushered in saw, as well as a flowering of technology and culture, Greco-Macedonian settlers established across the Near East in order to provide a pool of manpower for the phalanxes of the kingdoms, all of which formed their armies, however many subject or allied peoples or mercenaries they could also command, around a central core of phalangites. Eventually the rising power of Rome, its insatiable appetite for conquest, and its numerous and aggressive armies proved too much for the divided Hellenistic kingdoms and their phalanx armies; and yet in a sense the phalanx did outlast the legion, and the principle of massed heavy infantry armed with long spears, drilled and trained to fight in unison, lived on long after Macedon itself had become no more than another Roman province.

List of battles

The following is a list, in chronological order, of major battles involving a phalanx armed in the Macedonian fashion, with brief notes as to combatants and outcome (where known, and with particular reference to the actions of the phalanx) and the more important sources. The list is not exhaustive, since there were many smaller engagements in which elements of the phalanx will have taken part (I limit the list to those battles with around 10,000 or more men on each side), while even for the larger battles we often have only the most basic information (if that) about orders of battle or the course of events, rendering them of little value in assessing the role of the phalanx – I have indicated such 'lost battles' with (?). Several battles of the third and second centuries, known only by the combatants and an approximate date and location, are also not listed. In the combatants listing, I have indicated the side using a phalanx with (ph), or (ph?) if there is some doubt or only a small part were Macedonian-armed. Armies designated 'Macedonian' usually included large numbers of non-Macedonian allies and subjects. As usual, all dates are BC.

Battles of Philip II

358 – Lyncus Plain (?) – Macedonians (ph?) under Philip II defeat Dardanians (Illyrians).
Philip victorious primarily due to a flanking cavalry attack.
Diod. 16.4

353/2 – Crocus Field (?) – Macedonians (ph) and Thessalians under Philip II defeat Phocians.
Philip victorious chiefly due to Thessalian cavalry.
Diod. 16.35

338 – Chaeronea – Macedonians (ph) under Philip II defeat Boeotians and Athenians.
Philip (perhaps) conducts feint retreat with phalanx, then defeats Athenian hoplites. Boeotian hoplites (including Sacred Band) defeated either by cavalry or phalanx.
Diod. 16.85–87; Polyaen. 4.2.2, 7.

Battles of Alexander III

334 – Granicus – Macedonians (ph) under Alexander III defeat Persians.

Phalanx takes part in assault across river, and then in defeat of isolated Greek mercenary hoplites.

Arr. *Anab.* 1.13–17; Diod. 17.18–21; Plut. *Alex.* 16

333 – Issus – Macedonians (ph) under Alexander III defeat Persians under Darius III.

Phalanx takes part in assault across river against mercenary hoplites; suffers losses, but victorious following flanking attack.

Arr. *Anab.* 2.7–11; Diod. 17.32–5; Plut. *Alex.* 20

331 – Gaugamela (Arbela) – Macedonians (ph) under Alexander III defeat Persians under Darius III.

Phalanx resists attack by scythed chariots, and joins Companion cavalry in attacking Persian line (probably mainly facing mercenary hoplites). Gap opens in phalanx, exploited by Persian cavalry, but these are defeated by second line.

Arr. *Anab.* 3.8–15; Diod. 17.57–61; Q.C. 4.13–16; Plut. *Alex.* 32–3

331 – Megalopolis (?)— Macedonians (ph) under Antipater defeat Spartans and allies under Agis.

No details, but heavy losses on both sides.

Diod. 17.62–3; Q.C. 6.1

326 – Hydaspes – Macedonians (ph) and allies under Alexander III defeat Indians under Porus.

Phalanx engages Indian elephants and infantry, defeating them after a hard fight.

Arr. *Anab.* 5.15–18; Diod. 17.87–9; Plut. *Alex.* 60

Battles of the Successors

322 – Crannon (?) – Macedonians (ph) under Antipater defeat Athenians and allies.

Phalanx defeats hoplites, who are able to withdraw to rough ground.

Diod. 18.17.

321 – Hellespont - Macedonians (ph?) under Eumenes defeat Macedonians (ph) under Craterus.

Eumenes, fearing the better-quality phalanx of his opponents, relies on his cavalry to defeat the enemy cavalry (and kill Craterus); the phalanx then accepts terms.

Dio. 18.3–32

319 – Orkynia (?) – Macedonians (ph) under Antigonus Monophthalmus defeat Macedonians (ph) under Eumenes.

Antigonus victorious when Eumenes' cavalry desert.

Diod. 18.40

319 – Cretopolis – Macedonians (ph) under Antigonus Monophthalmus defeat Macedonians (ph) formerly under Perdiccas.

Antigonus makes forced march to surprise Perdiccans, defeats their cavalry and surrounds their phalanx with cavalry while attacking with his phalanx and elephants.

Diod. 18.44

317/6 – Paraetacene – Macedonians (ph) under Antigonus Monophthalmus in disputed defeat of Macedonians (ph) under Eumenes.

Phalanxes engage in centre, with Silver Shields leading Eumenes' phalanx to victory, but Antigonus claims victory after winning cavalry battles on wings.

Diod. 19.27–31

316/5 – Gabiene – Macedonians (ph) under Antigonus Monophthalmus defeat Macedonians (ph) under Eumenes.

Silver Shields again defeat Antigonus' phalanx, while Antigonus' cavalry again victorious; Eumenes' phalanx withdraws in square.

Diod. 19.38–43

312 – Gaza – Macedonians (ph) under Ptolemy and Seleucus defeat Macedonians (ph) under Demetrius.

Battle decided by cavalry and elephants.

Diod. 19.81–85

301 – Ipsus (?) – Macedonians (ph) under Lysimachus, Seleucus and Cassander defeat Macedonians (ph) under Antigonus Monophthalmus and Demetrius

Antigonus' cavalry, initially victorious, pursue off field and are blocked by elephants; isolated Antigonid phalanx is then defeated.

Plut. *Dem.* 28–29

281 – Corupedion (?) – Macedonians (ph?) under Seleucus I defeat Macedonians (ph?) under Lysimachus.

No details known.

App. *Syr.* 62

Battles of Pyrrhus

280 – Heraclea (?) – Epirotes and allies (ph) under Pyrrhus defeat Romans.

Phalanx engages indecisively with Romans; battle decided by cavalry and elephants.

Plut. *Pyrr.* 16–17

279 – Asculum (?) – Epirotes and allies (ph) under Pyrrhus defeat (?) Romans.
Phalanx drives back Romans, aided by cavalry and elephants; battle dissolves
    into confusion.

D.H. 20.1–3; Plut. *Pyrr.* 21

275 – Beneventum (?) – Romans defeat Epirotes and allies (ph) under Pyrrhus.
Failed night attack; Romans defend camp against elephants.

D.H. 20.12; Plut. *Pyrr.* 25

Hellenistic battles

222 – Sellasia – Antigonids (ph) under Antigonus III Doson defeat Spartans
    (ph) under Cleomenes III.
Fought over two hills; Macedonian phalanx in alternating units with Illyrians
    defeats Spartan left, while second phalanx defeats Spartan phalanx after long
    struggle.

Pol. 2.65–9

220 – Caphyae – Aetolians defeat Achaeans (ph?) under Aratus.
Achaean phalanx flees after defeat of light-armed infantry and cavalry.

Pol. 4.11–12

220 – Apollonia – Seleucids (ph) under Antioch III defeat Seleucid rebels
    (ph?) under Molon.
Rebel army broken when elements desert to Antiochus.

Pol. 5.52–54

217 – Raphia – Ptolemies (ph) under Ptolemy IV defeat Seleucids (ph) under
    Antiochus III.
Ptolemaic phalanx augmented by Egyptian recruits defeats Seleucid phalanx,
    while cavalry pursue off field.

Pol. 5.63–6, 5.79–86

207 – Mantinea – Achaeans (ph) under Philopoemen defeat Spartans (ph)
    under Machanidas.
Spartan phalanx falls into disorder crossing a ditch, and is routed by Achaean
    phalanx.

Pol. 11.11–18

200 (?) – Panion (?) – Seleucids (ph) under Antiochus III defeat Ptolemies (ph)
    under Scopas.
Fought over hilly terrain. Flank charge by Seleucid cavalry contributes to defeat
    of Ptolemaic phalanx.

Pol. 16.18–19

Battles against Rome

197 – Cynoscephalae – Romans under Flamininus defeat Antigonids (ph)
under Philip V.

Meeting engagement; Antigonid right flank drives back Roman left, but left
flank fails to deploy and is defeated by Roman right. Reserves from Roman
right then attack Macedonian right in the rear.

Pol. 18.20–7

191 – Thermopylae – Romans under Glabrio defeat Seleucids (ph) under
Antiochus III.

Seleucid phalanx holds off Romans in the pass until their position is turned.

Liv. 36.16–19; App. *Syr.* 16–20

190 – Magnesia – Romans and Pergamenes under Scipio defeat Seleucids (ph)
under Antiochus III.

Seleucid cavalry defeat Roman right and pursue off the field; Roman centre
and right surround Seleucid phalanx and shoot down the elephants stationed
within the phalanx.

Liv. 37.38–44; App. *Syr.* 30–6

168 – Pydna – Romans under Aemilius Paullus defeat Antigonids (ph) under
Perseus.

Antigonids attack in haste from camp; after initial success, phalanx is defeated
as Romans exploit developing gaps.

Liv. 44.40–2; Plut. *Aem.* 16–22

146 – Corinth (?) – Romans under Mummius defeat Achaeans (ph?).

Achaean phalanx holds Romans until outflanked.

Dio Cass. 21.72

86 – Chaeronea – Romans under Sulla defeat Pontics (ph) under Archelaus.

Initial clashes involving field fortifications and scythed chariots. Pontic phalanx
defeated by Romans after heavy fighting.

Plut. *Sull.* 18–19

List of rulers and generals

S ome of the minor rulers (such as the early third-century kings of Macedon, including Philip IV, and the later Seleucids and Ptolemies) are omitted. The dates shown are regnal dates, or for important figures who did not become king (here classed 'generals', though they held other ranks, such as satrap) the periods of their main independent activity. For the Successors, kingship (outside Macedon) was a personal rank rather than associated with a particular kingdom – I have indicated the main areas of power.

Argead kings of Macedon

Caranus, King of Macedon 808–778
    – mythical founder of the Argead dynasty
… numerous kings
Alexander I, King of Macedon 498–454
Perdiccas II, King of Macedon 454–413
Archelaus I, King of Macedon 413–399
… several minor kings
Alexander II, King of Macedon 370–368
    – brother of Philip II, assassinated
Perdiccas III,King of Macedon 365–359
    – brother of Philip II; killed in battle against Illyrians
Amyntas IV, King of Macedon 359
    – son of Perdiccas III, put aside by Philip II
Philip II, King of Macedon 358–336
    – invented Macedonian phalanx, brought Greece under Macedonian control
Alexander III the Great, King of Macedon 336–323
    – conquered Persian Empire
Philip III Arrhidaeus and **Alexander IV** – titular kings 323–317/310
    – half-brother and posthumous son of Alexander III

The Successors

Antigonus Monophthalmus ('One-eye'), general 323–306, King (in Asia) 305–301
- defeated Eumenes of Cardia, founded Antigonid dynasty

Antipater, regent of Macedon 334–319
- defeated Athens in Lamian War

Cassander, regent of Macedon 317–305, King of Macedon 305–297

Craterus, general 323–321

Demetrius Poliorcetes ('the Besieger'), general 312–306, King (in Greece and Asia) 306–294, King of Macedon 294–288
- son of Antigonus Monophthalmus, defeated by Ptolemy at Gaza

Eumenes of Cardia, general 323–316
- fought Antigonus Monopthalmus at Paraitacene and Gabiene

Lysimachus, general 323–306, King (in Thrace) 305–281, King of Macedon 286–281
- defeated and killed at Corupedion

Perdiccas, regent of the empire 323–321

Polyperchon, regent of Macedon 319–317

Ptolemy, general 323–306, King (in Egypt, as Ptolemy I Soter) 305–282
- founded Ptolemaic dynasty

Ptolemy Keraunos
- son of Ptolemy I, assassinated Seleucus I, killed during Gallic invasions

Pyrrhus, King of Epirus 306–272, King of Macedon 288–285
- invaded Italy and fought three battles against Romans

Seleucus, general 323–306, King (in Syria, as Seleucis I Nicator) 305–281
- founded Seleucid dynasty

Antigonid dynasty (Kings of Macedon)

Antigonus II Gonatas 276–239

Demetrius II 239–229

Antigonus III Doson 229–221
- defeated Spartans at Sellasia

Philip V 221–179
- defeated by Rome at Cynoscephalae

Perseus 179–168
- defeated by Rome at Pydna

Seleucid dynasty (kings in Syria)

Seleucus I Nicator 305–281
Antiochus I Soter 281–261
Antiochus II Theos 261–246
Seleucus II Callinicus 246–225
Seleucus II Ceraunus 225–223
Antiochus III the Great 223–187
      – defeated by Ptolemies at Raphia, defeated by Rome at Magnesia
Seleucus IV Philopator 187–175
Antiochus IV Epiphanes 175–163
Antiochus V Eupator 163–161
Demetrius I Soter 161–150
Alexander I Balas 150–145
… and further minor kings

Ptolemaic dynasty (kings in Egypt)

Ptolemy I Soter 303–282
Ptolemy II Philadelphus 285–246
Ptolemy III Euergetes 246–221
Ptolemy IV Philopator 221–203
      – defeated Seleucids at Raphia
Ptolemy V Epiphanes 203–181
Ptolemy VI Philometor 181–145
… and further minor kings and queens, ending with
Cleopatra VII Philopator, 51–30
      – defeated by Octavian (Augustus) at Actium

Attalid dynasty (Kings of Pergamon)

Attalus I Soter 241–197
Eumenes II 197–159
      – fought on Roman side at Magnesia
Attalus II Philadelphus 160–138
Attalus III 138–133
      – bequeathed kingdom to Rome

Notable Kings (or tyrants) of Sparta

Agis III 338–331
- defeated and killed by Antipater at Megalopolis
Cleomenes III 235–222
- equipped Spartan army as Macedonian phalanx, defeated at Sellasia
Machanidas 210–207
- defeated at Mantinea
Nabis 206–192
- allied with Rome against Philip V

Other important figures

Achaeus – Seleucid general 223–213
- led Asia Minor in revolt against Seleucid rule
Archelaus – Pontic general *c*. 88–63
- defeated at second Chaeronea
Mithridates VI – King of Pontus *c*. 113–63
Molon – Seleucid general *c*.220
- led eastern satrapies in revolt against Seleucid rule
Philopoemen – Achaean general active 223–183
- equipped Achaean army as Macedonian phalanx

Romans

Titus Quinctius **Flamininus**, consul 198
- victor at Cynoscephalae
Manius Acilius **Glabrio**, consul 191
- victor at Thermopylae
Lucius Cornelius **Scipio**, consul 190
- victor at Magnesia (with his brother Publius Cornelius **Scipio Africanus**)
Lucius **Aemilius Paullus**, consul 168
- victor at Pydna
Lucius Cornelius **Sulla**, consul 88
- victor at second Chaeronea

Glossary

Achaemenids – ruling dynasty of the Persian Empire, last of which, Darius III, was defeated and deposed by Alexander the Great.

Agema – 'vanguard', the lead or elite unit of an army; in the Hellenistic period, the senior guard unit of cavalry or **peltasts**.

Ala – the Italian Allied equivalent of the **legion**, probably armed and organized the same but with a slightly larger cavalry contingent. Often loosely referred to as a **legion**, especially by modern authors.

Antigonid – the **Hellenistic** kingdom centred on Macedon, founded by Antigonus Gonatas, grandson of Antigonus Monophthalmus, one of Alexander the Great's generals.

Argyraspides – see **Silver Shields**

Aspis – any type of shield, usually round, and also specifically the larger types of round shield carried by heavy infantry; the classical Greek *aspis* had a bowl-like shape and prominent rim.

Asthetairoi – Best Companions? (translation uncertain), a subset of the Macedonian phalanx under Alexander III. See also *Pezhetairoi*.

Auxiliaries – foreign, subject or allied troops, those who are not full citizens, usually serving as light or medium infantry.

Bronze Shields (Greek *Chalcaspides*) – name for several of the Macedonian phalanxes of the Hellenistic kingdoms, especially those of the **Antigonids**. Perhaps, in the Antigonid army, one half of the whole phalanx, alongside the **White Shields**.

Caetrati – Latin translation of **peltasts**.

Cataphracts – heavy cavalry, with horse and man armoured. Particularly used in the Seleucid army from the second century.

Century – one of two subunits of the **maniple**, around sixty (traditionally 100) men strong, and commanded by a centurion.

Chalcaspides – see **Bronze Shields**.

Chiliarchy (Greek *chiliarchia*) – unit of 1,000 men. Probably used in Persian armies and adopted by the Macedonian and **Hellenistic** armies, for infantry and cavalry. As part of the **phalanx**, made up of four *syntagmata*, and numbering (ideally) 1,024 men. Compare with *taxis*.

Classical – the period of Greek history from the early fifth century BC to the time of Alexander the Great (late fourth century BC). Characterized by numerous small city-states (**poleis**) throughout Greece and the Greek world (which included southern Italy and the coast of Asia Minor). Followed by the **Hellenistic** period.

Cleruch (*klerouchos*) – holder of a *kleros*, a plot of land; used for settlers granted plots of land on which to live, and, particularly in **Ptolemaic** Egypt, for the settled heavy infantry and cavalry.

Cohort – a grouping of three **maniples**. Probably developed in the second century and sometimes anachronistically applied to earlier **legions**, though *alae* were perhaps always organized into cohorts on a regional basis.

Column – a formation deeper than it is wide (with more **ranks** than **files**), usually used for marching. Compare with **phalanx**.

Companion (Greek *hetairos*) – originally one of the nobles in attendance on the Macedonian king. The title was extended by Philip II or Alexander (I, II or III) to the whole of the noble cavalry, and to some or all of the infantry (as Foot Companions, *Pezhetairoi*). In the Hellenistic kingdoms, the attendants of the king became known as **Friends**.

Consul – one (of two) of the highest elected officials of the Roman Republic, and commander of its field army.

Cubit – Greek measure of distance, approximately equivalent to 1½ feet or 45cm (roughly half a metre, for ease of calculations).

Cuirass – body armour, of unspecified construction but usually bronze or thickly padded linen.

Diadochi – Greek/Latin name for the **Successors**.

Doru – the general Greek word for **spear**, but can be used for both **spears** and **pikes**. Also transliterated *dory*.

Drachma – a coin or small measure of currency, of silver, and roughly equivalent to a day's pay. Consists of six **obols**.

Ekklesia – assembly; the popular assembly of democratic states such as Athens, and by extension a meeting of any politically enfranchised group (such as soldiers).

Ephebes (Greek *epheboi*) – 18 to 19-year-old youths undertaking a state-sponsored programme of military training.

File – line of men in a formation standing one behind another, from front to back of a formation (such as the **phalanx**). Compare with **rank**.

File closer – soldier at the rear of a **file**, selected for courage and experience after the **file leader**. The file closers of a formation collectively form the formation's rear **rank**. Also, a more senior officer of a **syntagma**, whose duty is to keep the men in their ranks and prevent any hesitation or running away.

File leader – soldier at the front of a **file**, specially selected for courage and experience, and receiving higher pay. Commands the file, equivalent to a modern NCO (non-commissioned officer). The file leaders of a formation collectively form the formation's front **rank**.

Friend (Greek *philos*) – companions and associates of the Successors, and later of the Hellenistic kings. The title became increasingly formalized, especially in Egypt, with a rank structure of First Friend, Honoured Friend and so on.

Greaves – shin protectors, armour for the lower leg.

Hamippos – light infantryman running and fighting alongside cavalry.

Hastati – the youngest of the age classes of the Roman heavy infantry, forming the front line of a **legion** or **ala** in battle.

Hegemon (plural *hegemones*) – Greek word for a leader or officer, which could be applied to men of various ranks. Sometimes used to refer to the **file leaders** collectively, or to more senior officers, but less senior than the **strategoi**.

Hellenistic – the period of Greek history from the time of Alexander the Great and extending traditionally to the Battle of Actium (late fourth century to late first century BC). Followed the **Classical** period, and characterized by a small number of Greco-Macedonian kingdoms ruling much of the Near East.

Helot – a Spartan serf.

Hoplite – English name for the Classical Greek heavy infantryman, armed with *aspis* and *doru*. In Greek, *hoplitai* were any sort of heavy infantry, including **hoplites**, **phalangites** and **legionaries**.

Hypaspists – originally a small body of personal attendants of the Macedonian kings, the name was, under Philip II and Alexander III, applied to the royal infantry guard. Probably equipped as **peltasts**, and known, later in Alexander's reign and under the **Seleucids**, as **Silver Shields** (*Argyraspides*), and under the **Antigonids** as **Peltasts**.

Javelin – a **spear** specifically designed for throwing.

Katoikia – settlement, used for a variety of non-city (**polis**) settlements, particularly settled soldiers or settled garrisons in the **Seleucid** kingdom.

Keras ('horn') – the flank or wing of a formation, so (*epi keras*) a marching **column**.

Lacedaemonians – Spartans, including the *Spartiates* (citizens proper) and *perioikoi* (subordinate inhabitants).

Lance – a **spear** carried by cavalry.

Legion – large Roman formation, an integrated force of heavy infantry, light infantry and cavalry, around 5,000 men strong.

Legionaries – Roman or Italian heavy infantry fighting in a **legion** or *ala*, divided into *hastati*, *principes* and *triarii*.

Leucaspides – see **White Shields**.

Lochos – general word for a military unit, often used to refer to a **file**, sometimes (especially in the **Classical** period) to a larger unit.

Maniple – the smallest tactical subunit of the Roman infantry, a force of around 120 men made up of two **centuries**; three maniples formed a **cohort**.

Misthos – pay, particularly military pay (whether paid to citizen soldiers, allies, subjects or mercenaries). Compare *sitos*.

Misthophoroi – receivers of pay, professionals; usually used to refer to mercenaries, non-citizen foreign soldiers, whether serving long term or for a specific contract. Compare with **xenoi**.

Obol – small bronze coin, one sixth of a **drachma**.

Othismos – 'thrust', 'push' or 'pushing', a word occasionally applied to battles when one side is 'pushed back' (defeated), and in the context of **hoplite** battles taken by some modern authors to refer to a particular tactic (a mass shove, scrum or crowd crush).

Peltasts (Greek *peltastai*) – infantry carrying a *pelte*. In the fifth and fourth centuries, applied to light infantry skirmishers typically armed with **javelins**. In the Hellenistic period, applied to medium infantry with equipment lighter than the **phalangites**, but heavier than the light infantry. Also specifically the name of the **Antigonid** infantry guard (probably equipped as light **phalangites**).

Pelte/pelta – a type of shield, lacking a rim and either smaller in diameter, or lighter in construction, than the larger shield (**aspis**) of the heavy infantry. Usually round, though in earlier periods often crescent-shaped.

Pergamene – the **Hellenistic** kingdom centred on the city of Pergamon (Pergamum) in Asia Minor. Originally part of the **Seleucid** kingdom, rose to power from the late third century.

Perioikoi – inhabitants of a city or state (typically Sparta) with reduced citizen rights.

Pezhetairoi – Foot Companions, originally the infantry guard of Philip II (and perhaps of earlier Macedonian kings), later the name was applied to some or most of the Macedonian phalanx of Alexander III. See also *Asthetairoi*.

Phalangite – English name for *sarissa*-carrying heavy infantry (in Greek, called *phalangitai* or *hoplitai*).

Phalanx – a close-order linear formation of heavy infantry. Also used in Greek to denote a line of battle, that could be made up of several types of soldiers. Often used to refer specifically to the entire heavy infantry force, of **hoplites** or **phalangites**, in an army.

Pike – a long **spear** held in both hands.

Pilum – Latin name for the heavy **javelin** carried by the **legionaries**.

Polis (plural *poleis*) – Greek word for city, and usually used to mean an independent city state particularly of **Classical** Greece or Asia Minor. In the **Hellenistic** period, *poleis* sometimes maintained a precarious independence, and sometimes were subject to one or other of the kings. Citizens of a *polis* were required to fight in the **phalanx** as **hoplites**.

Principes – the next older age class of the Roman heavy infantry after the **hastati**, forming the second line of a **legion** or **ala** in battle.

Psiloi – lightest-equipped of the infantry, unarmoured and using missile weapons.

Pteruges ('feathers') – flexible leather or linen strips attached to the bottom edges and arm holes of a **cuirass** to provide additional protection.

Ptolemaic – the **Hellenistic** kingdom centred on Egypt, founded by Ptolemy, one of Alexander the Great's generals.

Rank – line of men in a formation standing beside one another, from side to side of a formation (such as the **phalanx**). Compare with **file**.

Sarisa/sarissa – the Greek word for a **pike**, but perhaps also a dialect word for other types of **spear**.

Sarissophoroi – sarissa-carriers, usually meaning **phalangites**, but could also be applied to cavalry armed with long **lances**.

Satrap – governor of a province (satrapy) of the Persian Empire. Under Alexander and the **Successors**, Greek or Macedonian commanders were appointed to rule most satrapies.

Sauroter – a butt spike (that is, a spike at the opposite end of the spear from the spearhead that was used in combat) of a **spear** (**doru**) – it is not known for sure whether the **sarissa** also had a butt spike.

Scutum – the elliptical or rectangular shield of the Roman heavy infantry; called **thureos** in Greek.

Seleucid – the **Hellenistic** kingdom centred on Syria, founded by Seleucus, one of Alexander the Great's generals.

Semeia – name used especially by Polybius for the smallest subunit of the Macedonian phalanx, typically 256 men strong and roughly equivalent to the **maniple** of the Roman **legion**. Called **syntagma** by the Tacticians.

Silver Shields (Greek *Argyraspides*) – later name for the **Hypaspists** of Alexander III, and the equivalent royal guard of the **Seleucids**. Probably equipped as **peltasts**.

Sitos – 'food', particularly army rations. Compare *misthos*.

Spear – a shafted weapon with a blade at one end, and often though not always a butt spike at the other, wielded in one hand. A longer spear wielded in both hands is called a **pike**. A light spear for throwing is a **javelin**. A spear carried by cavalry is sometimes but not always called a **lance**.

Speira – name used by Polybius for the Roman **maniple**.

Strategos (plural *strategoi*) – Greek word for a general, often applied to more senior army commanders of various ranks. Also a specific administrative position over a region of a **Hellenistic** kingdom.

Successors – the generals of Alexander who in the last two decades of the fourth century fought for control of Alexander's empire. The three most successful founded the **Antigonid**, **Seleucid** and **Ptolemaic** kingdoms. Also called **Diadochi**.

Syntagma – name used by the **Tacticians** for the smallest independent subunit of the Macedonian phalanx, typically 256 men strong. Also called *semeia*.

Tacticians – writers of organization and drill manuals describing the Macedonian **phalanx** (and associated arms). Three such manuals have survived to the modern day, written by Asclepiodotus, Aelian and Arrian.

The names of several other authors are known but their works have not survived. The tradition of writing such manuals was continued under the Byzantines (Late Romans), using earlier manuals as a source for some of their material.

Talent – a measure of weight about 26kg, commonly used to measure large sums of money (usually as talents of silver). Equivalent to 6,000 **drachmae** or 36,000 **obols**.

Taxis – a general word for any organized body of soldiers (like 'unit' in English). Also used specifically for the largest subunit, probably 1,500 men strong, of the **phalanx** of Alexander, and for a unit of 128 men, one half of a **syntagma**.

Thureophoroi (*thureos*-carriers) – Greek infantry armed with the *thureos* and, probably, a long spear and/or javelins, and fighting as medium infantry, lighter than the **phalangites**. Also sometimes used to indicate the Roman heavy infantry (**legionaries**) armed with the *scutum*.

Thureos – a rectangular or elongated oval type of shield, traditionally carried by Gallic infantry and widely adopted in the Hellenistic world in the third century. Also used for the Roman *scutum*.

Triarii – the oldest age class of the Roman heavy infantry, forming the third line of a **legion** or **ala** in battle, and so the final reserve.

Velites – the light infantry component of the **legion** or **ala**, formed from the youngest soldiers.

White Shields (Greek *Leucaspides*) – name for one part (perhaps half) of the **Antigonid** phalanx, alongside the **Bronze Shields**.

Xenoi – 'foreigners', often used to refer to foreign mercenary soldiers (perhaps distinguished from **misthophoroi** by different terms of service).

Notes

Chapter 1: Origins

1. Danforth (2010) offers a brief history and some reflections on the Macedonian question. See also the thoughts of Billows (2018) pp.17–27.

2. Reflections on views of the Macedonians in Antiquity – which are mostly drawn from non-Macedonian (Greek or Roman sources) in Asirvatham (2010). Specifically on the subtle and complex relationship of Macedonians and Greeks, Engels (2010).

3. For fourth-century Panhellenism, Müller (2010) pp.175, 178–9, with references to further reading.

4. The Classical hoplite phalanx and the transition from 'Homeric' warfare, have a vast bibliography of their own, not strictly relevant to the current work. The best starting point, with extensive further reading, is Kagan and Viggiano (2013). For a good recent general account of the Classical hoplite, Bardunias and Rey (2016). Origin of the word 'phalanx', Krentz (2013) p.137.

5. For the several (and non-technical) meanings of the word 'phalanx', Juhel (2017a) pp.1–2 n.4.

6. For a recent overview of Philip's reforms, Billows (2018) esp. pp.103–16 (and pp.305–6 for references to further reading). The fundamental account is Griffith in Hammond and Griffith (1979), 'Philip and the Army' (pp.405–49). See also Worthington (2014) pp.33–36. Matthew (2015) pp.22–46 discuss Philip II's possible role in inventing the Macedonian phalanx, with useful references to many other scholars' views; however, his own conclusion that Philip could not have been the inventor, based in part on the close order of the tacticians being 'impossible' for a pike-armed phalanx – more on these matters below – is hard to take seriously. Karunanithy (2013) pp.8–16 usefully points out that Philip would not have been operating in a vacuum, as there was a considerable body of military literature, now mostly lost, to inform and inspire him.

7. The scattered literary references to Macedonian infantry before Philip II are gathered by Sekunda (2010) pp.448–9. See also Greenwalt (2015).

8. See Juhel (2017b) on evidence (from their absence from fourth-century tombs and standardized appearance) for state manufacture and issue of weapons, and further below.

9. Sekunda (2010) pp.447–8 decides in favour of Alexander I as the reformer, citing Achaemenid Persian influence for *Hetairoi* (Companions) and dekads (files of ten). Erskine (1989) pp.385–94 argues that the Anaximenes quote is taken out of context (necessarily, since the context is lost), and that it may be referring only to a select body, not the whole Macedonian infantry. In Hammond and Griffith (1979), Griffith (pp.705–13) argues for the reformer of Anaximenes being Alexander III, and that the reform was merely to extend the name *Pezhetairoi* to the whole of the infantry. Billows (2018) pp.104–6 and 149 also argues for Anaximenes' Alexander being Alexander III and that just a change of name is meant, but this requires ignoring the reference to organizational reform. Matthew (2015) pp.1–46 considers the question in detail (and with references to further bibliography) and finds in favour of Alexander II, but sees this as an adoption of 'Iphicratid peltast' equipment, on which more below.

10. In support of this early dating, Juhel (2017b) connects the reforms described by Anaximenes with the decline of individual weaponry in Macedonian tombs in the early fifth century, proposing that this was when arms started to be manufactured centrally under royal control.

11. On dekads see Juhel (2017b) and Sekunda (2010) p.448. The *dekas* continued to be the name of the file at least into the reign of Alexander, and Asclepiodotus *Tactics* 2.2 notes that the file was formerly called a *dekania*, long after it in fact contained sixteen men. So Persian influence was not required for the continuation of the tradition, but might have been for its origin.

12. Much of our knowledge of *Pezhetairoi* ('Foot Companions') comes from fragments in ancient lexicons and commentaries on other works, as the word only occurs in three extant sources, Arrian's *Anabasis of Alexander*, Demosthenes' *Olynthiac* 2 and (probably anachronistically) Plutarch *Flamininus* 17.5 (and *Moralia* 197C), and is otherwise known only from later definitions which sometimes quote fragments of earlier, now lost, historians (like Anaximenes and Theopompus). On *Pezhetairoi* and *Asthetairoi* as elements of Alexander's phalanx, see further in Chapter 3. For Hypaspists and their successors, the Peltasts, Juhel (2017a) pp.94–160, 'Antigonid Redcoats'.

13. Sekunda (2013b) pp.369–80 for Iphicrates' reforms, and for the view that Iphricatean peltast equipment was the same as Philip's new equipment

(so also, 'Philip equipped his infantry as "peltasts" of the "Iphicratean" type', Sekunda (2010) p.449). Ueda-Sarson (2002a) pp.30–36 provides a useful summary of the reform and literature. Matthew (2015) pp.11–19 discusses this reform at length, though I am unconvinced by his conclusions; for a highly critical view of Matthew's arguments, Juhel (2017a) pp.5–6.

14. Matthew (2015) translates Diodorus as 'as large again', but see Juhel's criticisms in note 13 above. For the length of spear that can still be wielded in one hand, Juhel (2017a) pp.29–31. See also Best (1969) and Markle (1977) for the possibility (it is no more than that) that the long spear was adopted (by Iphicrates and Philip alike) from the Thracians.

15. Ueda-Sarson (2002a) and (2002b) for peltasts and their equivalents in the fourth century and under the Successors.

16. For Iphicrates' equipment being the same as Philip's, Sekunda (2013b) and Matthew (2015) quoted in note 13 above. Matthew takes the Iphicratean peltast to be identical to the peltasts of the tacticians, and seems to think that these peltasts are identical to the Macedonian phalangites and therefore separate from the tacticians' hoplites, but this seems exceptionally unlikely. It is perfectly clear that the hoplites of the tacticians are phalangites (in our sense), and that the tacticians' peltasts are a lighter variant.

17. Hammond (1997) discusses what Philip may have learned from the Thebans. The Theban tactics at Leuctra in particular have attracted a large bibliography; Lendon (2005) pp.106–14 and bibliographic notes pp. 414–5 is a good starting point.

18. We might also note the tradition that saw Charidemus, the fourth-century mercenary general, introduce the phalanx to Macedon – according to the Byzantine scholar Eustathius' commentary on *Iliad* 13.128–33 (Lendon (2005) p.354 n.16). This is, however, part of a tradition linking Homer, famous generals and the foremost Greek armies (in Pope's words 'this manner of ordering the phalanx was afterwards introduced among the Spartans by Lycurgus, among the Argives by Lysander, among the Thebans by Epaminondas, and among the Macedonians by Charidemus'), so I do not believe it can be wholly trusted, other than in demonstrating the link the Greeks themselves saw (or imagined) between Homer and their own way of fighting. Lendon (2005) part 1, 'The Greeks', discusses this Homeric inspiration at length.

19. This idea – that Alexander's phalanx was not a pike phalanx at all, with the fully developed pike phalanx described by Polybius arising only much later – has been most recently and forcefully argued by Juhel (2017) ch.1

414 The Macedonian Phalanx

(pp.1–93, esp. 50–56) 'La nature de la phalange macédonienne ou quand la science recule', recalling with particular approval German scholarship of the late nineteenth and early twentieth century (not now familiar to many Anglophone scholars for obvious if unfortunate reasons – '*ignorance des études publiée dans une autre langue que l'anglais*', Juhel (2017a) p.67). While no doubt the contribution of this 'German school' is valuable, I still disagree with its conclusions. Other writers have adopted a middle position, such as Markle (1977, 1978), who sees the pike phalanx arising in the course of Alexander's campaigns (which seems to me inherently unlikely). It is true that there is no direct, incontrovertible evidence for a pike phalanx under Philip and Alexander (Juhel (2017) p.10 f.). Ultimately I do not think that this question is susceptible to a definitive answer, and can only give my own conclusions based on my reading. I do at any rate share the reservations of Juhel with the practice of taking Polybius' or Asclepiodotus' testimony as to equipment and applying it unquestioningly and in detail to the phalanx of Alexander.

20. Note, however, that Aelian's list of sources (1) – and those in the other tacticians – are all post-Alexander (except Aeneas and Homer), so we do not need to take too seriously the idea that any of the tacticians are specifically describing Alexander's army; rather they take it for granted that the Macedonian phalanx they describe was essentially the same as that of Alexander.

21. Note, however, that as for example Juhel (2017a) pp.40–2 (n.82) points out, the positive evidence that the Seleucid and Ptolemaic phalanxes were armed as described by Polybius (18.29–30), who is talking specifically of the Antigonid phalanx, is lacking, and the assumption that all Hellenistic phalanxes were similar is, at heart, just an assumption. I believe it is a sound assumption given the evidence we do have, and the common armament implied by the phrase 'armed in the Macedonian fashion', but like so much in ancient history, the case is not settled beyond all doubt.

Chapter 2: Arms and armour

1. Juhel (2017b) pp.48–50 on royal ownership of weapons (contrasting this situation with Archaic Macedonia where burial with weapons, presumably owned by the individual, is more common). Karunanithy (2013) pp.40–63 collects the evidence for centralized weapons manufacture and distribution.

2. The best (modern English) discussion of the sarissa is Sekunda (2001a), whose findings I generally follow here. For non-Macedonian uses of the

word 'sarisa', Matthew (2015) p.12 (with Markle (1978) and Head (2001)), quoting Didymos, *Demosthenes* 13.3–7 and Justin 9.3.1–3, where Philip II is wounded by a Triballian with a sarissa, and Lucian, *Dial Mort* 439–40, relating a tale where a Mede cavalryman and his horse are both killed by a Thracian with *pelte* and sarissa. See also Sekunda (2013a) p.84, quoting a dedication at Lindos by Philip V of 'ten *peltai*, ten *sarisai*, ten helmets ... on his victory over the Dardanians and Maidoi'. Since dedications were usually of captured enemy weapons, this shows the Dardanians and Maidoi were using *sarisai* and *peltai* (though not necessarily that they fought in a Macedonian phalanx). For the Macedonian use of *sarisa*, Noguera (1999) collects and discusses uses of the word, including those where a long pike does not seem to be meant. See also Juhel (2017a) esp. pp.29–30 for a short sarissa in Alexander's army – such discussions seem to me, however, to be flawed by the assumption that spears carried by guards at banquets, for example, would necessarily be the same as spears carried in battle by regular infantry. See Best (1969) for the use of long spears by Thracians; he suggests that the 'Iphicratean reform' and Macedonian equipment were in turn inspired by Thracian use of long spears. The evidence for the use of long spears by Thracians, whether called sarissas or not, is, it has to be said, not totally compelling, but it is inherently likely that Philip's innovation was inspired by some precedent.

3. For discussions and reconstructions of the cavalry spear, see Connolly (2000) and Markle (1978). Whether the infantry sarissa was necessarily carried in two hands will be considered further below.

4. Matthew (2015) pp.66–77 discusses the length of the sarissa and the units of measurement used in detail and collects the references; note, however, the criticisms of his methods and conclusions (and those of other scholars) in Juhel (2017a) p.21 n.34 and p.22 n.35.

5. Matthew (2015) pp.77–8 tabulates the references to sarissa length.

6. Some historians such as Matthew (2015) p.12 and Juhel (2017a) pp.45–9 take Arrian's 16 feet as evidence that Arrian is describing an earlier phalanx with shorter (12 cubit) sarissas, matching this to Theophrastus' 12 cubits, but I think this is wishful thinking. The similarity of the texts make it highly unlikely that Arrian is referring to some different period phalanx than the other tacticians, and the rank spacing of 'two feet' is to my mind decisive that Arrian means cubits throughout. For a different view, Juhel (2017a) pp.45–6 and nn.87–9. Devine (1995) for the sources of the tacticians, with the further discussion of Rance (2017a).

7. Devine (1994) for this suggestion.

8. For the size of spear that can be wielded one-handed (longer than might be expected), Juhel (2017a) pp.32 f., giving later (Byzantine and Medieval) examples. Macedonian cavalry spears are discussed by Connolly (2001); the best depictions are the Alexander Mosaic (Cohen (1997)) and the Kinch Tomb (known only from a reproduction, the original having been lost through neglect), Kinch (1920) (or search 'Kinch Tomb painting' online).

9. The Pergamon plaque (lost during the Second World War, originally published in Conze, *Altertümer von Pergamon* Bd. 1 Text 2 p.251) is (now) frequently reproduced, see e.g. Sekunda (2007) p.337 and Sekunda (2013a) pp.97–8, and also available online at https://digi.ub.uni-heidelberg.de/diglit/pergamon1913/0165/image. For the Alexander Mosaic and Kinch Tomb see note 8 above.

10. Agios Athanasios tomb – Tsimbidou-Avloniti (2004). The images are readily available online (search 'Agios Athanasios tomb'); also well reproduced in Karunanithy (2013) plates 10 and 11. Juhel (2017) pp.26–8 for the argument that the spears are to scale, and (p.29 f.) that Alexander's phalanx wielded its spears in one hand.

11. For Mycenaean spear holds see for example the well-known 'Lion hunt' dagger in the Athens Archaeological Museum, with many reproductions online (search 'lion hunt dagger'), or the silver krater from shaft grave IV, Mycenae.

12. The Vergina spear head, butt and 'connecting tube' (see below) are published in Andronikos (1970). The general point that the equipment of ordinary infantrymen is not often found in tombs is made by Juhel (2017b), perhaps because it was owned by the king and not the individual (pp.48–50).

13. For those with a more positive view of the value of such reconstructions, Matthew (2015) pp.47–93, with Connolly (2001) and Markle (1977). A good example online is https://hetairoi.de/en/the-phalangite and https://hetairoi.de/en/the-sarissa-experiment.

14. In this conclusion I follow Sekunda (2001a) and (2013b) pp.53–4. See also Juhel (2017a) p.24.

15. Sekunda (2001) for the wood, and (I am sure correct) identification of ash as the most likely.

16. The weapon in question is variously called a *longche*, a sarissa (both Arr. *Anab.* 4.8.8–9), an *aichme* (Plut. *Alex.* 51) or (in Latin) a *lancea* (Q.C. 8.1.45), the latter two being names for javelins. The nature of the *longche* is uncertain, though it is likely also a javelin, see below. Matthew's (2015) pp.58–9 suggestion that a *longche* was a half-sarissa is attractive if you are convinced that the sarissa came in two halves (which I am not).

17. Caracalla's phalanx is discussed by Karunanithy (2001). Caracalla may not have been the first, since Nero also raised a 'phalanx of Alexander' (Suetonius, *Nero* 19), though this might have been just a name applied to regularly equipped legionaries.

18. Juhel (2017a) reaches the conclusion (p.66) that early phalangites were multifunctional (though he does not think one of their functions was as pike-armed hoplites, as I do). As he notes, Diod. 19.93.2, where Demetrius 'with his soldiers in light equipment made a forced march', may provide another example. For ephebes see further Chapter 4.

19. For the identity of the Antigonid Peltasts, Walbank (1940) Appendix II. See also Juhel (2017a) pp.94–160. The traditional view has long been that the Hypaspists or Peltasts, not the hoplites of the phalanx, are the bearers of the Argive (hoplite) shield still seen in Hellenistic art, but I believe this is the wrong way round, see below; so also Liampi (1998) ch.3. The literature on the identity and armament of the Hypaspists (and Argyraspides) is large and inconclusive. Matthew (2015) p.418 n.217 collects many of the references (most of which do not add anything new to the discussion). Anson (1981) remains a good starting point.

20. A number of scholars argue that neither Philip's nor Alexander's phalanx were armed 'in the Macedonian fashion', that is with a pike wielded in two hands; for example Markle (1978) and Juhel (2017) pp.1–81. Hammond (1980) discusses (following Markle) the extremely limited evidence for phalanx armament under Philip.

21. On the Macedonian shield generally, particularly on the question of decoration and later occurrences, with all known examples (actual shields, and depictions in art and on coins) up to the time of publication, the standard work is Liampi (1998).

22. The quote is from Anderson (1976) p.2. Matthew (2015) p.432 n.4 collects further references to discussions of the shield. Markle (1999) provides the arguments for two types of shield (a small *pelte* for the phalanx and a larger *aspis* for the Hypaspists) in his reconstruction of a monument from ancient Beroea; I am not convinced by his detailed argument though the existence of the two types of shield seems clear enough. Sekunda (2013a) pp.82–3 lists sizes of surviving examples ranging from 66–74cm. The largest example is a second-century Pontic shield of Macedonian design, 80cm in diameter, but it is not certain it is a phalangite's shield (Melikian-Chirvani (1994) identifies it as a cavalry shield).

23. Aemilius Paullus monument – Taylor (2016); Kähler (1965). Judging the size of a shield from an artistic depiction is particularly fraught; Juhel (2017a)

p.38 and n.76, for example, estimates the Agios Athanasios frieze shields to be about 70cm in diameter; this may be so, but at any rate, to my eyes they do not look noticeably smaller than a hoplite shield, so the difference can only be small. Furthermore, each shield is of a slightly different size, but I would hesitate to conclude that three types of shield are depicted.

24. The Ptolemaic shield mould, from the Allard Pierson museum, is Liampi (1998) p.59 S9 (plate 5); Karunanithy (2013) plate 17; online at https://www.uniquecollection.org/shield. That it is a mould, rather than serving some other purpose such as a votive offering or simply decoration (and therefore not actually life size), is not certain, but a mould seems the most likely.

25. Though there is the one possible illustration of a very small shield in the painting from Pompeii noted below (n.36), possibly depicting an Antigonid Peltast, Sekunda (2013) pp.38–40; Karunanithy (2013) plate 34. The modern view is typically that the Hypaspists/Peltasts had the larger shields, the hoplites/phalangites the smaller; Sekunda (2013a) argues for the reverse, I'm sure correctly.

26. The Amphipolis regulations are discussed in Hatzopoulos (2001) and published in translation in Austin (1981) ~74.

27. Examples of *peltai* in a Macedonian context in Plutarch: Plut. *Alex.* 16.4, Alexander (on horseback) at the Granicus 'was conspicuous by his buckler [*pelte*] and by his helmet's crest'; Plut. *Alex.* 67.1–2, Alexander's procession, 'not a shield [*pelten*] was to be seen, not a helmet [*kranos*], not a spear [*sarisan*]'; Plut. *Flam.* 14.1, Macedonian spoil in Flamininus' triumph: 'Greek helmets [*krane*] and Macedonian bucklers [*peltai*] and pikes [*sarisai*]'. On the other hand, note Plut. *Aem.* 32.3, Macedonian spoil in Aemilius' triumph: 'helmets [*krane*] lying upon shields [*aspisi*] and breastplates [*thorakes*] upon greaves [*knemisi*]'; Plut. *Eum.* 14.5, Eumenes' army, 'when the soldiers saw him, they hailed him at once in their Macedonian speech, caught up their shields [*aspidas*], beat upon them with their spears [*sarisais*], and raised their battle-cry'. Note that in his account of Pydna, Plutarch never uses the word 'Peltasts', though he will certainly have found it in Polybius (as did Livy, translating it as *caetrati*, Liv. 41.9). Plutarch used the account of Nasica specifically to add to or correct the account of Polybius (e.g. Plut. *Aem.* 15.3), and Plutarch's colourful description of the Macedonian advance (Plut. *Aem.* 18.3–4) certainly comes from Nasica, who had ridden out to join the *promachoi* (18.2), outposts of allies including Paelignians and Marrucinians. Nasica will also have provided the vivid account of the defeat of the Paelignians at 20.1–2, compare with the

rather dismissive reference to their recklessness in Liv. 41.9. See further Chapter 9.

28. The inscriptions are: *IG* II² 1473 K. I Z. 6–11; *IG* II² 1487 B Z. 96–97; *IG* II² 1490 B Z. 30–31; C. Blinkenberg, Lindos II vol.1 p.181 para XLII n.2; reproduced in Liampi (1998) p.3 and (Lindos) Sekunda (2013a) p.84 (and see also note 2 above).

29. Markle (1999) for two sizes (and also styles) of shield – I will return to this question below. Also Sekunda (2013a) pp.81–87 listing the sizes of extant examples, with references. Sekunda finds two sizes of Macedonian shields (*c*. 66cm and 73cm) from extant examples, although these size variations do not seem to me to be very significant, or to cover the larger sizes seen in art. Sekunda assigns the larger shields to the main phalanx.

30. The Sarcophagus is published most completely, with colour illustrations depicting the original paintwork (still visible at that time), in Winter (1912); more easy to find in libraries is Schefold (1968); relevant images are also reproduced in Karunanithy (2013) plate 1.

31. Markle (1999) for the Beroea monument and Dion.

32. See note 19 above on the Hypaspists. Lazenby (2012) p.40, for example, reports hypaspists in the Spartan army as the shield-carrying servants of officers (at least).

33. Bosworth (1973) gives probably the most widely accepted interpretation of *asthetairoi*, that they are from the (newly absorbed) Upper Macedonian districts. See Sekunda (2010) p.457 for other possibilities, and further in Chapter 3.

34. The strap theory is most clearly proposed by Markle (1999) but seems to be almost universally accepted; Matthew (2015) p.95 f. raises objections (but still seems to accept the general idea).

35. Reconstructions of *pelte* with neck strap are described by Connolly (2000) and Matthew (2015) pp.93–104. Unfortunately both are rather sketchily described, and it is unclear how or why a neck strap is used.

36. The first/second-century AD historian Julius Africanus says of Classical Greek equipment: 'For the Greeks are fond of heavy, full armour: they have a double helmet, a breastplate covered with scales, a concave bronze shield held by two handles [*ochanois duo*] (of which the one surrounding the forearm avails for shoving [*eis othismon*], while the other is grasped by the end of the hand), two greaves, a hand-held javelin, and a spear for hand-to-hand combat' (*Kestoi* 7.1.10). While not too much faith can be placed in his understanding of Greek equipment (though note the combination of spear and javelin), this suggests that to him at least a *porpax*

is a type of *ochanon* – which suggests that the difference between *porpax* and *ochanon* may be rather slight. The significance of 'shoving' (*othismon*) is something to which we will return in Chapter 8. The identification of the Macedonians at Pydna as 'neo-hoplites' is to be found in Bardunias and Rey (2016) pp.155–6 (the idea seems to be based on the description of peltast equipment, but peltasts carried smaller shields, not larger). Another possible illustration of the handles of a Macedonian shield is the painting from Pompeii possibly depicting an Antigonid Peltast, so identified by Sekunda (2013a) pp.38–40; well illustrated in Karunanithy (2013) plate 34. I don't think the identification is secure enough to conclude much from this, though it is suggestive of a flexible, presumably leather, band over the arm.

37. See the catalogue of examples in Liampi (1998), with additional examples (of shields and other equipment) in Juhel (2017b). See Sekunda (2013a) pp.85–7, and Liampi (1998) ch.4 for Balkan use of the decoration. Also Karunanithy (2013) pp.108–12, and illustrations in Head (1982) p.113. Note also that Sekunda (2013 a) pp.118–9 identifies the funerary stele of Zoilos, sometimes cited as an example of a Macedonian phalangite, as a Paionian. Again, the equipment is similar to that of the Macedonian phalanx, but this does not require that the drill and tactics were.

38. Earlier shields with the 'Macedonian' surface decoration – examples collected in Ueda-Sarson (2002a). See also Sekunda (2013a) p.84.

39. For the 'linothorax', including details of reconstructions and tests of strength and weight, see Aldrete, Bartell and Aldrete (2013). The idea that this armour was made of linen (rather than, say, leather) is not universally accepted, but for our purposes it is enough that it was not made of metal and was still fairly effective protection. Armour is discussed by Matthew (2015) pp.114–25 and Karunanithy (2013) pp.105–8.

40. See Juhel (2017) pp.61–6 for the argument that the front ranks of the phalanx (not a true pike phalanx, in his understanding) were heavily armed (armoured).

41. The tomb of Lyson and Kallikles is described in Miller (1993) and discussed in Sekunda (2013a) Chapter 1.

42. For the *kotthybos*, Hatzopoulos (2001), concluding it is a non-metallic cuirass. The *hemithorax* is said by Polyaenus 4.3.13 to have been introduced by Alexander as a disincentive to running away in battle (a story not widely accepted), Karunanithy (2013) p.107.

43. For Hellenistic helmets generally, Dintsis (1986). Karunanithy (2013) pp.103–5 on blue or iron helmets.

44. Helmet types are discussed by Matthew (2015) pp.104–14 and Karunanithy (2013) pp.100–5. The adoption of the pilos helmet is proposed by Juhel (2009), and see also Sextus Julius Africanus, *Kestoi* 1.1.45–50. For the 'morion', Juhel (2017a) pp.219–62. For Lyson and Kallikles' tomb, Miller (1993) and discussion of the helmets in Sekunda (2013a) Chapter 1. Juhel (2017b) suggests that earlier Macedonian infantry standardized on the 'Illyrian' helmet.

45. For this suggestion – identifying the file leader as the wearer of the transverse crest – Juhel (2017c).

46. On the *kausia*, Saatsoglou-Paliadeli (1993), Fredricksmeyer (1986), Karunanithy (2013) esp. pp.81–3.

47. On greaves, Matthew (2015) pp.123—5, Karunanithy (2013) pp.112–5.

48. For swords, Matthew (2015) pp.125–8, Karunanithy (2013) pp.137–44. Lyson and Kallikles – Miller (1993) and Sekunda (2013 a) pp.18–9.

49. On clothing (including the *kausia*) Saatsoglou-Paliadeli (1993), and also Juhel (2009) and Sekunda, refs in n.51 below; Karunanithy (2013) pp.81–6 (discussing cavalry), 112–5 (infantry footwear).

50. For the Seleucid units Sekunda (1994) pp.12–9 and note there are problems with the text of Polybius in this passage; pp.14–5 Sekunda rejects the idea of Gold Shields. On the *Leucaspides* see further Chapter 3.

51. See especially Juhel (2017) pp.136–45 for the 'Antigonid Redcoats' (Peltasts in red tunics), confirmed by a range of depictions. Also pp.213–9 for the particular identification of the *phoinix* as the purple cuirass depicted on the Agios Athanasios frieze.

52. For an alternative view, with the identification of uniforms for various units of the Hellenistic armies, see particularly the illustrated works of Sekunda (1984, 1994, 1995, 2012). The equipment and colours depicted are certainly accurate, though I would be less confident in assigning them to particular units, and uniformity of dress (tunics), as opposed to cloaks and equipment, seems in greater doubt. Karunanithy (2013) pp.240–50 considers cavalry clothing colours, and notes that 'five different tunic colours are worn by six figures' on the Agios Athanasios tomb. Juhel (2009) argues for the introduction of uniform issue helmets at the end of the reign of Alexander. For the frequency of different colours see the analysis of Post (2010).

Chapter 3: Organization and drill

1. See the pertinent observations of Sekunda (1994) pp.6–8. The *Tactics* of Aelian formed a direct blueprint for the early seventeenth-century AD

military reforms of Maurice of Nassau. See also Matthew (2012) preface. Many aspects of the Greek *Taktika* are covered by the papers in Rance and Sekunda (2017), the introduction (by Rance) pp.9–64 being especially valuable.

2.   Sekunda (1994) pp.5–8 for sources for the tacticians, identifying Poseidonius. Sekunda (1995) p.14 for more on Philostephanos. See also (*ibid*. p.6 and Mooren (1975) p.25) Kallikles of Alexandria, called 'instructor in tactics of the king' (Ptolemy VI) among other titles, including possibly 'commander of the left wing'. Devine (1995) suggests (as I think very likely) that Poseidonius' source in turn was Polybius. See also the introduction to the Loeb edition of Asclepiodotus, and Rance and Sekunda (2017).

3.   Juhel (2017a) p.8 and n.16 on the supposed Homeric precedent; this could be applied also to the earlier Classical hoplite phalanx. Nevertheless, I think that in Hellenistic military thought there was supposed to have been a particular link, in inspiration if nothing else, between Homer and the Macedonian phalanx (a link perhaps promoted by Philip II, stressing his Hellenic credentials, and/or Alexander, citing his favourite writer). The Latin equivalent to 'buckler pressed on buckler; helm on helm; and man on man' is to be found in Quintus Curtius, in the mercenary Charidemus' description of the phalanx – 'They themselves call it the phalanx, a steadfast body of infantry: man stands close to man, weapons are joined to weapons [*vir viro, armis arma conserta sunt*]", Q.C. 3.2.13, and Livy, describing drill at Cynoscephalae – 'he also ordered the troops to lessen intervals, so that man stood close to man and arms to arms [*ut vir viro, arma armis iungerentur*]', Livy 33.8.14. This is the same Charidemus linked with the adoption of the phalanx by Macedon, Lendon (2005) p.354 n.16, and above ch.1 n.18.

4.   The size (depth) of files is discussed by Matthew (2015) pp.256–75, and see also Chapter 7 below.

5.   Usage of the noun *synaspismos*, or the verbs *synaspizo* or *synaspidoō*, goes back to Classical authors, but the word originally carried the meaning of fighting alongside (like 'comrade in arms'), as well as crowding together in a tight formation, and the technical meaning of the tacticians (Asclepiodotus, Aelian, Arrian) appears to be a later adoption. It is, however, also used by Plutarch, along with *proballo*, 'projection' (of spears) to describe one of the distinctive features of the Macedonian phalanx. Outside the tacticians, the noun *synaspismos* is used once by Diodorus (16.3.1–2, the passage quoted in ch.1 concerning the origins of the phalanx) and nine times by Plutarch – Plut. *Flam.* 8.2 and 8.4 (the phalanx at Cynoscephalae); Plut. *Aem.* 19.1 and 20.4 (the phalanx at Pydna), Plut. *Phil.* 9.2 (the Achaean phalanx);

Plut. *Sull.* 18.4 (the Pontic phalanx at second Chaeronea); but also at Plut. *Timol.* 27.6 (Greek mercenaries at Crimissus in 339); Plut. *Arist.* 18.3 (the Spartans at Plataea in 479); Plut. *Mar.* 20.6 (German tribesmen fighting the Romans); Plut. *Crass.* 24.3 (Romans fighting Parthians). I think it is clear that Plutarch's usage does not necessarily refer to the tactician's one cubit order (though it might, in a Macedonian context). The verb is more widely used, but with a range of meanings and contexts, e.g. Xen. *Hell.* 3.5.11 (fight alongside) and 7.4.23 (close order, of hoplites); Arr. *Anab.* 5.17.7 (of Alexander's phalanx); Diod. 17.27.2, 17.57.6, 17.58.3 (of Alexander's phalanx, but also 17.84.5 with the sense of fight alongside, mercenaries and their wives, and 15.55.5, Spartans at Leuctra); Polybius 4.64 (Antigonid Peltasts), and 12.21 (Callisthenes on Issus, where it means two cubits, as his calculations show). See further on this question in Chapter 7 below.

6. The bibliography on the question of Classical file intervals is quite large; Krentz (2013) pp.139–40 summarizes the issue; Pritchett (1971) pp.134–54 collected the evidence, finding in favour of a 3 foot interval, which is widely accepted, though Krentz and van Wees (2004) still favour a more open formation. Note also Krentz (2013) p.151 n.37 where he points out that in his own earlier paper, '6m and 3m are misprints for 6 feet and 3 feet' – something to bear in mind when reading Arrian on the length of the sarissa.

7. See Goldsworthy (1996) p.179 for the question of the Roman file interval – finding (tentatively) in favour of 3 feet, but with some variability.

8. Good starting points for this extensively discussed topic are Bardunias and Rey (2017) pp.117–20 or Matthew (2015) pp.133–56 and 354–9 (and *passim*), with notes. However, Matthew's conclusion that the closest order (one cubit) spacing is impossible for phalangites but was regularly used by hoplites is, I believe, wholly untenable, and does not appear to be based on any practical experimentation. Connolly (2000), in contrast, found the one cubit spacing perfectly practicable (though sadly he gives few details of how it was done – for example, how, or whether, the shields were angled). Going back further, Delbrück (1975) – writing in 1900 – conducted experiments (pp.404—6) with poles and students (he doesn't specify if they used shields) and also found the one cubit spacing practicable. As he waspishly remarks (p.409): 'Whoever has once seen and measured such a phalanx is immediately relieved of any further tortures of doubt concerning the interval between files. Scholars are remarkable people. Here for once we have the rare opportunity of solving a historical problem through a very

simple experiment; why doesn't one do it?' Why not indeed? For myself I can only plead poverty of time and resources. I hope that some day an enterprising researcher with access to a re-enactment group may design and properly document rigorous experiments to demonstrate the matter conclusively. The main problem with all such evidence is of course that proving something is possible does not prove it was actually done; but it can be useful nevertheless to establish that something is not impossible.

9. For the organization of the Spartan army, Lazenby (2012).

10. Amphipolis regulations – Austin (1981) ~74, ll. 10–14. Sekunda (2010) pp.460–1 summarizes the epigraphic evidence for the units of the Antigonid army. Matthew (2015) pp.276–96 for a discussion of the larger subunits of the phalanx generally. Polybius uses the word *syntagma* nine times, but either in a general sense ('whole force' or 'formation' e.g. Pol. 18.31.4, 18.32.13) or for cavalry (e.g. Pol. 10.22.6), or to translate cohort ('three maniples [*speirai*] (this body [*syntagma*] of infantry the Romans call a cohort)', Pol. 11.23.1). *Speira* is more common in Polybius, used some twenty-eight times for small units of all armies – including Roman maniples (2.33.7, 3.115.12), Illyrians (2.3.2), Gauls (2.29.8), as well as Macedonians (2.66.5). *Semeia* is Polybius' usual translation of maniple, e.g. Pol.6.33–4, while Pol. 15.9 shows *speira* and *semeia* being used interchangeably. Note also that in all the following discussion the sizes of units and whole armies for the Hellenistic kingdoms are assumed to be accurately recorded, broadly speaking. Army sizes in antiquity were notoriously subject to exaggeration, but this applied mostly to 'barbarian' armies (particularly 'eastern' armies such as the Persians), with ludicrous figures in the millions often recorded. Hellenistic armies have recorded numbers which fit with known unit organization (chiliarchies etc), so can be safely accepted.

11. That the *taxis* of Alexander's phalanx was 1,500 men strong is by no means a given, and Ueda-Sarson (2001) makes a good case for each *taxis* containing 2,000 men (a *merarchia* in Asclepiodotus' terminology). See also Matthew (2015) pp.281–2, reaching a similar conclusion via a different argument.

12. On the *Pezhetairoi* and *Asthetairoi*, Bosworth (1973). There are seven occurrences of the word *pezhetairoi* in modern texts of Arrian, but only three of these are in the original manuscripts, the rest being emendations of *asthetairoi*, which Bosworth argues should be retained. Bosworth argues for the *Asthetairoi* comprising that half of the phalanx recruited from Upper Macedonia, and for the name meaning 'Closest kin Companions'. Sekunda (2010) pp.456–8 summarizes the evidence and differing interpretations;

Sekunda (2013a) pp.88–98 covers the Antigonid army. For the identity of the Antigonid Peltasts, Walbank (1940) Appendix II and Juhel (2017a) pp.94–160, who (pp.120–5) collects all the references. Regional recruitment: Bosworth (1988) pp.259, 261–2; p.259 f. for a summary of Alexander's army generally.

13. The identification of the Argyraspides with the Hypasists is confirmed by Diod. 17.57.2 and QC 4.13.27, which refer to Argyraspides at Gaugamela as obviously the same unit as Arrian's Hypaspists of 3.11.9 (Bosworth (1973) p.246 n.6). For the origins of the Hypaspists generally, see Hammond (1991), with references to the extensive earlier discussions, Bosworth (1997), and Sekunda (2010) pp.454–6 for Hypaspists and Argyraspides (and their commanders). For the later careers of the Argyraspides, Roisman (2012).

14. Sekunda (2013a) ch.8 pp.108–27 changes his previous view that the *Leucaspides* were part of the phalanx, and identifies them instead as non-Macedonian allied or mercenary *thureophoroi*. Certainty on this point, as so often, is impossible, but I still prefer on balance the earlier theory that they are part of the phalanx.

15. For units of the Ptolemaic army, Fischer-Bovet (2014) esp. pp.155–9, and for more on eponymous officers see Chapter 6.

16. See the translation and comments on Aelian in Matthew (2012), particularly on Chapter 28, with notes. Matthew freely translates according to his understanding that the insertion of half-files is meant, though the text of Aelian is much less clear on this point (and in places is, as Matthew says, almost unintelligible). Arrian's version (*Tactics* 25) is similar to Aelian's (without being much clearer). In this case I prefer to follow the earlier text of Asclepiodotus. See also Matthew (2015) pp.256–75 on the various subdivisions of the file. Similar drills had existed for the Classical hoplite phalanx (although there are similar levels of uncertainty precisely how they worked) – see Bardunias and Rey (2016) esp. pp.113–7, and further in Chapter 7 below.

17. For the Spartan army, Lazenby (2012), specifically p.38. For this manoeuvre among Classical hoplites, Bardunias and Rey (2017) pp.113–7.

18. Karunanithy (2013) p.29, with some further references to military dances.

Chapter 4: The men in the phalanx

1. See Millett (2010) pp.488–500 for the economic aspects of Philip's reforms, and the social and economic underpinning of his new army. Details of

Antigonid conscription and recruitment, using the surviving documents (chiefly the Amphipolis code, Beroea gymnasium laws and conscription diagramma) are provided by Hatzopoulos (2001).

2. Fischer-Bovet (2014) covers all aspects of the Ptolemaic army, and particularly the cleruchic system. Note here ch.2 (pp.15–43) for an account of earlier mercenary service and colonization in Egypt – the system of granting land to foreign soldiers long predated the Ptolemies.

3. For example, land reclaimed on the death of the cleruch, *P.Hib.* 81; land re-let to royal labourers, *P.Lille* 30–8; Crawford (1971) p.55. Belonging to the cleruch – *P.Lille* 4 – the land is taken by the crown only until 'it is registered as that of his sons, if he has any, within the number of days allowed by the statute'; Crawford (1971) p.56; Lewis (1986) p.33. Private property – for these developments, Lesquier (1911) pp.227–52; Préaux (1939) pp.463–71; Crawford (1971) p.57 – examples of inheritance, *P.Tebt.* 5; *P.Tebt* 124; *BGU* 1185 16–19. A *kleros* inherited by the daughter of a soldier in the first century, *SB* 9790. Agricultural factors – Préaux (1939) p.469 f.; Crawford (1971) pp.58, 185. Cardaces – *Clara Rhodos* IX 190–207; Hansen (1971) p.184 f.; Walbank 3 (1979) p.173 f.

4. Cult of Arsinoe – *P.Revenue Laws* col.24, second century – Préaux (1939) pp.472–3; in the civil wars, the kings also rewarded their supporters with grants of confiscated land, p.467. Cyprus – *BCH* 80 (1976) pp.437–51. Benefactions – *C.Ord.Ptol.* 53 ll. 35–50; Rostovtzeff (1953) 2 p.878 f. There were many such *philanthropiai*, edicts granting exemptions and amnesties, in the second century. Billets – Fischer-Bovet (2014) pp.242–6; *P.Lond.* 2015; *P.Petrie* iii 12; 14; on billets, Préaux (1939) pp.477–81; Uebel (1968) p.41 n.2; another example of such a will in Clarysse (1971). Friction between soldiers and inhabitants over billeting – e.g. *P.Petrie* iii 20 = *C.Ord.Ptol.* 5–10; *C.Ord.Ptol. 24*; Lewis (1986) pp.22–3. For friction over billeting of Seleucid soldiers, Diod. 34/35.17.2 and Millar (1987) p.130.

5. For Hellenistic settlements and city foundations generally, Cohen (1995), (2006) and (2013). Smyrna-Magnesia – *OGIS* 229 ll. 100–109; Cohen (1978) p.77 f. Land ownership – Cohen (1978) pp.66–9; the law on the inheritance of the *kleros* from Doura-Europos (Welles (1959) pp.76–9 no.12), if it represents the Seleucid practice, shows the *kleros* reverting to the crown only in absence of any other heirs, including women. See also Cohen (1984).

6. Exemptions – Piejko, *AJP* 108 (1987) pp.707–28; Pritchett 5 (1991) pp.451–2, and Piejko pp.716–9 for other similar examples. For tax exemptions

as a means to the goodwill of the population in general and soldiers in particular, Sherwin-White (1987) p.15.

7. Ilium decree is *OGIS* 219 = Austin (1981) p.139.

8. A summary of the political institutions of Macedon in King (2010). The 'constitutional' position is best stated by Hammond (1989a) esp. pp.58–70. For the extensive debate on the nature of Macedonian kingship and the questions of 'constitutional rule' and of the role of the Macedonian subjects in the state – Hammond (1989a) p.382 f.; Papazoglou (1983); Errington (1978) pp.77–134, (1983) pp.89–101; Mooren (1983); Adams (1986). A summary of the arguments and further bibliography in Borza (1990) pp.231–52. Greenwalt (2015) for the political significance of the rise of an effective Macedonian infantry.

9. On the *koinon*, Papazoglou (1983) esp. p.198 f.; Hammond (1988). Its powers – Hammond (1989a) p.58 f. For the army assembly under Alexander, Lock (1977), and under the early Successors, Anson (1991). The functioning of an army in a fashion analogous to but not actually representative of the political forms of the state was a feature of the Greek city armies also, Mossé (1968).

10. The translation is based on the emended text, the manuscript reading that the army inquired into the cases, and not mentioning the king. Errington (1978) p.86 f. would reject this emendation, but in the light of the other examples discussed below it seems that it is correct. Discussion in Hammond-Griffith 2 (1979) p.389 n.3. The parallel passages in Arrian (3.26 f.) and Diodorus (17.79.5–80) refer to judgement before 'the Macedonians'. Apelles' conspiracy – Errington (1967), Walbank (1940) p.51 f.; Hammond-Walbank 3 (1988) p.382 f.

11. On succession and acclamation, Errington (1978) p.115 f.; Anson (1985); Hatzopoulos (1986); Borza (1990) pp.243—5, esp. p.245; Chaniotis (2005) pp.62–4.

12. On the question of legitimacy, Grainger (2017) ch.12. (and ch.1).

13. Borza (1990) p.238 notes that 'the king could do exactly what he could get away with'; but the list of things he could expect to get away with would itself be defined in part by Macedonian customs and expectations. For other non-absolutist ideas of kingship, for example Doson's '*eudoxos douleia*' (Ael. *VH*. 2.20), Aalders (1975) p.20.

14. On Macedonians in the Seleucid kingdom, Bar-Kochva (1989) pp.90–111; p.105 f. For exclusivity of the Greco-Macedonian population, e.g. Le Rider (1965) on Susa, cf. also Millar (1987) for Syria esp. p.132. Alexandrian mob – Fraser (1972) 1 p.128, 2 p.233 n.309 on the masses in Alexandria;

Hammond (1989) p.281 f. notes that these events echo Macedonian arrangements (but he excessively formalizes the Macedonian position).

15. Chaniotis (2005) pp.20–26 on the equivalent (though different) continuation of military service as the civic duty of the citizen in many (but not all) Greek cities (some of which instead placed their reliance on mercenaries).

16. *Aposkeue* – Launey (1987) p.788; Pomeroy (1990) p.99 f. On *aposkeue* of soldiers generally, Holleaux 3 (1942) pp.15–26; for Seleucid soldiers' wives, Cohen (1978) p.33 f. Exemptions – *P.Paris* 63 = *UPZ* 110; exemption is granted to the elite corps in Alexandria and the Egyptian soldiers posted there and their families; all other soldiers presumably are on their lands with their families and so are not exempted. Special privileges – *C.Ord. Ptol.* 22.17–20; Cohen (1978) p.34; Pomeroy (1990) p.124.

17. For the amount of pay, Launey (1987) pp.750–79. Mutinies over pay, examples in Préaux (1978) 1 pp.308–9; difficulties over keeping up payments, and ruses undertaken to solve shortages of cash, Launey (1987) p.735 f. The rate of pay for citizen forces was evidently the same as for mercenaries – as in the Rhodes-Hierapytna treaty (I.Cret III iii 1 a, ll. 19–20), assuming the half of the force that are not Hierapytnans are to be mercenaries. At any rate, Bar-Kochva (1989) p.228 seems unjustified in thinking that the regulars were paid less than the mercenaries. Crowns – Amphipolis, *Moretti* II 114 A 3; Gaza, *SEG* VIII 269. See for such rewards Pritchett 2 (1974) pp.276–90; 5 (1991) p.378. Medals and awards – Karunanithy (2013) pp.154–7, 163–4.

18. Amphipolis regulations – *Moretti* II 114 = Austin (1981) 74; Pritchett 5 (1991) pp.377–8. cf. the Roman methods of dividing spoils, Pol. 10.16–17, which may possibly be the model for Philip's code. Examples of the division of booty to soldiers collected by Pritchett 5 (1991) pp.375–98.

19. On religion and kingship, introductions and further links in Christesen and Murray (2010), particularly pp.440–3, along with Potter (2003) and Chaniotis (2003). Launey (1987) p.875 f. on festivals and processions, pp.945–6 on Eumenes' device; Lévêque (1968) p.284. Launey (1987) p.875 f. treats at length the religious life of the army and the importance of the dynastic cult; this will not be considered in detail here. Chaniotis (2005) ch.8 pp.143–65 for all aspects of war and religion. Naiden (2018) for a view of Alexander emphasizing his religious role.

20. Smyrna-Magnesia – *OGIS* 229 ll. 61 f = Austin (1981) p.182. Eumenes – *OGIS* 266 l. 24 f.

21. For the kingly qualities of the Successors in their relations with their armies as precursors of the ideals of kingship, Hornblower (1981) pp.210–1.

Chaniotis (2005) esp. pp.57–62 on the military ideals of kingship. Examples of personal leadership in Préaux (1978) 1 pp.197–8. Wheeler (1991) p.125 sees Alexander as a temporary retrogression to a more heroic style of leadership, (cf. Samuel (1988)) but it is apparent that the other kings also led in Alexander's style. Preaux (1978) 1 p.198 for examples of kings killed or wounded in combat.

22. On the 'kinship' style of leadership, sharing in the hardships of the men, Wheeler (1991) p.144 f.

23. For Antigonus' special care as regards provisions, Billows (1990) pp.316–8.

24. Pritchett 1 (1971), Vaughn (1991) pp.38–62 for burial of the dead by Greek cities.

25. For a summary of the development of the need for technical military skills in a commander, Wheeler (1991) esp. p.121 f.

26. Sekunda (2010) and Sekunda (2013a) pp.106–7 summarize the Antigonid evidence. Fischer-Bovet (2014) p.66 f. and table on p.76 calculates total costs of the Ptolemaic and Seleucid armies and navies around the time of Raphia; considerable uncertainties around total numbers and length of service mean the numbers can only be approximate, but the total (6,200–6,700 talents for the Ptolemaic army, 7,000–8,000 for the Seleucid) are doubtless approximately correct. Chaniotis (2005) ch.7 pp.115–42 considers economic aspects of war, with an emphasis on the costs (chiefly to cities).

27. Fischer-Bovet (2014) p.73 also suggests 1 drachma per day for infantry (6 obols = 1 drachma).

28. Fischer-Bovet (2014) pp.66–83 calculates figures for the total yearly tax revenue and military costs for the Ptolemaic and Seleucid kingdoms; the main imponderable remains the length of service and the proportion of men who were paid at any time. Fischer-Bovet assumes all Ptolemaic cleruchs provided three months' paid service a year, and the entire Seleucid reserve was paid at all times – I would disagree with both conclusions, though ultimately it is impossible to be sure.

29. Fischer-Bovet (2014) p.70 collects some figures for Ptolemaic plunder. Again, figures are plagued by likely exaggerations, and the difficulty of determining how much of the stated amounts went to the king, and how much to the army.

30. My conclusion here is contrary to the conventional wisdom, that military campaigns were intended in large part to seize plunder, and that income from plunder largely financed wars and the kingdoms generally. This idea was most clearly stated by Austin (1986) and has been widely accepted.

Fischer-Bovet's data for the Ptolemaic army and navy (n.28) shows that realistic figures for plunder are still much lower than the total costs of the army (Fischer-Bovet (2014) table p.76). While plunder no doubt was an attraction, I do not believe it could have been a primary motivation for war from the kings' point of view. As a way to satisfy the common soldiers, however, its effect cannot be doubted.

31. Hatzopoulos (2001) p.103 f. for the Antigonid Peltasts, p.106 for age classes. Bar-Kochva (1976) pp.59–65 for the identification of the Argyraspides as sons of settlers (which, if drawn from the younger age classes, they would be).

32. Sekunda (2013 a) pp.104–5, Hatzopoulos (2001) p.103 f. for conscription (and p.109 f. for the detailed rules concerning which family members would be liable).

33. Sekunda (2010) p.464 for a summary or evidence for the Antigonid army, with much greater detail in Hatzopoulos (2001) p.131 f., together with Sekunda (2013a) pp.103–4. Chaniotis (2005) pp.46–51 for the training of young men in the Greek cities of the Hellenistic world. For the (lack of) training among Classical armies (except the Spartans), Lendon (2005) pp.106–14 and notes. For the Spartan army, Lazenby (2012). Lloyd (1996) pp.170–7 for the training regimes of Philip and Alexander. Karunanithy (2013) ch.3 pp.19–39 gathers evidence for training and the role of the gymnasium. For the Seleucid army, Bar-Kochva (1976) pp.94–102.

34. See Carney (1996) for discipline, and making the point about the relative lack of harsh discipline in Greek and Macedonian armies. She also points out that the various 'mutinies' under Alexander are more a 'falling out', a breakdown of personal relationships, than is typically implied by modern use of the word 'mutiny'. See also Brice (2015) for a definition of types of insubordination. Roisman (2015) considers opposition to kings in all its forms, and Roisman (2012) pp.31–60 looks specifically at the 'mutinies' under Alexander, and makes (e.g. p.232) the valid point that 'whenever troops act in their own interests, rather than those of their generals, they are called mutinous, undisciplined or … treacherous', categorizing this as an elitist viewpoint – which is fair enough, as military organization and discipline is, by its nature, elitist, and a disciplined army is not usually the place to look for an egalitarian ethos.

35. For the Amphipolis code and booty distribution, Juhel (2002). Discipline – Hatzopoulos (2001) pp.141–3. Motivation generally, including training and discipline – Lloyd (1996) pp.177–87.

36. Chaniotis (2005) pp.172–81 considers other debates about and justifications for war (and the importance of at least seeming to be waging a just war).
37. For reflections on the ubiquity of war in the Hellenistic world and on many aspects of attitudes to war (particularly from the perspective of the Greek cities), Chaniotis (2005). See pp.184–7 for attitudes to peace (as a means to safety, for Greeks, not an end in itself).
38. Examples in Chaniotis (2004) pp.204–7. Menas' epigram on pp.204–5. For the painted tombstones from Sidon, Sekunda (1995) with full colour reconstructions.

Chapter 5: Manpower and recruitment

1. Many of the matters considered in this chapter are usefully summarized, with further references, by Sekunda (2007). The view of the relative importance of race or ethnicity survives, unfortunately, into modern times; see e.g. the comments on Launey's views on race in Launey (1987) 2 Postface pp.xx–xxiii. But for the genuine military importance of national characteristics, Bar-Kochva (1989) pp.91–2.
2. For more on the ongoing debate on the manpower of Macedon see further below; the key studies, arguing for each side of the argument of whether Alexander's campaigns caused permanent manpower shortages, are Bosworth (1986) and Hammond (1989b). See also the further references in Sekunda (2010) p.466, particularly Rostovtzeff (1953) 2 p.1136; Launey (1987) p.290; Tarn (1951) p.70 n.5; Hammond-Walbank 3 (1988) pp.188–9.
3. Sekunda (2010) pp.466–7 and (2013a) pp.106–7.
4. Ethnicity of cleruchs – Bagnall (1984); the average figure is given on p.14. The calculation is not strictly valid, of course; Bagnall's figures apply to cleruchs attested throughout the third century, while the army at Raphia consists only of a single group at a single moment in time. Nevertheless, the figures provide at least an approximation of the sort of numbers of Macedonians that might be present in any one army.
5. Continued emigration – as Bagnall (1984) p.18 notes, this view, taken by e.g. Launey (1987) p.675, Lesquier (1911) pp.113, 134, Griffith (1935) p.117, 'may be taken to be the prevailing dogma'. See also Hammond-Walbank 3 (1988) p.209 – Macedonians continued to slip away to the new kingdoms.
6. For a summary of the origins of the cleruchic system, Fischer-Bovet (2014) ch.6. Difficulties with the evidence – Bagnall (1984) p.9, Launey (1987) Postface p.ix. There are around 3,000 soldiers in *Pros.Ptol.* vol.ii and vol. viii, of whom 600 have an ethnic; Uebel (1968) provides a list of around

1,500 cleruchs up to 145 BC, of whom 453 have a clear ethnic. Problem of ethnic designations, e.g. Uebel (1968) pp.11–13; Oates (1963) p.63; Bagnall (1988) p.22; Goudriaan (1988). Dionysios – Boswinkel-Pestman (1982) p.48 f.; cf. Bagnall (1988) pp.22–3 – Dionysios also has an Egyptian name.

7. *Tes epigones* – Fischer-Bovet (2014) pp.178–91; Oates (1963); Mélèze-Modrzejewski (1983) esp. p.260 f.; Bingen (1978); but see also the views of Boswinkel-Pestman (1982) p.58 f.; Fraser (1972) 1 p.49 f. Bikerman (1938) p.75 notes that it was normal Greek practice for the descendants of an immigrant to keep his ethnic. See also Fischer-Bovet (2014) p.185 on '*wynn ms n kmy*', the Demotic term literally 'Greek born in Egypt' which however does not simply mean this, but is (or became) a technical designation for a particular military class.

8. See chiefly Bagnall (1984). Fischer-Bovet (2014) ch.5, esp. pp.166–91, favours a more continuous process of settlement, but still (apparently) mostly from the earlier period, particularly for Macedonians.

9. Seleucid city foundation – Aperghis (2004); Grainger (1990a) esp. p.37 f. for foundations in Syria by Antigonus and Seleucus I, with the conclusion pp.47–9 that the main cities were probably founded (or refounded by Seleucos) between 301 and 299; Grainger (1990b) esp. p.128 f.; Cohen (1978); Billows (1990) pp.292–305 considers the importance of Antigonus' precedent in Seleucid foundations. Doubt has recently been cast (Aperghis (2004) pp.195–6) on the traditional view (of e.g. Bar-Kochva (1976) p.52) that native peoples were not recruited into the Seleucid phalanx. I believe that the traditional view is correct for the reasons discussed in this chapter, although no doubt as in Egypt by the second century there was a greater degree of ethnic mixing.

10. Gaza prisoners – Griffith (1935) p.116. There is some third-century evidence also of prisoner-cleruchs in Egypt, e.g. *P.Petr*.iii 104; Launey (1987) p.47. Eupolemos-Theangala – Robert, *Coll. Froehner I Inscr. Grecques* (1936) pp.69–86 no.52; Launey (1987) p.43. Iasos – *Annuario* 29–30 (1967/8) pp.437–45 no.1; *BE* 1971, 620; *ZPE* 9 (1972) pp.223–4; Bagnall (1976) pp.89–90.

11. Dryton – Bagnall (1988) p.23 for a discussion of this case. As Bagnall remarks, p.21 – 'there is significant conceptual disarray, visible at the level of detail as well as of generalisation', on the question of ethnicity in Egypt (and indeed on many other aspects of the Ptolemaic army). Dual names – Clarysse (1985) pp.57–67; cf. Boswinkel-Pestman (1982) pp.54–6; two brothers, classed as Persian, become Macedonian on joining the army. Goudriaan (1988) p.92 observes that the differentiation between Greek

and Egyptian must have been based on language and so would have been in practice, as Egyptians began to learn Greek, very fluid. Egyptians in the army – notably a series of articles by Peremans, (1972), (1978), (1983); also Clarysse (1985); Winnicki (1985). For Peremans' method, see (1970) pp.33–8 and (1983) p.98.

12. On the *machimoi* as the Egyptian soldier class, Fischer-Bovet (2014) p.161 f.; Lesquier (1911) pp.4–10; Launey (1987) pp.26, 58 f.; Uebel (1968) p.32; Crawford (1971) pp.53–5, 82–4. Egyptians also formed two paramilitary classes, apparently acting as police – Winnicki (1977). High-ranking Egyptians – *PP* VIII 2109a; *PP* I 285; Peremans (1983) pp.94–5. Dionysios – *Pros.Ptol.*II 2158. Peremans (1972) p.69 f. lists the Egyptian officers found in Pros.Ptol.

13. For all these developments, Fischer-Bovet (2014) esp. ch.5 and 7; Van't Dack (1977) on Egyptians as cleruchs, and other changes generally. Lesquier (1911) p.48 on the Greeks as *katoikoi*. Peremans (1972) and *Pros.Ptol.* II 3726–3769 on Egyptian *katoikoi*; even two *katoikoi hippeis* (on which, Boswinkel-Pestman (1982) p.40 f.), usually thought of as strictly Greek, have double names.

14. Boeotia – Roesch (1982), and summary in Hatzopoulos (2001) p.132; Feyel (1942) Part 2 ch.1 pp.187–215; Sekunda (2007) pp.339–43.

15. On Philopoemen's reform, a starting point is Anderson (1967) though early discussions of the subject are confused by not appreciating the true nature of Hellenistic *thureophoroi*.

16. The fundamental study of Hellenistic mercenaries remains Griffith (1935). Other basic studies of Hellenistic military matters such as Launey (1987) are also very much concerned with mercenaries. However, the common conception that, to quote Baker (2003) p.378, 'most soldiers were mercenaries' is I believe totally wrong.

17. Parke (1933) covers mercenaries of the earlier period. For Isocrates' solutions to socio-economic problems in Greece, Fuks (1972). Chaniotis (2005) pp.80–82 on the social context of mercenary service.

18. Fourth-century mercenaries – Parke (1933) p.227 f.; Pritchett 5 (1991) pp.458–9. McKechnie (1989) ch.4 considers the same question proceeding from the question of ownership of arms (hoplite equipment) and finding that much was probably supplied by the employer, but Whitehead (1991) casts doubt on this idea. Parke believes that circumstances changed in the third century, and mercenary service became a lucrative career attracting volunteers abroad. Cretans – Launey (1987) pp.276–7, although Brûlé (1978) p.163 f. expresses reservations about this view. Launey (1987)

p.724 f. uses funerary depictions and references to the presence of servants to demonstrate that soldiers were well off. New Comedy (the style of comedy drama that became popular in the Hellenistic period) abounds with references to soldiers returning home with plenty of money to waste (Launey p.800 f. – although in fact the depiction of soldiers in Menander at least seems to have been quite sympathetic). In most cases, however, those referred to are clearly officers. Griffith (1935) pp.308–16 on the standard of living.

19. Magnesia at Myous – *I.Milet.* III nos.33–39 and pp.175–203; discussed by Launey (1987) pp.660–4, Brûlé (1978). p.165 f. Family structures – Pomeroy (1983) p.215; Brûlé (1978) p.168 sees the first group also as hired by *xenologoi* and bringing their families with them as *aposkeue*; it is unclear in fact why this first group are accompanied by their families, but they are far more likely to be an ally contingent.

20. Cretan settlers – *I.Cret.* I viii 9 (pp.63–5), IV 176 (pp.246–8); Launey (1987) p.664. The penalties imposed could perhaps be compared with those to be imposed on citizens who accept mercenary service overseas contrary to the wishes of the city in the various mercenary treaties discussed below.

21. Tylissos – listed in Pouilloux-Verdelis (1950); cf. also Launey (1987) pp.79, 618, 791, 1101. It is not certain that these are in fact mercenaries, but it is likely. For the *misthophoroi* in Egypt (which could also, confusingly, include *misthophoroi klerouchoi*, probably cleruchs performing professional internal security duties), Fischer-Bovet (2014) pp.118–22.

22. Lesquier (1911) p.16 f. on the two types – national units with national weapons, and the *misthophoroi*, identifying them as Greek hoplites or peltasts. For another attempt to identify a difference between *xenoi* and *misthophoroi* e.g. Bikerman (1938) p.69 – taking *xenoi* to be those hired for a single campaign and *misthophoroi* to be in permanent service. Lilaia – *F.Delphes* III 4 132–135. Mixed unit in Syria – Rey-Coquais, *Syria* 55 (1978) pp.313–25 = SEG XXVII 973. Sidon – Bagnall (1976) p.17 – ethnic origins are given for twenty-two foreigners. Samos – Robert (1938) p.113 f. Athens – *IG2* II 2 1956; Syll3 I 485 = *IG2* II 2 1958; *IG2* II 2 1957; Griffith (1935) pp.240–1 for these garrison lists. Seleucid garrisons are listed in Bikerman (1938) p.53 f. and Egyptian in Bagnall (1976) passim.

23. Treaties of Cretan cities with kings or cities concerning the sending of a military force – Antiochus II with Lyttos, *I.Cret.* I xviii 8 (p.186); Demetrius II with Gortyn, *I.Cret.* IV 167 (p.229) (with Launey I p.253 no.7); Antigonus Doson with Eleutherna, *I.Cret* II xii 20 (pp.158–61); Doson with Hierapytna, *I.Cret* III iii 1 A (pp.25–6); Rhodes with

Hierapytna, *I.Cret* III iii 3 A (pp.32–5); Rhodes with Olous, *Kret.Chron.* 15/16 (1961/2) pp.231–4 (with *REG* 77 (1964) p.217 no.421 and *BCH* 93 (1963) pp.160–1); Attalus I with Malla, *BCH* 94 (1970) pp.638–42; Attalus I with Lato, *BCH* 94 (1970) pp.637–8; Eumenes II with thirty-one Cretan cities, *I.Cret.* IV 179 (p.251). Launey (1987) p.37 f. for such recruitment treaties; Van Effenterre (1948) p.185 considers their prevalence during the early third century.

24. Taenarum – Couvenhes (2008). For the Ptolemies, Bagnall (1984) p.16 f. – Ptolemaic soldiers outside Egypt (that is, mercenary garrisons overseas) are drawn predominantly from areas within Ptolemaic influence and control – the islands, Asia Minor, Cyrenaica – unlike the settlers which, for example, contain a large proportion from Macedon. Launey (1987) p.31 and Griffith (1935) p.254 f. note that recruiting was commonly carried out through diplomatic channels and that permission was probably required from the supplying power, though Griffith believes that if such permission was not available rallying points for individual volunteers were available. Chaniotis (2005) pp.82–88 on conditions of service.

25. Chaniotis (2005) pp.88–93 on garrisons in Greek cities.

26. Summary of Macedonian manpower measures in Sekunda (2010) pp.466–7. Philip's manpower measures – Griffith (1935) p.73 for the view that the purpose of these movements was to establish a manpower reserve rather than for the political ends given by Polybius; also Hammond (1989) p.385. Griffith (1935) p.78 for settlers in Macedon generally, and Hammond-Walbank 3 (1988) p.458 f. for Philip's measures to increase the population. Letter to Larissa – *Syll 3* 543; *IG* IX (2) 517 = Austin (1981) p.60; Hammond-Walbank 3 (1988) p.391.

27. For the military reforms of the second century and the new types of recruitment in use, and the difference between this army structure and the third-century cleruchs, Fischer-Bovet (2014) esp. ch.5. Earlier studies include Van't Dack (1977) esp. pp.92–5; Winnicki (1978) collects the evidence for the units stationed in the Thebaid. Préaux (1978) p.466; Uebel (1968) pp.18–21; Lesquier (1911) pp.113, 134; Griffith (1935) p.117; all believe that mercenaries did become cleruchs as a matter of course, but this goes against the evidence collected by Bagnall and cited above.

28. Smyrna-Magnesia treaty – *OGIS* 229; Cohen (1978) pp.60–3, 77 f.; Griffith (1935) p.154 f. Antioch in Persis – *OGIS* 233 ll. 14–20, Briant (1982) pp.95–7 on Antioch; Strabo xvi.2.5 for the new building in Antioch, and Grainger (1990a) p.124 f. Cohen (1978) e.g. p.37 for the inclusion of natives in the city population, cf. Jos.Ant. xviii.373 for the population of Seleucia

consisting of Greeks, Macedonians and Syrians. On new settlements in Syria, Grainger (1990a) p.137 f.; most are either very small (such as Laodiceia ad Libanum, pp.139–40) or are not truly new settlements but the addition of a dynastic name to an existing settlement; cf. also Cohen (1978) p.14 and Morkholm (1966) pp.116–8 on the 'new' foundations of Antiochus IV.

29. Lilaia – *F.Delphes* III 4 132–135. Citizenship – *OGIS* 338; Hansen (1971) p.224 f. Mysians – *OGIS* 282. Citizenship grant – *OGIS* 338.

30. See Sekunda (2013a) pp.101–03 for summary of Alexander and Antigonid evidence.

31. For the question of the Seleucid military settlers in general and recruitment to the army in particular, Griffith (1935) p.147 f.; Bar-Kochva (1976), esp. p.22 f.; Bickerman (1938) pp.78–88; Cohen (1978); Launey (1987) pp.337–53. See also Sekunda (1994) pp.13–14, whose views I broadly follow here.

32. Bikerman (1938) p.67 believes that cities could not be used for recruiting purposes, but Bar-Kochva (1976) p.25 f. (with further evidence for the use of citizen soldiers) and Rostovtzeff (1953) 1 p.500, 3 pp.1437–8 conclude that they could. Walbank 3 (1979) p.451 believes that the cities had their own militias which could be contributed to royal armies. There is no inherent reason why the cities should not have been liable for service; many of the Seleucid foundations attained true city autonomy only at a later period. That the cities of Syria supplied men for the army does not of course imply that the Greek cities of Asia Minor were also liable to service.

33. Disputed role of *katoikiai* – the basic account (with *katoikiai* as equivalent to cleruchs) is from Bar-Kochva (1976) pp.59–62; for contrary arguments, see especially Cohen (1991), Sekunda (2007) pp.334–5. Leon – *SEG* VII 17; *SEG* VII 4. Lack of land holdings based on rank – Cohen (1978) p.55 f.; where there are *kleroi* of different sizes other factors seem to be involved – perhaps, for example, how soon after the establishment of the site colonists arrived, or as compensation for a grant of land further away from the central settlement. Babylonian Jews – Cohen (1978) pp.5–9 on this settlement, with references to discussions of its authenticity; see also Bickerman (1938) p.84; cf. Demetrius' offer to use 30,000 Jews in garrisons, *I Macc.* 10.36.

34. Levies of Thyatira, Susa or Seleucia – this is Bickerman's view for Thyatira, (1938) p.82. Bar-Kochva (1976) p.40 uses these cases as evidence of soldiers being settled as distinct units; either case is possible but it seems most likely that military obligation in the Seleucid kingdom was collective, on

the (probable) Macedonian model, rather than individual as in Egypt (so Bikerman p.78). Cohen (1978) p.51 believes that conscription was regional, not based on land. Argyraspides – Bar-Kochva (1976) pp.58–67 and (1989) pp.413–31 for this identification. Bar-Kochva's conclusion is that the guard were drawn from settlers' sons, and this of course is in practice the effect of their being drawn from the youngest age classes; but the system was probably based on age classes rather than on the paternal relationship. The army at Daphne – on how the numbers of this army were made up, Griffith (1935) p.146; Launey (1987) p.319; Bar-Kochva (1976) p.226 n.104.

35. The basic account of Ptolemaic recruitment is now provided by Fischer-Bovet (2014). Earlier views based on Lesquier (1911); see also Uebel (1968) for a listing of the cleruchs. Rowlandson (2003) provides a good introduction to settlement in Ptolemaic Egypt, with further links to the extensive literature. Problems with the evidence – Bagnall (1984) p.9 f. Specifically for ethnic origins, Fischer-Bovet (2014) pp.169 f. and passim.

36. Fischer-Bovet (2014) ch.4 and ch.6 for the cleruchs generally. Rank and land – Lesquier (1911) ch.6 and p.173 f.; pp.31–51 on the military role of the cleruchs. Alexandrian citizen cleruchs, e.g. Heracleides son of Maron, *P.Petrie* iii 15 and Clarysse (1971) pp.13, 18. See also Fraser (1972) 1 pp.50–1. Oates (1963) on the civilian population. Fischer-Bovet (2014) pp.212–6 on the sizes of *kleroi*. Also Lesquier (1911) pp.1–26; Van't Dack (1977) esp. p.83; Uebel (1968) p.380.

37. *P.Cairo Zen.* 59003 and Bagnall (1976) p.17 on Toubias and the cleruchic cavalry; cf. Bar-Kochva (1976) p.197. *AJA* 65 (1961) pp.134–5 no.35 and Bagnall (1976) p.57 on Cyprus settlers; these may, however, be the families of mercenaries, see above Chapter 2. Transfers – such a soldier is Dryton the Cretan, Lewis (1986) p.88 f. On the Thebaid garrisons, Winnicki (1978), and on the use of professional soldiers, Fischer-Bovet (2014) p.118 f. Van't Dack (1977) p.92 f.

38. On the *epigonoi*, Fischer-Bovet (2014) pp.184–5; as sons of settlers performing paid military service, Lesquier (1911) p.52 f.; so e.g. *P.Lond.* [1] 23, and cf. Pol.v.65.10, Thracian and Galatian settlers and *epigonoi* at Raphia. This institution has escaped the detailed analysis devoted to the *tes epigones* (though they may be closely related). For training of the young men in gymnasia, Fischer-Bovet (2014) pp.280–90; Launey (1987) pp.836–69. Boswinkel-Pestman (1982) pp.37, 46 for the career of Dionysios, and pp.56–61 for this identification of *tes epigones*. Old men – see, for example, the group of cleruchs in Clarysse (1971), with ages averaging around 50 and in some cases (such as Kephalon, a Macedonian *epilarch*) as much

as 70; they could still serve (cf. the Argyraspids under Eumenes, Diod. 19.41.2) but they will hardly have been the first choice as soldiers. *Exo taxeon* – for these, Holleaux 3 (1942) pp.1–14, on *hegemon ton exo taxeon* as a reserve officer without current assignment; Van't Dack (1969). *Exo taxeon* in general means 'those not enrolled' and so 'non-combatants' attached to an army, cf. Diod. 19.49.3, 34/35.17.

39. *Kleros* sizes – Fischer-Bovet (2014) p.212 f. Crawford (1971) p.76 f; Van't Dack (1977) p.87. For leasing of *kleroi*, Fischer-Bovet (2014) pp.225–35; Bingen (1973), (1978) – the cleruchs in this case leasing their land through civilians and being apparently the economically weaker party. Agricultural importance of the cleruchs, Crawford (1971) p.54.

40. Stressing the importance of the Egyptian phalanx to the 'Great Revolt' and subsequent upheaval in Egypt of course requires taking the analysis of Polybius (5.107) at face value; for alternatives, Véïsse (2004), Fischer-Bovet (2014) p.92 f. On the size of the Egyptian phalanx at Raphia, see opposing views of Bar-Kochva (1976) pp.139–40; Griffith (1935) pp.122–3; Launey (1987) pp.99–100; Walbank 1 (1957) p.590 but see also 3 (1979) p.773. Fischer-Bovet (2014) favours the figure of 25,000 cleruchs. On the second-century reforms, a rather different picture from the traditional view (that this represents a degradation of the army by a reduction of the Greek element) is painted by Fischer-Bovet (2014), instead emphasizing the positive aspects of greater integration and native Egyptian involvement. *Politeumata* – Fischer-Bovet (2014) pp.293–5. Lesquier (1911) pp.142–55, Launey (1987) pp.1064–85. Mixed marriages and ethnic mixing in the second century – Fischer-Bovet (2014) ch.7. Winnicki (1972), (1981); Mélèze-Modrzejewski (1984) pp.353–76, but this was probably not widespread – Bagnall (1988) p.21.

Chapter 6: Command and control

1. 'King, Friends and military forces' - examples in Austin (1981) nos. 139, 151. Army as supply of governors - eg. Lévêque (1968) p. 281 states that the army provided a pool of people which the king would appoint to all posts, civil and military, within the kingdom; so also Préaux (1978) 1 p. 318 - satraps and governors were chosen from among army officers. Sekunda (2013 a) ch. 3 (pp. 50–66) considers officers in the Antigonid army. King (2010) esp. pp. 379 f. on bodyguards and councils. Sawada (2010) considers specific aspects of the Macedonian aristocracy. Chaniotis (2005) pp. 64–68 on 'friends' generally. An alternative view is that the king used the army to

offset the power of an independent and potentially rebellious nobility, King (2010) p. 374.

2. Alexander's officers – summary in Bosworth (1988) pp. 273-277, and details in Heckel (1992). English (2009) ch. 8 provides an overview.

3. Ptolemaic evidence – Fischer-Bovet (2014) pp. 155-159; Van't Dack (1988), Lesquier (1911). Taxiarch/hecatontarch – Van't Dack (1988) pp. 56,. 58-9; Fischer-Bovet (2014) p. 144. Smyrna-Magnesia – *OGIS* 229 l. 103

4. Seleucids – Launey (1987) p. 25 f.; Bikerman (1938) p. 64. Recruitment treaties – eg. in Rhodes-Olous treaty, *Kret.Chron.* 15/16 (1961/2) pp. 231-4 ll. 39-40, the men receive eight Rhodian obols, the officers commanding at least fifty men two drachmas; in Attalos I-Malla treaty, *BCH* 94 (1970) pp. 638-42 ll. 21-5, the men receive one Aeginetan drachma and the officers two drachmas.

5. Antigonid army – Sekunda (2013a) ch. 3 and (2010) p. 459. Greia land grant – Welles, *AJA* 42 (1938); Walbank (1940) p. 291. Amphipolis army code – Moretti II 114; Walbank (1940) p. 291.

6. Retained ranks – if this is the correct interpretation of *hegemon exo taxeon*, Holleaux 3 (1942) pp. 1-14. Hereditary commands – Van't Dack (1985); Lesquier (1911) pp. 78-9. For the Bodyguards under Alexander as a *cursus honorum*, see Heckel (1986).

7. Rank v. office – on this distinction, eg. Bagnall (1976) p. 42; Lesquier (1911) p. 72.

8. Bengtson (1964-7) provides a detailed account of the *strategos*, and of the administrative role of the Seleucid satraps and the Ptolemaic *strategoi* of the nomes. Fischer-Bovet (2014) pp. 156-8 for Ptolemaic strategoi.

9. Formal ranks – Bengtson (1964-7) 2 p. 155 and Bikerman (1933) p. 64 conclude that there were no formal ranks; Bar Kochva (1976) p. 89 f. offers explanations for these cases. Contrast the situation in Alexander's army, where 'the positions in the hierarchy which mattered most were of course the commanders of individual contingents', Bosworth (1988) p. 274. Possibly the difference between ranking officers and high officials given various regional or military commands is reflected by the use of the terms *hegemon* and *strategos*; thus the combination in inscriptions of *hegemones* and *stratiotai*, the army, as opposed to generals, not part of the army.

10. Grades of 'Friend' – Bikerman (1938) p. 40 f. for Seleucids; Mooren (1977) for the Ptolemies. Strategoi and Friends – from the lists in Lesquier (1911) and Bengtson (1964-7); Bengtson 2 p. 109 for a hipparch who is a friend. Bagnall (1976) p. 53 notes that there are no sure examples from Cyprus of hegemons with aulic (honorific Friend) rank.

11. On the qualities required of a successful military leader, Beston (2000). For a summary of the growth in the 4th C of systematic instruction in war, Whitehead (1990) p. 34 f.

12. For the view that there was a powerful nobility in Macedonia, eg. Hammond-Griffith 2 (1979) p. 409; Errington (1978). Hammond (1989) p. 54 f. notes that the Companions were chosen by the king entirely according to his own desires – thus the possibility of foreigners becoming Companions, although it is not certain that all land was under the control of the king, and foreign Companions need not become wealthy landed Macedonians. Hammond notes that the king could review the grants of his predecessors, (1988) pp. 382-91 cf. the Greia grant reverting to the crown, Welles, *AJA* 42 (1938). Walbank (1940) p. 5 states that possession of land depended on a grant from the king and carried an obligation to serve in the army. Cf. also Alexander's distribution of land to his followers (Plut.*Alex*.15). Borza (1990) pp. 235, 237 remarks on the lack of evidence for a Macedonian aristocracy. Revocable land grants – Cohen (1984), who also gives some examples of private land ownership outside cities.

13. On councils, Hammond (1989) pp. 53-4; Préaux (1978) 1 p. 200. For the importance of personal intimacy to take part in councils, Bikerman (1938) p. 47, and p. 40 f. generally.

14. Banquets – Hammond (1989) p. 55 for the Macedonian tradition; Borza (1983); (1990) pp. 241-2. For Stoic philosophers at the symposia of Gonatas, Erskine (1990) eg. p. 80. Achaemenid kings also had their 'table sharers', eg. Xen.*Anab*.i.8.25. Hornblower (1982) p. 147 for the connection between dining with the king and military service.

15. Oaths - for example, Eumenes I's agreement with his mercenaries required them to swear to 'guard anything I receive from him, whether a city or a [fort or] ships or money' (*OGIS* 266 1. 36), while the settlers at Magnesia swear to Seleucus II that 'what I have received from king Seleucus I will preserve to the best of my ability' (*OGIS* 229 1. 63). This would apply to the commander as much as to the men.

16. On commanders other than the king in charge of armies, Bar Kochva (1976) p. 86 - all are important men in the kingdom; local commanders leading their own forces, p. 87-8.

17. For this subject see also Matthew (2015) pp. 343-353. On generalship in general, Lendon (2005) ch. 5 pp. 140-155 emphasises the Hellenistic concept of warfare as a contest of technical skill between generals. Grainger (2017) ch. 9 for a general discussion of kings and war.

18. Matthew (2015) pp. 296-311 goes into great detail on the positioning of officers in the phalanx; he does favour placing the officers in the front rank. Wrightson (2010) examines this question for the higher ranked officers, concluding that the higher ranks at least may have commanded from horseback (though the evidence is slight at best).

19. Matthew (2015) pp. 157 f. considers the holding and lowering of the sarissa, somewhat speculatively. See also chapters 2 and 8.

20. For trumpet (*salpinx* in Greek) signals in Greek armies, Krentz (1991), who identifies six basic trumpet calls – call to arms, reveille, form line of battle, silence, charge, retreat. For other types of signals in Greek armies, Anderson (1965), pointing out that often command would involve a 'cautionary' command being issued first (perhaps by word of mouth), informing the men or junior commanders what they were to do, and the trumpet would provide the 'executive' command, indicating the moment when they should do it. This is the nature of the flag signals at Sellasia also, below. Romans certainly had more complex signals – see Krentz (1991) p. 117, quoting Aristides Qunitilianus 62.6-19 – 'when the attack was by line and the approach was by column, she [Rome] set down special phrases [*mele*] and a different kind for retreat; and when the pivoting was to the left or the right, again there were specific phrases for each.' The Hellenistic phalanx had the same need, and the same means was at hand, so I suspect the same or a similar solution was adopted.

21. The exception being the Spartans – see Lazenby (2012) esp. pp. 35-40, Anderson (1970), and especially the manoeuvres described in [Xenophon] *Constitution of the Lacedaemonians*, though it is open to doubt whether Spartan command flexibility was as great as Macedonian.

22. Beston (2000) pp. 321-325 considers these aspects of battlefield command. As he observes, the question of whether a general was better leading by example or provide command oversight was still open in this period. Grainger (2017) p. 144-5 makes the point about limited battlefield control, perhaps slightly overstating it (the skill, as shown at Paraitacene, lay in deployment).

Chapter 7: Battles and tactics

1. For lists and analyses of battles of the period, Pietrykowski (2009) is useful if sometimes a trifle imaginative. Bar Kochva (1976) is a good place to start for the battles of the Seleucid army, though his reconstructions are also quite speculative. Sabin (2007b) covers all the major battles of

the period from the perspective of wargame scenarios, but with useful references and discussion of the evidence for each, with an emphasis on the numbers involved on each side.

2. Matthew (2015) pp.311–26 goes into impressive detail on the question of the deployment at Issus and Mantinea, though I am not wholly convinced that the symmetrical arrangement of officers by ranking (described by Aelian, *Tactics* 10) was as important as he believes. On deployment from column into line in the Spartan army, Lazenby (2012) p.38 and Anderson (1970) p.105 f. For Classical hoplites generally, Bardunias and Rey (2017) pp.113–7.

3. Cynoscephalae is covered in detail by Hammond (1988), though with an emphasis on the location of the battle (on which his conclusions, though widely accepted, are highly speculative); see also Sabin (2007b) pp.193–6.

4. For further speculation on the manoeuvres, see Matthew (2015) pp.311–26. Ilipa has a literature of its own – see Lazenby (1978) pp.147–50 and Walbank (1967) pp.299–304.

5. What information there is on Macedonian camps is gathered with admirable completeness in Karunanithy (2013) pp.186–206.

6. For Pydna see Hammond (1984), again with an emphasis on the location of the battle. His diagram shows both armies fully deployed; compare Sabin (2007b) pp.200–3 (favouring a deployment from camp).

7. For Magnesia, Bar-Kochva (1976) pp.163–73; Sabin (2007b) pp.197–200.

8. Raphia – Bar-Kochva (1976) pp.128–41; Sabin (2007b) pp.157–60.

9. Size of files (and so depth of phalanx), covered also in Chapter 3 above, is discussed by Matthew (2015) pp.256–75; see also pp.359–70 for considerations assuming a symmetrical deployment of officers was important.

10. See above ch.3 for this question. On the non-technical use of terms by Polybius, Walbank (1979) on Pol 18.29–30, or Pol 12.21 where his calculations show 30,000 men drawn up *sunaspizo* would be at two–cubit intervals. Non-technical usage in other sources e.g. Xen. *Hell.* 3.5.11, where the verb *sunaspidoō* is used to mean 'fight alongside', or 7.4.23, 'massed together' (we can assume that Classical hoplites did not adopt Hellenistic one-cubit spacing). But see also further examples below.

11. Sellasia – Hammond and Walbank (1988) pp.358–9; Morgan (1981) (concentrating on the location of the battle); Sabin (2007b) pp.154–7.

12. On Gaugamela, Marsden (1964); also Devine (1986); Sabin (2007b) pp.136–9.

13. On Paraitacene, Devine (1985); Sabin (2007b) pp.146–8.

14. Leuctra – Devine (1983), with the comments of Buckler (1985). Gaugamela – Devine (1986).

15. Pydna – Sabin (2007b) and note 6 above, and see also ch.9.

16. On the pace of advance, Matthew (2015) pp.350–2 reaching the same conclusion; though some advances are called 'rapid', the term is only relative and a fast (disciplined) walk could fit the description. Note, however, that Connolly (2000) reports that his experimental phalanx was able to run in formation (with some concerns as regards health and safety). On hoplites, Bardunias and Rey (2016) p.129.

17. Matthew (2015) pp.371–3 finds in favour of the 'hammer and anvil' concept, with references to other modern adherents. If all that is meant is that Alexander used his cavalry as a strike force, and that Hellenistic armies tended to open proceedings with cavalry engagements on the wings, then I have no objection. For proportions of infantry to cavalry, see the table in Matthew (2015) p.388 (quoting Snodgrass (1999)) – ratios dropping from 2:1 in the 'age of Alexander' (though this seems too low) to 8:1 in the later Antigonid army.

18. For *hamippoi* – in general Wheeler (2007) p.222.

19. Matthew (2015) pp.331–43 on terrain, also concluding that the unsuitability of the phalanx for anything other than flat clear terrain is overstated. See also Chapter 9.

20. See the thoughts of Sabin (2007a) p.405 on this question, suggesting that the command limitations on wide formations may have been the main consideration, though as discussed in Chapter 6 I believe command was routinely delegated anyway.

21. Bosworth (1980) pp.308–9 on the difficulties interpreting this passage in Arrian.

22. Matthew (2015) p.352 appears to accept the idea of a feigned, backwards, retreat. Delbrück (1990) describes the idea of a backward march as a 'monstrous idea' and a 'grotesque concept', and while he is sometimes rather limited in what he finds plausible, in this case I would have to agree with him.

23. See Sabin (2007a) pp.406, 408 – stressing command limitations on the ability to commit reserves at the needed point (something the Romans overcame by the size of their reserve forces and the initiative of their junior commanders).

24. For a discussion of combined arms with particular reference to elephants, Wrightson (2015a). More generally, Sabin (2007a).

25. Juhel (2017a) pp.10–18 uses these relatively even contests between hoplite and pike-phalangite to support his argument that Alexander's phalanx could not have been a phalanx of pikemen. But I think there are far too many imponderables in these battles to reach any such conclusion, and we cannot conclude that a pike phalanx would necessarily brush aside a hoplite phalanx. Hoplites, like Roman legionaries (Chapter 9) would have sought, and occasionally found, a way to improve the odds. See further Chapter 8 on methods for opposing a pike phalanx.

26. For the Hydaspes, Sabin (2007b) pp.139–43 refers to the extensive modern bibliography, mostly concerned with the obscure movements of the cavalry. For elephants, Wrightson (2015a), Sabin (2007a) pp.419–21 and more generally, Scullard (1974).

27. Sabin (2007a) pp.414–6 on the disproportion between losses to winners and losers (and reasons to believe such accounts may be accurate).

28. Sabin (2007a) pp.417–9 on chariots in Hellenistic warfare generally.

29. The 'agonal' (formal competitive) nature of Classical battle has long been a source of discussion; Wheeler (2007) pp.188–91 provides an introduction. Sabin (2007a) and Roth (2007) for overviews of battle and war and strategy generally.

Chapter 8: Fighting in the phalanx

1. The name of this 'face of battle' approach derives from its founder's seminal work, Keegan (1976), *The Face of Battle*, which examined more recent conflicts – Agincourt, Waterloo and the Somme – as well as making the more general points outlined above.

2. Leading the field in ancient history was Hanson (1989), whose work has been highly influential (and somewhat controversial) and has sparked a number of other works on hoplite warfare, notably Hanson (ed.) (1991) and many works since; Bardunias and Rey (2016) provide a recent summary. Sabin (2000) is one of the few to apply these techniques to Roman, specifically Roman Republican, warfare, emphasizing the 'mechanics' approach, which also influence Goldsworthy (1996). See also Sabin (2007a) for thoughts on the applicability of this approach to Hellenistic warfare generally.

3. Matthew (2015) pp.375–98 is one of the very few to consider the mechanics of sarissa combat, though I find his account overly mechanistic. The *'othismos* controversy' has attracted a large bibliography, much of

it sadly repetitious and lacking in insight. The best starting point and summary of the origins of the debate is Krentz (2013).

4. For all these matters and references to the considerable literature, Krentz (2013). Bardunias and Rey (2016) pp.132–8 provide a modern restatement (and slight modification) of the 'scrum' – a 'crowd crush *othismos*' – which clarifies some of the physical properties of such a scrum.

5. Among many examples of uses of *otheo* or compounds, Hdt. 9.25.1 (hoplites and archers v cavalry), Thuc. 4.11.3 (ships), Thuc. 4.35.3 (peltasts v fortified Spartan hoplites on Pylos), Thuc. 8.25.4 (hoplites v barbarians), Pol. 5.84.3 (elephants), Pol. 2.33.8 (Romans v. Gauls); Diod. 19.42.5 (cavalry), Diod. 20.88.5 (ships). The originally military user of *otheo* was of course Homer (*Iliad* 8.336, 13.193, 16.45, 5.691, 12.420, 8.295, 16.655); Krentz (2013) pp.146–8 points outs this Homeric origin, and also the resonances between Homer, *Iliad* 4.446f and Xenophon, *Agesilaus*, 2.12–14 (the latter describing the fighting at Coronea, and much quoted by scrum adherents); Xenophon's much-quoted phrase 'they pushed, they fought, they killed, they died' (see below) echoes Homer's 'they clashed their shields together and their spears ... men killing and men killed' and is even more closely echoed by Xenophon himself in the *Cyropaedia* describing Persian cavalry fighting Egyptians – 'leaping forward they fought, pushed and were pushed, gave and received blows', Xen. *Cyr.* 7.1.38

6. I collect the evidence of *othismos*, *otheo* and related words in Taylor (2016) and (2017). Note also the example (missed in the articles referenced) of Julius Africanus (*Kestoi* 7.1.10) mentioned in ch.2 n.36 above – 'a concave bronze shield held by two handles (of which the one surrounding the forearm avails for shoving [*eis othismon*])' – this seems to me to be further support for individual shield-bashing, similar to the pushing of Xenophon's Egyptians in the *Cyropaedia* (Xen. *Cyr.* 7.1.33, quoted below). In the standard scrum (or modified crowd crush) version of *othismos* the shield grip would be irrelevant, since the shield would be squashed firmly up against the bearer's body. Note also Julius Africanus' comment on Romans, who carry 'an oblong shield [*thureos*] for defence, borne by the end of one hand (which is less efficacious for the body in fighting in closed ranks [*sunaspismo*], because the soldier is unable to press on the weapon [*hoplon*] with his whole shoulder [or arm]).' This contrast – that the Roman *scutum* could not be braced with the shoulder/arm, unlike the Greek *aspis* or the Egyptian shield which could – seems again strong evidence against a scrum or crowd crush, in which a *thureos* would act just the same as any other type

of shield (that is, it would be squashed between the bodies of subsequent ranks, the nature of the grip irrelevant).

7. Bardunias and Rey (2016) pp.132–8 deal with the stance issue and provide the data for the non-lethal nature of the forces generated (but to my mind the crowd crush is still not much more plausible than the scrum).

8. The influence of the earlier tacticians on Maurice specifically is covered in detail in Rance (2017b).

9. This matter, particularly 'bear forward with the weight of their bodies', is considered by Burliga (2017), though his conclusions are almost the opposite of mine; I would take issue in particular with his statement (p.125) that 'the manoeuvre depicted here is the famous ὠθισμός – an operation know[n] from many (if not all) battlefields in the classical era'. It is known (by that name) from precisely one battle of hoplite against hoplite.

10. Matthew (2015) pp.241–5 on breaking the sarissa, though he does not consider breakage due to frontal pressure, even though (p.384) he finds that 'the primary function of the sarissa was to be pressed into an opponent's shield' (this in the context of the, to my mind untenable, view that the sarissa was made in two parts, and precautions were needed to prevent the enemy simply pulling the end off). Note that a sarissa could also be deliberately cut through, particularly by a sword-armed enemy, and Early Modern pikes often carried metal strips below the pike head to protect against this. Matthew also (pp.225–35) calculates the penetrative power of the sarissa, and (pp.167–206) the reach and likely target area – all of which seems to presuppose that the sarissa is thrust by the hands, not pressed by the force of sixteen men. For the bendiness of the sarissa, see for example plates 1 and 13–17 in Matthew (2015), or the experience of one re-enactment group at https://www.hetairoi.de/index.php/en/the-sarissa-experiment.

11. The translation of Arrian here comes from Juhel (2017c), and is preferable to that of DeVoto (Juhel also collects a number of alternative translations of each passage, and draws attention (p.174 n.2) to the passage of Xenophon).

12. On the question of charges into contact, often quoted is Keegan's (1976) analysis of cavalry v infantry (particularly at Waterloo) and of infantry v infantry at Agincourt, and there is a considerable literature on the question outside the Ancient period, particularly eighteenth century and Napoleonic warfare, where the evidence collected by Brent Nosworthy is of particular note, finding that some cavalry at least did expect to charge into full contact. As with other discussions of this type, I feel the analysis is sometimes too formalistic – more on this topic below.

13. On the Early Modern use of Aelian (in particular), Roberts (2017). To see literal pushes of pike in action, search YouTube for 'push of pike' (an example is https://www.youtube.com/watch?v=1t_4g5f04PA). I am convinced that hoplite or pike phalanx battle was nothing whatever like this, though it is fair to say that the re-enactment community are well aware of the limitations of this sort of fighting. That 'push of pike' involved fighting with the pike, not scrummaging, is made certain by the comments of Sir Thomas Kellie in *Pallas Armata* (1627, p.25) and Sir John Smythe, *Instructions, Observations and orders Mylitarie* (1591), quoted below.

14. The quote is from Georg Frundsberg's *Trewer Rath und Bedencken eines Alten wol versuchten und Erfahrenen Kriegsmans* ('True advice and reflections of an old well tested and experienced warrior') of 1522, quoted by Delbrück (1990) vol.4 p.63. Delbrück himself finds (p.55 f.) that 'if two such units [Swiss pikes and their enemies] with long spears clashed with one another there resulted a powerful pressure. The sources speak again and again of "pressure" or of "pressure from the rear" with which the deep units sought to surge over the enemy and press him down.' However, the only examples he quotes are fighting at Bicocca, where advancing pikes were blocked by a ditch and rampart (which Frundsberg witnessed), and Monluc's account of Cerisoles. He also opines that pikes would mostly break or be forced upward or backward through the bearer's hands as the two sides pushed into bodily contact, and that we do not hear of this in antiquity since 'the late Macedonian phalanx never had occasion to fight with a similar opponent' (this in the context of his belief that the phalanx of Philip, Alexander and the Successors was not a pike phalanx). I am not convinced by Delbrück's analysis, but suffice to say that there is a similar (though quieter) debate about the nature of 'push of pike' as there is about '*othismos*'.

15. Considerably more information and speculation on the wielding and use of the sarissa, approached from a re-enactment rather than a comparative historical perspective, is to be found in Matthew (2015), esp. pp.157–254. I have not followed this approach here partly because Matthew already covers this ground, and partly because I am not convinced of the value of the quantified results obtained. However, see pp.233–4 for some thoughts (and numbers) on momentum.

16. Lloyd (1996) pp.187–94 ('Who wins and why?') identifies leadership, superior discipline, superior will to win, superior weaponry and superior numbers as the key factors, not necessarily in that order. Sabin (2007a)

'Determinants of success' pp.429–33 stresses leadership, fear, psychological shock and fatigue; pp.413–6 for casualty figures.

17. Evidence for medical care (in the Macedonian army) is covered by Karunanithy (2013) pp.164–70.

18. Sabin (2007a) pp.413–7 on casualty figures.

19. For comparison, the psychology of the Classical (Athenian) hoplite is examined by Crowley (2012); much less evidence is available for the Macedonian phalangite, though I believe many of Crowley's findings are equally applicable. See also the thoughts of Heckel (2006) pp.50–3.

20. Roisman (2012) specifically for the exploits of the Argyraspides, though he feels (p.200) that our sources overstate their importance (at Paraitacene, at least).

21. For the evidence for Athenian hoplites, Crowley (2012). The Xenophon quote, and other examples, p.95.

22. For tentmates in the file, Sekunda (2010) pp.464–5; Lloyd (1996) p.180.

23. This aspect of Greek warfare is examined by Ogden (1996). Heckel (2006) pp.52–3 touches on the question in the context of the Macedonian phalanx.

Chapter 9: Legion and phalanx

1. For a recent and highly readable analysis of the encounter of legion and phalanx, with battle reconstructions (more imaginative than I would attempt, but reaching broadly similar conclusions), Cole (2018).

2. Champion (2009) for a recent account of the career of Pyrrhus. Cole (2018) provides speculative (if sensible) reconstructions of all three battles, as does Pietrykowski (2009). Sabin (2007b) covers only Asculum.

3. For a detailed analysis of Roman (and Italian) manpower, Brunt (1987).

4. Overview of the battle in Sabin (2007b) pp.193–6; Cole (2018) pp.150–76. Possible location – Hammond (1988).

5. Grainger (2015a) for an account of the war (and wider career of Antiochus III); also Taylor (2013). For the battles (Thermopylae and Magnesia), Bar-Kochva (1976) pp.158–73; Sabin (2007b) pp.197–200; Cole (2018) pp.177–207.

6. Bar-Kochva (1976) pp.166–7 for the position of the Seleucid light infantry, p.168 (and generally pp.63–6) for the Argyraspides. Bar-Kochva's suggestion (below) that a Roman (Allied) *ala* was the target of Antiochus' charge has also been widely accepted, correctly I am sure.

7. Lendon (2005) bases ch.9 (pp.193–211) on the battle, and emphasizes the two Roman qualities of *virtus* and *disciplina* – on which more below. Cole

(2018) pp.208–42 and Sabin (2007b) pp.200–3 for summaries. Hammond (1984) for the battle's (possible) location.

8. Bar-Kochva (1976) p.56 and n.8 on this question.

9. The theory of a widespread Hellenistic adoption of Roman equipment and organization has been proposed particularly by Sekunda (1994), (1995) and (2001b) but has not, it is probably fair to say, won many converts.

10. See Matyszak (2008) for the life of Mithridates (or Mithradates – both spellings were used in antiquity). The battles themselves, for which we do not have any good accounts, tend to be disregarded by modern battle compilations of the Hellenistic period.

11. Lendon (2005) pp.193–211 emphasizes the role of *virtus* (at least as the Romans told it). See also Sabin (2007a) pp.430, noting approvingly the Roman emphasis on psychological over technical factors. See also Lendon (2007) pp.508–16 on the warlike nature of Roman culture.

Epilogue

1. See Rance (2017b) for the use of Aelian and Arrian (the 'Ancients') in Byzantine tactical writing. Wheeler (1979) makes the case for phalanx-like deployments of later Roman armies.

2. Roberts (2017) for the later influence of the Classical tacticians.

3. Even though the pike was obsolete on the battlefield by the eighteenth century, there were further attempts, though none came to fruition, to revive its use. In 1862 there was a plan to equip Confederate armies in the American Civil War with pikes, while in 1941 the British manufactured 250,000 'pikes' (at 5 feet long, these were really spears) for distribution to the Home Guard. 'Boarding pikes' also continued in use as naval weapons through the nineteenth century, though these were much shorter than the pikes of the Macedonians, and pikes continue to serve a ceremonial function in several armies, such as the Company of Pikemen and Musketeers in the British Army reserve.

Bibliography and Abbreviations

I have not referenced (or read) every modern work dealing with the topics covered in this book; the modern literature just on the technical features of the phalanx is vast, and including the social, economic and political aspects touched on in earlier chapters would make it greater still. Instead I have aimed to reference those works which by virtue of being recent, accessible or original, or where a specific text or document is discussed, seem to provide the best starting point for those wishing to delve deeper into the topics covered in this book.

As well as the bibliographic notes for each chapter, I include some thematic recommendations for further reading below.

General histories

There are many general histories of the Hellenistic Age. The historical chapters in Roisman and Worthington (2010) provide the background specifically for Macedon, while Erskine (2003) covers the wider Hellenistic world. For Hellenistic history as a whole, general works include Walbank (1993), Green (1990) and Errington (2008). Recent accounts of the life of Philip II include Worthington (2010) and (2014). The bibliography for Alexander the Great is enormous and growing constantly; Lane Fox (1973) is still a good place to start, while Cartledge (2005) provides a more up-to-date, thematic approach. A good recent account of the age of the Successors is Waterfield (2011).

Military matters

The most important recent specialist work on the Macedonian phalanx is Matthew (2015), with extensive references and discussion of the primary and secondary literature. Matthew's emphasis is largely on technical aspects such as the hold, reach and penetrative power of the sarissa, incorporating results from experimental archaeology, and some of his conclusions are quite idiosyncratic. Two books aimed at general readers are particularly valuable for their illustrations:

Connolly (1998) and Warry (2002). The main academic studies of military institutions more broadly are the older works by Griffith (1935), Launey (1987 reprint) and Tarn (1930), all of which are now supplemented by Sabin, van Wees and Whitby (2007).

Specific armies

Head (1982) is perhaps the best summary of the armies of this period, though light on notes and references. There are a number of studies of particular armies: for the army of Alexander, English (2009) provides a readable introduction; for the Seleucids, Bar-Kochva (1976) remains the standard work; for the Antigonid army, see Sekunda (2013a). Fischer-Bovet (2014) covers many aspects of the Ptolemaic army, with an emphasis on social aspects. The illustrated books from Osprey and Montvert provide overviews of each army, and details of uniform and equipment with colour reconstructions; for Alexander's army, Sekunda (1984); for Antigonid armies (and Macedonian armies generally), Sekunda (2012) and Heckel (2006); for the later Seleucid and Ptolemaic armies, Sekunda (1994) and (1995).

Battles and tactics

Pietrykowski (2009) provides useful accounts of the major battles of the period, with references to the ancient sources, though I find his reconstructions a little too imaginative. Sabin (2007b) is also useful for the major battles (presenting each as a scenario for the wargame rules developed in the book). Cole (2018) is very readable for the clashes of legion and phalanx.

Online resources

A very large proportion of the ancient texts quoted in the book, often with translations, are available from the invaluable Perseus Digital Library at http://www.perseus.tufts.edu/hopper/.

Also useful is the collection of texts and translations at Lacus Curtius, http://penelope.uchicago.edu/Thayer/E/Roman/home.html.

Images of many of the archaeological discoveries referenced here are also online, and a search in your preferred search engine will often yield more and better results than hours in a specialist library. I refer in the notes to such searches where appropriate.

The Society of Ancients is an amateur society for the study of ancient and medieval military history and wargaming, and their website (http://www.soa.org.uk) provides useful resources and a forum for often lively discussions of ancient military history.

Bibliography

AALDERS, G.J.D. (1975), *Political Thought in Hellenistic Times*.

ADAMS, W.L. (1986), 'Macedonian Kingship and the Right of Petition', in *Ancient Macedonia* 4, pp.43–52.

ALDRETE, G.S., BARTELL, S. and ALDRETE, A. (2013), *Ancient Linen Body Armor: Unraveling the Linothorax Mystery*.

ANDERSON, J.K. (1965), 'Cleon's Orders at Amphipolis', in *The Journal of Hellenic Studies*, Vol.85, pp.1–4.

———, (1967), 'Philopoemen's Reform of the Achaean Army', in *Classical Philology* 62 2, pp.104–6.

———, (1970), *Military Theory and Practice in the Age of Xenophon*.

———, (1976), 'Shields of Eight Palms' Width', in *California Studies in Classical Antiquity* 9, pp.1–6.

ANDRONICOS, M. (1970), 'Sarissa', in *Bulletin de Correspondance Hellénique*, 94 1, pp.91–107.

ANSON, E.M. (1981), 'Alexander's Hypaspists and the Argyraspids', in *Historia* 30 1, pp.117–20.

———, (1985) 'Macedonia's Alleged Constitutionalism', in *Classical Journal* 80, pp.303–16.

———, (1991) 'The Evolution of the Macedonian Army Assembly (330–315 BC)', in *Historia* 40, pp.230–47.

APERGHIS, G.G. (2004), *The Seleukid Royal Economy: The Finances and Financial Administration of the Seleukid Empire*.

ASIRVATHAM, S.R. (2010), 'Perspectives on the Macedonians from Greece, Rome and Beyond', in J. Roisman and I. Worthington (ed.), *A Companion to Ancient Macedonia*, pp.99–124.

AUSTIN, M.M. (1981), *The Hellenistic World from Alexander to the Roman Conquest* (Cambridge).

———, (1986), 'Hellenistic kings, war and the economy', in *Classical Quarterly* 36, pp.450–66.

BAGNALL, R.S. (1976), *The Administration of the Ptolemaic Possessions Outside Egypt* (Leiden).

————, (1982) 'Papyrology and Ptolemaic History 1956–1980', in *CW* 76, pp.13–21.

————, (1984) 'The Origins of the Ptolemaic Cleruchs', *Bulletin of the American Society of Papyrologists* 21, pp.7–20.

————, (1988) 'Greeks and Egyptians: Ethnicity, Status and Culture', in *Cleopatra's Egypt: Age of the Ptolemies* (Brooklyn).

BAGNALL, R.S. and DEROW, P. (2004), *Historical Sources in Translation: The Hellenistic Period.*

BAKER, P. (2003), 'Warfare', in A. Erskine (ed.), *A Companion to the Hellenistic World*, pp.373–88.

BARDUNIAS, P. and REY, F. (2016), *Hoplites at War.*

BAR-KOCHVA, B. (1976), *The Seleucid Army* (Cambridge) (reissued 2011).

————, (1989), *Judas Maccabaeus* (Cambridge).

BENGTSON, H. (1964–7), *Die Strategie in der hellenistischen Zeit* (2nd ed.).

BEST, J.G.P. (1969), *Thracian Peltasts and their Influence of Greek Warfare.*

BESTON, P. (2000), 'Hellenistic military leadership', in H. van Wees (ed.), *War and Violence in Ancient Greece.*

BIKERMAN, E. (1938), *Institutions des Séleucides.*

BILLOWS, R.A. (1990), *Antigonos the One-Eyed and the Creation of the Hellenistic State.*

————, (2018) *Before & After Alexander.*

BINGEN, J. (1973), 'Présence grecque et milieu rural ptolémaïque', in M.I. Finley (ed.), *Problèmes de la terre en Grèce ancienne*, pp.215–22.

BORZA, E.N. (1983), 'The symposium at Alexander's court', in *Ancient Macedonia* 3, pp.45–55.

————, (1990), *In the Shadow of Olympus: the emergence of Macedon.*

BOSWINKEL, E. and PESTMAN, P.W. (1982), *Les archives privees de Dionysios fils de Kephalas.*

BOSWORTH, A.B. (1973), 'ΑΣΘΕΤΑΙΡΟΙ', in *Classical Quarterly* 23.2, pp.245–53.

————, (1980), *A Historical Commentary on Arrian's History of Alexander*, vol. 1.

————, (1986), 'Alexander the Great and the decline of Macedon', in *Journal of Hellenic Studies* 16, pp.1–12.

————, (1988), *Conquest and Empire. The Reign of Alexander the Great.*

————, (1997), 'A cut too many? Occam's razor and Alexander's footguard', in *Ancient History Bulletin* 11, pp.47–56.

BRIANT, P. (1978), 'Colonisation hellénistique et populations indigènes I', in *Klio* 60, pp.57–92.

————, (1982), 'Colonisation hellénistique et populations indigènes II: renforts grecs dans les cités hellénistiques d'Orient', in *Klio* 64, pp.83–98.

BRICE, L.L. (2015), 'Military unrest in the age of Philip and Alexander of Macedon: defining the terms of debate', in T. Howe, E.E. Garvin and G. Wrightson (eds), *Greece, Macedon and Persia*, pp.69–76.

BRÛLÉ, P. (1978), *La Piraterie Crétoise Hellénistique*.

BRUNT, P. (1987), *Italian Manpower 225 BC – AD 14*.

BUCKLER, J. (1985), 'Epaminondas and the *Embolon*', in *Phoenix* 39, pp.134–43.

BURLIGA, B. (2017), 'Asclepiodotus' τοῖς γε σώμασιν ἐπιβρίθοντες (Tact. 5.2) and Polybius' τῷ τοῦ σώματος βάρει (18.30.1–4)', in Rance and Sekunda (eds), (2017).

CARNEY, E. (1996), 'Macedonians and Mutiny: Discipline and Indiscipline in the Army of Philip and Alexander', in *Classical Philology* 91, 1, pp.19–44.

CARTLEDGE, P. (2005), *Alexander the Great: The Truth Behind the Myth*.

CHAMPION, J. (2009), *Pyrrhus of Epirus*.

CHANIOTIS, A. (2003), 'The divinity of Hellenistic rulers', in A. Erskine (ed.), *A Companion to the Hellenistic World*, pp.431–45.

————, (2005), *War in the Hellenistic World: A Social and Cultural History*.

CHRISTESEN, P. and MURRAY, S.C. (2010), 'Macedonian Religion', in J. Roisman and I. Worthington (eds), *A Companion to Ancient Macedonia*, pp.428–45.

CLARYSSE, W. (1971), 'Three soldiers' wills in the Petrie collection; a re-edition', in *Ancient Society* 2, pp.7–20.

————, (1985) 'Greeks and Egyptians in the Ptolemaic Army and Administration', in *Aegyptus* 65, pp.57–67.

COHEN, A. (1997), *The Alexander Mosaic*.

COHEN, G.M. (1978), *The Seleucid Colonies. Studies in founding, administration and organisation*, Hist. Einz. 30.

————, (1984) 'Property rights of Hellenistic colonists', in *Proc. 7th Int. Fed. Soc. Class. Stud.* Vol.1, pp.323–5.

————, (1991), '*Katoikiai, Katoikioi* and Macedonians in Asia Minor', in *Ancient Society* 22, pp.41–50.

————, (1995), *The Hellenistic Settlements in Europe, the Islands and Asia Minor*.

————, (2006), *The Hellenistic Settlements in Syria, the Red Sea Basin, and North Africa*.

————, (2013), *The Hellenistic Settlements in the East from Armenia and Mesopotamia to Bactria and India*.

COLE, M. (2018), *Legion versus Phalanx*.

CONNOLLY, P. (1998), *Greece and Rome at War*.

―――, (2000), 'Experiments with the Sarissa – the Macedonian pike and cavalry lance – a functional view', in *Journal of Roman Military Equipment Studies* 11, pp.103–12.

COUVENHES, J.-C. (2008), 'Le Ténare: un grand marché de mercenaires à la fin du IVe siècle?', in C. Grandjean (ed.), *Le Péloponnèse d'Epaminondas à Hadrien*, pp.279–315.

CRAWFORD, D. (1971), *Kerkeosiris: an Egyptian Village in the Ptolemaic Period*.

CROWLEY, J. (2012), *The Psychology of the Athenian Hoplite: The Culture of Combat in Classical Athens*.

DANFORTH, L.M. (2010), 'Ancient Macedonia, Alexander the Great and the star or sun of Vergina: national symbols and the conflict between Greece and the Republic of Macedonia', in J. Roisman and I. Worthington (eds), *A Companion to Ancient Macedonia*, pp.572–98.

DELBRÜCK, H. (1990) vol.1 *Warfare in Antiquity*; vol.4 *The Dawn of Modern Warfare* (English trans. by W.J. Renfroe of *Geschichte der Kriegskunst im Rahmen der Politiken Geschichte*, 1920).

DEVINE, A.M. (1983), 'Embolon: a study in tactical terminology', in *Phoenix* 37, pp.201–17.

―――, (1985), 'Diodorus' account of the battle of Paraitacene (317 BC)', in *Ancient World* 12, pp.75–86.

―――, (1986), 'The battle of Gaugamela: a tactical and source-critical study', in *Ancient World* 13, pp.87–115.

―――, (1994), 'The short sarissa: tactical reality or scribal error?', in *Ancient History Bulletin* 8, p.132.

―――, (1995), 'Polybius' lost *Tactica*: the ultimate source for the tactical manuals of Asclepiodotus, Aelian and Arrian?', in *Ancient History Bulletin* 9, pp.40–4.

DINTSIS, P. (1986), *Hellenistische Helme* (Rome).

ENGELS, J. (2010), 'Macedonians and Greeks', in J. Roisman and I. Worthington (eds.), *A Companion to Ancient Macedonia*, pp.81–98.

ENGLISH, S. (2009), *The Army of Alexander the Great*.

ERRINGTON, R.M. (1967), 'Philip V, Aratus and the "Conspiracy of Apelles"', in *Historia* 16, pp.19–36.

―――, (1974), 'Macedonian "Royal Style" and its historical significance', in *Journal of Hellenic Studies* 94, pp.20–37.

―――, (1978), 'The Nature of the Macedonian State under the Monarchy', in *Chiron* 8, pp.77–134.

————, (1983), 'The Historiographical origins of Macedonian Staatsrecht', in *Ancient Macedonia* 3 (Thessaloniki).

————, (2008), *A History of the Hellenistic World 323–30 BC*.

ERSKINE, A. (1989), 'The πεζέταιροι of Philip II and Alexander III', in *Historia: Zeitschrift für Alte Geschichte* 38, H. 4 (4th Qtr), pp.385–94.

————, (2003) (ed.), *A Companion to the Hellenistic World*.

FEYEL, M. (1942), *Polybe et l'Histoire de Béotie au IIIe siècle avant notre ère*.

FISCHER-BOVET, C. (2014), *Army and Society in Ptolemaic Egypt*.

FRASER, P.M. (1972), *Ptolemaic Alexandria*.

FREDRICKSMEYER, E. (1986), 'Alexander the Great and the Macedonian kausia', in *Transactions of the American Philological Society* 116, pp.215–27.

FUKS, A. (1972), 'Isokrates and the Social-Economic situation in Greece', in *Ancient Society* 3, pp.17–44.

GOLDSWORTHY, A.K. (1996), *The Roman Army at War 100 BC – AD 200*.

GOUDRIAAN, K. (1988), *Ethnicity in Ptolemaic Egypt*.

GRAINGER, J.D. (1990a), *The Cities of Seleucid Syria* (London).

————, (1990b), *Seleukos Nikator. Constructing a Hellenistic Kingdom* (London).

————, (2014), *The Rise of the Seleukid Empire (323–223 BC): Seleukos I to Seleukos III*.

————, (2015a), *The Seleukid Empire of Antiochus III (223–187 BC)*.

————, (2015b), *The Fall of the Seleukid Empire 187–75 BC*.

————, (2017), *Kings and Kingship in the Hellenistic World 350–30 BC*.

GREEN, P. (1990), *From Alexander to Actium: The Hellenistic Age*.

GREENWALT, W. (2015), 'Infantry and the evolution of Argead Macedonia', in T. Howe, E.E. Garvin and G. Wrightson (eds), *Greece, Macedon and Persia*, pp.41–46.

GRIFFITH G.T. (1935), *The Mercenaries of the Hellenistic World*.

HAMMOND, N.G.L. (1980), 'Training in the use of the sarissa and its effects in battle 359–333 BC', *Antichthon* 14, pp.53–63.

————, (1984), 'The Battle of Pydna', in *Journal of Hellenic Studies* 104, pp.31–47.

————, (1988), 'The campaign and battle of Cynoscephalae in 197 BC', in *Journal of Hellenic Studies* 108, pp.60–82.

————, (1989a), *The Macedonian State* (Oxford).

————, (1989b), 'Casualties and reinforcements of citizen soldiers in Greece and Macedonia', in *Journal of Hellenic Studies* 109, pp.56–68.

————, (1991), 'The various guards of Philip II and Alexander III', in *Historia* 40, pp.396–418.

——, (1997), 'What may Philip have learned as a hostage in Thebes?', in *Greek, Roman and Byzantine Studies* 38, pp.355–72.

HAMMOND, N.G.L. and GRIFFITH, G.T. (1972), (1979) *A History of Macedonia* vol.1, vol.2.

HAMMOND, N.G.L. and WALBANK, F.W. (1988), *A History of Macedonia* vol.3.

HANSEN, E. (1971), *The Attalids of Pergamum*.

HANSON, V.D. (1983), *Warfare and Agriculture in Classical Greece*.

——, (1989), *The Western Way of War*.

——, (1991) (ed.), *Hoplites; the Classical Greek battle experience*.

HATZOPOULOS, M.B. (1986), 'Succession and Regency in Classical Macedonia', in *Ancient Macedonia* 4, pp.279–92.

——, (2001), *L'organisation de l'armée macédonienne sous les Antigonides. Problèmes anciens et documents nouveaux*.

HEAD, D. (1982), *Armies of the Macedonian and Punic Wars*.

——, (2001), 'The Thracian Sarissa', in *Slingshot* 214, pp.10–13.

HECKEL, W. (1986), 'Somatophylakia: a Macedonian cursus honorum', in *Phoenix* 40, pp.279–94.

——, (1992), *Alexander's Marshals: A Study of the Makedonian Aristocracy and the Politics of Military Leadership*.

——, (2006) (with R. Jones and C. Hook), *Macedonian Warrior: Alexander's elite infantryman*.

HOLLEAUX, M. (1942), (1952), *Etudes d'Epigraphie et d'Histoire grecques* 3, 4.

HORNBLOWER, J. (1981), *Hieronymus of Cardia*.

HORNBLOWER, S. (1982), *Mausolus*.

HOWE, T., GARVIN, E.E. and WRIGHTSON, G (eds) (2015), *Greece, Macedon and Persia*.

JUHEL, P.O. (2002), 'On orderliness with respect to the prizes of war: the Amphipolis regulation and the management of booty in the army of the last Antigonids', in *Annual of the British School at Athens* 97, pp.401–12.

——, (2009), 'The regulation helmet of the phalanx and the introduction of the concept of uniform in the Macedonian army at the end of the reign of Alexander the Great', in *Klio* 91, pp.342–55.

——, (2017a), *Autour de l'infanterie d'élite macédonienne à l'époque du royaume antigonide*.

——, (2017b), *Armes, armement et context funéraire dans la Macédoine hellénistique*.

————, (2017c), 'The rank insignia of the officers of the Macedonian phalanx: the lessons of iconography and an indirect reference in Vegetius', in Rance and Sekunda, pp.167–79.

KAGAN, D. and VIGGIANO, G.F. (eds) (2013), *Men of Bronze: Hoplite Warfare in Ancient Greece*.

KÄHLER, H. (1965), *Der Fries vom Reiterdenkmal des Aemilius Paullus in Delphi*.

KARUNANITHY, D. (2001), 'Of ox-hide helmets and three-ply armour: the equipment of Macedonian phalangites as described through a Roman source', in *Slingshot* 213, pp.33–40.

————, (2013), *The Macedonian War Machine: neglected aspects of the armies of Philip, Alexander and the Successors*.

KEEGAN, J. (1976), *The Face of Battle*.

KINCH, K.F. (1920), 'Le tombeau de Niausta. Tombeau Macédonien', in *Memoires de l'Academie Royale des Sciences et des Lettres de Danemark, Copenhague, 7me Série Section des Lettres* Vol.IV. No.3, pp.285–8.

KING, C.J. (2010), 'Macedonian kingship and other political institutions', in J. Roisman and I. Worthington (eds), *A Companion to Ancient Macedonia*, pp.373–91.

KRENTZ, P. (1991), 'The *salpinx* in Greek battle', in V.D. Hanson, *Hoplites: the Classical Greek battle experience*, pp.110–20.

————, (2013), 'Hoplite hell: how hoplites fought', in Kagan and Viggiano, ch.7, pp.134—6.

LANE FOX, R. (1973), *Alexander the Great*.

LAUNEY, M. (1987), *Recherches sur les armées hellénistiques* (reprint).

LAZENBY, J.F. (1978), *Hannibal's War*.

————, (2012), *The Spartan Army* (reprint of 1975 edition).

LENDON, J.E. (2005), *Soldiers and Ghosts: A History of Battle in Classical Antiquity*.

————, (2007), 'War and society', in Sabin, Van Wees and Whitby, pp.498–516.

LESQUIER, J. (1911), *Les institutions militaires de l'Egypte des Lagides*.

LÉVÊQUE, P. (1968), 'La guerre à l'époque hellénistique', in Vernant, pp.261–90.

LEWIS, N. (1986), *Greeks in Ptolemaic Egypt* (Oxford).

LIAMPI, K. (1998), *Der makedonische Schild* (Bonn).

LLOYD, A.B. (1996), 'Philip II and Alexander the Great: the moulding of Macedon's army', in A.B. Lloyd (ed.), *Battle in Antiquity*, pp.169–98.

LOCK, R.A. (1977), 'The Origin of the Argyraspids', *Historia* 26, pp.373–8.

MARKLE, M.M. (1977), 'The Macedonian Sarissa, Spear and Related Armour', in *American Journal of Archaeology* 81.3.

———, (1978), 'Use of the Sarissa by Philip and Alexander of Macedon', in *American Journal of Archaeology* 82, pp.483–97.

———, (1999), 'A Shield Monument from Veria and the Chronology of Macedonian Shield Types', in *Hesperia* 68 2, pp.219–54.

MARSDEN, E.W. (1964), *The Campaign of Gaugamela*.

MATTHEW, C. (2012), *The Tactics of Aelian*.

———, (2015), *An Invincible Beast: understanding the Hellenistic pike-phalanx at war*.

MATYSZAK, P. (2008), *Mithridates the Great: Rome's Indomitable Enemy*.

McKECHNIE, P. (1989), *Outsiders in the Greek Cities in the Fourth Century BC*.

MÉLÈZE-MODRZEJEWSKI (1983a), 'Le statut de Hellenes dans l'Egypte lagide', in *Revue des études grecques* 96, pp.241–68.

———, (1983b), 'Recherches récentes sur Alexandre le Grand, 1978–82', in *Revue des études grecques* 96, pp.225–41.

———, 1984), 'Dryton le Crétois et sa famille', in *Aux Origines de l'Hellénisme: La Crète et la Grèce. Hommages a Henri Van Effenterre*, pp.353–76.

MELIKIAN-CHIRVANI, A.S. (1993), 'L'emblème de gloire solaire d'un roi iranien du Pont', in *Bulletin of the Asia Institute* Vol.7, pp.21–29.

MILLAR, F. (1987), 'The Problem of Hellenistic Syria', in S. Sherwin-White and C. Kuhrt (eds), *Hellenism in the East*.

MILLER, S.G. (1993), *The Tomb of Lyson and Kallikles: a Painted Macedonian Tomb*.

MILLETT, P. (2010), 'The political economy of Macedonia', in J. Roisman and I. Worthington (eds), *A Companion to Ancient Macedonia*, pp.472–504.

MOOREN, L. (1977), *The Aulic Titulature in Ptolemaic Egypt, Stud. Hell.* 23.

———, (1983), 'The Nature of the Hellenistic Monarchy', in Van't Dack, pp. 205–40.

MORGAN, J.D. (1981), 'Sellasia revisited', in *American Journal of Archaeology* 85, pp.328–30.

MØRKHOLM, O. (1966), *Antiochus IV of Syria*.

MOSSÉ, C. (1968), 'Le rôle politique des armées dans le monde grecque a l'époque classique', in Vernant, pp.221–9.

MÜLLER, S. (2010), 'Philip II', in J. Roisman and I. Worthington (eds), *A Companion to Ancient Macedonia*, pp.166–85.

NAIDEN, F.S. (2018), *Soldier, Priest, and God: A Life of Alexander the Great*.

NOGUERA BOREL, A. (1999), 'L'évolution de la phalange macédonienne: le cas de la sarisse', in *Ancient Macedonia* 6 vol.2, pp.839–50.

OATES, J.F. (1963), 'The status designation *perses tes epigones*', in *Yale Classical Studies* 18, pp.1–129.

OGDEN, D. (1996), 'Homsexuality and warfare in Ancient Greece', in A.B. LLoyd (ed.), *Battle in Antiquity*, pp.107–68.

OMAN, C. (1937), *A History of the Art of War in the Sixteenth Century*.

PAPAZOGLOU, F. (1983), 'Sur l'organisation de la Macédoine des Antigonides', in *Ancient Macedonia* 3, pp.195–210.

PARKE, H.W. (1933), *Greek Mercenary Soldiers from the Earliest Times to the Battle of Ipsus*.

PEREMANS, W. (1951), 'Notes sur le bataille de Raphia', in *Aegyptus* 31, pp.214–22.

———, (1970), 'Sur l'identification des Egyptiens et des étrangers dans l'Egypte des Lagides', in *Ancient Society* 1, pp.25–38.

———, (1972), 'Egyptiens et étrangers dans l'armée de terre et dans la police de l'Egypte Ptolemaique', *Ancient Society* 3, pp.67–76.

———, (1978), 'Les indigènes égyptiens dans l'armée de terre lagide: recherches anthroponymiques', in *Ancient Society* 9, pp.83–100.

———, (1983), 'Les Egyptiens dans l'armée de terre des Lagides', in *Hist. Einz* 40 (St. H. Bengtson), pp.22–102.

PIETRYKOWSKI, J. (2009), *Great Battles of the Hellenistic World*.

POMEROY, S. (1983), 'Infanticide in Hellenistic Greece', in A.Cameron and A. Kuhrt (eds), *Images of Women in Antiquity*, pp.207–23.

———, (1990), *Women in Hellenistic Egypt from Alexander to Cleopatra*.

POST, R. (2010), 'Bright colours and uniformity: Hellenistic military costume', in *Ancient Warfare* IV, 6, pp.14–9.

POTTER, D. (2003), 'Hellenistic religion', in A. Erskine (ed.), *A Companion to the Hellenistic World*, pp.407–30.

POUILLOUX, J. and VERDELIS, N.M. (1950), 'Deux inscriptions de Demetrias', in *Bulletin de correspondance hellénique* 74, pp.33–47.

PRÉAUX, C. (1978), *Le Monde Hellénistique. La Grèce et l'Orient (323–146 av. J.C.)*.

PRITCHETT, W.K. (1971), (1974), (1979), (1985), (1991), *The Greek State at War* vols 1–5 (Berkeley).

RANCE, P. (2017a), 'Introduction', in Rance and Sekunda, pp.9–64.

———, (2017b), 'Maurice's Strategikon and "the Ancients": the Late Antique reception of Aelian and Arrian', in Rance and Sekunda, pp.217–55.

RANCE, P. and SEKUNDA, N.V. (eds), (2017), *Greek Taktika: Ancient Military Writing and its Heritage*.

LE RIDER, G. (1965), *Suse sous les Séleucides et les Parthes*.

ROBERT, L. (1938), *Études epigraphiques et philologiques*.

ROBERTS, K. (2017), 'The practical use of classical texts for modern war in the sixteenth and seventeenth centuries', in Rance and Sekunda, pp.256–81.

ROESCH, P. (1982), *Études béotiennes* (Centre de recherches archéologiques, Institut Fernand-Courby, units recherches archéologiques, 15.) Paris.

ROISMAN, J. (2012), *Alexander's Veterans and the Early Wars of the Successors*.

———, (2015), 'Opposition to Macedonian kings: riots for rewards and verbal protests', in T. Howe, E.E. Garvin and G. Wrightson (eds), *Greece, Macedon and Persia*, pp.77–86.

ROISMAN, J. and WORTHINGTON, I. (eds) (2010), *A Companion to Ancient Macedonia*.

ROSTOVTZEFF, M. (1953), *The Social and Economic History of the Hellenistic World*, 2nd ed.

ROTH, J.P. (2007), 'War', in Sabin, Van Wees and Whitby, pp.368–98.

ROWLANDSON, J. (2003), 'Town and country in Ptolemaic Egypt', in A. Erskine (ed.), *A Companion to the Hellenistic World*, pp.249–63.

SAATSOGLOU-PALIADELI, C. (1993), 'Aspects of ancient Macedonian costume', in *The Journal of Hellenic Studies* 113, pp.122–47.

SABIN, P. (2000), 'The Face of Roman Battle', in *Journal of Roman Studies* 90, pp.1–17.

———, (2007a), 'Battle. A: Land Battles', in Sabin, Van Wees and Whitby, pp.399–433.

———, (2007b), *Lost Battles: Reconstructing the Great Clashes of the Ancient World*.

SABIN, P., VAN WEES, H. and WHITBY, M. (eds) (2007), *The Cambridge History of Greek and Roman Warfare*.

SAWADA, N. (2010), 'Social customs and institutions: aspects of Macedonian elite society', in J. Roisman and I. Worthington (eds), *A Companion to Ancient Macedonia*, pp.392–408.

SCHEFOLD, K. (1968), *Der Alexander-Sarkofag*.

SCULLARD, H.H. (1974), *The Elephant in the Greek and Roman World*.

SEKUNDA, N.V. (1984), *The Army of Alexander the Great*.

———, (1994), *Seleucid and Ptolemaic Reformed Armies 168–145 BC. Vol.1: The Seleucid Army under Antiochus IV Epiphanes*.

———, (1995), *Seleucid and Ptolemaic Reformed Armies 168–145 BC. Vol.2: The Ptolemaic Army under Ptolemy VI Philometor*.

———, (2001a), 'The Sarissa', in *Acta Universitatis Lodziensis, Folia Archaeologica* 23, pp.13–41.

————, (2001b), *Hellenistic Infantry Reform in the 160s BC.*

————, (2007), 'Military Forces. A: Land Forces', in Sabin, van Wees and Whitby, pp.325–57.

————, (2010), 'Macedonian Military Forces', in J. Roisman and I. Worthington (eds), *A Companion to Ancient Macedonia*, pp.446–71.

————, (2012) (with P. Dennis), *Macedonian Armies after Alexander 323–168 BC.*

————, (2013a), *The Antigonid Army.*

————, (2013b), 'The Iphicratean Peltast Reform', in A.A. Sinitsyn and M.M. Kholod (eds), *KOINON ΔΩPON. Studies and Essays in Honour of Valery P. Nikonorov on the Occasion of His Sixtieth Birthday Presented by His Friends and Colleagues.*

SHERWIN-WHITE, S. and KUHRT, C. (eds) (1987), *Hellenism in the East* (London).

SNODGRASS, A.M. (1999), *Arms and Armour of the Greeks.*

TARN, W.W. (1930), *Hellenistic Military and Naval Developments.*

————, (1951), *The Greeks in Bactria and India* (Cambridge) 2nd ed.

TAYLOR, M. (2013), *Antiochus The Great.*

————, (2016), 'The battle scene on Aemilius Paullus' monument: a re-evaluation', in *Hesperia* 85-3, pp.559–76.

TAYLOR, R. (2016), 'When push comes to shove: the meaning of "*othismos*"', in *Slingshot* 306, pp.19–29.

————, (2017), '"Bear forward with the weight of their bodies": pushing in Greek infantry formations', in *Slingshot* 311, pp.2–8.

TSIMBIDOU-AVLONITI, M. (2004), 'The Macedonian Tomb at Aghios Athanasios, Thessaloniki', in D. Pandermalis (ed.), *Alexander the Great: Treasures from an Epic Era of Hellenism*, pp.149–51.

TURNER, E. (1984), 'Ptolemaic Egypt', Chapter 5 in *Cambridge Ancient History* VII 1, pp.118–74.

UEBEL, F. (1968), *Die Kleruchen Ägyptens unter den ersten sechs Ptolemäern*, Abh. Akad. Berlin 3.

UEDA-SARSON, L. (2001), 'Macedonian Unit Organisations', in *Slingshot* 214, pp. 35–8, online at http://lukeuedasarson.com/GranicusNotes.html.

————, (2002a), 'The Reforms of Iphikrates', in *Slingshot* 222, pp.30–6, online at http://lukeuedasarson.com/Iphikrates1.html.

————, (2002b), 'Infantry of the Successors', in *Slingshot* 223, pp.23–8, online at http://lukeuedasarson.com/Iphikrates2.html.

VAN EFFENTERRE, H. (1948), *La Crète et le monde grec de Platon a Polybe.*

VAN'T DACK, E. (1969), '*Exo taxeon* et *semeia* dans les papyrus démotiques', in *Archiv für Papyrusforschung* 19, pp.155–65.

———, (1977), 'Sur l'évolution des institutions militaires lagides', in Armées et fiscalité dans le monde antique (Colloques Nationaux du CNRS 936), pp.77–105 = Van't Dack (1988), pp.1–46.

———, (1983), *Egypt and the Hellenistic World*.

———, (1985), 'La collégialité dans les commandements éponymes de l'armée lagide', in *Chronique d'Egypte* 60, pp.379–92.

———, (1988), *Ptolemaica Selecta*, Stud. Hell. 29.

VAN WEES, H., (2004), *Greek Warfare: Myths and Realities*.

VAUGHN, P. (1991), 'The identification and retrieval of the Hoplite battle dead', in Hanson, pp.38–62.

VÉÏSSE, A.-E. (2004), *Les 'révoltes Égyptiennes': recherches sur les troubles intérieur enEgypte du règne de Ptolémée III Euergète à la conquête romaine*.

VERNANT, J.P. (ed.) (1968), *Problèmes de la guerre en Grèce ancienne*.

WALBANK, F.W. (1940), *Philip V of Macedon* (Cambridge).

———, (1957), (1967), (1979), *A Historical Commentary on Polybius* 1–3 (Oxford).

———, (1993), *The Hellenistic World*.

WARRY, J. (2002), *Warfare in the Classical World* (2nd ed.).

WATERFIELD, R. (2011), *Dividing the Spoils: The War for Alexander the Great's Empire*.

WELLES, C.B. *et. al.* (eds) (1959), *The Excavations at Dura-Europus, Final Report v. 1: The parchments and papyri*.

WHEELER, E.L. (1979), 'The legion as phalanx', in *Chiron* 9, pp.303–18.

———, (1988), 'Stratagem and the vocabulary of military trickery', in *Mnemosyne Suppl.* 108.

———, (1991), 'The General as Hoplite', in Hanson, pp.121–70.

———, (2007), 'Land Battles', in Sabin, Van Wees and Whitby, pp.186–223.

WHITEHEAD, D. (1990), *Aineias the Tactician: How to Survive under Siege*.

———, (1991), 'Who equipped mercenary troops in Classical Greece?', in *Historia* 40, pp.105–13.

WINNICKI, J.K. (1972), 'Ein ptolemäischer Offizier in Thebais', in *Eos* 60, pp.343–53.

———, (1977), 'Die Kalasirier der spätdynastische und der ptolemäischen Zeit', in *Historia* 26, pp.257–68.

———, (1978), *Ptolemaerarmee in Thebais* (Wroclaw).

———, (1981), 'Griechisch-demotische Soldatenkorrespondenz aus Pathyris (Gebelen)', in *Proc. XVI Int. Congr. Papyr.*, pp.547–52.

WINTER, F. (1912), *Der Alexandersarkofag aus Sidon*.

WORTHINGTON, I. (2010), *Philip II of Macedonia*.

———, (2014), *By the Spear: Philip II, Alexander the Great, and the Rise and Fall of the Macedonian Empire*.

WRIGHTSON, G. (2010), 'The nature of command in the Macedonian sarissa phalanx', in *The Ancient History Bulletin* 24, pp.71–92.

———, (2015a), 'Macedonian armies, elephants and the perfection of combined arms', in T. Howe, E.E. Garvin and G. Wrightson (eds), *Greece, Macedon and Persia*, pp.59–68.

———, (2015b), 'To use or not to use: The practical and historical reliability of Asclepiodotus' "philosophical" tactical manual', in *Ancient Warfare: Introducing Current Research*, pp.65–93.

Abbreviations

Literary texts:

Ael.	Aelian, *Tactics*
App. *Mith.*	Appian, *Mithridatic Wars*
App. *Syr.*	Appian, *Syrian Wars*
Arist. *Pol.*	Aristotle, *Politics*
Arr. *Anab.*	Arrian, *Anabasis of Alexander*
Arr. *Tact*	Arrian, *Tactics*
Asclep.	Asclepiodotus, *Tactics*
Athen.	Athenaeus, *Deipnosophistae (Philosophers' Dinner Party)*
B.G.	Julius Caesar, *The Gallic War* (*Bellum Gallicum*)
D.H.	Dionysius of Halicarnassus, *Roman Antiquities*
D.L.	Diogenes Laertius, *Lives of Eminent Philosophers*
Dio Cass.	Dio Cassius (Cassius Dio), *Roman History*
Diod.	Diodorus Siculus, *Library of History*
Hdt.	Herodotus, *Histories*
Isoc. *Paneg.*	Isocrates, *Panegyricus*
Jos. *Ant.*	Flavius Josephus, *Antiquities of the Jews*
Just.	Justin, *Epitome of Pompeius Trogus*
Liv.	Livy, *From the Founding of the City* (*Ab Urbe Condita*)
Paus.	Pausanias, *Description of Greece*
Plut. *Aem.*	Plutarch, *Life of Aemilius Paulus*

Plut. *Alex.*	Plutarch, *Life of Alexander*
Plut. *Ant.*	Plutarch, *Life of Antony*
Plut. *Arat.*	Plutarch, *Life of Aratus*
Plut. *Cleom.*	Plutarch, *Life of Cleomenes*
Plut. *Dem.*	Plutarch, *Life of Demetrius*
Plut. *Eum.*	Plutarch, *Life of Eumenes*
Plut. *Flam.*	Plutarch, *Life of Flamininus*
Plut. *Mor.*	Plutarch, *On moral virtues* (*De virtute morali*)
Plut. *Peric.*	Plutarch, *Life of Pericles*
Plut. *Philop.*	Plutarh, *Life of Philopoemen*
Plut. *Pyrr.*	Plutarch, *Life of Pyrrhus*
Plut. *Sull.*	Plutarch, *Life of Sulla*
Pol.	Polybius, *Histories*
Polyaen.	Polyaenus, *Stratagems*
Q.C.	Quintus Curtius Rufus, *History of Alexander the Great*
Str.	Strabo, *Geography*
Thuc.	Thucydides, *The Peloponnesian War.*
Veg.	Vegetius, *Epitome of military science*
Xen. *Anab*	Xenophon, *Anabasis*
Xen. *Const.Lac.*	Xenophon, *Constitution of the Lacedaimonians*
Xen. *Cyrop.*	Xenophon, *Education of Cyrus (Cyropaedia)*
Xen. *Hell.*	Xenophon, *Hellenica*
Xen. *Hipp.*	Xenophon, *On the Cavalry Commander*
Xen. *Horse.*	Xenophon, *On Horsemanship*
Xen. *Hunt.*	Xenophon, *On Hunting*

Inscriptions and papyri

BGU	Aegyptische Urkunden aus den Staatlichen Museen zu Berlin, Griechische Urkunden (Berlin, 1895)
C.Ord.Ptol.	M.-Th. Lenger, Corpus des ordonnances des Ptolémées (Brussels, 1980)
F.Delphes	*Fouilles de Delphes* Vol III (Paris, 1909)
I.Cret.	*Inscriptiones Creticae*, ed. M. Guarducci (Rome, 1935–50)
IG	*Inscriptiones Graecae*

I.Milet	A.Rehm, Die Inschriften. *Das Delphinion in Milet*. Milet III (Berlin, 1914)
Moretti	L. Moretti, *Iscrizioni agonistiche greche* (Rome, 1953)
OGIS	*Orientis graeci inscriptiones selectae*, ed. W. Dittenberger (Leipzig, 1903)
Pros. Ptol.	W. Peremans, E. Van't Dack *et. al.*, *Prosopographia Ptolemaica*, 8 vols (Louvain, 1950–75)
P.Cairo Zen.	*Catalogue général des antiquités égyptiennes du Musée du Caire: Zenon Papyri* (Cairo, 1925–31)
P.Hib.	*The Hibeh Papyri* (London, 1906, 1955)
P.Lille	*Papyrus grecs* (Institut papyrologique de l'Universite de Lille, Paris, 1907–28)
P.Lond.	*Greek Papyri in the British Museum* (London, 1893)
P.Paris	*Notices et textes des papyrus grecs du Musée du Louvre et de la bibliothèque impériale* (Paris, 1865)
P.Petrie	*The Flinders Petrie Papyri* (Dublin, 1891–1905)
P.Rev.Laws	*Revenue Laws of Ptolemy Philadelphus*, ed. B.P. Grenfell (Oxford, 1896)
P.Tebt.	*The Tebtunis Papyri*, ed. B.P. Grenfell *et. al.* (London, 1902–76)
Syll3	W. Dittenberger, *Sylloge inscriptionum graecarum* (Leipzig, 1915–24) 3rd ed.
UPZ	*Urkunden der Ptolemäerzeit*, ed. U. Wilcken (Berlin–Leipzig, 1922–57)
W.Chrest.	U. Wilcken, *Grundzuge und Chrestomathie der Papyruskunde 1: Historischer Teil* (Leipzig–Berlin, 1912)

Index